Part of JIST's Top Careers™ Series

100 Fastest-Growing CAREERS

Your Complete Guidebook to Major Jobs with the Most Growth and Openings

NINTH EDITION

Michael Farr

America's Career Publisher

100 Fastest-Growing Careers, Ninth Edition

Your Complete Guidebook to Major Jobs with the Most Growth and Openings

Previous edition was titled *America's 101 Fastest Growing Jobs*

Published by JIST Works, an imprint of JIST Publishing, Inc.
8902 Otis Avenue
Indianapolis, IN 46216-1033
Phone: 1-800-648-JIST Fax: 1-800-JIST-FAX
E-mail: info@jist.com Web site: www.jist.com

Some books by Michael Farr:
Best Jobs for the 21st Century
Overnight Career Choice
Next-Day Job Interview
Same-Day Resume
The Quick Resume & Cover Letter Book
The Very Quick Job Search

JIST's Top Careers™ Series:
Top 300 Careers
Top 100 Health-Care Careers
100 Fastest-Growing Jobs
Top 100 Careers Without a Four-Year Degree
Top 100 Careers for College Graduates
Top 100 Computer and Technical Careers

Visit www.jist.com for free job search information, book excerpts, and ordering information on our many products. For free information on 14,000 job titles, visit www.careeroink.com.

Quantity discounts are available for JIST products. Have future editions of JIST books automatically delivered to you on publication through our convenient standing order program. Please call 1-800-648-JIST or visit www.jist.com for a free catalog and more information.

Acquisitions and Development Editor: Susan Pines
Database Work: Laurence Shatkin
Cover Layout: Trudy Coler
Interior Design and Layout: Marie Kristine Parial-Leonardo
Proofreader: Jeanne Clark

Printed in the United States of America

08 07 06 9 8 7 6 5 4 3 2 1

ISBN-13: 978-1-59357-317-1

ISBN-10: 1-59357-317-0

Relax. You Don't Have to Read This Whole Book!

You don't need to read this entire book. I've organized it into easy-to-use sections so you can get just the information you want. You will find everything you need to

- ★ Learn about the 100 fastest-growing jobs, including their daily tasks, pay, outlook, and required education and skills.
- ★ Match your personal skills to the jobs.
- ★ Take seven steps to land a good job in less time.

To get started, simply scan the table of contents to learn more about these sections and to see a list of the jobs described in this book. Really, this book is easy to use, and I hope it helps you.

Who Should Use This Book?

This is more than a book of job descriptions. I've spent quite a bit of time thinking about how to make its contents useful for a variety of situations, including

- ★ **Exploring career options.** The job descriptions in Part II give a wealth of information on many of the most desirable jobs in the labor market. The assessment in Part I can help you focus your career options.
- ★ **Considering more education or training.** The information helps you avoid costly mistakes in choosing a career or deciding on additional training or education—and it increases your chances of planning a bright future.
- ★ **Job seeking.** This book helps you identify new job targets, prepare for interviews, and write targeted resumes. The advice in Part III has been proven to cut job search time in half.
- ★ **Career planning.** The job descriptions help you explore your options, and Parts III and IV provide career planning advice and other useful information.

Source of Information

The job descriptions come from the good people at the U.S. Department of Labor, as published in the most recent edition of the *Occupational Outlook Handbook.* The *OOH* is the best source of career information available, and the descriptions include the most current, accurate data on jobs. Thank you to all the people at the Department of Labor who gather, compile, analyze, and make sense of this information. It's good stuff, and I hope you can make good use of it.

Mike Farr

Contents

Summary of Major Sections

Introduction. Provides an explanation of the job descriptions, how best to use the book, and other details. *Begins on page 1.*

Part I: Using the Job-Match Grid to Choose a Career. Match your skills and preferences to the jobs in this book. *Begins on page 15.*

Part II: Descriptions of the 100 Fastest-Growing Careers. Presents thorough descriptions of the 100 fastest-growing jobs. Education and training requirements for these jobs vary from on-the-job training to a four-year college degree or more. Each description gives information on the nature of the work, working conditions, employment, training, other qualifications, advancement, job outlook, earnings, related occupations, and sources of additional information. The jobs are presented in alphabetical order. The page numbers where specific descriptions begin are listed in the detailed contents. *Begins on page 31.*

Part III: Quick Job Search—Seven Steps to Getting a Good Job in Less Time. This relatively brief but important section offers results-oriented career planning and job search techniques. It includes tips on identifying your key skills, defining your ideal job, using effective job search methods, writing resumes, organizing your time, improving your interviewing skills, and following up on leads. The last part of this section features professionally written and designed resumes for some of the fastest-growing jobs. *Begins on page 299.*

Part IV: Important Trends in Jobs and Industries. This section includes two well-written articles and two charts on labor market trends. The articles and charts are worth your time. Titles of the articles are "Tomorrow's Jobs" and "Employment Trends in Major Industries." Titles of the charts are "High-Paying Occupations with Many Openings, Projected 2004–2014" and "Large Metropolitan Areas That Had the Fastest Employment Growth, 2004–2005." *Begins on page 361.*

Detailed Contents

Introduction 1

Part I: Using the Job-Match Grid to Choose a Career........................15

Part II: Descriptions of the 100 Fastest-Growing Careers 31

Accountants and Auditors 32
Administrative Services Managers 36
Advertising, Marketing, Promotions, Public Relations, and Sales Managers 39
Animal Care and Service Workers........41
Athletes, Coaches, Umpires, and Related Workers 44
Automotive Service Technicians and Mechanics 47
Barbers, Cosmetologists, and Other Personal Appearance Workers 51
Bill and Account Collectors........53
Bookkeeping, Accounting, and Auditing Clerks 55
Building Cleaning Workers 56
Bus Drivers 59
Carpenters 62
Cement Masons, Concrete Finishers, Segmental Pavers, and Terrazzo Workers 64
Chefs, Cooks, and Food Preparation Workers........67
Child Care Workers 71
Clinical Laboratory Technologists and Technicians 74
Computer and Information Systems Managers 76
Computer Scientists and Database Administrators 78
Computer Software Engineers........82
Computer Support Specialists and Systems Administrators 84
Computer Systems Analysts 87
Counselors 90
Counter and Rental Clerks........94
Customer Service Representatives........95
Demonstrators, Product Promoters, and Models........98
Dental Assistants 102
Dental Hygienists........103
Education Administrators........105
Electricians........108

Emergency Medical Technicians and Paramedics 111
Engineers 113
Financial Analysts and Personal Financial Advisors 122
Financial Managers 125
Fire Fighting Occupations 128
Fitness Workers 131
Food and Beverage Serving and Related Workers 133
Food Processing Occupations 137
Gaming Services Occupations 140
Graphic Designers 143
Grounds Maintenance Workers 145
Hazardous Materials Removal Workers 148
Heating, Air-Conditioning, and Refrigeration Mechanics and Installers 150
Hotel, Motel, and Resort Desk Clerks 153
Human Resources Assistants, Except Payroll and Timekeeping 155
Human Resources, Training, and Labor Relations Managers and Specialists 157
Instructional Coordinators 162
Lawyers 163
Licensed Practical and Licensed Vocational Nurses 167
Maintenance and Repair Workers, General 169
Management Analysts 170
Market and Survey Researchers 173
Massage Therapists 175
Material Moving Occupations 178
Medical and Health Services Managers 181
Medical Assistants 183
Medical Records and Health Information Technicians 185
Medical Scientists 187
Medical Transcriptionists 190
Nursing, Psychiatric, and Home Health Aides 192
Occupational Therapists 195
Office and Administrative Support Worker Supervisors and Managers 197
Office Clerks, General 199
Painters and Paperhangers 201
Paralegals and Legal Assistants 203
Payroll and Timekeeping Clerks 206
Personal and Home Care Aides 207
Pharmacists 209
Pharmacy Technicians 212
Physical Therapist Assistants and Aides 214
Physical Therapists 215
Physician Assistants 217
Physicians and Surgeons 219
Pipelayers, Plumbers, Pipefitters, and Steamfitters 222
Police and Detectives 225
Property, Real Estate, and Community Association Managers 229
Public Relations Specialists 232
Radiologic Technologists and Technicians 235
Real Estate Brokers and Sales Agents 237
Receptionists and Information Clerks 239
Recreation Workers 241
Registered Nurses 243
Respiratory Therapists 247
Retail Salespersons 249
Roofers 251
Sales Representatives, Wholesale and Manufacturing 253
Secretaries and Administrative Assistants 256
Security Guards and Gaming Surveillance Officers 259
Social and Human Service Assistants 261
Social Workers 263
Surgical Technologists 266
Taxi Drivers and Chauffeurs 268
Teacher Assistants 271
Teachers—Postsecondary 273
Teachers—Preschool, Kindergarten, Elementary, Middle, and Secondary 277
Teachers—Self-Enrichment Education 281
Teachers—Special Education 283
Top Executives 285
Truck Drivers and Driver/Sales Workers 288
Veterinary Technologists and Technicians 292
Writers and Editors 294

Part III: Quick Job Search—Seven Steps to Getting a Good Job in Less Time 299

Part IV: Important Trends in Jobs and Industries 361

Tomorrow's Jobs 363
Employment Trends in Major Industries 373
High-Paying Occupations with Many Openings, Projected 2004–2014 385
Large Metropolitan Areas That Had the Fastest Employment Growth, 2004–2005 387

Index 389

Introduction

This book is about improving your life, not just about selecting and getting a fast-growing job. The career you choose will have an enormous impact on how you live.

A huge amount of information is available on occupations, but most people don't know where to find accurate, reliable facts to help them make good career decisions—or they don't take the time to look. Important choices such as what to do with your career or whether to get additional training or education deserve your time.

If you are considering more training or education, this book will help with solid information. The education and training needed for the jobs described in this book vary enormously. You will notice that many of the better-paying jobs may require more training or education than you now have. Some require brief training or on-the-job experience. Many better-paying jobs, however, call for technical training lasting from a few months to a few years. Others require a four-year college degree or more. But some jobs, such as certain sales and management occupations, have high pay but do not always involve advanced education. This book is designed to give you facts to help you explore your options.

A certain type of work or workplace may interest you as much as a certain type of job. If your interests and values lead you to work in health care, for example, you can choose from a variety of work environments and a variety of industries. This book includes details to help you weigh your options.

The time you spend in career planning can pay off in higher earnings, but being satisfied with your work—and your life—is often more important than the amount you earn. For this reason, I suggest that you begin to explore alternatives by following your interests and finding a career path that allows you to use your skills and talents. This book can help you find the work that suits you best and that offers a promising future.

The 100 Fastest-Growing Careers List

I think it's important for you to understand how I developed the list of the fastest-growing careers for this book. I used the most recent data from the U.S. Department of Labor, which provides growth projections through 2014 for 268 major jobs that encompass 90 percent of the workforce. I started by sorting all of those jobs based on their percent of projected growth through 2014, from highest to lowest. I then sorted the jobs based on the projected number of annual new job openings, also from highest to lowest. For these 268 jobs, the average (mean) growth rate is 11.1 percent, and the average number of openings annually is 63,848.

From these two lists I created a third list based on the relative position of each job on the first two lists. I did this by adding the score for each job's position on the lists. For example, a job with a high percentage of growth and a high number of new job openings appears toward the top.

Perhaps you're wondering why I use figures for both job growth and number of openings. Aren't these two ways of saying the same thing? Actually, both are important. A job may have a fast growth rate overall, but it may be a relatively small occupation with not many people employed in it. So jobs with both a high rate of growth *and* many openings offer the best opportunity.

The 100 jobs with the most favorable combined scores for projected percent increase and annual number of job openings through 2014 appear in the following table. As you can see, the list includes a variety of jobs at all levels of education, training, and interest.

Notice that two of the top 10 fastest-growing jobs are computer related, and four are in the health-care area—two rapidly growing fields. Another point to notice is that most of the fastest-growing jobs require training or education beyond high school. While job opportunities at all levels of education and training are listed in the table, many better-paying jobs require postsecondary education or training. If you want more information on important labor market trends, consider reading the excellent and brief review of labor market trends in Part IV.

Note that you can find a complete description for each job listed below in Part II. You will also find these jobs listed in the table of contents along with the page number where each job description begins.

The 100 Fastest-Growing Careers

	Percent Growth Through 2014	Annual Job Openings
1. Nursing, Psychiatric, and Home Health Aides	31	487,000
2. Personal and Home Care Aides	40	230,000
3. Teachers—Postsecondary	32	329,000
4. Medical Assistants	52	93,000
5. Registered Nurses	29	229,000
6. Computer Software Engineers	46	91,000
7. Customer Service Representatives	22	510,000
8. Computer Support Specialists and Systems Administrators	28	121,000
9. Receptionists and Information Clerks	21	299,000
10. Counter and Rental Clerks	23	126,000
11. Human Resources, Training, and Labor Relations Managers and Specialists	23	114,000
12. Accountants and Auditors	22	157,000
13. Retail Salespersons	17	1,350,000
14. Social and Human Service Assistants	29	61,000
15. Dental Assistants	42	45,000
16. Teachers—Preschool, Kindergarten, Elementary, Middle, and Secondary	18	510,000
17. Computer Systems Analysts	31	56,000
18. Grounds Maintenance Workers	19	279,000
19. Teachers—Self-Enrichment Education	25	74,000
20. Food and Beverage Serving and Related Workers	16	2,359,000
21. Fitness Workers	27	50,000
22. Bill and Account Collectors	21	85,000
23. Building Cleaning Workers	16	863,000
24. Counselors	21	83,000
25. Top Executives	16	246,000
26. Social Workers	22	67,000
27. Advertising, Marketing, Promotions, Public Relations, and Sales Managers	20	77,000

		Percent Growth Through 2014	Annual Job Openings
28.	Athletes, Coaches, Umpires, and Related Workers	20	75,000
29.	Management Analysts	20	82,000
30.	Taxi Drivers and Chauffeurs	24	43,000
31.	Pharmacy Technicians	28	35,000
32.	Gaming Services Occupations	23	47,000
33.	Physicians and Surgeons	23	41,000
34.	Chefs, Cooks, and Food Preparation Workers	14	844,000
35.	Paralegals and Legal Assistants	29	28,000
36.	Animal Care and Service Workers	24	34,000
37.	Public Relations Specialists	22	38,000
38.	Licensed Practical and Licensed Vocational Nurses	17	84,000
39.	Recreation Workers	17	69,000
40.	Financial Analysts and Personal Financial Advisors	21	45,000
41.	Truck Drivers and Driver/Sales Workers	13	515,000
42.	Bus Drivers	15	110,000
43.	Maintenance and Repair Workers, General	15	154,000
44.	Child Care Workers	13	439,000
45.	Computer Scientists and Database Administrators	26	26,000
46.	Hotel, Motel, and Resort Desk Clerks	17	62,000
47.	Dental Hygienists	43	17,000
48.	Medical and Health Services Managers	22	33,000
49.	Teacher Assistants	14	252,000
50.	Teachers—Special Education	20	37,000
51.	Automotive Service Technicians and Mechanics	15	93,000
52.	Computer and Information Systems Managers	25	25,000
53.	Barbers, Cosmetologists, and Other Personal Appearance Workers	15	87,000
54.	Carpenters	13	210,000
55.	Education Administrators	16	58,000
56.	Medical Scientists	33	16,000
57.	Clinical Laboratory Technologists and Technicians	22	28,000
58.	Emergency Medical Technicians and Paramedics	27	21,000
59.	Physical Therapists	36	13,000
60.	Sales Representatives, Wholesale and Manufacturing	13	216,000
61.	Heating, Air-Conditioning, and Refrigeration Mechanics and Installers	19	33,000
62.	Physical Therapist Assistants and Aides	40	12,000
63.	Writers and Editors	17	35,000
64.	Fire Fighting Occupations	22	25,000
65.	Physician Assistants	49	10,000
66.	Police and Detectives	15	66,000
67.	Security Guards and Gaming Surveillance Officers	12	232,000
68.	Medical Transcriptionists	23	20,000
69.	Payroll and Timekeeping Clerks	17	36,000
70.	Pipelayers, Plumbers, Pipefitters, and Steamfitters	15	68,000
71.	Roofers	16	38,000
72.	Instructional Coordinators	27	15,000

(continued)

(continued)

The 100 Fastest-Growing Careers

		Percent Growth Through 2014	Annual Job Openings
73.	Medical Records and Health Information Technicians	28	14,000
74.	Engineers	13	111,000
75.	Property, Real Estate, and Community Association Managers	15	58,000
76.	Material Moving Occupations	8	1,190,000
77.	Office Clerks, General	8	695,000
78.	Pharmacists	24	16,000
79.	Financial Managers	14	63,000
80.	Radiologic Technologists and Technicians	23	17,000
81.	Surgical Technologists	29	12,000
82.	Hazardous Materials Removal Workers	31	11,000
83.	Veterinary Technologists and Technicians	35	9,000
84.	Food Processing Occupations	11	123,000
85.	Market and Survey Researchers	20	23,000
86.	Painters and Paperhangers	12	105,000
87.	Demonstrators, Product Promoters, and Models	16	33,000
88.	Massage Therapists	23	12,000
89.	Occupational Therapists	33	7,000
90.	Human Resources Assistants, Except Payroll and Timekeeping	16	28,000
91.	Secretaries and Administrative Assistants	6	545,000
92.	Lawyers	14	40,000
93.	Cement Masons, Concrete Finishers, Segmental Pavers, and Terrazzo Workers	15	33,000
94.	Graphic Designers	15	35,000
95.	Office and Administrative Support Worker Supervisors and Managers	8	167,000
96.	Administrative Services Managers	16	25,000
97.	Bookkeeping, Accounting, and Auditing Clerks	5	291,000
98.	Real Estate Brokers and Sales Agents	13	53,000
99.	Electricians	11	68,000
100.	Respiratory Therapists	23	9,000

Some Advice for Reviewing the Fastest-Growing Careers

Major changes are occurring in our labor market, and Part IV describes these changes. Rapidly growing jobs will often be more attractive career options than jobs that are not growing quickly. Rapidly growing jobs often offer better-than-average opportunities for employment and job security. For this reason, you should pay attention to jobs that are projected to grow rapidly.

But there most likely will be openings for new people in slower-growing or declining jobs. Some slower-growing jobs employ large numbers of people and will create many openings due to retirement, people leaving the field, and other reasons. Considering jobs that are generating large numbers of openings but that may not have high percentage growth rates will give you more options to consider. Information on all major occupational and industry groups is provided in Part IV, including those that are growing more slowly than average or even declining.

Keep in Mind That Your Situation Is Probably Not "Average"

Although the employment growth and earnings trends for many occupations and industries are quite positive, the averages in this book will not be true for many individuals. Earnings and job opportunities vary enormously in different parts of the country, in different occupations, and in different industries. My point is that your situation is probably not average. But this book's solid information is a great place to start. Good information will give you a strong foundation for good decisions.

Four Important Labor Market Trends That Will Affect Your Career

Our economy has changed over the past years, with profound effects on how we work and live. Here are four trends that you must consider in making your career plans.

1. Education Pays

I'm sure you won't be surprised to learn that people with higher levels of education and training have higher average earnings. The data that follows comes from the U.S. Department of Labor. I've selected data to show you the median earnings for people with various levels of education. (The median is the point where half earn more and half earn less.) Based on this information, I computed the earnings advantage of people at various education levels over those who did not graduate from high school. I've also included information showing the average percentage of people at that educational level who are unemployed.

Earnings for Year-Round, Full-Time Workers Age 25 and Over, by Educational Attainment

Level of Education	Median Annual Earnings	Premium Over High School Dropouts	Unemployment Rate
Master's degree	$53,200	$33,400	2.9%
Bachelor's degree	45,000	25,200	3.3
Associate degree	33,600	13,800	4.0
Some college, no degree	31,100	11,300	5.2
High school graduate	27,700	7,900	5.5
High school dropout	19,800	—	8.8

Source: Bureau of Labor Statistics

As you can see in the table, the earnings difference between a college graduate and someone with a high school education is $17,300 a year—enough to buy a nice car, make a down payment on a house, or even take a few months' vacation for two to Europe. As you see, over a lifetime, this earnings difference will make an enormous difference in lifestyle.

The table makes it very clear that those with more training and education earn more than those with less and experience lower levels of unemployment. Jobs that require education and training beyond high school are projected to grow significantly faster than jobs that do not. People with higher levels of education and training are less likely to be unemployed and, when they are, they tend to remain unemployed for shorter periods of time. There are always exceptions, but it is quite clear that a college education results in higher earnings and lower rates of unemployment.

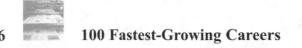

2. Knowledge of Computer and Other Technologies Is Increasingly Important

As you look over the jobs in this book, you may notice that many require computer or technical skills. Even jobs that do not appear to be technical often call for computer literacy. Managers, for example, are often expected to understand and use spreadsheet, word-processing, and database software.

In most fields, people without job-related technical and computer skills will have a more difficult time finding good opportunities because they are often competing with those who have these skills. Employers tend to hire people with the skills they need, and people without these abilities won't get the best jobs. So, no matter what your age, consider upgrading your job-related computer and technology skills if you need to—and plan to stay up-to-date.

3. Ongoing Education and Training Are Essential

School and work once were separate activities, and most people did not go back to school after they began working. But with rapid changes in technology, most people are now required to learn throughout their work lives. Jobs are constantly upgraded, and today's jobs often cannot be handled by people who have only the knowledge and skills that were adequate for workers a few years ago.

To remain competitive, you will need to constantly upgrade your technology and other job-related skills. This may include taking formal courses, reading work-related materials and Web sites, signing up for on-the-job training, or participating in other forms of education. Upgrading your work skills on an ongoing basis is no longer optional for most jobs.

4. Good Career Planning Is More Important Than Ever

Most people spend more time watching TV in a week than they spend on career planning during an entire year. Yet most people will change their jobs many times and make major career changes five to seven times. For this reason, it is important to spend time considering your career options and preparing to advance.

While you probably picked up this book for its information on jobs, it also provides a great deal of information on career planning. For example, Part I offers an assessment to match your skills to the fastest-growing jobs. Part III gives good career and job search advice. Part IV has useful information on labor market trends. I urge you to read these and related materials because career-planning and job-seeking skills are the keys to surviving in this economy.

Tips on Using This Book

This book is based on information from a variety of government sources and includes the most up-to-date and accurate data available. The job descriptions are well written and pack a lot of information into a brief format. *100 Fastest-Growing Careers* can be used in many ways, and this discussion provides tips for the following individuals:

★ Students and others exploring career, education, or training alternatives

★ Job seekers

★ Employers and business people

★ Counselors, instructors, career specialists, librarians, and other professionals

Tips for People Exploring Career, Education, or Training Alternatives

100 Fastest-Growing Careers is an excellent resource for anyone exploring career, education, or training alternatives. Many people do not have a good idea of what they want to do in their careers. Others may be considering additional training or education but may not know what sort of training they should get. If you are one of these people, this book can help in several ways.

Review the list of jobs. Trust yourself. Research studies indicate that most people have a good sense of their interests. Your interests can be used to guide you to career options you should consider in more detail.

Begin by looking over the occupations listed in the table of contents. Look at all the jobs, because you may identify previously overlooked possibilities. If other people will be using this book, please don't mark in it. Instead, on a separate sheet of paper, list the jobs that interest you. Or make a photocopy of the table of contents and use it to mark the jobs that interest you.

Next, look up and carefully read the descriptions of the jobs that most interest you in Part II. A quick review will often eliminate one or more of these jobs based on pay, working conditions, education required, or other considerations. After you have identified the three or four jobs that seem most interesting, research each one more thoroughly before making any important decisions.

Match your skills to the jobs in this book using the Job-Match Grid. Another way to identify possible job options is to answer questions about your skills and job preferences in Part I, "Using the Job-Match Grid to Choose a Career." This section will help you focus your job options and concentrate your research on a handful of job descriptions.

Study the jobs and their training and education requirements. Too many people decide to obtain additional training or education without knowing much about the jobs the training will lead to. Reviewing the descriptions in this book is one way to learn more about an occupation before you enroll in an education or training program. If you are currently a student, the job descriptions in this book can help you decide on a major course of study or learn more about the jobs for which your studies are preparing you.

Do not be too quick to eliminate a job that interests you. If a job requires more education or training than you currently have, you can obtain this training in many ways.

Don't abandon your past experience and education too quickly. If you have significant work experience, training, or education, do not abandon it too quickly. Many people have changed careers after carefully considering what they wanted to do and found that the skills they already had could still be used.

100 Fastest-Growing Careers can help you explore career options in several ways. First, on a separate sheet of paper, list the skills needed in the jobs you have held in the past. Then, using the descriptions in this book as a reference, do the same for jobs that interest you now. By comparing the lists, you will be able to identify skills you used in previous jobs that you could also use in jobs that interest you for the future. These "transferable" skills form the basis for moving to a new career.

You can also identify skills you have developed or used in nonwork activities, such as hobbies, family responsibilities, volunteer work, school, the military, and extracurricular involvements.

If you want to stay with your current employer, the job descriptions can also help. For example, you may identify jobs within your organization that offer more rewarding work, higher pay, or other advantages over your present job. Read the descriptions related to these jobs, because you may be able to transfer into another job rather than leave the organization.

performing routine tasks under close supervision. Experienced workers usually undertake more difficult tasks and are expected to perform with less supervision.

Some job descriptions mention common alternative job titles or occupational specialties. For example, the job description on accountants and auditors discusses a few specialties, such as public accountants, management accountants, and internal auditors.

Information in this section may be updated from earlier editions for several reasons. One is the emergence of occupational specialties. Information also may be updated due to changing technology that affects the way in which a job is performed. Or job duties may be affected by modifications to business practices, such as restructuring or changes in response to government regulations. An example is paralegals and legal assistants, who are increasingly being utilized by law firms in order to lower costs and increase the efficiency and quality of legal services.

Many sources are consulted in researching the nature of the work section or any other section of a job description. Usual sources include articles in newspapers, magazines, and professional journals. Useful information also appears on the Web sites of professional associations, unions, and trade groups. Information found on the Internet or in periodicals is verified through interviews with individuals employed in the occupation; professional associations; unions; and others with occupational knowledge, such as university professors and counselors in career centers.

Working Conditions

This section identifies the typical hours worked, the workplace environment, physical activities, susceptibility to injury, special equipment, and the extent of travel required. In many occupations, people work regular business hours—40 hours a week, Monday through Friday—but many do not. The work setting can range from a hospital, to a mall, to an outdoor site. Truck drivers might be susceptible to injury, while paramedics have high job-related stress. Some workers may wear protective clothing or equipment, do physically demanding work, or travel frequently.

Information on various worker characteristics, such as the average number of hours worked per week, is obtained from the Current Population Survey (CPS)—a survey of households conducted by the U.S. Census Bureau for the Bureau of Labor Statistics.

Training, Other Qualifications, and Advancement

After knowing what a job is all about, it is important to understand how to prepare for it. This section describes the most significant sources of education and training, including the education or training preferred by employers, the typical length of training, and the possibilities for advancement. Job skills sometimes are acquired through high school, informal on-the-job training, formal training (including apprenticeships), the U.S. Armed Forces, home study, hobbies, or previous work experience. For example, sales experience is particularly important for many sales jobs. Many professional jobs, on the other hand, require formal postsecondary education—postsecondary vocational or technical training, or college, postgraduate, or professional education.

In addition to training requirements, this book mentions desirable skills, aptitudes, and personal characteristics. For some entry-level jobs, personal characteristics are more important than formal training. Employers generally seek people who read, write, and speak well; compute accurately; think logically; learn quickly; get along with others; and demonstrate dependability.

Some occupations require certification or licensing for entry, advancement, or independent practice. Certification or licensing usually requires completing courses and passing examinations. Some occupations have numerous professional credentials granted by different organizations. In this case, the most widely recognized organizations are listed in this book.

Many occupations increasingly are requiring workers to participate in continuing education or training in relevant skills, either to keep up with the changes in their occupation or to improve their advancement opportunities.

Some job descriptions list the number of training programs. For example, the job description on pharmacists indicates the number of colleges of pharmacy accredited by the American Council on Pharmaceutical Education. The minimum requirements for federal government employment cited in some job descriptions are based on standards set by the U.S. Office of Personnel Management.

The training section may focus on changes in educational, certification, or licensing requirements, such as an increase in the number of hours of required training or in the number of states requiring a license.

Employment

This section reports the number of jobs that the occupation provides, the key industries in which those jobs were found, and the number or proportion of self-employed workers in the occupation, if significant. When significant, the geographic distribution of jobs and the proportion of part-time workers (those working less than 35 hours a week) are mentioned.

Job Outlook

In planning for the future, it is important to consider potential job opportunities. This section describes the factors that will result in employment change.

Many factors are examined in developing the employment projections. One is job growth or decline in industries that employ a significant percentage of workers in the occupation. If workers are concentrated in an industry that is growing rapidly, their employment will likely also grow rapidly. For example, the growing need for business expertise is fueling demand for consulting services. Hence, management, scientific, and technical consulting services is projected to be among the fastest-growing industries through 2014. Projected rapid growth in this industry helps to spur faster-than-average growth in employment of management analysts.

Demographic changes, which affect what services are required, can influence occupational growth or decline. For example, an aging population demands more health-care workers, from registered nurses to pharmacists.

Technological change is another key factor. New technology can either create new job opportunities or eliminate jobs by making workers obsolete. The Internet has increased the demand for workers in the computer and information technology fields, such as computer support specialists and systems administrators.

Another factor affecting job growth or decline is changes in business practices, such as restructuring businesses or outsourcing (contracting out) work. The substitution of one product or service for another can affect employment projections as well.

Competition from foreign trade usually has a negative impact on employment. Often, foreign manufacturers can produce goods more cheaply than they can be produced in the United States, and the cost savings can be passed on in the form of lower prices with which U.S. manufacturers cannot compete. Increased international competition is a major reason for the decline in employment among textile, apparel, and furnishings workers.

In some cases, this book mentions that an occupation is likely to provide numerous job openings. This information reflects the projected change in employment, as well as replacement needs. Large occupations that have high turnover generally provide the most job openings—reflecting the need to replace workers who transfer to other occupations or who stop working.

Some job descriptions discuss the relationship between the number of job seekers and the number of job openings. In some occupations, there is a rough balance between job seekers and job openings, resulting in good opportunities. In other occupations, employers may report difficulty finding qualified applicants, resulting in excellent job opportunities. Still other occupations are characterized by a surplus of applicants, leading to keen competition for jobs. Variation in job opportunities by industry, educational attainment, size of firm, or geographic location also may be discussed. Even in crowded occupations, job openings exist. Good students or highly qualified individuals should not be deterred from undertaking training for, or seeking entry into, those occupations.

Key Phrases Used in the Job Descriptions

The tables below explain how to interpret the key phrases used to describe projected changes in employment. They also explain the terms used to describe the relationship between the number of job openings and the number of job seekers.

Changing Employment Between 2004 and 2014

If the Statement Reads:	Employment Is Projected to:
Grow much faster than average	Increase 27 percent or more
Grow faster than average	Increase 18 to 26 percent
Grow about as fast as average	Increase 9 to 17 percent
Grow more slowly than average	Increase 0 to 8 percent
Decline	Decrease any amount

Opportunities and Competition for Jobs

If the Statement Reads:	Job Openings Compared with Job Seekers May Be:
Very good to excellent opportunities	More numerous
Good or favorable opportunities	In rough balance
May face or can expect keen competition	Fewer

Earnings

This section discusses typical earnings and how workers are compensated—by annual salaries, hourly wages, commissions, piece rates, tips, or bonuses. Within every occupation, earnings vary by experience, responsibility, performance, tenure, and geographic area. Almost every job description contains earnings data for wage and salary workers. Information on earnings in the major industries in which the occupation is employed may be given as well.

In addition to presenting earnings data from Bureau of Labor Statistics sources, some job descriptions contain additional earnings data from non-BLS sources. Starting and average salaries of federal workers are based on 2005 data from the U.S. Office of Personnel Management. The National Association of Colleges and Employers supplies information on average salary offers in 2005 for students graduating with a bachelor's, master's, or Ph.D. degree in certain fields. A few job descriptions contain additional earnings information from other sources, such as unions, professional associations, and private companies.

Benefits account for a significant portion of total compensation costs to employers. Benefits such as paid vacation, health insurance, and sick leave may not be mentioned, because they are so widespread. In some job descriptions, the absence of these traditional benefits is pointed out. Although not as common as traditional benefits, flexible hours and profit-sharing plans may be offered to attract and retain highly qualified workers. Less common benefits also include childcare, tuition for dependents, housing assistance, summers off, and free or discounted merchandise or services. For certain occupations, the percentage of workers affiliated with a union is listed.

Related Occupations

Occupations involving similar duties, skills, interests, education, and training are listed.

Sources of Additional Information

No single publication can describe all aspects of an occupation. Thus, this book lists the mailing addresses of associations, government agencies, unions, and other organizations that can provide occupational information. In some cases, toll-free telephone numbers and Internet addresses also are listed. Free or relatively inexpensive publications offering more information may be mentioned; some of these publications also may be available in libraries, in school career centers, in guidance offices, or on the Internet.

Part III: Quick Job Search—Seven Steps to Getting a Good Job in Less Time

For more than 20 years, I've been helping people find better jobs in less time. If you have ever experienced unemployment, you know that it is not pleasant. Unemployment is something most people want to get over quickly—in fact, the quicker the better. Part III will give you some techniques to help.

I know that most of you who read this book want to improve yourselves. You want to consider career and training options that lead to a better job and life in whatever way you define this—better pay, more flexibility, more-enjoyable or more-meaningful work, proving to your mom that you really can do anything you set your mind to, and other reasons. That is why I include advice on career planning and job search in Part III. It includes the basics that are most important in planning your career and in reducing the time it takes to get a job. I hope it will make you think about what is important to you in the long run.

Part III showcases professionally written resumes for some of America's fastest-growing jobs. Use these as examples when creating your own resume. I know you will resist completing the activities in Part III, but consider this: It is often not the best person who gets the job, but the best job seeker. People who do their career planning and job search homework often get jobs over those with better credentials because they have these distinct advantages:

1. **They get more interviews,** including many for jobs that will never be advertised.
2. **They do better in interviews.**

People who understand what they want and what they have to offer employers present their skills more convincingly and are much better at answering problem questions. And, because they have learned more about job search techniques, they are likely to get more interviews with employers who need the skills they have.

Doing better in interviews often makes the difference between getting a job offer and sitting at home. And spending time planning your career can make an enormous difference to your happiness and lifestyle over time. So please consider reading Part III and completing its activities. I suggest you schedule a time right now to at least read it. An hour or so spent there can help you do just enough better in your career planning, job seeking, and interviewing to make the difference.

Part IV: Important Trends in Jobs and Industries

This part is made up of very good articles and charts on labor market trends. These articles come directly from U.S. Department of Labor sources and are interesting, well written, and short. They will give you a good idea of factors that will impact your career in the years to come.

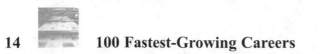

Other Major Career Information Sources

The information in this book will be very useful, but you may want or need additional facts and guidance. Keep in mind that the job descriptions here cover major jobs and not the many more-specialized jobs that are often related to them. Each job description in this book provides some sources of information related to that job, but here are additional resources to consider. All are available through JIST Publishing.

Occupational Outlook Handbook (or the *OOH*): Updated every two years by the U.S. Department of Labor, this book provides descriptions of about 270 major jobs covering more than 90 percent of the workforce. The *OOH* is the source of the job descriptions used in this book.

Enhanced Occupational Outlook Handbook: This resource includes all descriptions in the *OOH* plus descriptions of more than 6,000 more-specialized jobs that are related to them.

*O*NET Dictionary of Occupational Titles:* This book is the only printed source of the jobs described in the U.S. Department of Labor's Occupational Information Network (O*NET) database.

New Guide for Occupational Exploration: This important reference features an intuitive system based on extensive research to organize more than 900 jobs into 16 major interest areas and 117 more-specific work groups. The interest areas are based on U.S. Department of Education career clusters to closely link interests, learning, and occupations.

Best Jobs for the 21st Century: This best-selling book includes descriptions for the 500 jobs with the best combination of earnings, growth, and number of openings. Useful lists make jobs easy to explore (examples: highest-paying jobs by level of education or training; best jobs overall; and best jobs for different ages, personality types, interests, and more). Other books in the series include *200 Best Jobs for College Graduates, 300 Best Jobs Without a Four-Year Degree, 50 Best Jobs for Your Personality, 250 Best Jobs Through Apprenticeships, 40 Best Fields for Your Career, 225 Best Jobs for Baby Boomers,* and *250 Best-Paying Jobs.*

Exploring Careers—A Young Person's Guide to 1,000 Jobs: For youth in grades 7–12 exploring career and education opportunities, this book covers 1,000 job options in an interesting and useful format. Featured are profiles of real people at work, "skill samplers" that help youths better understand whether they have the skills required for certain jobs, and brief descriptions of jobs in logical groups.

Young Person's Occupational Outlook Handbook: This popular resource offers age-appropriate descriptions for each job in the *Occupational Outlook Handbook.* Very easy to use and understand, for grades 4 on.

www.CareerOINK.com: This Web site provides more than 14,000 job descriptions and a variety of useful ways to explore them.

Part I

Using the Job-Match Grid to Choose a Career

By the Editors at JIST

This book describes so many occupations—how can you choose the best job for you? This section is your answer! It can help you to identify the jobs where your abilities will be valued, and you can rule out jobs that have certain characteristics you'd rather avoid. You will respond to a series of statements and use the Job-Match Grid to match your skills and preferences to the most appropriate jobs in this book.

So grab a pencil and get ready to mark up the following sections. Or, if someone else will be using this book, find a sheet of paper and get ready to take notes.

Thinking About Your Skills

Everybody knows that skills are important for getting and keeping a job. Employers expect you to list relevant skills on your resume. They ask about your skills in interviews. And they expect you to develop skills on the job so that you will remain productive as new technologies and new work situations emerge.

But maybe you haven't thought about how closely skills are related to job satisfaction. For example, let's say you have enough communication skills to hold a certain job where these skills are used heavily, but you wouldn't really *enjoy* using them. In that case, this job probably would be a bad choice for you. You need to identify a job that will use the skills that you *do* enjoy using.

That's why you need to take a few minutes to think about your skills: the ones you're good at and the ones you like using. The checklists that follow can help you do this. On each of the seven skills checklists that follow, use numbers to indicate how much you agree with each statement:

3 = I strongly agree

2 = I agree

1 = There's some truth to this

0 = This doesn't apply to me

Artistic Skills

_________ I am an amateur artist.

_________ I have musical talent.

(continued)

(continued)

________ I enjoy planning home makeovers.
________ I am good at performing onstage.
________ I enjoy taking photos or shooting videos.
________ I am good at writing stories, poems, articles, or essays.
________ I have enjoyed taking ballet or other dance lessons.
________ I like to cook and plan meals.
________ I can sketch a good likeness of something or somebody.
________ Playing music or singing is a hobby of mine.
________ I have a good sense of visual style.
________ I have participated in amateur theater.
________ I like to express myself through writing.
________ I can prepare tasty meals better than most people.
________ I have a flair for creating attractive designs.
________ I learn new dance steps or routines easily.
________ **Total for Artistic Skills**

A note for those determined to work in the arts: Before you move on to the next skill, take a moment to decide whether working in some form of art is essential to you. Some people have exceptional talent and interest in a certain art form and are unhappy unless they are working in that art form—or until they have given their best shot at trying to break into it. If you are that kind of person, the total score shown above doesn't really matter. In fact, you may have given a 3 to just *one* of the statements above, but if you care passionately about your art form, you should toss out ordinary arithmetic and change the total to 100.

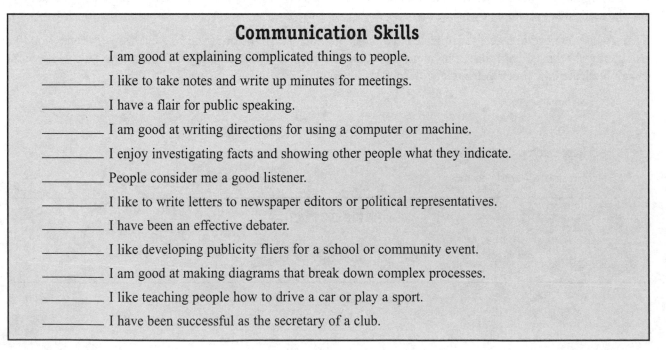

Communication Skills

________ I am good at explaining complicated things to people.
________ I like to take notes and write up minutes for meetings.
________ I have a flair for public speaking.
________ I am good at writing directions for using a computer or machine.
________ I enjoy investigating facts and showing other people what they indicate.
________ People consider me a good listener.
________ I like to write letters to newspaper editors or political representatives.
________ I have been an effective debater.
________ I like developing publicity fliers for a school or community event.
________ I am good at making diagrams that break down complex processes.
________ I like teaching people how to drive a car or play a sport.
________ I have been successful as the secretary of a club.

_________ I enjoy speaking at group meetings or worship services.

_________ I have a knack for choosing the most effective word.

_________ I enjoy tutoring young people.

_________ Technical manuals are not hard for me to understand.

_________ **Total for Communication Skills**

Interpersonal Skills

_________ I am able to make people feel that I understand their point of view.

_________ I enjoy working collaboratively.

_________ I often can make suggestions to people without sounding critical of them.

_________ I enjoy soliciting clothes, food, and other supplies for needy people.

_________ I am good at "reading" people to tell what's on their minds.

_________ I have a lot of patience with people who are doing something for the first time.

_________ People consider me outgoing.

_________ I enjoy taking care of sick relatives, friends, or neighbors.

_________ I am good at working out conflicts between friends or family members.

_________ I enjoy serving as a host or hostess for houseguests.

_________ People consider me a team player.

_________ I enjoy meeting new people and finding common interests.

_________ I am good at fundraising for school groups, teams, or community organizations.

_________ I like to train or care for animals.

_________ I often know what to say to defuse a tense situation.

_________ I have enjoyed being an officer or advisor for a youth group.

_________ **Total for Interpersonal Skills**

Managerial Skills

_________ I am good at inspiring people to work together toward a goal.

_________ I tend to use time wisely and not procrastinate.

_________ I usually know when I have enough information to make a decision.

_________ I enjoy planning and arranging programs for school or a community organization.

_________ I am not reluctant to take responsibility when things turn out wrong.

_________ I have enjoyed being a leader of a scout troop or other such group.

_________ I often can figure out what motivates somebody.

_________ People trust me to speak on their behalf and represent them fairly.

_________ I like to help organize things at home, such as shopping lists and budgets.

(continued)

(continued)

_________ I have been successful at recruiting members for a club or other organization.

_________ I have enjoyed helping run a school or community fair or carnival.

_________ People find me persuasive.

_________ I enjoy buying large quantities of food or other products for an organization.

_________ I have a knack for identifying abilities in other people.

_________ I am able to get past details and look at the big picture.

_________ I am good at delegating authority rather than trying to do everything myself.

_________ **Total for Managerial Skills**

Mathematics Skills

_________ I have always done well in math classes.

_________ I enjoy balancing checkbooks for family members.

_________ I can make mental calculations quickly.

_________ I enjoy calculating sports statistics or keeping score.

_________ Preparing family income tax returns is not hard for me.

_________ I like to tutor young people in math.

_________ I have taken or plan to take courses in statistics or calculus.

_________ I enjoy budgeting the family expenditures.

_________ **Subtotal for Mathematics Skills**

x 2 **Multiply by 2**

_________ **Total for Mathematics Skills**

Mechanical Skills

_________ I have a good sense of how mechanical devices work.

_________ I like to tinker with my car or motorcycle.

_________ I can understand diagrams of machinery or electrical wiring.

_________ I enjoy installing and repairing home stereo or computer equipment.

_________ I like looking at the merchandise in a building-supply warehouse store.

_________ I can sometimes fix household appliances when they break down.

_________ I have enjoyed building model airplanes, automobiles, or boats.

_________ I can do minor plumbing and electrical installations in the home.

_________ **Subtotal for Mechanical Skills**

x 2 **Multiply by 2**

_________ **Total for Mechanical Skills**

Science Skills

_________ Some of my best grades have been in science classes.

_________ I enjoy tweaking my computer's settings to make it run better.

_________ I have a good understanding of the systems and organs of the human body.

_________ I have enjoyed performing experiments for a science fair.

_________ I have taken or plan to take college-level courses in science.

_________ I like to read about new breakthroughs in science and technology.

_________ I know how to write programs in a computer language.

_________ I enjoy reading medical or scientific magazines.

_________ **Subtotal for Science Skills**

x 2 **Multiply by 2**

_________ **Total for Science Skills**

Finding Your Skills on the Job-Match Grid

Okay, you've made a lot of progress so far. Now it's time to review what you've said about skills so you can use these insights to sort through the jobs listed on the Job-Match Grid.

Look at your totals for the seven skills listed previously. Enter your totals in the left column on this scorecard:

Total	Skill	Rank
_________	Artistic	_________
_________	Communication	_________
_________	Interpersonal	_________
_________	Managerial	_________
_________	Mathematics	_________
_________	Mechanical	_________
_________	Science	_________

Next, enter the rank of each skill in the right column—that is, the highest-scored skill gets ranked #1, the next-highest #2, and so forth. **Important:** Keep in mind that *the numbers in the Total column are only a rough guideline*. If you feel that a skill should be ranked higher or lower than its numerical total would suggest, *go by your impressions rather than just by the numbers*.

Now turn to the Job-Match Grid and find the columns for your #1-ranked and #2-ranked skills. Move down through the grid, going from page to page, and notice what symbols appear in those columns. If a row of the grid has a black circle (●) in *both* columns, circle the occupation name—or, if someone else will be using this book, jot down the name on a piece of paper. These occupations use a high level of both skills, or the skills are essential to these jobs.

Go through the Job-Match Grid a second time, looking at the column for your #3-ranked skill. If a *job you have already circled* has a black circle (●) or a bull's-eye (◉) in the column for your #3-ranked skill, put a check mark next to the occupation name. If none of your selected jobs has a black circle or a bull's-eye in this column, look for a white circle (○) and mark these jobs with check marks.

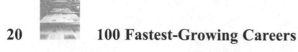

A second note for those determined to work in the arts: If a *particular* art form is essential for you to work in, you almost certainly know which occupations involve that art form and which don't. So not every job that has a black circle (●) in the "Artistic" column is going to interest you. Circle only the jobs that have a black circle in this column that *are* related to your art form (if you're not sure, look at the description of the occupation in this book) and that also have a symbol of some kind (●, ◉, or ○) in the column for your #2-ranked skill. As you circle each job, also give it a check mark, because there will be so few of them that you won't need to go through the Job-Match Grid a second time. If you have a more general interest in the arts, follow the general instructions.

Your Hot List of Possible Career Matches

Now that you have made a first and second cut of the jobs on the Job-Match Grid, you can focus on the occupations that look most promising at this point. Write the names of the occupations that are both *circled* and *checked:*

______________________________	______________________________
______________________________	______________________________
______________________________	______________________________
______________________________	______________________________
______________________________	______________________________
______________________________	______________________________
______________________________	______________________________

This is your Hot List of occupations that you are going to explore in detail *if* they are not eliminated by certain important job-related factors that you'll consider next.

Thinking About Other Job-Related Factors

Next, you need to consider four other job-related factors:

- ★ Economic sensitivity
- ★ Outdoor work
- ★ Physically demanding work
- ★ Hazardous conditions

Economic Sensitivity

You've read about how our nation's economy has gone up and down over the years. When the economy is on an upswing, there are more job openings, but when it veers downward toward recession, jobs are harder to find.

Are you aware that these trends affect some occupations more than others? For example, during an economic upswing, people do more vacation traveling and businesses send more workers on business trips. This keeps travel agencies very busy, so they need to hire more travel agents. When the economy is going down, people cut back on their vacation travel, businesses tell their workers to use teleconferencing instead of business trips, and travel agents are not in demand. Some may be laid off, and people who want to enter this field may find very few openings. By contrast, most jobs in the health-care field are not sensitive to the economy, and automotive mechanics are just as busy as ever during economic slowdowns because people want to keep their old cars running.

So this issue of economic sensitivity (and its opposite, job security) is one that may affect which occupation you choose. Some people want to avoid economically sensitive occupations because they don't want to risk losing their job (or having difficulty finding a job) during times of recession. Other people are willing to risk being in an economically sensitive occupation because they want to profit from the periods when both the economy and the occupation are booming.

How important is it to you to be in an occupation that *doesn't* go through periods of boom and bust along with the nation's economy? Check one:

_________ It doesn't matter to me.

_________ It's not important, but I'd consider it.

_________ It's somewhat important to me.

_________ It's very important to me.

If you answered "It doesn't matter to me," skip to the next section, "Outdoor Work." Otherwise, turn back to the Job-Match Grid and find the column for "Economically Sensitive."

If you answered "It's not important, but I'd consider it," see whether any of the jobs on your Hot List have a black circle (●) in this column. If so, cross them off and write an "E" next to them.

If you answered "It's somewhat important to me," see whether any of the jobs on your Hot List have a black circle (●) or a bull's-eye (◉) in this column. If so, cross them off and write an "E" next to them.

If you answered "It's very important to me," see whether any of the jobs on your Hot List have *any* symbol (●, ◉, or ○) in this column. If so, cross them off and write an "E" next to them.

Outdoor Work

Some people prefer to work indoors in a climate-controlled setting, such as an office, a classroom, a factory floor, a laboratory, or a hospital room. Other people would rather work primarily in an outdoor setting, such as a forest, an athletic field, or a city street. And some would enjoy a job that alternates between indoor and outdoor activities.

What is *your* preference for working indoors or outdoors? Check one:

_________ It's very important to me to work **indoors.**

_________ I'd prefer to work mostly **indoors.**

_________ Either indoors or outdoors is okay with me.

_________ I'd prefer to work mostly **outdoors.**

_________ It's very important to me to work **outdoors.**

If you answered "Either indoors or outdoors is okay with me," skip to the next section, "Physically Demanding Work." Otherwise, turn to the Job-Match Grid and find the column for "Outdoor Work."

If you answered "It's very important to me to work **indoors,**" see whether any of the jobs on your Hot List have *any* symbol (●, ◉, or ○) in this column. If so, cross them off and write an "O" next to them.

If you answered "I'd prefer to work mostly **indoors,**" see whether any of the jobs on your Hot List have a black circle (●) in this column. If so, cross them off and write an "O" next to them.

If you answered "I'd prefer to work mostly **outdoors,**" see whether any of the jobs on your Hot List have *no* symbol—just a blank—in this column. If so, cross them off and write an "O" next to them. All the jobs remaining on your Hot List should have some kind of symbol (●, ◉, or ○) in this column.

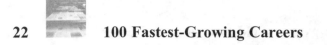

If you answered "It's very important to me to work **outdoors,**" see whether any of the jobs on your Hot List have either *no* symbol or just a white circle (○) in this column. If so, cross them off and write an "O" next to them. All the jobs remaining on your Hot List should have either a black circle (●) or a bull's-eye (◉) in this column.

Physically Demanding Work

Jobs vary by how much muscle power they require you to use. Some jobs require a lot of lifting heavy loads, standing for long times, climbing, or stooping. On other jobs, the heaviest thing you lift is a notebook or telephone handset, and most of the time you are sitting. Still other jobs require only a moderate amount of physical exertion.

What is *your* preference for the physical demands of work? Check one:

________ I don't care whether my work requires heavy or light physical exertion.

________ I want my work to require only light physical exertion.

________ I want my work to require no more than occasional moderate physical exertion.

________ I want my work to require moderate physical exertion, with occasional heavy exertion.

________ I want my work to require a lot of heavy physical exertion.

If you answered "I don't care whether my work requires heavy or light physical exertion," skip to the next section, "Hazardous Conditions." Otherwise, turn to the Job-Match Grid and find the column for "Physically Demanding Work."

If you answered "I want my work to require only light physical exertion," see whether any of the jobs on your Hot List have *any* symbol (●, ◉, or ○) in this column. If so, cross them off and write a "P" next to them.

If you answered "I want my work to require no more than occasional moderate physical exertion," see whether any of the jobs on your Hot List have either a black circle (●) or a bull's-eye (◉) in this column. If so, cross them off and write a "P" next to them.

If you answered "I want my work to require moderate physical exertion, with occasional heavy exertion," see whether any of the jobs on your Hot List have either a black circle (●), a white circle (○), or *no* symbol in this column. If so, cross them off and write a "P" next to them. All the jobs remaining on your Hot List should have a bull's-eye (◉) in this column.

If you answered "I want my work to require a lot of heavy physical exertion," see whether any of the jobs on your Hot List have either *no* symbol or just a white circle (○) or a bull's-eye (◉) in this column. If so, cross them off and write a "P" next to them. All the jobs remaining on your Hot List should have a black circle (●) in this column.

Hazardous Conditions

Every day about 9,000 Americans sustain a disabling injury on the job. Many workers have jobs that require them to deal with hazardous conditions, such as heat, noise, radiation, germs, toxins, or dangerous machinery. These workers need to wear protective clothing or follow safety procedures to avoid injury.

What is *your* preference regarding hazardous conditions on the job? Check one:

________ I want hazardous workplace conditions to be very unlikely.

________ I want hazardous conditions to be unlikely or minor.

________ I am willing to accept some major workplace hazards.

If you answered "I am willing to accept some major workplace hazards," skip to the section "Geographically Concentrated Jobs." Otherwise, turn to the Job-Match Grid and find the column for "Hazardous Conditions."

If you answered "I want hazardous workplace conditions to be very unlikely," see whether any of the jobs on your Hot List have *any* symbol (●, ⦿, or ○) in this column. If so, cross them off and write an "H" next to them.

If you answered "I want hazardous conditions to be unlikely or minor," see whether any of the jobs on your Hot List have a black circle (●) in this column. If so, cross them off and write an "H" next to them.

If Every Job on Your Hot List Is Now Crossed Off

It's possible that you have crossed off *all* the occupations on your Hot List. If so, consider these two options:

★ You may want to relax some of your requirements. Maybe you were too hasty in crossing off some of the jobs. Take another look at the four job-related factors and decide whether you could accept work that doesn't meet the requirements you set previously—for example, work that is not as much indoors or outdoors as you specified. If you change your mind now, you can tell by the letters in the margin which jobs you crossed off for which reasons.

★ You may want to add to your Hot List by considering additional skills. So far you have considered only occupations that involve your top three skills. You may want to add jobs that have a black circle (●) or a bull's-eye (⦿) in the column for your #4-ranked skill and possibly for your #5-ranked skill. If you do add any jobs, be sure to repeat your review of the four job-related factors.

Evaluating Occupations Described in This Book

You are now ready to make the jump from the checklists to the detailed information about jobs in this book. The first detailed issue you need to consider is whether you will be able to find work in your area or have to relocate.

Geographically Concentrated Jobs

Turn to the Job-Match Grid one more time and find the column for "Geographically Concentrated." Look at all the occupations on your Hot List that haven't been crossed off. If there is a symbol in this column, especially a bull's-eye (⦿) or a black circle (●), it means that employment for this occupation tends to be concentrated in certain geographic areas. For example, most acting jobs are found in big cities because that's where you'll find most theaters, TV studios, and movie studios. Most water transportation jobs are found on the coasts and beside major lakes and rivers.

If a symbol shows that a Hot List occupation *is* geographically concentrated, the location of the jobs may be obvious, as in the examples of acting and water transportation. If it's not clear to you where the jobs may be found, find the occupation in "The Job Descriptions" section and look for the facts under the heading "Employment" in the description. Once you understand where most of the jobs are, you have to make some decisions:

★ **Are most of the job openings in a geographic location where I am now or would enjoy living?** If you answered "yes" to this question, repeat this exercise for all the other occupations still on your Hot List. Then jump to the next heading, "Nature of the Work." If you answered "no," proceed to the next bulleted question.

★ **If most of the job openings are in a distant place where I don't want to relocate, am I willing to take a chance and hope to be one of the few workers who get hired in an *uncommon* location?** If you answered "yes," take a good look at the Job Outlook information in the job description. If the outlook for the occupation is very good and if you expect to have some of the advantages mentioned there (such as the right degree, in some cases), taking a chance on being hired in an unusual location may be a reasonable decision. On the other hand, if the outlook is only so-so or not good and if you have no special qualifications, you probably are setting yourself up for disappointment. You should seriously consider changing your mind about this decision. At least speak to people in your area who are knowledgeable about the occupation to determine whether you have any chance of success. If you answered "no"—you are not willing to take a chance—cross off this occupation and write a "G" next to it. (If you now have no jobs left on your Hot List, see the previous section titled "If Every Job on Your Hot List Is Now Crossed Off.")

Nature of the Work

When you read the job description for an occupation on your Hot List, you will see that the "Nature of the Work" section discusses what workers do on the job, what tools and equipment they use, and how closely they are supervised. Keep in mind that this is an overview of a diverse collection of workers, and in fact few workers perform the full set of tasks itemized here. In fact, in many cases the work force covered by the job description is so diverse that it actually divides into several occupational specialties, which are italicized.

Here are some things to think about as you read this section:

★ Note the kinds of problems, materials, and tools you will encounter on the job. Are these are a good match for your interests?

★ Also note the work activities mentioned here. Do you think they will be rewarding? Are there many that stand out as unpleasant or boring?

Working Conditions

This section in each job description identifies the typical hours worked, the workplace environment (both physical and psychological), physical activities and susceptibility to injury, special equipment, and the extent of travel required. If conditions vary between the occupational specialties, that is mentioned here. Here are some things to look for in the Working Conditions section:

★ If you have a disability, note the physical requirements that are mentioned here and consider whether you can meet these requirements with or without suitable accommodations.

★ If you're bothered by conditions such as heights, stress, or a cramped workspace, see whether this section mentions any conditions that would discourage you.

★ Note what this section says about the work schedule and the need for travel, if any. This information may be good to know if you have pressing family responsibilities or, on the other hand, a desire for unusual hours or travel.

★ If you find a working condition that bothers you, be sure to check the wording to see whether it *always* applies to the occupation or whether it only *may* apply. Even if it seems to be a condition that you cannot avoid, find out for sure by talking to people in the occupation or educators who teach related courses. Maybe you can carve out a niche that avoids the unappealing working condition.

Training, Other Qualifications, and Advancement

In the "Training, Other Qualifications, and Advancement" section, you can see how to prepare for the occupation and how to advance in it. It identifies the significant entry routes—those that are most popular and that are preferred by employers. It mentions any licensure or certification that may be necessary for entry or advancement. It also identifies the particular skills, aptitudes, and work habits that employers value. Look for these topics in this section:

★ Compare the entry requirements to your background and to the educational and training opportunities that are available to you. Be sure to consider nontraditional and informal entry routes, if any are possible, as well as the formal routes. Ask yourself, Am I willing to get the additional education or training that will be necessary? Do I have the time, money, ability, interest, and commitment?

★ Maybe you're already partway down the road to job entry. In general, you should try to use your previous education, training, and work experience rather than abandon it. Look for specifics that are already on your resume—educational accomplishments, skills, work habits—that will meet employers' expectations. If you have some of these qualifications already, this occupation may be a better career choice than some others.

Employment

The "Employment" section in the job description reports how many jobs the occupation currently provides, the industries that provide the most jobs, and the number or proportion of self-employed or part-time workers in the occupation, if significant. In this section, you'll want to pay attention to these facts:

★ Note the industries that provide most of the employment for the occupation. This knowledge can help you identify contacts who can tell you more about the work, and later it can help in your job hunting.

★ If you're interested in self-employment or part-time work, see whether these work arrangements are mentioned here.

Job Outlook

The "Job Outlook" section describes the economic forces that will affect future employment in the occupation. Here are some things to look for in this section:

★ The information here can help you identify occupations with a good job outlook so that you will have a better-than-average chance of finding work. Be alert for any mention of an advantage that you may have over other job seekers (for example, a college degree) or any other factor that might make your chances better or worse.

★ If you are highly motivated and highly qualified for a particular occupation, don't be discouraged by a bad employment outlook. Job openings occur even in shrinking or overcrowded occupations, and with exceptional talent or good personal connections, you may go on to great success.

★ These projections are the most definitive ones available, but they are not foolproof and apply only to a 10-year time span. No matter what occupation you choose, you will need to adapt to changes.

Earnings

The "Earnings" section discusses the wages for the occupation. Here are some things to keep in mind:

★ The wage figures are national averages. Actual wages in your geographic region may be considerably higher or lower. Also, an average figure means that half of the workers earn more and half earn less, and the actual salary any one worker earns can vary greatly from that average.

★ Remember to consider *all* the pluses and minuses of the job. Not every day of the work week is payday, so make your choice based on the whole occupation, not just the paycheck.

Related Occupations

The "Related Occupations" section identifies occupations that are similar to the one featured in the job description in terms of tasks, interests, skills, education, or training. You may find this section interesting for these reasons:

★ If you're interested in an occupation but not strongly committed to pursuing it, this section may suggest another occupation with similar rewards that may turn out to be a better fit. Try to research these related occupations, but keep in mind that they may not all be included in this book.

★ You may want to choose one of these occupations as your Plan B goal if your original goal should not work out. In that case, it helps to identify an occupation that involves similar kinds of problems and work settings but requires *less* education or training.

Sources of Additional Information

This section in each job description lists several sources and resources you can turn to for more information about the occupation. Try to consult at least some of these sources. This book should be only the beginning of your career decision-making process. You need more detailed information from several viewpoints to make an informed decision.

Don't rely entirely on the Web sites listed here. You especially need to talk to and observe individual workers to learn what their workdays are like, what the workers enjoy and dislike about the job, how they got hired, and what effects the job has had on other aspects of their lives. Maybe you can make contact with local workers through the local chapter of an organization listed here.

Narrowing Down Your Choices

The information in the job descriptions should help you cross more jobs off your Hot List. And what you learn by turning to other resources should help you narrow down your Hot List jobs to a few promising choices and maybe one best bet. Here are some final considerations: Have I talked to people who are actually doing this work? Am I fully aware of the pluses and minuses of this job? If there are aspects of the job that I don't like, how do I expect to avoid them or overcome them? If the odds of finding a job opening are not good, why do I expect to beat the odds? What is my Plan B goal if I lose interest in my original goal or don't succeed at it?

The Job-Match Grid

The grid on the following pages provides information about the personal skills and job characteristics for occupations covered in this book. Use the directions and questions that start at the beginning of this section to help you get the most from this grid.

Below is what the symbols on the grid represent. If a job has no symbol in a column, it means that the skill or job characteristic is not important or relevant to the job.

Personal Skills

- ● Essential or high-skill level
- ⦿ Somewhat essential or moderate-skill level
- ○ Basic-skill level

Job Characteristics

- ● Highly likely
- ⦿ Somewhat likely
- ○ A little likely

Job-Match Grid

	Personal Skills							Job Characteristics				
	Artistic	Communication	Interpersonal	Managerial	Mathematics	Mechanical	Science	Economically Sensitive	Outdoor Work	Physically Demanding Work	Hazardous Conditions	Geographically Concentrated
Accountants and auditors		○	○	⦿	●			○				
Administrative services managers	○	●	●	●	⦿			○				
Advertising, marketing, promotions, public relations, and sales managers	●	●	●	●	●	⦿		●				
Animal care and service workers		○	○		○	⦿	○	⦿	⦿	●	●	
Athletes, coaches, umpires, and related workers	⦿	⦿	⦿	●		○	○		●	●	○	
Automotive service technicians and mechanics		○	○		○	●	⦿		○	⦿	○	
Barbers, cosmetologists, and other personal appearance workers	●	⦿	○		○	⦿	○	⦿		○	○	
Bill and account collectors		○	●		●			⦿				
Bookkeeping, accounting, and auditing clerks		○	○		●			○				
Building cleaning workers	○	○			○	●		○		●	○	
Bus drivers		○	○			○			○	⦿	●	
Carpenters	⦿	○	○		⦿	●	○	●	⦿	●	●	
Cement masons, concrete finishers, segmental pavers, and terrazzo workers	○	○	○		○	●	○	●	⦿	●	○	
Chefs, cooks, and food preparation workers	●	⦿	⦿	●	○	⦿	○	●		⦿	○	
Child care workers	○	⦿	●	○	○	○			○	⦿		
Clinical laboratory technologists and technicians		⦿	○	○	●	●	●			○	○	
Computer and information systems managers		●	●	●	●	●	●	●				
Computer scientists and database administrators		⦿	○	○	●		●	○				
Computer software engineers		⦿	⦿	⦿	●	●	●	○				
Computer support specialists and systems administrators		⦿	⦿	○	⦿	●	⦿	○				
Computer systems analysts		⦿	○	○	●		●	○				
Counselors		●	●	○	○		○					
Counter and rental clerks		○	⦿		⦿			⦿		⦿		
Customer service representatives		●	●		⦿		○	○				
Demonstrators, product promoters, and models	●	●	●		○	○		⦿		⦿		
Dental assistants		⦿	⦿	○	○	●	⦿			⦿	⦿	
Dental hygienists		⦿	⦿	○	⦿	●	⦿			○	⦿	
Education administrators		●	●	●	⦿		○					
Electricians		○	○		⦿	●	⦿	●	○	⦿	●	
Emergency medical technicians and paramedics		●	●	●	○	●	●		●	●	●	

(continued)

Personal Skills: ●—Essential or high-skill level; ⦿—Somewhat essential or moderate-skill level; ○—Basic-skill level
Job Characteristics: ●—Highly likely; ⦿—Somewhat likely; ○—A little likely

(continued)

	Personal Skills							Job Characteristics				
	Artistic	Communication	Interpersonal	Managerial	Mathematics	Mechanical	Science	Economically Sensitive	Outdoor Work	Physically Demanding Work	Hazardous Conditions	Geographically Concentrated
Engineers	◉	◉	○	◉	●	●	●	◉	○	○	○	◉
Financial analysts and personal financial advisors		●	●	○	●		○	●				
Financial managers		●	●	●	●		○	◉				
Fire fighting occupations		●	○	○	○	●	○		●	●	●	
Fitness workers	○	●	●	○	○	○	○	◉	◉	●		
Food and beverage serving and related workers	○	◉	●		○			●	○	●		
Food processing occupations		○			○	●				●	●	
Gaming services occupations	○	◉	●	●	○	○		◉		●		●
Graphic designers	●	◉	◉	◉				○		○		○
Grounds maintenance workers	◉	○			○	●	○	○	●	●	◉	
Hazardous materials removal workers		○	○		○	●	●		●	●	●	
Heating, air conditioning, and refrigeration mechanics and installers		○	○		○	●	○	◉	○	◉	○	
Hotel, motel, and resort desk clerks	○	◉	●	○	○			●		◉		
Human resources assistants, except payroll and timekeeping		○	○		◉			○				
Human resources, training, and labor relations managers and specialists		●	●	●	○			○				
Instructional coordinators	○	●	●	◉	◉	◉	◉					
Lawyers		●	●	●	○		○	◉				
Licensed practical and licensed vocational nurses		◉	●	○	○	●	●			◉	◉	
Maintenance and repair workers, general		○	○		○	●	○		◉	◉	◉	
Management analysts		●	◉	○	●			○				
Market and survey researchers		●	●	○	●			◉				
Massage therapists			○							◉		
Material moving occupations		○				●		●	●	●	●	
Medical and health services managers		●	●	●	◉	◉	◉					
Medical assistants		◉	◉	○	◉	●	●			◉	◉	
Medical records and health information technicians		◉	○	○	◉		◉					
Medical scientists		◉	○	◉	●	●	●	○			○	
Medical transcriptionists		●	○	○	○	○	●					
Nursing, psychiatric, and home health aides		◉	◉	○	○	◉	○			●	●	
Occupational therapists		●	●	◉	◉	◉	◉			○	◉	
Office and administrative support worker supervisors and managers		●	●	●	◉	○		○				
Office clerks, general		○	◉		○			◉				
Painters and paperhangers	◉	○	○		○	●	○	●	●	●	○	
Paralegals and legal assistants		●	●	○	○		○	◉				

Personal Skills: ●—Essential or high-skill level; ◉—Somewhat essential or moderate-skill level; ○—Basic-skill level
Job Characteristics: ●—Highly likely; ◉—Somewhat likely; ○—A little likely

	Personal Skills							Job Characteristics				
	Artistic	Communication	Interpersonal	Managerial	Mathematics	Mechanical	Science	Economically Sensitive	Outdoor Work	Physically Demanding Work	Hazardous Conditions	Geographically Concentrated
Payroll and timekeeping clerks		○	○		◉			○				
Personal and home care aides		◉	●	○	○		○			●	◉	
Pharmacists		●	◉	◉	●	○	●			○		
Pharmacy technicians		◉	◉	○	◉	◉	◉			○		
Physical therapist assistants and aides		◉	◉	○	○	◉	◉			●	◉	
Physical therapists		●	●	○	◉	○	●			●	◉	
Physician assistants		●	●	○	●	◉	●			◉	◉	
Physicians and surgeons	◉	●	●	●	◉	●	●			◉	◉	
Pipelayers, plumbers, pipefitters, and steamfitters		○	○		○	●	◉	●	○	●	○	
Police and detectives		●	○	◉	○	●	○		●	●	●	
Property, real estate, and community association managers	○	●	●	●	○	○		○	○			
Public relations specialists	◉	●	●	○	○							◉
Radiologic technologists and technicians		◉	◉	○	●	●	◉			◉	◉	
Real estate brokers and sales agents	○	●	●	◉	◉			◉	○			
Receptionists and information clerks		●	●		◉	◉		○				
Recreation workers	○	●	●	○	○	○	○	◉	◉	●		
Registered nurses		●	●	◉	●	●	●			◉	◉	
Respiratory therapists		●	●	○	●	●	●			○	◉	
Retail salespersons	○	◉	●		○			◉				
Roofers	○	○	○		○	●	○	○	●	●	●	
Sales representatives, wholesale and manufacturing	○	●	●		◉		○	●				
Secretaries and administrative assistants	○	●	●	○	○			○				
Security guards and gaming surveillance officers		○	○	○		○		○	◉	○	●	
Social and human service assistants		◉	●				○					
Social workers		●	●	○	○		○					
Surgical technologists		◉	◉	○	●	●	●			◉	◉	
Taxi drivers and chauffeurs		○	○			○			○	◉	●	◉
Teacher assistants	◉	●	●	◉	○		◉					
Teachers—postsecondary	◉	●	●	●	●		◉					
Teachers—preschool, kindergarten, elementary, middle, and secondary	◉	●	●	●	◉	○	◉					
Teachers—self-enrichment education	◉	●	●	●	◉		◉					
Teachers—special education	◉	●	●	●	◉	○	◉					
Top executives	○	●	●	●	●		◉	○				
Truck drivers and driver/sales workers		○				○		●	○	●	●	
Veterinary technologists and technicians		◉	◉	◉	◉	●	◉	○	○	●	●	
Writers and editors	●	●	●	○	○		○					

Personal Skills: ●—Essential or high-skill level; ◉—Somewhat essential or moderate-skill level; ○—Basic-skill level
Job Characteristics: ●—Highly likely; ◉—Somewhat likely; ○—A little likely

Descriptions of the 100 Fastest-Growing Careers

This is the book's main section. It contains helpful descriptions of the 100 major occupations that have the most-favorable combined scores for projected percent increase and number of job openings through 2014. To learn a job's ranking, see the introduction.

The jobs are arranged in alphabetical order. Refer to the table of contents for a list of the jobs and the page numbers where their descriptions begin. Review the table of contents to discover occupations that interest you, and then find out more about them in this section. If you are interested in medical careers, for example, you can go through the list and quickly pinpoint those you want to learn more about. Or use the assessment in Part I to identify several possible career matches.

While the job descriptions in this part are easy to understand, the introduction provides additional information for interpreting them. Keep in mind that the descriptions present information that is average for the country. Conditions in your area and with specific employers may be quite different.

Also, you may come across jobs that sound interesting but require more education and training than you have or are considering. Don't eliminate them too soon. There are many ways to obtain education and training, and most people change careers many times. You probably have more skills than you realize that can transfer to new jobs. People often have more opportunities than barriers. Use the descriptions to learn more about possible jobs and look into the suggested resources to help you take the next step.

Accountants and Auditors

(O*NET 13-2011.01 and 13-2011.02)

Significant Points

- Most jobs require at least a bachelor's degree in accounting or a related field.
- Overall job opportunities should be favorable; jobseekers who obtain professional recognition through certification or licensure, a master's degree, proficiency in accounting and auditing computer software, or specialized expertise will have the best opportunities.
- An increase in the number of businesses, changing financial laws and regulations, and greater scrutiny of company finances will drive faster-than-average growth of accountants and auditors.

Nature of the Work

Accountants and auditors help to ensure that the nation's firms are run efficiently, its public records kept accurately, and its taxes paid properly and on time. They perform these vital functions by offering an increasingly wide array of business and accounting services, including public, management, and government accounting, as well as internal auditing, to their clients. Beyond carrying out the fundamental tasks of the occupation—preparing, analyzing, and verifying financial documents in order to provide information to clients—many accountants now are required to possess a wide range of knowledge and skills. Accountants and auditors are broadening the services they offer to include budget analysis, financial and investment planning, information technology consulting, and limited legal services.

Specific job duties vary widely among the four major fields of accounting: *public*, *management*, and *government accounting* and *internal auditing*.

Public accountants perform a broad range of accounting, auditing, tax, and consulting activities for their clients, which may be corporations, governments, nonprofit organizations, or individuals. For example, some public accountants concentrate on tax matters, such as advising companies about the tax advantages and disadvantages of certain business decisions and preparing individual income tax returns. Others offer advice in areas such as compensation or employee health care benefits, the design of accounting and data-processing systems, and the selection of controls to safeguard assets. Still others audit clients' financial statements and inform investors and authorities that the statements have been correctly prepared and reported. Public accountants, many of whom are Certified Public Accountants (CPAs), generally have their own businesses or work for public accounting firms.

Some public accountants specialize in forensic accounting—investigating and interpreting white-collar crimes such as securities fraud and embezzlement, bankruptcies and contract disputes, and other complex and possibly criminal financial transactions, including money laundering by organized criminals. Forensic accountants combine their knowledge of accounting and finance with law and investigative techniques in order to determine whether an activity is illegal. Many forensic accountants work closely with law enforcement personnel and lawyers during investigations and often appear as expert witnesses during trials.

In response to recent accounting scandals, new federal legislation restricts the nonauditing services that public accountants can provide to clients. If an accounting firm audits a client's financial statements, that same firm cannot provide advice on human resources, technology, investment banking, or legal matters, although accountants may still advise on tax issues, such as establishing a tax shelter. Accountants may still advise other clients in these areas or may provide advice within their own firm.

Management accountants—also called cost, managerial, industrial, corporate, or private accountants—record and analyze the financial information of the companies for which they work. Among their other responsibilities are budgeting, performance evaluation, cost management, and asset management. Usually, management accountants are part of executive teams involved in strategic planning or the development of new products. They analyze and interpret the financial information that corporate executives need in order to make sound business decisions. They also prepare financial reports for other groups, including stockholders, creditors, regulatory agencies, and tax authorities. Within accounting departments, management accountants may work in various areas, including financial analysis, planning and budgeting, and cost accounting.

Government accountants and auditors work in the public sector, maintaining and examining the records of government agencies and auditing private businesses and individuals whose activities are subject to government regulations or taxation. Accountants employed by federal, state, and local governments guarantee that revenues are received and expenditures are made in accordance with laws and regulations. Those employed by the federal government may work as Internal Revenue Service agents or in financial management, financial institution examination, or budget analysis and administration.

Internal auditors verify the accuracy of their organization's internal records and check for mismanagement, waste, or fraud. Internal auditing is an increasingly important area of accounting and auditing. Internal auditors examine and evaluate their firms' financial and information systems, management procedures, and internal controls to ensure that records are accurate and controls are adequate to protect against fraud and waste. They also review company operations, evaluating their efficiency, effectiveness, and compliance with corporate policies and procedures, laws, and government regulations. There are many types of highly specialized auditors, such as electronic data-processing, environmental, engineering, legal, insurance premium, bank, and health care auditors. As computer systems make information timelier, internal auditors help managers to base their decisions on actual data, rather than personal observation. Internal auditors also may recommend controls for their organization's computer system, to ensure the reliability of the system and the integrity of the data.

Computers are rapidly changing the nature of the work of most accountants and auditors. With the aid of special software packages, accountants summarize transactions in standard formats used by financial records and organize data in special formats employed in financial analysis. These accounting packages greatly reduce the amount of tedious manual work associated with data management and recordkeeping. Computers enable accountants and auditors to be more mobile and to use their clients' computer systems to extract information from databases and the Internet. As a result, a growing number of accountants and auditors with extensive computer skills are specializing in correcting problems with software or in developing software to meet unique data management and analytical needs. Accountants also are beginning to perform more technical duties, such as implementing, controlling, and auditing systems and networks, developing technology plans, and analyzing and devising budgets.

Increasingly, accountants also are assuming the role of a personal financial advisor. They not only provide clients with accounting and tax help, but also help them develop personal budgets, manage assets and investments, plan for retirement, and recognize and reduce their exposure to risks. This role is a response to clients' demands for a single trustworthy individual or firm to meet all of their financial needs. However, accountants are restricted from providing these services to clients whose financial statements they also prepare.

Working Conditions

Most accountants and auditors work in a typical office setting. Self-employed accountants may be able to do part of their work at home. Accountants and auditors employed by public accounting firms and government agencies may travel frequently to perform audits at branches of their firm, clients' places of business, or government facilities.

Most accountants and auditors generally work a standard 40-hour week, but many work longer hours, particularly if they are self-employed and have numerous clients. Tax specialists often work long hours during the tax season.

Training, Other Qualifications, and Advancement

Most accountant and auditor positions require at least a bachelor's degree in accounting or a related field. Beginning accounting and auditing positions in the federal government, for example, usually require 4 years of college (including 24 semester hours in accounting or auditing) or an equivalent combination of education and experience. Some employers prefer applicants with a master's degree in accounting, or with a master's degree in business administration with a concentration in accounting.

Previous experience in accounting or auditing can help an applicant get a job. Many colleges offer students an opportunity to gain experience through summer or part-time internship programs conducted by public accounting or business firms. In addition, practical knowledge of computers and their applications in accounting and internal auditing is a great asset for jobseekers in the accounting field.

Professional recognition through certification or licensure provides a distinct advantage in the job market. CPAs are licensed by a State Board of Accountancy. The vast majority of states require CPA candidates to be college graduates, but a few states substitute a number of years of public accounting experience for a college degree.

As of early 2005, on the basis of recommendations made by the American Institute of Certified Public Accountants (AICPA), 42 states and the District of Columbia required CPA candidates to complete 150 semester hours of college coursework—an additional 30 hours beyond the usual 4-year bachelor's degree. Another five states have adopted similar legislation that will become effective between 2006 and 2009. Colorado, Delaware, New Hampshire, and Vermont are the only states that do not require 150 semester hours. In response to this trend, many schools have altered their curricula accordingly, with most programs offering master's degrees as part of the 150 hours, so prospective accounting majors should carefully research accounting curricula and the requirements of any states in which they hope to become licensed.

All states use the four-part Uniform CPA Examination prepared by the AICPA. The 2-day CPA examination is rigorous, and only about one-quarter of those who take it each year pass every part they attempt. Candidates are not required to pass all four parts at once, but most states require candidates to pass at least two parts for partial credit and to complete all four sections within a certain period. The CPA exam is now computerized and is offered quarterly at various testing centers throughout the United States. Most states also require applicants for a CPA certificate to have some accounting experience.

The AICPA also offers members with valid CPA certificates the option to receive any or all of the Accredited in Business Valuation (ABV), Certified Information Technology Professional (CITP), or Personal Financial Specialist (PFS) designations. CPA's with these designations may claim a certain level of expertise in the nontraditional areas in which accountants are practicing ever more frequently. The ABV designation requires a written exam, as well as the completion of a minimum of 10 business valuation projects that demonstrate a candidate's experience and competence. The CITP requires payment of a fee, a written statement of intent, and the achievement of a set number of points awarded for business experience and education. Those who do not meet the required number of points may substitute a written exam. Candidates for the PFS designation also must achieve a certain level of points, based on experience and education, and must pass a written exam and submit references.

Nearly all states require CPAs and other public accountants to complete a certain number of hours of continuing professional education before their licenses can be renewed. The professional associations representing accountants sponsor numerous courses, seminars, group study programs, and other forms of continuing education.

Accountants and auditors also can seek to obtain other forms of credentials from professional societies on a voluntary basis. Voluntary certification can attest to professional competence in a specialized field of accounting and auditing. It also can certify that a recognized level of professional competence has been achieved by accountants and auditors who have acquired some skills on the job, without the formal education or public accounting work experience needed to meet the rigorous standards required to take the CPA examination.

The Institute of Management Accountants (IMA) confers the Certified Management Accountant (CMA) designation upon applicants who complete a bachelor's degree or who attain a minimum score or higher on specified graduate school entrance exams. Applicants, who must have worked at least 2 years in management accounting, also must pass a four-part examination, agree to meet continuing education requirements, and comply with standards of professional conduct. The CMA exam provides an in-depth measure of competence in areas such as financial statement analysis, working-capital policy, capital structure, valuation issues, and risk management. The CMA program is administered by the Institute of Certified Management Accountants, an affiliate of the IMA.

Graduates from accredited colleges and universities who have worked for 2 years as internal auditors and have passed a four-part examination may earn the Certified Internal Auditor (CIA) designation from the Institute of Internal Auditors (IIA). The IIA recently implemented three new specialty designations: Certification in Control Self-Assessment (CCSA), Certified Government Auditing Professional (CGAP), and Certified Financial Services Auditor (CFSA). Requirements are similar to those of the CIA. The Information Systems Audit and Control Association confers the Certified Information Systems Auditor (CISA) designation upon candidates who pass an examination and have 5 years of experience auditing information systems. Auditing or data-processing experience and a college education may be substituted for up to 2 years of work experience in this program. Accountants and auditors may hold multiple designations. For instance, an internal auditor might be a CPA, CIA, and CISA.

The Accreditation Council for Accountancy and Taxation, a satellite organization of the National Society of Public Accountants, confers four designations—Accredited Business Accountant (ABA), Accredited Tax Advisor (ATA), Accredited Tax Preparer (ATP) and Elder Care Specialist (ECS)—on accountants specializing in tax preparation for small and medium-sized businesses. Candidates for the ABA must pass an exam; candidates for the ATA, ATP, and ECS must complete the required coursework and pass an exam. Often, a practitioner will hold multiple licenses and designations.

The Association of Government Accountants grants the Certified Government Financial Manager (CGFM) designation for accountants, auditors, and other government financial personnel at the federal, state, and local levels. Candidates must have a minimum of a bachelor's degree, 24 hours of study in financial management, and 2 years' experience in government and must pass a series of three exams. The exams cover topics in governmental environment; governmental accounting, financial reporting, and budgeting; and financial management and control.

Persons planning a career in accounting should have an aptitude for mathematics and be able to analyze, compare, and interpret facts and figures quickly. They must be able to clearly communicate the results of their work to clients and managers both verbally and in writing. Accountants and auditors must be good at working with people, as well as with business systems and computers. At a minimum, accountants should be familiar with basic accounting software packages. Because financial decisions are made on the basis of their statements and services, accountants and auditors should have high standards of integrity.

Capable accountants and auditors may advance rapidly; those having inadequate academic preparation may be assigned routine jobs and find promotion difficult. Many graduates of junior colleges or business or correspondence schools, as well as bookkeepers and accounting clerks who meet the education and experience requirements set by their employers, can obtain junior accounting positions and advance to positions with more responsibilities by demonstrating their accounting skills on the job.

Beginning public accountants usually start by assisting with work for several clients. They may advance to positions with more responsibility in 1 or 2 years and to senior positions within another few years. Those who excel may become supervisors, managers, or partners; open their own public accounting firm; or transfer to executive positions in management accounting or internal auditing in private firms.

Management accountants often start as cost accountants, junior internal auditors, or trainees for other accounting positions. As they rise through the organization, they may advance to accounting manager, chief cost accountant, budget director, or manager of internal auditing. Some become controllers, treasurers, financial vice presidents, chief financial officers, or corporation presidents. Many senior corporation executives have a background in accounting, internal auditing, or finance.

In general, public accountants, management accountants, and internal auditors have much occupational mobility. Practitioners often shift into management accounting or internal auditing from public accounting, or between internal auditing and management accounting. It is less common for accountants and auditors to move from either management accounting or internal auditing into public accounting.

Employment

Accountants and auditors held about 1.2 million jobs in 2004. They worked throughout private industry and government, but 1 out of 4 wage and salary accountants worked for accounting, tax preparation, bookkeeping, and payroll services firms. Approximately 1 out of 10 accountants or auditors was self-employed.

Many accountants and auditors are unlicensed management accountants, internal auditors, or government accountants and auditors; however, a large number are licensed CPAs. Most accountants and auditors work in urban areas, where public accounting firms and central or regional offices of businesses are concentrated.

Some individuals with backgrounds in accounting and auditing are full-time college and university faculty; others teach part time while working as self-employed accountants or as accountants for private industry or government.

Job Outlook

Employment of accountants and auditors is expected to grow faster than average for all occupations through the year 2014. An increase in the number of businesses, changing financial laws and regulations, and increased scrutiny of company finances will drive growth. In addition to openings resulting from growth, the need to replace accountants and auditors who retire or transfer to other occupations will produce numerous job openings in this large occupation.

As the economy grows, the number of business establishments will increase, requiring more accountants and auditors to set up books, prepare taxes, and provide management advice. As these businesses grow, the volume and complexity of information developed by accountants and auditors regarding costs, expenditures, and taxes will increase as well. An increased need for accountants and auditors will arise from changes in legislation related to taxes, financial reporting standards, business investments, mergers, and other financial events. The growth of international business also has led to more demand for accounting expertise and services related to international trade and accounting rules, as well as to international mergers and acquisitions. These trends should create more jobs for accountants and auditors.

As a result of accounting scandals at several large corporate companies, Congress passed legislation in an effort to curb corporate accounting fraud. This legislation requires public companies to maintain well-functioning internal controls to ensure the accuracy and reliability of their financial reporting. It also holds the company's chief executive personally responsible for falsely reporting financial information.

These changes should lead to increased scrutiny of company finances and accounting procedures and should create opportunities for accountants and auditors, particularly CPAs, to audit financial records more thoroughly. In order to ensure that finances comply with the law before public accountants conduct audits, management accountants and internal auditors increasingly will be needed to discover and eliminate fraud. Also, in an effort to make government agencies more efficient and accountable, demand for government accountants should increase.

Increased awareness of financial crimes such as embezzlement, bribery, and securities fraud will increase the demand for forensic accountants, to detect illegal financial activity by individuals, companies, and organized crime rings. Computer technology has made these crimes easier to commit, and they are on the rise. At the same time, the development of new computer software and electronic surveillance technology has made tracking down financial criminals easier, thus increasing the ease with which, and likelihood that, forensic accountants will discover their crimes. As success rates of investigations grow, demand also will grow for forensic accountants.

The changing role of accountants and auditors also will spur job growth, although this growth will be limited as a result of financial scandals. In response to demand, some accountants were offering more financial management and consulting services as they assumed a greater advisory role and developed more sophisticated accounting systems. Because federal legislation now prohibits accountants from providing nontraditional services to clients whose books they audit, opportunities for accountants to offer such services could be limited. However, accountants will still be able to advise on other financial matters for clients that are not publicly traded companies and for nonaudit clients, but growth in these areas will be slower than in the past. Also, due to the increasing popularity of tax preparation firms and computer software, accountants will shift away from tax preparation. As computer programs continue to simplify some accounting-related tasks, clerical staff will increasingly handle many routine calculations.

Overall, job opportunities for accountants and auditors should be favorable. After most states instituted the 150-hour rule for CPAs, enrollment in accounting programs declined; however, enrollment is slowly beginning to grow again as more students become attracted to the profession because of the attention from the accounting scandals. Those who earn a CPA should have excellent job prospects. However, many accounting graduates are instead pursuing other certifications, such as the CMA and CIA, so job prospects may not be as favorable in management accounting and internal auditing as in public accounting. Regardless of specialty, accountants and auditors who have earned professional recognition through certification or licensure should have the best job prospects. Applicants with a master's degree in accounting, or a master's degree in business administration with a concentration in accounting, also will have an advantage. In the aftermath of the accounting scandals, professional certification is even more important in order to ensure that accountants' credentials and ethics are sound.

Proficiency in accounting and auditing computer software, or expertise in specialized areas such as international business, specific industries, or current legislation, may be helpful in landing certain accounting and auditing jobs. In addition, employers increasingly are seeking applicants with strong interpersonal and communication skills. Because many accountants work on teams with others from different backgrounds, they must be able to communicate accounting and financial information clearly and concisely. Regardless of one's qualifications, however, competition will remain keen for the most prestigious jobs in major accounting and business firms.

Earnings

Median annual wage and salary earnings of accountants and auditors were $50,770 in May 2004. The middle half of the occupation earned between $39,890 and $66,900. The top 10 percent of accountants and auditors earned more than $88,610, and the bottom 10 percent earned less than $32,320. In May 2004, median annual earnings in the industries employing the largest numbers of accountants and auditors were as follows:

Federal executive branch and United States Postal Service	$56,900
Accounting, tax preparation, bookkeeping and payroll services	53,870
Management of companies and enterprises	52,260
Local government	47,440
State government	43,400

According to a salary survey conducted by the National Association of Colleges and Employers, bachelor's degree candidates in accounting received starting offers averaging $43,269 a year in 2005; master's degree candidates in accounting were offered $46,251 initially.

According to a 2005 salary survey conducted by Robert Half International, a staffing services firm specializing in accounting and finance, accountants and auditors with up to 1 year of experience earned between $28,250 and $45,000 a year. Those with 1 to 3 years of experience earned between $33,000 and $52,000. Senior accountants and auditors earned between $40,750 and $69,750, managers between $48,000 and $90,000, and directors of accounting and auditing between $64,750 and $200,750. The variation in salaries reflects differences in size of firm, location, level of education, and professional credentials.

In the federal government, the starting annual salary for junior accountants and auditors was $24,677 in 2005. Candidates who had a superior academic record might start at $30,567, while applicants with a master's degree or 2 years of professional experience usually began at $37,390. Beginning salaries were slightly higher in selected areas where the prevailing local pay level was higher. Accountants employed by the federal government in nonsupervisory, supervisory, and managerial positions averaged $74,907 a year in 2005; auditors averaged $78,890.

Related Occupations

Accountants and auditors design internal control systems and analyze financial data. Others for whom training in accounting is valuable include budget analysts; cost estimators; loan officers; financial analysts and personal financial advisors; tax examiners, collectors, and revenue agents; bill and account collectors; and bookkeeping, accounting, and auditing clerks. Recently, accountants have assumed the role of management analysts and are involved in the design, implementation, and maintenance of accounting software systems. Others who perform similar work include computer programmers, computer software engineers, and computer support specialists and systems administrators.

Sources of Additional Information

Information on accredited accounting programs can be obtained from:

- AACSB International—Association to Advance Collegiate Schools of Business, 777 South Harbour Island Blvd., Suite 750, Tampa FL 33602-5730. Internet: http://www.aacsb.edu/accreditation/AccreditedMembers.asp

Information about careers in certified public accounting and CPA standards and examinations may be obtained from:

- American Institute of Certified Public Accountants, 1211 Avenue of the Americas, New York, NY 10036. Internet: http://www.aicpa.org

Information on CPA licensure requirements by state may be obtained from:

- National Association of State Boards of Accountancy, 150 Fourth Ave. North, Suite 700, Nashville, TN 37219-2417. Internet: http://www.nasba.org

Information on careers in management accounting and the CMA designation may be obtained from:

- Institute of Management Accountants, 10 Paragon Dr., Montvale, NJ 07645-1718. Internet: http://www.imanet.org

Information on the Accredited in Accountancy, Accredited Business Accountant, Accredited Tax Advisor, or Accredited Tax Preparer designation may be obtained from:

- Accreditation Council for Accountancy and Taxation, 1010 North Fairfax St., Alexandria, VA 22314-1574 Internet: http://www.acatcredentials.org

Information on careers in internal auditing and the CIA designation may be obtained from:

- The Institute of Internal Auditors, 247 Maitland Ave., Altamonte Springs, FL 32701-4201. Internet: http://www.theiia.org

Information on careers in information systems auditing and the CISA designation may be obtained from:

- Information Systems Audit and Control Association, 3701 Algonquin Rd., Suite 1010, Rolling Meadows, IL 60008. Internet: http://www.isaca.org

Information on careers in government accounting and the CGFM designation may be obtained from:

- Association of Government Accountants, 2208 Mount Vernon Ave., Alexandria, VA 22301. Internet: http://www.agacgfm.org

Information on obtaining positions as an accountant or auditor with the federal government is available from the Office of Personnel Management through USAJOBS, the federal government's official employment information system. This resource for locating and applying for job opportunities can be accessed through the Internet at http://www.usajobs.opm.gov or through an interactive voice response telephone system at (703) 724-1850 or TDD (978) 461-8404. These numbers are not toll free, and charges may result.

Administrative Services Managers

(O*NET 11-3011.00)

Significant Points

- Applicants will face keen competition because of the substantial supply of competent, experienced workers seeking managerial jobs.
- Administrative services managers work throughout private industry and government and have a wide range of responsibilities, experience, earnings, and education.
- Administrative services managers should be analytical, detail-oriented, flexible, and decisive and have good communication skills.

Nature of the Work

Administrative services managers perform a broad range of duties in virtually every sector of the economy. They coordinate and direct support services to organizations as diverse as insurance companies, computer manufacturers, and government offices. These workers manage the many services that allow organizations to operate efficiently, such as secretarial and reception; administration; payroll; conference planning and travel; information and data processing; mail; materials scheduling and distribution; printing and reproduction; records management; telecommunications management; security; parking; and personal property procurement, supply, and disposal.

Specific duties for these managers vary by degree of responsibility and authority. First-line administrative services managers directly supervise a staff that performs various support services. Mid-level managers, on the other hand, develop departmental plans, set goals and deadlines, implement procedures to improve productivity and customer service, and define the responsibilities of supervisory-level managers. Some mid-level administrative services managers oversee first-line supervisors from various departments, including the clerical staff. Mid-level managers also may be involved in the hiring and dismissal of employees, but they generally have no role in the formulation of personnel policy. Some of these managers advance to upper-level positions, such as vice president of administrative services.

In small organizations, a single administrative services manager may oversee all support services. In larger ones, however, first-line administrative services managers often report to mid-level managers who, in turn, report to owners or top-level managers. As the size of the firm increases, administrative services managers are more likely to specialize in specific support activities. For example, some administrative services managers work primarily as office managers, contract administrators, or unclaimed property officers. In many cases, the duties of these administrative services managers are similar to those of other managers and supervisors.

The nature of managerial jobs varies as significantly as the range of administrative services required by organizations. For example, administrative services managers who work as contract administrators oversee the preparation, analysis, negotiation, and review of contracts related to the purchase or sale of equipment, materials, supplies, products, or services. In addition, some administrative services managers acquire, distribute, and store supplies, while others dispose of surplus property or oversee the disposal of unclaimed property.

Administrative services managers who work as facility managers plan, design, and manage buildings and grounds in addition to people. This task requires integrating the principles of business administration, architecture, and behavioral and engineering science. Although the specific tasks assigned to facility managers vary substantially depending on the organization, the duties fall into several categories relating to operations and maintenance, real estate, project planning and management, communication, finance, quality assessment, facility function, technology integration, and management of human and environmental factors. Tasks within these broad categories may include space and workplace planning, budgeting, purchase and sale of real estate, lease management, renovations, or architectural planning and design. Facility managers may suggest and oversee renovation projects for a variety of reasons, ranging from improving efficiency to ensuring that facilities meet government regulations and environmental, health, and security standards. Additionally, facility managers continually monitor the facility to ensure that it remains safe, secure, and well-maintained. Often, the facility manager is responsible for directing staff, including maintenance, grounds, and custodial workers.

Working Conditions

Administrative services managers generally work in comfortable offices. Managers involved in contract administration and personal property procurement, use, and disposal may travel between their home office, branch offices, vendors' offices, and property sales sites. Also, facility managers who are responsible for the design of workspaces may spend time at construction sites and may travel between different facilities while monitoring the work of maintenance, grounds, and custodial staffs. However, new technology has increased the number of managers who telecommute from home or other offices, and teleconferencing has reduced the need for travel.

Most administrative services managers work a standard 40-hour week. However, uncompensated overtime frequently is required to resolve problems and meet deadlines. Facility managers often are "on call" to address a variety of problems that can arise in a facility during nonwork hours.

Training, Other Qualifications, and Advancement

Educational requirements for these managers vary widely, depending on the size and complexity of the organization. In small organizations, experience may be the only requirement needed to enter a position as office manager. When an opening in administrative services management occurs, the office manager may be promoted to the position based on past performance. In large organizations, however, administrative services managers normally are hired from outside, and each position has formal education and experience requirements. Some administrative services managers have advanced degrees.

Specific requirements vary by job responsibility. For first-line administrative services managers of secretarial, mailroom, and related support activities, many employers prefer an associate degree in business or management, although a high school diploma may suffice when combined with appropriate experience. For managers of audiovisual, graphics, and other technical activities, post-secondary technical school training is preferred. Managers of highly complex services, such as contract administration, generally need at least a bachelor's degree in business, human resources, or finance. Regardless of major, the curriculum should include courses in office technology, accounting, business mathematics, computer applications, human resources, and business law. Most facility managers have an undergraduate or graduate degree in engineering, architecture, construction management, business administration, or facility management. Many have a background in real estate, construction, or interior design in addition to managerial experience.

Whatever the manager's educational background, it must be accompanied by related work experience reflecting demonstrated ability. For this reason, many administrative services managers have advanced through the ranks of their organization, acquiring work experience in various administrative positions before assuming first-line supervisory duties. All managers who oversee departmental supervisors should be familiar with office procedures and equipment. Managers of personal property acquisition and disposal need experience in purchasing and sales and knowledge of a variety of supplies, machinery, and equipment. Managers concerned with supply, inventory, and distribution should be experienced in receiving, warehousing, packaging, shipping, transportation, and related operations. Contract administrators may have worked as contract specialists, cost analysts, or procurement specialists. Managers of unclaimed property often have experience in insurance claims analysis and records management.

Persons interested in becoming administrative services managers should have good communication skills and be able to establish effective working relationships with many different people, ranging from managers, supervisors, and professionals to clerks and blue-collar workers. They should be analytical, detail-oriented, flexible, and decisive. They must be able to coordinate several activities at once, quickly analyze and resolve specific problems, and cope with deadlines.

Most administrative services managers in small organizations advance by moving to other management positions or to a larger organization. Advancement is easier in large firms that employ several levels of administrative services managers. Attainment of the

Certified Manager (CM) designation offered by the Institute of Certified Professional Managers (ICPM), through education, work experience, and successful completion of examinations, can enhance a manager's advancement potential. In addition, a master's degree in business administration or a related field enhances a first-level manager's opportunities to advance to a mid-level management position, such as director of administrative services, and eventually to a top-level management position, such as executive vice president for administrative services. Those with enough money and experience can establish their own management consulting firm.

Advancement of facility managers is based on the practices and size of individual companies. Some facility managers transfer from other departments within the organization or work their way up from technical positions. Others advance through a progression of facility management positions that offer additional responsibilities. Completion of the competency-based professional certification program offered by the International Facility Management Association can give prospective candidates an advantage. In order to qualify for this Certified Facility Manager (CFM) designation, applicants must meet certain educational and experience requirements. People entering the profession also may obtain the Facility Management Professional (FMP) credential, a stepping stone to the CFM.

Employment

Administrative services managers held about 268,000 jobs in 2004. About 80 percent worked in service-providing industries, including federal, state, and local government; health care; financial services; professional, scientific, and technical services; administrative and support services; and education. Most of the remaining managers worked in wholesale and retail trade, in management of companies and enterprises, or in manufacturing.

Job Outlook

Employment of administrative services managers is projected to grow about as fast as the average for all occupations through 2014. Like persons seeking other managerial positions, applicants will face keen competition because there will be more competent, experienced workers seeking jobs than there will be positions available. However, demand should be strong for facility managers because businesses increasingly are realizing the importance of maintaining, securing, and efficiently operating their facilities, which are very large investments for most organizations. Administrative services managers employed in management services and management consulting also should be in demand, as public and private organizations continue to streamline and, in some cases, contract out administrative services functions in an effort to cut costs.

At the same time, continuing corporate restructuring and increasing utilization of office technology should result in a flatter organizational structure with fewer levels of management, reducing the need for some middle management positions. This should adversely affect administrative services managers who oversee first-line managers. However, the effects of these changes on employment should be less severe for administrative services managers, who have a wide range of responsibilities, than for other middle managers who specialize in certain functions. In addition to new administrative services management jobs created over the 2004–14 projection period, many job openings will stem from the need to replace workers who transfer to other jobs, retire, or leave the occupation for other reasons.

Earnings

Earnings of administrative services managers vary greatly depending on the employer, the specialty, and the geographic area. In general, however, median annual earnings of administrative services managers in May 2004 were $60,290. The middle 50 percent earned between $42,680 and $83,510. The lowest 10 percent earned less than $31,120, and the highest 10 percent earned more than $110,270. Median annual earnings in the industries employing the largest numbers of these managers in May 2004 were:

Management of companies and enterprises	$71,870
Elementary and secondary schools	65,850
Colleges, universities, and professional schools	61,020
Local government	59,380
State government	55,500

In the federal government, industrial specialists in nonsupervisory, supervisory, and managerial positions averaged $69,802 a year in 2005. Corresponding averages were $69,211 for facility operations services managers, $67,185 for industrial property managers, $63,614 for property disposal specialists, $67,855 for administrative officers, and $60,370 for support services administrators.

Related Occupations

Administrative services managers direct and coordinate support services and oversee the purchase, use, and disposal of personal property. Occupations with similar functions include office and administrative support worker supervisors and managers; cost estimators; property, real estate, and community association managers; purchasing managers, buyers, and purchasing agents; and top executives.

Sources of Additional Information

For information about careers and education and degree programs in facility management, as well as the Certified Facility Manager designation, contact:

- International Facility Management Association, 1 East Greenway Plaza, Suite 1100, Houston, TX 77046-0194. Internet: http://www.ifma.org

General information regarding facility management and a list of facility management education and degree programs may be obtained from:

- Association of Higher Education Facilities Officers, 1643 Prince St., Alexandria, VA 22314-2818. Internet: http://www.appa.org

For information about the Certified Manager (CM) designation, contact:

- Institute of Certified Professional Managers, James Madison University, MSC 5504, Harrisonburg, VA 22807.

Advertising, Marketing, Promotions, Public Relations, and Sales Managers

(O*NET 11-2011.00, 11-2021.00, 11-2022.00, and 11-2031.00)

Significant Points

- Keen competition for jobs is expected.
- College graduates with related experience, a high level of creativity, strong communication skills, and computer skills should have the best job opportunities.
- High earnings, substantial travel, and long hours, including evenings and weekends, are common.

Nature of the Work

The objective of any firm is to market and sell its products or services profitably. In small firms, the owner or chief executive officer might assume all advertising, promotions, marketing, sales, and public relations responsibilities. In large firms, which may offer numerous products and services nationally or even worldwide, an executive vice president directs overall advertising, promotions, marketing, sales, and public relations policies. Advertising, marketing, promotions, public relations, and sales managers coordinate the market research, marketing strategy, sales, advertising, promotion, pricing, product development, and public relations activities.

Advertising managers oversee advertising and promotion staffs, which usually are small, except in the largest firms. In a small firm, managers may serve as liaisons between the firm and the advertising or promotion agency to which many advertising or promotional functions are contracted out. In larger firms, advertising managers oversee in-house account, creative, and media services departments. The *account executive* manages the account services department, assesses the need for advertising, and, in advertising agencies, maintains the accounts of clients. The creative services department develops the subject matter and presentation of advertising. The *creative director* oversees the copy chief, art director, and associated staff. The *media director* oversees planning groups that select the communication media—for example, radio, television, newspapers, magazines, the Internet, or outdoor signs—to disseminate the advertising.

Promotions managers supervise staffs of promotion specialists. These managers direct promotion programs that combine advertising with purchase incentives to increase sales. In an effort to establish closer contact with purchasers—dealers, distributors, or consumers—promotion programs may use direct mail, telemarketing, television or radio advertising, catalogs, exhibits, inserts in newspapers, Internet advertisements or Web sites, in-store displays or product endorsements, and special events. Purchasing incentives may include discounts, samples, gifts, rebates, coupons, sweepstakes, and contests.

Marketing managers develop the firm's marketing strategy in detail. With the help of subordinates, including *product development managers* and *market research managers,* they estimate the demand for products and services offered by the firm and its competitors. In addition, they identify potential markets—for example, business firms, wholesalers, retailers, government, or the general public. Marketing managers develop pricing strategy to help firms maximize profits and market share while ensuring that the firm's customers are satisfied. In collaboration with sales, product development, and other managers, they monitor trends that indicate the need for new products and services and they oversee product development. Marketing managers work with advertising and promotion managers to promote the firm's products and services and to attract potential users.

Public relations managers supervise public relations specialists. These managers direct publicity programs to a targeted audience. They often specialize in a specific area, such as crisis management, or in a specific industry, such as health care. They use every available communication medium to maintain the support of the specific group upon whom their organization's success depends, such as consumers, stockholders, or the general public. For example, public relations managers may clarify or justify the firm's point of view on health or environmental issues to community or special-interest groups.

Public relations managers also evaluate advertising and promotion programs for compatibility with public relations efforts and serve as the eyes and ears of top management. They observe social, economic, and political trends that might ultimately affect the firm, and they make recommendations to enhance the firm's image on the basis of those trends.

Public relations managers may confer with labor relations managers to produce internal company communications—such as newsletters about employee–management relations and with financial managers to produce company reports. They assist company executives in drafting speeches, arranging interviews, and maintaining other forms of public contact; oversee company archives, and respond to requests for information. In addition, some of these managers handle special events, such as the sponsorship of races, parties introducing new products, or other activities that the firm supports in order to gain public attention through the press without advertising directly.

Sales managers direct the firm's sales program. They assign sales territories, set goals, and establish training programs for the sales representatives. Sales managers advise the sales representatives on ways to improve their sales performance. In large, multiproduct firms, they oversee regional and local sales managers and their staffs. Sales managers maintain contact with dealers and distributors. They analyze sales statistics gathered by their staffs to determine sales potential and inventory requirements and to monitor customers' preferences. Such information is vital in the development of products and the maximization of profits.

Working Conditions

Advertising, marketing, promotions, public relations, and sales managers work in offices close to those of top managers. Long hours, including evenings and weekends, are common. In 2004, about two-thirds of advertising, marketing, and public relations managers worked more than 40 hours a week. Working under pressure is unavoidable when schedules change and problems arise, but deadlines and goals must still be met.

Substantial travel may be involved. For example, attendance at meetings sponsored by associations or industries often is mandatory. Sales managers travel to national, regional, and local offices and to the offices of various dealers and distributors. Advertising and promotions managers may travel to meet with clients or representatives of communications media. At times, public relations managers travel to meet with special-interest groups or government officials. Job transfers between headquarters and regional offices are common, particularly among sales managers.

Training, Other Qualifications, and Advancement

A wide range of educational backgrounds is suitable for entry into advertising, marketing, promotions, public relations, and sales managerial jobs, but many employers prefer those with experience in related occupations plus a broad liberal arts background. A bachelor's degree in sociology, psychology, literature, journalism, or philosophy, among other subjects, is acceptable. However, requirements vary, depending upon the particular job.

For marketing, sales, and promotions management positions, some employers prefer a bachelor's or master's degree in business administration with an emphasis on marketing. Courses in business law, economics, accounting, finance, mathematics, and statistics are advantageous. In highly technical industries, such as computer and electronics manufacturing, a bachelor's degree in engineering or science, combined with a master's degree in business administration, is preferred.

For advertising management positions, some employers prefer a bachelor's degree in advertising or journalism. A course of study should include marketing, consumer behavior, market research, sales, communication methods and technology, and visual arts—for example, art history and photography.

For public relations management positions, some employers prefer a bachelor's or master's degree in public relations or journalism. The applicant's curriculum should include courses in advertising, business administration, public affairs, public speaking, political science, and creative and technical writing.

For all these specialties, courses in management and the completion of an internship while the candidate is in school are highly recommended. Familiarity with word-processing and database applications also is important for many positions. Computer skills are vital because marketing, product promotion, and advertising on the Internet are increasingly common. Also, the ability to communicate in a foreign language may open up employment opportunities in many rapidly growing areas around the country, especially cities with large Spanish-speaking populations.

Most advertising, marketing, promotions, public relations, and sales management positions are filled by promoting experienced staff or related professional personnel. For example, many managers are former sales representatives; purchasing agents; buyers; or product, advertising, promotions, or public relations specialists. In small firms, where the number of positions is limited, advancement to a management position usually comes slowly. In large firms, promotion may occur more quickly.

Although experience, ability, and leadership are emphasized for promotion, advancement can be accelerated by participation in management training programs conducted by larger firms. Many firms also provide their employees with continuing education opportunities—either in-house or at local colleges and universities—and encourage employee participation in seminars and conferences, often held by professional societies. In collaboration with colleges and universities, numerous marketing and related associations sponsor national or local management training programs. Course subjects include brand and product management, international marketing, sales management evaluation, telemarketing and direct sales, interactive marketing, promotion, marketing communication, market research, organizational communication, and data-processing systems procedures and management. Many firms pay all or part of the cost for employees who successfully complete courses.

Some associations offer certification programs for these managers. Certification—an indication of competence and achievement—is particularly important in a competitive job market. While relatively few advertising, marketing, promotions, public relations, and sales managers currently are certified, the number of managers who seek certification is expected to grow. Today, there are numerous management certification programs based on education and job performance. In addition, The Public Relations Society of America offers a certification program for public relations practitioners based on years of experience and performance on an examination.

Persons interested in becoming advertising, marketing, promotions, public relations, and sales managers should be mature, creative, highly motivated, resistant to stress, flexible, and decisive. The ability to communicate persuasively, both orally and in writing, with other managers, staff, and the public is vital. These managers also need tact, good judgment, and exceptional ability to establish and maintain effective personal relationships with supervisory and professional staff members and client firms.

Because of the importance and high visibility of their jobs, advertising, marketing, promotions, public relations, and sales managers often are prime candidates for advancement to the highest ranks. Well-trained, experienced, and successful managers may be promoted to higher positions in their own or another firm; some become top executives. Managers with extensive experience and sufficient capital may open their own businesses.

Employment

Advertising, marketing, promotions, public relations, and sales managers held about 646,000 jobs in 2004. The following tabulation shows the distribution of jobs by occupational specialty:

Sales managers	337,000
Marketing managers	188,000
Advertising and promotions managers	64,000
Public relations managers	58,000

These managers were found in virtually every industry. Sales managers held almost half of the jobs; most were employed in wholesale and retail trade and finance and insurance industries. Marketing managers held more than one-fourth of the jobs; the professional, scientific, and technical services industries employed almost one-third of marketing managers. About one-fourth of advertising and promotions managers worked in the professional, scientific, and technical services industries and the information industries, including advertising and related services and publishing industries. Most public relations managers were employed in service-providing industries, such as professional, scientific, and technical services; finance and insurance; health care and social assistance; and educational services.

Job Outlook

Advertising, marketing, promotions, public relations, and sales manager jobs are highly coveted and will be sought by other managers or highly experienced professionals, resulting in keen competition. College graduates with related experience, a high level of creativity, and strong communication skills should have the best job opportunities. In particular, employers will seek those who have the computer skills to conduct advertising, marketing, promotions, public relations, and sales activities on the Internet.

Employment of advertising, marketing, promotions, public relations, and sales managers is expected to increase faster than the average for all occupations through 2014, spurred by intense domestic and global competition in products and services offered to consumers. However, projected employment growth varies by industry. For example, employment is projected to grow much faster than average in scientific, professional, and related services, such as computer systems design and related services, and in advertising and related services, as businesses increasingly hire contractors for these services instead of additional full-time staff. By contrast, a decline in employment is expected in many manufacturing industries.

Earnings

Median annual earnings in May 2004 were $63,610 for advertising and promotions managers, $87,640 for marketing managers, $84,220 sales managers, and $70,000 for public relations managers.

Median annual earnings of advertising and promotions managers in May 2004 in the advertising and related services industry were $89,570.

Median annual earnings in the industries employing the largest numbers of marketing managers in May 2004 were as follows:

Computer systems design and related services	$107,030
Management of companies and enterprises	98,700
Insurance carriers	86,810
Architectural, engineering, and related services	83,610
Depository credit intermediation	76,450

Median annual earnings in the industries employing the largest numbers of sales managers in May 2004 were as follows:

Computer systems design and related services	$119,140
Wholesale electronic markets and agents and brokers	101,930
Automobile dealers	97,460
Management of companies and enterprises	95,410
Machinery, equipment, and supplies merchant wholesalers	84,680

According to a National Association of Colleges and Employers survey, starting salaries for marketing majors graduating in 2005 averaged $33,873; starting salaries for advertising majors averaged $31,340.

Salary levels vary substantially, depending upon the level of managerial responsibility, length of service, education, size of firm, location, and industry. For example, manufacturing firms usually pay these managers higher salaries than do nonmanufacturing firms. For sales managers, the size of their sales territory is another important determinant of salary. Many managers earn bonuses equal to 10 percent or more of their salaries.

Related Occupations

Advertising, marketing, promotions, public relations, and sales managers direct the sale of products and services offered by their firms and the communication of information about their firms' activities. Other workers involved with advertising, marketing, promotions, public relations, and sales include actors, producers, and directors; advertising sales agents; artists and related workers; demonstrators, product promoters, and models; market and survey researchers; public relations specialists; sales representatives, wholesale and manufacturing; and writers and editors.

Sources of Additional Information

For information about careers in advertising management, contact:

- American Association of Advertising Agencies, 405 Lexington Ave., New York, NY 10174-1801. Internet: http://www.aaaa.org

Information about careers and professional certification in public relations management is available from:

- Public Relations Society of America, 33 Maiden Lane, New York, NY 10038-5150. Internet: http://www.prsa.org

Animal Care and Service Workers

(O*NET 39-2011.00 and 39-2021.00)

Significant Points

- Animal lovers get satisfaction in this occupation, but the work can be unpleasant, physically and emotionally demanding, and sometimes dangerous.
- Most workers are trained on the job, but employers generally prefer to hire people who have some experience with animals; some jobs require a bachelor's degree in biology, animal science, or a related field.
- Good employment opportunities are expected for most positions; however, keen competition is expected for jobs as zookeepers. Earnings are relatively low.

Nature of the Work

Many people like animals. But, as pet owners can attest, taking care of them is hard work. Animal care and service workers—which include animal caretakers and animal trainers—train, feed, water, groom, bathe, and exercise animals and clean, disinfect, and repair their cages. They also play with the animals, provide companionship, and observe behavioral changes that could indicate illness or injury. Boarding kennels, animal shelters, veterinary hospitals and clinics, stables, laboratories, aquariums, and zoological parks all house animals and employ animal care and service workers. Job titles and duties vary by employment setting.

Kennel attendants care for pets while their owners are working or traveling out of town. Beginning attendants perform basic tasks, such as cleaning cages and dog runs, filling food and water dishes, and exercising animals. Experienced attendants may provide basic animal health care, as well as bathe animals, trim nails, and attend to other grooming needs. Attendants who work in kennels also may sell pet food and supplies, assist in obedience training, help with breeding, or prepare animals for shipping.

Animal caretakers who specialize in grooming or maintaining a pet's—usually a dog's or cat's—appearance are called *groomers*. Some groomers work in kennels, veterinary clinics, animal shelters, or pet-supply stores. Others operate their own grooming business, typically at a salon, or increasingly, by making house calls. Such mobile services are growing rapidly as it offers convenience for pet owners and flexible hours for groomers. Groomers answer telephones, schedule appointments, discuss pets' grooming needs with clients, and collect information on the pet's disposition and its veterinarian. Groomers often are the first to notice a medical problem, such as an ear or skin infection, that requires veterinary care.

Grooming the pet involves several steps: an initial brush-out is followed by an initial clipping of hair or fur using electric clippers, combs, and grooming shears; the groomer then cuts the nails, cleans the ears, bathes, and blow-dries the animal, and ends with a final clipping and styling.

Animal caretakers in animal shelters perform a variety of duties and work with a wide variety of animals. In addition to attending to the basic needs of the animals, caretakers also must keep records of the animals received and discharged and any tests or treatments done. Some vaccinate newly admitted animals under the direction of a veterinarian or veterinary technician, and euthanize (painlessly put to death) seriously ill, severely injured, or unwanted animals. Animal caretakers in animal shelters also interact with the public, answering telephone inquiries, screening applicants for animal adoption, or educating visitors on neutering and other animal health issues.

Caretakers in stables are called *grooms*. They saddle and unsaddle horses, give them rubdowns, and walk them to cool them off after a ride. They also feed, groom, and exercise the horses; clean out stalls and replenish bedding; polish saddles; clean and organize the tack (harness, saddle, and bridle) room; and store supplies and feed. Experienced grooms may help train horses.

In zoos, animal care and service workers, called *keepers*, prepare the diets and clean the enclosures of animals, and sometimes assist in raising them when they are very young. They watch for any signs of illness or injury, monitor eating patterns or any changes in behavior, and record their observations. Keepers also may answer questions and ensure that the visiting public behaves responsibly toward the exhibited animals. Depending on the zoo, keepers may be assigned to work with a broad group of animals such as mammals, birds, or reptiles, or they may work with a limited collection of animals such as primates, large cats, or small mammals.

Animal trainers train animals for riding, security, performance, obedience, or assisting persons with disabilities. Animal trainers do this by accustoming the animal to human voice and contact, and conditioning the animal to respond to commands. Trainers use several techniques to help them train animals. One technique, known as a bridge, is a stimulus that a trainer uses to communicate the precise moment an animal does something correctly. When the animal responds correctly, the trainer gives positive reinforcement in a variety of ways: food, toys, play, rubdowns, or speaking the word "good." Animal training takes place in small steps, and often takes months and even years of repetition. During the conditioning process, trainers provide animals mental stimulation, physical exercise, and husbandry care. In addition to their hands-on work with the animals, trainers often oversee other aspects of the animal's care, such as diet preparation. Trainers often work in competitions or shows, such as the circus or marine parks. Trainers who work in shows also may participate in educational programs for visitors and guests.

Working Conditions

People who love animals get satisfaction from working with and helping them. However, some of the work may be unpleasant, physically and emotionally demanding, and sometimes dangerous. Most animal care and service workers have to clean animal cages and lift, hold, or restrain animals, risking exposure to bites or scratches. Their work often involves kneeling, crawling, repeated bending, and lifting heavy supplies like bales of hay or bags of feed. Animal caretakers must take precautions when treating animals with germicides or insecticides. The work setting can be noisy. Caretakers of show and sports animals travel to competitions.

Animal care and service workers who witness abused animals or who assist in the euthanizing of unwanted, aged, or hopelessly injured animals may experience emotional distress. Those working for private humane societies and municipal animal shelters often deal with the public, some of whom might react with hostility to any implication that the owners are neglecting or abusing their pets. Such workers must maintain a calm and professional demeanor while they enforce the laws regarding animal care.

Animal care and service workers may work outdoors in all kinds of weather. Hours are irregular. Animals must be fed every day, so caretakers often work weekend and holiday shifts. In some animal hospitals, research facilities, and animal shelters, an attendant is on duty 24 hours a day, which means night shifts.

Training, Other Qualifications, and Advancement

Most animal care and service workers are trained on the job; however, employers generally prefer to hire people who have some experience with animals. Some training programs are available for specific types of animal caretakers, such as groomers, but formal training is usually not necessary for entry-level positions. Animal trainers often need to possess a high school diploma or GED equivalent. However, some animal training jobs may require a bachelor's degree and additional skills. For example, a marine mammal trainer usually needs a bachelor's degree in biology, marine biology, animal science, psychology, zoology, or related field, plus strong swimming skills and SCUBA certification. All animal trainers need patience, sensitivity, and experience with problem-solving and animal obedience. Certification is not mandatory for animal trainers, but several organizations offer training programs and certification for prospective animal trainers.

Most pet groomers learn their trade by completing an informal apprenticeship, usually lasting 6 to 10 weeks, under the guidance of an experienced groomer. Prospective groomers also may attend one of the 50 state-licensed grooming schools throughout the country, with programs varying in length from 2 to 18 weeks. The National Dog Groomers Association of America offers certification for master status as a groomer with a focus on four principle areas—nonsporting, sporting, terrier, and masters. The examination consists of 400 questions with a separate part testing practical skills. Beginning groomers often start by taking on one duty, such as bathing and drying the pet. They eventually assume responsibility for the entire grooming process, from the initial brush-out to the final clipping. Groomers who work in large retail establishments or kennels may, with experience, move into supervisory or managerial positions. Experienced groomers often choose to open their own salons.

Beginning animal caretakers in kennels learn on the job, and usually start by cleaning cages and feeding and watering animals. Kennel caretakers may be promoted to kennel supervisor, assistant manager, and manager, and those with enough capital and experience may open up their own kennels. The American Boarding Kennels Association (ABKA) offers a three-stage, home-study program for individuals interested in pet care. The first two stages address basic and advanced principles of animal care, while the third stage focuses on in depth animal care and good business procedures. Those who complete the third stage and pass oral and written examinations administered by the ABKA become Certified Kennel Operators (CKO).

Some zoological parks may require their caretakers to have a bachelor's degree in biology, animal science, or a related field. Most require experience with animals, preferably as a volunteer or paid keeper in a zoo. Zookeepers may advance to senior keeper, assistant head keeper, head keeper, and assistant curator, but very few openings occur, especially for the higher level positions.

Animal caretakers in animal shelters are not required to have any specialized training, but training programs and workshops are increasingly available through the Humane Society of the United States, the American Humane Association, and the National Animal Control Association. Workshop topics include cruelty investigations, appropriate methods of euthanasia for shelter animals, proper guidelines for capturing animals techniques for preventing problems with wildlife, and dealing with the general public. Because shelter workers often deal with individuals who abandon their pets, excellent communication skills, including the ability to handle emotional people, is vital. With experience and additional training, caretakers in animal shelters may become adoption coordinators, animal control officers, emergency rescue drivers, assistant shelter managers, or shelter directors.

Employment

Animal care and service workers held 172,000 jobs in 2004. Almost 3 out of 4 worked as nonfarm animal caretakers; the remainder worked as animal trainers. Nonfarm animal caretakers worked primarily in boarding kennels, animal shelters, stables, grooming shops, animal hospitals, and veterinary offices. A significant number also worked for animal humane societies, racing stables, dog and horse racetrack operators, zoos, theme parks, circuses, and other amusement and recreations services. In 2004, nearly 1 out of every 3 nonfarm animal caretakers was self-employed.

Employment of animal trainers was concentrated in animal services that specialize in training horses, pets, and other animal specialties; and in commercial sports, training racehorses and dogs. About 3 in 5 animal trainers were self-employed.

Job Outlook

Good job opportunities are expected for most positions because many workers leave this occupation each year. The need to replace workers leaving the field will create the overwhelming majority of job openings. Many animal caretaker jobs require little or no training and have flexible work schedules, attracting people seeking their first job, students, and others looking for temporary or part-time work, including retired people. The outlook for caretakers in zoos, however, is not favorable due to slow growth in zoo capacity and keen competition for the few positions. Job opportunities for animal care and service workers may vary from year to year, because the strength of the economy affects demand for these workers. Pet owners tend to spend more on animal services when the economy is strong.

In addition to replacement needs, employment of animal care and service workers is expected to grow faster than average for all occupations through 2014. The companion pet population—which drives employment of animal caretakers in kennels, grooming shops, animal shelters, and veterinary clinics and hospitals—is expected to increase. Pet owners—including a large number of baby boomers, whose disposable income is expected to increase as they age—are expected to increasingly take advantage of grooming services, daily and overnight boarding services, training services, and veterinary services, resulting in more jobs for animal care and service workers. As many pet owners increasingly consider their pet as part of the family, their demand for luxury animal services and willingness to spend greater amounts of money on their pet will continue to grow.

Demand for animal care and service workers in animal shelters is expected to remain steady. Communities are increasingly recognizing the connection between animal abuse and abuse toward humans, and will probably continue to commit private funds to animal shelters, many of which are working hand-in-hand with social service agencies and law enforcement teams. Employment growth of personal and group animal trainers will stem from an increased number of animal owners seeking training services for their pets, including behavior modification and feline behavior training. Job openings as shelter workers will continue to be driven by high turnover as the job is extremely demanding and stressful.

Earnings

Earnings are relatively low. Median hourly earnings of nonfarm animal caretakers were $8.39 in May 2004. The middle 50 percent earned between $7.16 and $10.50. The bottom 10 percent earned less than $6.17, and the top 10 percent earned more than $13.66.

Median hourly earnings in the industries employing the largest numbers of nonfarm animal caretakers in May 2004 were:

Spectator sports	$8.48
Other personal services	8.47
Social advocacy organizations	8.15
Other miscellaneous store retailers	7.95
Other professional, scientific, and technical services	7.86

Median hourly earnings of animal trainers were $10.60 in May 2004. The middle 50 percent earned between $8.10 and $15.23. The lowest 10 percent earned less than $7.07, and the top 10 percent earned more than $20.62.

Related Occupations

Others who work extensively with animals include farmers, ranchers, and agricultural managers; agricultural workers; veterinarians; veterinary technologists and technicians; veterinary assistants; biological scientists; and medical scientists.

Sources of Additional Information

For more information on jobs in animal caretaking and control, and the animal shelter and control personnel training program, write to:

- Humane Society of the United States, 2100 L St. NW, Washington, DC 20037-1598. Internet: http://www.hsus.org

For career information and information on training, certification, and earnings of animal control officers at federal, state, and local levels, contact:

- National Animal Control Association, P.O. Box 1480851, Kansas City, MO 64148-0851. Internet: http://www.nacanet.org

For information on becoming an advanced pet care technician at a kennel, contact:

- American Boarding Kennels Association, 1702 East Pikes Peak Ave., Colorado Springs, CO 80909.

Athletes, Coaches, Umpires, and Related Workers

(O*NET 27-2021.00, 27-2022.00, and 27-2023.00)

Significant Points

- Work hours are often irregular; travel may be extensive.
- Career-ending injuries are always a risk for athletes.
- Job opportunities will be best for part-time coaches, sports instructors, umpires, referees, and sports officials in high schools, sports clubs, and other settings.
- Competition for professional athlete jobs will continue to be extremely intense; athletes who seek to compete professionally must have extraordinary talent, desire, and dedication to training.

Nature of the Work

We are a nation of sports fans and sports players. Some of those who participate in amateur sports dream of becoming paid professional athletes, coaches, or sports officials, but very few beat the long and daunting odds of making a full-time living from professional athletics. Those athletes who do make it to professional levels find that careers are short and jobs are insecure. Even though the chances of employment as a professional athlete are slim, there are many opportunities for at least a part-time job as a coach, instructor, referee, or umpire in amateur athletics or in high school, college, or university sports.

Athletes and sports competitors compete in organized, officiated sports events to entertain spectators. When playing a game, athletes are required to understand the strategies of their game while obeying the rules and regulations of the sport. The events in which they compete include both team sports—such as baseball, basketball, football, hockey, and soccer—and individual sports—such as golf, tennis, and bowling. The level of play varies from unpaid high school athletics to professional sports, in which the best from around the world compete in events broadcast on international television.

Being an athlete involves more than competing in athletic events. Athletes spend many hours each day practicing skills and improving teamwork under the guidance of a coach or a sports instructor. They view videotapes to critique their own performances and techniques and to learn their opponents' tendencies and weaknesses to gain a competitive advantage. Some athletes work regularly with strength trainers to gain muscle and stamina and to prevent injury. Many athletes push their bodies to the limit during both practice and play, so career-ending injury always is a risk; even minor injuries may put a player at risk of replacement. Because competition at all levels is extremely intense and job security is always precarious, many athletes train year round to maintain excellent form and technique and peak physical condition. Very little downtime from the sport exists at the professional level. Athletes also must conform to regimented diets during their sports season to supplement any physical training program.

Coaches organize amateur and professional athletes and teach them the fundamentals of individual and team sports. (In individual sports, *instructors* sometimes may fill this role.) Coaches train athletes for competition by holding practice sessions to perform drills that improve the athletes' form, technique, skills, and stamina. Along with refining athletes' individual skills, coaches are responsible for instilling good sportsmanship, a competitive spirit, and teamwork and for managing their teams during both practice sessions and competitions. Before competition, coaches evaluate or scout the opposing team to determine game strategies and practice specific plays. During competition, coaches may call specific plays intended to surprise or overpower the opponent, and they may substitute players for optimum team chemistry and success. Coaches' additional tasks may include selecting, storing, issuing, and taking inventory of equipment, materials, and supplies.

Many coaches in high schools are primarily teachers of academic subjects who supplement their income by coaching part time. College coaches consider coaching a full-time discipline and may be away from home frequently as they travel to scout and recruit prospective players.

Sports instructors teach professional and nonprofessional athletes individually. They organize, instruct, train, and lead athletes in indoor and outdoor sports such as bowling, tennis, golf, and swimming. Because activities are as diverse as weight lifting, gymnastics, scuba diving, and karate, instructors tend to specialize in one or a few activities. Like coaches, sports instructors also may hold daily practice sessions and be responsible for any needed equipment and supplies. Using their knowledge of their sport and of physiology, they determine the type and level of difficulty of exercises, prescribe specific drills, and correct athletes' techniques. Some instructors also teach and demonstrate the use of training apparatus, such as trampolines or weights, for correcting athletes' weaknesses and enhancing their conditioning. As coaches do, sports instructors evaluate the athlete and the athlete's opponents to devise a competitive game strategy.

Coaches and sports instructors sometimes differ in their approaches to athletes because of the focus of their work. For example, while coaches manage the team during a game to optimize its chance for victory, sports instructors—such as those who work for professional tennis players—often are not permitted to instruct their athletes during competition. Sports instructors spend more of their time with athletes working one-on-one, which permits them to design customized training programs for each individual. Motivating athletes to play hard challenges most coaches and sports instructors but is vital for the athlete's success. Many coaches and instructors derive great satisfaction working with children or young adults, helping them to learn new physical and social skills, improve their physical condition, and achieve success in their sport.

Umpires, referees, and other sports officials officiate at competitive athletic and sporting events. They observe the play, detect infractions of rules, and impose penalties established by the rules and regulations of the various sports. Umpires, referees, and sports officials anticipate play and position themselves to best see the action, assess the situation, and determine any violations. Some sports officials, such as boxing referees, may work independently, while others such as umpires work in groups. Regardless of the sport, the job is highly stressful because officials are often required to make a decision in a split second, sometimes resulting in strong disagreement among competitors, coaches, and spectators.

Professional scouts evaluate the skills of both amateur and professional athletes to determine talent and potential. As a sports intelligence agent, the scout's primary duty is to seek out top athletic candidates for the team he or she represents. At the professional level, scouts typically work for scouting organizations or as freelance scouts. In locating new talent, scouts perform their work in secrecy so as not to "tip off" their opponents about their interest in certain players. At the college level, the head scout often is an assistant coach, although freelance scouts may aid colleges by reporting to coaches about exceptional players. Scouts at this level seek talented high school athletes by reading newspapers, contacting high school coaches and alumni, attending high school games, and studying videotapes of prospects' performances. They also evaluate potential players' background and personal characteristics, such as motivation and discipline, by talking to the players' coaches, parents, and teachers.

Working Conditions

Irregular work hours are the trademark of the athlete. They also are common for coaches, umpires, referees, and other sports officials. People in these occupations often work Saturdays, Sundays, evenings, and holidays. Athletes and full-time coaches usually work more than 40 hours a week for several months during the sports season, if not most of the year. Some coaches in educational institutions may coach more than one sport, particularly in high schools.

Athletes, coaches, and sports officials who participate in competitions that are held outdoors may be exposed to all weather conditions of the season; those involved in events that are held indoors tend to work in climate-controlled comfort, often in arenas, enclosed stadiums, or gymnasiums. Athletes, coaches, and some sports officials frequently travel to sporting events by bus or airplane. Scouts also travel extensively in locating talent, often by automobile.

Umpires, referees, and other sports officials regularly encounter verbal abuse by fans, coaches, and athletes. The officials also face possible physical assault and, increasingly, lawsuits from injured athletes based on their officiating decisions.

Training, Other Qualifications, and Advancement

Education and training requirements for athletes, coaches, umpires, and related workers vary greatly by the level and type of sport. Regardless of the sport or occupation, jobs require immense overall knowledge of the game, usually acquired through years of experience at lower levels. Athletes usually begin competing in their sports while in elementary or middle school, and continue through high school and sometimes college. They play in amateur tournaments and on high school and college teams, where the best attract the attention of professional scouts. Most schools require that participating athletes maintain specific academic standards to remain eligible to play. Becoming a professional athlete is the culmination of years of effort. Athletes who seek to compete professionally must have extraordinary talent, desire, and dedication to training.

For high school coaching and sports instructor jobs, schools usually prefer to hire teachers willing to take on the jobs part time. If no one suitable is found, schools hire someone from outside. Some entry-level positions for coaches or instructors require only experience derived as a participant in the sport or activity. Many coaches begin their careers as assistant coaches to gain the knowledge and experience needed to become a head coach. Head coaches at large schools that strive to compete at the highest levels of a sport require substantial experience as a head coach at another school or as an assistant coach. To reach the ranks of professional coaching, a person usually needs years of coaching experience and a winning record in the lower ranks.

Head coaches at public secondary schools and sports instructors at all levels usually must have a bachelor's degree. Those who are not teachers must meet state requirements for certification to become a head coach. Certification, however, may not be required for coaching and sports instructor jobs in private schools. Degree programs specifically related to coaching include exercise and sports science, physiology, kinesiology, nutrition and fitness, physical education, and sports medicine.

For those interested in becoming a tennis, golf, karate, or other kind of instructor, certification is highly desirable. Often, one must be at least 18 years old and certified in cardiopulmonary resuscitation (CPR). There are many certifying organizations specific to the various sports, and their training requirements vary. Participation in a clinic, camp, or school usually is required for certification. Part-time workers and those in smaller facilities are less likely to need formal education or training.

For example, there are two organizations that certify tennis instructors and coaches—the Professional Tennis Registry, an international organization, and the U.S. Professional Tennis Association. Both organizations offer three levels of certification, but the requirements are slightly different. Each level of certification is based on the candidate's National Tennis Rating Program rating, teaching experience, and score on the organization's written and practical certifying exams. There are also minimum age requirements for each level.

Each sport has specific requirements for umpires, referees, and other sports officials. Umpires, referees, and other sports officials often begin their careers by volunteering for intramural, community, and recreational league competitions. To officiate at high school athletic events, officials must register with the state agency that oversees high school athletics and pass an exam on the rules of the particular game. For college refereeing, candidates must be certified by an officiating school and be evaluated during a probationary period. Some larger college sports conferences require officials to have certification and other qualifications, such as residence in or near the conference boundaries, along with several years of experience officiating at high school, community college, or other college conference games.

Standards are even more stringent for officials in professional sports. Whereas umpires for high school baseball need a high school diploma or its equivalent, 20/20 vision, and quick reflexes, those seeking to officiate at minor or major league games must attend professional umpire training school. Currently, there are two schools whose curriculums have been approved by the Professional Baseball Umpires Corporation for training. Top graduates are selected for further evaluation while officiating in a rookie minor league. Umpires then usually need 8 to 10 years of experience in various minor leagues before being considered for major league jobs. Becoming an official for professional football also is competitive, as candidates must have at least 10 years of officiating experience, with 5 of them at a collegiate varsity or minor professional level. For the National Football League (NFL), prospective trainees are interviewed by clinical psychologists to determine levels of intelligence and ability to handle extremely stressful situations. In addition, the NFL's security department conducts thorough background checks. Potential candidates are likely to be interviewed by a panel from the NFL officiating department and are given a comprehensive examination on the rules of the sport.

Scouting jobs require experience playing a sport at the college or professional level that makes it possible to spot young players who possess extraordinary athletic ability and skills. Most beginning scouting jobs are as part-time talent spotters in a particular area or region. Hard work and a record of success often lead to full-time jobs responsible for bigger territories. Some scouts advance to scouting director jobs or various administrative positions in sports.

Athletes, coaches, umpires, and related workers must relate well to others and possess good communication and leadership skills. Coaches also must be resourceful and flexible to successfully instruct and motivate individuals and groups of athletes.

Employment

Athletes, coaches, umpires, and related workers held about 212,000 jobs in 2004. Coaches and scouts held 178,000 jobs; athletes, 17,000; and umpires, referees, and other sports officials, 16,000. Nearly 37 percent of athletes, coaches, umpires, and related workers worked part time, while 20 percent maintained variable schedules. Many sports officials and coaches receive such small and irregular payments for their services—occasional officiating at club games, for example—that they may not consider themselves employed in these occupations, even part time.

Among those employed in wage and salary jobs, 30 percent held jobs in private educational services. About 15 percent worked in amusement, gambling, and recreation industries, including golf and tennis clubs, gymnasiums, health clubs, judo and karate schools, riding stables, swim clubs, and other sports and recreation facilities. Another 9 percent worked in the spectator sports industry.

About 1 out of 4 workers in this occupation was self-employed, earning prize money or fees for lessons, scouting, or officiating assignments. Many other coaches and sports officials, although technically not self-employed, have such irregular or tenuous working arrangements that their working conditions resemble those of self-employment.

Job Outlook

Employment of athletes, coaches, umpires, and related workers is expected to increase faster than the average for all occupations through the year 2014. Employment will grow as the general public continues to participate in organized sports for entertainment, recreation, and physical conditioning. Increasing participation in organized sports by girls and women will boost demand for coaches, umpires, and related workers. Job growth also will be driven by the increasing number of baby boomers approaching retirement, during which they are expected to participate more and require instruction in leisure activities such as golf and tennis. The large number of children of baby boomers also will be active participants in high school and college athletics and will require coaches and instructors.

Employment of coaches and instructors also will increase with expansion of school and college athletic programs and growing demand for private sports instruction. Sports-related job growth within education also will be driven by the decisions of local school boards. Population growth dictates the construction of additional schools, particularly in the expanding suburbs, but funding for athletic programs often is cut first when budgets become tight. Still, the popularity of team sports often enables shortfalls to be offset somewhat by assistance from fundraisers, booster clubs, and parents. Persons who are state-certified to teach academic subjects in addition to physical education are likely to have the best prospects for obtaining coaching and instructor jobs. The need to replace the many high school coaches who change occupations or leave the labor force entirely also will provide some coaching opportunities.

Competition for professional athlete jobs will continue to be extremely intense. Opportunities to make a living as a professional in individual sports such as golf or tennis may grow as new tournaments are established and as prize money distributed to participants increases. Because most professional athletes' careers last only a few years due to debilitating injuries and age, annual turnover in these jobs is high, creating some job opportunities. However, the talented young men and women who dream of becoming sports superstars greatly outnumber and will compete aggressively for these openings.

Opportunities should be best for persons seeking part-time umpire, referee, and other sports official jobs at the high school level. Competition is expected for higher paying jobs at the college level and will be even greater for jobs in professional sports. Competition should be very keen for jobs as scouts, particularly for professional teams, because the number of available positions is limited.

Earnings

Median annual earnings of athletes were $48,310 in May 2004. However, the highest-paid professional athletes earn much more.

Median annual earnings of umpires and related workers were $21,260 in May 2004. The middle 50 percent earned between $16,870 and $31,390. The lowest-paid 10 percent earned less than $14,160, and the highest-paid 10 percent earned more than $44,140.

In May 2004, median annual earnings of coaches and scouts were $26,350. The middle 50 percent earned between $17,230 and $40,460. The lowest-paid 10 percent earned less than $13,320, and the highest-paid 10 percent earned more than $57,800. However, the highest-paid professional coaches earn much more. Median annual earnings in the industries employing the largest numbers of coaches and scouts in May 2004 are shown below:

Colleges, universities, and professional schools $36,610
Other amusement and recreation industries 26,340
Other schools and instruction 22,560
Elementary and secondary schools 21,970
Civic and social organizations 19,020

Earnings vary by level of education, certification, and geographic region. Some instructors and coaches are paid a salary, while others may be paid by the hour, per session, or based on the number of participants.

Related Occupations

Athletes and coaches use their extensive knowledge of physiology and sports to instruct, inform, and encourage sports participants. Other workers with similar duties include dietitians and nutritionists; physical therapists; recreation workers; fitness workers; recreational therapists; and teachers—preschool, kindergarten, elementary, middle, and secondary.

Sources of Additional Information

For information about sports officiating for team and individual sports, contact:

- National Association of Sports Officials, 2017 Lathrop Ave., Racine, WI 53405. Internet: http://www.naso.org

For more information about certification of tennis instructors and coaches, contact:

- Professional Tennis Registry, P.O. Box 4739, Hilton Head Island, SC 29938. Internet: http://www.ptrtennis.org
- U.S. Professional Tennis Association, 3535 Briarpark Dr., Suite One, Houston, TX 77042. Internet: http://www.uspta.org

Automotive Service Technicians and Mechanics

(O*NET 49-3023.01 and 49-3023.02)

Significant Points

- Formal automotive technician training is the best preparation for these challenging technology-based jobs.
- Opportunities should be very good for automotive service technicians and mechanics with diagnostic and problem-solving skills, knowledge of electronics and mathematics, and mechanical aptitude.
- Automotive service technicians and mechanics must continually adapt to changing technology and repair techniques as vehicle components and systems become increasingly sophisticated.

Nature of the Work

Anyone whose car or light truck has broken down knows the importance of the jobs of automotive service technicians and mechanics. The ability to diagnose the source of a problem quickly and accurately requires good reasoning ability and a thorough knowledge of automobiles. Many technicians consider diagnosing hard to find troubles one of their most challenging and satisfying duties.

The work of automotive service technicians and mechanics has evolved from mechanical repair to a high technology job. As a result, these workers are now usually called "technicians" in automotive services and the term "mechanic" is falling into disuse. Today, integrated electronic systems and complex computers run vehicles and measure their performance while on the road. Technicians must have an increasingly broad base of knowledge about how vehicles' complex components work and interact, as well as the ability to work with electronic diagnostic equipment and computer-based technical reference materials.

Automotive service technicians use their high-tech skills to inspect, maintain, and repair automobiles and light trucks that run on gasoline, ethanol and other alternative fuels, such as electricity. The increasing sophistication of automotive technology now requires workers who can use computerized shop equipment and work with electronic components while maintaining their skills with traditional hand tools.

When mechanical or electrical troubles occur, technicians first get a description of the symptoms from the owner or, if they work in a large shop, from the repair service estimator or service advisor who wrote the repair order. To locate the problem, technicians use a diagnostic approach. First, they test to see whether components and systems are proper and secure. Then, they isolate the components or systems that could not logically be the cause of the problem. For example, if an air-conditioner malfunctions, the technician's diagnostic approach can pinpoint a problem as simple as a low coolant level or as complex as a bad drive-train connection that has shorted out the air conditioner. Technicians may have to test drive the vehicle or use a variety of testing equipment, such as onboard and handheld diagnostic computers or compression gauges, to identify the source of the problem. These tests may indicate whether a component is salvageable or whether a new one is required to get the vehicle back in working order.

During routine service inspections, technicians test and lubricate engines and other major components. In some cases, the technician may repair or replace worn parts before they cause breakdowns that could damage critical components of the vehicle. Technicians usually follow a checklist to ensure that they examine every critical part. Belts, hoses, plugs, brake and fuel systems, and other potentially troublesome items are among those closely watched.

Service technicians use a variety of tools in their work—power tools, such as pneumatic wrenches to remove bolts quickly; machine tools like lathes and grinding machines to rebuild brakes; welding and flame-cutting equipment to remove and repair exhaust systems, and jacks and hoists to lift cars and engines. They also use common hand tools, such as screwdrivers, pliers, and wrenches, to work on small parts and in hard-to-reach places.

Computers also have become commonplace in modern repair shops. Service technicians compare the readouts from computerized diagnostic testing devices with the benchmarked standards given by the manufacturer of the components being tested. Deviations outside of acceptable levels are an indication to the technician that further attention to an area is necessary. A shop's computerized system provides automatic updates to technical manuals and unlimited access to manufacturers' service information, technical service bulletins, and other databases that allow technicians to keep current on problem spots and to learn new procedures.

Automotive service technicians in large shops have increasingly become specialized. For example, *transmission technicians and rebuilders* work on gear trains, couplings, hydraulic pumps, and other parts of transmissions. Extensive knowledge of computer controls, the ability to diagnose electrical and hydraulic problems, and other specialized skills are needed to work on these complex components, which employ some of the most sophisticated technology used in vehicles. *Tuneup technicians* adjust the ignition timing and valves, and adjust or replace spark plugs and other parts to ensure efficient engine performance. They often use electronic testing equipment to isolate and adjust malfunctions in fuel, ignition, and emissions control systems.

Automotive air-conditioning repairers install and repair air-conditioners and service their components, such as compressors, condensers, and controls. These workers require special training in federal and state regulations governing the handling and disposal of refrigerants. *Front-end mechanics* align and balance wheels and repair steering mechanisms and suspension systems. They frequently use special alignment equipment and wheel-balancing machines. *Brake repairers* adjust brakes, replace brake linings and pads, and make other repairs on brake systems. Some technicians specialize in both brake and front-end work. Even though electronics and electronic systems in automobiles were a specialty in the past, electronics are now so common that it is essential for all types of service technicians to be familiar with at least the basic principles of electronics.

Working Conditions

Nearly half of automotive service technicians work more than 40 hours a week. Some may also work evenings and weekends to satisfy customer service needs. Generally, service technicians work indoors in well-ventilated and -lighted repair shops. However, some shops are drafty and noisy. Although some problems can be fixed with simple computerized adjustments, technicians frequently work with dirty and greasy parts, and in awkward positions. They often lift heavy parts and tools. Minor cuts, burns, and bruises are common, but technicians can usually avoid serious accidents if the shop is kept clean and orderly, and safety practices are observed.

Training, Other Qualifications, and Advancement

Automotive technology is rapidly increasing in sophistication, and most training authorities strongly recommend that persons seeking automotive service technician and mechanic jobs complete a formal training program in high school, or in a postsecondary vocational school or community college. However, some service technicians still learn the trade solely by assisting and learning from experienced workers. Courses in automotive repair, electronics, physics, chemistry, English, computers, and mathematics provide a good educational background for a career as a service technician.

High school programs, while an asset, vary greatly in scope. Some aim to equip graduates with enough skills to get a job as a technician's helper or trainee technician. Other programs offer only an introduction to automotive technology and service for the future consumer or hobbyist. Some of the more extensive programs participate in Automotive Youth Education Service (AYES), which has about 500 participating schools and more than 4000 participating dealers. Students who complete these programs receive an AYES certification and upon high school graduation are better prepared to enter entry-level technician positions, or to advance their technical education.

Postsecondary automotive technician training programs vary greatly in format, but normally provide intensive career preparation through a combination of classroom instruction and hands-on practice. Some trade and technical school programs provide concentrated training for 6 months to a year, depending on how many hours the student attends each week, and award a certificate. Community college programs normally award an associate degree or certificate and usually spread the training over 2 years by supplementing the automotive training with instruction in English, basic mathematics, computers, and other subjects. Some students earn repair certificates in one particular skill and opt to leave the program to begin their career before graduation. Recently, some programs have added to their curriculums training on employability skills such as customer service and stress management. Employers find that these skills help technicians handle the additional responsibilities of dealing with the customers and parts vendors.

The various automobile manufacturers and their participating dealers sponsor 2-year associate degree programs at postsecondary schools across the nation. The Accrediting Commission of Career Schools and Colleges of Technology (ACCSCT) currently certifies a number of automotive and diesel technology schools. Schools update their curriculums frequently to reflect changing technology and equipment. Students in these programs typically spend alternate 6- to 12-week periods attending classes full time and working full time in the service departments of sponsoring dealers. At these dealerships, students get practical experience while assigned to an experienced worker who provides hands-on instruction and timesaving tips.

The ASE certification is a nationally recognized standard for programs offered by high schools, postsecondary trade schools, technical institutes, and community colleges that train automobile service technicians. Some automotive manufacturers provide ASE-certified instruction programs with service equipment and current-model cars on which students practice new skills and learn the latest automotive technology. While ASE certification is voluntary, it does signify that the program meets uniform standards for instructional facilities, equipment, staff credentials, and curriculum. To ensure that programs keep up with ever-changing technology, repair techniques, and ASE standards, the certified programs are subjected to periodic compliance reviews and mandatory recertification, as are the ASE standards themselves. In 2004, about 2000 high school and postsecondary automotive service technician training programs had been certified by ASE.

For trainee automotive service technician jobs, employers look for people with strong communication and analytical skills. Technicians need good reading, mathematics, and computer skills to study technical manuals and to keep abreast of new technology and learn new service and repair procedures and specifications. Trainees also must possess mechanical aptitude and knowledge of how automobiles work. Most employers regard the successful completion of a vocational training program in automotive service technology as the best preparation for trainee positions. Experience working on motor vehicles in the Armed Forces or as a hobby also is valuable. Because of the complexity of new vehicles, a growing number of employers require completion of high school and additional postsecondary training.

Many new cars have several onboard computers, operating everything from the engine to the radio. Engine controls and dashboard instruments were among the first components to use electronics, but today most automotive systems, such as braking, transmission, and steering systems, are controlled primarily by computers and electronic components. Some of the more advanced vehicles have global positioning systems, Internet access, and other high-tech features integrated into the functions of the vehicle. The training in electronics is vital because electrical components, or a series of related components, account for nearly all malfunctions in modern vehicles.

In addition to electronics and computers, automotive service technicians will have to learn and understand the science behind the alternate-fuel vehicles that have begun to enter the market. The fuel for these vehicles will come from the dehydrogenization of water, electric fuel cells, natural gas, solar power, and other non-petroleum-based sources. Hybrid vehicles, for example, use the energy from braking to recharge batteries that power an electric motor, which supplements a gasoline engine. As vehicles with these new technologies become more common, technicians will need additional training to learn the science and engineering that makes them possible. Currently, the manufacturers of these alternate-fuel vehicles are providing the necessary training. However, as the warrantees begin to expire, technicians in all industries will need to be trained to service these vehicles. As the number of these automobiles on the road increases, some technicians will likely specialize in the service and repair of these vehicles.

Those new to automotive service usually start as trainee technicians, technicians' helpers, or lubrication workers, and gradually acquire and practice their skills by working with experienced mechanics and technicians. With a few months' experience, beginners perform many routine service tasks and make simple repairs. While some graduates of postsecondary automotive training programs are often able to earn promotion to the journey level after only a few months on the job, it typically takes 2 to 5 years of experience to become a journey level service technician, who is expected to quickly perform the more difficult types of routine service and repairs. An additional 1 to 2 years of experience familiarizes technicians with all types of repairs. Complex specialties, such as transmission repair, require another year or two of training and experience. In contrast, brake specialists may learn their jobs in considerably less time because they do not need a complete knowledge of automotive repair.

At work, the most important possessions of technicians are their hand tools. Technicians usually provide their own tools, and many experienced workers have thousands of dollars invested in them. Employers typically furnish expensive power tools, engine analyzers, and other diagnostic equipment, but technicians accumulate hand tools with experience. Some formal training programs have alliances with tool manufacturers that help entry-level technicians accumulate tools during their training period.

Employers increasingly send experienced automotive service technicians to manufacturer training centers to learn to repair new models or to receive special training in the repair of components, such as electronic fuel injection or air-conditioners. Motor vehicle dealers and other automotive service providers also may send promising beginners to manufacturer-sponsored technician training programs; most employers periodically send experienced technicians to manufacturer-sponsored technician training programs for additional training to maintain or upgrade employees' skills and thus increase the employees' value to the employer. Factory representatives also visit many shops to conduct short training sessions.

Voluntary certification by the National Institute for Automotive Service Excellence (ASE) has become a standard credential for automotive service technicians. Certification is available in 1 or more of 8 different areas of automotive service, such as electrical systems, engine repair, brake systems, suspension and steering, and heating and air-conditioning. For certification in each area, technicians must have at least 2 years of experience and pass the examination. Completion of an automotive training program in high school, vocational or trade school, or community or junior college may be substituted for 1 year of experience. For ASE certification as a master automobile technician, technicians must be certified in all eight areas. Technicians must retake each examination once every 5 years to maintain their certifications.

Experienced technicians who have leadership ability sometimes advance to shop supervisor or service manager. Those who work well with customers may become automotive repair service estimators. Some with sufficient funds open independent repair shops.

Employment

Automotive service technicians and mechanics held about 803,000 jobs in 2004. The majority worked for automotive repair and maintenance shops, automobile dealers, and retailers and wholesalers of automotive parts, accessories, and supplies. Others found employment in gasoline stations; home and auto supply stores; automotive equipment rental and leasing companies; federal, state, and local governments; and other organizations. More than 16 percent of service technicians were self-employed, more than twice the proportion for all installation, maintenance, and repair occupations.

Job Outlook

Job opportunities in this occupation are expected to be very good for persons who complete automotive training programs in high school, vocational and technical schools, or community colleges as employers report difficulty in finding workers with the right skills. Persons with good diagnostic and problem-solving abilities, and whose training includes basic electronics and computer courses, should have the best opportunities. For well-prepared people with a technical background, automotive service technician careers offer an excellent opportunity for good pay and the satisfaction of highly skilled work with vehicles incorporating the latest in advanced technology. However, persons without formal automotive training are likely to face competition for entry-level jobs.

Employment of automotive service technicians and mechanics is expected to increase as fast as the average through the year 2014. Over the 2004–14 period, demand for technicians will grow as the number of vehicles in operation increases, reflecting continued growth in the number of multi-car families. Growth in demand will be offset somewhat by slowing population growth and the continuing increase in the quality and durability of automobiles, which will require less frequent service. Additional job openings will be due to the need to replace a growing number of retiring technicians, who tend to be the most experienced workers.

Most persons who enter the occupation can expect steady work, even through downturns in the economy. While car owners may postpone maintenance and repair on their vehicles when their budgets become strained, and employers of automotive technicians may cutback hiring new workers, changes in economic conditions generally have minor effects on the automotive service and repair business.

Employment growth will continue to be concentrated in automobile dealerships and independent automotive repair shops. Many new jobs also will be created in small retail operations that offer after-warranty repairs, such as oil changes, brake repair, air-conditioner service, and other minor repairs generally taking less than 4 hours to complete. Employment of automotive service technicians and mechanics in gasoline service stations will continue to decline, as fewer stations offer repair services.

Earnings

Median hourly earnings of automotive service technicians and mechanics, including commission, were $15.60 in May 2004. The middle 50 percent earned between $11.31 and $20.75 per hour. The lowest 10 percent earned less than $8.70, and the highest 10 percent earned more than $26.22 per hour. Median annual earnings in the industries employing the largest numbers of service technicians in May 2004 were as follows:

Local government	$38,160
Automobile dealers	38,060
Automotive repair and maintenance	28,810
Gasoline stations	28,030
Automotive parts, accessories, and tire stores	27,180

Many experienced technicians employed by automobile dealers and independent repair shops receive a commission related to the labor cost charged to the customer. Under this method, weekly earnings depend on the amount of work completed. Employers frequently guarantee commissioned technicians a minimum weekly salary.

Some automotive service technicians are members of labor unions such as the International Association of Machinists and Aerospace Workers; the International Union, United Automobile, Aerospace and Agricultural Implement Workers of America; the Sheet Metal Workers' International Association; and the International Brotherhood of Teamsters.

Related Occupations

Other workers who repair and service motor vehicles include automotive body and related repairers, diesel service technicians and mechanics, and small engine mechanics.

Sources of Additional Information

For more details about work opportunities, contact local automobile dealers and repair shops or local offices of the state employment service. The state employment service also may have information about training programs.

A list of certified automotive service technician training programs can be obtained from:

- National Automotive Technicians Education Foundation, 101 Blue Seal Dr. SE, Suite 101, Leesburg, VA 20175. Internet: http://www.natef.org

For a directory of accredited private trade and technical schools that offer programs in automotive service technician training, contact:

- Accrediting Commission of Career Schools and Colleges of Technology, 2101 Wilson Blvd., Suite 302, Arlington, VA 22201. Internet: http://www.accsct.org

Information on automobile manufacturer-sponsored programs in automotive service technology can be obtained from:

- Automotive Youth Educational Systems (AYES), 100 W. Big Beaver, Suite 300, Troy, MI 48084. Internet: http://www.ayes.org

Information on how to become a certified automotive service technician is available from:

- National Institute for Automotive Service Excellence (ASE), 101 Blue Seal Dr. SE, Suite 101, Leesburg, VA 20175. Internet: http://www.asecert.org

For general information about a career as an automotive service technician, contact:

- National Automobile Dealers Association, 8400 Westpark Dr., McLean, VA 22102. Internet: http://www.nada.org
- Automotive Retailing Today, 8400 Westpark Dr., MS #2, McLean, VA 22102. Internet: http://www.autoretailing.org
- Automotive Jobs Today, 8400 Westpark Dr., MS #2, McLean, VA 22102. Internet: http://www.autojobstoday.org
- Career Voyages, U.S. Department of Labor, 200 Constitution Ave. NW, Washington DC 20210. Internet: http://www.careervoyages.gov/automotive-main.cfm

Barbers, Cosmetologists, and Other Personal Appearance Workers

(O*NET 39-5011.00, 39-5012.00, 39-5091.00, 39-5092.00, 39-5093.00, and 39-5094.00)

Significant Points

- Job opportunities generally should be good, but competition is expected for jobs and clients at higher paying salons; opportunities will be best for those licensed to provide a broad range of services.
- A state license is required for barbers, cosmetologists, and most other personal appearance workers, with the exception of shampooers; qualifications vary by state.
- About 48 percent of workers are self-employed; many also work flexible schedules.

Nature of the Work

Barbers and cosmetologists, also called *hairdressers* and *hairstylists*, provide hair care services to enhance the appearance of consumers. Other personal appearance workers, such as *manicurists and pedicurists*, *shampooers*, and *skin care specialists* provide specialized services that help clients look and feel their best.

Barbers cut, trim, shampoo, and style hair. They also fit hairpieces and offer scalp treatments and facial shaving. In many states, barbers are licensed to color, bleach, or highlight hair and to offer permanent-wave services. Many barbers also provide skin care and nail treatments.

Hairdressers, hairstylists, and cosmetologists offer beauty services, such as shampooing, cutting, coloring, and styling hair. They may advise clients on how to care for their hair, how to straighten their hair or give it a permanent wave, or how to lighten or darken their hair color. In addition, cosmetologists may be trained to give manicures, pedicures, and scalp and facial treatments; provide makeup analysis; and clean and style wigs and hairpieces.

A number of workers offer specialized services. *Manicurists and pedicurists*, called *nail technicians* in some states, work exclusively on nails and provide manicures, pedicures, coloring, and nail extensions to clients. Another group of specialists is *skin care specialists*, or *estheticians*, who cleanse and beautify the skin by giving facials, full-body treatments, and head and neck massages and by removing hair through waxing. *Electrologists* use an electrolysis machine to remove hair. Finally, in some larger salons, *shampooers* specialize in shampooing and conditioning hair.

In addition to working with clients, personal appearance workers are expected to maintain clean work areas and sanitize all their work instruments. They may make appointments and keep records of hair color and permanent-wave formulas used by their regular clients. A growing number actively sell hair care products and other cosmetic supplies. Barbers, cosmetologists, and other personal appearance workers who operate their own salons have managerial duties that may include hiring, supervising, and firing workers, as well as keeping business and inventory records, ordering supplies, and arranging for advertising.

Working Conditions

Barbers, cosmetologists, and other personal appearance workers usually work in clean, pleasant surroundings with good lighting and ventilation. Good health and stamina are important, because these workers are on their feet for most of their shift. Prolonged exposure to some hair and nail chemicals may cause irritation, so protective clothing, such as plastic gloves or aprons, may be worn.

Most full-time barbers, cosmetologists, and other personal appearance workers put in a 40-hour week, but longer hours are common, especially among self-employed workers. Work schedules may include evenings and weekends, the times when beauty salons and barbershops are busiest. Barbers and cosmetologists generally work on weekends and during lunch and evening hours; as a result, they may arrange to take breaks during less busy times. About 32 percent of cosmetologists and 17 percent of barbers work part time, and 14 percent of cosmetologists and 17 percent of barbers have variable schedules.

Training, Other Qualifications, and Advancement

All states require barbers, cosmetologists, and most other personal appearance workers, with the exception of shampooers, to be licensed; however, qualifications for a license vary by state. Generally, a person must have graduated from a state-licensed barber or cosmetology school and be at least 16 years old. A few states require applicants to pass a physical examination. Some states require graduation from high school, while others require as little as an eighth-grade education. In a few states, the completion of an apprenticeship can substitute for graduation from a school, but very few barbers or cosmetologists learn their skills in this way. Applicants for a license usually are required to pass a written test and demonstrate an ability to perform basic barbering or cosmetology services.

Some states have reciprocity agreements that allow licensed barbers and cosmetologists to obtain a license in a different state without additional formal training. Such agreements are uncommon, however, and most states do not recognize training or licenses obtained from a different state. Consequently, persons who wish to work in a particular state should review the laws of that state before entering a training program.

Public and private vocational schools offer daytime or evening classes in barbering and cosmetology. Full-time programs in barbering and cosmetology usually last 9 to 24 months, but training for manicurists and pedicurists, skin care specialists, and electrologists requires significantly less time. An apprenticeship program can last from 1 to 3 years. Shampooers generally do not need formal training or a license. Formal training programs include classroom study, demonstrations, and practical work. Students study the basic services—cutting and styling hair, chemically treating hair, shaving customers, and giving hair and scalp treatments—and, under supervision, practice on customers in school "clinics." Students attend lectures on the use and care of instruments, sanitation and hygiene, chemistry, anatomy, physiology, and the recognition of simple skin ailments. Instruction also is provided in communication, sales, and general business practices. Experienced barbers and cosmetologists may take advanced courses in hairstyling, coloring, the sale and service of wigs and hairpieces, and sales and marketing.

After graduating from a training program, students can take a state licensing examination, which consists of a written test and, in some cases, a practical test of styling skills based on established performance criteria. A few states include an oral examination in which applicants are asked to explain the procedures they are following while taking the practical test. In many states, cosmetology training may be credited toward a barbering license, and vice versa. A few states combine the two licenses into one hairstyling license. Many states require separate licensing examinations for manicurists, pedicurists, and skin care specialists.

For many barbers, cosmetologists, and other personal appearance workers, formal training and a license are only the first steps in a career that requires years of continuing education. Personal appearance workers must keep abreast of the latest fashions and beauty techniques as hairstyles change, new products are developed, and services expand to meet clients' needs. They attend training at salons, cosmetology schools, or industry trade shows. Through workshops and demonstrations of the latest techniques, industry representatives introduce cosmetologists to a wide range of products and services. As retail sales become an increasingly important part of salons' revenue, the ability to be an effective salesperson becomes ever more vital for salon workers.

Successful personal appearance workers should have an understanding of fashion, art, and technical design. They should enjoy working with the public and be willing and able to follow clients' instructions. Communication, image, and attitude play an important role in career success. Some cosmetology schools consider "people skills" to be such an integral part of the job that they require coursework in that area. Business skills are important for those who plan to operate their own salons.

During their first months on the job, new workers are given relatively simple tasks or are assigned the simplest procedures. Once they have demonstrated their skills, they are gradually permitted to perform more complicated tasks, such as coloring hair or applying permanent waves. As they continue to work in the field, more training usually is required to learn the techniques particular to each salon and to build on the basics learned in cosmetology school.

Advancement usually takes the form of higher earnings as barbers and cosmetologists gain experience and build a steady clientele. Some barbers and cosmetologists manage large salons, lease booth space in salons, or open their own salons after several years of experience. Others teach in barber or cosmetology schools or provide training through vocational schools. Still others advance to become sales representatives, image or fashion consultants, or examiners for state licensing boards.

Employment

Barbers, cosmetologists, and other personal appearance workers held about 790,000 jobs in 2004. Of these, barbers, hairdressers, hairstylists, and cosmetologists held 670,000 jobs, manicurists and pedicurists 60,000, skin care specialists 30,000, and shampooers 27,000.

Most of these workers are employed in beauty salons or barber shops, but they also are found in nail salons, day and resort spas, department stores, nursing and other residential care homes, and drug and cosmetics stores. Nearly every town has a barbershop or beauty salon, but employment in this occupation is concentrated in the most populous cities and states.

About 48 percent of all barbers, cosmetologists, and other personal appearance workers are self-employed. Many own their own salon, but a growing number lease booth space or a chair from the salon's owner.

Job Outlook

Job opportunities generally should be good. However, competition is expected for jobs and clients at higher paying salons as applicants compete with a large pool of licensed and experienced cosmetologists for these positions. Opportunities will be best for those with previous experience and for those licensed to provide a broad range of services.

Overall employment of barbers, cosmetologists, and other personal appearance workers is projected to grow about as fast as the average for all occupations through 2014, because of an increasing population, rising incomes, and growing demand for personal appearance services. In addition to those arising from job growth, numerous job openings will come about from the need to replace workers who transfer to other occupations, retire, or leave the labor force for other reasons.

Employment trends are expected to vary among the different occupational specialties. On the one hand, slower-than-average growth is expected in employment of barbers because of the large number of retirements expected over the 2004–14 projection period and because of the relatively small number of cosmetology school graduates opting to obtain barbering licenses. On the other hand, employment of hairdressers, hairstylists, and cosmetologists should grow about as fast as the average for all workers because many now cut and style both men's and women's hair and because the demand for hair treatment by teens and aging baby boomers is expected to remain steady or even grow.

Continued growth in the number of nail salons and full-service day spas will generate numerous job openings for manicurists, pedicurists, skin care specialists, and shampooers. Employment of manicurists, pedicurists, and skin care specialists will grow faster than the average, while employment of shampooers will grow about as fast as the average. Nail salons specialize in providing manicures and pedicures. Day spas typically provide a full range of services, including beauty wraps, manicures and pedicures, facials, and massages.

Earnings

A number of factors, including the size and location of the salon, clients' tipping habits, and competition from other barber shops and salons, determine the total income of barbers, cosmetologists, and other personal appearance workers. They may receive commissions based on the price of the service, or a salary based on the number of hours worked, and many receive commissions on the products they sell. In addition, some salons pay bonuses to employees who bring in new business. A cosmetologist's or barber's initiative and ability to attract and hold regular clients also are key factors in determining his or her earnings. Earnings for entry-level workers are usually low; however, for those who stay in the profession, earnings can be considerably higher.

Although some salons offer paid vacations and medical benefits, many self-employed and part-time workers in this occupation do not enjoy such benefits.

Median annual earnings in May 2004 for salaried hairdressers, hairstylists, and cosmetologists, including tips and commission, were $19,800. The middle 50 percent earned between $ 15,480 and $26,600. The lowest 10 percent earned less than $12,920, and the highest 10 percent earned more than $35,990.

Median annual earnings in May 2004 for salaried barbers, including tips, were $21,200. The middle 50 percent earned between $15,380 and $30,390. The lowest 10 percent earned less than $12,950, and the highest 10 percent earned more than $43,170.

Among skin care specialists, median annual earnings, including tips, were $ 24,010, for manicurists and pedicurists $18,500, and for shampooers $14,610.

Related Occupations

Other workers who provide a personal service to clients and usually must be professionally licensed or certified include massage therapists and fitness workers.

Sources of Additional Information

A list of licensed training schools and licensing requirements for cosmetologists may be obtained from:

- National Accrediting Commission of Cosmetology Arts and Sciences, 4401 Ford Ave., Suite 1300, Alexandria, VA 22302. Internet: http://www.naccas.org

Information about a career in cosmetology is available from:

- National Cosmetology Association, 401 N. Michigan Ave., 22nd Floor, Chicago, IL 60611. Internet: http://www.ncacares.org

For details on state licensing requirements and approved barber or cosmetology schools, contact the state boards of barber or cosmetology examiners in your state.

Bill and Account Collectors

(O*NET 43-3011.00)

Significant Points

- About 1 in 5 collectors works for collection agencies; others work in banks, retail stores, government, physicians' offices, hospitals, and other institutions that lend money and extend credit.
- Most jobs in this occupation require only a high school diploma, though many employers prefer workers with some postsecondary training.
- Faster-than-average employment growth is expected as companies focus more efforts on collecting unpaid debts.

Nature of the Work

Bill and account collectors, called simply *collectors*, keep track of accounts that are overdue and attempt to collect payment on them. Some are employed by third-party collection agencies, while others—known as "in-house collectors"—work directly for the original creditors, such as department stores, hospitals, or banks.

The duties of bill and account collectors are similar in the many different organizations in which they are employed. First, collectors are called upon to locate and notify customers of delinquent accounts, usually over the telephone, but sometimes by letter. When customers move without leaving a forwarding address, collectors may check with the post office, telephone companies, credit bureaus, or former neighbors to obtain the new address. The attempt to find the new address is called "skip tracing." New computer systems assist in tracing by automatically tracking when customers change their address or contact information on any of their open accounts.

Once collectors find the debtor, they inform him or her of the overdue account and solicit payment. If necessary, they review the terms of the sale, service, or credit contract with the customer. Collectors also may attempt to learn the cause of the delay in payment. Where feasible, they offer the customer advice on how to pay off the debts, such as by taking out a bill consolidation loan. However, the collector's prime objective is always to ensure that the customer pays the debt in question.

If a customer agrees to pay, collectors record this commitment and check later to verify that the payment was indeed made. Collectors may have authority to grant an extension of time if customers ask for one. If a customer fails to respond, collectors prepare a statement indicating the customer's action for the credit department of the establishment. In more extreme cases, collectors may initiate repossession proceedings, disconnect the customer's service, or hand the account over to an attorney for legal action. Most collectors handle other administrative functions for the accounts assigned to them, including recording changes of addresses and purging the records of the deceased.

Collectors use computers and a variety of automated systems to keep track of overdue accounts. Typically, collectors work at video display terminals that are linked to computers. In sophisticated predictive dialer systems, a computer dials the telephone automatically, and the collector speaks only when a connection has been made.

Such systems eliminate time spent calling busy or nonanswering numbers. Many collectors use regular telephones, but others wear headsets like those used by telephone operators.

Working Conditions

In-house bill and account collectors typically are employed in an office environment, while those who work for third-party collection agencies may work in a call-center environment. Workers spend most of their time on the phone tracking down and contacting people with debts. The work can be stressful as some customers can be confrontational when pressed about their debts, although some appreciate assistance in resolving their outstanding debt. Collectors may also feel pressured to meet targets for the amount of debt they are expected to recover in a certain period.

Bill and account collectors often have to work evenings and weekends, when it usually is easier to reach people. As a result, it is not uncommon for workers to work part time or on flexible work schedules, though the majority work 40 hours per week.

Training, Other Qualifications, and Advancement

Most bill and account collectors are required to have at least a high school diploma. However, employers prefer workers who have completed some college or who have experience in other occupations that involve contact with the public. Workers should have good communication skills and be computer literate; experience with advanced telecommunications equipment is also useful.

Once hired, workers usually receive on-the-job training. Under the guidance of a supervisor or some other senior worker, new employees learn company procedures. Some formal classroom training also may be necessary, such as training in specific computer software. Additional training topics usually include telephone techniques and negotiation skills. Workers are also instructed in the laws governing the collection of debt as mandated by the Fair Debt Collection Practices Act (FDCPA), which applies to all third party and some in-house collectors.

Workers usually advance by taking on more duties in the same occupation for higher pay or by transferring to a closely related occupation. Many companies fill supervisory positions by promoting individuals from within the organization, and workers who acquire additional skills, experience, and training improve their advancement opportunities.

Employment

Bill and account collectors held about 456,000 jobs in 2004. About 1 in 5 collectors works for collection agencies. Many others work in banks, retail stores, government, physician's offices, hospitals, and other institutions that lend money and extend credit.

Job Outlook

Employment of bill and account collectors is expected to grow faster than the average for all occupations through 2014. Cash flow is becoming increasingly important to companies, which are now placing greater emphasis on collecting unpaid debts sooner. Thus, the workload for collectors is expected to continue to increase as they seek to collect not only debts that are relatively old, but ones that are more recent. Also, as more companies in a wide range of industries get involved in lending money and issuing their own credit cards, they will need to hire collectors because debt levels will likely continue to rise. In addition to job openings from employment growth, a significant number of openings will result from the high level of turnover in the occupation. As a result, job opportunities should be favorable.

Hospitals and physicians' offices are two of the fastest-growing industries requiring collectors. With insurance reimbursements not keeping up with cost increases, the health care industry is seeking to recover more money from patients. Government agencies also are making more use of collectors to collect on everything from parking tickets to child-support payments and past-due taxes. Finally, the Internal Revenue Service (IRS) is looking into outsourcing the collection of overdue federal taxes to third-party collection agencies. If the IRS does outsource, more collectors will be required for this large job.

Despite the increasing demand for bill collectors, employment growth may be limited due to an increased use of third-party debt collectors, who are generally more efficient than in-house collectors. Also, some firms are beginning to use offshore collection agencies, whose lower cost structures allow them to collect debts that are too small for domestic collection agencies. Contrary to the pattern in most occupations, employment of bill and account collectors tends to rise during recessions, reflecting the difficulty that many people have in meeting their financial obligations. However, collectors usually have more success at getting people to repay their debts when the economy is good.

Earnings

Median hourly earnings of bill and account collectors were $13.20 in May 2004. The middle 50 percent earned between $10.87 and $16.28. The lowest 10 percent earned less than $9.22, and the highest 10 percent earned more than $20.10. In addition to a basic rate of pay, many bill and account collectors earn commissions based on the amount of debt they recover.

Related Occupations

Bill and account collectors review and collect information on accounts. Other occupations with similar responsibilities include credit authorizers, checkers, and clerks; loan officers; and interviewers.

Sources of Additional Information

Career information on bill and account collectors is available from:

- ACA International, The Association of Credit and Collection Professionals, P.O. Box 390106, Minneapolis, MN 55439. Internet: http://www.acainternational.org

Bookkeeping, Accounting, and Auditing Clerks

(O*NET 43-3031.00)

Significant Points

- Bookkeeping, accounting, and auditing clerks held more than 2 million jobs in 2004 and are employed in every industry.
- Employment is projected to grow more slowly than average as the spread of office automation lifts worker productivity.
- The large size of this occupation ensures plentiful job openings, including many opportunities for temporary and part-time work; those who can carry out a wider range of bookkeeping and accounting activities will be in greater demand than specialized clerks.

Nature of the Work

Bookkeeping, accounting, and auditing clerks are an organization's financial recordkeepers. They update and maintain one or more accounting records, including those which tabulate expenditures, receipts, accounts payable and receivable, and profit and loss. They represent a wide range of skills and knowledge from full-charge bookkeepers who can maintain an entire company's books to accounting clerks who handle specific accounts. All of these clerks make numerous computations each day and increasingly must be comfortable using computers to calculate and record data.

In small establishments, *bookkeeping clerks* handle all financial transactions and recordkeeping. They record all transactions, post debits and credits, produce financial statements, and prepare reports and summaries for supervisors and managers. Bookkeepers also prepare bank deposits by compiling data from cashiers; verifying and balancing receipts; and sending cash, checks, or other forms of payment to the bank. They also may handle payroll, make purchases, prepare invoices, and keep track of overdue accounts.

In large offices and accounting departments, *accounting clerks* have more specialized tasks. Their titles, such as accounts payable clerk or accounts receivable clerk, often reflect the type of accounting they do. In addition, their responsibilities vary by level of experience. Entry-level accounting clerks post details of transactions, total accounts, and compute interest charges. They also may monitor loans and accounts to ensure that payments are up to date.

More advanced accounting clerks may total, balance, and reconcile billing vouchers; ensure the completeness and accuracy of data on accounts; and code documents according to company procedures. These workers post transactions in journals and on computer files and update the files when needed. Senior clerks also review computer printouts against manually maintained journals and make necessary corrections. They may review invoices and statements to ensure that all the information appearing on them is accurate and complete, and they may reconcile computer reports with operating reports.

Auditing clerks verify records of transactions posted by other workers. They check figures, postings, and documents to ensure that they are correct, mathematically accurate, and properly coded. They also correct or note errors for accountants or other workers to adjust.

As organizations continue to computerize their financial records, many bookkeeping, accounting, and auditing clerks are using specialized accounting software on personal computers. With manual posting to general ledgers becoming obsolete, these clerks increasingly are posting charges to accounts on computer spreadsheets and databases. They now enter information from receipts or bills into computers, and the information is then stored either electronically or as computer printouts (or both). The widespread use of computers also has enabled bookkeeping, accounting, and auditing clerks to take on additional responsibilities, such as payroll, procurement, and billing. Many of these functions require these clerks to write letters, make phone calls to customers or clients, and interact with colleagues. Therefore, good communication skills are becoming increasingly important in the occupation.

Working Conditions

Bookkeeping, accounting, and auditing clerks work in an office environment. They may experience eye and muscle strain, backaches, headaches, and repetitive motion injuries as a result of using computers on a daily basis. Clerks may have to sit for extended periods while reviewing detailed data.

Many bookkeeping, accounting, and auditing clerks work regular business hours and a standard 40-hour week. A substantial number work just part time. Full-time and part-time clerks may work some evenings and weekends. Bookkeeping, accounting, and auditing clerks may work longer hours to meet deadlines at the end of the fiscal year, during tax time, or when monthly or yearly accounting audits are performed. Those who work in hotels, restaurants, and stores may put in overtime during peak holiday and vacation seasons.

Training, Other Qualifications, and Advancement

Most bookkeeping, accounting, and auditing clerks are required to have a high school degree at a minimum. However, having some college is increasingly important, and an associate degree in business or accounting is required for some positions. Although a college degree is rarely required, graduates may accept bookkeeping, accounting, and auditing clerk positions to get into a particular company or to enter the accounting or finance field with the hope of eventually being promoted to professional or managerial positions.

Experience in a related job and working in an office environment also is recommended. Employers prefer workers who are computer-literate; knowledge of word-processing and spreadsheet software is especially valuable.

Once hired, bookkeeping, accounting, and auditing clerks usually receive on-the-job training. Under the guidance of a supervisor or other senior worker, new employees learn company procedures. Some formal classroom training also may be necessary, such as training in specific computer software. Bookkeeping, accounting, and auditing clerks must be careful, orderly, and detail-oriented in order to avoid making errors and to recognize errors made by others. These workers also should be discreet and trustworthy because they frequently come in contact with confidential material. In addition, all bookkeeping, accounting, and auditing clerks should have a strong aptitude for numbers.

Bookkeepers, particularly those who handle all the recordkeeping for companies, may find it beneficial to become certified. The Certified Bookkeeper designation, awarded by the American Institute of Professional Bookkeepers, assures employers that individuals have the skills and knowledge required to carry out all the bookkeeping and accounting functions up through the adjusted trial balance, including payroll functions. For certification, candidates must have at least 2 years of bookkeeping experience, pass three tests, and adhere to a code of ethics. More than 100 colleges and universities offer a preparatory course for certification and another 150 offer a course online. The Universal Accounting Center offers the Professional Bookkeeper designation. Bookkeeping, accounting, and auditing clerks usually advance by taking on more duties in the same occupation for higher pay or by transferring to a closely related occupation. Most companies fill office and administrative support supervisory and managerial positions by promoting individuals from within their organizations, so clerks who acquire additional skills, experience, and training improve their advancement opportunities. With appropriate experience and education, some bookkeeping, accounting, and auditing clerks may become accountants or auditors.

Employment

Bookkeeping, accounting, and auditing clerks held more than 2 million jobs in 2004. They are found in all industries and at all levels of government. Local government and the accounting, tax preparation, bookkeeping, and payroll services industry are among the individual industries employing the largest numbers of these clerks. A growing number work for employment services firms, the result of an increase in outsourcing of this occupation. About 1 out of 4 bookkeeping, accounting, and auditing clerks worked part time in 2004.

Job Outlook

Employment of bookkeeping, accounting, and auditing clerks is projected to grow more slowly than the average for all occupations through 2014. More job openings will stem from replacement needs than from job growth. Each year, numerous jobs will become available as these clerks transfer to other occupations or leave the labor force. The large size of this occupation ensures plentiful job openings, including many opportunities for temporary and part-time work.

Although a growing economy will result in more financial transactions and other activities that require these clerical workers, the continuing spread of office automation will lift worker productivity and contribute to the slower-than-average increase in employment. In addition, organizations of all sizes will continue to downsize and consolidate various recordkeeping functions, thus reducing the demand for bookkeeping, accounting, and auditing clerks. Furthermore, some work performed by these workers will be outsourced to lower-wage foreign countries. Those who can carry out a wider range of bookkeeping and accounting activities will be in greater demand than specialized clerks. Demand for full-charge bookkeepers is expected to increase because they are called upon to do much of the work of accountants as well as perform a wider variety of financial transactions, from payroll to billing. Certified bookkeepers and those with several years of accounting or bookkeeper experience will have the best job prospects.

Earnings

In May 2004, the median wage and salary annual earnings of bookkeeping, accounting, and auditing clerks were $28,570. The middle half of the occupation earned between $22,960 and $35,450. The top 10 percent of bookkeeping, accounting, and auditing clerks earned more than $43,570, and the bottom 10 percent earned less than $18,580.

Related Occupations

Bookkeeping, accounting, and auditing clerks work with financial records. Other clerks who perform similar duties include bill and account collectors; billing and posting clerks and machine operators; brokerage clerks; credit authorizers, checkers, and clerks; payroll and timekeeping clerks; procurement clerks; and tellers.

Sources of Additional Information

For information on the Certified Bookkeeper designation, contact:

- American Institute of Professional Bookkeepers, 6001 Montrose Rd., Suite 500, Rockville, MD 20852. Internet: http://www.aipb.org

For information on the Professional Bookkeeper designation, contact:

- Universal Accounting Center, 5250 South Commerce Dr., Salt Lake City, UT 84107.

Building Cleaning Workers

(O*NET 37-1011.01, 37-1011.02, 37-2011.00, and 37-2012.00)

Significant Points

- This very large occupation requires few skills to enter and has one of the largest numbers of job openings of any occupation each year.
- Most job openings result from the need to replace the many workers who leave these jobs because of their limited opportunities for training or advancement, low pay, and high incidence of only part-time or temporary work.
- Most new jobs will occur in businesses providing janitorial and cleaning services on a contract basis.

Nature of the Work

Building cleaning workers—including janitors, maids, housekeeping cleaners, window washers, and rug shampooers—keep office buildings, hospitals, stores, apartment houses, hotels, and residences clean, sanitary, and in good condition. Some do only cleaning, while others have a wide range of duties.

Janitors and cleaners perform a variety of heavy cleaning duties, such as cleaning floors, shampooing rugs, washing walls and glass, and removing rubbish. They may fix leaky faucets, empty trash cans, do painting and carpentry, replenish bathroom supplies, mow lawns, and see that heating and air conditioning equipment works properly. On a typical day, janitors may wet- or dry-mop floors, clean bathrooms, vacuum carpets, dust furniture, make minor repairs, and exterminate insects and rodents. They also clean snow or debris from sidewalks in front of buildings and notify management of the need for major repairs. While janitors typically perform most of the duties mentioned, cleaners tend to work for companies that specialize in one type of cleaning activity, such as washing windows.

Maids and housekeeping cleaners perform any combination of light cleaning duties to keep private households or commercial establishments such as hotels, restaurants, hospitals, and nursing homes clean and orderly. In hotels, aside from cleaning and maintaining the premises, maids and housekeeping cleaners may deliver ironing boards, cribs, and rollaway beds to guests' rooms. In hospitals, they also may wash bed frames, brush mattresses, make beds, and disinfect and sterilize equipment and supplies with germicides and sterilizing equipment.

Janitors, maids, and cleaners use many kinds of equipment, tools, and cleaning materials. For one job they may need standard cleaning implements; another may require an electric polishing machine and a special cleaning solution. Improved building materials, chemical cleaners, and power equipment have made many tasks easier and less time consuming, but cleaning workers must learn the proper use of equipment and cleaners to avoid harming floors, fixtures, and themselves.

Cleaning supervisors coordinate, schedule, and supervise the activities of janitors and cleaners. They assign tasks and inspect building areas to see that work has been done properly; they also issue supplies and equipment and inventory stocks to ensure that supplies on hand are adequate. They also screen and hire job applicants; train new and experienced employees; and recommend promotions, transfers, or dismissals. Supervisors may prepare reports concerning the occupancy of rooms, hours worked, and department expenses. Some also perform cleaning duties.

Cleaners and servants in private households dust and polish furniture; sweep, mop, and wax floors; vacuum; and clean ovens, refrigerators, and bathrooms. They also may wash dishes, polish silver, and change and make beds. Some wash, fold, and iron clothes; a few wash windows. General houseworkers also may take clothes and laundry to the cleaners, buy groceries, and perform many other errands.

Building cleaning workers in large office and residential buildings, and more recently in large hotels, often work in teams consisting of workers who specialize in vacuuming, picking up trash, and cleaning restrooms, among other things. Supervisors conduct inspections to ensure that the building is cleaned properly and the team is functioning efficiently. In hotels, one member of the team is responsible for reporting electronically to the supervisor when rooms are cleaned.

Working Conditions

Because most office buildings are cleaned while they are empty, many cleaning workers work evening hours. Some, however, such as school and hospital custodians, work in the daytime. When there is a need for 24-hour maintenance, janitors may be assigned to shifts. Most full time building cleaners work about 40 hours a week. Part-time cleaners usually work in the evenings and on weekends.

Building cleaning workers usually work inside heated, well-lighted buildings. However, they sometimes work outdoors, sweeping walkways, mowing lawns, or shoveling snow. Working with machines can be noisy, and some tasks, such as cleaning bathrooms and trashrooms, can be dirty and unpleasant. Janitors may suffer cuts, bruises, and burns from machines, hand tools, and chemicals. They spend most of their time on their feet, sometimes lifting or pushing heavy furniture or equipment. Many tasks, such as dusting or sweeping, require constant bending, stooping, and stretching. As a result, janitors also may suffer back injuries and sprains.

Training, Other Qualifications, and Advancement

No special education is required for most janitorial or cleaning jobs, but beginners should know simple arithmetic and be able to follow instructions. High school shop courses are helpful for jobs involving repair work.

Most building cleaners learn their skills on the job. Beginners usually work with an experienced cleaner, doing routine cleaning. As they gain more experience, they are assigned more complicated tasks. In some cities, programs run by unions, government agencies, or employers teach janitorial skills. Students learn how to clean buildings thoroughly and efficiently; how to select and safely use various cleansing agents; and how to operate and maintain machines, such as wet and dry vacuums, buffers, and polishers. Students learn to plan their work, to follow safety and health regulations, to interact positively with people in the buildings they clean, and to work without supervision. Instruction in minor electrical, plumbing, and other repairs also may be given. Those who come in contact with the public should have good communication skills. Employers usually look for dependable, hard-working individuals who are in good health, follow directions well, and get along with other people.

Building cleaners usually find work by answering newspaper advertisements, applying directly to organizations where they would like to work, contacting local labor unions, or contacting state employment service offices.

Advancement opportunities for workers usually are limited in organizations where they are the only maintenance worker. Where there is a large maintenance staff, however, cleaning workers can be promoted to supervisor or to area supervisor or manager. A high school diploma improves the chances for advancement. Some janitors set up their own maintenance or cleaning businesses.

Supervisors usually move up through the ranks. In many establishments, they are required to take some inservice training to improve their housekeeping techniques and procedures and to enhance their supervisory skills.

A small number of cleaning supervisors and managers are members of the International Executive Housekeepers Association, which offers two kinds of certification programs for cleaning supervisors and managers: Certified Executive Housekeeper (CEH) and Registered Executive Housekeeper (REH). The CEH designation is offered to those with a high school education, while the REH designation is offered to those who have a 4-year college degree. Both designations are earned by attending courses and passing exams, and both must be renewed every 2 years to ensure that workers keep abreast of new cleaning methods. Those with the REH designation usually oversee the cleaning services of hotels, hospitals, casinos, and other large institutions that rely on well-trained experts for their cleaning needs.

Employment

Building cleaning workers held more than 4 million jobs in 2004. More than 6 percent were self-employed.

Janitors and cleaners work in nearly every type of establishment and held about 2.4 million jobs. They accounted for more than 58 percent of all building cleaning workers. More than 29 percent worked for firms supplying building maintenance services on a contract basis, more than 20 percent were employed in public or private educational services, and 2 percent worked in hotels or motels. Other employers included hospitals; restaurants; religious institutions; manufacturing firms; government agencies; and operators of apartment buildings, office buildings, and other types of real estate.

First-line supervisors of housekeeping and janitorial workers held about 236,000 jobs. Approximately 23 percent worked in firms supplying building maintenance services on a contract basis, while approximately 13 percent were employed in hotels or motels. More than 20 percent worked for state and local governments, primarily at schools and colleges. Others worked for hospitals, nursing homes and other residential care facilities.

Maids and housekeepers held about 1.4 million jobs. Private households employed the most maids and housekeepers—almost 28 percent—while hotels, motels, and other traveler accommodations employed the second most—almost 27 percent. Hospitals, nursing homes, and other residential care facilities employed large numbers, also. Although cleaning jobs can be found in all cities and towns, most are located in highly populated areas where there are many office buildings, schools, apartment houses, nursing homes, and hospitals.

Job Outlook

Overall employment of building cleaning workers is expected to grow as fast as average for all occupations through 2014, as more office complexes, apartment houses, schools, factories, hospitals, and other buildings requiring cleaning are built to accommodate a growing population and economy. As many firms reduce costs by contracting out the cleaning and maintenance of buildings, businesses providing janitorial and cleaning services on a contract basis are expected to have the greatest number of new jobs in this field. Although there have been some improvements in productivity in the way buildings are cleaned and maintained—using teams of cleaners, for example, and better cleaning supplies—cleaning still is very much a labor-intensive job. Faster than average growth is expected among janitors and cleaners and among cleaning supervisors, but as fast as average growth is projected for maids and housekeeping cleaners. In addition to job openings arising due to growth, numerous openings should result from the need to replace those who leave this very large occupation each year. Limited promotion potential, low pay, and the fact that many jobs are part-time and temporary, induce many to leave the occupation, thereby contributing to the number of job openings and the need to replace these workers.

Much of the growth in these occupations will come from cleaning residential properties. As families become more pressed for time, they increasingly are hiring cleaning and handyman services to perform a variety of tasks in their homes. Also, as the population ages, older people will need to hire cleaners to help maintain their houses. In addition, housekeeping cleaners will be needed to clean the growing number of residential care facilities for the elderly. These facilities, including assisted-living residences, generally provide housekeeping services as part of the rent.

Earnings

Median annual earnings of janitors and cleaners, except maids and housekeeping cleaners, were $18,790 in May 2004. The middle 50 percent earned between $15,320 and $24,420. The lowest 10 percent earned less than $13,010 and the highest 10 percent earned more than $31,780. Median annual earnings in 2004 in the industries employing the largest numbers of janitors and cleaners, except maids and housekeeping cleaners, were as follows:

Elementary and secondary schools	$22,910
Local government	22,860
Colleges, universities, and professional schools	21,860
Lessors of real estate	21,050
Services to buildings and dwellings	16,820

Median annual earnings of maids and housekeepers were $16,900 in May 2004. The middle 50 percent earned between $14,570 and $20,570. The lowest 10 percent earned less than $12,530, and the highest 10 percent earned more than $25,220. Median annual earnings in 2004 in the industries employing the largest numbers of maids and housekeepers were as follows:

General medical and surgical hospitals	$18,770
Services to buildings and dwellings	17,130
Community care facilities for the elderly	17,010
Nursing care facilities	16,960
Traveler accommodation	16,250

Median annual earnings of first-line supervisors and managers of housekeeping and janitorial workers were $29,510 in May 2004. The middle 50 percent earned between $22,720 and $38,790. The lowest 10 percent earned less than $18,550, and the highest 10 percent earned more than $49,230. Median annual earnings in May 2004 in the industries employing the largest numbers of first-line supervisors and managers of housekeeping and janitorial workers were as follows:

Local government	$34,780
Elementary and secondary schools	33,760
Nursing care facilities	28,370
Services to buildings and dwellings	27,760
Traveler accommodation	24,310

Related Occupations

Workers who specialize in one of the many job functions of janitors and cleaners include pest control workers; general maintenance and repair workers; and grounds maintenance workers.

Sources of Additional Information

Information about janitorial jobs may be obtained from state employment service offices.

For information on certification in executive housekeeping, contact:

- International Executive Housekeepers Association, Inc., 1001 Eastwind Dr., Suite 301, Westerville, OH 43081-3361. Internet: http://www.ieha.org

Bus Drivers

(O*NET 53-3021.00 and 53-3022.00)

Significant Points

- Opportunities should be good, particularly for school bus driver jobs; applicants for higher-paying public transit bus driver positions may encounter competition.
- State and federal governments establish bus driver qualifications and standards, which include a commercial driver's license.
- Work schedules vary considerably among various types of bus drivers.
- Bus drivers must possess strong customer service skills, including communication skills and the ability to manage large groups of people with varying needs.

Nature of the Work

Bus drivers provide transportation for millions of people every year, from commuters to school children to vacationers. There are two major kinds of bus drivers: *transit and intercity bus drivers*, who transport people between regions of a state or of the country, along routes run within a metropolitan area or county, or on chartered excursions and tours; and *school bus drivers*, who take children to and from schools and related events.

Bus drivers pick up and drop off passengers at bus stops, stations, or—in the case of students—at regularly scheduled neighborhood locations, all according to strict time schedules. Drivers must operate vehicles safely, especially in heavy traffic. They cannot let light traffic put them ahead of schedule so that they miss passengers. Bus drivers drive a range of vehicles from 15-passenger buses to 60-foot articulated buses that can carry more than 100 passengers.

Local-transit and *intercity bus drivers* report to their assigned terminal or garage, where they stock up on tickets or transfers and prepare trip report forms. In some transportation firms, maintenance departments are responsible for keeping vehicles in good condition; in others, drivers may be expected to check their vehicle's tires, brakes, windshield wipers, lights, oil, fuel, and water supply before beginning their routes. Drivers usually verify that the bus has safety equipment, such as fire extinguishers, first aid kits, and emergency reflectors.

During the course of their shift, local-transit and intercity bus drivers collect fares; answer questions about schedules, routes, and transfer points; and sometimes announce stops. Intercity bus drivers may make only a single one-way trip to a distant city or a round trip each day. They may stop at towns just a few miles apart or only at large cities hundreds of miles apart. Local-transit bus drivers may make several trips each day over the same city and suburban streets, stopping as frequently as every few blocks.

Local-transit bus drivers submit daily trip reports with a record of trips, significant schedule delays, and mechanical problems. Intercity drivers who drive across state or national boundaries must comply with U.S. Department of Transportation regulations. These include completing vehicle inspection reports and recording distances traveled and the periods they spend driving, performing other duties, and off duty.

Some intercity drivers operate motor coaches which transport passengers on chartered trips and sightseeing tours. Drivers routinely interact with customers and tour guides to make the trip as comfortable and informative as possible. They are directly responsible for keeping to strict schedules, adhering to the guidelines of the tour's itinerary, and ensuring the overall success of the trip. These drivers act as customer service representative, tour guide, program director, and safety guide. Trips frequently last more than a day. The driver may be away for more than a week if assigned to an extended tour. As with all commercial drivers who drive across state or national boundaries, motor coach drivers must comply with U.S. Department of Transportation and state regulations.

School bus drivers usually drive the same routes each day, stopping to pick up pupils in the morning and return them to their homes in the afternoon. Some school bus drivers also transport students and teachers on field trips or to sporting events. In addition to driving, some school bus drivers work part time in the school system as janitors, mechanics, or classroom assistants when not driving buses.

Bus drivers must be alert to prevent accidents, especially in heavy traffic or in bad weather, and to avoid sudden stops or swerves that jar passengers. School bus drivers must exercise particular caution when children are getting on or off the bus. They must maintain order on their bus and enforce school safety standards by allowing only students to board. In addition, they must know and enforce the school system's rules regarding student conduct.

School bus drivers do not always have to report to an assigned terminal or garage. In some cases, they have the choice of taking their bus home or parking it in a more convenient area. School bus drivers do not collect fares. Instead, they prepare weekly reports on the number of students, trips or "runs," work hours, miles, and fuel consumption. Their supervisors set time schedules and routes for the day or week.

Working Conditions

Driving a bus through heavy traffic while dealing with passengers is more stressful and fatiguing than physically strenuous. Many drivers enjoy the opportunity to work without direct supervision, with full responsibility for their bus and passengers. To improve working conditions and retain drivers, many bus lines provide ergonomically designed seats and controls for drivers. Many bus companies use

Global Positioning Systems to help dispatchers manage their bus fleets and help drivers navigate.

Intercity bus drivers may work nights, weekends, and holidays and often spend nights away from home, during which they stay in hotels at company expense. Senior drivers with regular routes have regular weekly work schedules, but others do not have regular schedules and must be prepared to report for work on short notice. They report for work only when called for a charter assignment or to drive extra buses on a regular route. Intercity bus travel and charter work tend to be seasonal. From May through August, drivers may work the maximum number of hours per week that regulations allow. During winter, junior drivers may work infrequently, except for busy holiday travel periods, and may be furloughed at times.

School bus drivers work only when school is in session. Many work 20 hours a week or less, driving one or two routes in the morning and afternoon. Drivers taking field or athletic trips, or who also have midday kindergarten routes, may work more hours a week. As more students with a variety of physical and behavioral disabilities assimilate into mainstream schools, school bus drivers must learn how to accommodate their special needs.

Regular local-transit bus drivers usually have a 5-day workweek; Saturdays and Sundays are considered regular workdays. Some drivers work evenings and after midnight. To accommodate commuters, many work "split shifts"—for example, 6 a.m. to 10 a.m. and 3 p.m. to 7 p.m., with time off in between.

Intercity bus drivers operating tour and charter buses may work any day and all hours of the day, including weekends and holidays. Their hours are dictated by the destinations, schedules, and itineraries of chartered tours. Like all commercial drivers, their weekly hours must be consistent with the Department of Transportation's rules and regulations concerning hours of service. For example, drivers may drive for 10 hours and work for up to 15 hours—including driving and nondriving duties—before having 8 hours off duty. Drivers may not drive after having worked for 60 hours in the past 7 days or 70 hours in the past 8 days. Most drivers are required to document their time in a logbook.

Training, Other Qualifications, and Advancement

Many employers prefer high school graduates and require a written test of ability to follow complex bus schedules. Many intercity and public transit bus companies prefer applicants who are at least 24 years of age; some require several years of experience driving a bus or truck. In some states, school bus drivers must pass a background investigation to uncover any criminal record or history of mental problems.

Bus driver qualifications and standards are established by state and federal regulations. All drivers must comply with federal regulations and with any state regulations that exceed federal requirements. Federal regulations require drivers who operate commercial motor vehicles in excess of 26,000 pounds gross vehicle weight rating or designed to carry 16 or more persons, including the driver, to hold a commercial driver's license (CDL) with the appropriate endorsements from the state in which they live.

To qualify for a CDL, applicants must pass a knowledge test on rules and regulations and then demonstrate in a skills test that they can operate a bus safely. A national databank records all driving violations incurred by persons who hold commercial licenses, and a state may not issue a CDL to a person who has already had a license suspended or revoked in another state. To be issued a CDL, a driver must surrender all other driver's licenses. A driver with a CDL must accompany trainees until the trainees get their own CDL. In addition to having a CDL, all bus drivers must have a "passenger" endorsement for their CDL, which requires passing a knowledge test and demonstrating the necessary skills in a vehicle of the same type as the one they would be driving in their duties. Information on how to apply for a CDL and each type of endorsement can be obtained from state motor vehicle administrations.

While many states allow those who are 18 years of age and older to drive buses within state borders, the Department of Transportation establishes minimum qualifications for bus drivers engaged in interstate commerce. Federal Motor Carrier Safety Regulations require drivers to be at least 21 years old and to pass a physical examination once every 2 years. The main physical requirements include good hearing, at least 20/40 vision with or without glasses or corrective lenses, and a 70-degree field of vision in each eye. Drivers cannot be colorblind. They must be able to hear a forced whisper in one ear at not less than 5 feet, with or without a hearing aid. Drivers must have normal blood pressure as well as normal use of their arms and legs. They may not use any controlled substances unless prescribed by a licensed physician. Persons with epilepsy or with diabetes controlled by insulin are not permitted to be interstate bus drivers. Federal regulations also require employers to test their drivers for alcohol and drug use as a condition of employment and require periodic random tests of the drivers while they are on duty. In addition, a driver must not have been convicted of a felony involving the use of a motor vehicle, a crime involving drugs, driving under the influence of drugs or alcohol, refusing to submit to an alcohol test required by a state or its implied consent laws or regulations, leaving the scene of a crime, or causing a fatality through negligent operation of a commercial vehicle. All drivers must be able to read and speak English well enough to read road signs, prepare reports, and communicate with law enforcement officers and the public. In addition, drivers must take a written examination on the Motor Carrier Safety Regulations of the U.S. Department of Transportation.

Because bus drivers deal with passengers, they must be courteous. They need an even temperament and emotional stability because driving in heavy, fast-moving, or stop-and-go traffic and dealing with passengers can be stressful. Drivers must have strong customer service skills, including communication skills and the ability to coordinate and manage large groups of people.

Most intercity bus companies and local-transit systems give driver trainees 2 to 8 weeks of classroom and behind-the-wheel instruction. In the classroom, trainees learn Department of Transportation and company work rules, safety regulations, state and municipal driving regulations, and safe driving practices. They also learn to read schedules, determine fares, keep records, and deal courteously with passengers.

School bus drivers also are required to obtain a CDL from the state in which they live. They must additionally have a "school bus" endorsement for their CDL. To receive this endorsement, they must pass a written test and demonstrate necessary skills. The skills portion of the test is taken in a bus of the same type that they would be driving on their route. Both of these tests are specific to school buses and are in addition to the testing required to receive a CDL and the "passenger" endorsement. Many persons who become school bus drivers have never driven any vehicle larger than an automobile. They receive between 1 and 4 weeks of driving instruction and classroom training on state and local laws, regulations, and policies of operating school buses; safe driving practices; driver-pupil relations; first aid; special needs of disabled and emotionally troubled students; and emergency evacuation procedures. School bus drivers also must be aware of the school system's rules for discipline and conduct for bus drivers and the students they transport.

During training, bus drivers practice driving on set courses. They practice turns and zigzag maneuvers, backing up, and driving in narrow lanes. Then, they drive in light traffic and, eventually, on congested highways and city streets. They also make trial runs without passengers to improve their driving skills and learn the routes. Local-transit trainees memorize and drive each of the runs operating out of their assigned garage. New drivers make regularly scheduled trips with passengers, accompanied by an experienced driver who gives helpful tips, answers questions, and evaluates the new driver's performance. Most bus drivers get brief supplemental training at regular periods to keep abreast of safety issues and regulatory changes.

New intercity and local-transit drivers usually are placed on an "extra" list to drive chartered runs, extra buses on regular runs, and special runs (for example, during morning and evening rush hours and to sports events). They also substitute for regular drivers who are ill or on vacation. New drivers remain on the extra list and may work only part time, perhaps for several years, until they have enough seniority to be given a regular run.

Senior drivers may bid for the runs that they prefer, such as those with more work hours, lighter traffic, weekends off, or—in the case of intercity bus drivers—higher earnings or fewer workdays per week.

Opportunities for promotion are generally limited. However, experienced drivers may become supervisors or dispatchers—assigning buses to drivers, checking whether drivers are on schedule, rerouting buses to avoid blocked streets or other problems, and dispatching extra vehicles and service crews to scenes of accidents and breakdowns. In transit agencies with rail systems, drivers may become train operators or station attendants. Opportunities exist for bus drivers to become either instructors of new bus drivers or master-instructors, who train new instructors. A few drivers become managers. Promotion in publicly owned bus systems is often determined by competitive civil service examination. Some motor coach drivers purchase their own equipment and open their own business.

Employment

Bus drivers held about 653,000 jobs in 2004. About 35 percent worked part time. Around 71 percent of all bus drivers were school bus drivers working primarily for school systems or for companies providing school bus services under contract. Most of the remainder worked for private and local government transit systems; some also worked for intercity and charter bus lines.

Job Outlook

Persons seeking jobs as bus drivers likely will encounter many opportunities. Individuals who have good driving records and who are willing to work a part-time or irregular schedule probably will have the best job prospects. School bus driving jobs, particularly in rapidly growing suburban areas, should be easiest to acquire because most are part-time positions with high turnover and less training required than for other bus-driving jobs. Those seeking higher paying public transit bus driver positions may encounter competition. Opportunities for intercity driving positions should be good, although employment prospects for motor coach drivers will depend on tourism which fluctuates with the cyclical nature of the economy.

Employment of bus drivers overall is expected to increase about as fast as the average for all occupations through the year 2014, primarily to meet the transportation needs of the growing general population and the school-aged population. Most job openings are expected to occur each year because of the need to replace workers who take jobs in other occupations or who retire or leave the occupation for other reasons.

The number of school bus drivers is expected to increase as fast as average over the next 10 years, although at a decreasing rate. School enrollments are projected to increase in 30 states and to decrease in 20 states. The net effect will be a slowdown in school enrollment and, therefore, in employment growth of school bus drivers. This, as well as the part-time nature of the occupation, will result in most openings for school bus drivers being to replace those who leave the occupation.

Employment growth for local-transit bus drivers is expected to be faster than the average for all occupations in 2004, and will likely be the result of the increasing popularity of mass transit due to congestion and rising fuel prices, as well as the demand for transit services in expanding portions of metropolitan areas. There may be competition for positions with more regular hours and steady driving routes.

Competition from other modes of transportation—airplane, train, or automobile—will temper job growth among intercity bus drivers. Most growth in intercity bus transportation will occur in group charters to locations not served by other modes of transportation. Like automobiles, buses have a far greater number of possible destinations than airplanes or trains. Since they offer greater cost savings and convenience over automobiles, buses usually are the most economical option for tour groups traveling to out-of-the-way destinations.

Full-time bus drivers rarely are laid off during recessions. If the number of passengers decreases, however, employers might reduce the hours of part-time local-transit and intercity bus drivers since fewer extra buses would be needed. Seasonal layoffs are common. Many intercity bus drivers with little seniority, for example, are furloughed during the winter when regularly scheduled and charter business declines, while school bus drivers seldom work during the summer or school holidays.

Earnings

Median hourly earnings of transit and intercity bus drivers were $14.30 in May 2004. The middle 50 percent earned between $10.74 and $19.31 an hour. The lowest 10 percent earned less than $8.66, and the highest 10 percent earned more than $23.53 an hour. Median hourly earnings in the industries employing the largest numbers of transit and intercity bus drivers in May 2004 were as follows:

Local government	$17.10
Interurban and rural bus transportation	15.86
Urban transit systems	13.49
Charter bus industry	10.81
Other transit and ground passenger transportation	10.74

Median hourly earnings of school bus drivers were $11.18 in May 2004. The middle 50 percent earned between $8.10 and $13.92 an hour. The lowest 10 percent earned less than $6.23, and the highest 10 percent earned more than $16.81 an hour. Median hourly earnings in the industries employing the largest numbers of school bus drivers in May 2004 were as follows:

School and employee bus transportation	$11.97
Elementary and secondary schools	10.74
Other transit and ground passenger transportation	10.62
Child day care services	9.28
Individual and family services	8.75

The benefits bus drivers receive from their employers vary greatly. Most intercity and local-transit bus drivers receive paid health and life insurance, sick leave, vacation leave, and free bus rides on any of the regular routes of their line or system. School bus drivers receive sick leave, and many are covered by health and life insurance and pension plans. Because they generally do not work when school is not in session, they do not get vacation leave.

Many intercity and local-transit bus drivers are members of the Amalgamated Transit Union. Local-transit bus drivers in New York and several other large cities belong to the Transport Workers Union of America. Some drivers belong to the United Transportation Union or to the International Brotherhood of Teamsters.

Related Occupations

Other workers who drive vehicles on highways and city streets include taxi drivers and chauffeurs, and truck drivers and driver/sales workers.

Sources of Additional Information

For information on employment opportunities, contact local-transit systems, intercity bus lines, school systems, or the local offices of the state employment service.

General information on school bus driving is available from:

- National School Transportation Association, 113 South West St., 4th Floor, Alexandria, VA 22314.
- National Association of State Directors of Pupil Transportation Services, 6298 Rock Hill Road, The Plains, VA 20198-1916.

General information on motor coach driving is available from:

- United Motorcoach Association, 113 South West St., 4th Floor, Alexandria, VA 22314.
- American Bus Association, 700 13th Street NW, Suite 575, Washington, DC 20005.

Carpenters

(O*NET 47-2031.01, 47-2031.02, 47-2031.03, 47-2031.04, 47-2031.05, and 47-2031.06)

Significant Points

- About one-third of all carpenters—the largest construction trade—are self-employed.
- Job opportunities should be excellent for those with the most training and all-round skills.
- To become a skilled carpenter usually takes between 3 and 4 years of both on-the-job training and classroom instruction.

Nature of the Work

Carpenters are involved in many different kinds of construction activity, from the building of highways and bridges, to the installation of kitchen cabinets. Carpenters construct, erect, install, and repair structures and fixtures made from wood and other materials. Depending on the type of work and the employer, carpenters may specialize in one or two activities or may be required to know how to perform many different tasks. Small home builders and remodeling companies may require carpenters to learn about all aspects of building a house—framing walls and partitions, putting in doors and windows, building stairs, installing cabinets and molding, and many other tasks. Large construction contractors or specialty contractors, however, may require their carpenters to perform only a few regular tasks, such as framing walls, constructing wooden forms for pouring concrete, or erecting scaffolding. Carpenters also build tunnel bracing, or brattices, in underground passageways and mines to control the circulation of air through the passageways and to worksites.

Each carpentry task is somewhat different, but most involve the same basic steps. Working from blueprints or instructions from supervisors, carpenters first do the layout—measuring, marking, and arranging materials—in accordance with local building codes. They cut and shape wood, plastic, fiberglass, or drywall using hand and power tools, such as chisels, planes, saws, drills, and sanders. They then join the materials with nails, screws, staples, or adhesives. In the final step, carpenters check the accuracy of their work with levels, rules, plumb bobs, framing squares, or electronic versions of these tools, and make any necessary adjustments. When working with prefabricated components, such as stairs or wall panels, the carpenter's task is somewhat simpler because it does not require as much layout work or the cutting and assembly of as many pieces. Prefabricated components are designed for easy and fast installation and generally can be installed in a single operation.

Carpenters who remodel homes and other structures need a broad range of carpentry skills because they must be able to perform any of the many different tasks these jobs may require. Since they are so well-trained, these carpenters often can switch from residential building to commercial construction or remodeling work, depending on which offers the best work opportunities.

Carpenters employed outside the construction industry perform a variety of installation and maintenance work. They may replace panes of glass, ceiling tiles, and doors, as well as repair desks, cabinets, and other furniture. Depending on the employer, carpenters install partitions, doors, and windows; change locks; and repair broken furniture. In manufacturing firms, carpenters may assist in moving or installing machinery.

Working Conditions

As is true of other building trades, carpentry work is sometimes strenuous. Prolonged standing, climbing, bending, and kneeling often are necessary. Carpenters risk injury working with sharp or rough materials, using sharp tools and power equipment, and working in situations where they might slip or fall. Although many carpenters work indoors, those that work outdoors are subject to variable weather conditions.

Some carpenters change employers each time they finish a construction job. Others alternate between working for a contractor and working as contractors themselves on small jobs, depending on where the work is available.

Training, Other Qualifications, and Advancement

Carpenters learn their trade through formal and informal training programs. To become a skilled carpenter usually takes between 3 and 4 years of both classroom and on-the-job training. While there are a number of different ways to obtain this training, in general, the more formalized the process, the more skilled you will become, and the more in demand by employers. For some, this training can begin in a high school, where classes in English, algebra, geometry, physics, mechanical drawing, blueprint reading, and general shop are recommended. After high school, there are a number of different avenues that one can take to obtain the necessary training. One of the ways is to obtain a job with a contractor who will then provide on-the-job training. Entry-level workers generally start as helpers, assisting more experienced workers. During this time, the carpenter's helper may elect to attend a trade or vocational school, or community college to receive further trade-related training.

Some employers, particularly large nonresidential construction contractors with union membership, offer employees formal apprenticeships. These programs combine on-the-job training with related classroom instruction. Apprenticeship applicants usually must be at least 18 years old and meet local requirements; some union locals, for example, test an applicant's aptitude for carpentry. Apprenticeship programs are usually 3 to 4 years in length, but vary with the apprentice's skill. The number of apprenticeship programs is limited, however, so only a small proportion of carpenters learn their trade through these programs, mostly those working for commercial and industrial building contractors.

On the job, apprentices learn elementary structural design and become familiar with common carpentry jobs, such as layout, form building, rough framing, and outside and inside finishing. They also learn to use the tools, machines, equipment, and materials of the trade. Apprentices receive classroom instruction in safety, first aid, blueprint reading, freehand sketching, basic mathematics, and various carpentry techniques. Both in the classroom and on the job, they learn the relationship between carpentry and the other building trades.

Some persons aiming for carpentry careers choose to obtain their classroom training before seeking a job. There are a number of public and private vocational-technical schools and training academies affiliated with the unions and contractors that offer training to become a carpenter. Employers often look favorably upon these students and usually start them at a higher level than those without the training.

Some skills needed to become a carpenter include manual dexterity, eye-hand coordination, physical fitness, and a good sense of balance. The ability to solve arithmetic problems quickly and accurately also is required. In addition, a good work history or military service is viewed favorably by contractors.

Carpenters usually have greater opportunities than most other construction workers to become general construction supervisors because carpenters are exposed to the entire construction process. For those who would like to advance, it is increasingly important to be able to communicate in both English and Spanish in order to relay instructions and safety precautions to workers with limited understanding of English; Spanish-speaking workers make up a large part of the construction workforce in many areas. Carpenters may advance to carpentry supervisor or general construction supervisor positions. Others may become independent contractors. Supervisors and contractors need good communication skills to deal with clients and subcontractors, should be able to identify and estimate the quantity of materials needed to complete a job, and accurately estimate how long a job will take to complete and at what cost.

Employment

Carpenters are employed throughout the country in almost every community and make up the largest building trades occupation. They held about 1.3 million jobs in 2004. About one-third worked in building construction and about one-fifth worked for special trade contractors. Most of the rest of the wage and salary workers worked for manufacturing firms, government agencies, retail establishments and a wide variety of other industries. About one-third of all carpenters were self-employed.

Job Outlook

Job opportunities for carpenters are expected to be excellent over the 2004–14 period, particularly for those with the most skills. Employment of carpenters is expected to increase about as fast as average for all occupations through 2014, and turnover also creates a large number of openings each year. Contractors report having trouble finding skilled carpenters to fill many of their openings, due in part to the fact that many jobseekers are not inclined to go into construction, preferring work that is less strenuous with more comfortable working conditions. Also, many people with limited skills take jobs as carpenters but eventually leave the occupation because they dislike the work or cannot find steady employment.

The need for carpenters is expected to grow as construction activity increases in response to demand for new housing, office and retail space, and for modernizing and expanding schools and industrial plants. A strong home remodeling market also will create a large demand for carpenters.

Some of the demand for carpenters, however, will be offset by expected productivity gains resulting from the increasing use of prefabricated components and improved fasteners and tools. Prefabricated wall panels, roof assemblies and stairs and prehung doors and windows can be installed very quickly. Instead of having to be built on the worksite, prefabricated walls, partitions, and stairs can be lifted into place in one operation; beams—and, in some cases, entire roof assemblies—are lifted into place using a crane. As prefabricated components become more standardized, builders will use them more often. In addition, improved adhesives are reducing the time needed to join materials, and lightweight, cordless, and pneumatic tools—such as nailers and drills—will all continue to make carpenters more efficient. New and improved tools, equipment, techniques, and materials also have vastly increased carpenter versatility.

Carpenters with all-round skills will have better opportunities for steady work than carpenters who can perform only a few relatively simple, routine tasks. Carpenters can experience periods of unemployment because of the short-term nature of many construction projects, winter slowdowns in construction activity in northern areas, and the cyclical nature of the construction industry. During economic downturns, the number of job openings for carpenters declines. Building activity depends on many factors that vary with the state of the economy—interest rates, availability of mortgage funds, government spending, and business investment.

Job opportunities for carpenters also vary by geographic area. Construction activity parallels the movement of people and businesses and reflects differences in local economic conditions. The areas with the largest population increases will also provide the best job opportunities for carpenters and apprenticeship opportunities for persons seeking to enter carpentry.

Earnings

In May 2004, median hourly earnings of carpenters were $16.78. The middle 50 percent earned between $12.91 and $22.62. The lowest 10 percent earned less than $10.36, and the highest 10 percent earned more than $28.65. Median hourly earnings in the industries employing the largest numbers of carpenters in May 2004 were as follows:

Nonresidential building construction	$18.70
Building finishing contractors	17.51
Residential building construction	16.48
Foundation, structure, and building exterior contractors	16.40
Employment services	13.94

Earnings can be reduced on occasion because carpenters lose work time in bad weather and during recessions when jobs are unavailable.

Some carpenters are members of the United Brotherhood of Carpenters and Joiners of America.

Related Occupations

Carpenters are skilled construction workers. Other skilled construction occupations include brickmasons, blockmasons, and stonemasons; cement masons, concrete finishers, segmental pavers, and terrazzo workers; electricians; pipelayers, plumbers, pipefitters, and steamfitters; and plasterers and stucco masons.

Sources of Additional Information

For information about carpentry apprenticeships or other work opportunities in this trade, contact local carpentry contractors, locals of the union mentioned above, local joint union-contractor apprenticeship committees, or the nearest office of the state employment service or apprenticeship agency. You can also find information on the registered apprenticeship system with links to state apprenticeship programs on the U.S. Department of Labor's Web site: http://www.doleta.gov/atels_bat

For information on training opportunities and carpentry in general, contact:

- Associated Builders and Contractors, 4250 North Fairfax Dr., 9th Floor, Arlington, VA 22203. Internet: http://www.trytools.org
- Associated General Contractors of America, Inc., 2300 Wilson Boulevard, Suite 400, Arlington, VA 22201. Internet: http://www.agc.org
- National Center for Construction Education and Research, P.O. Box 141104, Gainesville, FL 32614-1104. Internet: http://www.nccer.org
- National Association of Home Builders, Home Builders Institute, 1201 15th St. NW, Washington, DC 20005. Internet: http://www.hbi.org
- United Brotherhood of Carpenters and Joiners of America, Carpenters Training Fund, 6801 Placid Street, Las Vegas, NV 89119. Internet: http://www.carpenters.org

Cement Masons, Concrete Finishers, Segmental Pavers, and Terrazzo Workers

(O*NET 47-2051.00, 47-2053.00, and 47-4091.00)

Significant Points

- Job opportunities are expected to be good due to a combination of job growth and a growing number of retirements.
- Most learn the job though a combination of classroom and on-the-job training that can take 3 to 4 years.
- Like many other construction trades, these workers may experience reduced earnings and layoffs during downturns in construction activity.
- Cement masons often work overtime, with premium pay, because once concrete has been placed, the job must be completed.

Nature of the Work

Cement masons, concrete finishers, and terrazzo workers all work with concrete, one of the most common and durable materials used in construction. Once set, concrete—a mixture of Portland cement, sand, gravel, and water—becomes the foundation for everything from decorative patios and floors to huge dams or miles of roadways.

Cement masons and *concrete finishers* place and finish the concrete. They also may color concrete surfaces; expose aggregate (small stones) in walls and sidewalks; or fabricate concrete beams, columns, and panels. In preparing a site for placing concrete, cement masons first set the forms for holding the concrete and properly align them. They then direct the casting of the concrete and supervise laborers who use shovels or special tools to spread it. Masons then guide a straightedge back and forth across the top of the forms to "screed," or level, the freshly placed concrete. Immediately after leveling the concrete, masons carefully smooth the concrete surface with a "bull float," a long-handled tool about 8 by 48 inches that covers the coarser materials in the concrete and brings a rich mixture of fine cement paste to the surface.

After the concrete has been leveled and floated, concrete finishers press an edger between the forms and the concrete and guide it along the edge and the surface. This produces slightly rounded edges and helps prevent chipping or cracking. Concrete finishers use a special tool called a "groover" to make joints or grooves at specific intervals that help control cracking. Next, they trowel the surface using either a powered or hand trowel, a small, smooth, rectangular metal tool.

Sometimes, cement masons perform all the steps of laying concrete, including the finishing. As the final step, they retrowel the concrete surface back and forth with powered and hand trowels to create a smooth finish. For a coarse, nonskid finish, masons brush the surface with a broom or stiff-bristled brush. For a pebble finish, they embed small gravel chips into the surface. They then wash any excess cement from the exposed chips with a mild acid solution. For color, they use colored premixed concrete. On concrete surfaces that will remain exposed after the forms are stripped, such as columns, ceilings, and wall panels, cement masons cut away high spots and loose concrete with hammer and chisel, fill any large indentations with a Portland cement paste, and smooth the surface with a carborundum stone. Finally, they coat the exposed area with a rich Portland cement mixture, using either a special tool or a coarse cloth to rub the concrete to a uniform finish.

Throughout the entire process, cement masons must monitor how the wind, heat, or cold affects the curing of the concrete. They must have a thorough knowledge of concrete characteristics so that, by using sight and touch, they can determine what is happening to the concrete and take measures to prevent defects.

Segmental pavers lay out, cut, and install pavers, which are flat pieces of masonry usually made from compacted concrete or brick. Pavers are used to pave paths, patios, playgrounds, driveways, and steps. They are manufactured in various textures and often interlock together to form an attractive pattern. Segmental pavers first prepare the site by removing the existing pavement or soil. They grade the remaining soil to the proper depth and determine the amount of base material that is needed, depending on the local soil conditions. They then install and compact the base material, a granular material that compacts easily, and lay the pavers from the center out, so that any trimmed pieces will be on the outside rather than in the center. Then, they install edging materials to prevent the pavers from shifting and fill the spaces between the pavers with dry sand.

Terrazzo workers create attractive walkways, floors, patios, and panels by exposing marble chips and other fine aggregates on the surface of finished concrete. Much of the preliminary work of terrazzo workers is similar to that of cement masons. Attractive, marble-chip terrazzo requires three layers of materials. First, cement masons or terrazzo workers build a solid, level concrete foundation that is 3 to 4 inches deep. After the forms are removed from the foundation, workers add a 1-inch layer of sandy concrete. Terrazzo workers partially embed, or attach with adhesive, metal divider strips in the concrete wherever there is to be a joint or change of color in the terrazzo. For the final layer, terrazzo workers blend and place into each of the panels a fine marble chip mixture that may be color-pigmented. While the mixture is still wet, workers add additional marble chips of various colors into each panel and roll a lightweight roller over the entire surface.

When the terrazzo is thoroughly set, helpers grind it with a terrazzo grinder, which is somewhat like a floor polisher, only much heavier. Any depressions left by the grinding are filled with a matching grout material and hand-troweled for a smooth, uniform surface. Terrazzo workers then clean, polish, and seal the dry surface for a lustrous finish.

Working Conditions

Concrete, segmental paving, or terrazzo work is fast-paced and strenuous and requires continuous physical effort. Because most finishing is done at floor level, workers must bend and kneel often. Many jobs are outdoors, and work is generally halted during inclement weather. The work, either indoors or outdoors, may be in areas that are muddy, dusty, or dirty. To avoid chemical burns from uncured concrete and sore knees from frequent kneeling, many workers wear kneepads. Workers usually also wear water-repellent boots while working in wet concrete.

Training, Other Qualifications, and Advancement

Most cement masons, concrete finishers, segmental pavers, and terrazzo workers learn their trades either through on-the-job training as helpers, or through 3-year or 4-year apprenticeship programs. Some workers also learn their jobs by attending trade or vocational-technical schools.

Many masons and finishers first gain experience as construction laborers. When hiring helpers and apprentices, employers prefer high school graduates who are at least 18 years old, possess a driver's license, and are in good physical condition. The ability to get along with others is also important because cement masons frequently work in teams. High school courses in general science, mathematics, and vocational-technical subjects, such as blueprint reading and mechanical drawing provide a helpful background.

On-the-job training programs consist of informal instruction, in which experienced workers teach helpers to use the tools, equipment, machines, and materials of the trade. Trainees begin with tasks such as edging, jointing, and using a straightedge on freshly placed concrete. As training progresses, assignments become more complex, and trainees can usually do finishing work within a short time.

Apprenticeship programs usually are sponsored by local contractors, trade associations, or by local union-management committees. They provide on-the-job training in addition to the recommended minimum of 144 hours of classroom instruction each year. A written test and a physical exam may be required. In the classroom, apprentices learn applied mathematics, blueprint reading, and safety. Apprentices generally receive special instruction in layout work and cost estimation.

Cement masons, concrete finishers, segmental pavers, and terrazzo workers should enjoy doing demanding work. They should take pride in craftsmanship and be able to work without close supervision.

With additional training, cement masons, concrete finishers, segmental pavers, or terrazzo workers may become supervisors for masonry contractors, or move into construction management, building inspection, or contract estimation. Some eventually become owners of businesses, where they may spend most of their time managing rather than practicing their original trade. For those who want to own their own business, taking business classes will help to prepare workers for operating a business.

Employment

Cement masons, concrete finishers, segmental pavers, and terrazzo workers held about 209,000 jobs in 2004; segmental pavers and terrazzo workers accounted for only a small portion of the total. Most cement masons and concrete finishers worked for specialty trade contractors, primarily foundation, structure, and building exterior contractors. They also worked for contractors in residential and nonresidential building construction and in heavy and civil engineering construction on projects such as highways; bridges; shopping malls; or large buildings such as factories, schools, and hospitals. A small number were employed by firms that manufacture concrete products. Most segmental pavers and terrazzo workers worked for specialty trade contractors who install decorative floors and wall panels.

Less than 5 percent of cement masons, concrete finishers, segmental pavers, and terrazzo workers were self-employed, a smaller proportion than in other building trades. Most self-employed masons specialized in small jobs, such as driveways, sidewalks, and patios.

Job Outlook

Opportunities for cement masons, concrete finishers, segmental pavers, and terrazzo workers are expected to be good, particularly for those with the most experience and skills. Employers report difficulty in finding workers with the right skills, as many qualified jobseekers often prefer work that is less strenuous and has more comfortable working conditions.

Employment of cement masons, concrete finishers, segmental pavers, and terrazzo workers is expected to grow as fast as average for all occupations through 2014. These workers will be needed to build new highways, bridges, factories, and other residential and nonresidential structures to meet the demand of a growing population. Additionally, cement masons will be needed to repair and renovate existing highways and bridges, which are deteriorating rapidly, and other aging structures. The increasing use of concrete as a building material, particularly since September 2001, will add to the demand. In addition to job growth, there are expected to be a significant number of retirements over the next decade, which will create more job openings.

Employment of cement masons, concrete finishers, segmental pavers, and terrazzo workers, like that of many other construction workers, is sensitive to the fluctuations of the economy. Workers in these trades may experience periods of unemployment when the overall level of construction falls. On the other hand, shortages of these workers may occur in some areas during peak periods of building activity.

Earnings

In May 2004, the median hourly earnings of cement masons and concrete finishers were $15.10. The middle 50 percent earned between $11.76 and $20.11. The bottom 10 percent earned less than $9.53, and the top 10 percent earned over $25.89. Median hourly earnings in the industries employing the largest numbers of cement masons and concrete finishers in May 2004 were as follows:

Industry	Earnings
Residential building construction	$16.28
Nonresidential building construction	15.91
Other specialty trade contractors	15.58
Foundation, structure, and building exterior contractors	14.98
Highway, street, and bridge construction	14.86

In May 2004, the median hourly earnings of terrazzo workers and finishers were $13.45. The middle 50 percent earned between $10.44 and $19.57. The bottom 10 percent earned less than $9.07, and the top 10 percent earned over $25.72.

Like those of other construction trades workers, earnings of cement masons, concrete finishers, segmental pavers, and terrazzo workers may be reduced on occasion because poor weather and slowdowns in construction activity limit the amount of time they can work. Nonunion workers generally have lower wage rates than union workers. Apprentices usually start at 50 to 60 percent of the rate paid to experienced workers. Cement masons often work overtime, with premium pay, because once concrete has been placed, the job must be completed.

Some cement masons, concrete finishers, segmental pavers, and terrazzo workers belong to unions, mainly the Operative Plasterers' and Cement Masons' International Association of the United States and Canada and the International Union of Bricklayers and Allied Craftworkers. A few terrazzo workers belong to the United Brotherhood of Carpenters and Joiners of the United States.

Related Occupations

Cement masons, concrete finishers, segmental pavers, and terrazzo workers combine skill with knowledge of building materials to construct buildings, highways, and other structures. Other occupations involving similar skills and knowledge include brickmasons, blockmasons, and stonemasons; carpet, floor, and tile installers and finishers; drywall installers, ceiling tile installers, and tapers; and plasterers and stucco masons.

Sources of Additional Information

For general information about cement masons, concrete finishers, segmental pavers, and terrazzo workers, contact:

- National Concrete Masonry Association, 13750 Sunrise Valley Dr., Herndon, VA 20171-3499. Internet: http://www.ncma.org
- Associated Builders and Contractors, Workforce Development Division, 4250 North Fairfax Dr., 9th Floor, Arlington, VA 22203. Internet: http://www.trytools.org

- Associated General Contractors of America, Inc., 2300 Wilson Boulevard, Suite 400, Arlington, VA 22201. Internet: http://www.agc.org
- International Union of Bricklayers and Allied Craftworkers, International Masonry Institute, The James Brice House, 42 East St., Annapolis, MD 21401. Internet: http://www.imiweb.org
- United Brotherhood of Carpenters and Joiners, 50 F St. NW, Washington, DC 20001. Internet: http://www.carpenters.org
- Operative Plasterers' and Cement Masons' International Association of the United States and Canada, 14405 Laurel Place, Suite 300, Laurel, MD 20707. Internet: http://www.opcmia.org
- National Terrazzo and Mosaic Association, 110 E. Market St., Suite 200 A, Leesburg, VA 20176.
- National Center for Construction Education and Research, P.O. Box 141104, Gainesville FL 32614-1104. Internet: http://www.nccer.org
- Portland Cement Association, 5420 Old Orchard Rd., Skokie, IL 60077. Internet: http://www.cement.org/

For information about apprenticeships and work opportunities, contact local concrete or terrazzo contractors, locals of unions previously mentioned, a local joint union-management apprenticeship committee, or the nearest office of the state employment service or apprenticeship agency. You may also check the U.S. Department of Labor's Web site for information on apprenticeships and links to state apprenticeship programs. Internet: http://www.doleta.gov/atels_bat

Chefs, Cooks, and Food Preparation Workers

(O*NET 35-1011.00, 35-2011.00, 35-2012.00, 35-2013.00, 35-2014.00, 35-2015.00, and 35-2021.00)

Significant Points

- Many young people work as cooks and food preparation workers—almost 19 percent were between 16 and 19 years old.
- More than 2 out of 5 food preparation workers are employed part time.
- Job openings are expected to be plentiful because many of these workers transfer to other occupations with higher earnings or burn out from the fast work pace and pressure to fill orders quickly.

Nature of the Work

Chefs, cooks, and food preparation workers prepare, season, and cook a wide range of foods—from soups, snacks, and salads to entrees, side dishes, and desserts—in a variety of restaurants and other food services establishments. Chefs and cooks create recipes and prepare meals, while food preparation workers peel and cut vegetables, trim meat, prepare poultry, and perform other duties such as keeping work areas clean and monitoring temperatures of ovens and stovetops.

In general, *chefs* and *cooks* measure, mix, and cook ingredients according to recipes, using a variety of pots; pans; cutlery; and other equipment, including ovens, broilers, grills, slicers, grinders, and blenders. Chefs and head cooks also are responsible for directing the work of other kitchen workers, estimating food requirements, and ordering food supplies.

Larger restaurants and food services establishments tend to have varied menus and larger kitchen staffs. They often include several chefs and cooks, sometimes called assistant or line cooks, along with other lesser-skilled kitchen workers, such as *food preparation workers*. Each chef or cook works an assigned station that is equipped with the types of stoves, grills, pans, and ingredients needed for the foods prepared at that station. Job titles often reflect the principal ingredient prepared or the type of cooking performed—*vegetable cook, fry cook,* or *grill cook*.

Executive chefs and *head cooks* coordinate the work of the kitchen staff and direct the preparation of meals. They determine serving sizes, plan menus, order food supplies, and oversee kitchen operations to ensure uniform quality and presentation of meals. The terms chef and cook often are used interchangeably, but generally reflect the different types of chefs and the organizational structure of the kitchen staff. For example, an *executive chef* is in charge of all food service operations and also may supervise the many kitchens of a hotel, restaurant group, or corporate dining operation. A *chef de cuisine* reports to an executive chef and is responsible for the daily operations of a single kitchen. A *sous chef*, or sub chef, is the second in command and runs the kitchen in the absence of the chef. Chefs tend to be more highly skilled and better trained than cooks. Many chefs earn fame both for themselves and for their kitchens because of the quality and distinctive nature of the food they serve.

The specific responsibilities of most cooks are determined by a number of factors, including the type of restaurant in which they work. *Institution and cafeteria cooks*, for example, work in the kitchens of schools, cafeterias, businesses, hospitals, and other institutions. For each meal, they prepare a large quantity of a limited number of entrees, vegetables, and desserts. *Restaurant cooks* usually prepare a wider selection of dishes, cooking most orders individually. *Short-order cooks* prepare foods in restaurants and coffee shops that emphasize fast service and quick food preparation. They grill and garnish hamburgers, prepare sandwiches, fry eggs, and cook French fries, often working on several orders at the same time. *Fast-food cooks* prepare a limited selection of menu items in fast-food restaurants. They cook and package batches of food, such as hamburgers and fried chicken, to be kept warm until served.

Some cooks do not work in restaurant or food service kitchens. *Private household cooks (or personal chefs)* plan and prepare meals in private homes according to the client's tastes or dietary needs. They order groceries and supplies, clean the kitchen, and wash dishes and utensils. They also may serve meals. *Research chefs* combine culinary skills with knowledge of food science to develop recipes and test new formulas, experiment with flavors and eye appeal of prepared foods, and test new products and equipment for chain restaurants, food growers and processors, and manufacturers and marketers.

Food preparation workers perform routine, repetitive tasks such as readying ingredients for complex dishes, slicing and dicing vegetables, and composing salads and cold items under the direction of chefs and cooks. They weigh and measure ingredients, go after pots and pans, and stir and strain soups and sauces. Food preparation workers may cut and grind meats, poultry, and seafood in preparation for cooking. Their responsibilities also include cleaning work areas, equipment, utensils, dishes, and silverware.

The number and types of workers employed in kitchens depends on the type of establishment. For example, fast-food establishments offer only a few items, which are prepared by fast-food cooks. Small, full-service restaurants offering casual dining often feature a limited number of easy-to-prepare items supplemented by short-order specialties and ready-made desserts. Typically, one cook prepares all the food with the help of a short-order cook and one or two other kitchen workers.

Grocery and specialty food stores employ chefs, cooks, and food preparation workers to develop recipes and prepare meals for customers to carry out. Typically, entrees, side dishes, salads, or other items are prepared in large quantities and stored at an appropriate temperature. Servers portion and package items according to customer orders for serving at home.

Working Conditions

Many restaurant and institutional kitchens have modern equipment, convenient work areas, and air conditioning, but kitchens in older and smaller eating places are often not as well designed. Kitchens must be well ventilated, appropriately lit, and properly equipped with sprinkler systems to protect against fires. Kitchen staffs invariably work in small quarters against hot stoves and ovens. They are under constant pressure to prepare meals quickly while ensuring that quality is maintained and safety and sanitation guidelines are observed.

Working conditions vary with the type and quantity of food prepared and the local laws governing food service operations. Workers usually must withstand the pressure and strain of standing for hours at a time, lifting heavy pots and kettles, and working near hot ovens and grills. Job hazards include slips and falls, cuts, and burns, but injuries are seldom serious.

Work hours in restaurants may include early mornings, late evenings, holidays, and weekends. Work schedules of chefs, cooks, and other kitchen workers in factory and school cafeterias may be more regular. In 2004, about 40 percent of cooks and 46 percent of food preparation workers had part-time schedules, compared to 16 percent of workers throughout the economy. Work schedules in fine-dining restaurants, however, tend to be longer because of the time required to prepare ingredients in advance. Many executive chefs regularly work 12-hour days because they oversee the delivery of foodstuffs early in the day, plan the menu, and start preparing those menu items that take the greatest amount of preparation time or skill.

The wide range in dining hours and the need for fully-staffed kitchens during all open hours creates work opportunities for individuals seeking supplemental income, flexible work hours, or variable schedules. For example, almost 19 percent of cooks and food preparation workers were 16–19 years old in 2004, and almost 11 percent had variable schedules. Kitchen workers employed by schools may work during the school year only, usually for 9 or 10 months. Similarly, resort establishments usually only offer seasonal employment.

Training, Other Qualifications, and Advancement

Most fast-food or short-order cooks and food preparation workers require little education or training; most skills are learned on the job. Training generally starts with basic sanitation and workplace safety subjects and continues with instruction on food handling, preparation, and cooking procedures.

A high school diploma is not required for beginning jobs, but it is recommended for those planning a career as a cook or chef. High school or vocational school programs may offer courses in basic food safety and handling procedures and general business and computer classes for those who want to manage or open their own place. Many school districts, in cooperation with state departments of education, provide on-the-job training and summer workshops for cafeteria kitchen workers who aspire to become cooks. Large corporations in the food services and hospitality industries also offer paid internships and summer jobs to those just starting out in the field. Internships provide valuable experience and can lead to placement in more formal chef training programs.

Executive chefs and head cooks who work in fine-dining restaurants require many years of training and experience and an intense desire to cook. Some chefs and cooks may start their training in high school or post–high school vocational programs. Others may receive formal training through independent cooking schools, professional culinary institutes, or 2- or 4-year college degree programs in hospitality or culinary arts. In addition, some large hotels and restaurants operate their own training and job-placement programs for chefs and cooks. Most formal training programs require some form of apprenticeship, internship, or outplacement program jointly offered by the school and affiliated restaurants. Professional culinary institutes, industry associations, and trade unions also may sponsor formal apprenticeship programs in coordination with the U.S. Department of Labor. Many chefs are trained on the job, receiving real work experience and training from chef mentors in the restaurants where they work.

People who have had courses in commercial food preparation may start in a cook or chef job without spending a lot of time in lower-skilled kitchen jobs. Their education may give them an advantage when looking for jobs in better restaurants. Some vocational programs in high schools may offer training, but employers usually prefer training given by trade schools, vocational centers, colleges, professional associations, or trade unions. Postsecondary courses range from a few months to 2 years or more. Degree-granting programs are open only to high school graduates. Chefs also may compete and test for certification as master chefs. Although certification is not required to enter the field, it can be a measure of accomplishment and lead to further advancement and higher-paying positions. The U.S. Armed Forces also are a good source of training and experience.

Although curricula may vary, students in formal culinary training programs spend most of their time in kitchens learning to use the appropriate equipment and to prepare meals through actual practice. They learn good knife techniques, safe food-handling procedures, and proper use and care of kitchen equipment. Training programs often include courses in nutrition, menu planning, portion control, purchasing and inventory methods, proper food storage procedures,

and use of leftover food to minimize waste. Students also learn sanitation and public health rules for handling food. Training in food service management, computer accounting and inventory software, and banquet service are featured in some training programs.

The number of formal and informal culinary training programs continues to increase to meet demand. Formal programs, which may offer training leading to a certificate or a 2- or 4-year degree, are geared more for training chefs for fine-dining or upscale restaurants. They offer a wider array of training options and specialties, such as advanced cooking techniques; cooking for banquets, buffets, or parties; and cuisines and cooking styles from around the world.

The American Culinary Federation accredits more than 100 formal training programs and sponsors apprenticeship programs around the country. Typical apprenticeships last three years and combine classroom training and work experience. Accreditation is an indication that a culinary program meets recognized standards regarding course content, facilities, and quality of instruction. The American Culinary Federation also certifies pastry professionals, personal chefs, and culinary educators in addition to various levels of chefs. Certification standards are based primarily on experience and formal training.

Vocational or trade-school programs typically offer more basic training in preparing food, such as food handling and sanitation procedures; nutrition, slicing and dicing methods for various kinds of meats and vegetables; and basic cooking methods, such as baking, broiling, and grilling.

Important characteristics for chefs, cooks, and food preparation workers include working well as part of a team, having a keen sense of taste and smell, and working efficiently to turn out meals rapidly. Personal cleanliness is essential because most states require health certificates indicating that workers are free from communicable diseases. Knowledge of a foreign language can be an asset because it may improve communication with other restaurant staff, vendors, and the restaurant's clientele.

Advancement opportunities for chefs, cooks, and food preparation workers depend on their training, work experience, and ability to perform more responsible and sophisticated tasks. Many food preparation workers, for example, may move into assistant or line cook positions. Chefs and cooks who demonstrate an eagerness to learn new cooking skills and to accept greater responsibility may move up within the kitchen and take on responsibility for training or supervising newer or lesser-skilled kitchen staff. Others may move from one kitchen or restaurant to another.

Some chefs and cooks go into business as caterers or personal chefs or they open their own restaurant. Others become instructors in culinary training programs. A number of cooks and chefs advance to executive chef positions or food service management positions, particularly in hotels; clubs; or larger, more elegant restaurants where they may oversee operations in a number of kitchens or restaurants.

Employment

Chefs, cooks and food preparation workers held nearly 3.1 million jobs in 2004. The distribution of jobs among the various types of chefs, cooks, and food preparation workers was as follows:

Food preparation workers	889,000
Cooks, restaurant	783,000
Cooks, fast food	662,000
Cooks, institution and cafeteria	424,000
Cooks, short order	230,000
Chefs and head cooks	125,000
Cooks, private household	9,200

Nearly two-thirds of all chefs, cooks, and food preparation workers were employed in restaurants and other food services and drinking places. Almost one-fifth worked in institutions such as schools, universities, hospitals, and nursing care facilities. Grocery stores, hotels, gasoline stations with convenience stores, and other organizations employed the remainder.

Job Outlook

Job openings for chefs, cooks, and food preparation workers are expected to be plentiful through 2014; however, competition should be keen for jobs in the top kitchens of higher-end restaurants. While job growth will create new positions, primarily due to the expansion of family-casual dining, the overwhelming majority of job openings will stem from the need to replace workers who leave this large occupational group. Many chef, cook, and food preparation worker jobs are attractive to people seeking first-time or short-term employment, additional income, or a flexible schedule. Employers typically hire a large number of part-time workers and require minimal education and training for these lesser-skilled entry-level positions. Many of these workers transfer to other occupations or stop working, creating numerous openings for those entering the field.

Overall employment of chefs, cooks, and food preparation workers is expected to increase about as fast as the average for all occupations over the 2004–14 period. Employment growth will be spurred by increases in population, household income, and leisure time that will allow people to more often dine out and take vacations. In addition, the large number of two-income households will lead more families to opt for the convenience of dining out.

Projected employment growth, however, varies by specialty. The number of higher-skilled chefs and cooks working in full-service restaurants—those that offer table service and more varied menus—is expected to increase about as fast as the average. Much of the increase in this segment, however, will come from job growth in more casual dining, rather than upscale full-service restaurants. Dining trends suggest increasing numbers of meals eaten away from home and growth in family dining restaurants but greater limits on expense-account meals. Similarly, employment of food preparation workers will grow faster than the average, reflecting diners' desires for convenience as they shop for carryout meals in a greater variety of places—full-service restaurants, limited-service eating places, or grocery stores.

Employment of fast-food cooks is expected to grow about as fast as the average. Duties of cooks in fast-food restaurants are limited; most workers are likely to be combined food preparation and serving workers rather than fast-food cooks. Employment of short-order cooks is expected to increase about as fast as the average. Short-order cooks may work a grill or sandwich station in a full-line restaurant but also may work in lunch counters or coffee shops that specialize in meals served quickly.

Employment of institution and cafeteria chefs and cooks will show little or no growth. Their employment will not keep pace with the rapid growth in the educational and health services industries—where their employment is concentrated. In an effort to make "institutional food" more attractive to office workers, students, staff, visitors, and patients, offices, schools, and hospitals increasingly contract out their food services. Employment of cooks, private household, however, is projected to decline, reflecting the general decline in private household service employment.

Employment of chefs, cooks, and food preparation workers who prepare meals to go, such as those who work in the prepared foods sections of grocery or specialty food stores, should increase much faster than the average as people continue to demand quality meals and convenience. Similarly, much faster than average growth also is expected among those who work in contract food service establishments, such as those that provide catering services and those who support employee dining rooms or staff hotel restaurants on a contract basis. These changes reflect a continuing trend among large establishments to contract out food services so they may better focus on their core business of running a hospital, hotel, factory, or school. Also, there is a growing consumer desire for healthier, made-from-scratch meals without sacrificing the convenience of pre-packaged prepared foods or fast-food dining.

Earnings

Wages of chefs, cooks, and food preparation workers vary greatly according to region of the country and the type of food services establishment in which they work. Wages usually are highest in elegant restaurants and hotels, where many executive chefs are employed, and in major metropolitan areas.

Median hourly earnings of chefs and head cooks were $14.75 in May 2004. The middle 50 percent earned between $10.71 and $20.28. The lowest 10 percent earned less than $8.28, and the highest 10 percent earned more than $26.75 per hour. Median hourly earnings in the industries employing the largest number of chefs and head cooks in May 2004 were:

Other amusement and recreation industries $19.27
Traveler accommodations 18.25
Special food services 15.06
Full-service restaurants 13.57
Limited-service eating places 12.00

Median hourly earnings of cooks, private household were $9.42 in May 2004. The middle 50 percent earned between $7.08 and $12.79. The lowest 10 percent earned less than $6.01, and the highest 10 percent earned more than $16.55 per hour.

Median hourly earnings of restaurant cooks were $9.39 in May 2004. The middle 50 percent earned between $7.79 and $11.13. The lowest 10 percent earned less than $6.76, and the highest 10 percent earned more than $13.37 per hour. Median hourly earnings in the industries employing the largest numbers of restaurant cooks in May 2004 were:

Traveler accommodations $10.69
Other amusement and recreation industries.............10.55
Special food services 10.00
Full-service restaurants 9.34
Drinking places (alcoholic beverages) 9.27
Limited-service eating places 8.25

Median hourly earnings of institution and cafeteria cooks were $9.10 in May 2004. The middle 50 percent earned between $7.20 and $11.22. The lowest 10 percent earned less than $6.08, and the highest 10 percent earned more than $13.72 per hour. Median hourly earnings in the industries employing the largest numbers of institution and cafeteria cooks in May 2004 were:

General medical and surgical hospitals $10.38
Special food services 10.11
Community care facilities for the elderly 9.60
Nursing care facilities 9.33
Elementary and secondary schools...........................8.06

Median hourly earnings of short-order cooks were $8.11 in May 2004. The middle 50 percent earned between $6.90 and $9.92. The lowest 10 percent earned less than $5.97, and the highest 10 percent earned more than $11.50 per hour. Median hourly earnings in the industries employing the largest number of short-order cooks in May 2004 were:

Full-service restaurants $8.53
Drinking places (alcoholic beverages) 8.08
Other amusement and recreation industries................7.79
Limited-service eating places 7.21
Gasoline stations 6.99

Median hourly earnings of food preparation workers were $8.03 in May 2004. The middle 50 percent earned between $6.89 and $9.78. The lowest 10 percent earned less than $5.97, and the highest 10 percent earned more than $11.90 per hour. Median hourly earnings in the industries employing the largest number of food preparation workers in May 2004 were:

Elementary and secondary schools..........................$9.04
Grocery stores 8.54
Nursing care facilities 8.10
Full-service restaurants 7.94
Limited-service eating places 7.27

Median hourly earnings of fast-food cooks were $7.07 in May 2004. The middle 50 percent earned between $6.20 and $8.22. The lowest 10 percent earned less than $5.68, and the highest 10 percent earned more than $9.63 per hour. Median hourly earnings in the industries employing the largest number of fast-food cooks in May 2004 were:

Grocery stores..$8.26
Special food services 7.97
Gasoline stations 7.18
Full-service restaurants 7.16
Limited-service eating places 7.02

Some employers provide employees with uniforms and free meals, but federal law permits employers to deduct from their employees' wages the cost or fair value of any meals or lodging provided, and some employers do so. Chefs, cooks, and food preparation workers who work full time often receive typical benefits, but part-time workers usually do not.

In some large hotels and restaurants, kitchen workers belong to unions. The principal unions are the Hotel Employees and Restaurant Employees International Union and the Service Employees International Union.

Related Occupations

Workers who perform tasks similar to those of chefs, cooks, and food preparation workers include food processing occupations, such as butchers and meat cutters, and bakers. Others who work closely with these workers include food service managers and food and beverage serving and related workers.

Sources of Additional Information

Information about job opportunities may be obtained from local employers and local offices of the state employment service.

Career information about chefs, cooks, and other kitchen workers, as well as a directory of 2- and 4-year colleges that offer courses or programs that prepare persons for food service careers, is available from:

- National Restaurant Association, 1200 17th St. NW, Washington, DC 20036-3097. Internet: http://www.restaurant.org

For information on the American Culinary Federation's apprenticeship and certification programs for cooks, as well as a list of accredited culinary programs, send a self-addressed, stamped envelope to:

- American Culinary Federation, 180 Center Place Way, St. Augustine, FL 32095. Internet: http://www.acfchefs.org

For information about becoming a personal chef, contact:

- American Personal Chef Association, 4572 Delaware St., San Diego, CA 92116.

For general information on hospitality careers, contact:

- International Council on Hotel, Restaurant, and Institutional Education, 2613 North Parham Rd., 2nd Floor, Richmond, VA 23294. Internet: http://www.chrie.org

Child Care Workers

(O*NET 39-9011.00 and 39-9011.01)

Significant Points

- About 1 out of 3 child care workers are self-employed; most of these are family child care providers.
- Training requirements vary from a high school diploma to a college degree, although a high school diploma and little or no experience are adequate for many jobs.
- Many workers leave these jobs every year, creating good job opportunities.

Nature of the Work

Child care workers nurture and care for children who have not yet entered formal schooling and also work with older children in before- and after-school situations. These workers play an important role in a child's development by caring for the child when parents are at work or away for other reasons. In addition to attending to children's basic needs, child care workers organize activities that stimulate children's physical, emotional, intellectual, and social growth. They help children explore individual interests, develop talents and independence, build self-esteem, and learn how to get along with others.

Child care workers generally are classified in three different groups, depending on the setting in which they work: Workers who care for children at the children's home, called private household workers; those who care for children in their own home, called family child care providers; and those that work at separate child care centers and centers that provide preschool services to 3- and 4-year-old children.

Private household workers who are employed on an hourly basis usually are called *babysitters*. These child care workers bathe, dress, and feed children; supervise their play; wash their clothes; and clean their rooms. Babysitters also may put children to bed and wake them, read to them, involve them in educational games, take them for doctors' visits, and discipline them. Those who are in charge of infants, sometimes called *infant nurses*, also prepare bottles and change diapers. *Nannies* work full or part time for a single family. They generally take care of children from birth to age 10 or 12, tending to the child's early education, nutrition, health, and other needs, and also may perform the duties of a housekeeper, including cleaning and laundry.

Family child care providers often work alone with a small group of children, though some work in larger settings with multiple adults. Child care centers generally have more than one adult per group of children; in groups of older children, a child care worker may assist a more experienced preschool teacher.

Most child care workers perform a combination of basic care and teaching duties, but the majority of their time is spent on caregiving activities. However, many basic care activities also are opportunities for children to learn. For example, a worker who shows a child how to tie a shoelace teaches the child while also providing for that child's basic care needs. Child care programs help children learn about trust and gain a sense of security.

Child care workers spend most of their day working with children. However, they do maintain contact with parents or guardians through informal meetings or scheduled conferences to discuss each child's progress and needs. Many child care workers keep records of each child's progress and suggest ways in which parents can stimulate their child's learning and development at home. Some child care centers and before- and after-school programs actively recruit parent volunteers to work with the children and participate in administrative decisions and program planning.

Young children learn mainly through play. Child care workers recognize this and capitalize on children's play to further language development (storytelling and acting games), improve social skills (working together to build a neighborhood in a sandbox), and introduce scientific and mathematical concepts (balancing and counting blocks when building a bridge or mixing colors when painting). Often a less structured approach is used to teach young children, including small-group lessons; one-on-one instruction; and creative activities such as art, dance, and music. Child care workers play a vital role in preparing children to build the skills they will need in school.

Child care workers in child care centers or family child care homes greet young children as they arrive, help them to remove outer garments, and select an activity of interest. When caring for infants, they feed and change them. To ensure a well-balanced program, child care workers prepare daily and long-term schedules of activities. Each day's activities balance individual and group play, as well as quiet and active time. Children are given some freedom to participate in activities in which they are interested.

Concern over school-aged children being home alone before and after school has spurred many parents to seek alternative ways for their children to constructively spend their time. The purpose of before- and after-school programs is to watch over school-aged children during the gap between school hours and their parents' work hours. These programs also may operate during the summer and on weekends. Workers in before- and after-school programs may help students with their homework or engage them in other extracurricular activities. These activities may include field trips, learning about computers, painting, photography, and participating in sports. Some child care workers may be responsible for taking children to school in the morning and picking them up from school in the afternoon. Before- and after-school programs may be operated by public school systems, local community centers, or other private organizations.

Helping keep young children healthy is an important part of the job. Child care workers serve nutritious meals and snacks and teach good eating habits and personal hygiene. They ensure that children have proper rest periods. They identify children who may not feel well and, in some cases, may help parents locate programs that will provide basic health services. Child care workers also watch for children who show signs of emotional or developmental problems and discuss these matters with their supervisor and the child's parents. Early identification of children with special needs—such as those with behavioral, emotional, physical, or learning disabilities—is important to improve their future learning ability. Special education teachers often work with these preschool children to provide the individual attention they need.

Working Conditions

Helping children grow, learn, and gain new skills can be very rewarding. Child care workers help to improve children's communication, learning, and other personal skills. The work is sometimes routine; however, new activities and challenges mark each day. Child care can be physically and emotionally taxing, as workers constantly stand, walk, bend, stoop, and lift to attend to each child's interests and problems.

To ensure that children in child care centers receive proper supervision, state or local regulations may require a certain ratio of workers to children. The ratio varies with the age of the children. Child development experts generally recommend that a single caregiver be responsible for no more than 3 or 4 infants (less than 1 year old), 5 or 6 toddlers (1 to 2 years old), or 10 preschool-aged children (between 2 and 5 years old). In before- and after-school programs, workers may be responsible for many school-aged children at a time.

Family child care providers work out of their own homes. While this arrangement provides convenience, it also requires that their homes be accommodating to young children. Private household workers usually work in the pleasant and comfortable homes or apartments of their employers. Most are day workers who live in their own homes and travel to work, though some live in the home of their employer, generally with their own room and bath. They often become part of their employer's family and may derive satisfaction from caring for the family.

The work hours of child care workers vary widely. Child care centers usually are open year round, with long hours so that parents can drop off and pick up their children before and after work. Some centers employ full-time and part-time staff with staggered shifts to cover the entire day. Some workers are unable to take regular breaks during the day due to limited staffing. Public and many private preschool programs operate during the typical 9- or 10-month school year, employing both full-time and part-time workers. Family child care providers have flexible hours and daily routines, but they may work long or unusual hours to fit parents' work schedules. Live-in nannies usually work longer hours than do those who have their own homes. However, although nannies may work evenings or weekends, they usually get other time off.

Training, Other Qualifications, and Advancement

The training and qualifications required of child care workers vary widely. Each state has its own licensing requirements that regulate caregiver training; these range from a high school diploma to community college courses to a college degree in child development or early childhood education. State requirements are generally higher for workers at child care centers than for family child care providers; child care workers in private settings who care for only a few children often are not regulated by states at all. Child care workers generally can obtain some form of employment with a high school diploma and little or no experience, but certain private firms and publicly funded programs have more demanding training and education requirements.

Some employers prefer to hire child care workers who have earned a nationally recognized Child Development Associate (CDA) credential or the Certified Childcare Professional designation, have taken secondary or postsecondary courses in child development and early childhood education, or have work experience in a child care setting. Other employers require their own specialized training. An increasing number of employers require an associate degree in early childhood education.

Child care workers must anticipate and prevent problems, deal with disruptive children, provide fair but firm discipline, and be enthusiastic and constantly alert. They must communicate effectively with the children and their parents, as well as with other teachers and child care workers. Workers should be mature, patient, understanding, and articulate and have energy and physical stamina. Skills in music, art, drama, and storytelling also are important. Self-employed child care workers must have business sense and management abilities.

Opportunities for advancement are limited. However, as child care workers gain experience, some may advance to supervisory or administrative positions in large child care centers or preschools. Often, these positions require additional training, such as a bachelor's or master's degree. Other workers move on to work in resource and referral agencies, consulting with parents on available child services. A few workers become involved in policy or advocacy work related to child care and early childhood education. With a bachelor's degree, workers may become preschool teachers or become certified to teach in public or private schools. Some workers set up their own child care businesses.

Employment

Child care workers held about 1.3 million jobs in 2004. Many worked part time. About 1 out of 3 child care workers were self-employed; most of these were family child care providers.

Seventeen percent of all child care workers are found in child day care services, and about 21 percent work for private households. The remainder worked primarily in local government educational services; nursing and residential care facilities; religious organizations; amusement and recreation industries; private educational services; civic and social organizations; individual and family services; and local government, excluding education and hospitals. Some child care programs are for-profit centers; some of these are affiliated with a local or national chain. Religious institutions, community agencies, school systems, and state and local governments operate nonprofit programs. A very small percentage of private industry establishments operate onsite child care centers for the children of their employees.

Job Outlook

High replacement needs should create good job opportunities for child care workers. Qualified persons who are interested in this work should have little trouble finding and keeping a job. Many child care workers must be replaced each year as they leave the occupation temporarily to fulfill family responsibilities, to study, or for other reasons. Others leave permanently because they are interested in pursuing other occupations or because of dissatisfaction with hours, low pay and benefits, and stressful conditions.

Employment of child care workers is projected to increase about as fast as the average for all occupations through the year 2014. The number of women in the labor force of childbearing age (widely considered to be ages 15 to 44) and the number of children under 5 years of age are both expected to rise over the next 10 years. Also, the proportion of children being cared for exclusively by parents or other relatives is likely to continue to decline, spurring demand for additional child care workers. Concern about the behavior of school-aged children during nonschool hours also should increase demand for before- and after-school programs and child care workers to staff them.

The growth in demand for child care workers will be moderated, however, by an increasing emphasis on early childhood education programs. While only a few states currently provide targeted or universal preschool programs, many more are considering or currently implementing such programs. There also is likely to be a rise in enrollment in private preschools as the value of formal education before kindergarten becomes more widely accepted. Since the majority of workers in these programs are classified as preschool teachers, this growth in preschool enrollment will mean that relatively fewer child care workers will be needed for children old enough to participate in preschool.

Earnings

Pay depends on the educational attainment of the worker and the type of establishment. Although the pay generally is very low, more education usually means higher earnings. Median hourly earnings of wage and salary child care workers were $8.06 in May 2004. The middle 50 percent earned between $6.75 and $10.01. The lowest 10 percent earned less than $5.90, and the highest 10 percent earned more than $12.34. Median hourly earnings in the industries employing the largest numbers of child care workers in 2004 were as follows:

Other residential care facilities	$9.66
Elementary and secondary schools	9.22
Civic and social organizations	7.62
Other amusement and recreation industries	7.58
Child day care services	7.34

Earnings of self-employed child care workers vary depending on the hours worked, the number and ages of the children, and the location.

Benefits vary, but are minimal for most child care workers. Many employers offer free or discounted child care to employees. Some offer a full benefits package, including health insurance and paid vacations, but others offer no benefits at all. Some employers offer seminars and workshops to help workers learn new skills. A few are willing to cover the cost of courses taken at community colleges or technical schools. Live-in nannies receive free room and board.

Related Occupations

Child care work requires patience; creativity; an ability to nurture, motivate, teach, and influence children; and leadership, organizational, and administrative skills. Others who work with children and need these qualities and skills include teacher assistants; teachers—preschool, kindergarten, elementary, middle, and secondary; and teachers—special education.

Sources of Additional Information

For an electronic question-and-answer service on child care, information on becoming a child care provider, and other resources, contact:

- National Child Care Information Center, 243 Church St. NW, 2nd Floor, Vienna, VA 22180. Internet: http://www.nccic.org

For information on becoming a family child care provider, send a stamped, self-addressed envelope to:

- The Children's Foundation, 725 15th St. NW, Suite 505, Washington, DC 20005-2109. Internet: http://www.childrensfoundation.net

For eligibility requirements and a description of the Child Development Associate credential, contact:

- Council for Professional Recognition, 2460 16th St. NW, Washington, DC 20009-3575. Internet: http://www.cdacouncil.org

For eligibility requirements and a description of the Certified Child-care Professional designation, contact:

- National Child Care Association, 1016 Rosser St., Conyers, GA 30012. Internet: http://www.nccanet.org

For information about a career as a nanny, contact:

- International Nanny Association, 191 Clarksville Rd., Princeton Junction, NJ 08550-3111. Telephone (toll free): 888-878-1477. Internet: http://www.nanny.org

State departments of human services or social services can supply state regulations and training requirements for child care workers.

Clinical Laboratory Technologists and Technicians

(O*NET 29-2011.00 and 29-2012.00)

Significant Points

- Faster than average employment growth is expected as the volume of laboratory tests continues to increase with both population growth and the development of new types of tests.
- Clinical laboratory technologists usually have a bachelor's degree with a major in medical technology or in one of the life sciences; clinical laboratory technicians generally need either an associate degree or a certificate.
- Job opportunities are expected to be excellent.

Nature of the Work

Clinical laboratory testing plays a crucial role in the detection, diagnosis, and treatment of disease. Clinical laboratory technologists, also referred to as clinical laboratory scientists or medical technologists, and clinical laboratory technicians, also known as medical technicians or medical laboratory technicians, perform most of these tests.

Clinical laboratory personnel examine and analyze body fluids, and cells. They look for bacteria, parasites, and other microorganisms; analyze the chemical content of fluids; match blood for transfusions; and test for drug levels in the blood to show how a patient is responding to treatment. Technologists also prepare specimens for examination, count cells, and look for abnormal cells in blood and body fluids. They use automated equipment and computerized instruments capable of performing a number of tests simultaneously, as well as microscopes, cell counters, and other sophisticated laboratory equipment. Then they analyze the results and relay them to physicians. With increasing automation and the use of computer technology, the work of technologists and technicians has become less hands-on and more analytical.

The complexity of tests performed, the level of judgment needed, and the amount of responsibility workers assume depend largely on the amount of education and experience they have.

Clinical laboratory technologists perform complex chemical, biological, hematological, immunologic, microscopic, and bacteriological tests. Technologists microscopically examine blood and other body fluids. They make cultures of body fluid and tissue samples, to determine the presence of bacteria, fungi, parasites, or other microorganisms. Clinical laboratory technologists analyze samples for chemical content or a chemical reaction and determine concentrations of compounds such as blood glucose and cholesterol levels. They also type and cross match blood samples for transfusions.

Clinical laboratory technologists evaluate test results, develop and modify procedures, and establish and monitor programs, to ensure the accuracy of tests. Some technologists supervise clinical laboratory technicians.

Technologists in small laboratories perform many types of tests, whereas those in large laboratories generally specialize. Technologists who prepare specimens and analyze the chemical and hormonal contents of body fluids are called clinical chemistry technologists. Those who examine and identify bacteria and other microorganisms are microbiology technologists. Blood bank technologists, or immunohematology technologists, collect, type, and prepare blood and its components for transfusions. Immunology technologists examine elements of the human immune system and its response to foreign bodies. Cytotechnologists prepare slides of body cells and examine these cells microscopically for abnormalities that may signal the beginning of a cancerous growth. Molecular biology technologists perform complex protein and nucleic acid testing on cell samples.

Clinical laboratory technicians perform less complex tests and laboratory procedures than technologists perform. Technicians may prepare specimens and operate automated analyzers, for example, or they may perform manual tests in accordance with detailed instructions. Like technologists, they may work in several areas of the clinical laboratory or specialize in just one. Histotechnicians cut and stain tissue specimens for microscopic examination by pathologists, and phlebotomists collect blood samples. They usually work under the supervision of medical and clinical laboratory technologists or laboratory managers.

Working Conditions

Hours and other working conditions of clinical laboratory technologists and technicians vary with the size and type of employment setting. In large hospitals or in independent laboratories that operate continuously, personnel usually work the day, evening, or night shift and may work weekends and holidays. Laboratory personnel in small facilities may work on rotating shifts, rather than on a regular shift. In some facilities, laboratory personnel are on call several nights a week or on weekends, in case of an emergency.

Clinical laboratory personnel are trained to work with infectious specimens. When proper methods of infection control and sterilization are followed, few hazards exist. Protective masks, gloves, and goggles are often necessary to ensure the safety of laboratory personnel.

Laboratories usually are well lighted and clean; however, specimens, solutions, and reagents used in the laboratory sometimes produce fumes. Laboratory workers may spend a great deal of time on their feet.

Training, Other Qualifications, and Advancement

The usual requirement for an entry-level position as a clinical laboratory technologist is a bachelor's degree with a major in medical technology or in one of the life sciences; although it is possible to qualify through a combination of education, on-the-job, and specialized training. Universities and hospitals offer medical technology programs.

Bachelor's degree programs in medical technology include courses in chemistry, biological sciences, microbiology, mathematics, and statistics, as well as specialized courses devoted to knowledge and skills used in the clinical laboratory. Many programs also offer or require courses in management, business, and computer applications. The Clinical Laboratory Improvement Act requires technologists who perform highly complex tests to have at least an associate degree.

Medical and clinical laboratory technicians generally have either an associate degree from a community or junior college or a certificate from a hospital, a vocational or technical school, or one of the U.S. Armed Forces. A few technicians learn their skills on the job.

The National Accrediting Agency for Clinical Laboratory Sciences (NAACLS) fully accredits 469 programs for medical and clinical laboratory technologists, medical and clinical laboratory technicians, histotechnologists and histotechnicians, cytogenetic technologists, and diagnostic molecular scientists. NAACLS also approves 57 programs in phlebotomy and clinical assisting. Other nationally recognized accrediting agencies that accredit specific areas for clinical laboratory workers include the Commission on Accreditation of Allied Health Education Programs and the Accrediting Bureau of Health Education Schools.

Some states require laboratory personnel to be licensed or registered. Information on licensure is available from state departments of health or boards of occupational licensing. Certification is a voluntary process by which a nongovernmental organization, such as a professional society or certifying agency, grants recognition to an individual whose professional competence meets prescribed standards. Widely accepted by employers in the health care industry, certification is a prerequisite for most jobs and often is necessary for advancement. Agencies certifying medical and clinical laboratory technologists and technicians include the Board of Registry of the American Society for Clinical Pathology, the American Medical Technologists, the National Credentialing Agency for Laboratory Personnel, and the Board of Registry of the American Association of Bioanalysts. These agencies have different requirements for certification and different organizational sponsors.

Clinical laboratory personnel need good analytical judgment and the ability to work under pressure. Close attention to detail is essential, because small differences or changes in test substances or numerical readouts can be crucial for patient care. Manual dexterity and normal color vision are highly desirable. With the widespread use of automated laboratory equipment, computer skills are important. In addition, technologists in particular are expected to be good at problem solving.

Technologists may advance to supervisory positions in laboratory work or may become chief medical or clinical laboratory technologists or laboratory managers in hospitals. Manufacturers of home diagnostic testing kits and laboratory equipment and supplies seek experienced technologists to work in product development, marketing, and sales. A graduate degree in medical technology, one of the biological sciences, chemistry, management, or education usually speeds advancement. A doctorate is needed to become a laboratory director; however, federal regulation allows directors of moderately complex laboratories to have either a master's degree or a bachelor's degree, combined with the appropriate amount of training and experience. Technicians can become technologists through additional education and experience.

Employment

Clinical laboratory technologists and technicians held about 302,000 jobs in 2004. More than half of jobs were in hospitals. Most of the remaining jobs were in offices of physicians and in medical and diagnostic laboratories. A small proportion was in educational services and in all other ambulatory health care services.

Job Outlook

Job opportunities are expected to be excellent, because the number of job openings is expected to continue to exceed the number of job seekers. Employment of clinical laboratory workers is expected to grow faster than average for all occupations through the year 2014, as the volume of laboratory tests continues to increase with both population growth and the development of new types of tests.

Technological advances will continue to have two opposing effects on employment. On the one hand, new, increasingly powerful diagnostic tests will encourage additional testing and spur employment. On the other hand, research and development efforts targeted at simplifying routine testing procedures may enhance the ability of nonlaboratory personnel—physicians and patients in particular—to perform tests now conducted in laboratories. Although hospitals are expected to continue to be the major employer of clinical laboratory workers, employment is expected to grow faster in medical and diagnostic laboratories, offices of physicians, and all other ambulatory health care services.

Although significant, job growth will not be the only source of opportunities. As in most occupations, many openings will result from the need to replace workers who transfer to other occupations, retire, or stop working for some other reason.

Earnings

Median annual earnings of medical and clinical laboratory technologists were $45,730 in May 2004. The middle 50 percent earned between $38,740 and $54,310. The lowest 10 percent earned less than $32,240, and the highest 10 percent earned more than $63,120. Median annual earnings in the industries employing the largest numbers of medical and clinical laboratory technologists in May 2004 were as follows:

General medical and surgical hospitals	$46,020
Medical and diagnostic laboratories	45,840
Offices of physicians	41,070

Median annual earnings of medical and clinical laboratory technicians were $30,840 in May 2004. The middle 50 percent earned between $24,890 and $37,770. The lowest 10 percent earned less than $20,410, and the highest 10 percent earned more than $45,680. Median annual earnings in the industries employing the largest numbers of medical and clinical laboratory technicians in May 2004 were as follows:

Colleges, universities, and professional schools	$32,410
General medical and surgical hospitals	31,830
Offices of physicians	29,620

Medical and diagnostic laboratories 29,220
Other ambulatory health care services 28,130

According to the American Society for Clinical Pathology, median hourly wages of staff clinical laboratory technologists and technicians in 2003 varied by specialty and laboratory type as follows:

	Hospital	Private clinic	Physician office laboratory
Cytotechnologist	$24.70	$24.07	$25.66
Histotechnologist	19.88	19.22	20.50
Medical technologist	20.40	19.00	18.00
Histotechnician	16.97	16.13	20.00
Medical laboratory technician	16.12	15.00	14.75
Phlebotomist	11.13	10.57	10.50

Related Occupations

Clinical laboratory technologists and technicians analyze body fluids, tissue, and other substances, using a variety of tests. Similar or related procedures are performed by chemists and materials scientists, science technicians, and veterinary technologists and technicians.

Sources of Additional Information

For a list of accredited and approved educational programs for clinical laboratory personnel, contact:

- National Accrediting Agency for Clinical Laboratory Sciences, 8410 W. Bryn Mawr Ave., Suite 670, Chicago, IL 60631. Internet: http://www.naacls.org

Information on certification is available from:

- American Association of Bioanalysts, Board of Registry, 906 Olive St., Suite 1200, St. Louis, MO 63101-1434. Internet: http://www.aab.org
- American Medical Technologists, 710 Higgins Rd., Park Ridge, IL 60068.
- American Society for Clinical Pathology, 2100 West Harrison St., Chicago, IL 60612. Internet: http://www.ascp.org
- National Credentialing Agency for Laboratory Personnel, P.O. Box 15945, Lenexa, KS 66285. Internet: http://www.nca-info.org

Additional career information is available from:

- American Association of Blood Banks, 8101 Glenbrook Rd., Bethesda, MD 20814-2749. Internet: http://www.aabb.org
- American Society for Clinical Laboratory Science, 6701 Democracy Blvd., Suite 300, Bethesda, MD 20817. Internet: http://www.ascls.org
- American Society for Cytopathology, 400 West 9th St., Suite 201, Wilmington, DE 19801. Internet: http://www.cytopathology.org
- Clinical Laboratory Management Association, 989 Old Eagle School Rd., Suite 815, Wayne, PA 19087. Internet: http://www.clma.org

Computer and Information Systems Managers

(O*NET 11-3021.00)

Significant Points

- Employment of computer and information systems managers is expected to grow faster than the average for all occupations through the year 2014.
- Many managers possess advanced technical knowledge gained from working in a computer occupation.
- Job opportunities will be best for applicants with computer-related work experience; a master's degree in business administration (MBA) with technology as a core component, or a management information systems degree; and strong communication and administrative skills.

Nature of the Work

How and when companies and organizations use technology are critical to remaining competitive. Computer and information systems managers play a vital role in the technological direction of their organizations. They do everything from constructing the business plan to overseeing network security to directing Internet operations.

Computer and information systems managers plan, coordinate, and direct research and facilitate the computer-related activities of firms. They help determine both technical and business goals in consultation with top management and make detailed plans for the accomplishment of these goals. For example, working with their staff, they may develop the overall concepts and requirements of a new product or service, or may identify how an organization's computing capabilities can effectively aid project management.

Computer and information systems managers direct the work of systems analysts, computer programmers, support specialists, and other computer-related workers. These managers plan and coordinate activities such as installation and upgrading of hardware and software, programming and systems design, development of computer networks, and implementation of Internet and intranet sites. They are increasingly involved with the upkeep, maintenance, and security of networks. They analyze the computer and information needs of their organizations from an operational and strategic perspective and determine immediate and long-range personnel and equipment requirements. They assign and review the work of their subordinates and stay abreast of the latest technology to ensure the organization does not lag behind competitors.

The duties of computer and information systems managers vary with their specific titles. *Chief technology officers*, for example, evaluate the newest and most innovative technologies and determine how these can help their organizations. The chief technology officer, who often reports to the organization's chief information officer, manages and plans technical standards and tends to the daily information technology issues of the firm. Because of the rapid pace of technological change, chief technology officers must constantly be on the lookout for developments that could benefit their organizations.

They are responsible for demonstrating to a company how information technology can be used as a competitive tool that not only cuts costs, but also increases revenue and maintains or increases competitive advantage.

Management information systems (MIS) directors manage information systems and computing resources for their organizations. They also may work under the chief information officer and plan and direct the work of subordinate information technology employees. These managers oversee a variety of user services such as an organization's help desk, which employees can call with questions or problems. MIS directors also may make hardware and software upgrade recommendations based on their experience with an organization's technology. Helping ensure the availability, continuity, and security of data and information technology services is the primary responsibility of these workers.

Project managers develop requirements, budgets, and schedules for their firms' information technology projects. They coordinate such projects from development through implementation, working with internal and external clients, vendors, consultants, and computer specialists. These managers are increasingly involved in projects that upgrade the information security of an organization.

LAN/WAN (local area network/wide area network) *managers* provide a variety of services, from design to administration of the local area network, which connects staff within an organization. These managers direct the network and its computing environment, including hardware, systems software, applications software, and all other computer-related configurations.

Computer and information systems managers need strong communication skills. They coordinate the activities of their unit with those of other units or organizations. They confer with top executives; financial, production, marketing, and other managers; and contractors and equipment and materials suppliers.

Working Conditions

Computer and information systems managers spend most of their time in an office. Most work at least 40 hours a week and may have to work evenings and weekends to meet deadlines or solve unexpected problems. Some computer and information systems managers may experience considerable pressure in meeting technical goals within short timeframes or tight budgets. As networks continue to expand and more work is done remotely, computer and information systems managers have to communicate with and oversee offsite employees using modems, laptops, e-mail, and the Internet.

Like other workers who sit continuously in front of a keyboard, computer and information systems managers are susceptible to eyestrain, back discomfort, and hand and wrist problems such as carpal tunnel syndrome.

Training, Other Qualifications, and Advancement

Advanced technical knowledge is essential for computer and information systems managers, who must understand and guide the work of their subordinates yet also explain the work in nontechnical terms to senior managers and potential customers. Therefore, many computer and information systems managers have experience in a computer occupation such as systems analyst; other managers may have worked as a computer support specialist, programmer, or other information technology professional.

A bachelor's degree usually is required for management positions, although employers often prefer a graduate degree, especially an MBA with technology as a core component. This degree differs from a traditional MBA in that there is a heavy emphasis on information technology in addition to the standard business curriculum. This preparation is becoming important because more computer and information systems managers are making important technology decisions as well as business decisions for their organizations. Some universities specialize in offering degrees in management information systems, which blend technical core subjects with business, accounting, and communications courses. A few computer and information systems managers attain their positions with only an associate degree, but they must have sufficient experience and must have acquired additional skills on the job. To aid their professional advancement, though, many managers with an associate degree eventually earn a bachelor's or master's degree while working.

Computer and information systems managers need a broad range of skills. Employers want managers who have experience with the specific software or technology used on the job, as well as a background in either consulting or business management. The expansion of electronic commerce has elevated the importance of business insight; many computer and information systems managers are called on to make important business decisions. Managers need a keen understanding of people, management processes, and customers' needs.

Computer and information systems managers must possess strong interpersonal, communication, and leadership skills because they are required to interact not only with their staff, but also with other people inside and outside their organizations. They also must possess team skills to work on group projects and other collaborative efforts. Computer and information systems managers increasingly interact with persons outside their organizations, reflecting their emerging role as vital parts of their firms' executive teams.

Computer and information systems managers may advance to progressively higher leadership positions in their field. Some may become managers in nontechnical areas such as marketing, human resources, or sales. In high-technology firms, managers in nontechnical areas often must possess the same specialized knowledge as do managers in technical areas.

Employment

Computer and information systems managers held about 280,000 jobs in 2004. About 9 in 10 computer managers worked in service-providing industries, mainly in computer systems design and related services. This industry provides services related to the commercial use of computers on a contract basis, including custom computer programming services; computer systems integration design services; computer facilities management services, including computer systems or data-processing facilities support services; and other computer-related services, such as disaster recovery services and software installation. Other large employers include insurance and financial firms, government agencies, and manufacturers.

Job Outlook

Employment of computer and information systems managers is expected to grow faster than the average for all occupations through the year 2014. Technological advancements will boost the employment of computer-related workers; as a result, the demand for managers to direct these workers also will increase. In addition, job openings will result from the need to replace managers who retire or move into other occupations. Opportunities for obtaining a management position will be best for those with computer-related work experience; an MBA with technology as a core component, or a management information systems degree; and strong communication and administrative skills.

Despite the downturn in the technology sector in the early part of the decade, the outlook for computer and information systems managers remains strong. To remain competitive, firms will continue to install sophisticated computer networks and set up more complex Internet and intranet sites. Keeping a computer network running smoothly is essential to almost every organization. Firms will be more willing to hire managers who can accomplish that.

Similarly, the security of computer networks will continue to increase in importance as more business is conducted over the Internet. The security of the nation's entire electronic infrastructure has come under renewed scrutiny in light of recent threats. Organizations need to understand how their systems are vulnerable and how to protect their infrastructure and Internet sites from hackers, viruses, and other acts of cyberterrorism. The emergence of cybersecurity as a key issue facing most organizations should lead to strong growth for computer managers. Firms will increasingly hire cybersecurity experts to fill key leadership roles in their information technology departments because the integrity of their computing environments is of utmost concern. As a result, there will be a high demand for managers proficient in computer security issues.

With the explosive growth of electronic commerce and the capacity of the Internet to create new relationships with customers, the role of computer and information systems managers will continue to evolve. Persons in these jobs will become increasingly vital to their companies. The expansion of the wireless Internet will spur the need for computer and information systems managers with both business savvy and technical proficiency.

Opportunities for those who wish to become computer and information systems managers should be closely related to the growth of the occupations they supervise and the industries in which they are found.

Earnings

Earnings for computer and information systems managers vary by specialty and level of responsibility. Median annual earnings of these managers in May 2004 were $92,570. The middle 50 percent earned between $71,650 and $118,330. Median annual earnings in the industries employing the largest numbers of computer and information systems managers in May 2004 were as follows:

Software publishers	$107,870
Computer systems design and related services	103,850
Management of companies and enterprises	99,880
Insurance carriers	97,900
Depository credit intermediation	86,450

According to Robert Half International, a professional staffing and consulting services firm, average starting salaries in 2005 for high-level information technology managers ranged from $80,250 to $112,250. According to a 2005 survey by the National Association of Colleges and Employers, starting salary offers for those with an MBA, a technical undergraduate degree, and 1 year or less of experience averaged $52,300; for those with a master's degree in management information systems/business data processing, the starting salary averaged $56,909.

In addition, computer and information systems managers, especially those at higher levels, often receive more employment-related benefits—such as expense accounts, stock option plans, and bonuses—than do nonmanagerial workers in their organizations.

Related Occupations

The work of computer and information systems managers is closely related to that of computer programmers, computer software engineers, computer systems analysts, computer scientists and database administrators, and computer support specialists and systems administrators. Computer and information systems managers also have some high-level responsibilities similar to those of top executives.

Sources of Additional Information

For information about a career as a computer and information systems manager, contact the sources of additional information for the various computer occupations discussed elsewhere this book.

Computer Scientists and Database Administrators

(O*NET 15-1011.00, 15-1061.00, and 15-1099.99)

Significant Points

- Education requirements range from an associate degree to a doctoral degree.
- Employment is expected to increase much faster than the average as organizations continue to adopt increasingly sophisticated technologies.
- Job prospects are favorable.

Nature of the Work

The rapid spread of computers and information technology has generated a need for highly trained workers proficient in various job functions. These workers—computer scientists, database administrators, and network systems and data communication analysts—include a wide range of computer specialists. Job tasks and occupational titles used to describe these workers evolve rapidly, reflecting new areas of specialization or changes in technology as well as the preferences and practices of employers.

Computer scientists work as theorists, researchers, or inventors. Their jobs are distinguished by the higher level of theoretical expertise and innovation they apply to complex problems and the creation or application of new technology. Those employed by academic institutions work in areas ranging from complexity theory to hardware to programming-language design. Some work on multidisciplinary projects, such as developing and advancing uses of virtual reality, extending human-computer interaction, or designing robots. Their counterparts in private industry work in areas such as applying theory; developing specialized languages or information technologies; or designing programming tools, knowledge-based systems, or even computer games.

With the Internet and electronic business generating large volumes of data, there is a growing need to be able to store, manage, and extract data effectively. *Database administrators* work with database management systems software and determine ways to organize and store data. They identify user requirements, set up computer databases, and test and coordinate modifications to the computer database systems. An organization's database administrator ensures the performance of the system, understands the platform on which the database runs, and adds new users to the system. Because they also may design and implement system security, database administrators often plan and coordinate security measures. With the volume of sensitive data generated every second growing rapidly, data integrity, backup systems, and database security have become increasingly important aspects of the job of database administrators.

Because networks are configured in many ways, *network systems and data communications analysts* are needed to design, test, and evaluate systems such as local area networks (LANs), wide area networks (WANs), the Internet, intranets, and other data communications systems. Systems can range from a connection between two offices in the same building to globally distributed networks, voice mail, and e-mail systems of a multinational organization. Network systems and data communications analysts perform network modeling, analysis, and planning; they also may research related products and make necessary hardware and software recommendations. *Telecommunications specialists* focus on the interaction between computer and communications equipment. These workers design voice and data communication systems, supervise the installation of the systems, and provide maintenance and other services to clients after the systems are installed.

The growth of the Internet and the expansion of the World Wide Web (the graphical portion of the Internet) have generated a variety of occupations related to the design, development, and maintenance of Web sites and their servers. For example, *webmasters* are responsible for all technical aspects of a Web site, including performance issues such as speed of access, and for approving the content of the site. *Internet developers* or *Web developers*, also called *Web designers*, are responsible for day-to-day site creation and design.

Working Conditions

Computer scientists and database administrators normally work in offices or laboratories in comfortable surroundings. They usually work about 40 hours a week—the same as many other professional or office workers do. However, evening or weekend work may be necessary to meet deadlines or solve specific problems. With the technology available today, telecommuting is common for computer professionals. As networks expand, more work can be done from remote locations through modems, laptops, electronic mail, and the Internet.

Like other workers who spend long periods in front of a computer terminal typing on a keyboard, computer scientists and database administrators are susceptible to eyestrain, back discomfort, and hand and wrist problems such as carpal tunnel syndrome or cumulative trauma disorder.

Training, Other Qualifications, and Advancement

Rapidly changing technology requires an increasing level of skill and education on the part of employees. Companies look for professionals with an ever-broader background and range of skills including not only technical knowledge, but also communication and other interpersonal skills. While there is no universally accepted way to prepare for a job as a network systems analyst, computer scientist, or database administrator, most employers place a premium on some formal college education. A bachelor's degree is a prerequisite for many jobs; however, some jobs may require only a 2-year degree. Relevant work experience also is very important. For more technically complex jobs, persons with graduate degrees are preferred.

For database administrator positions, many employers seek applicants who have a bachelor's degree in computer science, information science, or management information systems (MIS). MIS programs usually are part of the business school or college and differ considerably from computer science programs, emphasizing business and management-oriented coursework and business computing courses. Employers increasingly seek individuals with a master's degree in business administration (MBA), with a concentration in information systems, as more firms move their business to the Internet. For some network systems and data communication analysts, such as webmasters, an associate degree or certificate is sufficient, although more advanced positions might require a computer-related bachelor's degree. For computer and information scientists, a doctoral degree generally is required because of the highly technical nature of their work.

Despite employers' preference for those with technical degrees, persons with degrees in a variety of majors find employment in these occupations. The level of education and the type of training that employers require depend on their needs. One factor affecting these needs is changes in technology. Employers often scramble to find workers capable of implementing new technologies. Workers with formal education or experience in information security, for example, are in demand because of the growing need for their skills and services. Employers also look for workers skilled in wireless technologies as wireless networks and applications have spread into many firms and organizations.

Most community colleges and many independent technical institutes and proprietary schools offer an associate's degree in computer science or a related information technology field. Many of these programs may be geared more toward meeting the needs of local businesses and are more occupation-specific than are 4-year degree programs. Some jobs may be better suited to the level of training that such programs offer. Employers usually look for people who have broad knowledge and experience related to computer systems and technologies, strong problem-solving and analytical skills, and good interpersonal skills. Courses in computer science or systems design offer good preparation for a job in these computer occupations. For jobs in a business environment, employers usually want systems analysts to have business management or closely related skills, while a background in the physical sciences, applied mathematics, or engineering is preferred for work in scientifically oriented organizations. Art or graphic design skills may be desirable for webmasters or Web developers.

Jobseekers can enhance their employment opportunities by participating in internship or co-op programs offered through their schools. Because many people develop advanced computer skills in a noncomputer occupation and then transfer those skills to a computer occupation, a background in the industry in which the person's job is located, such as financial services, banking, or accounting, can be important. Others have taken computer science courses to supplement their study in fields such as accounting, inventory control, or other business areas.

Computer scientists and database administrators must be able to think logically and have good communication skills. Because they often deal with a number of tasks simultaneously, the ability to concentrate and pay close attention to detail is important. Although these computer specialists sometimes work independently, they frequently work in teams on large projects. They must be able to communicate effectively with computer personnel, such as programmers and managers, as well as with users or other staff who may have no technical computer background.

Computer scientists employed in private industry may advance into managerial or project leadership positions. Those employed in academic institutions can become heads of research departments or published authorities in their field. Database administrators may advance into managerial positions, such as chief technology officer, on the basis of their experience managing data and enforcing security. Computer specialists with work experience and considerable expertise in a particular subject or a certain application may find lucrative opportunities as independent consultants or may choose to start their own computer consulting firms.

Technological advances come so rapidly in the computer field that continuous study is necessary to keep one's skills up to date. Employers, hardware and software vendors, colleges and universities, and private training institutions offer continuing education. Additional training may come from professional development seminars offered by professional computing societies.

Certification is a way to demonstrate a level of competence in a particular field. Some product vendors or software firms offer certification and require professionals who work with their products to be certified. Many employers regard these certifications as the industry standard. For example, one method of acquiring enough knowledge to get a job as a database administrator is to become certified in a specific type of database management. Voluntary certification also is available through various organizations associated with computer specialists. Professional certification may afford a jobseeker a competitive advantage.

Employment

Computer scientists and database administrators held about 507,000 jobs in 2004, including about 66,000 who were self-employed. Employment was distributed among the detailed occupations as follows:

Network systems and data communication analysts	231,000
Database administrators	104,000
Computer and information scientists, research	22,000
Computer specialists, all other	149,000

Although they are increasingly employed in every sector of the economy, the greatest concentration of these workers is in the computer systems design and related services industry. Firms in this industry provide services related to the commercial use of computers on a contract basis, including custom computer programming services; computer systems integration design services; computer facilities management services, including computer systems or data processing facilities support services for clients; and other computer-related services, such as disaster recovery services and software installation. Many computer scientists and database administrators are employed by Internet service providers; Web search portals; and data processing, hosting, and related services firms. Others work for government, manufacturers of computer and electronic products, insurance companies, financial institutions, and universities.

A growing number of computer specialists, such as network and data communications analysts, are employed on a temporary or contract basis; many of these individuals are self-employed, working independently as contractors or consultants. For example, a company installing a new computer system may need the services of several network systems and data communication analysts just to get the system running. Because not all of the analysts would be needed once the system is functioning, the company might contract for such employees with a temporary help agency or a consulting firm or with the network systems analysts themselves. Such jobs may last from several months to 2 years or more. This growing practice enables companies to bring in people with the exact skills they need to complete a particular project instead of having to spend time or money training or retraining existing workers. Often, experienced consultants then train a company's in-house staff as a project develops.

Job Outlook

Computer scientists and database administrators should continue to enjoy favorable job prospects. As technology becomes more sophisticated and complex, however, employers demand a higher level of skill and expertise from their employees. Individuals with an advanced degree in computer science or computer engineering or with an MBA with a concentration in information systems should enjoy favorable employment prospects. College graduates with a bachelor's degree in computer science, computer engineering, information science, or MIS also should enjoy favorable prospects, particularly if they have supplemented their formal education with practical experience. Because employers continue to seek computer specialists who can combine strong technical skills with good interpersonal and business skills, graduates with degrees in fields other than computer science who have had courses in computer programming, systems analysis, and other information technology areas also should continue to find jobs in these computer fields. In fact, individuals with the right experience and training can work in these computer occupations regardless of their college major or level of formal education.

Computer scientists and database administrators are expected to be among the fastest growing occupations through 2014. Employment of these computer specialists is expected to grow much faster than the average for all occupations as organizations continue to adopt and integrate increasingly sophisticated technologies. Job increases will be driven by very rapid growth in computer systems design and related services, which is projected to be one of the fastest growing industries in the U.S. economy. Job growth will not be as rapid as during the previous decade, however, as the information technology sector begins to mature and as routine work is increasingly outsourced overseas. In addition to growth, many job openings will arise annually from the need to replace workers who move into managerial positions or other occupations or who leave the labor force.

The demand for networking to facilitate the sharing of information, the expansion of client–server environments, and the need for computer specialists to use their knowledge and skills in a problem-solving capacity will be major factors in the rising demand for computer scientists and database administrators. Moreover, falling prices of computer hardware and software should continue to induce more businesses to expand their computerized operations and integrate new technologies into them. To maintain a competitive edge and operate more efficiently, firms will keep demanding computer specialists who are knowledgeable about the latest technologies and are able to apply them to meet the needs of businesses.

Increasingly, more sophisticated and complex technology is being implemented across all organizations, fueling demand for computer scientists and database administrators. There is growing demand for network systems and data communication analysts to help firms maximize their efficiency with available technology. Expansion of electronic commerce—doing business on the Internet—and the continuing need to build and maintain databases that store critical information on customers, inventory, and projects are fueling demand for database administrators familiar with the latest technology. Also, the increasing importance placed on cybersecurity—the protection of electronic information—will result in a need for workers skilled in information security.

The development of new technologies usually leads to demand for various kinds of workers. The expanding integration of Internet technologies into businesses, for example, has resulted in a growing need for specialists who can develop and support Internet and intranet applications. The growth of electronic commerce means that more establishments use the Internet to conduct their business online. The introduction of the wireless Internet, known as WiFi, creates new systems to be analyzed and new data to be administered. The spread of such new technologies translates into a need for information technology professionals who can help organizations use technology to communicate with employees, clients, and consumers. Explosive growth in these areas also is expected to fuel demand for specialists who are knowledgeable about network, data, and communications security.

Earnings

Median annual earnings of computer and information scientists, research, were $85,190 in May 2004. The middle 50 percent earned between $64,860 and $108,440. The lowest 10 percent earned less than $48,930, and the highest 10 percent earned more than $132,700. Median annual earnings of computer and information scientists employed in computer systems design and related services in May 2004 were $85,530.

Median annual earnings of database administrators were $60,650 in May 2004. The middle 50 percent earned between $44,490 and $81,140. The lowest 10 percent earned less than $33,380, and the highest 10 percent earned more than $97,450. In May 2004, median annual earnings of database administrators employed in computer systems design and related services were $70,530, and for those in management of companies and enterprises, earnings were $65,990.

Median annual earnings of network systems and data communication analysts were $60,600 in May 2004. The middle 50 percent earned between $46,480 and $78,060. The lowest 10 percent earned less than $36,260, and the highest 10 percent earned more than $95,040. Median annual earnings in the industries employing the largest numbers of network systems and data communications analysts in May 2004 are shown below:

Wired telecommunications carriers	$65,130
Insurance carriers	64,660
Management of companies and enterprises	64,170
Computer systems design and related services	63,910
Local government	52,300

Median annual earnings of all other computer specialists were $59,480 in May 2004. Median annual earnings of all other computer specialists employed in computer systems design and related services were $57,430, and, for those in management of companies and enterprises, earnings were $68,590 in May 2004.

According to the National Association of Colleges and Employers, starting offers for graduates with a doctoral degree in computer science averaged $93,050 in 2005. Starting offers averaged $50,820 for graduates with a bachelor's degree in computer science; $46,189 for those with a degree in computer systems analysis; $44,417 for those with a degree in management information systems; and $44,775 for those with a degree in information sciences and systems.

According to Robert Half International, a firm providing specialized staffing services, starting salaries in 2005 ranged from $67,750 to $95,500 for database administrators. Salaries for networking and Internet-related occupations ranged from $47,000 to $68,500 for LAN administrators and from $51,750 to $74,520 for Web developers. Starting salaries for information security professionals ranged from $63,750 to $93,000 in 2005.

Related Occupations

Others who work with large amounts of data are computer programmers, computer software engineers, computer and information systems managers, engineers, mathematicians, and statisticians.

Sources of Additional Information

Further information about computer careers is available from:

- Association for Computing Machinery (ACM), 1515 Broadway, New York, NY 10036. Internet: http://www.acm.org
- Institute of Electrical and Electronics Engineers Computer Society, Headquarters Office, 1730 Massachusetts Ave. NW, Washington, DC 20036-1992. Internet: http://www.computer.org
- National Workforce Center for Emerging Technologies, 3000 Landerholm Circle SE, Bellevue, WA 98007. Internet: http://www.nwcet.org

Computer Software Engineers

(O*NET 15-1031.00 and 15-1032.00)

Significant Points

- Computer software engineers are projected to be one of the fastest growing occupations over the 2004–14 period.
- Very good opportunities are expected for college graduates with at least a bachelor's degree in computer engineering or computer science and with practical work experience.
- Computer software engineers must continually strive to acquire new skills in conjunction with the rapid changes that are occurring in computer technology.

Nature of the Work

The explosive impact of computers and information technology on our everyday lives has generated a need to design and develop new computer software systems and to incorporate new technologies into a rapidly growing range of applications. The tasks performed by workers known as computer software engineers evolve quickly, reflecting new areas of specialization or changes in technology as well as the preferences and practices of employers. Computer software engineers apply the principles and techniques of computer science, engineering, and mathematical analysis to the design, development, testing, and evaluation of the software and systems that enable computers to perform their many applications.

Software engineers working in applications or systems development analyze users' needs and design, construct, test, and maintain computer applications software or systems. Software engineers can be involved in the design and development of many types of software, including software for operating systems and network distribution and compilers, which convert programs for execution on a computer. In programming, or coding, software engineers instruct a computer, line by line, how to perform a function. They also solve technical problems that arise. Software engineers must possess strong programming skills but are more concerned with developing algorithms and analyzing and solving programming problems than with actually writing code.

Computer applications software engineers analyze users' needs and design, construct, and maintain general computer applications software or specialized utility programs. These workers use different programming languages, depending on the purpose of the program. The programming languages most often used are C, C++, and Java, with Fortran and COBOL used less commonly. Some software engineers develop both packaged systems and systems software or create customized applications.

Computer systems software engineers coordinate the construction and maintenance of a company's computer systems and plan their future growth. Working with the company, they coordinate each department's computer needs—ordering, inventory, billing, and payroll recordkeeping, for example—and make suggestions about its technical direction. They also might set up the company's intranets—networks that link computers within the organization and ease communication among the various departments.

Systems software engineers work for companies that configure, implement, and install complete computer systems. These workers may be members of the marketing or sales staff, serving as the primary technical resource for sales workers and customers. They also may be involved in product sales and in providing their customers with continuing technical support. Since the selling of complex computer systems often requires substantial customization for the purchaser's organization, software engineers help to explain the requirements necessary for installing and operating the new system in the purchaser's computing environment. In addition, systems software engineers are responsible for ensuring security across the systems they are configuring.

Computer software engineers often work as part of a team that designs new hardware, software, and systems. A core team may comprise engineering, marketing, manufacturing, and design people, who work together until the product is released.

Working Conditions

Computer software engineers normally work in well-lighted and comfortable offices or laboratories in which computer equipment is located. Most software engineers work at least 40 hours a week; however, due to the project-oriented nature of the work, they also may have to work evenings or weekends to meet deadlines or solve unexpected technical problems. Like other workers who sit for hours at a computer, typing on a keyboard, software engineers are susceptible to eyestrain, back discomfort, and hand and wrist problems such as carpal tunnel syndrome.

As they strive to improve software for users, many computer software engineers interact with customers and co-workers. Computer software engineers who are employed by software vendors and consulting firms, for example, spend much of their time away from their offices, frequently traveling overnight to meet with customers. They call on customers in businesses ranging from manufacturing plants to financial institutions.

As networks expand, software engineers may be able to use modems, laptops, e-mail, and the Internet to provide more technical support and other services from their main office, connecting to a customer's computer remotely to identify and correct developing problems.

Training, Other Qualifications, and Advancement

Most employers prefer to hire persons who have at least a bachelor's degree and broad knowledge of, and experience with, a variety of computer systems and technologies. The usual degree concentration for applications software engineers is computer science or software engineering; for systems software engineers, it is computer science or computer information systems. Graduate degrees are preferred for some of the more complex jobs.

Academic programs in software engineering emphasize software and may be offered as a degree option or in conjunction with computer science degrees. Increasing emphasis on computer security suggests that software engineers with advanced degrees that include mathematics and systems design will be sought after by software developers, government agencies, and consulting firms specializing in information assurance and security. Students seeking software engineering jobs enhance their employment opportunities by participating in internship or co-op programs offered through their schools. These experiences provide the students with broad knowledge and experience, making them more attractive candidates to employers. Inexperienced college graduates may be hired by large computer and consulting firms that train new employees in intensive company-based programs. In many firms, new hires are mentored, and their mentors have an input into the performance evaluations of these new employees.

For systems software engineering jobs that require workers to have a college degree, a bachelor's degree in computer science or computer information systems is typical. For systems engineering jobs that place less emphasis on workers having a computer-related degree, computer training programs leading to certification are offered by systems software vendors. Nonetheless, most training authorities feel that program certification alone is not sufficient for the majority of software engineering jobs.

Persons interested in jobs as computer software engineers must have strong problem-solving and analytical skills. They also must be able to communicate effectively with team members, other staff, and the customers they meet. Because they often deal with a number of tasks simultaneously, they must be able to concentrate and pay close attention to detail.

As is the case with most occupations, advancement opportunities for computer software engineers increase with experience. Entry-level computer software engineers are likely to test and verify ongoing designs. As they become more experienced, they may become involved in designing and developing software. Eventually, they may advance to become a project manager, manager of information systems, or chief information officer. Some computer software engineers with several years of experience or expertise find lucrative opportunities working as systems designers or independent consultants or starting their own computer consulting firms.

As technological advances in the computer field continue, employers demand new skills. Computer software engineers must continually strive to acquire such skills if they wish to remain in this extremely dynamic field. For example, computer software engineers interested in working for a bank should have some expertise in finance as they integrate new technologies into the computer system of the bank. To help them keep up with the changing technology, continuing education and professional development seminars are offered by employers, software vendors, colleges and universities, private training institutions, and professional computing societies.

Employment

Computer software engineers held about 800,000 jobs in 2004. Approximately 460,000 were computer applications software engineers, and around 340,000 were computer systems software engineers. Although they are employed in most industries, the largest concentration of computer software engineers—almost 30 percent—are in computer systems design and related services. Many computer software engineers also work for establishments in other industries, such as software publishers, government agencies, manufacturers of computers and related electronic equipment, and management of companies and enterprises.

Employers of computer software engineers range from startup companies to established industry leaders. The proliferation of Internet, e-mail, and other communications systems is expanding electronics to engineering firms that are traditionally associated with unrelated disciplines. Engineering firms specializing in building bridges and power plants, for example, hire computer software engineers to design and develop new geographic data systems and automated drafting systems. Communications firms need computer software engineers to tap into growth in the personal communications market. Major communications companies have many job openings for both computer software applications engineers and computer systems engineers.

An increasing number of computer software engineers are employed on a temporary or contract basis, with many being self-employed, working independently as consultants. Some consultants work for firms that specialize in developing and maintaining client companies' Web sites and intranets. About 23,000 computer software engineers were self-employed in 2004.

Job Outlook

Computer software engineers are projected to be one of the fastest-growing occupations from 2004 to 2014. Rapid employment growth in the computer systems design and related services industry, which employs the greatest number of computer software engineers, should result in very good opportunities for those college graduates with at least a bachelor's degree in computer engineering or computer science and practical experience working with computers. Employers will continue to seek computer professionals with strong programming, systems analysis, interpersonal, and business skills. With the software industry beginning to mature, however, and with routine software engineering work being increasingly outsourced overseas, job growth will not be as rapid as during the previous decade.

Employment of computer software engineers is expected to increase much faster than the average for all occupations as businesses and other organizations adopt and integrate new technologies and seek to maximize the efficiency of their computer systems. Competition among businesses will continue to create an incentive for increasingly sophisticated technological innovations, and organizations will need more computer software engineers to implement these changes. In addition to jobs created through employment growth, many job openings will result annually from the need to replace workers who move into managerial positions, transfer to other occupations, or leave the labor force.

Demand for computer software engineers will increase as computer networking continues to grow. For example, the expanding integration of Internet technologies and the explosive growth in electronic commerce—doing business on the Internet—have resulted in rising demand for computer software engineers who can develop Internet, intranet, and World Wide Web applications. Likewise, expanding electronic data-processing systems in business, telecommunications, government, and other settings continue to become more sophisticated and complex. Growing numbers of systems software engineers will be needed to implement, safeguard, and update systems and resolve problems. Consulting opportunities for computer software engineers also should continue to grow as businesses seek help to manage, upgrade, and customize their increasingly complicated computer systems.

New growth areas will continue to arise from rapidly evolving technologies. The increasing uses of the Internet, the proliferation of Web sites, and mobile technology such as the wireless Internet have created a demand for a wide variety of new products. As individuals and businesses rely more on hand-held computers and wireless networks, it will be necessary to integrate current computer systems with this new, more mobile technology. Also, information security concerns have given rise to new software needs. Concerns over "cyber security" should result in businesses and government continuing to invest heavily in software that protects their networks and vital electronic infrastructure from attack. The expansion of this technology in the next 10 years will lead to an increased need for computer engineers to design and develop the software and systems to run these new applications and integrate them into older systems.

As with other information technology jobs, employment growth of computer software engineers may be tempered somewhat as more software development is contracted out abroad. Firms may look to cut costs by shifting operations to lower-wage foreign countries with highly educated workers who have strong technical skills. At the same time, jobs in software engineering are less prone to being sent abroad compared with jobs in other computer specialties because the occupation requires innovation and intense research and development.

Earnings

Median annual earnings of computer applications software engineers who worked full time in May 2004 were about $74,980. The middle 50 percent earned between $59,130 and $92,130. The lowest 10 percent earned less than $46,520, and the highest 10 percent earned more than $113,830. Median annual earnings in the industries employing the largest numbers of computer applications software engineers in May 2004 were as follows:

Software publishers $79,930
Management, scientific, and technical consulting services 78,460
Computer systems design and related services 76,910
Management of companies and enterprises 70,520
Insurance carriers 68,440

Median annual earnings of computer systems software engineers who worked full time in May 2004 were about $79,740. The middle 50 percent earned between $63,150 and $98,220. The lowest 10 percent earned less than $50,420, and the highest 10 percent earned more than $118,350. Median annual earnings in the industries employing the largest numbers of computer systems software engineers in May 2004 are as follows:

Scientific research and development services $91,390
Computer and peripheral equipment manufacturing 87,800
Software publishers 83,670
Computer systems design and related services 79,950
Wired telecommunications carriers 74,370

According to the National Association of Colleges and Employers, starting salary offers for graduates with a bachelor's degree in computer engineering averaged $52,464 in 2005; offers for those with a master's degree averaged $60,354. Starting salary offers for graduates with a bachelor's degree in computer science averaged $50,820.

According to Robert Half International, starting salaries for software engineers in software development ranged from $63,250 to $92,750 in 2005. For network engineers, starting salaries in 2005 ranged from $61,250 to $88,250.

Related Occupations

Other workers who use mathematics and logic extensively include computer systems analysts, computer scientists and database administrators, computer programmers, computer hardware engineers, computer support specialists and systems administrators, engineers, statisticians, mathematicians, and actuaries.

Sources of Additional Information

Additional information on a career in computer software engineering is available from the following organizations:

- Association for Computing Machinery (ACM), 1515 Broadway, New York, NY 10036. Internet: http://www.acm.org
- Institute of Electronics and Electrical Engineers Computer Society, Headquarters Office, 1730 Massachusetts Ave. NW, Washington, DC 20036-1992. Internet: http://www.computer.org
- National Workforce Center for Emerging Technologies, 3000 Landerholm Circle SE, Bellevue, WA 98007. Internet: http://www.nwcet.org

Computer Support Specialists and Systems Administrators

(O*NET 15-1041.00, 15-1071.00, and 15-1071.01)

Significant Points

- Rapid job growth is projected over the 2004–14 period.
- There are many paths of entry to these occupations.
- Job prospects should be best for college graduates who are up to date with the latest skills and technologies; certifications and practical experience are essential for persons without degrees.

Nature of the Work

In the last decade, computers have become an integral part of everyday life, used for a variety of reasons at home, in the workplace, and at schools. Of course, almost every computer user encounters a problem occasionally, whether it is the disaster of a crashing hard drive or the annoyance of a forgotten password. The explosive use of computers has created a high demand for specialists to provide advice to users as well as for day-to-day administration, maintenance, and support of computer systems and networks.

Computer support specialists provide technical assistance, support, and advice to customers and other users. This occupational group includes *technical support specialists* and *help-desk technicians.* These troubleshooters interpret problems and provide technical support for hardware, software, and systems. They answer telephone calls, analyze problems by using automated diagnostic programs, and resolve recurring difficulties. Support specialists may work either within a company that uses computer systems or directly for a computer hardware or software vendor. Increasingly, these specialists work for help-desk or support services firms, for which they provide computer support to clients on a contract basis.

Technical support specialists answer telephone calls from their organizations' computer users and may run automatic diagnostics programs to resolve problems. Working on monitors, keyboards, printers, and mice, they install, modify, clean, and repair computer hardware and software. They also may write training manuals and train computer users in how to use new computer hardware and software. In addition, technical support specialists oversee the daily performance of their company's computer systems and evaluate software programs with regard to their usefulness.

Help-desk technicians assist computer users with the inevitable hardware and software questions that are not addressed in a product's instruction manual. Help-desk technicians field telephone calls and e-mail messages from customers who are seeking guidance on technical problems. In responding to these requests for guidance, help-desk technicians must listen carefully to the customer, ask questions to diagnose the nature of the problem, and then patiently walk the customer through the problem-solving steps.

Help-desk technicians deal directly with customer issues, and companies value them as a source of feedback on their products. These technicians are consulted for information about what gives customers the most trouble as well as other customer concerns. Most computer support specialists start out at the help desk.

Network administrators and *computer systems administrators* design, install, and support an organization's local-area network (LAN), wide-area network (WAN), network segment, Internet, or intranet system. They provide day-to-day onsite administrative support for software users in a variety of work environments, including professional offices, small businesses, government, and large corporations. They maintain network hardware and software, analyze problems, and monitor the network to ensure its availability to system users. These workers gather data to identify customer needs and then use the information to identify, interpret, and evaluate system and network requirements. Administrators also may plan, coordinate, and implement network security measures.

Systems administrators are the information technology employees responsible for the efficient use of networks by organizations. They ensure that the design of an organization's computer site allows all of the components, including computers, the network, and software, to fit together and work properly. Furthermore, they monitor and adjust the performance of existing networks and continually survey the current computer site to determine future network needs. Administrators also troubleshoot problems reported by users and by automated network monitoring systems and make recommendations for enhancements in the implementation of future servers and networks.

In some organizations, *computer security specialists* may plan, coordinate, and implement the organization's information security. These workers may be called upon to educate users about computer security, install security software, monitor the network for security breaches, respond to cyber attacks, and, in some cases, gather data and evidence to be used in prosecuting cyber crime. The responsibilities of computer security specialists has increased in recent years as there has been a large increase in the number of cyber attacks on data and networks. This and other growing specialty occupations reflect an increasing emphasis on client-server applications, the expansion of Internet and intranet applications, and the demand for more end-user support.

Working Conditions

Computer support specialists and systems administrators normally work in well-lighted, comfortable offices or computer laboratories. They usually work about 40 hours a week, but that may include being "on call" via pager or telephone for rotating evening or weekend work if the employer requires computer support over extended hours. Overtime may be necessary when unexpected technical problems arise. Like other workers who type on a keyboard for long periods, computer support specialists and systems administrators are susceptible to eyestrain, back discomfort, and hand and wrist problems such as carpal tunnel syndrome.

Due to the heavy emphasis on helping all types of computer users, computer support specialists and systems administrators constantly interact with customers and fellow employees as they answer questions and give valuable advice. Those who work as consultants are away from their offices much of the time, sometimes spending months working in a client's office.

As computer networks expand, more computer support specialists and systems administrators may be able to connect to a customer's computer remotely, using modems, laptops, e-mail, and the Internet, to provide technical support to computer users. This capability would reduce or eliminate travel to the customer's workplace. Systems administrators also can administer and configure networks and servers remotely, although this practice is not as common as it is among computer support specialists.

Training, Other Qualifications, and Advancement

Due to the wide range of skills required, there are many paths of entry to a job as a computer support specialist or systems administrator. While there is no universally accepted way to prepare for a job as a computer support specialist, many employers prefer to hire persons with some formal college education. A bachelor's degree in computer science or information systems is a prerequisite for some jobs; however, other jobs may require only a computer-related associate's degree. For systems administrators, many employers seek applicants with bachelor's degrees, although not necessarily in a computer-related field.

A number of companies are becoming more flexible about requiring a college degree for support positions. However, certification and practical experience demonstrating these skills will be essential for applicants without a degree. The completion of a certification training program, offered by a variety of vendors and product makers, may help some people to qualify for entry-level positions. Relevant computer experience may substitute for formal education.

Beginning computer support specialists usually work for organizations that deal directly with customers or in-house users. Then they may advance into more responsible positions in which they use what they have learned from customers to improve the design and efficiency of future products. Job promotions usually depend more on performance than on formal education. Eventually, some computer support specialists become applications developers, designing products rather than assisting users. Computer support specialists at hardware and software companies often enjoy great upward mobility; advancement sometimes comes within months of one's initial employment.

Entry-level network and computer systems administrators are involved in routine maintenance and monitoring of computer systems, typically working behind the scenes in an organization. After gaining experience and expertise, they often are able to advance into more senior-level positions in which they take on more responsibilities. For example, senior network and computer systems administrators may present recommendations to management on matters related to a company's network. They also may translate the needs of an organization into a set of technical requirements based on the available technology. As with support specialists, administrators may become software engineers, actually involved in the designing of the system or network and not just its day-to-day administration.

Persons interested in becoming a computer support specialist or systems administrator must have strong problem-solving, analytical, and communication skills because troubleshooting and helping others are vital parts of the job. The constant interaction with other computer personnel, customers, and employees requires computer support specialists and systems administrators to communicate effectively on paper, via e-mail, or in person. Strong writing skills are useful in preparing manuals for employees and customers.

As technology continues to improve, computer support specialists and systems administrators must keep their skills current and acquire new ones. Many continuing education programs are provided by employers, hardware and software vendors, colleges and universities, and private training institutions. Professional development seminars offered by computing services firms also can enhance one's skills and advancement opportunities.

Employment

Computer support specialists and systems administrators held about 797,000 jobs in 2004. Of these, approximately 518,000 were computer support specialists and around 278,000 were network and computer systems administrators. Although they worked in a wide range of industries, about 23 percent of all computer support specialists and systems administrators were employed in professional, scientific, and technical services industries, principally computer systems design and related services. Other organizations that employed substantial numbers of these workers include administrative and support services companies, banks, government agencies, insurance companies, educational institutions, and wholesale and retail vendors of computers, office equipment, appliances, and home electronic equipment. Many computer support specialists worked for manufacturers of computers, semiconductors, and other electronic components.

Employers of computer support specialists and systems administrators range from startup companies to established industry leaders. With the continued development of the Internet, telecommunications, and e-mail, industries not typically associated with computers—such as construction—increasingly need computer workers. Small and large firms across all industries are expanding or developing computer systems, creating an immediate need for computer support specialists and systems administrators.

Job Outlook

Job prospects should be best for college graduates who are up to date with the latest skills and technologies, particularly if they have supplemented their formal education with some relevant work experience. Employers will continue to seek computer specialists who possess a strong background in fundamental computer skills combined with good interpersonal and communication skills. Due to the demand for computer support specialists and systems administrators over the next decade, those who have strong computer skills but do not have a bachelor's degree should continue to qualify for some entry-level positions. However, certifications and practical experience are essential for persons without degrees.

Employment of computer support specialists is expected to increase faster than the average for all occupations through 2014 as organizations continue to adopt increasingly sophisticated technology and integrate it into their systems. Job growth will continue to be driven by the ongoing expansion of the computer system design and related services industry, which is projected to remain one of the fastest-growing industries in the U.S. economy. Growth will not be as explosive as during the previous decade, however, as the information technology industry matures and some of these jobs are increasingly outsourced overseas.

Job growth among computer support specialists reflects the rapid pace of improved technology. As computers and software become more complex, support specialists will be needed to provide technical assistance to customers and other users. New mobile technologies, such as the wireless Internet, will continue to create a demand for these workers to familiarize and educate computer users. Consulting opportunities for computer support specialists also should continue to grow as businesses increasingly need help managing, upgrading, and customizing ever more complex computer systems. However, growth in employment of support specialists may be tempered somewhat as firms continue to cut costs by shifting more routine work abroad to countries where workers are highly skilled and labor costs are lower. Physical location is not as important for computer support specialists as it is for others because these workers can provide assistance remotely and support services can be provided around the clock.

Employment of systems administrators is expected to increase much faster than the average for all occupations as firms continue to invest heavily in securing computer networks. Companies are looking for workers who are knowledgeable about the function and administration of networks. Such employees have become increasingly hard to find as systems administration has moved from being a separate function within corporations to one that forms a crucial element of business in an increasingly high-technology economy. Also, demand for computer security specialists will grow as businesses and government continue to invest heavily in "cyber security," protecting vital computer networks and electronic infrastructures from attack. The information security field is expected to generate many opportunities over the next decade as firms across all industries place a high priority on safeguarding their data and systems.

The growth of electronic commerce means that more establishments use the Internet to conduct their business online. This growth translates into a need for information technology specialists who can help organizations use technology to communicate with employees, clients, and consumers. Growth in these areas also is expected to fuel demand for specialists who are knowledgeable about network, data, and communications security.

Earnings

Median annual earnings of computer support specialists were $40,430 in May 2004. The middle 50 percent earned between $30,980 and $53,010. The lowest 10 percent earned less than $24,190, and the highest 10 percent earned more than $69,110. Median annual earnings in the industries employing the largest numbers of computer support specialists in May 2004 were as follows:

Software publishers	$44,890
Management of companies and enterprises	42,780
Computer systems design and related services	42,750
Colleges, universities, and professional Schools	37,940
Elementary and secondary schools	35,500

Median annual earnings of network and computer systems administrators were $58,190 in May 2004. The middle 50 percent earned between $46,260 and $73,620. The lowest 10 percent earned less than $37,100, and the highest 10 percent earned more than $91,300. Median annual earnings in the industries employing the largest numbers of network and computer systems administrators in May 2004 were as follows:

Wired telecommunications carriers	$65,120
Computer systems design and related services	63,710
Management of companies and enterprises	61,600
Elementary and secondary schools	51,420
Colleges, universities, and professional schools	51,170

According to Robert Half International, starting salaries in 2005 ranged from $26,250 to $53,750 for help-desk and technical support staff and from $44,500 to $63,250 for more senior technical support specialists. For systems administrators, starting salaries in 2005 ranged from $47,250 to $70,500.

Related Occupations

Other computer specialists include computer programmers, computer software engineers, computer systems analysts, and computer scientists and database administrators.

Sources of Additional Information

For additional information about a career as a computer support specialist, contact the following organizations:

- Association of Computer Support Specialists, 333 Mamaroneck Ave., #129, White Plains, NY 10605. Internet: http://www.acss.org
- Association of Support Professionals, 122 Barnard Ave., Watertown, MA 02472.

For additional information about a career as a systems administrator, contact:

- System Administrators Guild, 2560 9th St., Suite 215, Berkeley, CA 94710. Internet: http://www.sage.org

Further information about computer careers is available from:

- National Workforce Center for Emerging Technologies, 3000 Landerholm Circle SE, Bellevue, WA 98007. Internet: http://www.nwcet.org

Computer Systems Analysts

(O*NET 15-1051.00)

Significant Points

- Employers generally prefer applicants who have at least a bachelor's degree in computer science, information science, or management information systems (MIS).
- Employment is expected to increase much faster than the average as organizations continue to adopt increasingly sophisticated technologies.
- Job prospects are favorable.

Nature of the Work

All organizations rely on computer and information technology to conduct business and operate more efficiently. The rapid spread of technology across all industries has generated a need for highly trained workers to help organizations incorporate new technologies. The tasks performed by workers known as computer systems analysts evolve rapidly, reflecting new areas of specialization or changes in technology as well as the preferences and practices of employers.

Computer systems analysts solve computer problems and apply computer technology to meet the individual needs of an organization. They help an organization to realize the maximum benefit from its investment in equipment, personnel, and business processes. Systems analysts may plan and develop new computer systems or devise ways to apply existing systems' resources to additional operations. They may design new systems, including both hardware and software, or add a new software application to harness more of the computer's power. Most systems analysts work with specific types of systems—for example, business, accounting, or financial systems or scientific and engineering systems—that vary with the kind of organization. Some systems analysts also are known as *systems developers* or *systems architects*.

Systems analysts begin an assignment by discussing the systems problem with managers and users to determine its exact nature. Defining the goals of the system and dividing the solutions into individual steps and separate procedures, systems analysts use techniques such as structured analysis, data modeling, information engineering, mathematical model building, sampling, and cost accounting to plan the system. They specify the inputs to be accessed by the system, design the processing steps, and format the output to meet users' needs. They also may prepare cost-benefit and return-on-investment analyses to help management decide whether implementing the proposed technology will be financially feasible.

When a system is accepted, systems analysts determine what computer hardware and software will be needed to set the system up. They coordinate tests and observe the initial use of the system to ensure that it performs as planned. They prepare specifications, flow charts, and process diagrams for computer programmers to follow; then, they work with programmers to "debug," or eliminate, errors from the system. Systems analysts who do more in-depth testing of products may be referred to as *software quality assurance analysts*. In addition to running tests, these individuals diagnose problems, recommend solutions, and determine whether program requirements have been met.

In some organizations, *programmer-analysts* design and update the software that runs a computer. Because they are responsible for both programming and systems analysis, these workers must be proficient in both areas. As this dual proficiency becomes more commonplace, these analysts are increasingly working with databases and object-oriented programming languages as well as client–server applications development and multimedia and Internet technology.

One obstacle associated with expanding computer use is the need for different computer systems to communicate with each other. Because of the importance of maintaining up-to-date information—accounting records, sales figures, or budget projections, for example—systems analysts work on making the computer systems within an organization, or among organizations, compatible so that information can be shared among them. Many systems analysts are involved with "networking," connecting all the computers internally—in an individual office, department, or establishment—or externally because many organizations rely on e-mail or the Internet. A primary goal of networking is to allow users to retrieve data from a mainframe computer or a server and use it on their desktop computer. Systems analysts must design the hardware and software to allow the free exchange of data, custom applications, and the computer power to process it all. For example, analysts are called upon to ensure the compatibility of computing systems between and among businesses to facilitate electronic commerce.

Working Conditions

Computer systems analysts work in offices or laboratories in comfortable surroundings. They usually work about 40 hours a week—the same as many other professional or office workers do. However, evening or weekend work may be necessary to meet deadlines or solve specific problems. Given the technology available today, telecommuting is common for computer professionals. As networks expand, more work can be done from remote locations through modems, laptops, electronic mail, and the Internet.

Like other workers who spend long periods in front of a computer terminal typing on a keyboard, computer systems analysts are susceptible to eyestrain, back discomfort, and hand and wrist problems such as carpal tunnel syndrome or cumulative trauma disorder.

Training, Other Qualifications, and Advancement

Rapidly changing technology requires an increasing level of skill and education on the part of employees. Companies increasingly look for professionals with a broad background and range of skills, including not only technical knowledge but also communication and other interpersonal skills. This shift from requiring workers to possess solely sound technical knowledge emphasizes workers who can handle various responsibilities. While there is no universally accepted way to prepare for a job as a systems analyst, most employers place a premium on some formal college education. Relevant work experience also is very important. For more technically complex jobs, persons with graduate degrees are preferred.

Many employers seek applicants who have at least a bachelor's degree in computer science, information science, or management information systems (MIS). MIS programs usually are part of the business school or college and differ considerably from computer science programs, emphasizing business and management-oriented coursework and business computing courses. Employers are increasingly seeking individuals with a master's degree in business administration (MBA), with a concentration in information systems, as more firms move their business to the Internet.

Despite employers' preference for those with technical degrees, persons with degrees in a variety of majors find employment as system analysts. The level of education and type of training that employers require depend on their needs. One factor affecting these needs is changes in technology. Employers often scramble to find workers capable of implementing "hot" new technologies such as the wireless Internet. Those workers with formal education or experience in information security, for example, are in demand because of the growing need for their skills and services. Another factor driving employers' needs is the timeframe during which a project must be completed.

Employers usually look for people who have broad knowledge and experience related to computer systems and technologies, strong problem-solving and analytical skills, and good interpersonal skills. Courses in computer science or systems design offer good preparation for a job in these computer occupations. For jobs in a business environment, employers usually want systems analysts to have business management or closely related skills, while a background in the physical sciences, applied mathematics, or engineering is preferred for work in scientifically oriented organizations.

Job seekers can enhance their employment opportunities by participating in internship or co-op programs offered through their schools. Because many people develop advanced computer skills in a non-computer-related occupation and then transfer those skills to a computer occupation, a background in the industry in which the person's job is located, such as financial services, banking, or accounting, can be important. Others have taken computer science courses to supplement their study in fields such as accounting, inventory control, or other business areas.

Computer systems analysts must be able to think logically and have good communication skills. Because they often deal with a number of tasks simultaneously, the ability to concentrate and pay close attention to detail is important. Although these workers sometimes work independently, they frequently work in teams on large projects. They must be able to communicate effectively with computer personnel, such as programmers and managers, as well as with users or other staff who may have no technical computer background.

Systems analysts may be promoted to senior or lead systems analyst. Those who show leadership ability also can become project managers or advance into management positions such as manager of information systems or chief information officer. Workers with work experience and considerable expertise in a particular subject or a certain application may find lucrative opportunities as independent consultants or may choose to start their own computer consulting firms.

Technological advances come so rapidly in the computer field that continuous study is necessary to keep one's skills up to date. Employers, hardware and software vendors, colleges and universities, and private training institutions offer continuing education. Additional training may come from professional development seminars offered by professional computing societies.

Employment

Computer systems analysts held about 487,000 jobs in 2004; about 28,000 were self-employed.

Although they are increasingly employed in every sector of the economy, the greatest concentration of these workers is in the computer systems design and related services industry. Firms in this industry provide services related to the commercial use of computers on a contract basis, including custom computer programming services; computer systems integration design services; computer facilities management services, including computer systems or data processing facilities; support services for clients; and other computer services, such as disaster recovery services and software installation. Computer systems analysts are also employed by governments, insurance companies, financial institutions, Internet service providers, data processing services firms, and universities.

A growing number of systems analysts are employed on a temporary or contract basis; many of these individuals are self-employed, working independently as contractors or consultants. For example, a company installing a new computer system may need the services of several systems analysts just to get the system running. Because not all of the analysts would be needed once the system is functioning, the company might contract for such employees with a temporary help agency or a consulting firm or with the systems analysts themselves. Such jobs may last from several months up to 2 years or more. This growing practice enables companies to bring in people with the exact skills the firm needs to complete a particular project instead of having to spend time or money training or retraining existing workers. Often, experienced consultants then train a company's in-house staff as a project develops.

Job Outlook

Employment of computer systems analysts is expected to grow much faster than the average for all occupations through the year 2014 as organizations continue to adopt and integrate increasingly sophisticated technologies. Job increases will be driven by very rapid growth in computer system design and related services, which is projected to be among the fastest-growing industries in the U.S. economy. In addition, many job openings will arise annually from the need to replace workers who move into managerial positions or other occupations or who leave the labor force. Job growth will not be as rapid as during the previous decade, however, as the information technology sector begins to mature and as routine work is increasingly outsourced to lower-wage foreign countries.

Workers in the occupation should enjoy favorable job prospects. The demand for networking to facilitate the sharing of information, the expansion of client–server environments, and the need for computer specialists to use their knowledge and skills in a problem-solving capacity will be major factors in the rising demand for computer systems analysts. Moreover, falling prices of computer hardware and software should continue to induce more businesses to expand their computerized operations and integrate new technologies into them. In order to maintain a competitive edge and operate more efficiently, firms will keep demanding system analysts who are knowledgeable about the latest technologies and are able to apply them to meet the needs of businesses.

Increasingly, more sophisticated and complex technology is being implemented across all organizations, which should fuel the demand for these computer occupations. There is a growing demand for system analysts to help firms maximize their efficiency with available technology. Expansion of electronic commerce—doing business on the Internet—and the continuing need to build and maintain databases that store critical information on customers, inventory, and projects are fueling demand for database administrators familiar with the latest technology. Also, the increasing importance being placed on "cybersecurity"—the protection of electronic information—will result in a need for workers skilled in information security.

The development of new technologies usually leads to demand for various kinds of workers. The expanding integration of Internet technologies into businesses, for example, has resulted in a growing need for specialists who can develop and support Internet and intranet applications. The growth of electronic commerce means that more establishments use the Internet to conduct their business online. The introduction of the wireless Internet, known as WiFi, creates new systems to be analyzed. The spread of such new technologies translates into a need for information technology professionals who can help organizations use technology to communicate with employees, clients, and consumers. Explosive growth in these areas also is expected to fuel demand for analysts who are knowledgeable about network, data, and communications security.

As technology becomes more sophisticated and complex, employers demand a higher level of skill and expertise from their employees. Individuals with an advanced degree in computer science or computer engineering, or with an MBA with a concentration in information systems, should enjoy favorable employment prospects. College graduates with a bachelor's degree in computer science, computer engineering, information science, or MIS also should enjoy favorable prospects for employment, particularly if they have supplemented their formal education with practical experience. Because employers continue to seek computer specialists who can combine strong technical skills with good interpersonal and business skills, graduates with non-computer-science degrees who have had courses in computer programming, systems analysis, and other information technology subjects also should continue to find jobs in computer fields. In fact, individuals with the right experience and training can work in computer occupations regardless of their college major or level of formal education.

Earnings

Median annual earnings of computer systems analysts were $66,460 in May 2004. The middle 50 percent earned between $52,400 and $82,980 a year. The lowest 10 percent earned less than $41,730, and the highest 10 percent earned more than $99,180. Median annual earnings in the industries employing the largest numbers of computer systems analysts in May 2004 were:

Federal government	$71,770
Computer systems design and related services	69,560
Management of companies and enterprises	67,230
Insurance carriers	66,840
State government	57,040

According to the National Association of Colleges and Employers, starting offers for graduates with a master's degree in computer science averaged $62,727 in 2005. Starting offers averaged $50,820 for graduates with a bachelor's degree in computer science; $46,189 for those with a degree in computer systems analysis; $44,417 for those with a degree in management information systems; and $44,775 for those with a degree in information sciences and systems.

According to Robert Half International, starting salaries for systems analysts ranged from $61,500 to $82,500 in 2005.

Related Occupations

Other workers who use computers extensively and who use logic and creativity to solve business and technical problems include computer programmers, computer software engineers, computer and information systems managers, engineers, mathematicians, statisticians, operations research analysts, management analysts, and actuaries.

Sources of Additional Information

Further information about computer careers is available from:

- Association for Computing Machinery (ACM), 1515 Broadway, New York, NY 10036. Internet: http://www.acm.org
- Institute of Electrical and Electronics Engineers Computer Society, Headquarters Office, 1730 Massachusetts Ave. NW, Washington, DC 20036-1992. Internet: http://www.computer.org
- National Workforce Center for Emerging Technologies, 3000 Landerholm Circle SE, Bellevue, WA 98007. Internet: http://www.nwcet.org

Counselors

(O*NET 21-1011.00, 21-1012.00, 21-1013.00, 21-1014.00, 21-1015.00, and 21-1019.99)

Significant Points

- School counselors must be certified, and other counselors must be licensed to practice in all but two states. A master's degree generally is needed to become a licensed counselor.
- Job opportunities for counselors should be very good because job openings are expected to exceed the number of graduates from counseling programs.
- State and local governments employ about 4 in 10 counselors, and the health services industry employs most of the others.

Nature of the Work

Counselors assist people with personal, family, educational, mental health, and career decisions and problems. Their duties depend on the individuals they serve and on the settings in which they work.

Educational, vocational, and school counselors provide individuals and groups with career and educational counseling. In school settings—elementary through postsecondary—they usually are called school counselors, and they work with students, including those with academic and social development problems and those with special needs. They advocate for students and work with other individuals and organizations to promote the academic, career, personal, and social development of children and youths. School counselors help students evaluate their abilities, interests, talents, and personality characteristics in order to develop realistic academic and career goals. Counselors use interviews, counseling sessions, interest and aptitude assessment tests, and other methods to evaluate and advise students. They also operate career information centers and career education programs. High school counselors advise students regarding college majors, admission requirements, entrance exams, financial aid, trade or technical schools, and apprenticeship programs. They help students develop job search skills, such as resume writing and interviewing techniques. College career planning and placement counselors assist alumni or students with career development and job-hunting techniques.

Elementary school counselors observe younger children during classroom and play activities and confer with their teachers and parents to evaluate the children's strengths, problems, or special needs. In conjunction with teachers and administrators, they make sure that the curriculum addresses both the academic and the emotional development needs of students. Elementary school counselors do less vocational and academic counseling than do secondary school counselors.

School counselors at all levels help students to understand and deal with social, behavioral, and personal problems. These counselors emphasize preventive and developmental counseling to provide students with the life skills needed to deal with problems before they occur and to enhance students' personal, social, and academic growth. Counselors provide special services, including alcohol and drug prevention programs and conflict resolution classes. They also try to identify cases of domestic abuse and other family problems that can affect a student's development. Counselors interact with students individually, in small groups, or with entire classes. They consult and collaborate with parents, teachers, school administrators, school psychologists, medical professionals, and social workers in order to develop and implement strategies to help students be successful in the education system.

Vocational counselors who provide mainly career counseling outside the school setting are also referred to as *employment counselors* or *career counselors*. Their chief focus is helping individuals with career decisions. Vocational counselors explore and evaluate the client's education, training, work history, interests, skills, and personality traits, and arrange for aptitude and achievement tests to assist the client in making career decisions. They also work with individuals to develop their job-search skills, and they assist clients in locating and applying for jobs. In addition, career counselors provide support to persons experiencing job loss, job stress, or other career transition issues.

Rehabilitation counselors help people deal with the personal, social, and vocational effects of disabilities. They counsel people with disabilities resulting from birth defects, illness or disease, accidents, or the stress of daily life. They evaluate the strengths and limitations of individuals, provide personal and vocational counseling, and arrange for medical care, vocational training, and job placement. Rehabilitation counselors interview both individuals with disabilities and their families, evaluate school and medical reports, and confer and plan with physicians, psychologists, occupational therapists, and employers to determine the capabilities and skills of the individual. Conferring with the client, they develop a rehabilitation program that often includes training to help the person develop job skills. Rehabilitation counselors also work toward increasing the client's capacity to live independently.

Mental health counselors Work with individuals, families, and groups to address and treat mental and emotional disorders and to promote optimum mental health. They are trained in a variety of therapeutic techniques used to address a wide range of issues, including depression, addiction and substance abuse, suicidal impulses, stress management, problems with self-esteem, issues associated with aging, job and career concerns, educational decisions, issues related to mental and emotional health, and family, parenting, and marital or other relationship problems. Mental health counselors often work closely with other mental health specialists, such as psychiatrists, psychologists, clinical social workers, psychiatric nurses, and school counselors.

Substance abuse and behavioral disorder counselors help people who have problems with alcohol, drugs, gambling, and eating disorders. They counsel individuals who are addicted to drugs, helping them to identify behaviors and problems related to their addiction. They also conduct programs aimed at preventing addictions from occurring in the first place. These counselors hold sessions designed for individuals, families, or groups.

Marriage and family therapists apply principles, methods, and therapeutic techniques to individuals, families, couples, or organizations in order to resolve emotional conflicts. In doing so, they modify people's perceptions and behaviors, enhance communication and understanding among family members, and help to prevent family and individual crises. Marriage and family therapists also may engage in psychotherapy of a nonmedical nature, make appropriate referrals to psychiatric resources, perform research, and teach courses about human development and interpersonal relationships.

Other counseling specialties include gerontological, multicultural, and genetic counseling. A gerontological counselor provides services to elderly persons and their families when they face changing lifestyles as they grow older. A multicultural counselor helps employers adjust to an increasingly diverse workforce. Genetic counselors provide information and support to families who have members with birth defects or genetic disorders and to families who may be at risk for a variety of inherited conditions. These counselors identify families at risk, investigate the problem that is present in the family, interpret information about the disorder, analyze inheritance patterns and risks of recurrence, and review available options with the family.

Working Conditions

Some school counselors work the traditional 9- to 10-month school year with a 2- to 3-month vacation, but increasing numbers, especially those working in middle and high schools, are employed on 11-month or full-year contracts. They usually work the same hours as teachers, but may travel more frequently to attend conferences and conventions. College career planning and placement counselors work long and irregular hours during student recruiting periods.

Rehabilitation counselors usually work a standard 40-hour week. Self-employed counselors and those working in mental health and community agencies, such as substance abuse and behavioral disorder counselors, frequently work evenings in order to counsel clients who work during the day. Both mental health counselors and marriage and family therapists also often work flexible hours to accommodate families in crisis or working couples who must have evening or weekend appointments.

Counselors must possess high physical and emotional energy to handle the array of problems that they address. Dealing daily with these problems can cause stress. Although the risk of litigation is relatively low, it is still prudent for counselors in all fields to hold some form of personal liability insurance. Because privacy is essential for confidential and frank discussions with clients, counselors usually have private offices.

Training, Other Qualifications, and Advancement

All states require school counselors to hold a state school counseling certification and to have completed at least some graduate course work; most require the completion of a master's degree. Some states require public school counselors to have both counseling and teaching certificates and to have had some teaching experience before receiving certification. For counselors based outside of schools, 48 states and the District of Columbia have some form of counselor licensure that governs their practice of counseling. Requirements typically include the completion of a master's degree in counseling, the accumulation of 2 years or 3,000 hours of supervised clinical experience beyond the master's degree level, the passage of a state-recognized exam, adherence to ethical codes and standards, and the completion of annual continuing education requirements.

Counselors must be aware of educational and training requirements that are often very detailed and that vary by area and by counseling specialty. Prospective counselors should check with state and local governments, employers, and national voluntary certification organizations in order to determine which requirements apply.

As mentioned, a master's degree is typically required to be licensed as a counselor. A bachelor's degree often qualifies a person to work as a counseling aide, rehabilitation aide, or social service worker. Some states require counselors in public employment to have a master's degree; others accept a bachelor's degree with appropriate counseling courses. Counselor education programs in colleges and universities usually are found in departments of education or psychology. Fields of study include college student affairs, elementary or secondary school counseling, education, gerontological counseling, marriage and family counseling, substance abuse counseling, rehabilitation counseling, agency or community counseling, clinical mental health counseling, counseling psychology, career counseling, and related fields. Courses are grouped into eight core areas: Human growth and development, social and cultural diversity, relationships, group work, career development, assessment, research and program evaluation, and professional identity. In an accredited master's degree program, 48 to 60 semester hours of graduate study, including a period of supervised clinical experience in counseling, are required.

Graduate programs in career, community, gerontological, mental health, school, student affairs, and marriage and family counseling are accredited by the Council for Accreditation of Counseling and Related Educational Programs (CACREP). While completion of a CACREP-accredited program is not necessary to become a counselor, it makes it easier to fulfill the requirements for state licensing. Another organization, the Council on Rehabilitation Education (CORE), accredits graduate programs in rehabilitation counseling. Accredited master's degree programs include a minimum of 2 years of full-time study, including 600 hours of supervised clinical internship experience.

Some counselors elect to be nationally certified by the National Board for Certified Counselors, Inc. (NBCC), which grants the general practice credential "National Certified Counselor." To be certified, a counselor must hold a master's degree with a concentration in counseling from a regionally accredited college or university; must have at least 2 years of supervised field experience in a counseling setting (graduates from counselor education programs accredited by CACREP are exempted); must provide two professional endorsements, one of which must be from a recent supervisor; and must have a passing score on the NBCC's National Counselor Examination for Licensure and Certification (NCE). This national certification is voluntary and is distinct from state licensing. However, in some states, those who pass the national exam are exempted from taking a state certification exam. NBCC also offers specialty certifications in school, clinical mental health, and addiction counseling, which supplement the national certified counselor designation. These specialty certifications require passage of a supplemental exam. To maintain their certification, counselors retake and pass the NCE or complete 100 credit hours of acceptable continuing education every 5 years.

Another organization, the Commission on Rehabilitation Counselor Certification, offers voluntary national certification for rehabilitation counselors. Some employers may require rehabilitation counselors to be nationally certified. To become certified, rehabilitation counselors usually must graduate from an accredited educational program, complete an internship, and pass a written examination. (Certification requirements vary according to an applicant's educational history. Employment experience, for example, is required for those with a counseling degree in a specialty other than rehabilitation.) After meeting these requirements, candidates are designated "Certified Rehabilitation Counselors." To maintain their certification, counselors must successfully retake the certification exam or complete 100 credit hours of acceptable continuing education every 5 years.

Other counseling organizations also offer certification in particular counseling specialties. Usually, becoming certified is voluntary, but having certification may enhance one's job prospects.

Some employers provide training for newly hired counselors. Others may offer time off or provide help with tuition if it is needed to complete a graduate degree. Counselors must participate in graduate studies, workshops, and personal studies to maintain their certificates and licenses.

Persons interested in counseling should have a strong desire to help others and should possess the ability to inspire respect, trust, and confidence. They should be able to work independently or as part of a team. Counselors must follow the code of ethics associated with their respective certifications and licenses.

Prospects for advancement vary by counseling field. School counselors can move to a larger school; become directors or supervisors of counseling, guidance, or pupil personnel services; or, usually with further graduate education, become counselor educators, counseling psychologists, or school administrators. Some counselors choose to work for a state's department of education. For marriage and family therapists, doctoral education in family therapy emphasizes the training of supervisors, teachers, researchers, and clinicians in the discipline.

Counselors can become supervisors or administrators in their agencies. Some counselors move into research, consulting, or college teaching or go into private or group practice.

Employment

Counselors held about 601,000 jobs in 2004. Employment was distributed among the counseling specialties as follows:

Educational, vocational, and school counselors 248,000
Rehabilitation counselors 131,000
Mental health counselors 96,000
Substance abuse and behavioral disorder counselors 76,000
Marriage and family therapists............................24,000
Counselors, all other 25,000

Educational, vocational, and school counselors work primarily in elementary and secondary schools and colleges and universities. Other types of counselors work in a wide variety of public and private establishments, including health care facilities; job training, career development, and vocational rehabilitation centers; social agencies; correctional institutions; and residential care facilities, such as halfway houses for criminal offenders and group homes for children, the elderly, and the disabled. Some substance abuse and behavioral disorder counselors work in therapeutic communities where addicts live while undergoing treatment. Counselors also work in organizations engaged in community improvement and social change, drug and alcohol rehabilitation programs, and state and local government agencies. A growing number of counselors are self-employed and work in group practices or private practice, due in part to new laws allowing counselors to be paid for their services by insurance companies and to the growing recognition that counselors are well-trained, effective professionals.

Job Outlook

Overall employment of counselors is expected to grow faster than the average for all occupations through 2014. In addition, numerous job openings will occur as many counselors retire or leave the profession. While job prospects will vary with location and specialization, opportunities generally should be very good because the number of job openings that arise should exceed the number of graduates of counseling programs. Rehabilitation counselors and substance abuse and behavioral disorder counselors, in particular, should experience excellent prospects.

Employment of school counselors is expected to grow with increases in student enrollments at postsecondary schools and colleges and as more states require elementary schools to employ counselors. Expansion of the responsibilities of school counselors should also lead to increases in their employment. For example, counselors are becoming more involved in crisis and preventive counseling, helping students deal with issues ranging from drug and alcohol abuse to death and suicide. Although schools and governments realize the value of counselors in helping their students to achieve academic success, budget constraints at every school level will dampen job growth of school counselors. However, federal grants and subsidies may help to offset tight budgets and allow the reduction in student-to-counselor ratios to continue. Job prospects should be more favorable in rural and inner-city schools.

Demand for vocational or career counselors should grow as multiple job and career changes become common for workers and as workers become increasingly aware of the counselors' services. In addition, state and local governments will employ growing numbers of counselors to assist beneficiaries of welfare programs who exhaust their eligibility and must find jobs. Other opportunities for employment counselors will arise in private job-training centers that provide training and other services to laid-off workers and others seeking to acquire new skills or new careers.

Demand is expected to be strong for substance abuse and behavioral disorder counselors because drug offenders are increasingly being sent to treatment programs rather than to jail. Mental health counselors will be needed to staff statewide networks that are being established to improve services for children and adolescents with serious emotional disturbances and for their family members. Under managed care systems, insurance companies are increasingly providing for reimbursement of counselors as a less costly alternative to psychiatrists and psychologists.

The number of people who will need rehabilitation counseling is expected to grow as advances in medical technology allow more people to survive injury or illness and live independently again. In addition, legislation requiring equal employment rights for people with disabilities will spur demand for counselors, who not only help these people make a transition into the workforce but also help companies to comply with the law.

Employment of mental health counselors and marriage and family therapists will grow as more people become comfortable with seeking professional help for a variety of health, personal, and family problems. Employers are also increasingly offering employee assistance programs that provide mental health and alcohol and drug abuse counseling. More people are expected to use these services as society focuses on ways of developing mental well-being, such as controlling stress associated with job and family responsibilities.

Earnings

Median annual earnings of educational, vocational, and school counselors in May 2004 were $45,570. The middle 50 percent earned between $34,530 and $58,400. The lowest 10 percent earned less than $26,260, and the highest 10 percent earned more than $72,390. School counselors can earn additional income working summers in the school system or in other jobs. Median annual earnings in the industries employing the largest numbers of educational, vocational, and school counselors in 2004 were as follows:

Elementary and secondary schools	$51,160
Junior colleges	45,730
Colleges, universities, and professional schools	39,110
Individual and family services	30,240
Vocational rehabilitation services	27,800

Median annual earnings of substance abuse and behavioral disorder counselors in May 2004 were $32,130. The middle 50 percent earned between $25,840 and $40,130. The lowest 10 percent earned less than $21,060, and the highest 10 percent earned more than $49,600.

Median annual earnings of mental health counselors in May 2004 were $32,960. The middle 50 percent earned between $25,660 and $43,370. The lowest 10 percent earned less than $20,880, and the highest 10 percent earned more than $55,810.

Median annual earnings of rehabilitation counselors in May 2004 were $27,870. The middle 50 percent earned between $22,110 and $36,120. The lowest 10 percent earned less than $18,560, and the highest 10 percent earned more than $48,130.

For substance abuse, mental health, and rehabilitation counselors, government employers generally pay the highest wages, followed by hospitals and social service agencies. Residential care facilities often pay the lowest wages.

Median annual earnings of marriage and family therapists in May 2004 were $38,980. The middle 50 percent earned between $30,260 and $49,990. The lowest 10 percent earned less than $23,460, and the highest 10 percent earned more than $65,080. Median annual earnings in May 2004 were $33,620 in individual and family social services, the industry employing the largest number of marriage and family therapists.

Self-employed counselors who have well-established practices, as well as counselors employed in group practices, usually have the highest earnings.

Related Occupations

Counselors help people evaluate their interests, abilities, and disabilities and deal with personal, social, academic, and career problems. Others who help people in similar ways include teachers, social and human service assistants, social workers, psychologists, physicians and surgeons, registered nurses, members of the clergy, occupational therapists, and human resources, training, and labor relations managers and specialists.

Sources of Additional Information

For general information about counseling, as well as information on specialties such as college, mental health, rehabilitation, multicultural, career, marriage and family, and gerontological counseling, contact:

- American Counseling Association, 5999 Stevenson Ave., Alexandria, VA 22304-3300. Internet: http://www.counseling.org

For information on school counselors, contact:

- American School Counselors Association, 1101 King St., Suite 625, Alexandria, VA 22314. Internet: http://www.schoolcounselor.org

For information on accredited counseling and related training programs, contact:

- Council for Accreditation of Counseling and Related Educational Programs, American Counseling Association, 5999 Stevenson Ave., 4th floor, Alexandria, VA 22304. Internet: http://www.cacrep.org

For information on national certification requirements for counselors, contact:

- National Board for Certified Counselors, Inc., 3 Terrace Way, Suite D, Greensboro, NC 27403-3660. Internet: http://www.nbcc.org

State departments of education can supply information on those colleges and universities offering guidance and counseling training that meets state certification and licensure requirements.

State employment service offices have information about job opportunities and entrance requirements for counselors.

Counter and Rental Clerks

(O*NET 41-2021.00)

Significant Points

- Jobs primarily are entry level and require little or no experience and minimal formal education.
- Faster-than-average employment growth is expected as businesses strive to improve customer service.
- Part-time employment opportunities should be plentiful.

Nature of the Work

Whether renting videos, air compressors, or moving vans or dropping off clothes to be drycleaned or appliances to be serviced, customers rely on counter and rental clerks to handle their transactions efficiently. Although the specific duties of these workers vary by establishment, counter and rental clerks answer questions involving product availability, cost, and rental provisions. Counter and rental clerks also take orders, calculate fees, receive payments, and accept returned merchandise.

Regardless of where they work, counter and rental clerks must be knowledgeable about the company's goods and services, policies, and procedures. Depending on the type of establishment, counter and rental clerks use their special knowledge to give advice on a wide variety of products and services, ranging from hydraulic tools to shoe repair. For example, in the car rental industry, these workers inform customers about the features of different types of automobiles and about daily and weekly rental costs. They also ensure that customers meet age and other requirements for renting cars, and they indicate when and in what condition the cars must be returned. Those in the equipment rental industry have similar duties but also must know how to operate and care for the machinery rented. In drycleaning establishments, counter clerks inform customers when items will be ready and about the effects, if any, of the chemicals used on garments. In video rental stores, counter clerks advise customers about the use of video and game players and the length of a rental, scan returned movies and games, restock shelves, handle money, and log daily reports.

When taking orders, counter and rental clerks use various types of equipment. In some establishments, they write out tickets and order forms, although most use computers or barcode scanners. Most of these computer systems are user friendly, require very little data entry, and are customized for each firm. Scanners read the product code and display a description of the item on a computer screen. However, clerks must ensure that the data on the screen pertain to the product.

Working Conditions

Firms employing counter and rental clerks usually operate nights and weekends for the convenience of their customers. As a result, many employers offer flexible schedules. Some counter and rental clerks work 40-hour weeks, but about half are on part-time schedules—usually during rush periods, such as weekends, evenings, and holidays.

Working conditions usually are pleasant; most stores and service establishments are clean, well lighted, and temperature controlled. However, clerks are on their feet much of the time and may be confined behind a small counter area or may be required to move, lift, or carry heavy machinery or other equipment. The job requires constant interaction with the public and can be stressful, especially during busy periods.

Training, Other Qualifications, and Advancement

Most counter and rental clerk jobs are entry-level positions that require little or no experience and minimal formal education. However, many employers prefer workers with at least a high school diploma.

In most companies, counter and rental clerks are trained on the job, sometimes through the use of videos, brochures, and pamphlets. Clerks usually learn how to operate a firm's equipment and become familiar with the firm's policies and procedures under the observation of a more experienced worker. However, some employers have formal classroom training programs lasting from a few hours to a few weeks. Topics covered in this training include the nature of the industry, the company and its policies and procedures, operation of equipment, sales techniques, and customer service. Counter and rental clerks also must become familiar with the different products and services rented or provided by their company to give customers the best possible service.

Counter and rental clerks should enjoy working with people and should have the ability to deal tactfully with difficult customers. They also should be able to handle several tasks at once, while continuing to provide friendly service. In addition, good oral and written communication skills are essential.

Advancement opportunities depend on the size and type of company. Many establishments that employ counter or rental clerks tend to be small businesses, making advancement difficult. In larger establishments, however, jobs such as counter and rental clerks offer good opportunities for workers to learn about their company's products and business practices. These jobs can lead to more responsible positions. It is common in many establishments to promote counter and rental clerks to event planner, assistant manager, or salesperson. Workers may choose to pursue related positions, such as mechanic, or even establish their own business.

In certain industries, such as equipment repair, counter and rental jobs may be an additional or alternative source of income for workers who are unemployed or semiretired. For example, retired mechanics could prove invaluable at tool rental centers because of their knowledge of, and familiarity with, tools.

Employment

Counter and rental clerks held 451,000 jobs in 2004. About 23 percent of clerks worked in consumer goods rental, which includes video rental stores. Other large employers included drycleaning and laundry services; automotive equipment rental and leasing services; automobile dealers; amusement, gambling, and recreation industries; and grocery stores.

Counter and rental clerks are employed throughout the country, but are concentrated in metropolitan areas, where personal services and renting and leasing services are in greater demand.

Job Outlook

Employment of counter and rental clerks is expected to increase faster than average for all occupations through the year 2014, as all types of businesses strive to improve customer service by hiring more clerks. In addition, some industries employing counter and rental clerks—for example, rental and leasing services and amusement and recreation industries—are expected to grow rapidly. Nevertheless, most job openings will arise from the need to replace experienced workers who transfer to other occupations or leave the labor force. Part-time employment opportunities are expected to be plentiful.

Earnings

Counter and rental clerks typically start at the minimum wage, which, in establishments covered by federal law, was $5.15 an hour in 2004. In some states, the law sets the minimum wage higher, and establishments must pay at least that amount. Wages also tend to be higher in areas where there is intense competition for workers. In addition to wages, some counter and rental clerks receive commissions based on the number of contracts they complete or services they sell.

Median hourly earnings of counter and rental clerks in May 2004 were $8.79. The middle 50 percent earned between $7.21 and $11.99 an hour. The lowest 10 percent earned less than $6.15 an hour, and the highest 10 percent earned more than $16.79 an hour. Median hourly earnings in the industries employing the largest number of counter and rental clerks in May 2004 were as follows:

Automobile dealers	$17.87
Automotive equipment rental and leasing	10.42
Lessors of real estate	9.92
Consumer goods rental	7.78
Drycleaning and laundry services	7.62

Full-time workers typically receive health and life insurance, paid vacation, and sick leave. Benefits for counter and rental clerks who work part time or work for independent stores tend to be significantly less than for those who work full time. Many companies offer discounts to both full-time and part-time employees on the goods or services they provide.

Related Occupations

Counter and rental clerks take orders and receive payment for services rendered. Other workers with similar duties include tellers, cashiers, food and beverage serving and related workers, gaming cage workers, Postal Service workers, and retail salespersons.

Sources of Additional Information

For general information on employment in the equipment rental industry, contact:

- American Rental Association, 1900 19th St., Moline, IL 61265. Internet: http://www.ararental.org

For more information about the work of counter clerks in drycleaning and laundry establishments, contact:

- International Fabricare Institute, 14700 Sweitzer Lane, Laurel, MD 20707. Internet: http://www.ifi.org

Customer Service Representatives

(O*NET 43-4051.01 and 43-4051.02)

Significant Points

- Job prospects are expected to be excellent.
- Most jobs require only a high school diploma but educational requirements are rising.
- Strong verbal communication and listening skills are important.

Nature of the Work

Customer service representatives are employed by many different types of companies throughout the country to serve as a direct point of contact for customers. They are responsible for ensuring that their company's customers receive an adequate level of service or help with their questions and concerns. These customers may be individual consumers or other companies, and the nature of their service needs can vary considerably.

All customer service representatives interact with customers to provide information in response to inquiries about products or services and to handle and resolve complaints. They communicate with customers through a variety of means—by telephone; by e-mail, fax, or regular mail correspondence; or in person. Some customer service representatives handle general questions and complaints, whereas others specialize in a particular area.

Many customer inquiries involve routine questions and requests. For example, customer service representatives may be asked to provide a customer with their credit card balance, or to check on the status of an order that has been placed. Obtaining the answers to such questions usually requires simply looking up information on their computer. Other questions are more involved, and may call for additional research or further explanation on the part of the customer service representative. In handling customers' complaints, customer service representatives must attempt to resolve the problem according to guidelines established by the company. These procedures may involve asking questions to determine the validity of a complaint; offering possible solutions; or providing customers with refunds, exchanges, or other offers, such as discounts or coupons. In some cases, customer service representatives are required to follow up with an individual customer until a question is answered or an issue is resolved.

Some customer service representatives help people decide what types of products or services would best suit their needs. They may even aid customers in completing purchases or transactions. Although the primary function of customer service representatives is not sales, some may spend a part of their time with customers encouraging them to purchase additional products or services. Customer service representatives also may make changes or updates to a customer's profile or account information. They may keep records of transactions and update and maintain databases of information.

Most customer service representatives use computers and telephones extensively in their work. Customer service representatives frequently enter information into a computer as they are speaking to customers. Often, companies have large amounts of data, such as account information, that can be pulled up on a computer screen while the representative is talking to a customer so that he or she can answer specific questions relating to the account. Customer service representatives also may have access to information such as answers to the most common customer questions, or guidelines for dealing with complaints. In the event that they encounter a question or situation to which they do not know how to respond, workers consult with a supervisor to determine the best course of action. Customer service representatives use multiline telephones systems, which often route calls directly to the most appropriate representative. However, at times, the customer service representative must transfer a call to someone who may be better able to respond to the customer's needs.

In some organizations, customer service representatives spend their entire day on the telephone. In others, they may spend part of their day answering e-mails and the remainder of the day taking calls. For some, most of their contact with the customer is face to face. Customer service representatives need to remain aware of the amount of time spent with each customer so that they can fairly distribute their time among the people who require their assistance. This is particularly important for customer service representatives whose primary activities are answering telephone calls and whose conversations often are required to be kept within set time limits. For customer service representatives working in call centers, there usually is very little time between telephone calls; as soon as representatives have finished with one call, they must move on to another. When working in call centers, customer service representatives are likely to be under close supervision. Telephone calls may be taped and reviewed by supervisors to ensure that company policies and procedures are being followed, or a supervisor may listen in on conversations.

Job responsibilities can differ, depending on the industry in which a customer service representative is employed. For example, a customer service representative working in the branch office of a bank may assume the responsibilities of other workers, such as teller or new account clerk, as needed. In insurance agencies, a customer service representative interacts with agents, insurance companies, and policyholders. These workers handle much of the paperwork related to insurance policies, such as policy applications and changes and renewals to existing policies. They answer questions regarding policy coverage, help with reporting claims, and do anything else that may need to be done. Although they must know as much as insurance agents about insurance products, and usually must have credentials equal to those of an agent in order to sell products and make changes to policies, the duties of a customer service representative differ from those of an agent in that customer service representatives are not responsible for actively seeking potential customers. Customer service representatives employed by utilities and communications companies assist individuals interested in opening accounts for various utilities such as electricity and gas, or for communication services such as cable television and telephone. They explain various options and receive orders for services to be installed, turned on, turned off, or changed. They also may look into and resolve complaints about billing and service provided by utility, telephone, and cable television companies.

Working Conditions

Although customer service representatives can work in a variety of settings, most work in areas that are clean and well lit. Many work in call or customer contact centers. In this type of environment, workers generally have their own workstation or cubicle space equipped with a telephone, headset, and computer. Because many call centers are open extended hours, beyond the traditional work day, or are staffed around the clock, these positions may require workers to take on early morning, evening, or late night shifts. Weekend or holiday work also may be necessary. As a result, the occupation is well suited to flexible work schedules. Nearly 1 out of 5 customer service representatives work part time. The occupation also offers the opportunity for seasonal work in certain industries, often through temporary help agencies.

Call centers may be crowded and noisy, and work may be repetitious and stressful, with little time between calls. Workers usually must attempt to minimize the length of each call while still providing excellent service. To ensure that these procedures are followed, conversations may be monitored by supervisors, something that can be stressful. Also, long periods spent sitting, typing, or looking at a computer screen may cause eye and muscle strain, backaches, headaches, and repetitive motion injuries.

Customer service representatives working outside of a call center environment may interact with customers through several different means. For example, workers employed by an insurance agency or in a grocery store may have customers approach them in person or contact them by telephone, computer, mail, or fax. Many of these customer service representatives work a standard 40-hour week; however, their hours generally depend on the hours of operation of the establishment in which they are employed. Work environments outside of a call center also vary accordingly. Most customer service representatives work either in an office or at a service or help desk.

For virtually all types of customer service representatives, dealing with difficult or irate customers can be a trying task; however, the ability to resolve customers' problems has the potential to be very rewarding.

Training, Other Qualifications, and Advancement

Most customer service representative jobs require only a high school diploma. However, due to employers demanding a higher skilled workforce, many customer service jobs now require an associate or bachelor's degree. Basic to intermediate computer knowledge and good interpersonal skills also are important qualities for people who wish to be successful in the field. Because customer service representatives constantly interact with the public, good communication and problem-solving skills are a must. Verbal communication and listening skills are especially important. Additionally, for workers who communicate through e-mail, good typing, spelling, and written communication skills are necessary. High school courses in computers, English, or business are helpful in preparing for a job in customer service.

Customer service representatives play a critical role in providing an interface between customer and company, and for this reason employers seek out people who come across in a friendly and professional manner. The ability to deal patiently with problems and complaints and to remain courteous when faced with difficult or angry people is very important. Also, a customer service representative needs to be able to work independently within specified time constraints. Workers should have a clear and pleasant speaking voice and be fluent in English. However, the ability to speak a foreign language is becoming increasingly necessary, and bilingual skills are considered a plus.

Training requirements vary by industry. Almost all customer service representatives are provided with some training prior to beginning work, and training continues once on the job. This training generally covers customer service and phone skills, products and services and common customer problems with them, the use or operation of the telephone and/or computer systems, and company policies and regulations. Length of training varies, but it usually lasts at least several weeks. Because of a constant need to update skills and knowledge, most customer service representatives continue to receive instruction and training throughout their career. This is particularly true of workers in industries such as banking, in which regulations and products are continually changing.

Although some positions may require previous industry, office, or customer service experience, many customer service jobs are entry level. Customer service jobs are often good introductory positions into a company or an industry. In some cases, experienced workers can move up within the company into supervisory or managerial positions or they may move into areas such as product development, in which they can use their knowledge to improve products and services.

Within insurance agencies and brokerages, however, a customer service representative job usually is not an entry-level position. Workers must have previous experience in insurance and are often required by state regulations to be licensed like insurance sales agents. A variety of designations are available to demonstrate that a candidate has sufficient knowledge and skill, and continuing education and training are often offered through the employer. As they gain more knowledge of industry products and services, customer service representatives in insurance may advance to other, higher level positions, such as insurance sales agent.

Employment

Customer service representatives held about 2.1 million jobs in 2004. Although they were found in a variety of industries, about 1 in 4 customer service representatives worked in finance and insurance. The largest numbers were employed by insurance carriers, insurance agencies and brokerages, and banks and credit unions.

About 1 in 8 customer service representatives were employed in administrative and support services. These workers were concentrated in the business support services industry (which includes telephone call centers) and employment services (which includes temporary help services and employment placement agencies). Another 1in 8 customer service representatives were employed in retail trade establishments such as general merchandise stores, food and beverage stores, or nonstore retailers. Other industries that employ significant numbers of customer service representatives include information, particularly the telecommunications industry; manufacturing, such as printing and related support activities; and wholesale trade.

Although they are found in all states, customer service representatives who work in call centers tend to be concentrated geographically. Four states—California, Texas, Florida, and New York—employ 30 percent of customer service representatives. Delaware, Arizona, South Dakota, and Utah, have the highest concentration of workers in this occupation, with customer service representatives comprising over 2 percent of total employment in these states.

Job Outlook

Prospects for obtaining a job in this field are expected to be excellent, with more job openings than jobseekers. Bilingual jobseekers, in particular, may enjoy favorable job prospects. In addition to many new openings occurring as businesses and organizations expand, numerous job openings will result from the need to replace experienced customer service representatives who transfer to other occupations or leave the labor force. Replacement needs are expected to be significant in this large occupation because many young people work as customer service representatives before switching to other jobs. This occupation is well suited to flexible work schedules, and many opportunities for part-time work will continue to be available, particularly as organizations attempt to cut labor costs by hiring more temporary workers.

Employment of customer service representatives is expected to increase faster than the average for all occupations through the year 2014. Beyond growth stemming from expansion of the industries in which customer service representatives are employed, a need for additional customer service representatives is likely to result from heightened reliance on these workers. Customer service is critical to the success of any organization that deals with customers, and strong customer service can build sales and visibility as companies try to distinguish themselves from competitors. In many industries, gaining a competitive edge and retaining customers will be increasingly important over the next decade. This is particularly true in industries such as financial services, communications, and utilities, which already employ numerous customer service representatives. As the trend toward consolidation in industries continues, centralized call centers will provide an effective method for delivering a high level of customer service. As a result, employment of customer service representatives may grow at a faster rate in call centers than in other areas. However, this growth may be tempered: a variety of factors, including technological improvements, make it increasingly feasible and cost-effective for call centers to be built or relocated outside of the United States.

Technology is affecting the occupation in many ways. The Internet and automated teller machines have provided customers with means of obtaining information and conducting transactions that do not entail interacting with another person. Technology also allows for a greater streamlining of processes, while at the same time increasing the productivity of workers. The use of computer software to filter e-mails, generating automatic responses or directing messages to the appropriate representative, and the use of similar systems to answer or route telephone inquiries are likely to become more prevalent in the future. Also, with rapidly improving telecommunications, some organizations have begun to position their call centers overseas.

Despite such developments, the need for customer service representatives is expected to remain strong. In many ways, technology has heightened consumers' expectations for information and services, and availability of information online seems to have generated more need for customer service representatives, particularly to respond to e-mail. Also, technology cannot replace human skills. As more sophisticated technologies are able to resolve many customers' questions and concerns, the nature of the inquiries to be handled by customer service representatives is likely to become increasingly complex.

Furthermore, the job responsibilities of customer service representatives are expanding. As companies downsize or take other measures to increase profitability, workers are being trained to perform additional duties such as opening bank accounts or cross-selling products. As a result, employers may increasingly prefer customer service representatives who have education beyond high school, such as some college or even a college degree.

While jobs in some industries, such as retail trade, may be affected by economic downturns, the customer service occupation is generally resistant to major fluctuations in employment.

Earnings

In May 2004, median annual earnings for wage and salary customer service representatives were $27,020. The middle 50 percent earned between $21,510 and $34,560. The lowest 10 percent earned less than $17,680, and the highest 10 percent earned more than $44,160.

Earnings for customer service representatives vary according to level of skill required, experience, training, location, and size of firm. Median annual earnings in the industries employing the largest numbers of these workers in May 2004 are shown below.

Insurance carriers	$29,790
Agencies, brokerages, and other insurance related activities	28,800
Depository credit intermediation	26,140
Employment services	23,100
Business support services	21,390

In addition to receiving an hourly wage, full-time customer service representatives who work evenings, nights, weekends, or holidays may receive shift differential pay. Also, because call centers are often open during extended hours, or even 24 hours a day, some customer service representatives have the benefit of being able to work a schedule that does not conform to the traditional workweek. Other benefits can include life and health insurance, pensions, bonuses, employer-provided training, and discounts on the products and services the company offers.

Related Occupations

Customer service representatives interact with customers to provide information in response to inquiries about products and services and to handle and resolve complaints. Other occupations in which workers have similar dealings with customers and the public are information and record clerks; financial clerks, such as tellers and new-account clerks; insurance sales agents; securities, commodities, and financial services sales agents; retail salespersons; computer support specialists; and gaming services workers.

Sources of Additional Information

State employment service offices can provide information about employment opportunities for customer service representatives.

Demonstrators, Product Promoters, and Models

(O*NET 41-9011.00 and 41-9012.00)

Significant Points

- Job openings should be plentiful for demonstrators and product promoters, but keen competition is expected for modeling jobs.

- Most jobs are part time or have variable work schedules, and many jobs require frequent travel.
- Formal training and education requirements are limited.

Nature of the Work

Demonstrators, product promoters, and models create public interest in buying products such as clothing, cosmetics, food items, and housewares. The information they provide helps consumers make educated choices among the wide variety of products and services available.

Demonstrators and product promoters create public interest in buying a product by demonstrating it to prospective customers and answering their questions. They may sell the demonstrated merchandise, or gather names of prospects to contact at a later date or to pass on to a sales staff. *Demonstrators* promote sales of a product to consumers, while *product promoters* try to induce retail stores to sell particular products and market them effectively. Product demonstration is an effective technique used by both to introduce new products or promote sales of old products because it allows face-to-face interaction with potential customers.

Demonstrators and product promoters build current and future sales of both sophisticated and simple products, ranging from computer software to mops. They attract an audience by offering samples, administering contests, distributing prizes, and using direct-mail advertising. They must greet and catch the attention of possible customers and quickly identify those who are interested and qualified. They inform and educate customers about the features of products and demonstrate their use with apparent ease to inspire confidence in the product and its manufacturer. They also distribute information, such as brochures and applications. Some demonstrations are intended to generate immediate sales through impulse buying, while others are considered an investment to generate future sales and increase brand awareness.

Demonstrations and product promotions are conducted in retail and grocery stores, shopping malls, trade shows, and outdoor fairs. Locations are selected based on both the nature of the product and the type of audience. Demonstrations at large events may require teams of demonstrators to efficiently handle large crowds. Some demonstrators promote products on videotape or on television programs, such as "infomercials" or home shopping programs.

Demonstrators and product promoters may prepare the content of a presentation and alter it to target a specific audience or to keep it current. They may participate in the design of an exhibit or customize exhibits for particular audiences. Results obtained by demonstrators and product promoters are analyzed, and presentations are adjusted to make them more effective. Demonstrators and product promoters also may be involved in transporting, assembling, and disassembling materials used in demonstrations.

A demonstrator's presentation may include visuals, models, case studies, testimonials, test results, and surveys. The equipment used for a demonstration varies with the product being demonstrated. A food product demonstration might require the use of cooking utensils, while a software demonstration could require the use of a multimedia computer. Demonstrators must be familiar with the product to be able to relate detailed information to customers and to answer any questions that arise before, during, or after a demonstration. Therefore, they may research the product to be presented, the products of competitors, and the interests and concerns of the target audience before conducting a demonstration. Demonstrations of complex products can require practice.

Models pose for photos or as subjects for paintings or sculptures. They display clothing, such as dresses, coats, underclothing, swimwear, and suits, for a variety of audiences and in various types of media. They model accessories, such as handbags, shoes, and jewelry, and promote beauty products, including fragrances and cosmetics. The most successful models, called supermodels, hold celebrity status and often use their image to sell products such as books, calendars, and fitness videos. In addition to modeling, they may appear in movies and television shows.

Models' clients use printed publications, live modeling, and television to advertise and promote products and services. There are different categories of modeling jobs within these media, and the nature of a model's work may vary with each. Most modeling jobs are for printed publications, and models usually do a combination of editorial, commercial, and catalog work. Editorial print modeling uses still photographs of models for fashion magazine covers and to accompany feature articles, but does not include modeling for advertisements. Commercial print modeling includes work for advertisements in magazines and newspapers, and for outdoor advertisements such as billboards. Catalog models appear in department store and mail order catalogs.

During a photo shoot, a model poses to demonstrate the features of clothing and products. Models make small changes in posture and facial expression to capture the look desired by the client. As they shoot film, photographers instruct models to pose in certain positions and to interact with their physical surroundings. Models work closely with photographers, hair and clothing stylists, makeup artists, and clients to produce the desired look and to finish the photo shoot on schedule. Stylists and makeup artists prepare the model for the photo shoot, provide touchups, and change the look of models throughout the day. If stylists are not provided, models must apply their own makeup and bring their own clothing. Because the client spends time and money planning for and preparing an advertising campaign, the client usually is present to ensure that the work is satisfactory. The client also may offer suggestions.

Editorial printwork generally pays less than other types of modeling, but provides exposure for a model and can lead to commercial modeling opportunities. Often, beginning fashion models work in foreign countries where fashion magazines are more plentiful.

Live modeling is done in a variety of locations. Live models stand, turn, and walk to demonstrate clothing to a variety of audiences. At fashion shows and in showrooms, garment buyers are the primary audience. Runway models display clothes that either are intended for direct sale to consumers or are the artistic expressions of the designer. High fashion, or haute couture, runway models confidently walk a narrow runway before an audience of photographers, journalists, designers, and garment buyers. Live modeling also is done in apparel marts, department stores, and fitting rooms of clothing designers. In retail establishments, models display clothing directly for shoppers and may be required to describe the features and price of the clothing. Other models pose for sketching artists, painters, and sculptors.

Models may compete with actors and actresses for work in television and may even receive speaking parts. Television work includes commercials, cable television programs, and even game shows. However, competition for television work is intense because of the potential for high earnings and extensive exposure.

Because advertisers need to target very specific segments of the population, models may specialize in a certain area. Petite and plus-size fashions are modeled by women whose dress size is smaller or larger than that worn by the typical model. Models who are disabled may be used to model fashions or products for disabled consumers. "Parts" models have a body part, such as a hand or foot, that is particularly well-suited to model products such as fingernail polish or shoes.

Almost all models work through agents. Agents provide a link between models and clients. Clients pay models, while the agency receives a portion of the model's earnings for its services. Agents scout for new faces, advise and train new models, and promote them to clients. A typical modeling job lasts only 1 day, so modeling agencies differ from other employment agencies in that they maintain an ongoing relationship with the model. Agents find and nurture relationships with clients, arrange auditions called "go-sees," and book shoots if a model is hired. They also provide bookkeeping and billing services to models and may offer them financial planning services. Relatively short careers and variable incomes make financial planning an important issue for many models.

With the help of agents, models spend a considerable amount of time promoting and developing themselves. Models assemble and maintain portfolios, print composite cards, and travel to go-sees. A portfolio is a collection of a model's previous work that is carried to all go-sees and bookings. A composite card, or comp card, contains the best photographs from a model's portfolio, along with his or her measurements.

Models must gather information before a job. From an agent, they learn the pay, date, time, and length of the shoot. Also, models need to ask if hair, makeup, and clothing stylists will be provided. It is helpful to know what product is being promoted and what image they should project. Some models research the client and the product being modeled to prepare for a shoot. Models use a document called a voucher to record the rate of pay and the actual duration of the job. The voucher is used for billing purposes after both the client and model sign it. Once a job is completed, models must check in with their agency and plan for the next appointment.

Working Conditions

More than half of all demonstrators, product promoters, and models work part time and about 1 in 4 have variable work schedules. Many positions last 6 months or less.

Demonstrators and product promoters may work long hours while standing or walking, with little opportunity to rest. Some of them travel frequently, and night and weekend work often is required. The atmosphere of a crowded trade show or state fair is often hectic, and demonstrators and product promoters may feel pressure to influence the greatest number of consumers possible in a very limited amount of time. However, many enjoy the opportunity to interact with a variety of people.

Models work under a variety of conditions, which can often be both difficult and glamorous. The coming season's fashions may be modeled in a comfortable, climate-controlled studio or in a cold, damp outdoor location. Schedules can be demanding, and models must keep in constant touch with an agent so that they do not miss an opportunity for work. Being away from friends and family, and needing to focus on the photographer's instructions despite constant interruption for touchups, clothing, and set changes can be stressful. Yet, successful models interact with a variety of people and enjoy frequent travel. They may meet potential clients at several go-sees in one day and often travel to work in distant cities, foreign countries, and exotic locations.

Training, Other Qualifications, and Advancement

Formal training and education requirements are limited for demonstrators, product promoters, and models. Training usually is moderate term, lasting a month or more. Postsecondary education, while helpful, usually is not required: only 1 in 5 of these workers has a bachelor's degree or higher.

Demonstrators and product promoters usually receive on-the-job training. Training is primarily product oriented because a demonstrator must be familiar with the product to demonstrate it properly. The length of training varies with the complexity of the product. Experience with the product or familiarity with similar products may be required for demonstration of complex products, such as computers. During the training process, demonstrators may be introduced to the manufacturer's corporate philosophy and preferred methods for dealing with customers.

Employers look for demonstrators and product promoters with good communication skills and a pleasant appearance and personality. Demonstrators and product promoters must be comfortable with public speaking. They should be able to entertain an audience and use humor, spontaneity, and personal interest in the product as promotional tools. Foreign language skills are helpful.

While no formal training is required to begin a modeling career, models should be photogenic and have a basic knowledge of hair styling, makeup, and clothing. Some local governments require models under the age of 18 to hold a work permit. An attractive physical appearance is necessary to become a successful model. A model should have flawless skin, healthy hair, and attractive facial features. Specific requirements depend on the client, but most models must be within certain ranges for height, weight, and dress or coat size in order to meet the practical needs of fashion designers, photographers, and advertisers. Requirements may change slightly from time to time as our society's perceptions about physical beauty change; however, most fashion designers feel that their clothing looks its best on tall, thin models. Although physical requirements may be relaxed for some types of modeling jobs, opportunities are limited for those who do not meet these basic requirements.

Because a model's career depends on preservation of his or her physical characteristics, models must control their diet, exercise regularly, and get enough sleep in order to stay healthy. Haircuts, pedicures, and manicures are necessary work-related expenses for models.

In addition to being attractive, models must be photogenic. The ability to relate to the camera in order to capture the desired look on film is essential, and agents test prospective models using snapshots or professional photographs. For photographic and runway work, models must be able to move gracefully and confidently. Training in acting, voice, and dance is useful and allows a model to be considered for television work. Foreign language skills are useful because successful models travel frequently to foreign countries.

Because models must interact with a large number of people, personality plays an important role in success. Models must be professional, polite, and prompt; every contact could lead to future employment. Organizational skills are necessary to manage personal lives, financial matters, and busy work and travel schedules. Because competition for jobs is stiff and clients' needs are very specific, patience and persistence are essential.

Modeling schools provide training in posing, walking, makeup application, and other basic tasks, but attending such schools does not necessarily lead to job opportunities. In fact, many agents prefer beginning models with little or no previous experience and discourage models from attending modeling schools and purchasing professional photographs. A model's selection of an agency is an important factor for advancement in the occupation. The better the reputation and skill of the agency, the more assignments a model is likely to get. Because clients prefer to work with agents, it is very difficult for a model to pursue a freelance career.

Agents continually scout for new faces, and many of the top models are discovered in this way. Most agencies review snapshots or have "open calls", during which models are seen in person; this service usually is provided free of charge. Some agencies sponsor modeling contests and searches. Very few people who send in snapshots or attend open calls are offered contracts.

Agencies advise models on how to dress, wear makeup, and conduct themselves properly during go-sees and bookings. Because models' advancement depends on their previous work, development of a good portfolio is key to getting assignments. Models accumulate and display current tear sheets—examples of a model's editorial print work—and photographs in the portfolio. The higher the quality and currency of the photos in the portfolio, the more likely it is that the model will find work.

Demonstrators and product promoters who perform well and show leadership ability may advance to other marketing and sales occupations or open their own businesses. Because modeling careers are relatively short, most models eventually transfer to other occupations.

Employment

Demonstrators, product promoters, and models held about 120,000 jobs in 2004. Of these, models held only about 2,200 jobs in 2004. About 23 percent of all salaried jobs for demonstrators, product promoters, and models were in retail trade, especially general merchandise stores, and 14 percent were in administrative and support services—which includes employment services. Other jobs were found in advertising and related services.

Demonstrator and product promoter jobs may be found in communities throughout the nation, but modeling jobs are concentrated in New York, Chicago, Miami, and Los Angeles.

Job Outlook

Employment of demonstrators, product promoters, and models is expected to grow about as fast as average for all occupations through 2014. Job growth should be driven by increases in the number and size of trade shows and greater use of these workers in department stores and various retail shops for in-store promotions. Additional job openings will arise from the need to replace demonstrators, product promoters, and models that transfer to other occupations, retire, or stop working for other reasons.

Job openings should be plentiful for demonstrators and product promoters. Employers may have difficulty finding qualified demonstrators who are willing to fill part-time, short-term positions. Product demonstration is considered a very effective marketing tool. New jobs should arise as firms devote a greater percentage of marketing budgets to product demonstration.

On the other hand, modeling is considered a glamorous occupation, with limited formal entry requirements. Consequently, those who wish to pursue a modeling career can expect keen competition for jobs. The modeling profession typically attracts many more jobseekers than there are job openings available. Only models who closely meet the unique requirements of the occupation will achieve regular employment. The increasing diversification of the general population should boost demand for models more representative of diverse racial and ethnic groups. Work for male models also should increase as society becomes more receptive to the marketing of men's fashions. Because fashions change frequently, demand for a model's look may fluctuate. Most models experience periods of unemployment.

Employment of demonstrators, product promoters, and models is affected by downturns in the business cycle. Many firms tend to reduce advertising budgets during recessions.

Earnings

Demonstrators and product promoters had median hourly earnings of $9.95 in May 2004. The middle 50 percent earned between $8.18 and $13.29. The lowest 10 percent earned less than $7.25, and the highest 10 percent earned more than $20.08. Employers of demonstrators, product promoters, and models generally pay for job-related travel expenses.

Median hourly earnings of models were $10.50 in May 2004. The middle 50 percent earned between $8.44 and $14.34. The lowest 10 percent earned less than $7.16, and the highest 10 percent earned more than $17.17. Earnings vary for different types of modeling and depend on the experience and reputation of the model. Female models typically earn more than male models for similar work. Hourly earnings can be relatively high, particularly for supermodels and others in high demand, but models may not have work every day, and jobs may last only a few hours. Models occasionally receive clothing or clothing discounts instead of, or in addition to, regular earnings. Almost all models work with agents and pay 15 to 20 percent of their earnings in return for an agent's services. Models who do not find immediate work may receive payments, called advances, from agents to cover promotional and living expenses. Models must provide their own health and retirement benefits.

Related Occupations

Demonstrators, product promoters, and models create public interest in buying clothing, products, and services. Others who create interest in a product or service include actors, producers, and directors; insurance sales agents; real estate brokers; retail salespersons; sales representatives, wholesale and manufacturing; and reservation and transportation ticket agents and travel clerks.

Sources of Additional Information

For information about modeling schools and agencies in your area, contact a local consumer affairs organization such as the Better Business Bureau.

Dental Assistants

(O*NET 31-9091.00)

Significant Points

- Job prospects should be excellent.
- Dentists are expected to hire more assistants to perform routine tasks so that they may devote their own time to more complex procedures.
- Most assistants learn their skills on the job, although an increasing number are trained in dental-assisting programs; most programs take 1 year or less to complete.

Nature of the Work

Dental assistants perform a variety of patient care, office, and laboratory duties. They work chairside as dentists examine and treat patients. They make patients as comfortable as possible in the dental chair, prepare them for treatment, and obtain their dental records. Assistants hand instruments and materials to dentists and keep patients' mouths dry and clear by using suction or other devices. Assistants also sterilize and disinfect instruments and equipment, prepare trays of instruments for dental procedures, and instruct patients on postoperative and general oral health care.

Some dental assistants prepare materials for impressions and restorations, take dental X rays, and process X-ray film as directed by a dentist. They also may remove sutures, apply topical anesthetics to gums or cavity-preventive agents to teeth, remove excess cement used in the filling process, and place rubber dams on the teeth to isolate them for individual treatment.

Those with laboratory duties make casts of the teeth and mouth from impressions, clean and polish removable appliances, and make temporary crowns. Dental assistants with office duties schedule and confirm appointments, receive patients, keep treatment records, send bills, receive payments, and order dental supplies and materials.

Dental assistants should not be confused with dental hygienists, who are licensed to perform different clinical tasks.

Working Conditions

Dental assistants work in a well-lighted, clean environment. Their work area usually is near the dental chair so that they can arrange instruments, materials, and medication and hand them to the dentist when needed. Dental assistants must wear gloves, masks, eyewear, and protective clothing to protect themselves and their patients from infectious diseases. Assistants also follow safety procedures to minimize the risks associated with the use of X-ray machines.

About half of dental assistants have a 35- to 40-hour workweek, which may include work on Saturdays or evenings.

Training, Other Qualifications, and Advancement

Most assistants learn their skills on the job, although an increasing number are trained in dental-assisting programs offered by community and junior colleges, trade schools, technical institutes, or the Armed Forces. Assistants must be a second pair of hands for a dentist; therefore, dentists look for people who are reliable, work well with others, and have good manual dexterity. High school students interested in a career as a dental assistant should take courses in biology, chemistry, health, and office practices.

The Commission on Dental Accreditation within the American Dental Association (ADA) approved 265 dental-assisting training programs in 2005. Programs include classroom, laboratory, and preclinical instruction in dental-assisting skills and related theory. In addition, students gain practical experience in dental schools, clinics, or dental offices. Most programs take 1 year or less to complete and lead to a certificate or diploma. Two-year programs offered in community and junior colleges lead to an associate degree. All programs require a high school diploma or its equivalent, and some require science or computer-related courses for admission. A number of private vocational schools offer 4-month to 6-month courses in dental assisting, but the Commission on Dental Accreditation does not accredit these programs.

Most states regulate the duties that dental assistants are allowed to perform through licensure or registration. Licensure or registration may require passing a written or practical examination. States offering licensure or registration have a variety of schools offering courses—approximately 10 to 12 months in length—that meet their state's requirements. Other states require dental assistants to complete state-approved education courses of 4 to 12 hours in length. Some states offer registration of other dental assisting credentials with little or no education required. Some states require continuing education to maintain licensure or registration. A few states allow dental assistants to perform any function delegated to them by the dentist.

Individual states have adopted different standards for dental assistants who perform certain advanced duties, such as radiological procedures. Completion of the Radiation Health and Safety examination offered by the Dental Assisting National Board (DANB) meets those standards in more than 30 states. Some states require completion of a state-approved course in radiology as well.

Certification is available through DANB and is recognized or required in more than 30 states. Other organizations offer registration, most often at the state level. Certification is an acknowledgment of an assistant's qualifications and professional competence and may be an asset when one is seeking employment. Candidates may qualify to take the DANB certification examination by graduating from an ADA-accredited dental assisting education program or by having 2 years of full-time, or 4 years of part-time, experience as a dental assistant. In addition, applicants must have current certification in cardiopulmonary resuscitation. For annual recertification, individuals must earn continuing education credits.

Without further education, advancement opportunities are limited. Some dental assistants become office managers, dental-assisting instructors, or dental product sales representatives. Others go back to school to become dental hygienists. For many, this entry-level occupation provides basic training and experience and serves as a stepping-stone to more highly skilled and higher paying jobs.

Employment

Dental assistants held about 267,000 jobs in 2004. Almost all jobs for dental assistants were in offices of dentists. A small number of jobs were in the federal, state, and local governments or in offices of physicians. About 2 out of 5 dental assistants worked part time, sometimes in more than one dental office.

Job Outlook

Job prospects for dental assistants should be excellent. Employment is expected to grow much faster than average for all occupations through the year 2014. In fact, dental assistants is expected to be one of the fastest-growing occupations over the 2004–14 projection period.

In addition to job openings due to employment growth, numerous job openings will arise out of the need to replace assistants who transfer to other occupations, retire, or leave for other reasons. Many opportunities are for entry-level positions offering on-the-job training.

Population growth and greater retention of natural teeth by middle-aged and older people will fuel demand for dental services. Older dentists, who have been less likely to employ assistants, are leaving the occupation and will be replaced by recent graduates, who are more likely to use one or even two assistants. In addition, as dentists' workloads increase, they are expected to hire more assistants to perform routine tasks so that they may devote their own time to more complex procedures.

Earnings

Median hourly earnings of dental assistants were $13.62 in May 2004. The middle 50 percent earned between $11.06 and $16.65 an hour. The lowest 10 percent earned less than $9.11, and the highest 10 percent earned more than $19.97 an hour.

Benefits vary substantially by practice setting and may be contingent upon full-time employment. According to the American Dental Association (ADA), almost all full-time dental assistants employed by private practitioners received paid vacation time. The ADA also found that 9 out of 10 full-time and part-time dental assistants received dental coverage.

Related Occupations

Other workers supporting health practitioners include medical assistants, occupational therapist assistants and aides, pharmacy aides, pharmacy technicians, and physical therapist assistants and aides.

Sources of Additional Information

Information about career opportunities and accredited dental assistant programs is available from:

- Commission on Dental Accreditation, American Dental Association, 211 East Chicago Ave., Suite 1814, Chicago, IL 60611. Internet: http://www.ada.org

For information on becoming a Certified Dental Assistant and a list of state boards of dentistry, contact:

- Dental Assisting National Board, Inc., 676 North Saint Clair St., Suite 1880, Chicago, IL 60611. Internet: http://www.danb.org

For more information on a career as a dental assistant and general information about continuing education, contact:

- American Dental Assistants Association, 35 East Wacker Dr., Suite 1730, Chicago, IL 60601. Internet: http://www.dentalassistant.org

For more information about continuing education courses, contact:

- National Association of Dental Assistants, 900 South Washington St., Suite G-13, Falls Church, VA 22046.

Dental Hygienists

(O*NET 29-2021.00)

Significant Points

- Most dental hygiene programs grant an associate degree; others offer a certificate, a bachelor's degree, or a master's degree.
- Dental hygienists rank among the fastest growing occupations.
- Job prospects are expected to remain excellent.
- More than half work part time, and flexible scheduling is a distinctive feature of this job.

Nature of the Work

Dental hygienists remove soft and hard deposits from teeth, teach patients how to practice good oral hygiene, and provide other preventive dental care. Hygienists examine patients' teeth and gums, recording the presence of diseases or abnormalities. They remove calculus, stains, and plaque from teeth; perform root planing as a periodontal therapy; take and develop dental X rays; and apply cavity-preventive agents such as fluorides and pit and fissure sealants. In some states, hygienists administer anesthetics; place and carve filling materials, temporary fillings, and periodontal dressings; remove sutures; and smooth and polish metal restorations. Although hygienists may not diagnose diseases, they can prepare clinical and laboratory diagnostic tests for the dentist to interpret. Hygienists sometimes work chairside with the dentist during treatment.

Dental hygienists also help patients develop and maintain good oral health. For example, they may explain the relationship between diet and oral health or inform patients how to select toothbrushes and show them how to brush and floss their teeth.

Dental hygienists use hand and rotary instruments and ultrasonics to clean and polish teeth, X-ray machines to take dental pictures, syringes with needles to administer local anesthetics, and models of teeth to explain oral hygiene.

Working Conditions

Flexible scheduling is a distinctive feature of this job. Full-time, part-time, evening, and weekend schedules are widely available. Dentists frequently hire hygienists to work only 2 or 3 days a week, so hygienists may hold jobs in more than one dental office.

Dental hygienists work in clean, well-lighted offices. Important health safeguards include strict adherence to proper radiological procedures, and the use of appropriate protective devices when administering anesthetic gas. Dental hygienists also wear safety glasses, surgical masks, and gloves to protect themselves and patients from infectious diseases.

Training, Other Qualifications, and Advancement

Dental hygienists must be licensed by the state in which they practice. To qualify for licensure in nearly all states, a candidate must graduate from an accredited dental hygiene school and pass both a written and clinical examination. The American Dental Association's Joint Commission on National Dental Examinations administers the written examination, which is accepted by all states and the District of Columbia. State or regional testing agencies administer the clinical examination. In addition, most states require an examination on the legal aspects of dental hygiene practice. Alabama allows candidates to take its examinations if they have been trained through a state-regulated on-the-job program in a dentist's office.

In 2004, the Commission on Dental Accreditation accredited 266 programs in dental hygiene. Most dental hygiene programs grant an associate degree, although some also offer a certificate, a bachelor's degree, or a master's degree. A minimum of an associate degree or certificate in dental hygiene is generally required for practice in a private dental office. A bachelor's or master's degree usually is required for research, teaching, or clinical practice in public or school health programs.

A high school diploma and college entrance test scores are usually required for admission to a dental hygiene program. Also, some dental hygiene programs prefer applicants who have completed at least 1 year of college. Requirements vary from one school to another. Schools offer laboratory, clinical, and classroom instruction in subjects such as anatomy, physiology, chemistry, microbiology, pharmacology, nutrition, radiography, histology (the study of tissue structure), periodontology (the study of gum diseases), pathology, dental materials, clinical dental hygiene, and social and behavioral sciences.

Dental hygienists should work well with others and must have good manual dexterity, because they use dental instruments within a patient's mouth, with little room for error. High school students interested in becoming a dental hygienist should take courses in biology, chemistry, and mathematics.

Employment

Dental hygienists held about 158,000 jobs in 2004. Because multiple jobholding is common in this field, the number of jobs exceeds the number of hygienists. More than half of all dental hygienists worked part time—less than 35 hours a week.

Almost all jobs for dental hygienists were in offices of dentists. A very small number worked for employment services or in offices of physicians.

Job Outlook

Employment of dental hygienists is expected to grow much faster than average for all occupations through 2014, ranking among the fastest growing occupations, in response to increasing demand for dental care and the greater utilization of hygienists to perform services previously performed by dentists. Job prospects are expected to remain excellent.

Population growth and greater retention of natural teeth will stimulate demand for dental hygienists. Older dentists, who have been less likely to employ dental hygienists, are leaving the occupation and will be replaced by recent graduates, who are more likely to employ one or even two hygienists. In addition, as dentists' workloads increase, they are expected to hire more hygienists to perform preventive dental care, such as cleaning, so that they may devote their own time to more profitable procedures.

Earnings

Median hourly earnings of dental hygienists were $28.05 in May 2004. The middle 50 percent earned between $22.72 and $33.82 an hour. The lowest 10 percent earned less than $18.05, and the highest 10 percent earned more than $40.70 an hour.

Earnings vary by geographic location, employment setting, and years of experience. Dental hygienists may be paid on an hourly, daily, salary, or commission basis.

Benefits vary substantially by practice setting and may be contingent upon full-time employment. According to the American Dental Association (ADA), almost all full-time dental hygienists employed by private practitioners received paid vacation. The ADA also found that 9 out of 10 full-time and part-time dental hygienists received dental coverage. Dental hygienists who work for school systems, public health agencies, the federal government, or state agencies usually have substantial benefits.

Related Occupations

Other workers supporting health practitioners in an office setting include dental assistants, medical assistants, occupational therapist assistants and aides, physical therapist assistants and aides, physician assistants, and registered nurses.

Sources of Additional Information

For information on a career in dental hygiene, including educational requirements, contact:

- Division of Education, American Dental Hygienists Association, 444 N. Michigan Ave., Suite 3400, Chicago, IL 60611. Internet: http://www.adha.org

For information about accredited programs and educational requirements, contact:

- Commission on Dental Accreditation, American Dental Association, 211 E. Chicago Ave., Suite 1814, Chicago, IL 60611. Internet: http://www.ada.org

The State Board of Dental Examiners in each state can supply information on licensing requirements.

Education Administrators

(O*NET 11-9031.00, 11-9032.00, 11-9033.00, and 11-9039.99)

Significant Points

- Many jobs require a master's or doctoral degree and experience in a related occupation, such as a teacher or admissions counselor.
- Strong interpersonal and communication skills are essential because much of an administrator's job involves working and collaborating with others.
- Excellent opportunities are expected since a large proportion of education administrators is expected to retire over the next 10 years.

Nature of the Work

Smooth operation of an educational institution requires competent administrators. *Education administrators* provide instructional leadership as well as manage the day-to-day activities in schools, preschools, daycare centers, and colleges and universities. They also direct the educational programs of businesses, correctional institutions, museums, and job training and community service organizations. Education administrators set educational standards and goals and establish the policies and procedures to carry them out. They also supervise managers, support staff, teachers, counselors, librarians, coaches, and others. They develop academic programs; monitor students' educational progress; train and motivate teachers and other staff; manage career counseling and other student services; administer recordkeeping; prepare budgets; handle relations with parents, prospective and current students, employers, and the community; and perform many other duties. In an organization such as a small daycare center, one administrator may handle all these functions. In universities or large school systems, responsibilities are divided among many administrators, each with a specific function.

Educational administrators who manage elementary, middle, and secondary schools are called *principals*. They set the academic tone and hire, evaluate, and help improve the skills of teachers and other staff. Principals confer with staff to advise, explain, or answer procedural questions. They visit classrooms, observe teaching methods, review instructional objectives, and examine learning materials. They actively work with teachers to develop and maintain high curriculum standards, develop mission statements, and set performance goals and objectives. Principals must use clear, objective guidelines for teacher appraisals, because pay often is based on performance ratings.

Principals also meet and interact with other administrators, students, parents, and representatives of community organizations. Decision-making authority has increasingly shifted from school district central offices to individual schools. School principals have greater flexibility in setting school policies and goals, but when making administrative decisions they must pay attention to the concerns of parents, teachers, and other members of the community.

Principals prepare budgets and reports on various subjects, including finances and attendance, and oversee the requisition and allocation of supplies. As school budgets become tighter, many principals have become more involved in public relations and fundraising to secure financial support for their schools from local businesses and the community.

Principals must take an active role to ensure that students meet national, state, and local academic standards. Many principals develop school/business partnerships and school-to-work transition programs for students. Increasingly, principals must be sensitive to the needs of the rising number of non-English-speaking and culturally diverse students. In some areas growing enrollments also are a cause for concern because they are leading to overcrowding at many schools. When addressing problems of inadequate resources, administrators serve as advocates for the building of new schools or the repair of existing ones. During summer months, principals are responsible for planning for the upcoming year, overseeing summer school, participating in workshops for teachers and administrators, supervising building repairs and improvements, and working to be sure the school has adequate staff for the school year.

Schools continue to be involved with students' emotional welfare as well as their academic achievement. As a result, principals face responsibilities outside the academic realm. For example, in response to the growing numbers of dual-income and single-parent families and teenage parents, schools have established before- and after-school childcare programs or family resource centers, which also may offer parenting classes and social service referrals. With the help of community organizations, some principals have established programs to combat increases in crime, drug and alcohol abuse, and sexually transmitted diseases among students.

Assistant principals aid the principal in the overall administration of the school. Some assistant principals hold this position for several years to prepare for advancement to principal jobs; others are career assistant principals. They are primarily responsible for scheduling student classes, ordering textbooks and supplies, and coordinating transportation, custodial, cafeteria, and other support services. They usually handle student discipline and attendance problems, social and recreational programs, and health and safety matters. They also may counsel students on personal, educational, or vocational matters. With the advent of site-based management, assistant principals are playing a greater role in ensuring the academic success of students by helping to develop new curriculums, evaluating teachers, and dealing with school-community relations—responsibilities previously assumed solely by the principal. The number of assistant principals that a school employs may vary, depending on the number of students.

Administrators in school district central offices oversee public schools under their jurisdiction. This group includes those who direct subject-area programs such as English, music, vocational education, special education, and mathematics. They supervise instructional coordinators and curriculum specialists, and work with them to evaluate curriculums and teaching techniques and improve them. Administrators also may oversee career counseling programs and testing that measures students' abilities and helps to place them in appropriate classes. Others may also direct programs such as school psychology, athletics, curriculum and instruction, and professional development. With site-based management, administrators have transferred primary responsibility for many of these programs to the principals, assistant principals, teachers, instructional coordinators, and other staff in the schools.

In preschools and childcare centers, education administrators are the director or supervisor of the school or center. Their job is similar to that of other school administrators in that they oversee daily activities and operation of the schools, hire and develop staff, and make sure that the school meets required regulations.

In colleges and universities, *provosts* also known as *chief academic officers* assist presidents, make faculty appointments and tenure decisions, develop budgets, and establish academic policies and programs. With the assistance of *academic deans* and *deans of faculty,* they also direct and coordinate the activities of deans of individual colleges and chairpersons of academic departments. Fundraising is the chief responsibility of the *director of development* and also is becoming an essential part of the job for all administrators.

College or university department heads or *chairpersons* are in charge of departments that specialize in particular fields of study, such as English, biological science, or mathematics. In addition to teaching, they coordinate schedules of classes and teaching assignments; propose budgets; recruit, interview, and hire applicants for teaching positions; evaluate faculty members; encourage faculty development; serve on committees; and perform other administrative duties. In overseeing their departments, chairpersons must consider and balance the concerns of faculty, administrators, and students.

Higher education administrators also direct and coordinate the provision of student services. *Vice presidents of student affairs* or *student life, deans of students,* and *directors of student services* may direct and coordinate admissions, foreign student services, health and counseling services, career services, financial aid, and housing and residential life, as well as social, recreational, and related programs. In small colleges, they may counsel students. In larger colleges and universities, separate administrators may handle each of these services. *Registrars* are custodians of students' records. They register students, record grades, prepare student transcripts, evaluate academic records, assess and collect tuition and fees, plan and implement commencement, oversee the preparation of college catalogs and schedules of classes, and analyze enrollment and demographic statistics. *Directors of admissions* manage the process of recruiting, evaluating, and admitting students, and work closely with *financial aid directors*, who oversee scholarship, fellowship, and loan programs. Registrars and admissions officers at most institutions need computer skills because they use electronic student information systems. For example, for those whose institutions present college catalogs, schedules, and other information on the Internet, knowledge of online resources, imaging, and other computer skills is important. *Athletic directors* plan and direct intramural and intercollegiate athletic activities, seeing to publicity for athletic events, preparation of budgets, and supervision of coaches. Other increasingly important administrators direct public relations, distance learning, and technology.

Working Conditions

Education administrators hold leadership positions with significant responsibility. Most find working with students extremely rewarding, but as the responsibilities of administrators have increased in recent years, so has the stress. Coordinating and interacting with faculty, parents, students, community members, business leaders, and state and local policymakers can be fast-paced and stimulating, but also stressful and demanding. Principals and assistant principals, whose varied duties include discipline, may find working with difficult students to be challenging. They are also increasingly being held accountable for ensuring that their schools meet recently imposed state and federal guidelines for student performance and teacher qualifications.

Many education administrators work more than 40 hours a week, often including school activities at night and on weekends. Most administrators work 11 or 12 months out of the year. Some jobs include travel.

Training, Other Qualifications, and Advancement

Most education administrators begin their careers in related occupations, often as teachers, and prepare for advancement into education administration by completing a master's or doctoral degree. Because of the diversity of duties and levels of responsibility, their educational backgrounds and experience vary considerably. Principals, assistant principals, central office administrators, academic deans, and preschool directors usually have held teaching positions before moving into administration. Some teachers move directly into principal positions; others first become assistant principals, or gain experience in other administrative jobs at either the school or district level in positions such as department head, curriculum specialist, or subject matter advisor. In some cases, administrators move up from related staff jobs such as recruiter, school counselor, librarian, residence hall director, or financial aid or admissions counselor.

To be considered for education administrator positions, workers must first prove themselves in their current jobs. In evaluating candidates, supervisors look for leadership, determination, confidence, innovativeness, and motivation. The ability to make sound decisions and to organize and coordinate work efficiently is essential. Because much of an administrator's job involves interacting with others—such as students, parents, teachers, and the community— a person in such a position must have strong interpersonal skills and be an effective communicator and motivator. Knowledge of leadership principles and practices, gained through work experience and formal education, is important. A familiarity with computer technology is a necessity for principals, who are required to gather information and coordinate technical resources for their students, teachers, and classrooms.

In most public schools, principals, assistant principals, and school district administrators need a master's degree in education administration or educational leadership. Some principals and central office administrators have a doctorate or specialized degree in education administration. Most states require principals to be licensed as school administrators. License requirements vary by state, but nearly all states require either a master's degree or some other graduate-level training. Some states also require candidates for licensure to pass a test. Increasingly, on-the-job training, often with a mentor, is required or recommended for new school leaders. Some states require administrators to take continuing education courses to keep their license, thus ensuring that administrators have the most up-to-date skills. The number and types of courses required to maintain licensure vary by state. In private schools, which are not subject to state licensure requirements, some principals and assistant principals hold only a bachelor's degree, but the majority have a master's or doctoral degree.

Educational requirements for administrators of preschools and childcare centers vary depending on the setting of the program and the state of employment. Administrators who oversee preschool programs in public schools are often required to have at least a bachelor's degree. Child care directors are generally not required to have a degree; however, most states require a general preschool education credential, such as the Child Development Associate credential (CDA) sponsored by the Council for Professional Recognition, or a credential specifically designed for administrators. The National Child Care Association, offers a National Administration Credential, which some recent college graduates voluntarily earn to better qualify for positions as childcare center directors.

Academic deans and chairpersons usually have a doctorate in their specialty. Most have held a professorship in their department before advancing. Admissions, student affairs, and financial aid directors and registrars sometimes start in related staff jobs with bachelor's degrees—any field usually is acceptable—and obtain advanced degrees in college student affairs, counseling, or higher education administration. A Ph.D. or Ed.D. usually is necessary for top student affairs positions. Computer literacy and a background in accounting or statistics may be assets in admissions, records, and financial work.

Advanced degrees in higher education administration, educational leadership, and college student affairs are offered in many colleges and universities. Education administration degree programs include courses in school leadership, school law, school finance and budgeting, curriculum development and evaluation, research design and data analysis, community relations, politics in education, and counseling. The National Council for Accreditation of Teacher Education and the Educational Leadership Constituent Council accredit programs designed for elementary and secondary school administrators. While completion of an accredited program is not required, it may assist in fulfilling licensure requirements.

Education administrators advance through promotion to more responsible administrative positions or by transferring to more responsible positions at larger schools or systems. They also may become superintendents of school systems or presidents of educational institutions.

Employment

Education administrators held about 442,000 jobs in 2004. Of these, 58,000 were preschool or child care administrators, 225,000 were elementary or secondary school administrators, and 132,000 were postsecondary administrators. About 2 in 10 worked for private education institutions, and 6 in 10 worked for state and local governments, mainly in schools, colleges and universities, and departments of education. Less than 4 percent were self-employed. The rest worked in child daycare centers, religious organizations, job training centers, and businesses and other organizations that provided training for their employees.

Job Outlook

Employment of education administrators is projected to grow as fast as the average for all occupations through 2014. As education and training take on greater importance in everyone's lives, the need for people to administer education programs will grow. Job opportunities for many of these positions should also be excellent because a large proportion of education administrators are expected to retire over the next 10 years.

Enrollments of school-age children are the primary factor determining the demand for education administrators. Enrollment of students in elementary and secondary schools is expected to grow slowly over the next decade, which will limit the growth of principals and other administrators in these schools. However, preschool and childcare center administrators are expected to experience substantial growth as enrollments in formal child care programs continue to expand as fewer private households care for young children. Additionally, as more states begin implementing public preschool programs, more preschool directors will be needed. The number of postsecondary school students is projected to grow more rapidly than other student populations, creating significant demand for administrators at that level. Opportunities may vary by geographical area, as enrollments are expected to increase the fastest in the West and South, where the population is growing, and to decline or remain stable in the Northeast and the Midwest. School administrators also are in greater demand in rural and urban areas, where pay is generally lower than in the suburbs.

Principals and assistant principals should have very favorable job prospects. A sharp increase in responsibilities in recent years has made the job more stressful, and has discouraged some teachers from taking positions in administration. Principals are now being held more accountable for the performance of students and teachers, while at the same time they are required to adhere to a growing number of government regulations. In addition, overcrowded classrooms, safety issues, budgetary concerns, and teacher shortages in some areas all are creating additional stress for administrators. Many teachers feel the higher pay of administrators is not high enough to compensate for the greater responsibilities.

Job prospects also are expected to be favorable for college and university administrators, particularly those seeking nonacademic positions. Public colleges and universities may be subject to funding shortfalls during economic downturns, but increasing enrollments over the projection period will require that institutions replace the large numbers of administrators who retire, and even hire additional administrators. In addition, a significant portion of growth will stem from growth in the private and for-profit segments of higher education. Many of these schools cater to working adults who might not ordinarily participate in postsecondary education. These schools allow students to earn a degree, receive job-specific training, or update their skills in a convenient manner, such as through part-time programs or distance learning. As the number of these schools continues to grow, more administrators will be needed to oversee them.

While competition among faculty for prestigious positions as academic deans and department heads is likely to remain keen, fewer applicants are expected for nonacademic administrative jobs, such as director of admissions or student affairs. Furthermore, many people are discouraged from seeking administrator jobs by the requirement that they have a master's or doctoral degree in education administration—as well as by the opportunity to earn higher salaries in other occupations.

Earnings

In May 2004, elementary and secondary school administrators had median annual earnings of $74,190; postsecondary school administrators had median annual earnings of $68,340, while preschool and childcare center administrators earned a median of $35,730 per year. Salaries of education administrators depend on several factors, including the location and enrollment level in the school or school district. According to a survey of public schools, conducted by the Educational Research Service, average salaries for principals and assistant principals in the 2004–05 school year were as follows:

Principals:	
Senior high school	$82,225
Jr. high/middle school	78,160
Elementary school	74,062
Assistant principals:	
Senior high school	$68,945
Jr. high/middle school	66,319
Elementary school	63,398

According to the College and University Professional Association for Human Resources, median annual salaries for selected administrators in higher education in 2004–05 were as follows:

Chief academic officer	$127,066
Academic deans:	
Business	$120,460
Arts and sciences	110,412
Graduate programs	109,309
Education	107,660
Nursing	100,314
Health-related professions	100,185
Continuing education	91,800
Occupational or vocational education	79,845
Other administrators:	
Chief development officer	$114,400
Dean of students	75,245
Director, student financial aid	63,130
Registrar	61,953
Director, student activities	45,636

Benefits for education administrators are generally very good. Many get 4 or 5 weeks vacation every year and have generous health and pension packages. Many colleges and universities offer free tuition to employees and their families.

Related Occupations

Education administrators apply organizational and leadership skills to provide services to individuals. Workers in related occupations include administrative services managers; office and administrative support worker supervisors and managers; and human resource, training, and labor relations managers and specialists. Education administrators also work with students and have backgrounds similar to those of counselors; librarians; instructional coordinators; teachers—preschool, kindergarten, elementary, middle, and secondary; and teachers—postsecondary.

Sources of Additional Information

For information on principals, contact:

- The National Association of Elementary School Principals, 1615 Duke St., Alexandria, VA 22314-3483. Internet: http://www.naesp.org
- The National Association of Secondary School Principals, 1904 Association Drive, Reston, VA 20191-1537. Internet: http://www.nassp.org

For a list of nationally recognized programs in elementary and secondary educational administration, contact:

- The Educational Leadership Constituent Council, 1904 Association Drive, Reston, VA 20191. Internet: http://www.npbea.org/ELCC/index.html

For information on collegiate registrars and admissions officers, contact:

- American Association of Collegiate Registrars and Admissions Officers, One Dupont Circle NW, Suite 520, Washington, DC 20036-1171. Internet: http://www.aacrao.org

For information on professional development and graduate programs for college student affairs administrators, contact:

- NASPA, Student Affairs Administrators in Higher Education, 1875 Connecticut Ave. NW, Suite 418, Washington, DC 20009. Internet: http://www.naspa.org

Electricians

(O*NET 47-2111.00)

Significant Points

- Job opportunities are expected to be good, especially for those with the right skills.
- Most electricians acquire their skills by completing an apprenticeship program lasting 4 to 5 years.
- Nearly three-fourths of electricians work for building contractors or are self-employed, but there also will be many job openings for electricians in other industries.

Nature of the Work

Electricity is essential for light, power, air-conditioning, and refrigeration. Electricians install, connect, test, and maintain electrical systems for a variety of purposes, including climate control, security, and communications. They also may install and maintain the electronic controls for machines in business and industry.

Electricians generally specialize in construction or maintenance work, although a growing number do both. Electricians specializing in construction work primarily install wiring systems into new homes, businesses, and factories, but they also rewire or upgrade existing electrical systems as needed. Electricians specializing in maintenance work primarily maintain and upgrade existing electrical systems and repair electrical equipment.

Electricians work with blueprints when they install electrical systems. Blueprints indicate the locations of circuits, outlets, load centers, panel boards, and other equipment. Electricians must follow the National Electrical Code and comply with state and local building codes when they install these systems. Regulations vary depending on the setting and require various types of installation procedures.

When electricians install wiring systems in factories and commercial settings, they first place conduit (pipe or tubing) inside partitions, walls, or other concealed areas as designated by the blueprints. They also fasten to the walls small metal or plastic boxes that will house electrical switches and outlets. They pull insulated wires or cables through the conduit to complete circuits between these boxes. In residential construction, electricians usually install plastic encased insulated wire, which does not need to be run through conduit. The gauge and number of wires installed in all settings depends upon the load and end use of that part of the electrical system. The greater the diameter of the wire, the higher the voltage and amperage that can flow through it.

Electricians connect all types of wire to circuit breakers, transformers, outlets, or other components. They join the wires in boxes with various specially designed connectors. During installation, electricians use hand tools such as conduit benders, screwdrivers, pliers, knives, hacksaws, and wire strippers, as well as power tools such as drills and saws. After they finish installing the wiring, they use testing equipment, such as ammeters, ohmmeters, voltmeters, and oscilloscopes, to check the circuits for proper connections, ensuring electrical compatibility, and safety of components.

Maintenance work varies greatly, depending on where the electrician is employed. Electricians who specialize in residential work perform a wide variety of electrical work for homeowners. They may rewire a home and replace an old fuse box with a new circuit breaker box to accommodate additional appliances, or they may install new lighting and other electric household items, such as ceil ing fans. Those who work in large factories may repair motors, transformers, generators, and electronic controllers on machine tools and industrial robots. Those in office buildings and small plants may repair all types of electrical equipment.

Maintenance electricians working in factories, hospitals, and other settings repair electric and electronic equipment when breakdowns occur and install new electrical equipment. When breakdowns occur, they must make the necessary repairs as quickly as possible in order to minimize inconvenience. They may replace items such as circuit breakers, fuses, switches, electrical and electronic components, or wire. Electricians also periodically inspect all equipment to ensure it is operating properly, and locate and correct problems before breakdowns occur. Electricians also advise management whether continued operation of equipment could be hazardous. When working with complex electronic devices, they may work with engineers, engineering technicians, line installers and repairers, or industrial machinery installation, repair, and maintenance workers.

Although primarily classified as work for line installers and repairers, electricians also may install low voltage wiring systems in addition to wiring a building's electrical system. Low voltage wiring involves voice, data, and video wiring systems, such as those for telephones, computers and related equipment, intercoms, and fire alarm and security systems. Electricians also may install coaxial or fiber optic cable for computers and other telecommunications equipment and electronic controls for industrial uses.

Working Conditions

Electricians work both indoors and out; at construction sites, in homes, and in businesses or factories. Work may be strenuous at times and include bending conduit, lifting heavy objects, and standing, stooping, and kneeling for long periods of time. When working outdoors, they may be subject to inclement weather conditions. Some electricians may have to travel long distances to jobsites. Electricians risk injury from electrical shock, falls, and cuts; they must follow strict safety procedures to avoid injuries.

Most electricians work a standard 40-hour week, although overtime may be required. Those in maintenance work may work nights or weekends, and be on call to go to the worksite when needed. Electricians working in industrial settings may also have periodic extended overtime during scheduled maintenance or retooling periods. Companies that operate 24 hours a day may employ three shifts of electricians.

Training, Other Qualifications, and Advancement

Most electricians learn their trade through apprenticeship programs. These programs combine on-the-job training with related classroom instruction. Apprenticeship programs may be sponsored by joint training committees made up of local unions of the International Brotherhood of Electrical Workers and local chapters of the National Electrical Contractors Association; company management committees of individual electrical contracting companies; or local chapters of the Associated Builders and Contractors and the Independent Electrical Contractors Association. Because of the comprehensive training received, those who complete apprenticeship programs qualify to do both maintenance and construction work.

Applicants for apprenticeships usually must be at least 18 years old and have a high school diploma or a G.E.D. They should have good math and English skills, since most instruction manuals are in English. They also may have to pass a test and meet other requirements. Apprenticeship programs usually last 4 years and each year include at least 144 hours of classroom instruction and 2,000 hours of on-the-job training. In the classroom, apprentices learn electrical theory and installing and maintaining electrical systems. There also take classes in blueprint reading, mathematics, electrical code requirements, and safety and first aid practices also may receive specialized training in soldering, communications, fire alarm systems, and cranes and elevators. On the job, apprentices work under the supervision of experienced electricians. At first, they drill holes, set anchors, and attach conduit. Later, they measure, fabricate, and install conduit, as well as install, connect, and test wiring, outlets, and switches. They also learn to set up and draw diagrams for entire electrical systems. To complete the apprenticeship and become electricians, apprentices must demonstrate mastery of the electrician's work.

Some persons seeking to become electricians choose to obtain their classroom training before seeking a job. Training to become an electrician is offered by a number of public and private vocational-technical schools and training academies in affiliation with local unions and contractor organizations. Employers often hire students who complete these programs and usually start them at a more advanced level than those without the training. A few persons become electricians by first working as helpers, assisting electricians setting up job sites, gathering materials, and doing other non-electrical work, before entering an apprenticeship program.

Skills needed to become an electrician include manual dexterity, eye-hand coordination, physical fitness, and a good sense of balance. The ability to solve arithmetic problems quickly and accurately also is required. Good color vision is needed because workers frequently must identify electrical wires by color. In addition, a good work history or military service is viewed favorably by apprenticeship committees and employers.

Most localities require electricians to be licensed. Although licensing requirements vary from area to area, electricians usually must pass an examination that tests their knowledge of electrical theory, the National Electrical Code, and local electric and building codes. Experienced electricians periodically take courses offered by their employer or union to keep abreast of changes in the National Electrical Code and new materials or methods of installation. For example, classes on installing low voltage voice, data, and video systems have recently become common as these systems have become more prevalent.

Experienced electricians can advance to jobs as supervisors. In construction they also may become project managers or construction superintendents. Those with sufficient capital and management skills may start their own contracting business, although this may require an electrical contractor's license. Many electricians also become electrical inspectors. Supervisors and contractors should be able to identify and estimate the correct type and quantity of materials needed to complete a job, and accurately estimate how long a job will take to complete and at what cost. For those who seek to advance, it is increasingly important to be able to communicate in both English and Spanish in order to relay instructions and safety precautions to workers with limited understanding of English; Spanish-speaking workers make up a large part of the construction workforce in many areas. Spanish-speaking workers who want to advance in this occupation need very good English skills to understand instruction presented in classes and installation instructions, which are usually written in English and are highly technical.

Employment

Electricians held about 656,000 jobs in 2004. Nearly two-thirds of wage and salary workers were employed in the construction industry; while the remainder worked as maintenance electricians in other industries. In addition, about one in ten electricians were self-employed.

Because of the widespread need for electrical services, electrician jobs are found in all parts of the country.

Job Outlook

Employment of electricians is expected to increase as fast as average for all occupations through the year 2014. As the population and economy grow, more electricians will be needed to install and maintain electrical devices and wiring in homes, factories, offices, and other structures. New technologies also are expected to continue to stimulate the demand for these workers. For example, buildings need to increasingly accommodate the use of computers and telecommunications equipment. Also, the increasing prevalence in factories of robots and other automated manufacturing systems will require more complex wiring systems be installed and maintained. Additional jobs will be created as older structures are rehabilitated and retrofitted, which usually requires that they be brought up to meet existing electrical codes.

In addition to jobs created by the increased demand for electrical work, many openings are expected to occur over the next decade as a large number of electricians are expected to retire. This will create good job opportunities for the most qualified jobseekers. Job openings for electricians, though, will vary by area and will be greatest in the fastest growing regions of the country.

Employment of construction electricians, like that of many other construction workers, is sensitive to changes in the economy. This results from the limited duration of construction projects and the cyclical nature of the construction industry. During economic downturns, job openings for electricians are reduced as the level of construction activity declines. Apprenticeship opportunities also are less plentiful during these periods.

Although employment of maintenance electricians is steadier than that of construction electricians, those working in the automotive and other manufacturing industries that are sensitive to cyclical swings in the economy may be laid off during recessions. Also, opportunities for maintenance electricians may be limited in many industries by the increased contracting out for electrical services in an effort to reduce operating costs and increase productivity. However, increased job opportunities for electricians in electrical contracting firms should partially offset job losses in other industries.

Earnings

In May 2004, median hourly earnings of electricians were $20.33. The middle 50 percent earned between $15.43 and $26.90. The lowest 10 percent earned less than $12.18, and the highest 10 percent earned more than $33.63. Median hourly earnings in the industries employing the largest numbers of electricians in May 2004 were as follows:

Motor vehicle parts manufacturing	$30.04
Local government	22.24
Nonresidential building construction	19.99
Building equipment contractors	19.76
Employment services	15.62

Apprentices usually start at between 40 and 50 percent of the rate paid to fully trained electricians, depending on experience. As apprentices become more skilled, they receive periodic pay increases throughout the course of their training.

Some electricians are members of the International Brotherhood of Electrical Workers. Among unions representing maintenance electricians are the International Brotherhood of Electrical Workers; the International Union of Electronic, Electrical, Salaried, Machine, and Furniture Workers; the International Association of Machinists and Aerospace Workers; the International Union, United Automobile, Aircraft and Agricultural Implement Workers of America; and the United Steelworkers of America.

Related Occupations

To install and maintain electrical systems, electricians combine manual skill and knowledge of electrical materials and concepts. Workers in other occupations involving similar skills include heating, air-conditioning, and refrigeration mechanics and installers; line installers and repairers; electrical and electronics installers and repairers; electronic home entertainment equipment installers and repairers; and elevator installers and repairers.

Sources of Additional Information

For details about apprenticeships or other work opportunities in this trade, contact the offices of the state employment service, the state apprenticeship agency, local electrical contractors or firms that employ maintenance electricians, or local union-management electrician apprenticeship committees. This information also may be available from local chapters of the Independent Electrical Contractors, Inc.; the National Electrical Contractors Association; the Home Builders Institute; the Associated Builders and Contractors; and the International Brotherhood of Electrical Workers.

For information about union apprenticeship and training programs, contact:

- National Joint Apprenticeship Training Committee (NJATC), 301 Prince George's Blvd., Upper Marlboro, MD 20774. Internet: http://www.njatc.org
- National Electrical Contractors Association (NECA), 3 Metro Center, Suite 1100, Bethesda, MD 20814. Internet: http://www.necanet.org
- International Brotherhood of Electrical Workers (IBEW), 1125 15th St. NW, Washington, DC 20005. Internet: http://www.ibew.org

For information about independent apprenticeship programs, contact:

- Associated Builders and Contractors, Workforce Development Department, 4250 North Fairfax Dr., 9th Floor, Arlington, VA 22203. Internet: http://www.trytools.org
- Independent Electrical Contractors, Inc., 4401 Ford Ave., Suite 1100, Alexandria, VA 22302. Internet: http://www.ieci.org
- National Association of Home Builders, Home Builders Institute, 1201 15th St. NW, Washington, DC 20005. Internet: http://www.hbi.org
- National Center for Construction Education and Research, P.O. Box 141104, Gainesville, FL 32614-1104. Internet: http://www.nccer.org

Emergency Medical Technicians and Paramedics

(O*NET 29-2041.00)

Significant Points

- Because emergency services function 24 hours a day, emergency medical technicians and paramedics have irregular working hours.
- Emergency medical technicians and paramedics need formal training and certification, but requirements vary by state.
- Employment is projected to grow much faster than average as paid emergency medical technician positions replace unpaid volunteers.
- Competition will be greater for jobs in local fire, police, and rescue squad departments than in private ambulance services; opportunities will be best for those who have advanced certification.

Nature of the Work

People's lives often depend on the quick reaction and competent care of emergency medical technicians (EMTs) and paramedics—EMTs with additional advanced training to perform more difficult prehospital medical procedures. Incidents as varied as automobile accidents, heart attacks, drownings, childbirth, and gunshot wounds all require immediate medical attention. EMTs and paramedics provide this vital attention as they care for and transport the sick or injured to a medical facility.

In an emergency, EMTs and paramedics typically are dispatched to the scene by a 911 operator, and often work with police and fire department personnel. Once they arrive, they determine the nature and extent of the patient's condition while trying to ascertain whether the patient has preexisting medical problems. Following strict rules and guidelines, they give appropriate emergency care and, when necessary, transport the patient. Some paramedics are trained to treat patients with minor injuries on the scene of an accident or at their home without transporting them to a medical facility. Emergency treatment for more complicated problems is carried out under the direction of medical doctors by radio preceding or during transport.

EMTs and paramedics may use special equipment, such as backboards, to immobilize patients before placing them on stretchers and securing them in the ambulance for transport to a medical facility. Usually, one EMT or paramedic drives while the other monitors the patient's vital signs and gives additional care as needed. Some EMTs work as part of the flight crew of helicopters that transport critically ill or injured patients to hospital trauma centers.

At the medical facility, EMTs and paramedics help transfer patients to the emergency department, report their observations and actions to emergency room staff, and may provide additional emergency treatment. After each run, EMTs and paramedics replace used supplies and check equipment. If a transported patient had a contagious disease, EMTs and paramedics decontaminate the interior of the ambulance and report cases to the proper authorities.

Beyond these general duties, the specific responsibilities of EMTs and paramedics depend on their level of qualification and training. To determine this, the National Registry of Emergency Medical Technicians (NREMT) registers emergency medical service (EMS) providers at four levels: First Responder, EMT-Basic, EMT-Intermediate, and EMT-Paramedic. Some states, however, do their own certification and use numeric ratings from 1 to 4 to distinguish levels of proficiency.

The lowest-level workers—First Responders—are trained to provide basic emergency medical care because they tend to be the first persons to arrive at the scene of an incident. Many fire fighters, police officers, and other emergency workers have this level of training. The EMT-Basic, also known as EMT-1, represents the first component of the emergency medical technician system. An EMT-1 is trained to care for patients at the scene of an accident and while transporting patients by ambulance to the hospital under medical direction. The EMT-1 has the emergency skills to assess a patient's condition and manage respiratory, cardiac, and trauma emergencies.

The EMT-Intermediate (EMT-2 and EMT-3) has more advanced training that allows the administration of intravenous fluids, the use of manual defibrillators to give lifesaving shocks to a stopped heart, and the application of advanced airway techniques and equipment to assist patients experiencing respiratory emergencies. EMT-Paramedics (EMT-4) provide the most extensive prehospital care. In addition to carrying out the procedures already described, paramedics may administer drugs orally and intravenously, interpret electrocardiograms (EKGs), perform endotracheal intubations, and use monitors and other complex equipment.

Working Conditions

EMTs and paramedics work both indoors and outdoors, in all types of weather. They are required to do considerable kneeling, bending, and heavy lifting. These workers risk noise-induced hearing loss from sirens and back injuries from lifting patients. In addition, EMTs and paramedics may be exposed to diseases such as hepatitis-B and AIDS, as well as violence from drug overdose victims or mentally unstable patients. The work is not only physically strenuous, but can be stressful, sometimes involving life-or-death situations and suffering patients. Nonetheless, many people find the work exciting and challenging and enjoy the opportunity to help others.

EMTs and paramedics employed by fire departments work about 50 hours a week. Those employed by hospitals frequently work between 45 and 60 hours a week, and those in private ambulance services, between 45 and 50 hours. Some of these workers, especially those in police and fire departments, are on call for extended periods. Because emergency services function 24 hours a day, EMTs and paramedics have irregular working hours.

Training, Other Qualifications, and Advancement

Formal training and certification is needed to become an EMT or paramedic. A high school diploma is typically required to enter a formal training program. Some programs offer an associate degree along with the formal EMT training. All 50 states have a certification procedure. In most states and the District of Columbia, registration with the NREMT is required at some or all levels of certification. Other states administer their own certification examination or provide the option of taking the NREMT examination. To maintain certification, EMTs and paramedics must reregister, usually every 2 years. In order to reregister, an individual must be working as an EMT or paramedic and meet a continuing education requirement.

Training is offered at progressive levels: EMT-Basic, also known as EMT-1; EMT-Intermediate, or EMT-2 and EMT-3; and EMT-Paramedic, or EMT-4. EMT-Basic coursework typically emphasizes emergency skills, such as managing respiratory, trauma, and cardiac emergencies, and patient assessment. Formal courses are often combined with time in an emergency room or ambulance. The program also provides instruction and practice in dealing with bleeding, fractures, airway obstruction, cardiac arrest, and emergency childbirth. Students learn how to use and maintain common emergency equipment, such as backboards, suction devices, splints, oxygen delivery systems, and stretchers. Graduates of approved EMT basic training programs who pass a written and practical examination administered by the state certifying agency or the NREMT earn the title "Registered EMT-Basic." The course also is a prerequisite for EMT-Intermediate and EMT-Paramedic training.

EMT-Intermediate training requirements vary from state to state. Applicants can opt to receive training in EMT-Shock Trauma, wherein the caregiver learns to start intravenous fluids and give certain medications, or in EMT-Cardiac, which includes learning heart rhythms and administering advanced medications. Training commonly includes 35 to 55 hours of additional instruction beyond EMT-Basic coursework, and covers patient assessment as well as the use of advanced airway devices and intravenous fluids. Prerequisites for taking the EMT-Intermediate examination include registration as an EMT-Basic, required classroom work, and a specified amount of clinical experience.

The most advanced level of training for this occupation is EMT-Paramedic. At this level, the caregiver receives additional training in body function and learns more advanced skills. The Technology program usually lasts up to 2 years and results in an associate degree in applied science. Such education prepares the graduate to take the NREMT examination and become certified as an EMT-Paramedic. Extensive related coursework and clinical and field experience is required. Because of the longer training requirement, almost all EMT-Paramedics are in paid positions, rather than being volunteers. Refresher courses and continuing education are available for EMTs and paramedics at all levels.

EMTs and paramedics should be emotionally stable, have good dexterity, agility, and physical coordination, and be able to lift and carry heavy loads. They also need good eyesight (corrective lenses may be used) with accurate color vision.

Advancement beyond the EMT-Paramedic level usually means leaving fieldwork. An EMT-Paramedic can become a supervisor, operations manager, administrative director, or executive director of emergency services. Some EMTs and paramedics become instructors, dispatchers, or physician assistants, while others move into sales or marketing of emergency medical equipment. A number of people become EMTs and paramedics to assess their interest in health care, and then decide to return to school and become registered nurses, physicians, or other health workers.

Employment

EMTs and paramedics held about 192,000 jobs in 2004. Most career EMTs and paramedics work in metropolitan areas. Volunteer EMTs and paramedics are more common in small cities, towns, and rural areas. These individuals volunteer for fire departments, emergency medical services (EMS), or hospitals, and may respond to only a few calls for service per month or may answer the majority of calls, especially in smaller communities. EMTs and paramedics work closely with fire fighters, who often are certified as EMTs as well and act as first responders. A large number of EMTs or paramedics belong to a union.

Full-time and part-time paid EMTs and paramedics were employed in a number of industries. About 4 out of 10 worked as employees of private ambulance services. About 3 out of 10 worked in local government for fire departments, public ambulance services, and EMS. Another 2 out of 10 were found in hospitals, working full time within the medical facility or responding to calls in ambulances or helicopters to transport critically ill or injured patients. The remainder worked in various industries providing emergency services.

Job Outlook

Employment of emergency medical technicians and paramedics is expected to grow much faster than the average for all occupations through 2014, as full-time paid EMTs and paramedics replace unpaid volunteers. As population and urbanization increase, and as a large segment of the population—aging baby boomers—becomes more likely to have medical emergencies, demand will increase for EMTs and paramedics. There will still be demand for part-time, volunteer EMTs and paramedics in rural areas and smaller metropolitan areas. In addition to jobs arising from growth, openings will occur because of replacement needs; turnover is relatively high in this occupation because of the limited potential for advancement and the modest pay and benefits in private-sector jobs.

Job opportunities should be best in private ambulance services. Competition will be greater for jobs in local government, including fire, police, and independent third-service rescue squad departments, in which salaries and benefits tend to be slightly better. EMTs and paramedics who have advanced certifications, such as EMT-Intermediate and EMT-Paramedic, should enjoy the most favorable job prospects as clients and patients demand higher levels of care before arriving at the hospital.

Earnings

Earnings of EMTs and paramedics depend on the employment setting and geographic location as well as the individual's training and experience. Median annual earnings of EMTs and paramedics were $25,310 in May 2004. The middle 50 percent earned between $19,970 and $33,210. The lowest 10 percent earned less than $16,090, and the highest 10 percent earned more than $43,240. Median annual earnings in the industries employing the largest numbers of EMTs and paramedics in May 2004 were:

Local government	$27,710
General medical and surgical hospitals	26,590
Other ambulatory health care services	23,130

Those in emergency medical services who are part of fire or police departments receive the same benefits as fire fighters or police officers. For example, many are covered by pension plans that provide retirement at half pay after 20 or 25 years of service or if the worker is disabled in the line of duty.

Related Occupations

Other workers in occupations that require quick and level-headed reactions to life-or-death situations are air traffic controllers, fire fighting occupations, physician assistants, police and detectives, and registered nurses.

Sources of Additional Information

General information about emergency medical technicians and paramedics is available from:

- National Association of Emergency Medical Technicians, P.O. Box 1400, Clinton, MS 39060-1400. Internet: http://www.naemt.org
- National Registry of Emergency Medical Technicians, Rocco V. Morando Bldg., 6610 Busch Blvd., P.O. Box 29233, Columbus, OH 43229. Internet: http://www.nremt.org
- National Highway Transportation Safety Administration, EMS Division, 400 7th St. SW, NTS-14, Washington, DC 20590. Internet: http://www.nhtsa.dot.gov/portal/site/nhtsa/menuitem.2a0771e91315babbbf30811060008a0c/

Engineers

(O*NET 17-2011.00, 17-2021.00, 17-2031.00, 17-2041.00, 17-2051.00, 17-2061.00, 17-2071.00, 17-2072.00, 17-2081.00, 17-2111.01, 17-2111.02, 17-2111.03, 17-2112.00, 17-2121.01, 17-2121.02, 17-2131.00, 17-2141.00, 17-2151.00, 17-2161.00, 17-2171.00, and 17-2199.99)

Significant Points

- Overall job opportunities in engineering are expected to be good, but will vary by specialty.
- A bachelor's degree is required for most entry-level jobs.
- Starting salaries are significantly higher than those of college graduates in other fields.
- Continuing education is critical for engineers wishing to enhance their value to employers as technology evolves.

Nature of the Work

Engineers apply the principles of science and mathematics to develop economical solutions to technical problems. Their work is the link between perceived social needs and commercial applications.

Engineers consider many factors when developing a new product. For example, in developing an industrial robot, engineers precisely specify the functional requirements; design and test the robot's components; integrate the components to produce the final design; and evaluate the design's overall effectiveness, cost, reliability, and safety. This process applies to the development of many different products, such as chemicals, computers, gas turbines, helicopters, and toys.

In addition to design and development, many engineers work in testing, production, or maintenance. These engineers supervise production in factories, determine the causes of component failure, and test manufactured products to maintain quality. They also estimate the time and cost to complete projects. Some move into engineering management or into sales. In sales, an engineering background enables them to discuss technical aspects and assist in product planning, installation, and use. Supervisory engineers are responsible for major components or entire projects.

Engineers use computers extensively to produce and analyze designs; to simulate and test how a machine, structure, or system operates; and to generate specifications for parts. Many engineers also use computers to monitor product quality and control process efficiency. The field of nanotechnology, which involves the creation of high-performance materials and components by integrating atoms and molecules, also is introducing entirely new principles to the design process.

Most engineers specialize. This section provides details on the 17 engineering specialties covered in the federal government's Standard Occupational Classification system and on engineering in general. Numerous specialties are recognized by professional societies, and the major branches of engineering have numerous subdivisions. Some examples include structural and transportation engineering, which are subdivisions of civil engineering; and ceramic, metallurgical, and polymer engineering, which are subdivisions of materials engineering. Engineers also may specialize in one industry, such as motor vehicles, or in one type of technology, such as turbines or semiconductor materials.

- **Aerospace engineers** design, develop, and test aircraft, spacecraft, and missiles and supervise the manufacture of these products. Those who work with aircraft are called *aeronautical engineers*, and those working specifically with spacecraft are *astronautical engineers.* Aerospace engineers develop new technologies for use in aviation, defense systems, and space exploration, often specializing in areas such as structural design, guidance, navigation and control, instrumentation and communication, or production methods. They also may specialize in a particular type of aerospace product, such as commercial aircraft, military fighter jets, helicopters, spacecraft, or missiles and rockets, and may become experts in aerodynamics, thermodynamics, celestial mechanics, propulsion, acoustics, or guidance and control systems.
- **Agricultural engineers** apply knowledge of engineering technology and science to agriculture and the efficient use of biological resources. They design agricultural machinery and equipment and agricultural structures. Some specialize in areas such as power systems and machinery design; structures and environment engineering; and food and bioprocess engineering. They develop ways to conserve soil and water and to improve the processing of agricultural products. Agricultural engineers often work in research and development, production, sales, or management.
- **Biomedical engineers** develop devices and procedures that solve medical and health-related problems by combining their knowledge of biology and medicine with engineering principles and practices. Many do research, along with life scientists, chemists, and medical scientists, to develop and evaluate systems and products such as artificial organs, prostheses (artificial devices that replace missing body parts), instrumentation, medical information systems, and health management and care delivery systems. Biomedical engineers may also design devices used in various medical procedures, imaging systems such as magnetic resonance imaging (MRI), and devices for automating insulin injections or controlling body functions. Most engineers in this specialty need a sound background in another engineering specialty, such as mechanical or electronics engineering, in addition to specialized biomedical training. Some specialties within biomedical engineering include biomaterials, biomechanics, medical imaging, rehabilitation engineering, and orthopedic engineering.
- **Chemical engineers** apply the principles of chemistry to solve problems involving the production or use of chemicals and biochemicals. They design equipment and processes for large-scale chemical manufacturing, plan and test methods of manufacturing products and treating byproducts, and supervise production. Chemical engineers also work in a variety of manufacturing industries other than chemical manufacturing, such as those producing energy, electronics, food, clothing, and paper. They also work in health care, biotechnology, and business services. Chemical engineers apply principles of chemistry, physics, mathematics, and mechanical and electrical engineering. Some may specialize in a particular chemical process, such as oxidation or polymerization. Others specialize in a particular field, such as materials science, or in the development of specific products. They must be aware of all aspects of chemicals manufacturing and how the manufacturing process affects the environment and the safety of workers and consumers.
- **Civil engineers** design and supervise the construction of roads, buildings, airports, tunnels, dams, bridges, and water supply and sewage systems. They must consider many factors in the design process, from the construction costs and expected lifetime of a project to government regulations and potential environmental hazards such as earthquakes. Civil engineering, considered one of the oldest engineering disciplines, encompasses many specialties. The major specialties are structural, water resources, construction, environmental, transportation, and geotechnical engineering. Many civil engineers hold supervisory or administrative positions, from supervisor of a construction site to city engineer. Others may work in design, construction, research, and teaching.
- **Computer hardware engineers** research, design, develop, test, and oversee the installation of computer hardware and supervise its manufacture and installation. Hardware refers to computer chips, circuit boards, computer systems, and related equipment such as keyboards, modems, and printers. The work of computer hardware engineers is very similar to that of electronics engineers, but, unlike electronics engineers, computer hardware engineers work exclusively with computers and computer-related equipment. The rapid advances in computer technology are largely a result of the research, development, and design efforts of computer hardware engineers.
- **Electrical engineers** design, develop, test, and supervise the manufacture of electrical equipment. Some of this equipment includes electric motors; machinery controls, lighting, and wiring in buildings; automobiles; aircraft; radar and navigation systems; and power-generating, -controlling, and transmission devices used by electric utilities. Although the terms "electrical" and "electronics" engineering often are used interchangeably in academia and industry, electrical engineers have traditionally focused on the generation and supply of power, whereas electronics engineers have worked on applications of electricity to control systems or signal processing. Electrical engineers specialize in areas such as power systems engineering or electrical equipment manufacturing.

- **Electronics engineers, except computer,** are responsible for a wide range of technologies, from portable music players to the global positioning system (GPS), which can continuously provide the location of a vehicle. Electronics engineers design, develop, test, and supervise the manufacture of electronic equipment such as broadcast and communications systems. Many electronics engineers also work in areas closely related to computers. However, engineers whose work is related exclusively to computer hardware are considered computer hardware engineers. Electronics engineers specialize in areas such as communications, signal processing, and control systems or have a specialty within one of these areas industrial robot control systems or aviation electronics, for example.
- **Environmental engineers** develop solutions to environmental problems using the principles of biology and chemistry. They are involved in water and air pollution control, recycling, waste disposal, and public health issues. Environmental engineers conduct hazardous-waste management studies in which they evaluate the significance of the hazard, advise on treatment and containment, and develop regulations to prevent mishaps. They design municipal water supply and industrial wastewater treatment systems. They conduct research on the environmental impact of proposed construction projects, analyze scientific data, and perform quality-control checks. Environmental engineers are concerned with local and worldwide environmental issues. They study and attempt to minimize the effects of acid rain, global warming, automobile emissions, and ozone depletion. They may also be involved in the protection of wildlife. Many environmental engineers work as consultants, helping their clients to comply with regulations and to clean up hazardous sites.
- **Health and safety engineers, except mining safety engineers and inspectors,** promote worksite or product safety by applying knowledge of industrial processes and mechanical, chemical, and human performance principles. Using this specialized knowledge, they identify and measure potential hazards to people or property, such as the risk of fires or the dangers involved in the handling of toxic chemicals. Health and safety engineers develop procedures and designs to reduce the risk of injury or damage. Some work in manufacturing industries to ensure the designs of new products do not create unnecessary hazards. They must be able to anticipate, recognize, and evaluate hazardous conditions, as well as develop hazard control methods.
- **Industrial engineers** determine the most effective ways to use the basic factors of production—people, machines, materials, information, and energy—to make a product or to provide a service. They are mostly concerned with increasing productivity through the management of people, methods of business organization, and technology. To solve organizational, production, and related problems efficiently, industrial engineers carefully study the product requirements, use mathematical methods to meet those requirements, and design manufacturing and information systems. They develop management control systems to aid in financial planning and cost analysis, and design production planning and control systems to coordinate activities and ensure product quality. They also design or improve systems for the physical distribution of goods and services, as well as determine the most efficient plant locations. Industrial engineers develop wage and salary administration systems and job evaluation programs. Many industrial engineers move into management positions because the work is closely related to the work of managers.
- **Marine engineers and naval architects** are involved in the design, construction, and maintenance of ships, boats, and related equipment. They design and supervise the construction of everything from aircraft carriers to submarines, and from sailboats to tankers. Naval architects work on the basic design of ships, including hull form and stability. Marine engineers work on the propulsion, steering, and other systems of ships. Marine engineers and naval architects apply knowledge from a range of fields to the entire design and production process of all water vehicles. Workers who operate or supervise the operation of marine machinery on ships and other vessels also may be called marine engineers or, more frequently, ship engineers.
- **Materials engineers** are involved in the development, processing, and testing of the materials used to create a range of products, from computer chips and television screens to golf clubs and snow skis. They work with metals, ceramics, plastics, semiconductors, and composites to create new materials that meet certain mechanical, electrical, and chemical requirements. They also are involved in selecting materials for new applications. Materials engineers have developed the ability to create and then study materials at an atomic level, using advanced processes to replicate the characteristics of materials and their components with computers. Most materials engineers specialize in a particular material. For example, metallurgical engineers specialize in metals such as steel, and ceramic engineers develop ceramic materials and the processes for making ceramic materials into useful products such as glassware or fiber-optic communication lines.
- **Mechanical engineers** research, develop, design, manufacture, and test tools, engines, machines, and other mechanical devices. They work on power-producing machines such as electric generators, internal combustion engines, and steam and gas turbines, as well as power-using machines such as refrigeration and air-conditioning equipment, machine tools, material handling systems, elevators and escalators, industrial production equipment, and robots used in manufacturing. Mechanical engineers also design tools that other engineers need for their work. Mechanical engineering is one of the broadest engineering disciplines. Mechanical engineers may work in production operations in manufacturing or agriculture, maintenance, or technical sales; many are administrators or managers.
- **Mining and geological engineers, including mining safety engineers,** find, extract, and prepare coal, metals, and minerals for use by manufacturing industries and utilities. They design open-pit and underground mines, supervise the construction of mine shafts and tunnels in underground operations, and devise methods for transporting minerals to processing plants. Mining engineers are responsible for the safe, economical, and environmentally sound operation of mines. Some mining engineers work with geologists and metallurgical engineers to locate and

appraise new ore deposits. Others develop new mining equipment or direct mineral- processing operations that separate minerals from the dirt, rock, and other materials with which they are mixed. Mining engineers frequently specialize in the mining of one mineral or metal, such as coal or gold. With increased emphasis on protecting the environment, many mining engineers work to solve problems related to land reclamation and water and air pollution. Mining safety engineers use their knowledge of mine design and practices to ensure the safety of workers and to comply with state and federal safety regulations. They inspect walls and roof surfaces, monitor air quality, and examine mining equipment for compliance with safety practices.

- **Nuclear engineers** research and develop the processes, instruments, and systems used to derive benefits from nuclear energy and radiation. They design, develop, monitor, and operate nuclear plants to generate power. They may work on the nuclear fuel cycle—the production, handling, and use of nuclear fuel and the safe disposal of waste produced by the generation of nuclear energy—or on the development of fusion energy. Some specialize in the development of nuclear power sources for spacecraft; others find industrial and medical uses for radioactive materials, as in equipment used to diagnose and treat medical problems.
- **Petroleum engineers** search the world for reservoirs containing oil or natural gas. Once these resources are discovered, petroleum engineers work with geologists and other specialists to understand the geologic formation and properties of the rock containing the reservoir, determine the drilling methods to be used, and monitor drilling and production operations. They design equipment and processes to achieve the maximum profitable recovery of oil and gas. Because only a small proportion of oil and gas in a reservoir flows out under natural forces, petroleum engineers develop and use various enhanced recovery methods. These include injecting water, chemicals, gases, or steam into an oil reservoir to force out more of the oil and doing computer-controlled drilling or fracturing to connect a larger area of a reservoir to a single well. Because even the best techniques in use today recover only a portion of the oil and gas in a reservoir, petroleum engineers research and develop technology and methods to increase recovery and lower the cost of drilling and production operations.

Working Conditions

Most engineers work in office buildings, laboratories, or industrial plants. Others may spend time outdoors at construction sites and oil and gas exploration and production sites, where they monitor or direct operations or solve onsite problems. Some engineers travel extensively to plants or worksites.

Many engineers work a standard 40-hour week. At times, deadlines or design standards may bring extra pressure to a job, requiring engineers to work longer hours.

Training, Other Qualifications, and Advancement

A bachelor's degree in engineering is required for almost all entry-level engineering jobs. College graduates with a degree in a physical science or mathematics occasionally may qualify for some engineering jobs, especially in specialties in high demand. Most engineering degrees are granted in electrical, electronics, mechanical, or civil engineering. However, engineers trained in one branch may work in related branches. For example, many aerospace engineers have training in mechanical engineering. This flexibility allows employers to meet staffing needs in new technologies and specialties in which engineers may be in short supply. It also allows engineers to shift to fields with better employment prospects or to those that more closely match their interests.

Most engineering programs involve a concentration of study in an engineering specialty, along with courses in both mathematics and the physical and life sciences. General courses not directly related to engineering, such as those in the social sciences or humanities, are often a required component of programs. Many programs also include courses in general engineering. A design course, sometimes accompanied by a computer or laboratory class or both, is part of the curriculum of most programs.

In addition to the standard engineering degree, many colleges offer 2- or 4-year degree programs in engineering technology. These programs, which usually include various hands-on laboratory classes that focus on current issues in the application of engineering principles, prepare students for practical design and production work, rather than for jobs that require more theoretical and scientific knowledge. Graduates of 4-year technology programs may get jobs similar to those obtained by graduates with a bachelor's degree in engineering. Engineering technology graduates, however, are not qualified to register as professional engineers under the same terms as graduates with degrees in engineering. Some employers regard technology program graduates as having skills between those of a technician and an engineer.

Graduate training is essential for engineering faculty positions and many research and development programs, but is not required for the majority of entry-level engineering jobs. Many engineers obtain graduate degrees in engineering or business administration to learn new technology and broaden their education. Many high-level executives in government and industry began their careers as engineers.

About 360 colleges and universities offer bachelor's degree programs in engineering that are accredited by the Accreditation Board for Engineering and Technology, Inc. (ABET), and about 230 colleges offer accredited programs in engineering technology. ABET accreditation is based on an examination of an engineering program's student achievement, program improvement, faculty, curriculum, facilities, and institutional commitment to certain principles of quality and ethics. Although most institutions offer programs in the major branches of engineering, only a few offer programs in the smaller specialties. Also, programs of the same title may vary in content. For example, some programs emphasize industrial practices, preparing students for a job in industry, whereas others are more theoretical and are designed to prepare students for graduate work. Therefore, students should investigate curriculums and check accreditations carefully before selecting a college.

Admissions requirements for undergraduate engineering schools include a solid background in mathematics (algebra, geometry, trigonometry, and calculus) and science (biology, chemistry, and physics), with courses in English, social studies, and humanities. Bachelor's degree programs in engineering typically are designed to last 4 years, but many students find that it takes between 4 and 5 years to complete their studies. In a typical 4-year college curriculum, the first 2 years are spent studying mathematics, basic sciences, introductory engineering, humanities, and social sciences. In the last 2 years, most courses are in engineering, usually with a concentration in one specialty. Some programs offer a general engineering curriculum; students then specialize on the job or in graduate school.

Some engineering schools and 2-year colleges have agreements whereby the 2-year college provides the initial engineering education, and the engineering school automatically admits students for their last 2 years. In addition, a few engineering schools have arrangements that allow students who spend 3 years in a liberal arts college studying pre-engineering subjects and 2 years in an engineering school studying core subjects to receive a bachelor's degree from each school. Some colleges and universities offer 5-year master's degree programs. Some 5-year or even 6-year cooperative plans combine classroom study and practical work, permitting students to gain valuable experience and to finance part of their education.

All 50 states and the District of Columbia require licensure for engineers who offer their services directly to the public. Engineers who are licensed are called professional engineers (PE). This licensure generally requires a degree from an ABET-accredited engineering program, 4 years of relevant work experience, and successful completion of a state examination. Recent graduates can start the licensing process by taking the examination in two stages. The initial Fundamentals of Engineering (FE) examination can be taken upon graduation. Engineers who pass this examination commonly are called engineers in training (EIT) or engineer interns (EI). After acquiring suitable work experience, EITs can take the second examination, the Principles and Practice of Engineering exam. Several states have imposed mandatory continuing education requirements for relicensure. Most states recognize licensure from other states, provided that the manner in which the initial license was obtained meets or exceeds their own licensure requirements. Many civil, electrical, mechanical, and chemical engineers are licensed PEs. Independent of licensure, various certification programs are offered by professional organizations to demonstrate competency in specific fields of engineering.

Engineers should be creative, inquisitive, analytical, and detail oriented. They should be able to work as part of a team and to communicate well, both orally and in writing. Communication abilities are important because engineers often interact with specialists in a wide range of fields outside engineering.

Beginning engineering graduates usually work under the supervision of experienced engineers and, in large companies, also may receive formal classroom or seminar-type training. As new engineers gain knowledge and experience, they are assigned more difficult projects with greater independence to develop designs, solve problems, and make decisions. Engineers may advance to become technical specialists or to supervise a staff or team of engineers and technicians. Some may eventually become engineering managers or enter other managerial or sales jobs.

Employment

In 2004 engineers held 1.4 million jobs. The distribution of employment by engineering specialty is as follows:

Total, all engineers	1,449,000	100%
Civil	237,000	16.4
Mechanical	226,000	15.6
Industrial	177,000	12.2
Electrical	156,000	10.8
Electronics, except computer	143,000	9.9
Computer hardware	77,000	5.3
Aerospace	76,000	5.2
Environmental	49,000	3.4
Chemical	31,000	2.1
Health and safety, except mining safety	27,000	1.8
Materials	21,000	1.5
Nuclear	17,000	1.2
Petroleum	16,000	1.1
Biomedical	9,700	0.7
Marine engineers and naval architects	6,800	0.5
Mining and geological, including mining safety	5,200	0.4
Agricultural	3,400	0.2
All other engineers	172,000	11.8

About 555,000 engineering jobs were found in manufacturing industries, and another 378,000 wage and salary jobs were in the professional, scientific, and technical services sector, primarily in architectural, engineering, and related services and in scientific research and development services. Many engineers also worked in the construction and transportation, telecommunications, and utilities industries.

Federal, state, and local governments employed about 194,000 engineers in 2004. About 91,000 of these were in the federal government, mainly in the U.S. Departments of Defense, Transportation, Agriculture, Interior, and Energy and in the National Aeronautics and Space Administration. Most engineers in state and local government agencies worked in highway and public works departments. In 2004, about 41,000 engineers were self-employed, many as consultants.

Engineers are employed in every state, in small and large cities and in rural areas. Some branches of engineering are concentrated in particular industries and geographic areas for example, petroleum engineering jobs tend to be located in areas with sizable petroleum deposits, such as Texas, Louisiana, Oklahoma, Alaska, and California. Others, such as civil engineering, are widely dispersed, and engineers in these fields often move from place to place to work on different projects.

Engineers are employed in every major industry. The industries employing the most engineers in each specialty are given in the table below, along with the percent of occupational employment in the industry.

Table 1. Percent concentration of engineering specialty employment in key industries, 2004

Specialty/Industry	Percent
Aerospace	
Aerospace product and parts manufacturing	59.6
Agricultural	
State and local government	22.6
Biomedical	
Scientific research and development services	18.7
Pharmaceutical and medicine manufacturing	15.6
Chemical	
Chemical manufacturing	27.8
Architectural, engineering, and related services	16.3
Civil	
Architectural, engineering, and related services	46.0
Computer hardware	
Computer and electronic product manufacturing	43.2
Computer systems design and related services	15.0
Electrical	
Architectural, engineering, and related services	19.6
Navigational, measuring, electromedical, and control instruments manufacturing	10.8
Electronics, except computer	
Telecommunications	17.5
Federal government	14.4
Environmental	
Architectural, engineering, and related services	28.9
State and local government	19.6
Health and safety, except mining safety	
State and local government	12.4
Industrial	
Machinery manufacturing	7.8
Motor vehicle parts manufacturing	7.1
Marine engineers and naval architects	
Architectural, engineering, and related services	34.5
Materials	
Computer and electronic product manufacturing	14.3
Mechanical	
Architectural, engineering, and related services	18.1
Machinery manufacturing	13.4
Mining and geological, including mining safety	
Mining	49.9
Nuclear	
Electric power generation, transmission and distribution	36.1
Petroleum	
Oil and gas extraction	47.4

Job Outlook

Overall engineering employment is expected to grow about as fast as the average for all occupations over the 2004–14 period. Engineers have traditionally been concentrated in slow-growing manufacturing industries, in which they will continue to be needed to design, build, test, and improve manufactured products. However, increasing employment of engineers in faster growing service industries should generate most of the employment growth. Overall job opportunities in engineering are expected to be favorable because the number of engineering graduates should be in rough balance with the number of job openings over this period. However, job outlook varies by specialty, as discussed later in this section.

Competitive pressures and advancing technology will force companies to improve and update product designs and to optimize their manufacturing processes. Employers will rely on engineers to further increase productivity as investment in plant and equipment increases to expand output of goods and services. New technologies continue to improve the design process, enabling engineers to produce and analyze various product designs much more rapidly than in the past. Unlike in other fields, however, technological advances are not expected to limit employment opportunities substantially, because they will permit the development of new products and processes.

There are many well-trained, often English-speaking engineers available around the world willing to work at much lower salaries than are U.S. engineers. The rise of the Internet has made it relatively easy for much of the engineering work previously done by engineers in this country to be done by engineers in other countries, a factor that will tend to hold down employment growth. Even so, the need for onsite engineers to interact with other employees and with clients will remain.

Compared with most other workers, a smaller proportion of engineers leave their jobs each year. Nevertheless, many job openings will arise from replacement needs, reflecting the large size of this profession. Numerous job openings will be created by engineers who transfer to management, sales, or other professional occupations; additional openings will arise as engineers retire or leave the labor force for other reasons.

Many engineers work on long-term research and development projects or in other activities that continue even during economic slowdowns. In industries such as electronics and aerospace, however, large cutbacks in defense expenditures and in government funding for research and development have resulted in significant layoffs of engineers in the past. The trend toward contracting for engineering work with engineering services firms, both domestic and foreign, has had the same result.

It is important for engineers, as it is for those working in other technical and scientific occupations, to continue their education throughout their careers because much of their value to their employer depends on their knowledge of the latest technology. Engineers in high-technology areas, such as advanced electronics or information technology, may find that technical knowledge can become outdated rapidly. By keeping current in their field, engineers are able to deliver the best solutions and greatest value to their employers. Engineers who have not kept current in their field may find themselves passed over for promotions or vulnerable to layoffs.

The following section discusses job outlook by engineering specialty.

- **Aerospace engineers** are expected to have slower-than-average growth in employment over the projection period. Although increases in the number and scope of military aerospace projects likely will generate new jobs, increased efficiency will limit the number of new jobs in the design and production of commercial aircraft. Even with slow growth, the employment outlook for aerospace engineers through 2014 appears favorable: the number of degrees granted in aerospace engineering declined for many years because of a perceived lack of opportunities in this field, and, although this trend is reversing, new graduates continue to be needed to replace aerospace engineers who retire or leave the occupation for other reasons.
- **Agricultural engineers** are expected to have employment growth about as fast as the average for all occupations through 2014. The growing interest in worldwide standardization of agricultural equipment should result in increased employment of agricultural engineers. Job opportunities also should result from the need to feed a growing population, develop more efficient agricultural production, and conserve resources.
- **Biomedical engineers** are expected to have employment growth that is much faster than the average for all occupations through 2014. The aging of the population and the focus on health issues will drive demand for better medical devices and equipment designed by biomedical engineers. Along with the demand for more sophisticated medical equipment and procedures, an increased concern for cost- effectiveness will boost demand for biomedical engineers, particularly in pharmaceutical manufacturing and related industries. However, because of the growing interest in this field, the number of degrees granted in biomedical engineering has increased greatly. Biomedical engineers, particularly those with only a bachelor's degree, may face competition for jobs. Unlike the case for many other engineering specialties, a graduate degree is recommended or required for many entry-level jobs.
- **Chemical engineers** are expected to have employment growth about as fast as the average for all occupations though 2014. Although overall employment in the chemical manufacturing industry is expected to decline, chemical companies will continue to research and develop new chemicals and more efficient processes to increase output of existing chemicals. Among manufacturing industries, pharmaceuticals may provide the best opportunities for jobseekers. However, most employment growth for chemical engineers will be in service industries such as scientific research and development services, particularly in energy and the developing fields of biotechnology and nanotechnology.
- **Civil engineers** are expected to see average employment growth through 2014. Spurred by general population growth and an increased emphasis on infrastructure security, more civil engineers will be needed to design and construct safe and higher capacity transportation, water supply, and pollution control systems, as well as large buildings and building complexes. They also will be needed to repair or replace existing roads, bridges, and other public structures. Because construction and related industries—including those providing design services—employ many civil engineers, employment opportunities will vary by geographic area and may decrease during economic slowdowns, when construction often is curtailed.
- **Computer hardware engineers** are expected to have average employment growth through 2014. Although the use of information technology continues to expand rapidly, the manufacture of computer hardware is expected to be adversely affected by intense foreign competition. As computer and semiconductor manufacturing contract out more of their engineering needs, much of the growth in employment should occur in the computer systems design and related services industry. However, use of foreign computer hardware engineering services also will serve to limit job growth. Computer engineers should still have favorable employment opportunities, as the number of new entrants is expected to be in balance with demand.
- **Electrical engineers** should have favorable employment opportunities. The number of job openings resulting from employment growth and from the need to replace electrical engineers who transfer to other occupations or leave the labor force is expected to be in rough balance with the supply of graduates. Employment of electrical engineers is expected to increase about as fast as the average for all occupations through 2014. Although international competition and the use of engineering services performed in other countries may limit employment growth, strong demand for electrical devices such as giant electric power generators or wireless phone transmitters should boost growth. Prospects should be particularly good for electrical engineers working in engineering services firms providing technical expertise to other companies on specific projects.
- **Electronics engineers, except computer,** should have good job opportunities, and employment is expected to increase about as fast as the average for all occupations through 2014. Although rising demand for electronic goods—including advanced communications equipment, defense-related electronic equipment, medical electronics, and consumer products—should continue to increase employment, foreign competition in electronic products development and the use of engineering services performed in other countries will act to limit employment growth. Job growth is expected to be fastest in service-providing industries—particularly consulting firms that provide expertise in electronics engineering.
- **Environmental engineers** should have favorable job opportunities. Employment of environmental engineers is expected to increase much faster than the average for all occupations through 2014. More environmental engineers will be needed to comply with environmental regulations and to develop methods of cleaning up existing hazards. A shift in emphasis toward preventing problems rather than controlling those that already exist, as well as increasing public health concerns, also will spur demand for environmental engineers. Even though employment of environmental engineers should be less affected by economic conditions than that of most other types of engineers, a significant economic downturn could reduce the emphasis on environmental protection, reducing environmental engineers' job opportunities.
- **Health and safety engineers, except mining safety engineers and inspectors,** are projected to experience average employ-

ment growth through 2014. Because the main function of health and safety engineers is to make products and production processes as safe as possible, their services should be in demand as concern for health and safety within work environments increases. As new technologies for production or processing are developed, health and safety engineers will be needed to ensure their safety.

- **Industrial engineers** are expected to have employment growth about as fast as the average for all occupations through 2014. As firms seek to reduce costs and increase productivity, they increasingly will turn to industrial engineers to develop more efficient processes to reduce costs, delays, and waste. Because their work is similar to that done in management occupations, many industrial engineers leave the occupation to become managers. Many openings will be created by the need to replace industrial engineers who transfer to other occupations or leave the labor force.
- **Marine engineers and naval architects** likely will experience employment growth that is slower than the average for all occupations. Strong demand for naval vessels and for yachts and other small craft should more than offset the long-term decline in the domestic design and construction of large ocean-going vessels. There should be good prospects for marine engineers and naval architects because of growth in employment, the need to replace workers who retire or take other jobs, and the limited number of students pursuing careers in this occupation.
- **Materials engineers, including mining safety engineers,** are expected to have employment growth about as fast as the average for all occupations through 2014. Although many of the manufacturing industries in which materials engineers are concentrated are expected to experience declining employment, materials engineers still will be needed to develop new materials for electronics, biotechnology, and plastics products. Growth should be particularly strong for materials engineers working on nanomaterials and biomaterials. As manufacturing firms contract for their materials engineering needs, employment growth is expected in professional, scientific, and technical services industries.
- **Mechanical engineers** are projected to have an average rate of employment growth through 2014. Although total employment in manufacturing industries—in which employment of mechanical engineers is concentrated—is expected to decline, employment of mechanical engineers in manufacturing should increase as the demand for improved machinery and machine tools grows and as industrial machinery and processes become increasingly complex. Also, emerging technologies in biotechnology, materials science, and nanotechnology will create new job opportunities for mechanical engineers. Additional opportunities for mechanical engineers will arise because the skills acquired through earning a degree in mechanical engineering often can be applied in other engineering specialties.
- **Mining and geological engineers, including mining safety engineers**, are expected to have good employment opportunities, despite a projected decline in employment. Many mining engineers currently employed are approaching retirement age, a factor that should create some job openings over the 2004–14 period. In addition, relatively few schools offer mining engineering programs, and the small number of yearly graduates is not expected to increase substantially. Favorable job opportunities also may be available worldwide as mining operations around the world recruit graduates of U.S. mining engineering programs. As a result, some graduates may travel frequently or even live abroad. Employment of mining and geological engineers, including mining safety engineers, is projected to decline through 2014, primarily because most of the industries in which mining engineers are concentrated—such as coal, metal, and copper mining—are expected to experience declines in employment.
- **Nuclear engineers** are expected to have good opportunities because the small number of nuclear engineering graduates is likely to be in rough balance with the number of job openings. Employment of nuclear engineers is expected to grow more slowly than the average for all occupations through 2014. Most openings will result from the need to replace nuclear engineers who transfer to other occupations or leave the labor force. Although no commercial nuclear power plants have been built in the United States for many years, nuclear engineers will be needed to operate existing plants. In addition, nuclear engineers may be needed to research and develop future nuclear power sources. They also will be needed to work in defense-related areas, to develop nuclear medical technology, and to improve and enforce waste management and safety standards.
- **Petroleum engineers** are expected to have a decline in employment through 2014 because most of the potential petroleum-producing areas in the United States already have been explored. Even so, favorable opportunities are expected for petroleum engineers because the number of job openings is likely to exceed the relatively small number of graduates. All job openings should result from the need to replace petroleum engineers who transfer to other occupations or leave the labor force. Petroleum engineers work around the world and, in fact, the best employment opportunities may be in other countries. Many foreign employers seek U.S.-trained petroleum engineers, and many U.S. employers maintain overseas branches.

Earnings

Earnings for engineers vary significantly by specialty, industry, and education. Even so, as a group, engineers earn some of the highest average starting salaries among those holding bachelor's degrees. The following tabulation shows average starting salary offers for engineers, according to a 2005 survey by the National Association of Colleges and Employers.

Curriculum	Bachelor's	Master's	Ph.D.
Aerospace/aeronautical/ astronautical	$50,993	$62,930	$72,529
Agricultural	46,172	53,022	
Bioengineering & biomedical	48,503	59,667	
Chemical	53,813	57,260	79,591
Civil	43,679	48,050	59,625
Computer	52,464	60,354	69,625

Curriculum	Bachelor's	Master's	Ph.D.
Electrical/electronics & communications	51,888	64,416	80,206
Environmental/ environmental health	47,384		
Industrial/manufacturing	49,567	56,561	85,000
Materials	50,982		
Mechanical	50,236	59,880	68,299
Mining & mineral	48,643		
Nuclear	51,182	58,814	
Petroleum	61,516	58,000	

Variation in median earnings and in the earnings distributions for engineers in the various branches of engineering also is significant. For engineers in specialties covered in this statement, earnings distributions by percentile in May 2004 are shown in the following tabulation.

Specialty	10%	25%	50%	75%	90%
Aerospace	$52,820	$64,380	$79,100	$94,900	$113,520
Agricultural	37,680	43,270	56,520	77,740	90,410
Biomedical	41,260	51,620	67,690	86,400	107,530
Chemical	49,030	60,920	76,770	94,740	115,180
Civil	42,610	51,430	64,230	79,920	94,660
Computer hardware	50,490	63,730	81,150	102,100	123,560
Electrical	47,310	57,540	71,610	88,400	108,070
Electronics, except computer	49,120	60,280	75,770	92,870	112,200
Environmental	40,620	50,740	66,480	83,690	100,050
Health and safety, except mining safety	39,930	49,900	63,730	79,500	92,870
Industrial	42,450	52,210	65,020	79,830	93,950
Marine engineers and naval architects	43,790	54,530	72,040	89,900	109,190
Materials	44,130	53,510	67,110	83,830	101,120
Mechanical	43,900	53,070	66,320	82,380	97,850
Mining and geological, including mining safety	39,700	50,500	64,690	83,050	103,790
Nuclear	61,790	73,340	84,880	100,220	118,870
Petroleum	48,260	65,350	88,500	113,180	140,800

In the federal government, mean annual salaries for engineers ranged from $100,059 in ceramic engineering to $70,086 in agricultural engineering in 2005.

Related Occupations

Engineers apply the principles of physical science and mathematics in their work. Other workers who use scientific and mathematical principles include architects, except landscape and naval; engineering and natural sciences managers; computer and information systems managers; computer programmers; Computer software engineers; mathematicians; drafters; engineering technicians; sales engineers; science technicians; and physical and life scientists, including agricultural and food scientists, biological scientists, conservation scientists and foresters, atmospheric scientists, chemists and materials scientists, environmental scientists and hydrologists, geoscientists, and physicists and astronomers.

Sources of Additional Information

Information about careers in engineering is available from:

- JETS, 1420 King St., Suite 405, Alexandria, VA 22314-2794. Internet: http://www.jets.org

Information on ABET-accredited engineering programs is available from:

- Accreditation Board for Engineering and Technology, Inc., 111 Market Place, Suite 1050, Baltimore, MD 21202-4012. Internet: http://www.abet.org

Those interested in information on the Professional Engineer licensure should contact:

- National Society of Professional Engineers, 1420 King St., Alexandria, VA 22314-2794. Internet: http://www.nspe.org
- National Council of Examiners for Engineering and Surveying, P.O. Box 1686, Clemson, SC 29633-1686. Internet: http://www.ncees.org

Information on general engineering education and career resources is available from:

- American Society for Engineering Education, 1818 N St. NW, Suite 600, Washington, DC 20036 2479. Internet: http://www.asee.org

Information on obtaining positions as engineers with the federal government is available from the Office of Personnel Management through USAJOBS, the federal government's official employment information system. This resource for locating and applying for job opportunities can be accessed through the Internet at http://www.usajobs.opm.gov or through an interactive voice response telephone system at (703) 724-1850 or TDD (978) 461-8404. These numbers are not toll free, and charges may result.

For more detailed information on an engineering specialty, contact societies representing the individual branches of engineering. Each can provide information about careers in the particular branch.

Aerospace engineers

- Aerospace Industries Association, 1000 Wilson Blvd., Suite 1700, Arlington, VA 22209-3901. Internet: http://www.aia-aerospace.org
- American Institute of Aeronautics and Astronautics, Inc., 1801 Alexander Bell Dr., Suite 500, Reston, VA 20191-4344. Internet: http://www.aiaa.org

Agricultural engineers

- American Society of Agricultural and Biological Engineers, 2950 Niles Rd., St. Joseph, MI 49085-9659. Internet: http://www.asabe.org

Biomedical engineers

- Biomedical Engineering Society, 8401 Corporate Dr., Suite 225, Landover, MD 20785-2224. Internet: http://www.bmes.org

Chemical engineers

- American Institute of Chemical Engineers, 3 Park Ave., New York, NY 10016-5991. Internet: http://www.aiche.org
- American Chemical Society, Department of Career Services, 1155 16th St. NW, Washington, DC 20036. Internet: http://www.chemistry.org/portal/Chemistry

Civil engineers

- American Society of Civil Engineers, 1801 Alexander Bell Dr., Reston, VA 20191-4400. Internet: http://www.asce.org

Computer hardware engineers

- IEEE Computer Society, 1730 Massachusetts Ave. NW, Washington, DC 20036-1992. Internet: http://www.computer.org

Electrical and electronics engineers

- Institute of Electrical and Electronics Engineers—USA, 1828 L St. NW, Suite 1202, Washington, DC 20036. Internet: http://www.ieeeusa.org

Environmental engineers

- American Academy of Environmental Engineers, 130 Holiday Court, Suite 100, Annapolis, MD 21401. Internet: http://www.aaee.net

Health and safety engineers

- American Society of Safety Engineers, 1800 E Oakton St., Des Plaines, IL 60018. Internet: http://www.asse.org
- Board of Certified Safety Professionals, 208 Burwash Ave., Savoy, IL 61874. Internet: http://www.bcsp.org

Industrial engineers

- Institute of Industrial Engineers, 3577 Parkway Lane, Suite 200, Norcross, GA 30092. Internet: http://www.iienet.org

Materials engineers

- The Minerals, Metals, & Materials Society, 184 Thorn Hill Rd., Warrendale, PA 15086-7514. Internet: http://www.tms.org
- ASM International, 9639 Kinsman Rd., Materials Park, OH 44073-0002. Internet: http://www.asminternational.org

Mechanical engineers

- The American Society of Mechanical Engineers, 3 Park Ave., New York, NY 10016-5990. Internet: http://www.asme.org
- American Society of Heating, Refrigerating, and Air-Conditioning Engineers, Inc., 1791 Tullie Circle NE, Atlanta, GA 30329. Internet: http://www.ashrae.org
- Society of Automotive Engineers, 400 Commonwealth Dr., Warrendale, PA 15096-0001. Internet: http://www.sae.org

Marine engineers and naval architects

- Society of Naval Architects and Marine Engineers, 601 Pavonia Ave., Jersey City, NJ 07306. Internet: http://www.sname.org

Mining and geological engineers, including mining safety engineers

- The Society for Mining, Metallurgy, and Exploration, Inc., 8307 Shaffer Parkway, Littleton, CO 80127-4102. Internet: http://www.smenet.org

Nuclear engineers

- American Nuclear Society, 555 North Kensington Ave., LaGrange Park, IL 60526. Internet: http://www.ans.org

Petroleum engineers

- Society of Petroleum Engineers, P.O. Box 833836, Richardson, TX 75083-3836. Internet: http://www.spe.org

Financial Analysts and Personal Financial Advisors

(O*NET 13-2051.00 and 13-2052.00)

Significant Points

- A college degree and good interpersonal skills are among the most important qualifications for these workers.
- Although both occupations will benefit from an increase in investing by individuals, personal financial advisors will benefit more.
- Financial analysts and personal financial advisors who have earned a professional designation are expected to have the best opportunities; competition is anticipated to be keen for highly lucrative positions in investment banking.
- About 4 out of 10 personal financial advisors are self-employed.

Nature of the Work

Financial analysts and personal financial advisors provide analysis and guidance to businesses and individuals to help them with their investment decisions. Both types of specialists gather financial information, analyze it, and make recommendations to their clients. However, their job duties differ because of the type of investment information they provide and the clients for whom they work. *Financial analysts* assess the economic performance of companies and industries for firms and institutions with money to invest. *Personal financial advisors* generally assess the financial needs of individuals, offering them a wide range of options.

Financial analysts, also called *securities analysts* and *investment analysts*, work for banks, insurance companies, mutual and pension funds, securities firms, and other businesses, helping these companies or their clients make investment decisions. Financial analysts read company financial statements and analyze commodity prices, sales, costs, expenses, and tax rates in order to determine a company's value and to project its future earnings. They often meet with company officials to gain a better insight into the firm's prospects and to determine its managerial effectiveness. Usually, financial analysts study an entire industry, assessing current trends in business practices, products, and industry competition. They must keep abreast of new regulations or policies that may affect the industry, as well as monitor the economy to determine its effect on earnings.

Financial analysts use spreadsheet and statistical software packages to analyze financial data, spot trends, and develop forecasts. On the basis of their results, they write reports and make presentations, usually making recommendations to buy or sell a particular investment or security. Senior analysts may even be the ones who decide to buy or sell if they are responsible for managing the company's or client's assets. Other analysts use the data they find to measure the financial risks associated with making a particular investment decision.

Financial analysts in investment banking departments of securities or banking firms often work in teams, analyzing the future prospects of companies that want to sell shares to the public for the first time. They also ensure that the forms and written materials necessary for compliance with Securities and Exchange Commission regulations are accurate and complete. They may make presentations to prospective investors about the merits of investing in the new company. Financial analysts also work in mergers and acquisitions departments, preparing analyses on the costs and benefits of a proposed merger or takeover.

Some financial analysts, called *ratings analysts*, evaluate the ability of companies or governments that issue bonds to repay their debts. On the basis of their evaluation, a management team assigns a rating to a company's or government's bonds. Other financial analysts perform budget, cost, and credit analysis as part of their responsibilities.

Personal financial advisors, also called *financial planners* or *financial consultants*, use their knowledge of investments, tax laws, and insurance to recommend financial options to individuals in accordance with the individual's short-term and long-term goals. Some of the issues that planners address are retirement and estate planning, funding for college, and general investment options. While most planners offer advice on a wide range of topics, some specialize in areas such as retirement and estate planning or risk management.

An advisor's work begins with a consultation with the client, from whom the advisor obtains information on the client's finances and financial goals. The advisor then develops a comprehensive financial plan that identifies problem areas, makes recommendations for improvement, and selects appropriate investments compatible with the client's goals, attitude toward risk, and expectation or need for a return on the investment. Sometimes this plan is written, but more often it is in the form of verbal advice. Financial advisors usually meet with established clients at least once a year to update them on potential investments and to determine whether the clients have been through any life changes—such as marriage, disability, or retirement—that might affect their financial goals. Financial advisors also answer questions from clients regarding changes in benefit plans or the consequences of a change in their jobs or careers. A large part of the success of financial planners depends on their ability to educate their clients about risks and various possible scenarios so that the clients don't harbor unrealistic expectations.

Some advisors buy and sell financial products, such as mutual funds or insurance, or refer clients to other companies for products and services—for example, the preparation of taxes or wills. A number of advisors take on the responsibility of managing the clients' investments for them.

Finding clients and building a customer base is one of the most important of a financial advisor's job, because referrals from satisfied clients are an important source of new business. Many advisors also contact potential clients by giving seminars or lectures or meet clients through business and social contacts.

Working Conditions

Financial analysts and personal financial advisors usually work indoors in safe, comfortable offices or their own homes. Many of these workers enjoy the challenge of helping firms or people make financial decisions. However, financial analysts may face long hours, frequent travel to visit companies and talk to potential investors, and the pressure of deadlines. Much of their research must be done after office hours, because their day is filled with telephone calls and meetings. Personal financial advisors usually work standard business hours, but they also schedule meetings with clients in the evenings or on weekends. Many teach evening classes or hold seminars in order to bring in more clients.

Training, Other Qualifications, and Advancement

A college education is required for financial analysts and is strongly preferred for personal financial advisors. Most companies require financial analysts to have at least a bachelor's degree in business administration, accounting, statistics, or finance. Coursework in statistics, economics, and business is required, and knowledge of accounting policies and procedures, corporate budgeting, and financial analysis methods is recommended. A master's degree in business administration is desirable. Advanced courses in options pricing or bond valuation and knowledge of risk management also are suggested.

Employers usually do not require a specific field of study for personal financial advisors, but a bachelor's degree in accounting, finance, economics, business, mathematics, or law provides good preparation for the occupation. Courses in investments, taxes, estate planning, and risk management also are helpful. Programs in financial planning are becoming more widely available in colleges and universities. Working for a broker-dealer is a good way to gain experience that can help individuals pass the security license exams needed to practice financial planning. Individuals who start out as independent financial planners may find it more difficult to build their client base, and they often start by servicing their family members and friends. However, many financial planners enter the field after working in a related occupation, such as accountant; auditor; insurance sales agent; lawyer; or securities, commodities, and financial services sales agent.

Mathematical, computer, analytical, and problem-solving skills are essential qualifications for financial analysts and personal financial advisors. Good communication skills also are necessary, because these workers must present complex financial concepts and strategies in easy-to-understand language to clients and other professionals. Self-confidence, maturity, and the ability to work independently are important as well. Financial analysts must be detail oriented, motivated to seek out obscure information, and familiar with the workings of the economy, tax laws, and money markets. Strong interpersonal skills and sales ability are crucial to the success of both financial analysts and personal financial advisors.

Although not required for financial analysts or personal financial advisors to practice, certification can enhance one's professional standing and is strongly recommended by many employers. Financial analysts may receive the Chartered Financial Analyst (CFA) designation, sponsored by the CFA Institute. To qualify for this designation, applicants need a bachelor's degree and 3 years of work experience in a related field and must pass a series of three examinations. These essay exams, administered once a year for 3 years, cover subjects such as accounting, economics, securities analysis, financial markets and instruments, corporate finance, asset valuation, and portfolio management. Personal financial advisors may obtain the Certified Financial Planner credential, often referred to as CFP (R), demonstrating extensive training and competency in financial planning. This certification, issued by the Certified Financial Planner Board of Standards, requires relevant experience, the completion of education requirements, passing a comprehensive examination, and adherence to an enforceable code of ethics. The CFP (R) exams test the candidate's knowledge of the financial planning process, insurance and risk management, employee benefits planning, taxes and retirement planning, and investment and estate planning. The exam has been revised in recent years. Candidates are now required to have a working knowledge of debt management, planning liability, emergency fund reserves, and statistical modeling. It may take from 2 to 3 years of study to complete these programs.

Personal financial advisors also may obtain the Chartered Financial Consultant (ChFC) designation, issued by the American College in Bryn Mawr, Pennsylvania, which requires experience and the completion of an eight-course program of study. The ChFC designation and other professional designations have continuing education requirements.

A license is not required to work as a personal financial advisor, but advisors who sell stocks, bonds, mutual funds, insurance, or real estate may need licenses to perform these additional services. Also, if legal advice is provided, a license to practice law may be required. Financial advisors who do not offer these additional services often refer clients to those who are qualified to provide them.

Financial analysts may advance by becoming portfolio managers or financial managers, directing the investment portfolios of their companies or of clients. Personal financial advisors who work in firms also may move into managerial positions, but most advisors advance by accumulating clients and managing more assets.

Employment

Financial analysts and personal financial advisors held 355,000 jobs in 2004, of which financial analysts held 197,000. Many financial analysts work at the headquarters of large financial companies, several of which are based in New York City. More than 4 out of 10 financial analysts work for finance and insurance industries, including securities and commodity brokers, banks and credit institutions, and insurance carriers. Others worked throughout private industry and government.

Personal financial advisors held 158,000 jobs in 2004. Much like financial analysts, more than half work for finance and insurance industries, including securities and commodity brokers, banks, insurance carriers, and financial investment firms. However, 4 out of 10 personal financial advisors are self-employed, operating small investment advisory firms, usually in urban areas.

Job Outlook

Overall employment of financial analysts and personal financial advisors is expected to increase faster than average for all occupations through 2014, resulting from increased investment by businesses and individuals. Personal financial advisors will benefit even more than financial analysts as baby boomers save for retirement and as a generally better educated and wealthier population requires investment advice. In addition, people are living longer and must plan to finance more years of retirement. The globalization of the securities markets also will increase the need for analysts and advisors to help investors make financial choices. Financial analysts and personal financial advisors who have earned a professional designation are expected to have the best opportunities.

Deregulation of the financial services industry is expected to spur demand for financial analysts and personal financial advisors. In recent years, banks, insurance companies, and brokerage firms have been allowed to broaden their financial services. Many firms are adding investment advice to their list of services and are expected to increase their hiring of personal financial advisors. Many banks are entering the securities brokerage and investment banking fields and will increasingly need the skills of financial analysts.

Employment of personal financial advisors is projected to grow faster than the average for all occupations. The rapid expansion of self-directed retirement plans, such as 401(k) plans, is expected to continue. As the number and complexity of investments rises, more individuals will look to financial advisors to help manage their money.

Employment of financial analysts is expected to grow about as fast as the average for all occupations. As the number of mutual funds and the amount of assets invested in the funds increase, mutual fund companies will need increased numbers of financial analysts to recommend which financial products the funds should buy or sell.

Financial analysts also will be needed in the investment banking field, where they help companies raise money and work on corporate mergers and acquisitions. However, growth in demand for financial analysts to do company research has been, and will continue to be, constrained by regulations that require investment firms to separate research from investment banking. As a result, firms have eliminated research jobs in an effort to contain the costs of implementing these regulations.

Demand for financial analysts in investment banking fluctuates because investment banking is sensitive to changes in the stock market. In addition, further consolidation in the finance industries may eliminate some financial analyst positions, dampening overall employment growth somewhat. Competition is expected to be keen for these highly lucrative positions, with many more applicants than jobs.

Earnings

Median annual earnings of financial analysts were $61,910 in May 2004. The middle 50 percent earned between $47,410 and $82,730. The lowest 10 percent earned less than $37,580, and the highest 10 percent earned more than $113,490. Median annual earnings in the industries employing the largest numbers of financial analysts in 2004 were as follows:

Other financial investment activities $74,580
Securities and commodity contracts
intermediation and brokerage 67,730

Management of companies and enterprises 62,890
Insurance carriers 58,120
Depository credit intermediation 56,860

Median annual earnings of personal financial advisors were $62,700 in May 2004. The middle 50 percent earned between $41,860 and $108,280. Median annual earnings in the industries employing the largest number of personal financial advisors in 2004 were as follows:

Other financial investment activities $78,350
Securities and commodity contracts intermediation and brokerage 63,310
Depository credit intermediation 57,180
Agencies, brokerages, and other insurance related activities..56,950

Many financial analysts receive a bonus in addition to their salary, and the bonus can add substantially to their earnings. Usually, the bonus is based on how well their predictions compare to the actual performance of a benchmark investment. Personal financial advisors who work for financial services firms are generally paid a salary plus bonus. Advisors who work for financial investment or planning firms or who are self-employed either charge hourly fees for their services or charge one set fee for a comprehensive plan, based on its complexity. Advisors who manage a client's assets may charge a percentage of those assets. Advisors generally receive commissions for financial products they sell, in addition to charging a fee.

Related Occupations

Other jobs requiring expertise in finance and investment or in the sale of financial products include accountants and auditors; financial managers, insurance sales agents, real estate brokers and sales agents; and securities, commodities, and financial services sales agents.

Sources of Additional Information

For information on a career in financial planning, contact:

- The Financial Planning Association, 4100 E. Mississippi Ave., Suite 400, Denver, CO 80246-3053. Internet: http://www.fpanet.org

For information about the Certified Financial Planner (CFP) (R) certification, contact:

- Certified Financial Planner Board of Standards, Inc., 1670 Broadway, Suite 600, Denver, CO 80202-4809. Internet: http://www.cfp.net/become

For information about the Chartered Financial Consultant (ChFC) designation, contact:

- The American College, 270 South Bryn Mawr Ave., Bryn Mawr, PA 19010. Internet: http://www.theamericancollege.edu

For information on a career as a financial analyst, contact either of the following organizations:

- American Academy of Financial Management, 2 Canal St., Suite 2317, New Orleans, LA 70130. Internet: http://www.financialanalyst.org
- CFA Institute, P.O. Box 3668, 560 Ray C. Hunt Dr., Charlottesville, VA 22903. Internet: http://www.cfainstitute.org

Financial Managers

(O*NET 11-3031.01 and 11-3031.02)

Significant Points

- About 3 out of 10 work in finance and insurance industries.
- A bachelor's degree in finance, accounting, or a related field is the minimum academic preparation, but many employers increasingly seek graduates with a master's degree in business administration, economics, finance, or risk management.
- Experience may be more important than formal education for some financial manager positions—most notably, branch managers in banks.
- Jobseekers are likely to face competition.

Nature of the Work

Almost every firm, government agency, and other type of organization has one or more financial managers who oversee the preparation of financial reports, direct investment activities, and implement cash management strategies. Because computers are increasingly used to record and organize data, many financial managers are spending more time developing strategies and implementing the long-term goals of their organization.

The duties of financial managers vary with their specific titles, which include controller, treasurer or finance officer, credit manager, cash manager, and risk and insurance manager. *Controllers* direct the preparation of financial reports that summarize and forecast the organization's financial position, such as income statements, balance sheets, and analyses of future earnings or expenses. Controllers also are in charge of preparing special reports required by regulatory authorities. Often, controllers oversee the accounting, audit, and budget departments. *Treasurers* and *finance officers* direct the organization's financial goals, objectives, and budgets. They oversee the investment of funds, manage associated risks, supervise cash management activities, execute capital-raising strategies to support a firm's expansion, and deal with mergers and acquisitions. *Credit managers* oversee the firm's issuance of credit, establishing credit-rating criteria, determining credit ceilings, and monitoring the collections of past-due accounts. Managers specializing in international finance develop financial and accounting systems for the banking transactions of multinational organizations.

Cash managers monitor and control the flow of cash receipts and disbursements to meet the business and investment needs of the firm. For example, cash flow projections are needed to determine whether loans must be obtained to meet cash requirements or whether surplus cash should be invested in interest-bearing instruments. *Risk* and *insurance managers* oversee programs to minimize risks and losses that might arise from financial transactions and business operations undertaken by the institution. They also manage the organization's insurance budget.

Financial institutions, such as commercial banks, savings and loan associations, credit unions, and mortgage and finance companies, employ additional financial managers who oversee various functions, such as lending, trusts, mortgages, and investments, or programs, including sales, operations, or electronic financial services. These managers may be required to solicit business, authorize loans, and direct the investment of funds, always adhering to federal and state laws and regulations.

Branch managers of financial institutions administer and manage all of the functions of a branch office, which may include hiring personnel, approving loans and lines of credit, establishing a rapport with the community to attract business, and assisting customers with account problems. The trend is for branch managers to become more oriented toward sales and marketing. It is important that they have substantial knowledge about all types of products that the bank sells. Financial managers who work for financial institutions must keep abreast of the rapidly growing array of financial services and products.

In addition to carrying out the preceding general duties, all financial managers perform tasks unique to their organization or industry. For example, government financial managers must be experts on the government appropriations and budgeting processes, whereas health care financial managers must be knowledgeable about issues surrounding health care financing. Moreover, financial managers must be aware of special tax laws and regulations that affect their industry.

Financial managers play an increasingly important role in mergers and consolidations and in global expansion and related financing. These areas require extensive, specialized knowledge on the part of the financial manager to reduce risks and maximize profit. Financial managers increasingly are hired on a temporary basis to advise senior managers on these and other matters. In fact, some small firms contract out all their accounting and financial functions to companies that provide such services.

The role of the financial manager, particularly in business, is changing in response to technological advances that have significantly reduced the amount of time it takes to produce financial reports. Financial managers now perform more data analysis and use it to offer senior managers ideas on how to maximize profits. They often work on teams, acting as business advisors to top management. Financial managers need to keep abreast of the latest computer technology in order to increase the efficiency of their firm's financial operations.

Working Conditions

Working in comfortable offices, often close to top managers and to departments that develop the financial data those managers need, financial managers typically have direct access to state-of-the-art computer systems and information services. They commonly work long hours, often up to 50 or 60 per week. Financial managers generally are required to attend meetings of financial and economic associations and may travel to visit subsidiary firms or to meet customers.

Training, Other Qualifications, and Advancement

A bachelor's degree in finance, accounting, economics, or business administration is the minimum academic preparation for financial managers. However, many employers now seek graduates with a master's degree, preferably in business administration, economics, finance, or risk management. These academic programs develop analytical skills and provide knowledge of the latest financial analysis methods and technology.

Experience may be more important than formal education for some financial manager positions—most notably, branch managers in banks. Banks typically fill branch manager positions by promoting experienced loan officers and other professionals who excel at their jobs. Other financial managers may enter the profession through formal management training programs offered by the company. The American Institute of Banking, which is affiliated with the American Bankers Association, sponsors educational and training programs for bank officers through a wide range of banking schools and educational conferences.

Continuing education is vital to financial managers, who must cope with the growing complexity of global trade, changes in federal and state laws and regulations, and the proliferation of new and complex financial instruments. Firms often provide opportunities for workers to broaden their knowledge and skills by encouraging them to take graduate courses at colleges and universities or attend conferences related to their specialty. Financial management, banking, and credit union associations, often in cooperation with colleges and universities, sponsor numerous national and local training programs. Persons enrolled prepare extensively at home and then attend sessions on subjects such as accounting management, budget management, corporate cash management, financial analysis, international banking, and information systems. Many firms pay all or part of the costs for employees who successfully complete courses. Although experience, ability, and leadership are emphasized for promotion, advancement may be accelerated by this type of special study.

In some cases, financial managers also may broaden their skills and exhibit their competency by attaining professional certification. Many different associations offer professional certification programs. For example, the CFA Institute confers the Chartered Financial Analyst designation on investment professionals who have a bachelor's degree, pass three sequential examinations, and meet work experience requirements. The Association for Financial Professionals (AFP) confers the Certified Cash Manager credential to those who pass a computer-based exam and have a minimum of 2 years of relevant experience. The Institute of Management Accountants offers a Certified in Financial Management designation to members with a bachelor's degree, with at least 2 years of work experience, and who pass the institute's four-part examination and fulfill continuing education requirements. Also, financial managers who specialize in accounting may earn the Certified Public Accountant (CPA) or Certified Management Accountant (CMA) designation.

Candidates for financial management positions need a broad range of skills. Interpersonal skills are important because these jobs involve managing people and working as part of a team to solve problems. Financial managers must have excellent communication skills to explain complex financial data. Because financial managers work extensively with various departments in their firm, a broad overview of the business is essential.

Financial managers should be creative thinkers and problem-solvers, applying their analytical skills to business. They must be comfortable with the latest computer technology. Financial operations are increasingly being affected by the global economy, so financial managers must have knowledge of international finance. Proficiency in a foreign language also may be important.

Because financial management is critical to efficient business operations, well-trained, experienced financial managers who display a strong grasp of the operations of various departments within their organization are prime candidates for promotion to top management positions. Some financial managers transfer to closely related positions in other industries. Those with extensive experience and access to sufficient capital may start their own consulting firms.

Employment

Financial managers held about 528,000 jobs in 2004. Although they can be found in every industry, approximately 3 out of 10 are employed by finance and insurance establishments, such as banks, savings institutions, finance companies, credit unions, insurance carriers, and securities dealers. About 1 in 10 works for federal, state, or local government.

Job Outlook

Employment of financial managers is expected to grow about as fast as average for all occupations through 2014. The increasing need for financial expertise as a result of regulatory reforms and the expansion of the economy will drive job growth over the next decade. As the economy expands, both the growth of established companies and the creation of new businesses will spur demand for financial managers. However, mergers, acquisitions, and corporate downsizing are likely to restrict the employment growth to some extent.

As in other managerial occupations, jobseekers are likely to face competition, because the number of job openings is expected to be less than the number of applicants. Candidates with expertise in accounting and finance—particularly those with a master's degree—should enjoy the best job prospects. Strong computer skills and knowledge of international finance are important; so are excellent communication skills, because financial management jobs involve working on strategic planning teams. In addition, a good knowledge of compliance procedures is essential because of the many regulatory changes instituted in recent years.

Over the short term, employment growth in this occupation may slow or even reverse due to economic downturns, during which companies are more likely to close departments or even go out of business—decreasing the need for financial managers.

The banking industry will continue to consolidate, although at a slower rate than in previous years. In spite of this trend, employment of bank branch managers is expected to increase, because banks are refocusing on the importance of their existing branches and are creating new branches to service a growing population. As banks expand the range of products and services they offer to include insurance and investment products, branch managers with knowledge in these areas will be needed. As a result, candidates who are licensed to sell insurance or securities will have the most favorable prospects.

The long-run prospects for financial managers in the securities and commodities industry should be favorable, because more people will be needed to handle increasingly complex financial transactions and manage a growing amount of investments. Financial managers also will be needed to handle mergers and acquisitions, raise capital, and assess global financial transactions. Risk managers, who assess risks for insurance and investment purposes, also will be in demand.

Some companies may hire financial managers on a temporary basis, to see the organization through a short-term crisis or to offer suggestions for boosting profits. Other companies may contract out all accounting and financial operations. Even in these cases, however, financial managers may be needed to oversee the contracts.

Computer technology has reduced the amount of time and the staff required to produce financial reports. As a result, forecasting earnings, profits, and costs and generating ideas and creative ways to increase profitability will become a major role of corporate financial managers over the next decade. Financial managers who are familiar with computer software that can assist them in this role will be needed.

Earnings

Median annual earnings of financial managers were $81,880 in May 2004. The middle 50 percent earned between $59,490 and $112,320. Median annual earnings in the industries employing the largest numbers of financial managers in 2004 were as follows:

Securities and commodity contracts intermediation and brokerage	$129,770
Management of companies and enterprises	97,730
Nondepository credit intermediation	88,870
Local government	67,260
Depository credit intermediation	64,530

According to a 2005 survey by Robert Half International, a staffing services firm specializing in accounting and finance professionals, directors of finance earned between $78,500 and $178,250, and corporate controllers earned between $61,250 and $147,250.

A 2004 survey of manufacturing firms conducted by Abbot, Langer, and Associates, Inc., a human resources management consulting firm, reported the following median annual incomes: chief corporate financial officers, $130,000; corporate controllers, $86,150; cost accounting managers, $67,161; and general accounting managers, $64,100.

Large organizations often pay more than small ones, and salary levels also can depend on the type of industry and location. Many financial managers in both public and private industry receive additional compensation in the form of bonuses, which, like salaries, vary substantially by size of firm. Deferred compensation in the form of stock options is becoming more common, especially for senior-level executives.

Related Occupations

Financial managers combine formal education with experience in one or more areas of finance, such as asset management, lending, credit operations, securities investment, or insurance risk and loss control. Workers in other occupations requiring similar training and skills include accountants and auditors; budget analysts; financial analysts and personal financial advisors; insurance sales agents; insurance underwriters; loan officers; securities, commodities, and financial services sales agents; and real estate brokers and sales agents.

Sources of Additional Information

For information about careers and certification in financial management, contact:

- Financial Management Association International, College of Business Administration, University of South Florida, Tampa, FL 33620-5500. Internet: http://www.fma.org

For information about careers in financial and treasury management and the Certified Cash Manager program, contact:

- Association for Financial Professionals, 7315 Wisconsin Ave., Suite 600 West, Bethesda, MD 20814. Internet: http://www.afponline.org

For information about the Chartered Financial Analyst program, contact:

- CFA Institute, P.O. Box 3668, 560 Ray Hunt Dr., Charlottesville, VA 22903-0668. Internet: http://www.cfainstitute.org

For information on the Financial Risk Manager program, contact:

- Global Association of Risk Professionals, 100 Pavonia Ave., Suite 405, Jersey City, NJ 07310.

For information about the Certified in Financial Management designation, contact:

- Institute of Management Accountants, 10 Paragon Dr., Montvale, NJ, 07645-1718 Internet: http://www.imanet.org

Fire Fighting Occupations

(O*NET 33-1021.01, 33-1021.02, 33-2011.01, 33-2011.02, 33-2021.01, 33-2021.02, and 33-2022.00)

Significant Points

- Fire fighting involves hazardous conditions and long, irregular hours.
- About 9 out of 10 fire fighting workers are employed by municipal or county fire departments.
- Applicants for municipal fire fighting jobs generally must pass written, physical, and medical examinations.
- Although employment is expected to grow faster than the average, keen competition for jobs is expected because this occupation attracts many qualified candidates.

Nature of the Work

Every year, fires and other emergencies take thousands of lives and destroy property worth billions of dollars. Fire fighters help protect the public against these dangers by rapidly responding to a variety of emergencies. They are frequently the first emergency personnel at the scene of a traffic accident or medical emergency and may be called upon to put out a fire, treat injuries, or perform other vital functions.

During duty hours, fire fighters must be prepared to respond immediately to a fire or any other emergency that arises. Because fighting fires is dangerous and complex, it requires organization and teamwork. At every emergency scene, fire fighters perform specific duties assigned by a superior officer. At fires, they connect hose lines to hydrants, operate a pump to send water to high-pressure hoses, and position ladders to enable them to deliver water to the fire. They also rescue victims, provide emergency medical attention as needed, ventilate smoke-filled areas, and attempt to salvage the contents of buildings. Their duties may change several times while the company is in action. Sometimes they remain at the site of a disaster for days at a time, rescuing trapped survivors and assisting with medical treatment.

Fire fighters work in a variety of settings, including urban and suburban areas, airports, chemical plants, other industrial sites, and rural areas like grasslands and forests. They have also assumed a range of responsibilities, including emergency medical services. In fact, most calls to which fire fighters respond involve medical emergencies, and 65 percent of all fire departments provide emergency medical service. In addition, some fire fighters work in hazardous materials units that are trained for the control, prevention, and cleanup of materials; for example, these fire fighters respond to oil spills. Workers in urban and suburban areas, airports, and industrial sites typically use conventional fire fighting equipment and tactics, while forest fires and major hazardous materials spills call for different methods.

In national forests and parks, *forest fire inspectors and prevention specialists* spot fires from watchtowers and report their findings to headquarters by telephone or radio. Forest rangers patrol to ensure that travelers and campers comply with fire regulations. When fires break out, crews of fire fighters are brought in to suppress the blaze with heavy equipment, hand tools, and water hoses. Fighting forest fires, like fighting urban fires, is rigorous work. One of the most effective means of battling a blaze is creating fire lines—cutting down trees and digging out grass and all other combustible vegetation in the path of the fire—to deprive it of fuel. Elite fire fighters called smoke jumpers parachute from airplanes to reach otherwise inaccessible areas. This tactic, however, can be extremely hazardous because the crews have no way to escape if the wind shifts and causes the fire to burn toward them.

Between alarms, fire fighters clean and maintain equipment, conduct practice drills and fire inspections, and participate in physical fitness activities. They also prepare written reports on fire incidents and review fire science literature to keep abreast of technological developments and changing administrative practices and policies.

Most fire departments have a fire prevention division, usually headed by a fire marshal and staffed by *fire inspectors*. Workers in this division conduct inspections of structures to prevent fires and ensure compliance with fire codes. These fire fighters also work with developers and planners to check and approve plans for new buildings. Fire prevention personnel often speak on these subjects in schools and before public assemblies and civic organizations.

Some fire fighters become *fire investigators*, who determine the origin and causes of fires. They collect evidence, interview witnesses, and prepare reports on fires in cases where the cause may be arson or criminal negligence. They often are called upon to testify in court.

Working Conditions

Fire fighters spend much of their time at fire stations, which usually have features in common with a residential facility like a dormitory. When an alarm sounds, fire fighters respond rapidly, regardless of the weather or hour. Fire fighting involves the risk of death or injury from sudden cave-ins of floors, toppling walls, traffic accidents when responding to calls, and exposure to flames and smoke. Fire fighters also may come in contact with poisonous, flammable, or explosive gases and chemicals, as well as radioactive or other hazardous materials that may have immediate or long-term effects on their health. For these reasons, they must wear protective gear that can be very heavy and hot.

Work hours of fire fighters are longer and vary more widely than hours of most other workers. Many work more than 50 hours a week, and sometimes they may work even longer. In some agencies, fire fighters are on duty for 24 hours, then off for 48 hours, and receive an extra day off at intervals. In others, they work a day shift of 10 hours for 3 or 4 days, work a night shift of 14 hours for 3 or 4 nights, have 3 or 4 days off, and then repeat the cycle. In addition, fire fighters often work extra hours at fires and other emergencies and are regularly assigned to work on holidays. Fire lieutenants and fire captains often work the same hours as the fire fighters they supervise. Duty hours include time when fire fighters study, train, and perform fire prevention duties.

Training, Other Qualifications, and Advancement

Applicants for municipal fire fighting jobs generally must pass a written exam; tests of strength, physical stamina, coordination, and agility; and a medical examination that includes drug screening. Workers may be monitored on a random basis for drug use after accepting employment. Examinations are generally open to persons who are at least 18 years of age and have a high school education or the equivalent. Those who receive the highest scores in all phases of testing have the best chances for appointment. The completion of community college courses in fire science may improve an applicant's chances for appointment. In recent years, an increasing proportion of entrants to this occupation have had some postsecondary education.

As a rule, entry-level workers in large fire departments are trained for several weeks at the department's training center or academy. Through classroom instruction and practical training, the recruits study fire fighting techniques, fire prevention, hazardous materials control, local building codes, and emergency medical procedures, including first aid and cardiopulmonary resuscitation.

They also learn how to use axes, chain saws, fire extinguishers, ladders, and other fire fighting and rescue equipment. After successfully completing this training, the recruits are assigned to a fire company, where they undergo a period of probation.

Almost all departments require fire fighters to be certified as emergency medical technicians. While most fire departments require the lowest level of certification, EMT-Basic, larger departments in major metropolitan areas are increasingly requiring paramedic certification. Some departments include this training in the fire academy, while others prefer that recruits have EMT certification beforehand, but will give them up to 1 year to become certified on their own.

A number of fire departments have accredited apprenticeship programs lasting up to 4 years. These programs combine formal, technical instruction with on-the-job training under the supervision of experienced fire fighters. Technical instruction covers subjects such as fire fighting techniques and equipment, chemical hazards associated with various combustible building materials, emergency medical procedures, and fire prevention and safety.

In addition to participating in advanced training programs conducted by local fire departments, some fire fighters attend training sessions sponsored by the U.S. National Fire Academy. These training sessions cover topics such as executive development, anti-arson techniques, disaster preparedness, hazardous materials control, and public fire safety and education. Some states also have either voluntary or mandatory fire fighter training and certification programs. In addition, a number of colleges and universities offer courses leading to 2- or 4-year degrees in fire engineering or fire science. Many fire departments offer fire fighters incentives such as tuition reimbursement or higher pay for completing advanced training.

Among the personal qualities fire fighters need are mental alertness, self-discipline, courage, mechanical aptitude, endurance, strength, and a sense of public service. Initiative and good judgment also are extremely important because fire fighters make quick decisions in emergencies. Members of a crew live and work closely together under conditions of stress and danger for extended periods, so they must be dependable and able to get along well with others. Leadership qualities are necessary for officers, who must establish and maintain discipline and efficiency as well as direct the activities of fire fighters in their companies.

Most experienced fire fighters continue studying to improve their job performance and prepare for promotion examinations. To progress to higher-level positions, they acquire expertise in advanced fire fighting equipment and techniques, building construction, emergency medical technology, writing, public speaking, management and budgeting procedures, and public relations.

Opportunities for promotion depend upon the results of written examinations as well as job performance, interviews, and seniority. Increasingly, fire departments are using assessment centers, which simulate a variety of actual job performance tasks, to screen for the best candidates for promotion. The line of promotion usually is to engineer, lieutenant, captain, battalion chief, assistant chief, deputy chief, and, finally, chief. For promotion to positions higher than battalion chief, many fire departments now require a bachelor's degree, preferably in fire science, public administration, or a related field. An associate's degree is required for executive fire officer certification from the National Fire Academy.

Employment

Employment figures in this description include only paid career fire fighters—they do not cover volunteer fire fighters, who perform the same duties and may constitute the majority of fire fighters in a residential area. According to the U.S. Fire Administration, 70 percent of fire companies are staffed by volunteer fire fighters. In 2004, total employment in fire fighting occupations was about

353,000. Fire fighters held about 282,000 jobs, first-line supervisors/managers of fire fighting and prevention workers held about 56,000, and fire inspectors held about 15,000.

About 9 out of 10 fire fighting workers were employed by municipal or county fire departments. Some large cities have thousands of career fire fighters, while many small towns have only a few. Most of the remainder worked in fire departments on federal and state installations, including airports. Private fire fighting companies employ a small number of fire fighters and usually operate on a subscription basis.

In response to the expanding role of fire fighters, some municipalities have combined fire prevention, public fire education, safety, and emergency medical services into a single organization commonly referred to as a public safety organization. Some local and regional fire departments are being consolidated into countywide establishments in order to reduce administrative staffs, cut costs, and establish consistent training standards and work procedures.

Job Outlook

Prospective fire fighters are expected to face keen competition for available job openings. Many people are attracted to fire fighting because (1) it is challenging and provides the opportunity to perform an essential public service, (2) a high school education is usually sufficient for entry, and (3) a pension is guaranteed upon retirement after 25 years. Consequently, the number of qualified applicants in most areas exceeds the number of job openings, even though the written examination and physical requirements eliminate many applicants. This situation is expected to persist in coming years. Applicants with the best opportunities are those who are physically fit and score the highest on physical conditioning and mechanical aptitude exams. Those who have completed some fire fighter education at a community college and have EMT certification will have an additional advantage.

Employment of fire fighters is expected to grow faster than the average for all occupations through 2014. Most job growth will occur as volunteer fire fighting positions are converted to paid positions in growing suburban areas. In addition to job growth, openings are expected to result from the need to replace fire fighters who retire, stop working for other reasons, or transfer to other occupations.

Layoffs of fire fighters are uncommon. Fire protection is an essential service, and citizens are likely to exert considerable pressure on local officials to expand or at least preserve the level of fire protection. Even when budget cuts do occur, local fire departments usually trim expenses by postponing purchases of equipment or by not hiring new fire fighters rather than through staff reductions.

Earnings

Median hourly earnings of fire fighters were $18.43 in May 2004. The middle 50 percent earned between $13.65 and $24.14. The lowest 10 percent earned less than $9.71, and the highest 10 percent earned more than $29.21. Median hourly earnings were $18.78 in local government, $17.34 in the federal government, and $14.94 in state government.

Median annual earnings of first-line supervisors/managers of fire fighting and prevention workers were $58,920 in May 2004. The middle 50 percent earned between $46,880 and $72,600. The lowest 10 percent earned less than $36,800, and the highest 10 percent earned more than $90,860. First-line supervisors/managers of fire fighting and prevention workers employed in local government earned about $60,800 a year.

Median annual earnings of fire inspectors and investigators were $46,340 in May 2004. The middle 50 percent earned between $36,030 and $58,260 a year. The lowest 10 percent earned less than $28,420, and the highest 10 percent earned more than $71,490. Fire inspectors and investigators employed in local government earned about $48,020 a year.

According to the International City-County Management Association, average salaries in 2004 for sworn full-time positions were as follows:

	Minimum annual base salary	Maximum annual base salary
Fire chief	$68,701	$89,928
Deputy chief	63,899	79,803
Assistant fire chief	57,860	73,713
Battalion chief	58,338	73,487
Fire captain	49,108	59,374
Fire lieutenant	44,963	53,179
Fire prevention/ code inspector	43,297	54,712
Engineer	41,294	52,461

Fire fighters who average more than a certain number of hours a week are required to be paid overtime. The hours threshold is determined by the department during the fire fighter's work period, which ranges from 7 to 28 days. Fire fighters often earn overtime for working extra shifts to maintain minimum staffing levels or for special emergencies.

Fire fighters receive benefits that usually include medical and liability insurance, vacation and sick leave, and some paid holidays. Almost all fire departments provide protective clothing (helmets, boots, and coats) and breathing apparatus, and many also provide dress uniforms. Fire fighters generally are covered by pension plans, often providing retirement at half pay after 25 years of service or if the individual is disabled in the line of duty.

Related Occupations

Like fire fighters, emergency medical technicians and paramedics and police and detectives respond to emergencies and save lives.

Sources of Additional Information

Information about a career as a fire fighter may be obtained from local fire departments and from either of the following organizations:

- International Association of Fire Fighters, 1750 New York Ave. NW, Washington, DC 20006. Internet: http://www.iaff.org
- U.S. Fire Administration, 16825 South Seton Ave., Emmitsburg, MD 21727. Internet: http://www.usfa.fema.gov

Information about professional qualifications and a list of colleges and universities offering 2- or 4-year degree programs in fire science or fire prevention may be obtained from:

- National Fire Academy, 16825 South Seton Ave., Emmitsburg, MD 21727. Internet: http://www.usfa.fema.gov/nfa/index.htm

Fitness Workers

(O*NET 39-9031.00)

Significant Points

- Many group fitness and personal training jobs are part time, but many workers increase their hours by working at several different facilities or at clients' homes.
- Night and weekend working hours are common.
- Most fitness workers need to be certified.
- Employment prospects are expected to be good because of rapid growth in the fitness industry.

Nature of the Work

Fitness workers lead, instruct, and motivate individuals or groups in exercise activities, including cardiovascular exercise, strength training, and stretching. They work in commercial and nonprofit health clubs, country clubs, hospitals, universities, yoga and Pilates studios, resorts, and clients' homes. Increasingly, fitness workers also are found in workplaces, where they organize and direct health and fitness programs for employees of all ages.

Although gyms and health clubs offer a variety of exercise activities such as weightlifting, yoga, cardiovascular training, and karate, fitness workers typically specialize in only a few areas.

Personal trainers work one-on-one with clients either in a gym or in the client's home. Trainers help clients assess their level of physical fitness and set and reach fitness goals. Trainers also demonstrate various exercises and help clients improve their exercise techniques. Trainers may keep records of their clients' exercise sessions to assess clients' progress toward physical fitness.

Group exercise instructors conduct group exercise sessions that involve aerobic exercise, stretching, and muscle conditioning. Because cardiovascular conditioning classes often involve movement to music, outside of class instructors must choose and mix the music and choreograph a corresponding exercise sequence. Pilates and yoga are two increasingly popular conditioning methods taught in exercise classes. Instructors demonstrate the different moves and positions of the particular method; they also observe students and correct those who are doing the exercises improperly. Group exercise instructors are responsible for ensuring that their classes are motivating, safe, and challenging, yet not too difficult for the participants.

Fitness directors oversee the fitness-related aspects of a health club or fitness center. Their work involves creating and maintaining programs that meet the needs of the club's members, including new member orientations, fitness assessments, and workout incentive programs. They also select fitness equipment; coordinate personal training and group exercise programs; hire, train, and supervise fitness staff; and carry out administrative duties.

Fitness workers in smaller facilities with few employees may perform a variety of functions in addition to their fitness duties, such as tending the front desk, signing up new members, giving tours of the fitness center, writing newsletter articles, creating posters and flyers, and supervising the weight training and cardiovascular equipment areas. In larger commercial facilities, personal trainers are often required to sell their services to members and to make a specified number of sales. Some fitness workers may combine the duties of group exercise instructors and personal trainers, and in smaller facilities, the fitness director may teach classes and do personal training.

Working Conditions

Most fitness workers spend their time indoors at fitness centers and health clubs. Fitness directors and supervisors, however, typically spend most of their time in an office, planning programs and special events and tending to administrative issues. Those in smaller fitness centers may split their time among the office, personal training, and teaching classes. Directors and supervisors generally engage in less physical activity than do lower-level fitness workers. Nevertheless, workers at all levels risk suffering injuries during physical activities.

Since most fitness centers are open long hours, fitness workers often work nights and weekends and even occasional holidays. Some may have to travel from place to place throughout the day, to different gyms or to clients' homes, to maintain a full work schedule.

Fitness workers generally enjoy a lot of autonomy. Group exercise instructors choreograph or plan their own classes, and personal trainers have the freedom to design and implement their clients' workout routines.

Training, Other Qualifications, and Advancement

Personal trainers must obtain certification in the fitness field to gain employment, while group fitness instructors do not necessarily need certification to begin working. The most important characteristic that an employer looks for in a new group fitness instructor is the ability to plan and lead a class that is motivating and safe. Group fitness instructors often get started by participating in exercise classes, and some become familiar enough to successfully audition and begin teaching class. They also may improve their skills by taking training courses or attending fitness conventions. Most organizations encourage their group instructors to become certified, and many require it.

In the fitness field, there are many organizations—some of which are listed in the last section of this statement—that offer certification. Becoming certified by one of the top certification organizations is increasingly important, especially for personal trainers. One way to ensure that a certifying organization is reputable is to see whether it is accredited or seeking accreditation by the National Commission for Certifying Agencies.

Most certifying organizations require candidates to have a high school diploma, be certified in cardiopulmonary resuscitation (CPR), and pass an exam. All certification exams have a written component, and some also have a practical component. The exams measure knowledge of human physiology, proper exercise techniques, assessment of client fitness levels, and development of appropriate exercise programs. There is no particular training program required for certifications; candidates may prepare however they prefer. Certifying organizations do offer study materials, including books, CD-ROMs, other audio and visual materials, and exam preparation workshops and seminars, but exam candidates are not required to purchase materials to sit for the exams. Certification generally is good for 2 years, after which workers must become recertified by attending continuing education classes. Some organizations offer more advanced certification, requiring an associate or bachelor's degree in an exercise-related subject for individuals interested in training athletes, working with people who are injured or ill, or advising clients on whole-life health.

Training for Pilates and yoga teachers is changing. Because interest in these forms of exercise has exploded in recent years, the demand for teachers has grown faster than the ability to train them properly. However, because inexperienced teachers have contributed to student injuries, there has been a push toward more standardized, rigorous requirements for teacher training.

Pilates and yoga teachers usually do not need group exercise certifications like the ones described above. It is more important that they have specialized training in their particular method of exercise. For Pilates, training options range from weekend-long workshops to year-long programs, but the trend is toward requiring more training. The Pilates Method Alliance has established training standards that recommend at least 200 hours of training; the group also has standards for training schools and maintains a list of training schools that meet the requirements. However, some Pilates teachers are certified group exercise instructors who go through short Pilates workshops; currently, many fitness centers hire people with minimal Pilates training if the applicants have a fitness certification and group fitness experience.

Training requirements for yoga teachers are similar to those for Pilates teachers. Training programs range from a few days to more than 2 years. Many people get their start by taking yoga; eventually, their teachers may consider them suited to assist or to substitute teach. Some students may begin teaching their own classes when their yoga teachers think they are ready; the teachers may even provide letters of recommendation. Those who wish to pursue teaching more seriously usually then pursue formal teacher training. Currently, there are many training programs through the yoga community as well as programs through the fitness industry. The Yoga Alliance has established training standards of at least 200 training hours, with a specified number of hours in areas including techniques, teaching methodology, anatomy, physiology, and philosophy. The Yoga Alliance also registers schools that train students to the standards. Because some schools may meet the standards but not be registered, prospective students should check the requirements and decide if particular schools meet them.

An increasing number of employers require fitness workers to have a bachelor's degree in a field related to health or fitness, such as exercise science or physical education. Some employers allow workers to substitute a college degree for certification, but most employers who require a bachelor's degree require both a degree and certification.

People planning fitness careers should be outgoing, good at motivating people, and sensitive to the needs of others. Excellent health and physical fitness are important due to the physical nature of the job. Those who wish to be personal trainers in a large commercial fitness center should have strong sales skills.

Fitness workers usually do not receive much on-the-job training; they are expected to know how to do their jobs when they are hired. The exception is newly certified personal trainers with no work experience, who sometimes begin by working alongside an experienced trainer before being allowed to train clients alone. Workers may receive some organizational training to learn about the operations of their new employer. They occasionally receive specialized training if they are expected to teach or lead a specific method of exercise or focus on a particular age or ability group.

A bachelor's degree, and in some cases a master's degree, in exercise science, physical education, kinesiology, or a related area, along with experience, usually is required to advance to management positions in a health club or fitness center. As in many fields, managerial skills are needed to advance to supervisory or managerial positions. College courses in management, business administration, accounting, and personnel management may be helpful for advancement to supervisory or managerial jobs, but many fitness companies have corporate universities in which they train employees for management positions.

Personal trainers may advance to head trainer, with responsibility for hiring and overseeing the personal training staff and for bringing in new personal training clients. Group fitness instructors may be promoted to group exercise director, responsible for hiring instructors and coordinating exercise classes. A next possible step is the fitness director, who manages the fitness budget and staff. The general manager's main focus is on the financial aspect of the organization, particularly setting and achieving sales goals; in a small fitness center, however, the general manager usually is involved with all aspects of running the facility.

Some workers go into business for themselves and open their own fitness centers.

Employment

Fitness workers held about 205,000 jobs in 2004. Almost all personal trainers and group exercise instructors worked in physical fitness facilities, health clubs, and fitness centers, mainly in the amusement and recreation industry or in civic and social organizations. About 7 percent of fitness workers were self-employed; many of these were personal trainers, while others were group fitness instructors working on a contract basis with fitness centers. Many fitness jobs are part time, and many workers hold multiple jobs, teaching and/or doing personal training at several different fitness centers and at clients' homes.

Job Outlook

Opportunities are expected to be good for fitness workers because of rapid growth in the fitness industry. Many job openings also will stem from the need to replace the large numbers of workers who leave these occupations each year.

Employment of fitness workers—who are concentrated in the rapidly growing arts, entertainment, and recreation industry—is expected to increase much faster than the average for all occupations through 2014. An increasing number of people spend more time and money on fitness, and more businesses are recognizing the benefits of health and fitness programs and other services such as wellness programs for their employees.

Aging baby boomers are concerned with staying healthy, physically fit, and independent. They have become the largest demographic group of health club members. The reduction of physical education programs in schools, combined with parents' growing concern about childhood obesity, has resulted in rapid increases in children's health club membership. Increasingly, athletic youth also are hiring personal trainers, and weight-training gyms for children younger than 18 are expected to continue to grow. Health club membership among young adults also has grown steadily, driven by concern with physical fitness and by rising incomes.

As health clubs strive to provide more personalized service to keep their members motivated, they will continue to offer personal training and a wide variety of group exercise classes. Participation in yoga and Pilates is expected to continue to grow, driven partly by the aging population demanding low-impact forms of exercise and relief from ailments such as arthritis.

Earnings

Median annual earnings of personal trainers and group exercise instructors in May 2004 were $25,470. The middle 50 percent earned between $17,380 and $40,030. The bottom 10 percent earned less than $14,530 while the top 10 percent earned $55,560 or more. Earnings of successful self-employed personal trainers can be much higher. Median annual earnings in the industries employing the largest numbers of fitness workers in May 2004 were as follows:

Other amusement and recreation industries $28,670
Other schools and instruction 22,320
Civic and social organizations 20,530

Because many fitness workers work part time, they often do not receive benefits such as health insurance or retirement plans from their employers. They do get the unusual benefit of the use of fitness facilities at no cost.

Related Occupations

Occupations that focus on physical fitness, as do fitness workers, include athletes, coaches, umpires, and related workers.

Sources of Additional Information

For more information about fitness careers, and to find universities and other institutions offering programs in health and fitness, contact:

- IDEA Health and Fitness Association, 10455 Pacific Center Crt., San Diego, CA 92121-4339.

For information about personal trainer and group fitness instructor certifications, contact:

- American Council on Exercise, 4851 Paramount Dr., San Diego, CA 92123. Internet: http://www.acefitness.org
- American College of Sports Medicine, P.O. Box 1440, Indianapolis, IN 46206-1440. Internet: http://www.acsm.org
- National Academy of Sports Medicine, 26632 Agoura Rd., Calabasas, CA 91302. Internet: http://www.nasm.org
- National Strength and Conditioning Association Certification Commission, 3333 Landmark Circle, Lincoln, NE 68504. Internet: http://www.nsca-cc.org

For information about Pilates certification, and to find training programs, contact:

- Pilates Method Alliance, P.O. Box 370906, Miami, FL 33137-0906. Internet: http://www.pilatesmethodalliance.org

For information on yoga teacher training, and to find training programs, contact:

- Yoga Alliance, 7801 Old Branch Ave., Suite 400, Clinton, MD 20735. Internet: http://www.yogaalliance.org

To find accredited fitness certification programs, contact:

- National Commission for Certifying Agencies, 2025 M St. NW, Suite 800, Washington, DC 20036. Internet: http://www.noca.org/ncca/accredorg.htm

Food and Beverage Serving and Related Workers

(O*NET 35-3011.00, 35-3021.00, 35-3022.00, 35-3031.00, 35-3041.00, 35-9011.00, 35-9021.00, 35-9031.00, and 35-9099.99)

Significant Points

- Most jobs are part time, so many opportunities exist for young people—about one-fourth of these workers were 16 to 19 years old, almost six times the proportion for all workers.
- Job openings are expected to be abundant through 2014 because many of these workers transfer to other occupations or stop working, creating numerous openings.
- Tips comprise a major portion of earnings, so keen competition is expected for jobs where potential earnings from tips are greatest—bartenders, waiters and waitresses, and other jobs in popular restaurants and fine dining establishments.

Nature of the Work

Food and beverage serving and related workers are the front line of customer service in restaurants, coffee shops, and other food service establishments. These workers greet customers, escort them to seats and hand them menus, take food and drink orders, and serve food and beverages. They also answer questions, explain menu items and specials, and keep tables and dining areas clean and set for new diners. Most work as part of a team, helping co-workers to improve workflow and customer service.

Waiters and waitresses, the largest group of these workers, take customers' orders, serve food and beverages, prepare itemized checks, and sometimes accept payment. Their specific duties vary considerably, depending on the establishment. In coffee shops serving routine, straightforward fare, such as salads, soups, and sandwiches, servers are expected to provide fast, efficient, and courteous service. In fine dining restaurants, where more complicated meals are prepared and often served over several courses, waiters and waitresses provide more formal service, emphasizing personal, attentive treatment and a more leisurely pace. They may recommend certain dishes and identify ingredients or explain how various items on the menu are prepared. Some prepare salads, desserts, or other menu items tableside. Additionally, they may check the identification of patrons to ensure they meet the minimum age requirement for the purchase of alcohol and tobacco products.

Waiters and waitresses sometimes perform the duties of other food and beverage service workers. These tasks may include escorting guests to tables, serving customers seated at counters, clearing and setting up tables, or operating a cash register. However, full-service restaurants frequently hire other staff, such as hosts and hostesses, cashiers, or dining room attendants, to perform these duties.

Bartenders fill drink orders either taken directly from patrons at the bar or through waiters and waitresses who place drink orders for dining room customers. Bartenders check identification of customers seated at the bar to ensure they meet the minimum age requirement for the purchase of alcohol and tobacco products. They prepare mixed drinks, serve bottled or draught beer, and pour wine or other beverages. Bartenders must know a wide range of drink recipes and be able to mix drinks accurately, quickly, and without waste. Besides mixing and serving drinks, bartenders stock and prepare garnishes for drinks; maintain an adequate supply of ice, glasses, and other bar supplies; and keep the bar area clean for customers. They also may collect payment, operate the cash register, wash glassware and utensils, and serve food to customers seated at the bar. Bartenders usually are responsible for ordering and maintaining an inventory of liquor, mixes, and other bar supplies.

The majority of bartenders directly serve and interact with patrons. Bartenders should be friendly and enjoy talking with customers. Bartenders at service bars, on the other hand, have less contact with customers. They work in small bars often located off the kitchen in restaurants, hotels, and clubs where only waiters and waitresses place drink orders. Some establishments, especially larger, higher-volume ones, use equipment that automatically measures, pours, and mixes drinks at the push of a button. Bartenders who use this equipment, however, still must work quickly to handle a large volume of drink orders and be familiar with the ingredients for special drink requests. Much of a bartender's work still must be done by hand to fill each individual order.

Hosts and hostesses welcome guests and maintain reservation or waiting lists. They may direct patrons to coatrooms or restrooms or to a place to wait until their table is ready. Hosts and hostesses assign guests to tables suitable for the size of their group, escort patrons to their seats, and provide menus. They also schedule dining reservations, arrange parties, and organize any special services that are required. In some restaurants, they act as cashiers.

Dining room and cafeteria attendants and bartender helpers assist waiters, waitresses, and bartenders by cleaning tables, removing dirty dishes, and keeping serving areas stocked with supplies. Sometimes called backwaiters or runners, they bring meals out of the kitchen and assist waiters and waitresses by distributing dishes to individual diners. They also replenish the supply of clean linens, dishes, silverware, and glasses in the dining room and keep the bar stocked with glasses, liquor, ice, and drink garnishes. Dining room attendants set tables with clean tablecloths, napkins, silverware, glasses, and dishes and serve ice water, rolls, and butter. At the conclusion of meals, they remove dirty dishes and soiled linens from tables. Cafeteria attendants stock serving tables with food, trays, dishes, and silverware and may carry trays to dining tables for patrons. *Bartender helpers* keep bar equipment clean and wash glasses. *Dishwashers* clean dishes, cutlery, and kitchen utensils and equipment.

Counter attendants take orders and serve food in cafeterias, coffee shops, and carryout eateries. In cafeterias, they serve food displayed on steam tables, carve meat, dish out vegetables, ladle sauces and soups, and fill beverage glasses. In lunchrooms and coffee shops, counter attendants take orders from customers seated at the counter, transmit orders to the kitchen, and pick up and serve food. They also fill cups with coffee, soda, and other beverages and prepare fountain specialties, such as milkshakes and ice cream sundaes. Counter attendants also take carryout orders from diners and wrap or place items in containers. They clean counters, write itemized checks, and sometimes accept payment. Some counter attendants may prepare short-order items, such as sandwiches and salads.

Some food and beverage serving workers take orders from customers at counters or drive-through windows at fast-food restaurants. They assemble orders, hand them to customers, and accept payment. Many of these are *combined food preparation and serving workers* who also cook and package food, make coffee, and fill beverage cups using drink-dispensing machines.

Other workers serve food to patrons outside of a restaurant environment, such as in hotels, hospital rooms, or cars.

Working Conditions

Food and beverage service workers are on their feet most of the time and often carry heavy trays of food, dishes, and glassware. During busy dining periods, they are under pressure to serve customers quickly and efficiently. The work is relatively safe, but care must be taken to avoid slips, falls, and burns.

Part-time work is more common among food and beverage serving and related workers than among workers in almost any other occupation. In 2004, those on part-time schedules included half of all waiters and waitresses and 40 percent of all bartenders.

Food service and drinking establishments typically maintain long dining hours and offer flexible and varied work opportunities. Many food and beverage serving and related workers work evenings, weekends, and holidays. Many students and teenagers seek part time or seasonal work as food and beverage serving and related workers as a first job to gain work experience or to earn spending money while in school. Around one-fourth of food and beverage serving and related workers were 16 to 19 years old—about six times the proportion for all workers.

Training, Other Qualifications, and Advancement

There are no specific educational requirements for food and beverage service jobs. Many employers prefer to hire high school graduates for waiter and waitress, bartender, and host and hostess positions, but completion of high school usually is not required for fast-food workers, counter attendants, dishwashers, and dining room attendants and bartender helpers. For many people a job as a food and beverage service worker serves as a source of immediate income rather than a career. Many entrants to these jobs are in their late teens or early twenties and have a high school education or less. Usually, they have little or no work experience. Many are full-time students or homemakers. Food and beverage service jobs are a major source of part-time employment for high school and college students.

Restaurants rely on good food and quality customer service to retain loyal customers and succeed in a competitive industry. Food and beverage serving and related workers who exhibit excellent personal qualities—such as a neat, clean appearance; a well-spoken manner; an ability to work as a member of a team; and a pleasant way with patrons—will be highly sought after.

Waiters and waitresses need a good memory to avoid confusing customers' orders and to recall faces, names, and preferences of frequent patrons. These workers also should be comfortable using computers to place orders and generate customers' bills. Some may need to be quick at arithmetic so they can total bills manually. Knowledge of a foreign language is helpful to communicate with a diverse clientele and staff. Prior experience waiting on tables is preferred by restaurants and hotels that have rigid table service standards. Jobs at these establishments often offer higher wages and have greater income potential from tips, but they may also have stiffer employment requirements than other establishments, such as prior table service experience or higher education.

Usually, bartenders must be at least 21 years of age, but employers prefer to hire people who are 25 or older. Bartenders should be familiar with state and local laws concerning the sale of alcoholic beverages.

Most food and beverage serving and related workers pick up their skills on the job by observing and working with more-experienced workers. Some full-service restaurants also provide new dining room employees with some form of classroom-type training that alternates with periods of actual on-the-job work experience. These training programs communicate the operating philosophy of the restaurant, help establish a personal rapport with other staff, and instill a desire to work as a team. They also provide an opportunity to discuss customer service situations and the proper ways of handling unpleasant circumstances or unruly patrons with new employees. Additionally, managers, chefs, and servers may meet before each shift to discuss the menu and any new items or specials; review ingredients for any potential food allergies; and talk about any food safety, coordination between the kitchen and the dining room, and customer service issues from the previous day or shift.

Some employers, particularly those in fast-food restaurants, use self-instruction or online programs with audiovisual presentations and instructional booklets to teach new employees food preparation and service skills. Some public and private vocational schools, restaurant associations, and large restaurant chains provide classroom training in a generalized food service curriculum. All employees receive training on safe food handling procedures and sanitation practices.

Some bartenders acquire their skills by attending a bartending or vocational and technical school. These programs often include instruction on state and local laws and regulations, cocktail recipes, proper attire and conduct, and stocking a bar. Some of these schools help their graduates find jobs. Although few employers require any minimum level of educational attainment, some specialized training is usually needed in food handling and legal issues surrounding serving alcoholic beverages and tobacco. Employers are more likely to hire and promote based on people skills and personal qualities rather than education.

Due to the relatively small size of most food-serving establishments, opportunities for promotion are limited. After gaining experience, some dining room and cafeteria attendants and bartender helpers advance to waiter, waitress, or bartender jobs. For waiters, waitresses, and bartenders, advancement usually is limited to finding a job in a busier or more expensive restaurant or bar where prospects for tip earnings are better. Some bartenders, hosts and hostesses, and waiters and waitresses advance to supervisory jobs, such as dining room supervisor, maitre d'hotel, assistant manager, or restaurant general manager. A few bartenders open their own businesses. In larger restaurant chains, food and beverage service workers who excel at their work often are invited to enter the company's formal management training program.

Employment

Food and beverage serving and related workers held 6.8 million jobs in 2004. The distribution of jobs among the various food and beverage serving workers was as follows:

Waiters and waitresses	2,252,000
Combined food preparation and serving workers, including fast food	2,150,000
Dishwashers	507,000
Bartenders	474,000
Counter attendants, cafeteria, food concession, and coffee shop	465,000
Dining room and cafeteria attendants and bartender helpers	401,000
Hosts and hostesses, restaurant, lounge, and coffee shop	328,000
Food servers, nonrestaurant	189,000
All other food preparation and serving related workers	64,000

The overwhelming majority of jobs for food and beverage serving and related workers were found in food services and drinking places, such as restaurants, coffee shops, and bars. Other jobs were found primarily in traveler accommodation (hotels); amusement, gambling, and recreation industries; educational services; grocery stores; nursing care facilities; civic and social organizations; and hospitals.

Jobs are located throughout the country but are typically plentiful in large cities and tourist areas. Vacation resorts offer seasonal employment, and some workers alternate between summer and winter resorts instead of remaining in one area the entire year.

Job Outlook

Job openings are expected to be abundant for food and beverage serving and related workers. Overall employment of these workers is expected to increase as fast as the average over the 2004–14 period as population, personal incomes, and employment expand. While employment growth will create many new jobs, the overwhelming majority of openings will arise from the need to replace the high proportion of workers who leave the occupations each year. There is substantial movement into and out of these occupations because education and training requirements are minimal and the predominance of part-time jobs is attractive to people seeking a short-term source of income rather than a career. However, keen competition is expected for bartender, waiter and waitress, and other food and beverage service jobs in popular restaurants and fine dining establishments, where potential earnings from tips are greatest.

Projected employment growth between 2004 and 2014 varies somewhat by type of job; however, average employment growth is expected for almost all food and beverage serving and related occupations. Employment of combined food preparation and serving workers, which includes fast-food workers, is expected to increase as fast as the average in response to the continuing fast-paced lifestyle of many Americans and the addition of healthier foods at many fast-food restaurants. Average employment growth is expected for waiters and waitresses and hosts and hostesses because increases in the number of families and the more affluent 55-and-older population will result in more restaurants that offer table service and more varied menus. Employment of bartenders, dining room attendants, and dishwashers will grow more slowly than other food and beverage serving and related workers because diners increasingly are eating at more casual dining spots, such as coffee bars and sandwich shops, rather than at the full-service restaurants and drinking places that employ more of these workers.

Earnings

Food and beverage serving and related workers derive their earnings from a combination of hourly wages and customer tips. Earnings vary greatly, depending on the type of job and establishment. For example, fast-food workers and hosts and hostesses usually do not receive tips, so their wage rates may be higher than those of waiters and waitresses and bartenders in full-service restaurants, who typically earn more from tips than from wages. In some restaurants, workers contribute all or a portion of their tips to a tip pool, which is distributed among qualifying workers. Tip pools allow workers who don't usually receive tips directly from customers, such as dining room attendants, to feel a part of a team and to share in the rewards of good service.

In May 2004, median hourly earnings (including tips) of waiters and waitresses were $6.75. The middle 50 percent earned between $6.04 and $8.34. The lowest 10 percent earned less than $5.60, and the highest 10 percent earned more than $11.27 an hour. For most waiters and waitresses, higher earnings are primarily the result of receiving more in tips rather than higher hourly wages. Tips usually average between 10 and 20 percent of guests' checks; waiters and waitresses working in busy, expensive restaurants earn the most.

Bartenders had median hourly earnings (including tips) of $7.42 in May 2004. The middle 50 percent earned between $6.34 and $9.26. The lowest 10 percent earned less than $5.72, and the highest 10 percent earned more than $12.47 an hour. Like waiters and waitresses, bartenders employed in public bars may receive more than half of their earnings as tips. Service bartenders often are paid higher hourly wages to offset their lower tip earnings.

Median hourly earnings (including tips) of dining room and cafeteria attendants and bartender helpers were $7.10 in May 2004. The middle 50 percent earned between $6.24 and $8.25. The lowest 10 percent earned less than $5.68, and the highest 10 percent earned more than $9.88 an hour. Most received over half of their earnings as wages; the rest of their income was a share of the proceeds from tip pools.

Median hourly earnings of hosts and hostesses were $7.52 in May 2004. The middle 50 percent earned between $6.48 and $8.63. The lowest 10 percent earned less than $5.77, and the highest 10 percent earned more than $10.49 an hour. Wages comprised the majority of their earnings. In some cases, wages were supplemented by proceeds from tip pools.

Median hourly earnings of combined food preparation and serving workers, including fast food, were $7.06 in May 2004. The middle 50 percent earned between $6.18 and $8.25. The lowest 10 percent earned less than $5.65, and the highest 10 percent earned more than $9.85 an hour. Although some combined food preparation and serving workers receive a part of their earnings as tips, fast-food workers usually do not.

Median hourly earnings of counter attendants in cafeterias, food concessions, and coffee shops (including tips) were $7.53 in May 2004. The middle 50 percent earned between $6.50 and $8.59 an hour. The lowest 10 percent earned less than $5.80, and the highest 10 percent earned more than $10.38 an hour.

Median hourly earnings of dishwashers were $7.35 in May 2004. The middle 50 percent earned between $6.41 and $8.37. The lowest 10 percent earned less than $5.76, and the highest 10 percent earned more than $9.81 an hour.

Median hourly earnings of nonrestaurant food servers were $7.95 in May 2004. The middle 50 percent earned between $6.64 and $9.98. The lowest 10 percent earned less than $5.86, and the highest 10 percent earned more than $12.53 an hour.

Many beginning or inexperienced workers start earning the federal minimum wage of $5.15 an hour. However, a few states set minimum wages higher than the federal minimum. Also, various minimum wage exceptions apply under specific circumstances to disabled workers, full-time students, youth under age 20 in their first 90 days of employment, tipped employees, and student-learners. Tipped employees are those who customarily and regularly receive more than $30 a month in tips. The employer may consider tips as part of wages, but the employer must pay at least $2.13 an hour in direct wages. Employers also are permitted to deduct from wages the cost, or fair value, of any meals or lodging provided. Many employers, however, provide free meals and furnish uniforms. Food and beverage service workers who work full time often receive typical benefits, while part-time workers usually do not.

In some large restaurants and hotels, food and beverage serving and related workers belong to unions—principally the Hotel Employees and Restaurant Employees International Union and the Service Employees International Union.

Related Occupations

Other workers whose job involves serving customers and handling money include flight attendants, gaming services workers, and retail salespersons.

Sources of Additional Information

Information about job opportunities may be obtained from local employers and local offices of state employment services agencies.

A guide to careers in restaurants plus a list of 2- and 4-year colleges offering food service programs and related scholarship information is available from:

- National Restaurant Association, 1200 17th St. NW, Washington, DC 20036-3097. Internet: http://www.restaurant.org

For general information on hospitality careers, contact:

- International Council on Hotel, Restaurant, and Institutional Education, 2613 North Parham Rd., 2nd Floor, Richmond, VA 23294. Internet: http://www.chrie.org

Food Processing Occupations

(O*NET 51-3011.01, 51-3011.02, 51-3021.00, 51-3022.00, 51-3023.00, 51-3091.00, 51-3092.00, and 51-3093.00)

Significant Points

- Most employees in manual food-processing jobs require little or no training prior to being hired.
- As more jobs involving cutting and processing meat shift from retail stores to food-processing plants, job growth will be concentrated among lesser skilled workers, who are employed primarily in manufacturing.

Nature of the Work

Food processing occupations include many different types of workers who process raw food products into the finished goods sold by grocers or wholesalers, restaurants, or institutional food services. These workers perform a variety of tasks and are responsible for producing many of the food products found in every household.

Butchers as well as meat, poultry, and fish cutters and trimmers are employed at different stages in the process by which animal carcasses are converted into manageable pieces of meat, known as boxed meat, that are suitable for sale to wholesalers and retailers. Meat, poultry, and fish cutters and trimmers commonly work in animal slaughtering and processing plants, while butchers and meatcutters usually are employed in retail establishments. As a result, the nature of these jobs varies significantly.

In animal slaughtering and processing plants, *slaughterers and meatpackers* slaughter cattle, hogs, goats, and sheep and cut the carcasses into large wholesale cuts, such as rounds, loins, ribs, and chucks, to facilitate the handling, distribution, and marketing of meat. In some of these plants, slaughterers and meatpackers also further process the large parts into cuts that are ready for retail use. These workers also produce hamburger meat and meat trimmings, which are used to prepare sausages, luncheon meats, and other fabricated meat products. Slaughterers and meatpackers usually work on assembly lines, with each individual responsible for only a few of the many cuts needed to process a carcass. Depending on the type of cut, these workers use knives; cleavers; meat saws; band saws; or other potentially dangerous equipment.

In grocery stores, wholesale establishments that supply meat to restaurants, and institutional food service facilities, *butchers and meatcutters* separate wholesale cuts of meat into retail cuts or individually sized servings. These workers cut meat into steaks and chops, shape and tie roasts, and grind beef for sale as chopped meat. Boneless cuts are prepared with the use of knives, slicers, or power cutters, while band saws are required to carve bone-in pieces of meat. Butchers and meatcutters in retail food stores also may weigh, wrap, and label the cuts of meat; arrange them in refrigerated cases for display; and prepare special cuts to fill unique orders by customers.

Poultry cutters and trimmers slaughter and cut up chickens, turkeys, and other types of poultry. Although the poultry processing industry is becoming increasingly automated, many jobs, such as trimming, packing, and deboning, are still done manually. As in the animal slaughtering and processing industry, most poultry cutters and trimmers perform routine cuts on poultry as it moves along production lines.

Unlike some of the other occupations just listed, *fish cutters and trimmers,* also called *fish cleaners,* are likely to be employed in both manufacturing and retail establishments. These workers primarily scale, cut, and dress fish by removing the head, scales, and other inedible portions and cutting the fish into steaks or fillets. In retail markets, these workers may also wait on customers and clean fish to order.

Meat, poultry, and fish cutters and trimmers also prepare ready-to-heat foods. This preparation often entails filleting meat or fish; cutting it into bite-sized pieces; preparing and adding vegetables; and applying sauces, marinades, or breading.

Bakers mix and bake ingredients in accordance with recipes to produce varying quantities of breads, pastries, and other baked goods. Bakers commonly are employed in grocery stores and specialty shops, and produce small quantities of breads, pastries, and other baked goods for consumption on premises or for sale as specialty baked goods. In manufacturing, bakers produce goods in large quantities, using high-volume mixing machines, ovens, and other equipment. Goods produced in large quantities usually are available for sale through distributors, grocery stores, or manufacturers' outlets.

Others in food processing occupations include *food batchmakers,* who set up and operate equipment that mixes, blends, or cooks ingredients used in the manufacture of food products, according to formulas or recipes; *food cooking machine operators and tenders,* who operate or tend to cooking equipment, such as steam-cooking vats, deep-fry cookers, pressure cookers, kettles, and boilers to prepare food products, such as meat, sugar, cheese, and grain; and *food and tobacco roasting, baking, and drying machine operators and tenders,* who use equipment to reduce the moisture content of food or tobacco products or to process food in preparation for canning. Some of the machines that are used include hearth ovens, kiln driers, roasters, char kilns, steam ovens, and vacuum drying equipment.

Working Conditions

Working conditions vary by type and size of establishment. In animal slaughtering and processing plants and large retail food establishments, butchers and meatcutters work in large meatcutting rooms equipped with power machines and conveyors. In small retail markets, the butcher or fish cleaner may work in a cramped space behind the meat or fish counter. To prevent viral and bacterial infections, work areas must be kept clean and sanitary.

Butchers and meatcutters, poultry and fish cutters and trimmers, and slaughterer and meatpackers often work in cold, damp rooms. The work areas are refrigerated to prevent meat from spoiling and are damp because meat cutting generates large amounts of blood, condensation, and fat. Cool, damp floors increase the likelihood of slips and falls. In addition, cool temperatures, long periods of standing, and repetitious physical tasks make the work tiring. As a result, butchers as well as meat, poultry, and fish cutters and trimmers are more susceptible to injury than are most other workers.

Injuries include cuts and occasional amputations, which occur when knives, cleavers, or power tools are used improperly. Also, repetitive slicing and lifting often lead to cumulative trauma injuries, such as carpal tunnel syndrome. To reduce the incidence of cumulative trauma injuries, some employers have reduced employee workloads, added prescribed rest periods, redesigned jobs and tools, and promoted increased awareness of early warning signs so that steps can be taken to prevent further injury. Nevertheless, workers in the occupation still face the serious threat of disabling injuries.

Most traditional bakers work in bakeries, cake shops, hot-bread shops, hotels, restaurants, and cafeterias, and in the bakery departments of supermarkets. Bakers may work under hot and noisy conditions. Also, bakers typically work under strict order deadlines and critical time-sensitive baking requirements, both of which can induce stress. Bakers usually work in shifts and may work early mornings, evenings, weekends, and holidays. While many bakers often work as part of a team, they also may work alone when baking particular items. These workers may supervise assistants and teach apprentices and trainees. Bakers in retail establishments may be required to serve customers.

Other food processing workers—such as food batchmakers; food and tobacco roasting, baking, and drying machine operators and tenders; and food cooking machine operators and tenders—typically work in production areas that are specially designed for food preservation or processing. Food batchmakers, in particular, work in kitchen-type, assembly-line production facilities. Because this work involves food, work areas must meet governmental sanitary regulations. The ovens, as well as the motors of blenders, mixers, and other equipment, often make work areas very warm and noisy. There are some hazards, such as burns, created by the equipment that these workers use. Food batchmakers; food and tobacco roasting, baking, and drying machine operators; and food cooking machine operators and tenders spend a great deal of time on their feet and generally work a regular 40-hour week that may include evening and night shifts.

Training, Other Qualifications, and Advancement

Training varies widely among food processing occupations. However, most manual food processing workers require little or no training prior to being hired.

Most butchers as well as poultry and fish cutters and trimmers acquire their skills on the job through formal and informal training programs. The length of training varies significantly. Simple cutting operations require a few days to learn, while more complicated tasks, such as eviscerating slaughtered animals, generally require several months to learn. The training period for highly skilled butchers at the retail level may be 1 or 2 years.

Generally, on-the-job trainees begin by doing less difficult jobs, such as making simple cuts or removing bones. Under the guidance of experienced workers, trainees learn the proper use and care of tools and equipment and how to prepare various cuts of meat. After demonstrating skill with various meatcutting tools, trainees learn to divide carcasses into wholesale cuts and wholesale cuts into retail and individual portions. Trainees also may learn to roll and tie roasts, prepare sausage, and cure meat. Those employed in retail food establishments often are taught operations, such as inventory control, meat buying, and recordkeeping. In addition, growing concern about food-borne pathogens in meats has led employers to offer numerous safety seminars and extensive training in food safety to employees.

Skills that are important to meat, poultry, and fish cutters and trimmers include manual dexterity, good depth perception, color discrimination, and good hand-eye coordination. Physical strength often is needed to lift and move heavy pieces of meat. Butchers and fish cleaners who wait on customers should have a pleasant personality, a neat appearance, and the ability to communicate clearly. In some states, a health certificate is required for employment.

Bakers often start as apprentices or trainees. Apprentice bakers usually start in craft bakeries, while trainees usually begin in store bakeries, such as those in supermarkets. Bakers need to be skilled in baking, icing, and decorating. They also need to be able to follow instructions, have an eye for detail, and communicate well with others. Knowledge of bakery products and ingredients, as well as mechanical mixing and baking equipment, is important. Many apprentice bakers participate in correspondence study and may work towards a certificate in baking. Working as a baker's assistant or at other activities that involve handling food also is a useful tool for training. The complexity of the skills required for certification as a baker often is underestimated. Bakers need to know about applied chemistry; ingredients and nutrition; government health and sanitation regulations; business concepts; and production processes, including how to operate and maintain machinery. Modern food plants typically use high-speed automated equipment that often is operated by computers.

Food machine operators and tenders usually are trained on the job. They learn to run the different types of equipment by watching and helping other workers. Training can last anywhere from a month to a year, depending on the complexity of the tasks and the number of products involved. A degree in the appropriate area—dairy processing for those working in dairy product operations, for example—is helpful for advancement to a lead worker or a supervisory role. Most food batchmakers participate in on-the-job training, usually from about a month to a year. Some food batchmakers learn their trade through an approved apprenticeship program.

Food processing workers in retail or wholesale establishments may progress to supervisory jobs, such as department managers or team leaders in supermarkets. A few of these workers may become buyers for wholesalers or supermarket chains. Some food processing workers go on to open their own markets or bakeries. In processing plants, workers may advance to supervisory positions or become team leaders.

Employment

Food processing workers held 725,000 jobs in 2004. Employment among the various types of food processing occupations was distributed as follows:

Bakers	166,000
Meat, poultry, and fish cutters and trimmers	140,000
Slaughterers and meat packers	136,000
Butchers and meat cutters	134,000
Food batchmakers	87,000
Food cooking machine operators and tenders	43,000
Food and tobacco roasting, baking, and drying machine operators and tenders	18,000

Thirty-five percent of all food processing workers were employed in animal slaughtering and processing plants. Another 23 percent were employed at grocery stores. Most of the remainder worked in other food manufacturing industries. Butchers, meatcutters, and bakers are employed in almost every city and town in the nation, while most other food processing jobs are concentrated in communities with food-processing plants.

Job Outlook

Overall employment in the food processing occupations is projected to grow about as fast as average for all occupations through 2014. Increasingly, cheaper meat imports from abroad will have a negative effect on domestic employment in many food processing occupations. As more jobs involving cutting and processing meat shift from retail stores to food-processing plants, job growth will be concentrated among lesser skilled workers, who are employed primarily in manufacturing. Nevertheless, job opportunities should be available at all levels of the occupation due to the need to replace experienced workers who transfer to other occupations or leave the labor force.

As the nation's population grows, the demand for meat, poultry, and seafood should continue to increase. Successful marketing by the poultry industry is likely to increase demand for chicken and ready-to-heat products. Similarly, the development of prepared food products that are lower in fat and more nutritious promises to stimulate the consumption of red meat. The trend toward preparing meat in containers at the processing level also should contribute to demand for animal slaughterers and meatpackers.

Lesser skilled meat, poultry, and fish cutters and trimmers—who work primarily in animal slaughtering and processing plants—should experience average employment growth. With the growing popularity of labor-intensive, ready-to-heat poultry products, demand for poultry workers should remain firm. Fish cutters also will be in demand, as the task of preparing ready-to-heat fish goods gradually shifts from retail stores to processing plants. Also, advances in fish farming, or "aquaculture," should help meet the growing demand for fish and produce opportunities for fish cutters.

Employment of more highly skilled butchers and meatcutters, who work primarily in retail stores, is expected to grow more slowly than average. Automation and the consolidation of the animal slaughtering and processing industries are enabling employers to transfer employment from higher paid butchers to lower wage slaughterers and meatpackers in meatpacking plants. At present, most red meat arrives at grocery stores partially cut up, but a growing share of meat is being delivered prepackaged, with additional fat removed, to wholesalers and retailers. This trend is resulting in less work and, thus, fewer jobs for retail butchers.

While high-volume production equipment limits the demand for bakers in manufacturing, overall employment of bakers is expected to increase about as fast as average due to growing numbers of large wholesale bakers in stores, specialty shops, and traditional bakeries. In addition to the growing numbers of cookie, muffin, and cinnamon roll bakeries, the numbers of specialty bread and bagel shops have been growing, spurring demand for bread and pastry bakers.

Employment of food batchmakers, food cooking machine operators and tenders, and food and tobacco cooking and roasting machine operators and tenders, is expected to grow more slowly than average. As more of this work is being done at the manufacturing level rather than at the retail level, potential employment gains will be offset by productivity gains from automated cooking and roasting equipment.

Earnings

Earnings vary by industry, skill, geographic region, and educational level. Median annual earnings of butchers and meatcutters were $25,890 in May 2004. The middle 50 percent earned between $19,780 and $34,260. The highest 10 percent earned more than $41,980 annually, while the lowest 10 percent earned less than $15,920. Butchers and meatcutters employed at the retail level typically earn more than those in manufacturing. Median annual earnings in the industries employing the largest numbers of butchers and meatcutters in May 2004 were as follows:

Other general merchandise stores	$31,900
Grocery stores	27,030
Specialty food stores	22,010
Animal slaughtering and processing	21,440

Meat, poultry, and fish cutters and trimmers typically earn less than butchers and meatcutters. In May 2004, median annual earnings for these lower skilled workers were $18,900. The middle 50 percent earned between $16,240 and $22,360. The highest 10 percent earned more than $27,430, while the lowest 10 percent earned less than $14,410. Median annual earnings in the industries employing the largest numbers of meat, poultry, and fish cutters and trimmers in May 2004 are shown in the following tabulation:

Grocery and related product wholesalers $20,790
Grocery stores 20,650
Animal slaughtering and processing 18,660
Seafood product preparation and packaging 18,040

Median annual earnings of bakers were $21,330 in May 2004. The middle 50 percent earned between $17,070 and $27,210. The highest 10 percent earned more than $34,410, and the lowest 10 percent earned less than $14,680. Median annual earnings in the industries employing the largest numbers of bakers in May 2004 are given in the following tabulation:

Other general merchandise stores $23,390
Bakeries and tortilla manufacturing 22,170
Grocery stores 21,340
Full-service restaurants.......................................19,980
Limited-service eating places 18,690

Median annual earnings of food batchmakers were $22,090 in May 2004. The middle 50 percent earned between $17,010 and $28,790. The highest 10 percent earned more than $35,540, and the lowest 10 percent earned less than $14,370. Median annual earnings in the industries employing the largest numbers of food batchmakers in May 2004 are presented in the following tabulation:

Dairy product manufacturing $26,550
Other food manufacturing...................................23,970
Fruit and vegetable preserving and specialty food manufacturing 23,230
Sugar and confectionery product manufacturing......21,420
Bakeries and tortilla manufacturing 20,890

In May 2004, median annual earnings for slaughterers and meatpackers were $20,860. The middle 50 percent earned between $18,120 and $23,920. The highest 10 percent earned more than $27,910, and the lowest 10 percent earned less than $15,520. Median annual earnings in animal slaughtering and processing, the industry employing the largest number of slaughterers and meatpackers, were $20,900 in May 2004.

Median annual earnings for food cooking machine operators and tenders were $20,850 in May 2004. The middle 50 percent earned between $16,680 and $26,670. The highest 10 percent earned more than $33,780, and the lowest 10 percent earned less than $13,930. Median annual earnings in fruit and vegetable preserving and specialty food manufacturing, the industry employing the largest number of food cooking machine operators and tenders, were $24,370 in May 2004.

In May 2004, median annual earnings for food and tobacco roasting, baking, and drying machine operators and tenders were $23,840. The middle 50 percent earned between $18,600 and $30,590. The highest 10 percent earned more than $37,000, and the lowest 10 percent earned less than $15,000.

Food processing workers generally received typical benefits, including pension plans for union members or those employed by grocery stores. However, poultry workers rarely earned substantial benefits. In 2004, 21 percent of all food processing workers were union members or were covered by a union contract. Many food processing workers are members of the United Food and Commercial Workers International Union.

Related Occupations

Food processing workers must be skilled at both hand and machine work and must have some knowledge of processes and techniques that are involved in handling and preparing food. Other occupations that require similar skills and knowledge include chefs, cooks, and food preparation workers.

Sources of Additional Information

State employment service offices can provide information about job openings for food processing occupations.

Gaming Services Occupations

(O*NET 39-1011.00, 39-1012.00, 39-3011.00, 39-3012.00, 39-3019.99, and 39-3099.99)

Significant Points

- Job opportunities are available nationwide and are no longer limited to Nevada and New Jersey.
- Workers need a license issued by a regulatory agency, such as a state casino control board or commission; licensure requires proof of residency in the state in which gaming workers are employed.
- Employment is projected to grow faster than average.
- Job prospects are best for those with a degree or certification in gaming or a hospitality-related field, previous training or experience in casino gaming, and strong interpersonal and customer service skills.

Nature of the Work

Legalized gambling in the United States today includes casino gaming, state lotteries, pari-mutuel wagering on contests such as horse or dog racing, and charitable gaming. Gaming, the playing of games of chance, is a multibillion-dollar industry that is responsible for the creation of a number of unique service occupations.

The majority of all gaming services workers are employed in casinos. Their duties and titles may vary from one establishment to another. Despite differences in job title and task, however, workers perform many of the same basic functions in all casinos. Some positions are associated with oversight and direction—supervision, surveillance, and investigation—while others involve working with the games or patrons themselves, performing such activities as tending slot machines, handling money, writing and running tickets, and dealing cards or running games.

Like nearly every business establishment, casinos have workers who direct and oversee day-to-day operations. *Gaming supervisors* oversee the gaming operations and personnel in an assigned area. They circulate among the tables and observe the operations to ensure that all of the stations and games are covered for each shift. It is not uncommon for gaming supervisors to explain and interpret the operating rules of the house to patrons who may have difficulty understanding the rules. Gaming supervisors also may plan and organize activities to create a friendly atmosphere for the guests staying in their hotels or in casino hotels. Periodically, they address and adjust complaints about service.

Some gaming occupations demand specially acquired skills—dealing blackjack, for example—that are unique to casino work. Others require skills common to most businesses, such as the ability to conduct financial transactions. In both capacities, the workers in these jobs interact directly with patrons in attending to slot machines, making change, cashing or selling tokens and coins, writing and running for other games, and dealing cards at table games. Part of their responsibility is to make those interactions enjoyable.

Slot key persons coordinate and supervise the slot department and its workers. Their duties include verifying and handling payoff winnings to patrons, resetting slot machines after completing the payoff, and refilling machines with money. Slot key persons must be familiar with a variety of slot machines and be able to make minor repairs and adjustments to the machines as needed. If major repairs are required, slot key persons determine whether the slot machine should be removed from the floor. Working the floor as frontline personnel, they enforce safety rules and report hazards.

Gaming and sportsbook writers and runners assist in the operations of games such as bingo and keno, in addition to taking bets on sporting events. They scan tickets presented by patrons and calculate and distribute winnings. Some writers and runners operate the equipment that randomly selects the numbers. Others may announce numbers selected, pick up tickets from patrons, collect bets, or receive, verify, and record patrons' cash wagers.

Gaming dealers operate table games such as craps, blackjack, and roulette. Standing or sitting behind the table, dealers provide dice, dispense cards to players, or run the equipment. Some dealers also monitor the patrons for infractions of casino rules. Gaming dealers must be skilled in customer service and in executing their game. Dealers determine winners, calculate and pay winning bets, and collect losing bets. Because of the fast-paced work environment, most gaming dealers are competent in at least two games, usually blackjack and craps.

Working Conditions

The atmosphere in casinos is generally filled with fun and often considered glamorous. However, casino work can also be physically demanding. Most occupations require that workers stand for long periods; some require the lifting of heavy items. The atmosphere in casinos exposes workers to certain hazards, such as cigarette, cigar, and pipe smoke. Noise from slot machines, gaming tables, and talking workers and patrons may be distracting to some, although workers wear protective headgear in areas where loud machinery is used to count money.

Most casinos are open 24 hours a day, seven days a week and offer three staggered shifts.

Training, Other Qualifications, and Advancement

There usually are no minimum educational requirements for entry-level gaming jobs, although most employers prefer at least a high school diploma or GED. Each casino establishes its own requirements for education, training, and experience. Some of the major casinos and slot manufacturers run their own training schools, and almost all provide some form of in-house training in addition to requiring certification. The type and quantity of classes needed may vary. Many institutions of higher learning give training toward certificates in gaming, as well as offer an associate, bachelor's, or master's degree in a hospitality-related field such as hospitality management, hospitality administration, or hotel management. Some schools offer training in games, gaming supervision, slot attendant and slot repair technician work, slot department management, and surveillance and security.

Gaming services workers are required to have a license issued by a regulatory agency, such as a state casino control board or commission. Applicants for a license must provide photo identification, offer proof of residency in the state in which they anticipate working, and pay a fee. Age requirements vary by state. The licensing application process also includes a background investigation.

In addition to possessing a license, gaming services workers need superior customer service skills. Casino gaming workers provide entertainment and hospitality to patrons, and the quality of their service contributes to an establishment's success or failure. Therefore, gaming workers need good communication skills, an outgoing personality, and the ability to maintain their composure even when dealing with angry or demanding patrons. Personal integrity also is important, because workers handle large amounts of money.

Gaming services workers who manage money should have some experience handling cash or using calculators or computers. For such positions, most casinos administer a math test to assess an applicant's level of competency.

Most gaming supervisors have experience in other gaming occupations, typically as dealers, and have a broad knowledge of casino rules, regulations, procedures, and games. While an associate or bachelor's degree is beneficial, it is not a requirement for most positions. Gaming supervisors must have strong leadership, organizational, and communication skills. Excellent customer service and employee skills also are necessary.

Slot key persons do not need to meet formal educational requirements to enter the occupation, but completion of slot attendant or slot technician training is helpful. As with most other gaming workers, slot key persons receive on-the-job training during the first several weeks of employment.

Gaming and sportsbook writers and runners must have at least a high school diploma or GED. Most of these workers receive on-the-job training. Because gaming and sportsbook writers and runners work closely with patrons, they need excellent customer service skills.

Most gaming dealers acquire their skills by attending a dealer school or vocational and technical school. Most of these schools are found in Nevada and New Jersey. They teach the rules and procedures of the games as well as state and local laws and regulations. Graduation from one of these schools does not guarantee a job at many casinos, however, as most casinos require prospective dealers to also audition for open positions. During the audition, personal qualities are assessed along with knowledge of the games. Experienced dealers, who often are able to attract new or return business, have the best job prospects. Dealers with more experience are placed at the "high-roller" tables.

Advancement opportunities in casino gaming depend less on workers' previous casino duties and titles than on their ability and eagerness to learn new jobs. For example, an entry-level gaming worker eventually might advance to become a dealer or card room manager or to assume some other supervisory position.

Employment

Gaming services occupations provided 177,000 jobs in 2004. Employment by occupational specialty was distributed as follows:

Gaming dealers	83,000
Gaming supervisors	38,000
Slot key persons	23,000
Gaming and sports book writers and runners	18,000
Gaming service workers, all other	15,000

Gaming services workers are found mainly in the traveler accommodation and gaming industries. Most are employed in commercial casinos, including land-based or riverboat casinos, in 11 states: Colorado, Illinois, Indiana, Iowa, Louisiana, Michigan, Mississippi, Missouri, Nevada, New Jersey, and South Dakota. The largest number works in casinos in Nevada, and the second-largest group works in similar establishments in Atlantic City, New Jersey. Mississippi, which boasts the greatest number of riverboat casinos in operation, employs the most workers in that venue. In addition, there are 28 states with Indian casinos. Legal lotteries are held in 40 states and the District of Columbia, and pari-mutuel wagering is legal in 40 states. Forty-seven states and the District of Columbia also allow charitable gaming. Other states have recently passed legislation to permit gambling, but no casinos have been opened as of yet.

For most workers, gaming licensure requires proof of residency in the state in which gaming workers are employed. But some gaming services workers do not limit themselves to one state or even one country, finding jobs on the small number of casinos located on luxury cruise liners that travel the world. These individuals live and work aboard the vessel.

Job Outlook

With demand for gaming showing no sign of waning, employment in gaming services occupations is projected to grow faster than average for all occupations through 2014. Even during the recent downturn in the economy, revenues at casinos have risen. In addition, the increasing popularity and prevalence of Indian casinos, particularly in California, and pari-mutuel casinos will provide substantial job openings that were not available in the past. With many states benefiting from casino gambling in the form of tax revenue or agreements with Indian tribes, additional states are reconsidering their opposition to legalized gambling and will likely approve the construction of more casinos and other gaming establishments during the next decade. Some job growth will occur in established gaming areas in Nevada and Atlantic City, New Jersey, but most of the openings in these locations will come from job turnover.

The increase in gaming reflects growth in the population and in its disposable income, both of which are expected to continue. Higher expectations for customer service among gaming patrons also should result in more jobs for gaming services workers.

Job prospects in gaming services occupations will be best for those with previous casino gaming experience, a degree or technical or vocational training in gaming or a hospitality-related field, and strong interpersonal and customer service skills. As a direct result of increasing demand for additional table games in gaming establishments, the most rapid growth is expected among gaming dealers. However, there are generally more applicants than jobs for dealers, creating keen competition for jobs. In addition to job openings arising from employment growth, opportunities will result from the need to replace workers transferring to other occupations or leaving the labor force.

Earnings

Wage earnings for gaming services workers vary according to occupation, level of experience, training, location, and size of the gaming establishment. The following were median earnings for various gaming services occupations in May 2004:

Gaming supervisors	$40,840
Slot key persons	23,010
Gaming service workers, all other	20,820
Gaming and sports book writers and runners	18,390
Gaming dealers	14,340

Gaming dealers generally receive a large portion of their earnings from tokes, which are tips in the form of tokens received from players. Earnings from tokes can vary depending on the table games the dealer operates and the personal traits of the dealer.

Related Occupations

Many other occupations provide hospitality and customer service. Some examples of related occupations are security guards and gaming surveillance officers, sales worker supervisors, cashiers, gaming change persons and booth cashiers, retail salespersons, gaming cage workers, and tellers.

Sources of Additional Information

For additional information on careers in gaming, visit your public library and your state gaming regulatory agency or casino control commission.

Information on careers in gaming also is available from:

- American Gaming Association, 555 13th St. NW, Suite 1010 East, Washington, DC 20004. Internet: http://www.americangaming.org

Graphic Designers

(O*NET 27-1024.00)

Significant Points

- Among the five design occupations, graphic designers are expected to have the most new jobs through 2014; however, job seekers are expected to face keen competition for available positions.
- Graphic designers with Web site design and animation experience will have the best opportunities.
- A bachelor's degree is required for most entry-level positions; however, an associate degree may be sufficient for technical positions.
- About 3 out of 10 designers are self-employed; many do freelance work in addition to holding a salaried job in design or in another occupation.

Nature of the Work

Graphic designers—or graphic artists—plan, analyze, and create visual solutions to communications problems. They decide the most effective way of getting a message across in print, electronic, and film media using a variety of methods such as color, type, illustration, photography, animation, and various print and layout techniques. Graphic designers develop the overall layout and production design of magazines, newspapers, journals, corporate reports, and other publications. They also produce promotional displays, packaging, and marketing brochures for products and services, design distinctive logos for products and businesses, and develop signs and signage systems—called environmental graphics—for business and government. An increasing number of graphic designers also are developing material for Internet Web pages, interactive media, and multimedia projects. Graphic designers also may produce the credits that appear before and after television programs and movies.

The first step in developing a new graphic design is to determine the needs of the client, the message the design should portray, and its appeal to customers or users. Graphic designers consider cognitive, cultural, physical, and social factors in planning and executing designs for the target audience. Designers gather relevant information by meeting with clients, creative or art directors, and by performing their own research. Identifying the needs of consumers is becoming increasingly important for graphic designers as the scope of their work continues to focus on creating corporate communication strategies in addition to technical design and layout work.

Graphic designers prepare sketches or layouts—by hand or with the aid of a computer—to illustrate the vision for the design. They select colors, sound, artwork, photography, animation, style of type, and other visual elements for the design. Designers also select the size and arrangement of the different elements on the page or screen. They also may create graphs and charts from data for use in publications, and often consult with copywriters on any text that may accompany the visual part of the design. Designers then present the completed design to their clients or art or creative director for approval. In printing and publishing firms, graphic designers also may assist the printers by selecting the type of paper and ink for the publication and reviewing the mock-up design for errors before final publication.

Graphic designers use a variety of graphics and layout computer software to assist in their designs. Designers creating Web pages or other interactive media designs also will use computer animation and programming packages. Computer software programs allow ease and flexibility in exploring a greater number of design alternatives, thus reducing design costs and cutting the time it takes to deliver a product to market.

Graphic designers sometimes supervise assistants who carry out their creations. Designers who run their own businesses also may devote a considerable amount of time to developing new business contacts, examining equipment and space needs, and performing administrative tasks, such as reviewing catalogues and ordering samples. The need for up-to-date computer and communications equipment is an ongoing consideration for graphic designers.

Working Conditions

Working conditions and places of employment vary. Graphic designers employed by large advertising, publishing, or design firms generally work regular hours in well-lighted and comfortable settings. Designers in smaller design consulting firms, or those who freelance, generally work on a contract, or job, basis. They frequently adjust their workday to suit their clients' schedules and deadlines. Consultants and self-employed designers tend to work longer hours and in smaller, more congested, environments.

Designers may transact business in their own offices or studios or in clients' offices. Designers who are paid by the assignment are under pressure to please clients and to find new ones in order to maintain a steady income. All designers sometimes face frustration when their designs are rejected or when their work is not as creative as they wish. Graphic designers may work evenings or weekends to meet production schedules, especially in the printing and publishing industries where deadlines are shorter and more frequent.

Training, Other Qualifications, and Advancement

A bachelor's degree is required for most entry-level and advanced graphic design positions; although some entry-level technical positions may only require an associate degree. In addition to postsecondary training in graphic design, creativity, and communication and problem-solving skills are crucial. Graphic designers also need to be familiar with computer graphics and design software. A good portfolio—a collection of examples of a person's best work—often is the deciding factor in getting a job.

Bachelor's of fine arts degree programs in graphic design are offered at many colleges, universities, and private design schools. The curriculum includes studio art, principles of design, computerized design, commercial graphics production, printing techniques, and Web site design. In addition to design courses, a liberal arts education or a program that includes courses in art history, writing, psychology, sociology, foreign languages and cultural studies, marketing, and business are useful in helping designers work effectively with the content of their work. Graphic designers must effectively communicate complex subjects to a variety of audiences. Increasingly, clients rely on graphic designers to develop the content and the context of the message in addition to performing technical layout work.

Associate degrees and certificates in graphic design also are available from 2- and 3-year professional schools. These programs usually focus on the technical aspects of graphic design and include very few liberal arts courses. Graduates of 2-year programs normally qualify as assistants to graphic designers or for positions requiring technical skills only. Individuals who wish to pursue a career in graphic design—and who already possess a bachelor's degree in another field—can complete a 2-year or 3-year program in graphic design to learn the technical requirements.

The National Association of Schools of Art and Design accredits about 250 postsecondary institutions with programs in art and design. Most of these schools award a degree in graphic design. Many schools do not allow formal entry into a bachelor's degree program until a student has successfully finished a year of basic art and design courses. Applicants may be required to submit sketches and other examples of their artistic ability.

Increasingly, employers expect new graphic designers to be familiar with computer graphics and design software. Graphic designers must continually keep up to date with the development of new and updated software, usually either on their own or through software training programs.

Graphic designers also must be creative and able to communicate their ideas in writing, visually, and verbally. Because consumer tastes can change quickly, designers need to be well read, open to new ideas and influences, and quick to react to changing trends. Problem-solving skills, paying attention to detail, and the ability to work independently and under pressure also are important traits. People in this field need self-discipline to start projects on their own, to budget their time, and to meet deadlines and production schedules. Good business sense and sales ability also are important, especially for those who freelance or run their own business.

Beginning graphic designers usually receive on-the-job training and normally need 1 to 3 years of training before they can advance to higher level positions. Experienced graphic designers in large firms may advance to chief designer, art or creative director, or other supervisory positions. Some designers leave the occupation to become teachers in design schools or in colleges and universities. Many faculty members continue to consult privately or operate small design studios to complement their classroom activities. Some experienced designers open their own firms or choose to specialize in one area of graphic design.

Employment

Graphic designers held about 228,000 jobs in 2004. About 7 out of 10 were wage and salary designers. Most worked in specialized design services; advertising and related services; printing and related support activities; or newspaper, periodical, book, and directory publishers. Other graphic designers produced computer graphics for computer systems design firms or motion picture production firms. A small number of designers also worked in engineering services or for management, scientific, and technical consulting firms.

About 3 out of 10 designers were self-employed. Many did freelance work—full time or part time—in addition to holding a salaried job in design or in another occupation.

Job Outlook

Employment of graphic designers is expected to grow about as fast as average for all occupations through the year 2014, as demand for graphic design continues to increase from advertisers, publishers, and computer design firms. Among the five different design occupations, graphic designers will have the most new jobs. However, graphic designers are expected to face keen competition for available positions. Many talented individuals are attracted to careers as graphic designers. Individuals with a bachelor's degree and knowledge of computer design software, particularly those with Web site design and animation experience, will have the best opportunities.

Demand for graphic designers should increase because of the rapidly expanding market for Web-based information and expansion of the video entertainment market, including television, movies, video, and made-for-Internet outlets. Graphic designers with Web site design and animation experience will especially be needed as demand for design projects increase for interactive media—Web sites, video games, cellular telephones, personal digital assistants (PDAs), and other technology. Demand for graphic designers also will increase as advertising firms create print and Web marketing and promotional materials for a growing number of products and services.

In recent years, some computer, printing, and publishing firms have outsourced basic layout and design work to design firms overseas. This trend is expected to continue and may have a negative impact on employment growth for lower level, technical graphic design workers. However, most higher-level graphic design jobs will remain in the U.S. and will focus on developing communication strategies, called strategic design, for clients and firms in order for them to gain competitive advantages in the market. Strategic design work requires close proximity to the consumer in order to identify and target their needs and interests. Graphic designers with a broad liberal arts education and experience in marketing and business management will be best suited for these positions.

Earnings

Median annual earnings for graphic designers were $38,030 in May 2004. The middle 50 percent earned between $29,360 and $50,840. The lowest 10 percent earned less than $23,220, and the highest 10 percent earned more than $65,940. Median annual earnings in the industries employing the largest numbers of graphic designers were:

Architectural, engineering, and related services $42,740
Specialized design services 41,620
Advertising and related services 40,010
Printing and related support activities 32,830
Newspaper, periodical, book, and directory publishers 32,390

The American Institute of Graphic Arts reported 2005 median annual total cash compensation for graphic designers according to level of responsibility. Entry-level designers earned a median salary of $32,000 in 2005, while staff-level graphic designers earned $42,500. Senior designers, who may supervise junior staff or have some decision-making authority that reflects their knowledge of graphic design, earned $56,000. Solo designers, who freelanced or worked under contract to another company, reported median earnings of $60,000. Design directors, the creative heads of design firms or in-house corporate design departments, earned $90,000. Graphic designers with ownership or partnership interests in a firm or who were principals of the firm in some other capacity earned $100,000.

Related Occupations

Workers in other occupations in the art and design field include artists and related workers; commercial and industrial designers; fashion designers; floral designers; and interior designers. Other occupations that require computer-aided design skills include computer software engineers, drafters, and desktop publishers. Other occupations involved in the design, layout, and copy of publications include advertising, marketing, promotions, public relations, and sales managers; photographers; writers and editors; and prepress technicians and workers.

Sources of Additional Information

For general information about art and design and a list of accredited college-level programs, contact:

- National Association of Schools of Art and Design, 11250 Roger Bacon Dr., Suite 21, Reston, VA 20190-5248. Internet: http://nasad.arts-accredit.org

For information about graphic, communication, or interaction design careers, contact:

- American Institute of Graphic Arts, 164 Fifth Ave., New York, NY 10010. Internet: http://www.aiga.org

For information on workshops, scholarships, internships, and competitions for graphic design students interested in advertising careers, contact:

- Art Directors Club, 106 West 29th St., New York, NY 10001. Internet: http://www.adcglobal.org

Grounds Maintenance Workers

(O*NET 37-1012.01, 37-1012.02, 37-3011.00, 37-3012.00, 37-3013.00, and 37-3019.99)

Significant Points

- Opportunities should be very good, especially for workers willing to work seasonal or variable schedules, because of significant job turnover and increasing demand by landscaping services companies.
- Many beginning jobs have low earnings and are physically demanding.
- Most workers learn through short-term on-the-job training.

Nature of the Work

Attractively designed, healthy, and well-maintained lawns, gardens, and grounds create a positive first impression, establish a peaceful mood, and increase property values. Grounds maintenance workers perform the variety of tasks necessary to achieve a pleasant and functional outdoor environment. They also care for indoor gardens and plantings in commercial and public facilities, such as malls, hotels, and botanical gardens.

The duties of *landscaping workers* and *groundskeeping workers* are similar and often overlap. Landscaping workers physically install and maintain landscaped areas. They grade property, install lighting or sprinkler systems, and build walkways, terraces, patios, decks, and fountains. In addition to initially transporting and planting new vegetation, they transplant, mulch, fertilize, and water flowering plants, trees, and shrubs and mow and water lawns. A growing number of residential and commercial clients, such as managers of office buildings, shopping malls, multiunit residential buildings, and hotels and motels, favor full-service landscape maintenance. Landscaping workers perform a range of duties, including mowing, edging, trimming, fertilizing, dethatching, and mulching for such clients on a regular basis during the growing season.

Groundskeeping workers, also called *groundskeepers*, maintain a variety of facilities, including athletic fields, golf courses, cemeteries, university campuses, and parks. In addition to caring for sod, plants, and trees, they rake and mulch leaves, clear snow from walkways and parking lots, and use irrigation methods to adjust the amount of water consumption and prevent waste. They see to the proper upkeep and repair of sidewalks, parking lots, groundskeeping equipment, pools, fountains, fences, planters, and benches.

Groundskeeping workers who care for athletic fields keep natural and artificial turf in top condition, mark out boundaries, and before events paint turf with team logos and names. They must make sure that the underlying soil on fields with natural turf has the required composition to allow proper drainage and to support the grasses used on the field. Groundskeeping workers mow, water, fertilize, and aerate the fields regularly. They also vacuum and disinfect synthetic turf after its use, in order to prevent the growth of harmful bacteria, and they remove the turf and replace the cushioning pad periodically.

Workers who maintain golf courses are called *greenskeepers*. Greenskeepers do many of the same things as other groundskeepers. In addition, greenskeepers periodically relocate the holes on putting greens to eliminate uneven wear of the turf and to add interest and challenge to the game. Greenskeepers also keep canopies, benches, ball washers, and tee markers repaired and freshly painted.

Some groundskeeping workers specialize in caring for cemeteries and memorial gardens. They dig graves to specified depths, generally using a backhoe. They mow grass regularly, apply fertilizers and other chemicals, prune shrubs and trees, plant flowers, and remove debris from graves.

Groundskeeping workers in parks and recreation facilities care for lawns, trees, and shrubs, maintain athletic fields and playgrounds, clean buildings, and keep parking lots, picnic areas, and other public spaces free of litter. They also may remove snow and ice from roads and walkways, erect and dismantle snow fences, and maintain swimming pools. These workers inspect buildings and equipment, make needed repairs, and keep everything freshly painted.

Landscaping and groundskeeping workers use hand tools such as shovels, rakes, pruning and regular saws, hedge and brush trimmers, and axes, as well as power lawnmowers, chain saws, snowblowers, and electric clippers. Some use equipment such as tractors and twin-axle vehicles. Landscaping and groundskeeping workers at parks, schools, cemeteries, and golf courses may use sod cutters to harvest sod that will be replanted elsewhere.

Pesticide handlers, sprayers, and applicators, vegetation, mix pesticides, herbicides, fungicides, or insecticides and apply them through sprays, dusts, vapors into the soil, or onto trees, shrubs, lawns, or botanical crops. Those working for chemical lawn service firms are more specialized, inspecting lawns for problems and applying fertilizers , herbicides, pesticides, and other chemicals to stimulate growth and prevent or control weeds, diseases, or insect infestation. Many practice integrated pest-management techniques.

Tree trimmers and pruners cut away dead or excess branches from trees or shrubs either to maintain rights-of-way for roads, sidewalks, or utilities or to improve the appearance, health, and value of trees. Some of these workers also specialize in pruning trim and shape ornamental trees and shrubs for private residences, golf courses, or other institutional grounds. Tree trimmers and pruners use handsaws, pruning hooks, shears, and clippers. When trimming near power lines, they usually use truck-mounted lifts and power pruners.

Supervisors of landscaping and groundskeeping workers perform various functions. They prepare cost estimates, schedule work for crews on the basis of weather conditions or the availability of equipment, perform spot checks to ensure the quality of the service, and suggest changes in work procedures. In addition, supervisors train workers in their tasks; keep employees' time records and record work performed; and even assist workers when deadlines are near. Supervisors who own their own business are also known as *landscape contractors*. They may also call themselves *landscape designers* if they create landscape design plans.

Supervisors of tree trimmers and pruners are often referred to as arborists. Arborists specialize in the care of individual trees and are trained and equipped to provide proper care. Some arborists plant trees, and most can recommend types of trees that are appropriate for a specific location, as the wrong tree in the wrong location could lead to future problems as a result of limited growing space, insects, diseases, or poor growth. Arborists are employed by cities to improve urban green space, utilities to maintain power distribution networks, companies to care for residential and commercial properties, as well as many other settings.

Working Conditions

Many of the jobs for grounds maintenance workers are seasonal, meaning that they are in demand mainly in the spring, summer, and fall, when most planting, mowing, trimming, and cleanup are necessary. Most of the work is performed outdoors in all kinds of weather. It can be physically demanding and repetitive, involving much bending, lifting, and shoveling. Workers in landscaping and groundskeeping may be under pressure to get the job completed, especially when they are preparing for scheduled events such as athletic competitions.

Those who work with pesticides, fertilizers, and other chemicals, as well as dangerous equipment and tools such as power lawnmowers, chain saws, and power clippers, must exercise safety precautions. Workers who use motorized equipment must take care to protect themselves against hearing damage.

Training, Other Qualifications, and Advancement

There usually are no minimum educational requirements for entry-level positions in grounds maintenance, although a diploma is necessary for some jobs. In 2004, most workers had a high school education or less. Short-term on-the-job training generally is sufficient to teach new hires how to operate equipment such as mowers, trimmers, leaf blowers, and small tractors and to follow correct safety procedures. Entry-level workers must be able to follow directions and learn proper planting and maintenance procedures for their localities. They also must learn how to repair the equipment they're using. If driving is an essential part of a job, employers look for applicants with a good driving record and some experience driving a truck. Employers also look for responsible, self-motivated individuals because grounds maintenance workers often work with little supervision. Workers who deal directly with customers must get along well with people.

Laborers who demonstrate a willingness to work hard and quickly, have good communication skills, and take an interest in the business may advance to crew leader or other supervisory positions. Advancement or entry into positions such as grounds manager and landscape contractor usually requires some formal education beyond high school and several years of progressively more responsible experience.

Most states require certification for workers who apply pesticides. Certification requirements vary, but usually include passing a test on the proper and safe use and disposal of insecticides, herbicides, and fungicides. Some states require that landscape contractors be licensed.

The Professional Grounds Management Society (PGMS) offers certification to grounds managers who have a combination of 8 years of experience and formal education beyond high school and who pass an examination covering subjects such as equipment management, personnel management, environmental issues, turf care, ornamentals, and circulatory systems. The PGMS also offers certification to groundskeepers who have a high school diploma or equivalent, plus 2 years of experience in the grounds maintenance field.

The Professional Landcare Network (PLANET) offers the designations "Certified Landscape Professional" (Exterior and Interior) and "Certified Landscape Technician" (Exterior or Interior) to those who meet established education and experience standards and who pass a specific examination. The hands-on test for technicians covers areas such as the operation of maintenance equipment and the installation of plants by reading a plan. A written safety test also is administered. PLANET also offers the designations "Certified Turfgrass Professional" (CTP) and "Certified Ornamental Landscape Professional" (COLP), which require written exams.

Some workers with groundskeeping backgrounds may start their own businesses after several years of experience.

Employment

Grounds maintenance workers held about 1.5 million jobs in 2004. Employment was distributed as follows:

Landscaping and groundskeeping workers	1,177,000
First-line supervisors/managers of landscaping, lawn service, and groundskeeping workers	184,000
Tree trimmers and pruners	55,000
Pesticide handlers, sprayers, and applicators, vegetation	30,000
Grounds maintenance workers, all other	21,000

About one-third of the workers in grounds maintenance were employed in companies providing landscaping services to buildings and dwellings. Others worked for property management and real-estate development firms, lawn and garden equipment and supply stores, and amusement and recreation facilities, such as golf courses and racetracks. Some were employed by local governments, installing and maintaining landscaping for parks, schools, hospitals, and other public facilities.

Almost 1 out of every 4 grounds maintenance workers was self-employed, providing landscape maintenance directly to customers on a contract basis. About 1 of every 7 worked part time; about 8% were of school age.

Job Outlook

Those interested in grounds maintenance occupations should find plentiful job opportunities in the future. Demand for their services is growing, and because wages for beginners are low and the work is physically demanding, many employers have difficulty attracting enough workers to fill all openings, creating very good job opportunities. In addition, high turnover will generate a large number of job openings, including at the supervisory and managerial level.

More workers also will be needed to keep up with increasing demand by lawn care and landscaping companies. Employment of grounds maintenance workers is expected to grow faster than the average for all occupations through the year 2014. Expected growth in the construction of all types of buildings, from office buildings to shopping malls and residential housing, plus more highways and parks, will increase demand for grounds maintenance workers. In addition, the upkeep and renovation of existing landscaping and grounds are continuing sources of demand for grounds maintenance workers. Owners of many buildings and facilities recognize the importance of "curb appeal" in attracting business and maintaining the value of the property and are expected to use grounds maintenance services more extensively to maintain and upgrade their properties. Grounds maintenance workers working for state and local governments, however, may face budget cuts, which may affect hiring.

Homeowners are a growing source of demand for grounds maintenance workers. Many two-income households lack the time to take care of their lawn so they are increasingly hiring people to maintain it for them. They also know that a nice yard will increase the property's value. In addition, there is a growing interest by homeowners in their backyards, as well as a desire to make the yards more attractive for outdoor entertaining. With many newer homes having more and bigger windows overlooking the yard, it becomes more important to maintain and beautify the grounds. Also, as the population ages, more elderly homeowners will require lawn care services to help maintain their yards.

Job opportunities for tree trimmers and pruners should also increase as utility companies step up pruning of trees around electric lines to prevent power outages. Additionally, tree trimmers and pruners will be needed to help combat infestations caused by new species of insects from other countries. Ash trees in Michigan, for example, have been especially hurt by a pest from China.

Job opportunities for nonseasonal work are more numerous in regions with temperate climates, where landscaping and lawn services are required all year. However, opportunities may vary with local economic conditions.

Earnings

Median hourly earnings in May 2004 of grounds maintenance workers were as follows:

First-line supervisors/managers of landscaping, lawn service, and groundskeeping workers	$16.99
Tree trimmers and pruners	12.57
Pesticide handlers, sprayers, and applicators, vegetation	12.30
Landscaping and groundskeeping workers	9.82
Grounds maintenance workers, all other	9.57

Median hourly earnings in the industries employing the largest numbers of landscaping and groundskeeping workers in May 2004 were as follows:

Elementary and secondary schools	$13.25
Local government	11.25
Services to buildings and dwellings	9.78
Other amusement and recreation industries	9.14
Employment services	8.64

Related Occupations

Grounds maintenance workers perform most of their work outdoors and have some knowledge of plants and soils. Others whose jobs may require that they work outdoors are agricultural workers; farmers, ranchers, and agricultural managers; forest, conservation, and logging workers; landscape architects; and biological scientists.

Sources of Additional Information

For career and certification information on tree trimmers and pruners, contact

- Tree Care Industry Association, 3 Perimeter Rd., Unit I, Manchester, NH 03103-3341. Internet: http://www.TreeCareIndustry.org
- International Society of Arboriculture, P.O. Box 3129, Champaign, IL 61826-3129.

For information on work as a landscaping and groundskeeping worker, contact either of the following organizations:

- Professional Landcare Network, 950 Herndon Parkway, Suite 450, Herndon, VA 20170-5528. Internet: http://www.landcarenetwork.org/

- Professional Grounds Management Association, 720 Light Street, Baltimore, MD 21230-3850 Internet: http://www.pgms.org

For information on becoming a licensed pesticide applicator, contact your state's Department of Agriculture or Department of Environmental Protection or Conservation.

Hazardous Materials Removal Workers

(O*NET 47-4041.00)

Significant Points

- Working conditions can be hazardous, and the use of protective clothing often is required.
- Formal education beyond high school is not required, but a training program leading to a federal license is mandatory.
- Excellent job opportunities are expected.

Nature of the Work

Increased public awareness and federal and state regulations are resulting in the removal of hazardous materials from buildings, facilities, and the environment to prevent further contamination of natural resources and to promote public health and safety. Hazardous materials removal workers identify, remove, package, transport, and dispose of various hazardous materials, including asbestos, lead, and radioactive and nuclear materials. They also respond to emergencies where harmful substances are present. The removal of hazardous materials, or "hazmats," from public places and the environment also is called abatement, remediation, and decontamination.

Hazardous materials removal workers use a variety of tools and equipment, depending on the work at hand. Equipment ranges from brooms to personal protective suits that completely isolate workers from the hazardous material. The equipment required varies with the threat of contamination and can include disposable or reusable coveralls, gloves, hardhats, shoe covers, safety glasses or goggles, chemical-resistant clothing, face shields, and devices to protect one's hearing. Most workers also are required to wear respirators while working, to protect them from airborne particles. The respirators range from simple versions that cover only the mouth and nose to self-contained suits with their own air supply.

Asbestos and lead are two of the most common contaminants that hazardous materials removal workers encounter. In the past, asbestos was used to fireproof roofing and flooring, for heat insulation, and for a variety of other purposes. Today, asbestos is rarely used in buildings, but there still are structures that contain the material. Embedded in materials, asbestos is fairly harmless; airborne, however, it can cause several lung diseases, including lung cancer and asbestosis. Similarly, lead was a common building component found in paint and plumbing fixtures and pipes until the late 1970s. Because lead is easily absorbed into the bloodstream, often from breathing lead dust or from eating chips of paint containing lead, it can cause serious health risks, especially in children. Due to these risks, it has become necessary to remove lead-based products and asbestos from buildings and structures.

Asbestos abatement workers and *lead abatement workers* remove asbestos, lead, and other materials from buildings scheduled to be renovated or demolished. Using a variety of hand and power tools, such as vacuums and scrapers, these workers remove the asbestos and lead from surfaces. A typical residential lead abatement project involves the use of a chemical to strip the lead-based paint from the walls of the home. Lead abatement workers apply the compound with a putty knife and allow it to dry. Then they scrape the hazardous material into an impregnable container for transport and storage. They also use sandblasters and high-pressure water sprayers to remove lead from large structures. The vacuums utilized by asbestos abatement workers have special, highly efficient filters designed to trap the asbestos, which later is disposed of or stored. During the abatement, special monitors measure the amount of asbestos and lead in the air, to protect the workers; in addition, lead abatement workers wear a personal air monitor that indicates the amount of lead to which a worker has been exposed. Workers also use monitoring devices to identify the asbestos, lead, and other materials that need to be removed from the surfaces of walls and structures.

Transportation of hazardous materials is safer today than it was in the past, but accidents still occur. *Emergency and disaster response workers* clean up hazardous materials after train derailments and trucking accidents. These workers also are needed when an immediate cleanup is required, as would be the case after an attack by biological or chemical weapons.

Radioactive materials are classified as either high- or low-level wastes. High-level wastes are primarily nuclear-reactor fuels used to produce electricity. Low-level wastes include any radioactively contaminated protective clothing, tools, filters, medical equipment, and other items. *Decontamination technicians* perform duties similar to those of janitors and cleaners. They use brooms, mops, and other tools to clean exposed areas and remove exposed items for decontamination or disposal. Some of these jobs are now being done by robots controlled by persons away from the contamination site.

With experience, decontamination technicians can advance to *radiation-protection technician* jobs and use radiation survey meters to locate and evaluate materials, operate high-pressure cleaning equipment for decontamination, and package radioactive materials for transportation or disposal.

Decommissioning and decontamination workers remove and treat radioactive materials generated by nuclear facilities and power plants. With a variety of hand tools, they break down contaminated items such as "gloveboxes," which are used to process radioactive materials. At decommissioning sites, the workers clean and decontaminate the facility, as well as remove any radioactive or contaminated materials.

Treatment, storage, and disposal workers transport and prepare materials for treatment or disposal. To ensure proper treatment of the materials, laws require these workers to be able to verify shipping manifests. At incinerator facilities, treatment, storage, and disposal workers transport materials from the customer or service center to the incinerator. At landfills, they follow a strict procedure for the processing and storage of hazardous materials. They organize and track the location of items in the landfill and may help change the state of a material from liquid to solid in preparation for its storage. These workers typically operate heavy machinery, such as forklifts, earthmoving machinery, and large trucks and rigs.

Mold remediation is a new and growing part of the work of some hazardous materials removal workers. Some types of mold can cause allergic reactions, especially in people who are susceptible to them. Although mold is present in almost all structures, some mold—especially the types that cause allergic reactions—can infest a building to such a degree that extensive efforts must be taken to remove it safely. Mold typically grows in damp areas, in heating and air-conditioning ducts, within walls, and in attics and basements. Although some mold remediation work is undertaken by other construction workers, mold often must be removed by hazardous materials removal workers, who take special precautions to protect themselves and surrounding areas from being contaminated.

Hazardous materials removal workers also may be required to construct scaffolding or erect containment areas prior to abatement or decontamination. In most cases, government regulation dictates that hazardous materials removal workers be closely supervised on the worksite. The standard usually is 1 supervisor to every 10 workers. The work is highly structured, sometimes planned years in advance, and team oriented. There is a great deal of cooperation among supervisors and workers. Because of the hazard presented by the materials being removed, work areas are restricted to licensed hazardous materials removal workers, thus minimizing exposure to the public.

Working Conditions

Hazardous materials removal workers function in a highly structured environment to minimize the danger they face. Each phase of an operation is planned in advance, and workers are trained to deal with safety breaches and hazardous situations. Crews and supervisors take every precaution to ensure that the worksite is safe. Whether they work with asbestos, mold, lead abatement or in radioactive decontamination, hazardous materials removal workers must stand, stoop, and kneel for long periods. Some must wear fully enclosed personal protective suits for several hours at a time; these suits may be hot and uncomfortable and may cause some individuals to experience claustrophobia.

Hazardous materials removal workers face different working conditions, depending on their area of expertise. Although many work a standard 40-hour week, overtime and shift work are common, especially in asbestos and lead abatement. Asbestos abatement and lead abatement workers are found primarily in structures such as office buildings and schools. Because they are under pressure to complete their work within certain deadlines, workers may experience fatigue. Completing projects frequently requires night and weekend work, because hazardous materials removal workers often work around the schedules of others. Treatment, storage, and disposal workers are employed primarily at facilities such as landfills, incinerators, boilers, and industrial furnaces. These facilities often are located in remote areas, due to the kinds of work being done. As a result, workers employed by treatment, storage, or disposal facilities may commute long distances to their jobs.

Decommissioning and decontamination workers, decontamination technicians, and radiation protection technicians work at nuclear facilities and electric power plants. Like treatment, storage, and disposal facilities, these sites often are far from urban areas. Workers, who often perform jobs in cramped conditions, may need to use sharp tools to dismantle contaminated objects. A hazardous materials removal worker must have great self-control and a level head to cope with the daily stress associated with handling hazardous materials.

Hazardous materials removal workers may be required to travel outside their normal working areas in order to respond to emergencies, the cleanup of which sometimes take several days or weeks to complete. During the cleanup, workers may be away from home for the entire time.

Training, Other Qualifications, and Advancement

No formal education beyond a high school diploma is required for a person to become a hazardous materials removal worker. Federal regulations require an individual to have a license to work in the occupation, although, at present, there are few laws regulating mold removal. Most employers provide technical training on the job, but a formal 32- to 40-hour training program must be completed if one is to be licensed as an asbestos abatement and lead abatement worker or a treatment, storage, and disposal worker. The program covers health hazards, personal protective equipment and clothing, site safety, recognition and identification of hazards, and decontamination. In some cases, workers discover one hazardous material while abating another. If they are not licensed to work with the newly discovered material, they cannot continue to work with it. Many experienced workers opt to take courses in additional disciplines to avoid this situation. Some employers prefer to hire workers licensed in multiple disciplines.

For decommissioning and decontamination workers employed at nuclear facilities, training is more extensive. In addition to the standard 40-hour training course in asbestos, lead, and hazardous waste, workers must take courses dealing with regulations governing nuclear materials and radiation safety. These courses add up to approximately 3 months of training, although most are not taken consecutively. Many agencies, organizations, and companies throughout the country provide training programs that are approved by the U.S. Environmental Protection Agency, the U.S. Department of Energy, and other regulatory bodies. Workers in all fields are required to take refresher courses every year in order to maintain their license.

Workers must be able to perform basic mathematical conversions and calculations, and should have good physical strength and manual dexterity. Because of the nature of the work and the time constraints sometimes involved, employers prefer people who are dependable, prompt, and detail-oriented. Because much of the work is done in buildings, a background in construction is helpful.

Employment

Hazardous materials removal workers held about 38,000 jobs in 2004. About 8 in 10 were employed in waste management and remediation services. About 1 in 20 was employed in construction, primarily in asbestos abatement and lead abatement. A small number worked at nuclear and electric plants as decommissioning and decontamination workers and radiation safety and decontamination technicians.

Job Outlook

Job opportunities are expected to be excellent for hazardous materials removal workers. The occupation is characterized by a relatively high rate of turnover, resulting in a number of job openings each year stemming from experienced workers leaving the occupation. In addition, many potential workers are not attracted to this occupation, because they may prefer work that is less strenuous and has safer working conditions. Experienced workers will have especially favorable opportunities, particularly in the private sector, as more state and local governments contract out hazardous materials removal work to private companies.

Employment of hazardous materials removal workers is expected to grow much faster than average for all occupations through the year 2014, reflecting increasing concern for a safe and clean environment. Special-trade contractors will have strong demand for the largest segment of these workers, namely, asbestos abatement and lead abatement workers; lead abatement should offer particularly good opportunities. Mold remediation is a growing part of the occupation at the present time, but it is unclear whether the growth will continue as builders find ways to prevent moisture from entering homes.

Employment of decontamination technicians, radiation safety technicians, and decommissioning and decontamination workers is expected to grow in response to increased pressure for safer and cleaner nuclear and electric generator facilities. Renewed interest in nuclear power production could lead to the construction of additional facilities. However, the number of older closed facilities that need decommissioning may continue to grow due to federal legislation. These workers are less affected by economic fluctuations because the facilities in which they work must operate, regardless of the state of the economy.

Earnings

Median hourly earnings of hazardous materials removal workers were $16.02 in May 2004. The middle 50 percent earned between $12.52 and $22.27 per hour. The lowest 10 percent earned less than $10.48 per hour, and the highest 10 percent earned more than $27.25 per hour. The median hourly earnings in remediation and other waste management services, the largest industry employing hazardous materials removal workers in May 2004, were $15.46.

According to the limited data available, treatment, storage, and disposal workers usually earn slightly more than asbestos abatement and lead abatement workers. Decontamination and decommissioning workers and radiation protection technicians, though constituting the smallest group, tend to earn the highest wages.

Related Occupations

Asbestos abatement workers and lead abatement workers share skills with other construction trades workers, including painters and paperhangers; insulation workers; and sheet metal workers. Treatment, storage, and disposal workers, decommissioning and decontamination workers, and decontamination and radiation safety technicians work closely with plant and system operators, such as power-plant operators, distributors, and dispatchers and water and wastewater treatment plant operators. Police officers and fire fighters also respond to emergencies and often are the first ones to respond to incidents where hazardous materials may be present.

Sources of Additional Information

For more information on hazardous materials removal workers that work in the construction industry, including information on training, contact:

- Laborers-AGC Education and Training Fund, 37 Deerfield Rd., P.O. Box 37, Pomfret, CT 06259. Internet: http://www.laborerslearn.org
- Heat and Frost Insulators and Asbestos Workers, 9602 M. L. King Jr. Hwy., Lanham, MD 20706. Internet: http://www.insulators.org

Heating, Air-Conditioning, and Refrigeration Mechanics and Installers

(O*NET 49-9021.01 and 49-9021.02)

Significant Points

- Employment is projected to grow faster than average.
- Job prospects are expected to be excellent, particularly for those with training from an accredited technical school or with formal apprenticeship training.
- Obtaining certification through one of several organizations is increasingly recommended by employers and may increase advancement opportunities.

Nature of the Work

Heating and air-conditioning systems control the temperature, humidity, and the total air quality in residential, commercial, industrial, and other buildings. Refrigeration systems make it possible to store and transport food, medicine, and other perishable items. Heating, air-conditioning, and refrigeration mechanics and installers—also called technicians—install, maintain, and repair such systems. Because heating, ventilation, air-conditioning, and refrigeration systems often are referred to as HVACR systems, these workers also may be called HVACR technicians.

Heating, air-conditioning, and refrigeration systems consist of many mechanical, electrical, and electronic components, such as motors, compressors, pumps, fans, ducts, pipes, thermostats, and switches. In central forced air heating systems, for example, a furnace heats air that is distributed throughout the building via a system of metal or fiberglass ducts. Technicians must be able to maintain, diagnose, and correct problems throughout the entire system. To do this, they adjust system controls to recommended settings and test the performance of the entire system using special tools and test equipment.

Technicians often specialize in either installation or maintenance and repair, although they are trained to do both. They also may specialize in doing heating work or air-conditioning or refrigeration work. Some specialize in one type of equipment—for example, hydronics (water-based heating systems), solar panels, or commercial refrigeration. Technicians also try to sell service contracts to their clients. Service contracts provide for regular maintenance of the heating and cooling systems and they help to reduce the seasonal fluctuations of this type of work.

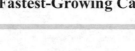

Technicians follow blueprints or other specifications to install oil, gas, electric, solid-fuel, and multiple-fuel heating systems and air conditioning systems. After putting the equipment in place, they install fuel and water supply lines, air ducts and vents, pumps, and other components. They may connect electrical wiring and controls and check the unit for proper operation. To ensure the proper functioning of the system, furnace installers often use combustion test equipment, such as carbon dioxide testers, carbon monoxide testers, combustion analyzers and oxygen testers.

After a furnace or air-conditioning unit has been installed, technicians often perform routine maintenance and repair work to keep the systems operating efficiently. They may adjust burners and blowers and check for leaks. If the system is not operating properly, they check the thermostat, burner nozzles, controls or other parts to diagnose and then correct the problem.

During the summer, when the heating system is not being used, heating equipment technicians do maintenance work, such as replacing filters, ducts, and other parts of the system that may accumulate dust and impurities during the operating season. During the winter, air-conditioning mechanics inspect the systems and do required maintenance, such as overhauling compressors.

Refrigeration mechanics install, service, and repair industrial and commercial refrigerating systems and a variety of refrigeration equipment. They follow blueprints, design specifications, and manufacturers' instructions to install motors, compressors, condensing units, evaporators, piping, and other components. They connect this equipment to the ductwork, refrigerant lines, and electrical power source. After making the connections, they charge the system with refrigerant, check it for proper operation, and program control systems.

When air-conditioning and refrigeration technicians service equipment, they must use care to conserve, recover, and recycle chlorofluorocarbon (CFC), hydrochlorofluorocarbon (HCFC), hydrofluorocarbon (HFC), and other refrigerants used in air-conditioning and refrigeration systems. The release of these refrigerants can be harmful to the environment. Technicians conserve the refrigerant by making sure that there are no leaks in the system; they recover it by venting the refrigerant into proper cylinders; they recycle it for reuse with special filter-dryers; or they insure that the refrigerant is properly disposed.

Heating, air-conditioning, and refrigeration mechanics and installers are adept at using a variety of tools, including hammers, wrenches, metal snips, electric drills, pipe cutters and benders, measurement gauges, and acetylene torches, to work with refrigerant lines and air ducts. They use voltmeters, thermometers, pressure gauges, manometers, and other testing devices to check airflow, refrigerant pressure, electrical circuits, burners, and other components.

Other craftworkers sometimes install or repair cooling and heating systems. For example, on a large air-conditioning installation job, especially where workers are covered by union contracts, ductwork might be done by sheet metal workers and duct installers; electrical work by electricians; and installation of piping, condensers, and other components by pipelayers, plumbers, pipefitters, and steamfitters. Home appliance repairers usually service room air-conditioners and household refrigerators.

Working Conditions

Heating, air-conditioning, and refrigeration mechanics and installers work in homes, retail establishments, hospitals, office buildings, and factories—anywhere there is climate-control equipment. They may be assigned to specific job sites at the beginning of each day or may be dispatched to a variety of locations if they are making service calls.

Technicians may work outside in cold or hot weather or in buildings that are uncomfortable because the air-conditioning or heating equipment is broken. In addition, technicians might have to work in awkward or cramped positions and sometimes are required to work in high places. Hazards include electrical shock, burns, muscle strains, and other injuries from handling heavy equipment. Appropriate safety equipment is necessary when handling refrigerants because contact can cause skin damage, frostbite, or blindness. Inhalation of refrigerants when working in confined spaces also is a possible hazard.

The majority of mechanics and installers work at least a 40-hour week. During peak seasons they often work overtime or irregular hours. Maintenance workers, including those who provide maintenance services under contract, often work evening or weekend shifts and are on call. Most employers try to provide a full workweek year-round by scheduling both installation and maintenance work, and many manufacturers and contractors now provide or even require service contracts. In most shops that service both heating and air-conditioning equipment, employment is stable throughout the year.

Training, Other Qualifications, and Advancement

Because of the increasing sophistication of heating, air-conditioning, and refrigeration systems, employers prefer to hire those with technical school training or those who have completed an apprenticeship. Some mechanics and installers, however, still learn the trade informally on the job.

Many secondary and postsecondary technical and trade schools, junior and community colleges, and the U.S. Armed Forces offer 6-month to 2-year programs in heating, air-conditioning, and refrigeration. Students study theory, design, and equipment construction, as well as electronics. They also learn the basics of installation, maintenance, and repair. There are three accrediting agencies that have set academic standards for HVACR programs. These accrediting bodies are HVAC Excellence, the National Center for Construction Education and Research (NCCER) and the Partnership for Air Conditioning, Heating, and Refrigeration Accreditation (PHARA). After completing these programs, new technicians generally need between an additional 6 months and 2 years of field experience before they can be considered proficient.

Apprenticeship programs frequently are run by joint committees representing local chapters of the Air-Conditioning Contractors of America, the Mechanical Contractors Association of America, Plumbing-Heating-Cooling Contractors—National Association, and locals of the sheet metal workers' International Association or the United Association of Journeymen and Apprentices of the Plumbing and Pipefitting Industry of the United States and Canada. Other apprenticeship programs are sponsored by local chapters of the Associated Builders and Contractors and the National Association of Home Builders. Formal apprenticeship programs normally last 3 to 5 years and combine on-the-job training with classroom instruction. Classes include subjects such as the use and care of tools, safety practices, blueprint reading, and the theory and design of heating, ventilation, air-conditioning, and refrigeration systems. Applicants for these programs must have a high school diploma or equivalent. Math and reading skills are essential. After completing an apprenticeship program, technicians are considered skilled trades workers and capable of working alone. These programs are also a pathway to certification and in some cases college credits.

Those who acquire their skills on the job usually begin by assisting experienced technicians. They may begin by performing simple tasks such as carrying materials, insulating refrigerant lines, or cleaning furnaces. In time, they move on to more difficult tasks, such as cutting and soldering pipes and sheet metal and checking electrical and electronic circuits.

Courses in shop math, mechanical drawing, applied physics and chemistry, electronics, blueprint reading, and computer applications provide a good background for those interested in entering this occupation. Some knowledge of plumbing or electrical work also is helpful. A basic understanding of electronics is becoming more important because of the increasing use of this technology in equipment controls. Because technicians frequently deal directly with the public, they should be courteous and tactful, especially when dealing with an aggravated customer. They also should be in good physical condition because they sometimes have to lift and move heavy equipment.

All technicians who purchase or work with refrigerants must be certified in their proper handling. To become certified to purchase and handle refrigerants, technicians must pass a written examination specific to the type of work in which they specialize. The three possible areas of certification are: Type I—servicing small appliances, Type II—high-pressure refrigerants, and Type III—low-pressure refrigerants. Exams are administered by organizations approved by the U.S. Environmental Protection Agency, such as trade schools, unions, contractor associations, or building groups.

Several organizations have begun to offer basic self-study, classroom, and Internet courses for individuals with limited experience. In addition to understanding how systems work, technicians also must learn about refrigerant products and the legislation and regulations that govern their use.

Throughout the learning process, job candidates may have to take a number of tests that measure their skills in the field. For those with less than 1 year of experience and taking classes, the industry has developed a series of exams to test basic competency in residential heating and cooling, light commercial heating and cooling, and commercial refrigeration. These are referred to as "entry-level" certification exams and are commonly conducted at both secondary and postsecondary technical and trade schools. For HVACR technicians who have at least one year of experience performing installations and 2 years of experience performing maintenance and repair, they can take a number of different tests to certify their competency in working with more specific types of equipment, such as oil-burning furnaces. The tests are offered through Refrigeration Service Engineers Society (RSES), HVAC Excellence, The Carbon Monoxide Safety Association (COSA), Air Conditioning and Refrigeration Safety Coalition, and North American Technician Excellence, Inc. (NATE), among others. Passing these tests and obtaining certification is increasingly recommended by employers and may increase advancement opportunities.

Advancement usually takes the form of higher wages. Some technicians, however, may advance to positions as supervisor or service manager. Others may move into areas such as sales and marketing. Still others may become building superintendents, cost estimators, or, with the necessary certification, teachers. Those with sufficient money and managerial skill can open their own contracting business.

Employment

Heating, air-conditioning, and refrigeration mechanics and installers held about 270,000 jobs in 2004; almost half worked for plumbing, heating, and air conditioning contractors. The remainder was employed in a variety of industries throughout the country, reflecting a widespread dependence on climate-control systems. Some worked for fuel oil dealers, refrigeration and air-conditioning service and repair shops, schools, and stores that sell heating and air-conditioning systems. Local governments, the federal government, hospitals, office buildings, and other organizations that operate large air-conditioning, refrigeration, or heating systems employed others. About 15 percent of mechanics and installers were self-employed.

Job Outlook

Job prospects for heating, air-conditioning, and refrigeration mechanics and installers are expected to be excellent, particularly for those with training from an accredited technical school or with formal apprenticeship training, and especially in the fastest growing areas of the country. A growing number of retirements of highly skilled technicians are expected to generate many job openings. In addition, employment of heating, air-conditioning, and refrigeration mechanics and installers is projected to increase faster than average for all occupations through the year 2014. As the population and stock of buildings grows, so does the demand for residential, commercial, and industrial climate-control systems. The increased complexity of HVACR systems, increasing the possibility that equipment may malfunction, also will create opportunities for service technicians. Technicians who specialize in installation work may experience periods of unemployment when the level of new construction activity declines, but maintenance and repair work usually remains relatively stable. People and businesses depend on their climate-control systems and must keep them in good working order, regardless of economic conditions.

Concern for the environment has prompted the development of new energy-saving heating and air-conditioning systems. An emphasis on better energy management should lead to the replacement of older systems and the installation of newer, more efficient systems in existing homes and buildings. Also, demand for maintenance and service work should increase as businesses and homeowners strive to keep increasingly complex systems operating at peak efficiency.

Regulations prohibiting the discharge and production of CFC and HCFC refrigerants should continue to result in the need to replace many existing air conditioning systems or modify them to use new environmentally safe refrigerants. The pace of replacement in the commercial and industrial sectors will quicken if Congress or individual states cut the time needed to fully depreciate the cost of new HVACR systems, which is being considered.

A growing focus on improving indoor air quality, as well as the increasing use of refrigerated equipment by a growing number of stores and gasoline stations that sell food, also should contribute to the creation of more jobs for heating, air-conditioning, and refrigeration technicians.

Earnings

Median hourly earnings of heating, air-conditioning, and refrigeration mechanics and installers were $17.43 in May 2004. The middle 50 percent earned between $13.51 and $22.21 an hour. The lowest 10 percent earned less than $10.88, and the top 10 percent earned more than $27.11. Median hourly earnings in the industries employing the largest numbers of heating, air-conditioning, and refrigeration mechanics and installers in May 2004 were:

Hardware and plumbing and heating equipment and supplies merchant wholesalers	$19.51
Direct selling establishments	17.81
Elementary and secondary schools	17.56
Commercial and industrial machinery and equipment (except automotive and electronic) repair and maintenance	17.52
Building equipment contractors	16.80

Apprentices usually begin at about 50 percent of the wage rate paid to experienced workers. As they gain experience and improve their skills, they receive periodic increases until they reach the wage rate of experienced workers.

Heating, air-conditioning, and refrigeration mechanics and installers enjoy a variety of employer-sponsored benefits. In addition to typical benefits such as health insurance and pension plans, some employers pay for work-related training and provide uniforms, company vans, and tools.

About 16 percent of heating, air-conditioning, and refrigeration mechanics and installers are members of a union. The unions to which the greatest numbers of mechanics and installers belong are the sheet metal workers International Association and the United Association of Journeymen and Apprentices of the Plumbing and Pipefitting Industry of the United States and Canada.

Related Occupations

Heating, air-conditioning, and refrigeration mechanics and installers work with sheet metal and piping, and repair machinery, such as electrical motors, compressors, and burners. Other workers who have similar skills include boilermakers; home appliance repairers; electricians; sheet metal workers; and pipelayers, plumbers, pipefitters, and steamfitters.

Sources of Additional Information

For more information about opportunities for training, certification, and employment in this trade, contact local vocational and technical schools; local heating, air-conditioning, and refrigeration contractors; a local of the unions or organizations previously mentioned; a local joint union-management apprenticeship committee; or the nearest office of the state employment service or apprenticeship agency.

For information on career opportunities, training, and technician certification, contact:

- Air-Conditioning Contractors of America (ACCA), 2800 Shirlington Rd., Suite 300, Arlington, VA 22206. Internet: http://www.acca.org
- Refrigeration Service Engineers Society (RSES), 1666 Rand Rd., Des Plaines, IL 60016-3552. Internet: http://www.rses.org
- Plumbing-Heating-Cooling Contractors (PHCC), 180 S. Washington St., P.O. Box 6808, Falls Church, VA 22046. Internet: http://www.phccweb.org
- Sheet Metal and Air-Conditioning Contractors National Association, 4201 Lafayette Center Dr., Chantilly, VA 20151-1209. Internet: http://www.smacna.org
- HVAC Excellence, P.O. Box 491, Mt. Prospect, IL 60056. Internet: http://www.hvacexcellence.org
- North American Technician Excellence (NATE), 4100 North Fairfax Dr., Suite 210, Arlington, VA 22203. Internet: http://www.natex.org
- Air-Conditioning and Refrigeration Institute, 4100 North Fairfax Dr., Suite 200, Arlington, VA 22203. Internet: http://www.coolcareers.org or http://www.ari.org
- Carbon Monoxide Safety Association, P.O. Box 669, Eastlake, CO 80614. Internet: http://www.cosafety.org
- National Occupational Competency Testing Institute. Internet: http://www.nocti.org
- Associated Builders and Contractors, Workforce Development Department, 4250 North Fairfax Dr., 9th Floor, Arlington, VA 22203. Internet: http://www.trytools.org
- Home Builders Institute, National Association of Home Builders, 1201 15th St. NW, 6th Floor, Washington, DC 20005-2800. Internet: http://www.hbi.org
- Mechanical Contractors Association of America, 1385 Piccard Dr., Rockville, MD 20850-4329. Internet: http://www.mcaa.org
- National Center for Construction Education and Research, P.O. Box 141104, Gainesville FL, 32601. Internet: http://www.nccer.org

Hotel, Motel, and Resort Desk Clerks

(O*NET 43-4081.00)

Significant Points

- Job opportunities should be plentiful, because of substantial replacement needs.
- Evening, weekend, and part-time work hours create potential for flexible schedules.
- Professional appearance and personality are more important than formal academic training in landing a job.

Nature of the Work

Hotel, motel, and resort desk clerks perform a variety of services for guests of hotels, motels, and other lodging establishments. Regardless of the type of accommodation, most desk clerks have similar responsibilities. They register arriving guests, assign rooms, and check out guests at the end of their stay. They also keep records of room assignments and other registration-related information on computers. When guests check out, desk clerks prepare and explain the charges, as well as process payments.

Front-desk clerks always are in the public eye and typically are the first line of customer service for a lodging property. Their attitude and behavior greatly influence the public's impressions of the establishment. And as such, they always must be courteous and helpful. Desk clerks answer questions about services, checkout times, the local community, or other matters of public interest. Clerks also report problems with guest rooms or public facilities to members of the housekeeping or maintenance staff for them to correct the problems. In larger hotels or in larger cities, desk clerks may refer queries about area attractions to a concierge and may direct more complicated questions to the appropriate manager.

In some smaller hotels and motels, where smaller staffs are employed, clerks may take on a variety of additional responsibilities, such as bringing fresh linens to rooms, which usually are performed by employees in other departments of larger lodging establishments. In the smaller places, desk clerks often are responsible for all front-office operations, information, and services. For example, they may perform the work of a bookkeeper, advance reservation agent, cashier, laundry attendant, and telephone switchboard operator.

Working Conditions

Hotels are open around the clock, creating the need for night and weekend work. Extended hours of operation also afford the many part-time job seekers an opportunity to find work in these establishments, especially on evenings and late-night shifts or on weekends and holidays. About half of all desk clerks work a 35 to 40 hour week—most of the rest work fewer hours—so the jobs are attractive to persons seeking part-time work or jobs with flexible schedules. Most clerks work in areas that are clean, well lit, and relatively quiet, although lobbies can become crowded and noisy when busy. Many hotels have stringent dress guidelines for desk clerks.

Desk clerks may experience particularly hectic times during check-in and check-out times or incur the pressures encountered when dealing with convention guests or large groups of tourists at one time. Moreover, dealing with irate guests can be stressful. Computer failures can further complicate an already busy time and add to stress levels. Hotel desk clerks may be on their feet most of the time and may occasionally be asked to lift heavy guest luggage.

Training, Other Qualifications, and Advancement

Hotel, motel, and resort desk clerks deal directly with the public, so a professional appearance and a pleasant personality are important. A clear speaking voice and fluency in English also are essential, because these employees talk directly with hotel guests and the public and frequently use the telephone or public-address systems. Good spelling and computer literacy are needed, because most of the work involves use of a computer. In addition, speaking a foreign language fluently is increasingly helpful, because of the growing international clientele of many properties.

Most hotel, motel, and resort desk clerks receive orientation and training on the job. Orientation may include an explanation of the job duties and information about the establishment, such as the arrangement of sleeping rooms, availability of additional services, such as a business or fitness center, and location of guest facilities, such as ice and vending machines, restaurants and other nearby retail stores. New employees learn job tasks through on-the-job training under the guidance of a supervisor or an experienced desk clerk. They often receive additional training on interpersonal or customer service skills and on how to use the computerized reservation, room assignment, and billing systems and equipment. Desk clerks typically continue to receive instruction on new procedures and on company policies after their initial training ends.

Formal academic training generally is not required so many students take jobs as desk clerks on evening or weekend shifts or during school vacation periods. Most employers look for people who are friendly and customer-service oriented, well groomed, and display the maturity and self confidence to demonstrate good judgment. Desk clerks, especially in high-volume and higher-end properties should be quick-thinking, show initiative, and be able to work as a member of a team. Hotel managers typically look for these personal characteristics when hiring first-time desk clerks, because it is easier to teach company policy and computer skills than personality traits.

Large hotel and motel chains may offer better opportunities for advancement than small, independently owned establishments. The large chains have more extensive career ladder programs and may offer desk clerks an opportunity to participate in a management training program. Also, the Educational Institute of the American Hotel and Motel Association offers home-study or group-study courses in lodging management, which may help some obtain promotions more rapidly.

Employment

Hotel, motel, and resort desk clerks held about 195,000 jobs in 2004. Virtually all were in hotels, motels, and other establishments in the accommodation industry. Few were self employed.

Job Outlook

Employment of hotel, motel, and resort desk clerks is expected to grow about as fast as the average for all occupations through 2014 as more hotels, motels, and other lodging establishments are built and occupancy rates rise. Job opportunities for hotel and motel desk clerks also will result from a need to replace workers, because many of these clerks either transfer to other occupations that offer better pay and advancement opportunities or simply leave the workforce altogether. Opportunities for part-time work should continue to be plentiful, because these businesses typically are staffed 24 hours a day, 7 days a week.

Employment of hotel and motel desk clerks should benefit from an increase in business and leisure travel. Shifts in preferences away from long vacations and toward long weekends and other, more frequent, shorter trips also should boost demand for these workers, because such stays increase the number of nights spent in hotels. While many lower budget and extended-stay establishments are being built to cater to families and the leisure traveler, many new luxury and resort accommodations also are opening to serve the upscale client. With the increased number of units requiring staff, employment opportunities for desk clerks should be good.

Growth of hotel, motel, and resort desk clerk jobs will be moderated by technology. Automated check-in and check-out procedures reduce the backlog of guests waiting for desk service and may reduce peak front desk staffing needs in many establishments. Nevertheless, the front desk remains the principal point of contact for guests at most properties and most will continue to have clerks on duty.

Employment of desk clerks is sensitive to cyclical swings in the economy. During recessions, vacation and business travel declines, and hotels and motels need fewer desk clerks. Similarly, employment is affected by special events, business and convention business, and seasonal fluctuations.

Earnings

Median annual earnings of hotel, motel and resort desk clerks were 17,700 in May 2004. The middle 50 percent earned between $15,190 and $21,270. The lowest 10 percent earned less than $13,040, while the highest 10 percent earned more than $25,200.

Earnings of hotel, motel and resort desk clerks vary by a number of seasonal or geographic factors, such as whether the establishment is in a major metropolitan area, a resort community, or other economic or regional characteristic. Earnings also will vary according to the size of the hotel and the level of service offered. For example, luxury hotels that offer guests more personal attention and a greater number of services typically have stricter and more demanding requirements for their desk staff. However, these higher standards of service also result in higher earnings for employees.

Related Occupations

Other positions in the hospitality industry include lodging managers. Occupations that also require workers to deal face-to-face with the public include counter and rental clerks, customer service representatives, receptionists and information clerks, and retail salespersons.

Sources of Additional Information

Information on careers in the lodging industry, as well as information about professional development and training programs, may be obtained from:

- Educational Institute of the American Hotel and Lodging Association, 800 N. Magnolia Ave., Suite 1800, Orlando, FL 32803. Internet: http://www.ei-ahma.org

Human Resources Assistants, Except Payroll and Timekeeping

(O*NET 43-4161.00)

Significant Points

- About 1 out of 4 work for federal, state, and local governments.
- Employment will grow as human resources assistants assume more responsibilities.
- Computer, communication, and interpersonal skills are important.

Nature of the Work

Human resources assistants maintain the human resource records of an organization's employees. These records include information such as name, address, job title, and earnings; benefits such as health and life insurance; and tax withholding. On a daily basis, these assistants record information and answer questions about employee absences and supervisory reports on employees' job performance. When an employee receives a promotion or switches health insurance plans, the human resources assistant updates the appropriate form. Human resources assistants also may prepare reports for managers elsewhere within the organization. For example, they might compile a list of employees eligible for an award.

In small organizations, some human resources assistants perform a variety of other clerical duties, including answering telephone or written inquiries from the public, sending out announcements of job openings or job examinations, and issuing application forms. When credit bureaus and finance companies request confirmation of a person's employment, the human resources assistant provides authorized information from the employee's personnel records. Assistants also may contact payroll departments and insurance companies to verify changes to records.

Some human resources assistants are involved in hiring. They screen job applicants to obtain information such as their education and work experience; administer aptitude, personality, and interest tests; explain the organization's employment policies and refer qualified applicants to the employing official; and request references from present or past employers. Also, human resources assistants inform job applicants, by telephone or letter, of their acceptance for or denial of employment.

In some job settings, human resources assistants have specific job titles. For example, *assignment clerks* notify a firm's existing employees of upcoming vacancies, identify applicants who qualify for the vacancies, and assign those who are qualified to various positions. They also keep track of vacancies that arise throughout the organization, and they complete and distribute forms advertising vacancies. When filled-out applications are returned, these clerks review and verify the information in them, using personnel records. After a selection for a position is made, they notify all of the applicants of their acceptance or rejection.

As another example, *identification clerks* are responsible for security matters at defense installations. They compile and record personal data about vendors, contractors, and civilian and military personnel and their dependents. The identification clerk's job duties include interviewing applicants; corresponding with law enforcement authorities; and preparing badges, passes, and identification cards.

Working Conditions

Human resources assistants usually work in clean, pleasant, and comfortable office settings. Assistants usually work a standard 35- to 40-hour week. Prolonged exposure to video display terminals may lead to eyestrain for assistants who work with computers.

Training, Other Qualifications, and Advancement

Most employers prefer applicants with a high school diploma or GED. Generally, training beyond high school is not required. However, training in computers, in filing and maintaining filing systems, in organizing, and in human resources practices is desirable. Proficiency using Microsoft Word, Excel, and other computer applications also is very desirable. Many of these skills can be learned in a vocational high school program aimed at office careers, and the remainder can be learned on the job.

Formal training is available at a small number of colleges, most of which offer diploma programs in office automation. Many proprietary schools also offer such programs.

Human resources assistants must be able to interact and communicate with individuals at all levels of the organization. In addition, assistants should demonstrate poise, tactfulness, diplomacy, and good interpersonal skills in order to handle sensitive and confidential situations.

Employment

Human resources assistants held about 172,000 jobs in 2004. About 1 out of 4 work for federal, state, and local governments. Other jobs for human resources assistants were in various industries such as health care; management of companies and enterprises; finance and insurance; and administrative and support services.

Job Outlook

Employment of human resources assistants is expected to grow about as fast as average for all occupations through 2014, as assistants assume more responsibilities. For example, workers conduct Internet research to locate resumes, they must be able to scan resumes of job candidates quickly and efficiently, and they must be increasingly sensitive to confidential information such as salaries and Social Security numbers. In a favorable job market, more emphasis is placed on human resources departments, thus increasing the demand for assistants. However, even in economic downturns there is demand for assistants, as human resources departments in all industries try to make their organizations more efficient by determining what type of employees to hire and strategically filling job openings. Human resources assistants may play an instrumental role in their organization's human resources policies. For example, they may talk to staffing firms and consulting firms, conduct other research, and then offer their ideas on issues such as whether to hire temporary contract workers or full-time staff.

As with other office and administrative support occupations, the growing use of computers in human resources departments means that much of the data entry that is done by human resources assistants can be eliminated, as employees themselves enter the data and send the electronic file to the human resources office. Such an arrangement, which is most feasible in large organizations with multiple human resources offices, could limit job growth among human resources assistants.

In addition to positions arising from job growth, replacement needs will account for many job openings for human resources assistants as they advance within the human resources department, take jobs unrelated to human resources administration, or leave the labor force.

Earnings

Median annual earnings of human resources assistants in May 2004 were $31,750. The middle 50 percent earned between $25,780 and $38,770. The lowest 10 percent earned less than $21,250 and the highest 10 percent earned more than $45,780. Median annual earnings in the industries employing the largest number of human resources assistants in May 2004 were:

Federal government	$35,490
Elementary and secondary schools	33,030
Local government	32,460
Management of companies and enterprises	30,930
General medical and surgical hospitals	29,390

In 2005, the federal government typically paid salaries ranging from $20,984 to $88,103 a year. Beginning human resources assistants with a high school diploma or 6 months of experience were paid an average annual salary of $20,984. The average salary for all human resources assistants employed by the federal government was $36,576 in 2005.

Some employers offer educational assistance to human resources assistants.

Related Occupations

Human resources assistants maintain the personnel records of an organization's employees. On a daily basis, these assistants record information and answer questions about employee absences and supervisory reports on employees' job performance. Other workers with similar skills and expertise in interpersonal relations include bookkeeping, accounting, and auditing clerks; communications equipment operators; customer service representatives; data entry and information processing workers; order clerks; receptionists and information clerks; secretaries and administrative assistants; stock clerks and order fillers; and tellers.

Sources of Additional Information

For information about human resource careers and certification, contact:

- Society for Human Resource Management, 1800 Duke St., Alexandria, VA 22314. Internet: http://www.shrm.org

Human Resources, Training, and Labor Relations Managers and Specialists

(O*NET 11-3040.00, 11-3041.00, 11-3042.00, 11-3049.99, 13-1071.01, 13-1071.02, 13-1072.00, 13-1073.00, and 13-1079.99)

Significant Points

- In filling entry-level jobs, many employers seek college graduates who have majored in human resources, human resources administration, or industrial and labor relations; other employers look for college graduates with a technical or business background or a well-rounded liberal arts education.
- For many specialized jobs, previous experience is an asset; for more advanced positions, including those of managers, arbitrators, and mediators, it is essential.
- Keen competition for jobs is expected because of the plentiful supply of qualified college graduates and experienced workers.

Nature of the Work

Attracting the most qualified employees and matching them to the jobs for which they are best suited is significant for the success of any organization. However, many enterprises are too large to permit close contact between top management and employees. Human resources, training, and labor relations managers and specialists provide this connection. In the past, these workers have been associated with performing the administrative function of an organization, such as handling employee benefits questions or recruiting, interviewing, and hiring new staff in accordance with policies and requirements that have been established in conjunction with top management. Today's human resources workers manage these tasks and, increasingly, consult top executives regarding strategic planning. They have moved from behind-the-scenes staff work to leading the company in suggesting and changing policies. Senior management is recognizing the significance of the human resources department to their financial success.

In an effort to enhance morale and productivity, limit job turnover, and help organizations increase performance and improve business results, they also help their firms effectively use employee skills, provide training and development opportunities to improve those skills, and increase employees' satisfaction with their jobs and working conditions. Although some jobs in the human resources field require only limited contact with people outside the office, dealing with people is an important part of the job.

In a small organization, a *human resources generalist* may handle all aspects of human resources work, and thus require an extensive range of knowledge. The responsibilities of human resources generalists can vary widely, depending on their employer's needs. In a large corporation, the top human resources executive usually develops and manages human resources programs and policies. These policies usually are implemented by a director or manager of human resources and, in some cases, a director of industrial relations.

The *director of human resources* may supervise several departments, each headed by an experienced manager who most likely specializes in one human resources activity, such as employment, compensation, benefits, training and development, or employee relations.

Employment and placement managers supervise the hiring and separation of employees and supervise various workers, including equal employment opportunity specialists and recruitment specialists. *Employment, recruitment,* and *placement specialists* recruit and place workers.

Recruiters maintain contacts within the community and may travel considerably, often to college campuses, to search for promising job applicants. Recruiters screen, interview, and occasionally test applicants. They also may check references and extend job offers. These workers must be thoroughly familiar with the organization and its human resources policies in order to discuss wages, working conditions, and promotional opportunities with prospective employees. They also must keep informed about equal employment opportunity (EEO) and affirmative action guidelines and laws, such as the Americans with Disabilities Act.

EEO officers, representatives, or *affirmative action coordinators* handle EEO matters in large organizations. They investigate and resolve EEO grievances, examine corporate practices for possible violations, and compile and submit EEO statistical reports.

Employer relations representatives, who usually work in government agencies, maintain working relationships with local employers and promote the use of public employment programs and services. Similarly, *employment interviewers*—whose many job titles include *human resources consultants, human resources development specialists,* and *human resources coordinators*—help to match employers with qualified jobseekers.

Compensation, benefits, and job analysis specialists conduct programs for employers and may specialize in specific areas such as position classifications or pensions. *Job analysts,* occasionally called *position classifiers,* collect and examine detailed information about job duties in order to prepare job descriptions. These descriptions explain the duties, training, and skills that each job requires. Whenever a large organization introduces a new job or reviews existing jobs, it calls upon the expert knowledge of the job analyst.

Occupational analysts conduct research, usually in large firms. They are concerned with occupational classification systems and study the effects of industry and occupational trends upon worker relationships. They may serve as technical liaison between the firm and other firms, government, and labor unions.

Establishing and maintaining a firm's pay system is the principal job of the *compensation manager.* Assisted by staff specialists, compensation managers devise ways to ensure fair and equitable pay rates. They may conduct surveys to see how their firm's rates compare with others and to see that the firm's pay scale complies with changing laws and regulations. In addition, compensation managers often manage their firm's performance evaluation system, and they may design reward systems such as pay-for-performance plans.

Employee benefits managers and specialists manage the company's employee benefits program, notably its health insurance and pension plans. Expertise in designing and administering benefits programs continues to take on importance as employer-provided benefits account for a growing proportion of overall compensation costs, and as benefit plans increase in number and complexity. For example, pension benefits might include savings and thrift, profit-sharing, and stock ownership plans; health benefits might include long-term catastrophic illness insurance and dental insurance. Familiarity with health benefits is a top priority for employee benefits managers and specialists, as more firms struggle to cope with the rising cost of health care for employees and retirees. In addition to health insurance and pension coverage, some firms offer employees life and accidental death and dismemberment insurance, disability insurance, and relatively new benefits designed to meet the needs of a changing workforce, such as parental leave, child and elder care, long-term nursing home care insurance, employee assistance and wellness programs, and flexible benefits plans. Benefits managers must keep abreast of changing federal and state regulations and legislation that may affect employee benefits.

Employee assistance plan managers, also called *employee welfare managers*, are responsible for a wide array of programs covering occupational safety and health standards and practices; health promotion and physical fitness, medical examinations, and minor health treatment, such as first aid; plant security; publications; food service and recreation activities; carpooling and transportation programs, such as transit subsidies; employee suggestion systems; child care and elder care; and counseling services. Child care and elder care are increasingly significant because of growth in the number of dual-income households and the elderly population. Counseling may help employees deal with emotional disorders, alcoholism, or marital, family, consumer, legal, and financial problems. Some employers offer career counseling as well. In large firms, certain programs, such as those dealing with security and safety, may be in separate departments headed by other managers.

Training and development managers and specialists conduct and supervise training and development programs for employees. Increasingly, management recognizes that training offers a way of developing skills, enhancing productivity and quality of work, and building worker loyalty to the firm, and most importantly, increasing individual and organizational performance to achieve business results. While training is widely accepted as an employee benefit and a method of improving employee morale, enhancing employee skills has become a business imperative. Increasingly, managers and leaders realize that the key to business growth and success is through developing the skills and knowledge of its workforce.

Other factors involved in determining whether training is needed include the complexity of the work environment, the rapid pace of organizational and technological change, and the growing number of jobs in fields that constantly generate new knowledge, and thus, require new skills. In addition, advances in learning theory have provided insights into how adults learn, and how training can be organized most effectively for them.

Training managers provide worker training either in the classroom or onsite. This includes setting up teaching materials prior to the class, involving the class, and issuing completion certificates at the end of the class. They have the responsibility for the entire learning process, and its environment, to ensure that the course meets its objectives and is measured and evaluated to understand how learning impacts business results.

Training specialists plan, organize, and direct a wide range of training activities. Trainers respond to corporate and worker service requests. They consult with onsite supervisors regarding available performance improvement services and conduct orientation sessions and arrange on-the-job training for new employees. They help all employees maintain and improve their job skills, and possibly prepare for jobs requiring greater skill. They help supervisors improve their interpersonal skills in order to deal effectively with employees. They may set up individualized training plans to strengthen an employee's existing skills or teach new ones. Training specialists in some companies set up leadership or executive development programs among employees in lower level positions. These programs are designed to develop leaders to replace those leaving the organization and as part of a succession plan. Trainers also lead programs to assist employees with job transitions as a result of mergers and acquisitions, as well as technological changes. In government-supported training programs, training specialists function as case managers. They first assess the training needs of clients and then guide them through the most appropriate training method. After training, clients may either be referred to employer relations representatives or receive job placement assistance.

Planning and program development is an essential part of the training specialist's job. In order to identify and assess training needs within the firm, trainers may confer with managers and supervisors or conduct surveys. They also evaluate training effectiveness to ensure that the training employees receive, helps the organization meet its strategic business goals and achieve results.

Depending on the size, goals, and nature of the organization, trainers may differ considerably in their responsibilities and in the methods they use. Training methods include on-the-job training; operating schools that duplicate shop conditions for trainees prior to putting them on the shop floor; apprenticeship training; classroom training; and electronic learning, which may involve interactive Internet-based training, multimedia programs, distance learning, satellite training, other computer-aided instructional technologies, videos, simulators, conferences, and workshops.

An organization's *director of industrial relations* forms labor policy, oversees industrial labor relations, negotiates collective bargaining agreements, and coordinates grievance procedures to handle complaints resulting from management disputes with unionized employees. The director of industrial relations also advises and collaborates with the director of human resources, other managers, and members of their staff, because all aspects of human resources policy—such as wages, benefits, pensions, and work practices—may be involved in drawing up a new or revised union contract.

Labor relations managers and their staffs implement industrial labor relations programs. Labor relations specialists prepare information for management to use during collective bargaining agreement negotiations, a process that requires the specialist to be familiar with economic and wage data and to have extensive knowledge of labor law and collective bargaining trends. The labor relations staff interprets and administers the contract with respect to grievances, wages and salaries, employee welfare, health care, pensions, union and management practices, and other contractual stipulations. As union membership continues to decline in most industries, industrial relations personnel are working more often with employees who are not members of a labor union.

Dispute resolution—attaining tacit or contractual agreements—has become increasingly significant as parties to a dispute attempt to avoid costly litigation, strikes, or other disruptions. Dispute resolution also has become more complex, involving employees, management, unions, other firms, and government agencies. Specialists involved in dispute resolution must be highly knowledgeable and experienced, and often report to the director of industrial relations. *Conciliators*, or *mediators*, advise and counsel labor and management to prevent and, when necessary, resolve disputes over labor agreements or other labor relations issues. *Arbitrators*, occasionally called umpires or referees, decide disputes that bind both labor and management to specific terms and conditions of labor contracts. Labor relations specialists who work for unions perform many of the same functions on behalf of the union and its members.

Other emerging specialties include *international human resources managers*, who handle human resources issues related to a company's foreign operations; and *human resources information system specialists*, who develop and apply computer programs to process human resources information, match job seekers with job openings, and handle other human resources matters.

Working Conditions

Human resources work usually takes place in clean, pleasant, and comfortable office settings. Arbitrators and mediators may work out of their homes. Many human resources, training, and labor relations managers and specialists work a standard 35- to 40-hour week. However, longer hours might be necessary for some workers—for example, labor relations managers and specialists, arbitrators, and mediators—when contract agreements are being prepared and negotiated.

Although most human resources, training, and labor relations managers and specialists work in the office, some travel extensively. For example, recruiters regularly attend professional meetings and visit college campuses to interview prospective employees; arbitrators and mediators often must travel to the site chosen for negotiations.

Training, Other Qualifications, and Advancement

The educational backgrounds of human resources, training, and labor relations managers and specialists vary considerably because of the diversity of duties and levels of responsibility. In filling entry-level jobs, many employers seek college graduates who have majored in human resources, human resources administration, or industrial and labor relations. Other employers look for college graduates with a technical or business background or a well-rounded liberal arts education.

Many colleges and universities have programs leading to a degree in personnel, human resources, or labor relations. Some offer degree programs in human resources administration or human resources management, training and development, or compensation and benefits. Depending on the school, courses leading to a career in human resources management may be found in departments of business administration, education, instructional technology, organizational development, human services, communication, or public administration, or within a separate human resources institution or department.

Because an interdisciplinary background is appropriate in this field, a combination of courses in the social sciences, business, and behavioral sciences is useful. Some jobs may require a more technical or specialized background in engineering, science, finance, or law, for example. Most prospective human resources specialists should take courses in compensation, recruitment, training and development, and performance appraisal, as well as courses in principles of management, organizational structure, and industrial psychology. Other relevant courses include business administration, public administration, psychology, sociology, political science, economics, and statistics. Courses in labor law, collective bargaining, labor economics, labor history, and industrial psychology also provide a valuable background for the prospective labor relations specialist. As in many other fields, knowledge of computers and information systems also is useful.

An advanced degree is increasingly important for some jobs. Many labor relations jobs require graduate study in industrial or labor relations. A strong background in industrial relations and law is highly desirable for contract negotiators, mediators, and arbitrators; in fact, many people in these specialties are lawyers. A background in law also is desirable for employee benefits managers and others who must interpret the growing number of laws and regulations. A master's degree in human resources, labor relations, or in business administration with a concentration in human resources management is highly recommended for those seeking general and top management positions.

For many specialized jobs in the human resources field, previous experience is an asset; for more advanced positions, including those of managers as well as arbitrators and mediators, it is essential. Many employers prefer entry-level workers who have gained some experience through an internship or work-study program while in school. Human resources administration and human resources development require the ability to work with individuals as well as a commitment to organizational goals. This field also demands other skills that people may develop elsewhere—using computers, selling, teaching, supervising, and volunteering, among others. The field offers clerical workers opportunities for advancement to professional positions. Responsible positions occasionally are filled by experienced individuals from other fields, including business, government, education, social services administration, and the military.

The human resources field demands a range of personal qualities and skills. Human resources, training, and labor relations managers and specialists must speak and write effectively. The growing diversity of the workforce requires that they work with or supervise people with various cultural backgrounds, levels of education, and experience. They must be able to cope with conflicting points of view, function under pressure, and demonstrate discretion, integrity, fair-mindedness, and a persuasive, congenial personality.

The duties given to entry-level workers will vary, depending on whether the new workers have a degree in human resource management, have completed an internship, or have some other type of human resources-related experience. Entry-level employees commonly learn the profession by performing administrative duties—helping to enter data into computer systems, compiling employee handbooks, researching information for a supervisor, or answering the phone and handling routine questions. Entry-level workers often enter formal or on-the-job training programs in which they learn how to classify jobs, interview applicants, or administer employee benefits. They then are assigned to specific areas in the human resources department to gain experience. Later, they may advance to a managerial position, supervising a major element of the human resources program—compensation or training, for example.

Exceptional human resources workers may be promoted to director of human resources or industrial relations, which can eventually lead to a top managerial or executive position. Others may join a consulting firm or open their own business. A Ph.D. is an asset for teaching, writing, or consulting work.

Most organizations specializing in human resources offer classes intended to enhance the marketable skills of their members. Some organizations offer certification programs, which are signs of competence and can enhance one's advancement opportunities. For example, the International Foundation of Employee Benefit Plans confers a designation to persons who complete a series of college-level courses and pass exams covering employee benefit plans. The American Society for Training & Development Certification Institute offers certification; it requires passing a knowledge-based exam and successful work product. The Society for Human Resource Management has two levels of certification; both require experience and a passing score on a comprehensive exam.

Employment

Human resources, training, and labor relations managers and specialists held about 820,000 jobs in 2004. The following tabulation shows the distribution of jobs by occupational specialty:

Training and development specialists	216,000
Employment, recruitment, and placement specialists	182,000
Human resources, training, and labor relations specialists, all other	166,000
Human resources managers	157,000
Compensation, benefits, and job analysis specialists	99,000

Human resources, training, and labor relations managers and specialists were employed in virtually every industry. About 21,000 specialists were self-employed, working as consultants to public and private employers.

The private sector accounted for more than 8 out of 10 salaried jobs, including 11 percent in administrative and support services; 9 percent in professional, scientific, and technical services; 9 percent in manufacturing; 9 percent in health care and social assistance; and 9 percent in finance and insurance firms.

Government employed 17 percent of human resources managers and specialists. They handled the recruitment, interviewing, job classification, training, salary administration, benefits, employee relations, and other matters related to the nation's public employees.

Job Outlook

The abundant supply of qualified college graduates and experienced workers should create keen competition for jobs. Overall employment of human resources, training, and labor relations managers and specialists is expected to grow faster than the average for all occupations through 2014. In addition to openings due to growth, many job openings will arise from the need to replace workers who transfer to other occupations or leave the labor force.

Legislation and court rulings setting standards in various areas—occupational safety and health, equal employment opportunity, wages, health care, pensions, and family leave, among others—will increase demand for human resources, training, and labor relations experts. Rising health care costs should continue to spur demand for specialists to develop creative compensation and benefits packages that firms can offer prospective employees. Employment of labor relations staff, including arbitrators and mediators, should grow as firms become more involved in labor relations, and attempt to resolve potentially costly labor-management disputes out of court. Additional job growth may stem from increasing demand for specialists in international human resources management and human resources information systems.

Demand may be particularly strong for certain specialists. For example, employers are expected to devote greater resources to job-specific training programs in response to the increasing complexity of many jobs, the aging of the workforce, and technological advances that can leave employees with obsolete skills. This should result in strong demand for training and development specialists. In addition, increasing efforts throughout industry to recruit and retain quality employees should create many jobs for employment, recruitment, and placement specialists.

Among industries, firms involved in management, consulting, and employment services should offer many job opportunities, as businesses increasingly contract out human resources functions or hire human resources specialists on a temporary basis in order to deal with the increasing cost and complexity of training and development programs. Demand also should increase in firms that develop and administer complex employee benefits and compensation packages for other organizations.

Demand for human resources, training, and labor relations managers and specialists also are governed by the staffing needs of the firms for which they work. A rapidly expanding business is likely to hire additional human resources workers—either as permanent employees or consultants—while a business that has experienced a merger or a reduction in its workforce will require fewer human resources workers. Also, as human resources management becomes increasingly important to the success of an organization, some small and medium-size businesses that do not have a human resources department may assign employees various human resources duties together with other unrelated responsibilities. In any particular firm, the size and the job duties of the human resources staff are determined by the firm's organizational philosophy and goals, skills of its workforce, pace of technological change, government regulations, collective bargaining agreements, standards of professional practice, and labor market conditions.

Job growth could be limited by the widespread use of computerized human resources information systems that make workers more productive. Like that of other workers, employment of human resources, training, and labor relations managers and specialists, particularly in larger firms, may be adversely affected by corporate downsizing, restructuring, and mergers.

Earnings

Annual salary rates for human resources workers vary according to occupation, level of experience, training, location, and size of the firm, and whether they are union members.

Median annual earnings of compensation and benefits managers were $66,530 in May 2004. The middle 50 percent earned between $49,970 and $89,340. The lowest 10 percent earned less than $39,250, and the highest 10 percent earned more than $118,880. In May 2004, median annual earnings were $ 81,080 in the management of companies and enterprises industry.

Median annual earnings of training and development managers were $67,460 in May 2004. The middle 50 percent earned between $49,060 and $91,020. The lowest 10 percent earned less than $36,430, and the highest 10 percent earned more than $119,580.

Median annual earnings of human resources managers, all other were $81,810 in May 2004. The middle 50 percent earned between $62,080 and $106,440. The lowest 10 percent earned less than $48,060, and the highest 10 percent earned more than $136,600. In May 2004, median annual earnings were $92,590, in the management of companies and enterprises industry.

Median annual earnings of employment, recruitment, and placement specialists were $41,190 in May 2004. The middle 50 percent earned between $31,820 and $55,540. The lowest 10 percent earned less than $25,690, and the highest 10 percent earned more than $76,230. In May 2004, median annual earnings in the industries employing the largest numbers of employment, recruitment, and placement specialists were:

Management, scientific, and technical consulting services	$52,800
Management of companies and enterprises	46,780
Local government	40,540
Employment services	37,780
State government	35,390

Median annual earnings of compensation, benefits, and job analysis specialists were $47,490 in May 2004. The middle 50 percent earned between $37,050 and $59,860. The lowest 10 percent earned less than $30,030, and the highest 10 percent earned more than $74,650. In May 2004, median annual earnings in the industries employing the largest numbers of compensation, benefits, and job analysis specialists were:

Local government	$51,430
Management of companies and enterprises	50,970
State government	39,150

Median annual earnings of training and development specialists were $44,570 in May 2004. The middle 50 percent earned between $33,530 and $58,750. The lowest 10 percent earned less than $25,800, and the highest 10 percent earned more than $74,650. In May 2004, median annual earnings in the industries employing the largest numbers of training and development specialists were:

Management of companies and enterprises	$49,540
Insurance carriers	47,300
Local government	45,320
State government	41,770
Federal government	38,930

According to a 2005 salary survey conducted by the National Association of Colleges and Employers, bachelor's degree candidates majoring in human resources, including labor relations, received starting offers averaging $36,967 a year.

The average salary for human resources managers employed by the federal government was $71,232 in 2005; for employee relations specialists, $84,847; for labor relations specialists, $93,895; and for employee development specialists, $80,958. Salaries were slightly higher in areas where the prevailing local pay level was higher. There are no formal entry-level requirements for managerial positions. Applicants must possess a suitable combination of educational attainment, experience, and record of accomplishment.

Related Occupations

All human resources occupations are closely related. Other workers with skills and expertise in interpersonal relations include counselors, education administrators, public relations specialists, lawyers, psychologists, social and human service assistants, and social workers.

Sources of Additional Information

For information about human resource management careers and certification, contact:

- Society for Human Resource Management, 1800 Duke St., Alexandria, VA 22314. Internet: http://www.shrm.org

For information about careers in employee training and development and certification, contact:

- American Society for Training &Development, 1640 King St., Box 1443, Alexandria, VA 22313-2043. Internet: http://www.astd.org

For information about careers and certification in employee compensation and benefits, contact:

- International Foundation of Employee Benefit Plans, 18700 W. Bluemound Rd., P.O. Box 69, Brookfield, WI 53008-0069. Internet: http://www.ifebp.org
- World at Work, 14040 N. Northsight Blvd., Scottsdale, AZ 85260. Internet: http://www.worldatwork.org

For information about academic programs in labor and employment relations, write to:

- Labor and Employment Relations Association, University of Illinois at Urbana-Champaign, 121 Labor and Industrial Relations Bldg., 504 E. Armory Ave., Champaign, IL 61820. Internet: http://www.lera.uiuc.edu

Information about human resources careers in the health care industry is available from:

- American Society for Healthcare Human Resources Administration, One North Franklin, 31st Floor, Chicago, IL 60606. Internet: http://www.ashhra.org

Instructional Coordinators

(O*NET 25-9031.00)

Significant Points

- Many instructional coordinators have experience as teachers or education administrators.
- A bachelor's degree is the minimum educational requirement, but a graduate degree is preferred.
- The need to meet new educational standards will create more demand for instructional coordinators to train teachers and develop new materials.

Nature of the Work

Instructional coordinators, also known as curriculum specialists, staff development specialists, or directors of instructional material, play a large role in improving the quality of education in the classroom. They develop curricula, select textbooks and other materials, train teachers, and assess educational programs in terms of quality and adherence to regulations and standards. They also assist in implementing new technology in the classroom. Instructional coordinators often specialize in specific subjects, such as reading, language arts, mathematics, or social studies.

Instructional coordinators evaluate how well a school or training program's curriculum, or plan of study, meets students' needs. They research teaching methods and techniques and develop procedures to determine whether program goals are being met. To aid in their evaluation, they may meet with members of educational committees and advisory groups to learn about subjects—English, history, or mathematics, for example—and to relate curriculum materials to these subjects, to students' needs, and to occupations for which these subjects are good preparation. They also may develop questionnaires and interview school staff about the curriculum. Based on their research and observations of instructional practice, they recommend instruction and curriculum improvements.

Another duty some instructional coordinators have is to review textbooks, software, and other educational materials and make recommendations on purchases. They monitor materials ordered and the ways in which teachers use them in the classroom. They also supervise workers who catalogue, distribute, and maintain a school's educational materials and equipment.

Instructional coordinators develop effective ways to use technology to enhance student learning. They monitor the introduction of new technology, including the Internet, into a school's curriculum. In addition, instructional coordinators might recommend installing educational computer software, such as interactive books and exercises designed to enhance student literacy and develop math skills. Instructional coordinators may invite experts—such as computer hardware, software, and library or media specialists—into the classroom to help integrate technological materials into a school's curriculum.

Many instructional coordinators plan and provide onsite education for teachers and administrators. They may train teachers about the use of materials and equipment or help them to improve their skills. Instructional coordinators also mentor new teachers and train experienced ones in the latest instructional methods. This role becomes especially important when a school district introduces new content, program innovations, or a different organizational structure. For example, when a state or school district introduces standards or tests that must be met by students in order to pass to the next grade, instructional coordinators often must advise teachers on the content of the standards and provide instruction on implementing the standards in the classroom.

Working Conditions

Instructional coordinators, including those employed by school districts, often work year round, usually in offices or classrooms. Some spend much of their time traveling between schools meeting with teachers and administrators. The opportunity to shape and improve instructional curricula and work in an academic environment can be satisfying. However, some instructional coordinators find the work stressful because the occupation requires continual accountability to school administrators and it is not uncommon for people in this occupation to work long hours.

Training, Other Qualifications, and Advancement

The minimum educational requirement for instructional coordinators is a bachelor's degree, usually in education. Most employers, however, prefer candidates with a master's or higher degree. State licensing is necessary for instructional coordinators in public school systems, although specific requirements vary by state. In some states, a teaching license is needed, while in others instructional coordinators need an education administrator license. Instructional coordinators should have training in curriculum development and instruction, or in the specific field for which they are responsible, such as mathematics or history. Instructional coordinators must have a good understanding of how to teach specific groups of students, in addition to expertise in developing educational materials. As a result, many persons transfer into instructional coordinator jobs after working for several years as teachers. Work experience in an education administrator position, such as principal or assistant principal, also can be beneficial.

Helpful college courses may include those in curriculum development and evaluation, instructional approaches, or research design, which teaches how to create and implement research studies to determine the effectiveness of a given method of instruction or curriculum, or to measure and improve student performance. Moreover, instructional coordinators usually are required to take continuing education courses to keep their skills current. Topics for continuing education courses may include teacher evaluation techniques, curriculum training, new teacher induction, consulting and teacher support, and observation and analysis of teaching.

Instructional coordinators must be able to make sound decisions about curriculum options and to organize and coordinate work efficiently. They should have strong interpersonal and communication skills. Familiarity with computer technology also is important for instructional coordinators, who are increasingly involved in gathering and coordinating technical information for students and teachers.

Depending on experience and educational attainment, instructional coordinators may advance to higher administrative positions in a school system, or to management or executive positions in private industry.

Employment

Instructional coordinators held about 117,000 jobs in 2004. More than 2 in 5 worked for local governments, mainly in public schools and school district offices. One in 5 worked in private education, primarily in private elementary, secondary, and postsecondary schools and educational consulting firms. About 1 in 5 worked for state governments in public colleges and universities or state departments of education. The remainder worked mostly in the following industries: Individual and family services; child day care services; scientific research and development services; and management, scientific, and technical consulting services.

Job Outlook

Employment of instructional coordinators is expected to grow much faster than the average for all occupations through the year 2014. Over the next decade, instructional coordinators will be instrumental in developing new curricula to meet the demands of a changing society and in training the teacher workforce. Although budget constraints may limit employment growth to some extent, a continuing emphasis on improving the quality of education is expected to result in an increasing demand for these workers. Also, as an increased emphasis on accountability at all levels of government causes more schools to focus on improving educational quality and student performance, growing numbers of coordinators will be needed to incorporate the standards into existing curricula and make sure teachers and administrators are informed of the changes. Opportunities are expected to be best for those who specialize in subject areas that have been targeted for improvement by the No Child Left Behind Act—namely, reading, math, and science.

Instructional coordinators also will be needed to provide classes on using technology in the classroom, to keep teachers up-to-date on changes in their fields, and to demonstrate new teaching techniques. Additional job growth for instructional coordinators will stem from the increasing emphasis on lifelong learning and on programs for students with special needs, including those for whom English is a second language. These students often require more educational resources and consolidated planning and management within the educational system.

Earnings

Median annual earnings of instructional coordinators in May 2004 were $48,790. The middle 50 percent earned between $35,940 and $65,040. The lowest 10 percent earned less than $27,300, and the highest 10 percent earned more than $81,210.

Related Occupations

Instructional coordinators are professionals involved in education and training and development, which requires organizational, administrative, teaching, research, and communication skills. Occupations with similar characteristics include preschool, kindergarten, elementary, middle, and secondary school teachers; postsecondary teachers; education administrators; counselors; and human resources, training, and labor relations managers and specialists.

Sources of Additional Information

Information on requirements and job opportunities for instructional coordinators is available from local school systems and state departments of education.

Lawyers

(O*NET 23-1011.00)

Significant Points

- Competition for job openings should be keen because of the large number of students graduating from law school each year.
- Formal requirements to become a lawyer generally include a 4-year college degree, 3 years of law school, and passing a written bar examination; however, some requirements may vary by state.
- Competition for admission to most law schools is intense.
- About 3 out of 4 lawyers practice privately, either as partners in law firms or in solo practices.

Nature of the Work

The legal system affects nearly every aspect of our society, from buying a home to crossing the street. Lawyers form the backbone of this vital system, linking it to society in numerous ways. For that reason, they hold positions of great responsibility and are obligated to adhere to a strict code of ethics.

Lawyers, also called *attorneys*, act as both advocates and advisors in our society. As advocates, they represent one of the parties in criminal and civil trials by presenting evidence and arguing in court to support their client. As advisors, lawyers counsel their clients concerning their legal rights and obligations and suggest particular courses of action in business and personal matters. Whether acting as an advocate or an advisor, all attorneys research the intent of laws and judicial decisions and apply the law to the specific circumstances faced by their client.

The more detailed aspects of a lawyer's job depend upon his or her field of specialization and position. Although all lawyers are licensed to represent parties in court, some appear in court more frequently than others. Trial lawyers, who specialize in trial work, must be able to think quickly and speak with ease and authority. In addition, familiarity with courtroom rules and strategy is particularly important in trial work. Still, trial lawyers spend the majority of their time outside the courtroom, conducting research, interviewing clients and witnesses, and handling other details in preparation for a trial.

Lawyers may specialize in a number of areas, such as bankruptcy, probate, international, or elder law. Those specializing in environmental law, for example, may represent interest groups, waste disposal companies, or construction firms in their dealings with the U.S. Environmental Protection Agency (EPA) and other federal and state agencies. These lawyers help clients prepare and file for licenses and applications for approval before certain activities may occur. In addition, they represent clients' interests in administrative adjudications.

Some lawyers specialize in the growing field of intellectual property, helping to protect clients' claims to copyrights, artwork under contract, product designs, and computer programs. Still other lawyers advise insurance companies about the legality of insurance transactions, guiding the company in writing insurance policies to conform with the law and to protect the companies from unwarranted claims. When claims are filed against insurance companies, these attorneys review the claims and represent the companies in court.

Most lawyers are in private practice, concentrating on criminal or civil law. In criminal law, lawyers represent individuals who have been charged with crimes and argue their cases in courts of law. Attorneys dealing with civil law assist clients with litigation, wills, trusts, contracts, mortgages, titles, and leases. Other lawyers handle only public-interest cases—civil or criminal—which may have an impact extending well beyond the individual client.

Lawyers are sometimes employed full time by a single client. If the client is a corporation, the lawyer is known as "house counsel" and usually advises the company concerning legal issues related to its business activities. These issues might involve patents, government regulations, contracts with other companies, property interests, or collective bargaining agreements with unions.

A significant number of attorneys are employed at the various levels of government. Lawyers who work for state attorneys general, prosecutors, public defenders, and courts play a key role in the criminal justice system. At the federal level, attorneys investigate cases for the U.S. Department of Justice and other agencies. Government lawyers also help develop programs, draft and interpret laws and legislation, establish enforcement procedures, and argue civil and criminal cases on behalf of the government.

Other lawyers work for legal aid societies—private, nonprofit organizations established to serve disadvantaged people. These lawyers generally handle civil, rather than criminal, cases. A relatively small number of trained attorneys work in law schools. Most are faculty members who specialize in one or more subjects; however, some serve as administrators. Others work full time in nonacademic settings and teach part time.

Lawyers are increasingly using various forms of technology to perform their varied tasks more efficiently. Although all lawyers continue to use law libraries to prepare cases, some supplement conventional printed sources with computer sources, such as the Internet and legal databases. Software is used to search this legal literature automatically and to identify legal texts relevant to a specific case. In litigation involving many supporting documents, lawyers may use computers to organize and index material. Lawyers also utilize electronic filing, videoconferencing, and voice-recognition technology to share information more effectively with other parties involved in a case.

Working Conditions

Lawyers do most of their work in offices, law libraries, and courtrooms. They sometimes meet in clients' homes or places of business and, when necessary, in hospitals or prisons. They may travel to attend meetings; gather evidence; and appear before courts, legislative bodies, and other authorities.

Salaried lawyers usually have structured work schedules. Lawyers who are in private practice may work irregular hours while conducting research, conferring with clients, or preparing briefs during nonoffice hours. Lawyers often work long hours, and of those who regularly work full time, about half work 50 hours or more per week. They may face particularly heavy pressure when a case is being tried. Preparation for court includes keeping abreast of the latest laws and judicial decisions.

Although legal work generally is not seasonal, the work of tax lawyers and other specialists may be an exception. Because lawyers in private practice often can determine their own workload and the point at which they will retire, many stay in practice well beyond the usual retirement age.

Training, Other Qualifications, and Advancement

To practice law in the courts of any state or other jurisdiction, a person must be licensed, or admitted to its bar, under rules established by the jurisdiction's highest court. All states require that applicants for admission to the bar pass a written bar examination; most states also require applicants to pass a separate written ethics examination. Lawyers who have been admitted to the bar in one state occasionally may be admitted to the bar in another without taking an examination if they meet the latter jurisdiction's standards of good moral character and a specified period of legal experience. In most cases, however, lawyers must pass the bar examination in each state in which they plan to practice. Federal courts and agencies set their own qualifications for those practicing before or in them.

To qualify for the bar examination in most states, an applicant usually must earn a college degree and graduate from a law school accredited by the American Bar Association (ABA) or the proper state authorities. ABA accreditation signifies that the law school—particularly its library and faculty—meets certain standards developed to promote quality legal education. As of 2005, there were 191 ABA-accredited law schools; others were approved by state authorities only. With certain exceptions, graduates of schools not approved by the ABA are restricted to taking the bar examination and practicing in the state or other jurisdiction in which the school is located; most of these schools are in California. In 2005, seven states—California, Maine, New York, Vermont, Virginia, Washington, and Wyoming—accepted the study of law in a law office as qualification for taking the bar examination; three jurisdictions—

California, the District of Columbia, and New Mexico—now accept the study of law by correspondence. Several states require registration and approval of students by the State Board of Law Examiners, either before the students enter law school or during their early years of legal study.

Although there is no nationwide bar examination, 48 states, the District of Columbia, Guam, the Northern Mariana Islands, Puerto Rico, and the Virgin Islands require the 6-hour Multistate Bar Examination (MBE) as part of the overall bar examination; the MBE is not required in Louisiana or Washington. The MBE covers a broad range of issues, and sometimes a locally prepared state bar examination is given in addition to it. The 3-hour Multistate Essay Examination (MEE) is used as part of the bar examination in several states. States vary in their use of MBE and MEE scores.

Many states also require Multistate Performance Testing (MPT) to test the practical skills of beginning lawyers. Requirements vary by state, although the test usually is taken at the same time as the bar exam and is a one-time requirement.

The required college and law school education usually takes 7 years of full-time study after high school—4 years of undergraduate study, followed by 3 years of law school. Law school applicants must have a bachelor's degree to qualify for admission. To meet the needs of students who can attend only part time, a number of law schools have night or part-time divisions, which usually require 4 years of study; about 1 in 10 graduates from ABA-approved schools attended part time.

Although there is no recommended "prelaw" major, prospective lawyers should develop proficiency in writing and speaking, reading, researching, analyzing, and thinking logically—skills needed to succeed both in law school and in the profession. Regardless of major, a multidisciplinary background is recommended. Courses in English, foreign languages, public speaking, government, philosophy, history, economics, mathematics, and computer science, among others, are useful. Students interested in a particular aspect of law may find related courses helpful. For example, prospective patent lawyers need a strong background in engineering or science, and future tax lawyers must have extensive knowledge of accounting.

Acceptance by most law schools depends on the applicant's ability to demonstrate an aptitude for the study of law, usually through good undergraduate grades, the Law School Admission Test (LSAT), the quality of the applicant's undergraduate school, any prior work experience, and sometimes, a personal interview. However, law schools vary in the weight they place on each of these and other factors.

All law schools approved by the ABA require applicants to take the LSAT. Nearly all law schools require applicants to have certified transcripts sent to the Law School Data Assembly Service, which then submits the applicants' LSAT scores and their standardized records of college grades to the law schools of their choice. Both this service and the LSAT are administered by the Law School Admission Council. Competition for admission to many law schools—especially the most prestigious ones—generally is intense, with the number of applicants greatly exceeding the number that can be admitted.

During the first year or year and a half of law school, students usually study core courses, such as constitutional law, contracts, property law, torts, civil procedure, and legal writing. In the remaining time, they may elect specialized courses in fields such as tax, labor, or corporate law. Law students often acquire practical experience by participating in school-sponsored legal clinic activities; in the school's moot court competitions, in which students conduct appellate arguments; in practice trials under the supervision of experienced lawyers and judges; and through research and writing on legal issues for the school's law journal.

A number of law schools have clinical programs in which students gain legal experience through practice trials and projects under the supervision of practicing lawyers and law school faculty. Law school clinical programs might include work in legal aid clinics, for example, or on the staff of legislative committees. Part-time or summer clerkships in law firms, government agencies, and corporate legal departments also provide valuable experience. Such training can lead directly to a job after graduation and can help students decide what kind of practice best suits them. Clerkships also may be an important source of financial aid.

In 2004, law school graduates in 52 jurisdictions were required to pass the Multistate Professional Responsibility Examination (MPRE), which tests their knowledge of the ABA codes on professional responsibility and judicial conduct. In some states, the MPRE may be taken during law school, usually after completing a course on legal ethics.

Law school graduates receive the degree of *juris doctor* (J.D.) as the first professional degree. Advanced law degrees may be desirable for those planning to specialize, research, or teach. Some law students pursue joint degree programs, which usually require an additional semester or year of study. Joint degree programs are offered in a number of areas, including law and business administration or public administration.

After graduation, lawyers must keep informed about legal and nonlegal developments that affect their practices. Currently, 40 states and jurisdictions mandate continuing legal education (CLE). Many law schools and state and local bar associations provide continuing education courses that help lawyers stay abreast of recent developments. Some states allow CLE credits to be obtained through participation in seminars on the Internet.

The practice of law involves a great deal of responsibility. Individuals planning careers in law should like to work with people and be able to win the respect and confidence of their clients, associates, and the public. Perseverance, creativity, and reasoning ability also are essential to lawyers, who often analyze complex cases and handle new and unique legal problems.

Most beginning lawyers start in salaried positions. Newly hired salaried attorneys usually start as associates and work with more experienced lawyers or judges. After several years of gaining more responsibilities, some lawyers are admitted to partnership in their firm or go into practice for themselves. Some experienced lawyers are nominated or elected to judgeships. Others become full-time law school faculty or administrators; a growing number of these lawyers have advanced degrees in other fields as well.

Some attorneys use their legal training in administrative or managerial positions in various departments of large corporations. A transfer from a corporation's legal department to another department often is viewed as a way to gain administrative experience and rise in the ranks of management.

Employment

Lawyers held about 735,000 jobs in 2004. Approximately 3 out of 4 lawyers practiced privately, either as partners in law firms or in solo practices. Most salaried lawyers held positions in government or with corporations or nonprofit organizations. The greatest number of lawyers working in government were employed at the local level. In the federal government, lawyers work for many different agencies, but are concentrated in the Departments of Justice, Treasury, and Defense. Many salaried lawyers working outside of government are employed as house counsel by public utilities, banks, insurance companies, real estate agencies, manufacturing firms, and other business firms and nonprofit organizations. Some also have part-time independent practices, while others work part time as lawyers and full time in another occupation.

Job Outlook

Employment of lawyers is expected to grow about as fast as average for all occupations through 2014, primarily as a result of growth in the population and in the general level of business activities. Job growth among lawyers also will result from increasing demand for legal services in such areas as health care, intellectual property, venture capital, energy, elder, antitrust, and environmental law. In addition, the wider availability and affordability of legal clinics should result in increased use of legal services by middle-income people. However, growth in demand for lawyers will be limited as businesses, in an effort to reduce costs, increasingly use large accounting firms and paralegals to perform some of the same functions that lawyers do. For example, accounting firms may provide employee-benefit counseling, process documents, or handle various other services previously performed by a law firm. Also, mediation and dispute resolution increasingly are being used as alternatives to litigation.

Competition for job openings should continue to be keen because of the large number of students graduating from law school each year. Graduates with superior academic records from highly regarded law schools will have the best job opportunities. Perhaps as a result of competition for attorney positions, lawyers are increasingly finding work in nontraditional areas for which legal training is an asset, but not normally a requirement—for example, administrative, managerial, and business positions in banks, insurance firms, real estate companies, government agencies, and other organizations. Employment opportunities are expected to continue to arise in these organizations at a growing rate.

As in the past, some graduates may have to accept positions in areas outside of their field of interest or for which they feel overqualified. Some recent law school graduates who have been unable to find permanent positions are turning to the growing number of temporary staffing firms that place attorneys in short-term jobs until they are able to secure full-time positions. This service allows companies to hire lawyers on an "as-needed" basis and permits beginning lawyers to develop practical skills while looking for permanent positions.

Because of the keen competition for jobs, a law graduate's geographic mobility and work experience assume greater importance. The willingness to relocate may be an advantage in getting a job, but to be licensed in another state, a lawyer may have to take an additional state bar examination. In addition, employers are increasingly seeking graduates who have advanced law degrees and experience in a specialty, such as tax, patent, or admiralty law.

Employment growth for lawyers will continue to be concentrated in salaried jobs, as businesses and all levels of government employ a growing number of staff attorneys and as employment in the legal services industry grows. Most salaried positions are in urban areas where government agencies, law firms, and big corporations are concentrated. The number of self-employed lawyers is expected to decrease slowly, reflecting the difficulty of establishing a profitable new practice in the face of competition from larger, established law firms. Moreover, the growing complexity of law, which encourages specialization, along with the cost of maintaining up-to-date legal research materials, favors larger firms.

For lawyers who wish to work independently, establishing a new practice will probably be easiest in small towns and expanding suburban areas. In such communities, competition from larger, established law firms is likely to be less keen than in big cities, and new lawyers may find it easier to become known to potential clients.

Some lawyers are adversely affected by cyclical swings in the economy. During recessions, demand declines for some discretionary legal services, such as planning estates, drafting wills, and handling real estate transactions. Also, corporations are less likely to litigate cases when declining sales and profits result in budgetary restrictions. Some corporations and law firms will not hire new attorneys until business improves, and these establishments may even cut staff to contain costs. Several factors, however, mitigate the overall impact of recessions on lawyers; during recessions, for example, individuals and corporations face other legal problems, such as bankruptcies, foreclosures, and divorces requiring legal action.

Earnings

In May 2004, the median annual earnings of all lawyers were $94,930. The middle half of the occupation earned between $64,620 and $143,620. Median annual earnings in the industries employing the largest numbers of lawyers in May 2004 were as follows:

Management of companies and enterprises	$126,250
Federal government	108,090
Legal services	99,580
Local government	73,410
State government	70,280

Median salaries of lawyers 9 months after graduation from law school in 2004 varied by type of work, as indicated in table 1.

Table 1. Median salaries of lawyers 9 months after graduation, 2004

Type of work	Salary
All graduates	$55,000
Private practice	80,000
Business/industry	60,000
Judicial clerkship and government	44,700
Academe	40,000

Source: National Association of Law Placement

Salaries of experienced attorneys vary widely according to the type, size, and location of their employer. Lawyers who own their own practices usually earn less than those who are partners in law firms. Lawyers starting their own practice may need to work part time in other occupations to supplement their income until their practice is well established.

Most salaried lawyers are provided health and life insurance, and contributions are made to retirement plans on their behalf. Lawyers who practice independently are covered only if they arrange and pay for such benefits themselves.

Related Occupations

Legal training is necessary in many other occupations, including paralegals and legal assistants; law clerks; title examiners, abstractors, and searchers; and judges, magistrates, and other judicial workers.

Sources of Additional Information

Information on law schools and a career in law may be obtained from the following organizations:

- American Bar Association, 321 North Clark St., Chicago, IL 60610. Internet: http://www.abanet.org
- National Association for Law Placement, 1025 Connecticut Ave. NW, Suite 1110, Washington, DC 20036. Internet: http://www.nalp.org

Information on the LSAT, the Law School Data Assembly Service, the law school application process, and financial aid available to law students may be obtained from:

- Law School Admission Council, P.O. Box 40, Newtown, PA 18940. Internet: http://www.lsac.org

Information on obtaining positions as occupational health and safety specialists and technicians with the federal government is available from the Office of Personnel Management through USAJOBS, the federal government's official employment information system. This resource for locating and applying for job opportunities can be accessed through the Internet at http://www.usajobs.opm.gov or through an interactive voice response telephone system at (703) 724-1850 or TDD (978) 461-8404. These numbers are not toll free, and charges may result.

The requirements for admission to the bar in a particular state or other jurisdiction also may be obtained at the state capital, from the clerk of the Supreme Court, or from the administrator of the State Board of Bar Examiners.

Licensed Practical and Licensed Vocational Nurses

(O*NET 29-2061.00)

Significant Points

- Training lasting about 1 year is available in about 1,200 state-approved programs, mostly in vocational or technical schools.
- Applicants for jobs in hospitals may face competition as the number of hospital jobs for licensed practical nurses declines; however, rapid employment growth is projected in other health care industries, with the best job opportunities occurring in nursing care facilities and in home health care services.
- Replacement needs will be a major source of job openings, as many workers leave the occupation permanently.

Nature of the Work

Licensed practical nurses (LPNs), or licensed vocational nurses (LVNs), care for the sick, injured, convalescent, and disabled under the direction of physicians and registered nurses.

Most LPNs provide basic bedside care, taking vital signs such as temperature, blood pressure, pulse, and respiration. They also prepare and give injections and enemas, monitor catheters, apply dressings, treat bedsores, and give alcohol rubs and massages. LPNs monitor their patients and report adverse reactions to medications or treatments. They collect samples for testing, perform routine laboratory tests, feed patients, and record food and fluid intake and output. To help keep patients comfortable, LPNs assist with bathing, dressing, and personal hygiene. In states where the law allows, they may administer prescribed medicines or start intravenous fluids. Some LPNs help to deliver, care for, and feed infants. Experienced LPNs may supervise nursing assistants and aides.

In addition to providing routine bedside care, LPNs in nursing care facilities help to evaluate residents' needs, develop care plans, and supervise the care provided by nursing aides. In doctors' offices and clinics, they also may make appointments, keep records, and perform other clerical duties. LPNs who work in private homes may prepare meals and teach family members simple nursing tasks.

Working Conditions

Most licensed practical nurses in hospitals and nursing care facilities work a 40-hour week, but because patients need round-the-clock care, some work nights, weekends, and holidays. They often stand for long periods and help patients move in bed, stand, or walk.

LPNs may face hazards from caustic chemicals, radiation, and infectious diseases such as hepatitis. They are subject to back injuries when moving patients and shock from electrical equipment. They often must deal with the stress of heavy workloads. In addition, the patients they care for may be confused, irrational, agitated, or uncooperative.

Training, Other Qualifications, and Advancement

All states and the District of Columbia require LPNs to pass a licensing examination, known as the NCLEX-PN, after completing a state-approved practical nursing program. A high school diploma or its equivalent usually is required for entry, although some programs accept candidates without a diploma, and some are designed as part of a high school curriculum.

In 2004, approximately 1,200 state-approved programs provided training in practical nursing. Most training programs are available from technical and vocational schools, or from community and junior colleges. Other programs are available through high schools, hospitals, and colleges and universities.

Most practical nursing programs last about 1 year and include both classroom study and supervised clinical practice (patient care). Classroom study covers basic nursing concepts and patient care-related subjects, including anatomy, physiology, medical-surgical nursing, pediatrics, obstetrics, psychiatric nursing, the administration of drugs, nutrition, and first aid. Clinical practice usually is in a hospital, but sometimes includes other settings.

In some employment settings, such as nursing homes, LPNs can advance to become charge nurses who oversee the work of other LPNs and of nursing aides. Some LPNs also choose to become registered nurses through numerous LPN-to-RN training programs.

LPNs should have a caring, sympathetic nature. They should be emotionally stable because working with the sick and injured can be stressful. They also should have keen observational, decision-making, and communication skills. As part of a health care team, they must be able to follow orders and work under close supervision.

Employment

Licensed practical nurses held about 726,000 jobs in 2004. About 27 percent of LPNs worked in hospitals, 25 percent in nursing care facilities, and another 12 percent in offices of physicians. Others worked for home health care services; employment services; community care facilities for the elderly; public and private educational services; outpatient care centers; and federal, state, and local government agencies. About 1 in 5 worked part time.

Job Outlook

Employment of LPNs is expected to grow about as fast as average for all occupations through 2014 in response to the long-term care needs of an increasing elderly population and the general growth of health care services. Replacement needs will be a major source of job openings, as many workers leave the occupation permanently. Applicants for jobs in hospitals may face competition as the number of hospital jobs for LPNs declines; however, rapid employment growth is projected in other health care industries, with the best job opportunities occurring in nursing care facilities and in home health care services.

Employment of LPNs in hospitals is expected to continue to decline. Sophisticated procedures once performed only in hospitals are being performed in physicians' offices and in outpatient care centers such as ambulatory surgical and emergency medical centers, largely because of advances in technology. Consequently, employment of LPNs in most health care industries outside the traditional hospital setting is projected to grow faster than average.

Employment of LPNs is expected to grow much faster than average in home health care services. Home health care agencies also will offer the most new jobs for LPNs because of an increasing number of older persons with functional disabilities, consumer preference for care in the home, and technological advances that make it possible to bring increasingly complex treatments into the home.

Employment of LPNs in nursing care facilities is expected to grow about as fast as average because of the growing number of aged and disabled persons in need of long-term care. In addition, LPNs in nursing care facilities will be needed to care for the increasing number of patients who have been discharged from the hospital but who have not recovered enough to return home. However, changes in consumer preferences towards less restrictive and more cost-effective care from assisted living facilities and home health care agencies will limit employment growth.

Earnings

Median annual earnings of licensed practical nurses were $33,970 in May 2004. The middle 50 percent earned between $28,830 and $40,670. The lowest 10 percent earned less than $24,480, and the highest 10 percent earned more than $46,270. Median annual earnings in the industries employing the largest numbers of licensed practical nurses in May 2004 were:

Employment services	$41,550
Nursing care facilities	35,460
Home health care services	35,180
General medical and surgical hospitals	32,570
Offices of physicians	30,400

Related Occupations

LPNs work closely with people while helping them. So do emergency medical technicians and paramedics; medical assistants; nursing, psychiatric, and home health aides; registered nurses; social and human service assistants; and surgical technologists.

Sources of Additional Information

For information about practical nursing, contact any of the following organizations:

- National Association for Practical Nurse Education and Service, Inc., P.O. Box 25647, Alexandria, VA 22313. Internet: http://www.napnes.org
- National League for Nursing, 61 Broadway, New York, NY 10006. Internet: http://www.nln.org
- National Federation of Licensed Practical Nurses, Inc., 605 Poole Dr., Garner, NC 27529. Internet: http://www.nflpn.org

Information on the NCLEX-PN licensing exam is available from:

- National Council of State Boards of Nursing, 111 East Wacker Dr., Suite 2900, Chicago, IL 60611. Internet: http://www.ncsbn.org

A list of state-approved LPN programs is available from individual state boards of nursing.

Maintenance and Repair Workers, General

(O*NET 49-9042.00)

Significant Points

- General maintenance and repair workers are employed in almost every industry.
- Many workers learn their skills informally on the job; others learn by working as helpers to other repairers or to construction workers such as carpenters, electricians, or machinery repairers.
- Job opportunities should be favorable, with many openings occurring as a result of turnover in this large occupation.

Nature of the Work

Most craft workers specialize in one kind of work, such as plumbing or carpentry. General maintenance and repair workers, however, have skills in many different crafts. They repair and maintain machines, mechanical equipment, and buildings and work on plumbing, electrical, and air-conditioning and heating systems. They build partitions, make plaster or drywall repairs, and fix or paint roofs, windows, doors, floors, woodwork, and other parts of building structures. They also maintain and repair specialized equipment and machinery found in cafeterias, laundries, hospitals, stores, offices, and factories. Typical duties include troubleshooting and fixing faulty electrical switches, repairing air-conditioning motors, and unclogging drains. New buildings sometimes have computer-controlled systems that allow maintenance workers to make adjustments in building settings and monitor for problems from a central location. For example, they can remotely control light sensors that turn off lights automatically after a set amount of time or identify a broken ventilation fan that needs to be replaced.

General maintenance and repair workers inspect and diagnose problems and determine the best way to correct them, frequently checking blueprints, repair manuals, and parts catalogs. They obtain supplies and repair parts from distributors or storerooms. Using common hand and power tools such as screwdrivers, saws, drills, wrenches, and hammers, as well as specialized equipment and electronic testing devices, these workers replace or fix worn or broken parts, where necessary, or make adjustments to correct malfunctioning equipment and machines.

General maintenance and repair workers also perform routine preventive maintenance and ensure that machines continue to run smoothly, building systems operate efficiently, and the physical condition of buildings does not deteriorate. Following a checklist, they may inspect drives, motors, and belts, check fluid levels, replace filters, and perform other maintenance actions. Maintenance and repair workers keep records of their work.

Employees in small establishments, where they are often the only maintenance worker, make all repairs, except for very large or difficult jobs. In larger establishments, their duties may be limited to the general maintenance of everything in a workshop or a particular area.

Working Conditions

General maintenance and repair workers often carry out several different tasks in a single day, at any number of locations. They may work inside of a single building or in several different buildings. They may have to stand for long periods, lift heavy objects, and work in uncomfortably hot or cold environments, in awkward and cramped positions, or on ladders. They are subject to electrical shock, burns, falls, cuts, and bruises. Most general maintenance workers work a 40-hour week. Some work evening, night, or weekend shifts or are on call for emergency repairs.

Those employed in small establishments often operate with only limited supervision. Those working in larger establishments frequently are under the direct supervision of an experienced worker.

Training, Other Qualifications, and Advancement

Many general maintenance and repair workers learn their skills informally on the job. They start as helpers, watching and learning from skilled maintenance workers. Helpers begin by doing simple jobs, such as fixing leaky faucets and replacing light bulbs, and progress to more difficult tasks, such as overhauling machinery or building walls. Some learn their skills by working as helpers to other repair or construction workers, including carpenters, electricians, or machinery repairers.

Necessary skills also can be learned in high school shop classes and postsecondary trade or vocational schools. It generally takes from 1 to 4 years of on-the-job training or school, or a combination of both, to become fully qualified, depending on the skill level required. Because a growing number of new buildings rely on computers to control various systems, general maintenance and repair workers may need basic computer skills, such as how to log onto a central computer system and navigate through a series of menus. Usually, companies that install computer-controlled equipment provide on-site training for general maintenance and repair workers.

Graduation from high school is preferred for entry into this occupation. High school courses in mechanical drawing, electricity, woodworking, blueprint reading, science, mathematics, and computers are useful. Mechanical aptitude, the ability to use shop mathematics, and manual dexterity are important. Good health is necessary because the job involves much walking, standing, reaching, and heavy lifting. Difficult jobs require problem-solving ability, and many positions require the ability to work without direct supervision.

Many general maintenance and repair workers in large organizations advance to maintenance supervisor or become a craftworker such as an electrician, a heating and air-conditioning mechanic, or a plumber. Within small organizations, promotion opportunities are limited.

Employment

General maintenance and repair workers held 1.3 million jobs in 2004. They were employed in almost every industry. Around 1 in 5 worked in manufacturing industries, almost evenly distributed through all sectors, while about 1 in 6 worked for different government bodies. Others worked for wholesale and retail firms and for real estate firms that operate office and apartment buildings.

Job Outlook

Job opportunities should be favorable, especially for those with experience in maintenance or related fields. General maintenance and repair is a large occupation with significant turnover. Additionally, many job openings are expected to result from the retirement of many experienced maintenance workers over the next decade.

Employment of general maintenance and repair workers is expected to grow about as fast as average for all occupations through 2014. Employment is related to the number of buildings—for example, office and apartment buildings, stores, schools, hospitals, hotels, and factories—and the amount of equipment needing maintenance and repair. However, as machinery becomes more advanced and requires less maintenance, the need for general maintenance and repair workers diminishes. Also, as more buildings are controlled by computers, buildings can be monitored more efficiently.

Earnings

Median hourly earnings of general maintenance and repair workers were $14.76 in May 2004. The middle 50 percent earned between $11.11 and $19.17. The lowest 10 percent earned less than $8.70, and the highest 10 percent earned more than $23.40. Median hourly earnings in the industries employing the largest numbers of general maintenance and repair workers in May 2004 are shown in the following tabulation:

Local government	$15.70
Elementary and secondary schools	14.93
Activities related to real estate	12.71
Lessors of real estate	11.96
Traveler accommodation	11.19

Some general maintenance and repair workers are members of unions, including the American Federation of State, County, and Municipal Employees and the United Auto Workers.

Related Occupations

Some duties of general maintenance and repair workers are similar to those of carpenters; pipelayers, plumbers, pipefitters, and steamfitters; electricians; and heating, air-conditioning, and refrigeration mechanics. Other duties are similar to those of coin, vending, and amusement machine servicers and repairers; electrical and electronics installers and repairers; electronic home entertainment equipment installers and repairers; and radio and telecommunications equipment installers and repairers.

Sources of Additional Information

Information about job opportunities may be obtained from local employers and local offices of the state employment service.

Management Analysts

(O*NET 13-1111.00)

Significant Points

- Despite fast employment growth, keen competition is expected for jobs; opportunities should be best for those with a graduate degree, specific industry expertise, and a talent for salesmanship and public relations.
- About 29 percent, more than 3 times the average for all occupations, are self-employed.
- Most positions in private industry require a master's degree and additional years of specialized experience; a bachelor's degree is sufficient for entry-level government jobs.

Nature of the Work

As business becomes more complex, the nation's firms are continually faced with new challenges. Firms increasingly rely on management analysts to help them remain competitive amidst these changes. Management analysts, often referred to as *management consultants* in private industry, analyze and propose ways to improve an organization's structure, efficiency, or profits. For example, a small but rapidly growing company that needs help improving the system of control over inventories and expenses may decide to employ a consultant who is an expert in just-in-time inventory management. In another case, a large company that has recently acquired a new division may hire management analysts to help reorganize the corporate structure and eliminate duplicate or nonessential jobs. In recent years, information technology and electronic commerce have provided new opportunities for management analysts. Companies hire consultants to develop strategies for entering and remaining competitive in the new electronic marketplace.

Firms providing management analysis range in size from a single practitioner to large international organizations employing thousands of consultants. Some analysts and consultants specialize in a specific industry, such as health care or telecommunications, while others specialize by type of business function, such as human resources, marketing, logistics, or information systems. In government, management analysts tend to specialize by type of agency. The work of management analysts and consultants varies with each client or employer, and from project to project. Some projects require a team of consultants, each specializing in one area. In other projects, consultants work independently with the organization's managers. In all cases, analysts and consultants collect, review, and analyze information in order to make recommendations to managers.

Both public and private organizations use consultants for a variety of reasons. Some lack the internal resources needed to handle a project, while others need a consultant's expertise to determine what resources will be required and what problems may be encountered if they pursue a particular opportunity. To retain a consultant, a company first solicits proposals from a number of consulting firms specializing in the area in which it needs assistance. These proposals include the estimated cost and scope of the project, staffing requirements, references from a number of previous clients, and a completion deadline. The company then selects the proposal that best suits its needs.

After obtaining an assignment or contract, management analysts first define the nature and extent of the problem. During this phase, they analyze relevant data—which may include annual revenues, employment, or expenditures—and interview managers and employees while observing their operations. The analyst or consultant then develops solutions to the problem. While preparing their recommendations, they take into account the nature of the organization, the relationship it has with others in the industry, and its internal organization and culture. Insight into the problem often is gained by building and solving mathematical models.

Once they have decided on a course of action, consultants report their findings and recommendations to the client. These suggestions usually are submitted in writing, but oral presentations regarding findings also are common. For some projects, management analysts are retained to help implement the suggestions they have made.

Like their private-sector colleagues, management analysts in government agencies try to increase efficiency and worker productivity, and to control costs. For example, if an agency is planning to purchase personal computers, it must first determine which type to buy, given its budget and data-processing needs. In this case, management analysts would assess the prices and characteristics of various machines and determine which ones best meet the agency's needs. Analysts may manage contracts for a wide range of goods and services to ensure quality performance and to prevent cost overruns.

Working Conditions

Management analysts usually divide their time between their offices and the client's site. In either situation, much of an analyst's time is spent indoors in clean, well-lit offices. Because they must spend a significant portion of their time with clients, analysts travel frequently.

Analysts and consultants generally work at least 40 hours a week. Uncompensated overtime is common, especially when project deadlines are approaching. Analysts may experience a great deal of stress as a result of trying to meet a client's demands, often on a tight schedule.

Self-employed consultants can set their workload and hours and work at home. On the other hand, their livelihood depends on their ability to maintain and expand their client base. Salaried consultants also must impress potential clients to get and keep clients for their company.

Training, Other Qualifications, and Advancement

Educational requirements for entry-level jobs in this field vary widely between private industry and government. Most employers in private industry generally seek individuals with a master's degree in business administration or a related discipline. Some employers also require additional years of experience in the field or industry in which the worker plans to consult, in addition to a master's degree. Some will hire workers with a bachelor's degree as a research analyst or associate. Research analysts usually need to pursue a master's degree in order to advance to a consulting position. Most government agencies hire people with a bachelor's degree and no pertinent work experience for entry-level management analyst positions.

Few universities or colleges offer formal programs of study in management consulting; however, many fields of study provide a suitable educational background for this occupation because of the wide range of areas addressed by management analysts. Common educational backgrounds include most academic programs in business and management, such as accounting and marketing, as well as economics, computer and information sciences, and engineering. In addition to the appropriate formal education, most entrants to this occupation have years of experience in management, human resources, information technology, or other specialties. Analysts also routinely attend conferences to keep abreast of current developments in their field.

Management analysts often work with minimal supervision, so they need to be self-motivated and disciplined. Analytical skills, the ability to get along with a wide range of people, strong oral and written communication skills, good judgment, time management skills, and creativity are other desirable qualities. The ability to work in teams also is an important attribute as consulting teams become more common.

As consultants gain experience, they often become solely responsible for a specific project, taking on more responsibility and managing their own hours. At the senior level, consultants may supervise teams working on more complex projects and become more involved in seeking out new business. Those with exceptional skills may eventually become a partner in the firm. Others with entrepreneurial ambition may open their own firm.

A high percentage of management consultants are self-employed, partly because business startup costs are low. Self-employed consultants also can share office space, administrative help, and other resources with other self-employed consultants or small consulting firms, thus reducing overhead costs. Since many small consulting firms fail each year because of lack of managerial expertise and clients, persons interested in opening their own firm must have good organizational and marketing skills and several years of consulting experience.

The Institute of Management Consultants USA, Inc. (IMC USA) offers a wide range of professional development programs and resources, such as meetings and workshops, which can be helpful for management consultants. The IMC USA also offers the Certified Management Consultant (CMC) designation to those who meet minimum levels of education and experience, submit client reviews, and pass an interview and exam covering the IMC USA's Code of Ethics. Management consultants with a CMC designation must be recertified every 3 years. Certification is not mandatory for management consultants, but it may give a jobseeker a competitive advantage.

Employment

Management analysts held about 605,000 jobs in 2004. About 29 percent of these workers, more than 3 times the average for all occupations, were self-employed. Management analysts are found throughout the country, but employment is concentrated in large metropolitan areas. Management analyst jobs are found in a wide range of industries, including management, scientific, and technical consulting firms; computer systems design and related services firms; and federal, state, and local governments. The majority of those working for the federal government are in the U.S. Department of Defense.

Job Outlook

Despite projected rapid employment growth, keen competition is expected for jobs as management analysts. The pool of applicants from which employers can draw is quite large since analysts can come from very diverse educational backgrounds. Furthermore, the independent and challenging nature of the work, combined with high earnings potential, makes this occupation attractive to many. Job opportunities are expected to be best for those with a graduate degree, specific industry expertise, and a talent for salesmanship and public relations.

Employment of management analysts is expected to grow faster than the average for all occupations through 2014, as industry and government increasingly rely on outside expertise to improve the performance of their organizations. Job growth is projected in very large consulting firms with international expertise and in smaller consulting firms that specialize in specific areas, such as biotechnology, health care, information technology, human resources, engineering, and marketing. Growth in the number of individual practitioners may be hindered by increasing use of consulting teams that can expedite solutions to a variety of different issues and problems within an organization.

Employment growth of management analysts has been driven by a number of changes in the business environment that have forced firms to take a closer look at their operations. These changes include developments in information technology and the growth of electronic commerce. Traditional companies hire analysts to help design intranets or company Web sites, or to establish online businesses. New Internet startup companies hire analysts not only to design Web sites but also to advise them in more traditional business practices, such as pricing strategies, marketing, and inventory and human resource management. In order to offer clients better quality and a wider variety of services, consulting firms are partnering with traditional computer software and technology firms. Also, many computer firms are developing consulting practices of their own in order to take advantage of this expanding market. Although information technology consulting should remain one of the fastest growing consulting areas, the volatility of the computer services industry necessitates that the most successful management analysts have knowledge of traditional business practices in addition to computer applications, systems integration, Web design, and management skills.

The growth of international business also has contributed to an increase in demand for management analysts. As U.S. firms expand their business abroad, many will hire management analysts to help them form the right strategy for entering the market; to advise them on legal matters pertaining to specific countries; or to help them with organizational, administrative, and other issues, especially if the U.S. company is involved in a partnership or merger with a local firm. These trends provide management analysts with more opportunities to travel or work abroad but also require them to have a more comprehensive knowledge of international business and foreign cultures and languages.

Furthermore, as international and domestic markets have become more competitive, firms have needed to use resources more efficiently. Management analysts increasingly are sought to help reduce costs, streamline operations, and develop marketing strategies. As this process continues and businesses downsize, even more opportunities will be created for analysts to perform duties that previously were handled internally. Finally, more management analysts also will be needed in the public sector, as federal, state, and local government agencies seek ways to become more efficient.

Though management consultants are continually expanding their services, employment growth could be hampered by increasing competition for clients from occupations that do not traditionally perform consulting work, such as accountants, financial analysts, lawyers, and computer systems analysts. Furthermore, economic downturns also can have adverse effects on employment for some management consultants. In these times, businesses look to cut costs, and consultants may be considered an excess expense. On the other hand, some consultants might experience an increase in work during recessions because they advise businesses on how to cut costs and remain profitable.

Earnings

Salaries for management analysts vary widely by years of experience and education, geographic location, sector of expertise, and size of employer. Generally, management analysts employed in large firms or in metropolitan areas have the highest salaries. Median annual wage and salary earnings of management analysts in May 2004 were $63,450. The middle 50 percent earned between $48,340 and $86,650. The lowest 10 percent earned less than $37,680, and the highest 10 percent earned more than $120,220. Median annual earnings in the industries employing the largest numbers of management analysts in May 2004 were:

Management, scientific, and technical consulting services	$72,480
Federal government	72,440
Computer systems design and related services	69,800
Management of companies and enterprises	59,420
State government	48,070

According to a the Association of Management Consulting Firms, typical earnings in 2004—including bonuses and profit sharing—averaged $52,482 for research associates in member firms; $65,066 for entry-level consultants; $89,116 for management consultants; $123,305 for senior consultants; $191,664 for junior partners; and $317,339 for senior partners. Only the most experienced workers in highly successful management consulting firms earn these top salaries.

Salaried management analysts usually receive common benefits, such as health and life insurance, a retirement plan, vacation, and sick leave, as well as less common benefits, such as profit sharing and bonuses for outstanding work. In addition, all travel expenses usually are reimbursed by the employer. Self-employed consultants have to maintain their own office and provide their own benefits.

Related Occupations

Management analysts collect, review, and analyze data; make recommendations; and implement their ideas. Occupations with similar duties include accountants and auditors; budget analysts; cost estimators; financial analysts and personal financial advisors; operations research analysts; economists; and market and survey researchers. Some management analysts specialize in information technology and work with computers, as do computer systems analysts and computer scientists and database administrators. Most management analysts also have managerial experience similar to that of administrative services managers; advertising, marketing, promotions, public relations, and sales managers; financial managers; human resources, training, and labor relations managers and specialists; and top executives.

Sources of Additional Information

Information about career opportunities in management consulting is available from:

- Association of Management Consulting Firms, 380 Lexington Ave., Suite 1700, New York, NY 10168. Internet: http://www.amcf.org

Information about the Certified Management Consultant designation can be obtained from:

- Institute of Management Consultants USA, Inc., 2025 M St. NW, Suite 800, Washington, DC 20036. Internet: http://www.imcusa.org

Information on obtaining a management analyst position with the federal government is available from the Office of Personnel Management (OPM) through USAJOBS, the federal government's official employment information system. This resource for locating and applying for job opportunities can be accessed through the Internet at http://www.usajobs.opm.gov or through an interactive voice response telephone system at (703) 724-1850 or TDD (978) 461-8404. These numbers are not toll free, and charges may result.

Market and Survey Researchers

(O*NET 19-3021.00 and 19-3022.00)

Significant Points

- Market and survey researchers need at least a bachelor's degree, but a master's degree may be required for employment; continuing education also is important.
- Employment is expected to grow faster than average.
- Job opportunities should be best for those with a master's or Ph.D. degree in marketing or a related field and strong quantitative skills.

Nature of the Work

Market, or *marketing, research analysts* are concerned with the potential sales of a product or service. Gathering statistical data on competitors and examining prices, sales, and methods of marketing and distribution, they analyze data on past sales to predict future sales. Market research analysts devise methods and procedures for obtaining the data they need. Often, they design telephone, mail, or Internet surveys to assess consumer preferences. They conduct some surveys as personal interviews, going door-to-door, leading focus group discussions, or setting up booths in public places such as shopping malls. Trained interviewers usually conduct the surveys under the market research analyst's direction.

After compiling and evaluating the data, market research analysts make recommendations to their client or employer on the basis of their findings. They provide a company's management with information needed to make decisions on the promotion, distribution, design, and pricing of products or services. The information also may be used to determine the advisability of adding new lines of merchandise, opening new branches, or otherwise diversifying the company's operations. Market research analysts also might develop advertising brochures and commercials, sales plans, and product promotions such as rebates and giveaways.

Survey researchers design and conduct surveys for a variety of clients, such as corporations, government agencies, political candidates, and providers of various services. The surveys collect information that is used for performing research, making fiscal or policy decisions, measuring the effectiveness of those decisions, or improving customer satisfaction. Analysts may conduct opinion research to determine public attitudes on various issues; the research results may help political or business leaders and others assess public support for their electoral prospects or social policies. Like market research analysts, survey researchers may use a variety of mediums to conduct surveys, such as the Internet, personal or telephone interviews, or questionnaires sent through the mail. They also may supervise interviewers who conduct surveys in person or over the telephone.

Survey researchers design surveys in many different formats, depending upon the scope of their research and the method of collection. Interview surveys, for example, are common because they can increase participation rates. Survey researchers may consult with economists, statisticians, market research analysts, or other data users in order to design surveys. They also may present survey results to clients.

Working Conditions

Market and survey researchers generally have structured work schedules. Some often work alone, writing reports, preparing statistical charts, and using computers, but they also may be an integral part of a research team. Market researchers who conduct personal interviews have frequent contact with the public. Most work under pressure of deadlines and tight schedules, which may require overtime. Their routine may be interrupted by special requests for data, as well as by the need to attend meetings or conferences. Travel may be necessary.

Training, Other Qualifications, and Advancement

A bachelor's degree is the minimum educational requirement for many market and survey research jobs. However, a master's degree may be required, especially for technical positions, and increases opportunities for advancement to more responsible positions. Also, continuing education is important in order to keep current with the latest methods of developing, conducting, and analyzing surveys and other data. Market and survey researchers may earn advanced degrees in business administration, marketing, statistics, communications, or some closely related discipline. Some schools help graduate students find internships or part-time employment in government agencies, consulting firms, financial institutions, or marketing research firms prior to graduation.

In addition to completing courses in business, marketing, and consumer behavior, prospective market and survey researchers should take other liberal arts and social science courses, including economics, psychology, English, and sociology. Because of the importance of quantitative skills to market and survey researchers, courses in mathematics, statistics, sampling theory and survey design, and computer science are extremely helpful. Many corporation and government executives have a strong background in marketing.

A master's degree is usually the minimum educational requirement for a job as a marketing or survey research instructor in junior and community colleges. In most colleges and universities, however, a Ph.D. is necessary for appointment as an instructor. A Ph.D. and extensive publications in academic journals are required for a professorship, tenure, and promotion.

While in college, aspiring market and survey researchers should gain experience gathering and analyzing data, conducting interviews or surveys, and writing reports on their findings. This experience can prove invaluable later in obtaining a full-time position in the field, because much of the initial work may center on these duties. With experience, market and survey researchers eventually are assigned their own research projects.

Much of the market and survey researcher's time is spent on precise data analysis, so those considering careers in the occupation should be able to pay attention to detail. Patience and persistence are necessary qualities because these workers must spend long hours on independent study and problem solving. At the same time, they must work well with others: often, market and survey researchers oversee interviews of a wide variety of individuals. Communication skills are important, too, because researchers must be able to present their findings both orally and in writing, in a clear, concise manner.

While certification currently is not required for market and survey researchers, the Marketing Research Association (MRA) offers a certification program for professional researchers. Certification is based on education and experience requirements, as well as on continuing education.

Employment

Market and survey researchers held about 212,000 jobs in 2004, most of which—190,000—were held by market research analysts. Because of the applicability of market research to many industries, market research analysts are employed throughout the economy. The industries that employ the largest number of market research analysts were management of companies and enterprises; management, scientific, and technical consulting services; insurance carriers; credit intermediation and related activities; computer systems design and related services; marketing research and public opinion polling; software publishers; professional and commercial equipment and supplies merchant wholesalers; securities and commodity contracts intermediation and brokerage; and advertising and related services.

Survey researchers held about 22,000 jobs in 2004. Survey researchers were employed mainly by professional, scientific, and technical services firms, especially in market research and public opinion polling; scientific research and development services; and management, scientific, and technical consulting services. State government also provided many jobs for survey researchers.

A number of market and survey researchers combine a full-time job in government, academia, or business with part-time or consulting work in another setting. About nine percent of market and survey researchers are self-employed.

Besides holding the previously mentioned jobs, many market and survey researchers held faculty positions in colleges and universities. Marketing faculties have flexible work schedules and may divide their time among teaching, research, consulting, and administration.

Job Outlook

Employment of market and survey researchers is expected to grow faster than average for all occupations through 2014. Many job openings are likely to result from the need to replace experienced workers who transfer to other occupations or who retire or leave the labor force for other reasons.

Job opportunities should be best for those with a master's or Ph.D. degree in marketing or a related field and strong quantitative skills. Bachelor's degree holders may face competition, as many positions, especially the more technical ones, require a master's or higher degree. Among bachelor's degree holders, those with good quantitative skills, including a strong background in mathematics, statistics, survey design, and computer science, will have the best opportunities. Ph.D. degree holders in marketing and related fields should have a range of opportunities in industry and consulting firms. Like those in many other disciplines, however, Ph.D. holders probably will face keen competition for tenured teaching positions in colleges and universities.

Demand for market research analysts should be strong because of an increasingly competitive economy. Marketing research provides organizations valuable feedback from purchasers, allowing companies to evaluate consumer satisfaction and plan more effectively for the future. As companies seek to expand their market and as consumers become better informed, the need for marketing professionals will increase. In addition, as globalization of the marketplace continues, market researchers will increasingly be utilized to analyze foreign markets and competition for goods and services.

Market research analysts should have the best opportunities in consulting firms and marketing research firms as companies find it more profitable to contract for market research services rather than support their own marketing department. Increasingly, market research analysts not only are collecting and analyzing information, but also are helping clients implement the analysts' ideas and recommendations. Other organizations, including computer systems design companies, software publishers, financial services organizations, health care institutions, advertising firms, and insurance companies, may offer job opportunities for market research analysts. Survey researchers will be needed to meet the growing demand for market and opinion research as an increasingly competitive economy requires businesses to allocate advertising funds more effectively and efficiently.

Earnings

Median annual earnings of market research analysts in May 2004 were $56,140. The middle 50 percent earned between $40,510 and $79,990. The lowest 10 percent earned less than $30,890, and the highest 10 percent earned more than $105,870. Median annual earnings in the industries employing the largest numbers of market research analysts in May 2004 were:

Management of companies and enterprises	$58,440
Computer systems design and related services	58,100
Insurance carriers	51,030
Other professional, scientific, and technical services	50,950
Management, scientific, and technical consulting services	49,080

Median annual earnings of survey researchers in May 2004 were $26,490. The middle 50 percent earned between $17,920 and $41,390. The lowest 10 percent earned less than $15,330, and the highest 10 percent earned more than $56,740. Median annual earnings of survey researchers in other professional, scientific, and technical services were $22,880.

Related Occupations

Market and survey researchers perform research to find out how well the market receives products or services. Such research may include planning, implementing, and analyzing surveys to determine the needs and preferences of people. Other jobs using these skills include economists, psychologists, sociologists, statisticians, and urban and regional planners.

Sources of Additional Information

For information about careers and certification in market research, contact:

- Marketing Research Association, 110 National Dr., Glastonbury, CT 06033. Internet: http://www.mra-net.org

For information about careers in survey research, contact:

- Council of American Survey Research Organizations, 170 North Country Rd., Suite 4, Port Jefferson, NY 11777. Internet: http://www.casro.org

Massage Therapists

(O*NET 31-9011.00)

Significant Points

- Employment is expected to grow faster than average over the 2004–2014 period as more people learn about the benefits of massage therapy.
- Many states require formal training and a national certification in order to practice massage therapy.
- This occupation contains a large number of part-time and self-employed workers.

Nature of the Work

Many physicians have been recommending massage therapy for nearly 2,400 years. The medical benefits of "friction" were first documented in Western culture by the Greek physician Hippocrates around 400 BC. Today, massage therapy is being used as a means of treating painful ailments, decompressing tired and overworked muscles, reducing stress, rehabilitating sports injuries, and promoting general health. This is accomplished by manipulating a client's soft tissues in order to improve the body's circulation and remove waste products from the muscles.

While massage therapy is done for medical benefit, a massage can be given to simply relax or rejuvenate the person being massaged. It is important to note that this type of massage is not intended for a medical purpose and provides medical value only through general stress reduction and increased energy levels. Massage therapy, on the other hand, is practiced by thoroughly trained individuals who provide specialized care with their client's medical health in mind.

Massage therapists can specialize in over 80 different types of massage, called modalities. Swedish massage, deep tissue massage, reflexology, acupressure, sports massage, and neuromuscular massage are just a few of the many approaches to massage therapy. Most massage therapists specialize in several modalities, which require different techniques. Some use exaggerated strokes ranging the length of a body part, while others use quick, percussion-like strokes with a cupped or closed hand. A massage can be as long as two hours or as short as five or ten minutes. Usually, the type of massage therapists give depends on the client's needs and the client's physical condition. For example, they use special techniques for elderly clients that they would not use for athletes, and they would use approaches for clients with injuries that would not be appropriate for clients seeking relaxation. There are also some forms of massage that are given solely to one type of client (for example, prenatal massage and infant massage).

Massage therapists work by appointment. Before beginning a massage therapy session, therapists conduct an informal interview with the client to find out about the person's medical history and desired results from the massage. This gives therapists a chance to discuss which techniques could be beneficial to the client and which could be harmful. Because massage therapists tend to specialize in only a few areas of massage, customers will often be referred or seek a therapist with a certain type of massage in mind. Based on the person's goals, ailments, medical history, and stress- or pain-related problem areas, a massage therapist will conclude whether a massage would be harmful, and if not, move forward with the session while concentrating on any areas of particular discomfort to the client. While giving the massage, therapists alter their approach or concentrate on a particular area as necessary.

Many modalities of massage therapy use massage oils, lotions, or creams to massage and rub the client's muscles. Most massage therapists, particularly those who are self-employed, supply their own table or chair, sheets, pillows, and body lotions or oils. Most modalities of massage require clients to be covered in a sheet or blanket and require clients to be undressed or to wear loose-fitting clothing. The therapist only exposes the body part on which he or she is currently massaging. Some types of massage are done without oils or lotions and are performed with the client fully clothed.

Massage can be a delicate issue for some clients, and those clients may indicate that they are comfortable with contact only in specified areas. For this reason—and also for general purpose business risks—about half of all massage therapists have liability insurance, either through a professional association membership or through other insurance carriers.

Massage therapists must develop a rapport with their clients if repeat customers are to be secured. Because those who seek a therapist tend to make regular visits, developing a loyal clientele is an important part of becoming successful.

Working Conditions

Massage therapists work in an array of settings both private and public: private offices, studios, hospitals, nursing homes, fitness centers, sports medicine facilities, airports, and shopping malls, for example. Some massage therapists also travel to clients' homes or offices to provide a massage. It is not uncommon for full-time massage therapists to divide their time among several different settings, depending on the clients and locations scheduled.

Most massage therapists give massages in dimly lit settings. Using candles and/or incense is not uncommon. Ambient or other calm, soothing music is often played. The dim lighting, smells, and background noise are meant to put clients at ease. On the other hand, when visiting a client's office, a massage therapist may not have those amenities. The working conditions depend heavily on a therapist's location and what the client wants.

Because massage is physically demanding, massage therapists can succumb to injury if the proper technique is not used. Repetitive motion problems and fatigue from standing for extended periods of time are most common. This risk can be limited by use of good technique, proper spacing between sessions, exercise, and in many cases by the therapists themselves receiving a massage on a regular basis.

Because of the physical nature of the work and time needed in between sessions, massage therapists typically give massages less than 40 hours per week. Therapists who give massages anywhere from 15 to 30 hours per week usually consider themselves to be full-time workers.

Training, Other Qualifications, and Advancement

Training standards and requirements for massage therapists vary greatly by state and locality. In 2004, 33 states and the District of Columbia had passed laws regulating massage therapy in some way. Most of the boards governing massage therapy in these states require practicing massage therapists to complete a formal education program and pass the national certification examination or a state exam. Some state regulations require that therapists keep up on their knowledge and technique through continuing education. It is best to check information on licensing, certification, and accreditation on a state-by-state basis.

There are roughly 1,300 massage therapy postsecondary schools, college programs, and training programs throughout the country. Massage therapy programs generally cover subjects such as anatomy; physiology, the study of organs and tissues; kinesiology, the study of motion and body mechanics; business; and ethics, as well as hands-on practice of massage techniques. Most formal training programs require an application and some require an in-person interview. Training programs may concentrate on certain modalities of massage. Several programs also provide alumni services such as post-graduate job placement and continuing educational services. Both full- and part-time programs are available.

These programs vary in accreditation. Massage therapy training programs are generally accredited by a state board or other accrediting agency. Of the many massage therapy programs in the country, about 300 are accredited by a state board or department of education–certified accrediting agency. In states that regulate massage therapy, graduation from an approved school or training program is usually required in order to practice massage therapy.

After completion of a training program, many massage therapists opt to take the national certification examination for therapeutic massage and bodywork. This exam is administered by the National Certification Board for Therapeutic Massage and Bodywork (NCBTMB), which has eligibility requirements of its own. Several states require that a massage therapist pass this test in order to practice massage therapy. In states that require massage therapy program accreditation, an exam candidate must graduate from a state-licensed training institute with at least 500 hours of training or submit a portfolio of training experience for NCBTMB review; in locations that do not require accredited training programs, this is unnecessary. After the applicant is approved for testing, the applicant may schedule a test time at a local testing center. Tests are available six or seven days a week, depending on the test site, and are entirely computer based with multiple-choice questions. The exam covers six areas of content: general knowledge of the body systems; detailed knowledge of anatomy, physiology, and kinesiology; pathology; therapeutic massage assessment; therapeutic massage application; and professional standards, ethics, business, and legal practices.

When a therapist passes the national certification exam for therapeutic massage and bodywork, he or she can use the recognized national credential Nationally Certified in Therapeutic Massage and Bodywork (NCTMB). The credential must be renewed every four years.

In order to remain certified, a therapist must perform at least 200 hours of therapeutic massage during the four-year period and complete a minimum of 48 credit hours of continuing education. In 2005, the NCBTMB introduced a new national certification test and corresponding professional credential. These are the national certification exam for therapeutic massage and the Nationally Certified in Therapeutic Massage (NCTM) credential. The new test covers the same topics as the traditional national certification exam, but covers fewer modalities of massage therapy. Recognition of this new national certification varies by state.

Many of the national, state, and local requirements coincide. States that require the national credential also require accredited training programs to comply with NCBTMB standards of training. Professional associations require that a professional member graduate from a training program that meets NCBTMB standards, have a state license, and/or have a national certification from the NCBTMB. Actual requirements differ on a state-by-state basis.

Because of the nature of massage therapy, opportunities for advancement are limited. However, with increased experience and an expanding client base, there are opportunities for therapists to increase client fees and therefore income. Both strong communication skills and a friendly, empathetic personality are extremely helpful qualities for fostering a trusting relationship with clients and in turn expanding one's client base. In addition, those who are well organized and have an entrepreneurial spirit may even go into business for themselves. Self-employed massage therapists with a large client base have the highest earnings.

Employment

Massage therapists held about 97,000 jobs in 2004. About two-thirds were self-employed. Of those self-employed, most owned their own business, and the rest worked as independent contractors. Others found employment in salons and spas, the offices of physicians and chiropractors, fitness and recreational sports centers, and hotels. About three-quarters of all massage therapists worked part time or had variable schedules, although as mentioned earlier many massage therapists who work 15 to 30 hours per week consider themselves to be full-time workers.

Job Outlook

Employment for massage therapists is expected to increase faster than average over the period from 2004 to 2014 as more people learn about the benefits of massage therapy. In states that regulate massage therapy, therapists who complete formal training programs and pass the national certification exam are likely to have very good job opportunities. Because referrals are a very important source of work for massage therapists, networking will increase the number of job opportunities. Joining a state or local chapter of a professional association can also help build strong contacts and further increase the likelihood of steady work.

Massage is an increasingly popular technique for relaxation and reduction of stress. As workplaces try to distinguish themselves as employee-friendly, providing professional in-office, seated massages for employees is becoming a popular on-the-job benefit.

Increased interest in alternative medicine and holistic healing will mean increased opportunities for those skilled in massage therapy. Health care providers and medical insurance companies are beginning to recognize massage therapy as a legitimate treatment and preventative measure for several types of injuries and illnesses. The health care industry is using massage therapy more often as a supplement to conventional medical techniques for ailments such as muscle problems, some sicknesses and diseases, and stress-related health problems. Massage therapy's growing acceptance as a medical tool, particularly by the medical provider and insurance industries, will greatly increase employment opportunities.

Older citizens who are in nursing homes or assisted living homes are also finding benefits from massage, such as increased energy levels and reduced health problems. Demand for massage therapy should grow among older age groups because they increasingly enjoy longer, more active lives, and persons age 55 and older are projected to be the most rapidly growing segment of the U.S. population over the next decade. However, demand for massage therapy is presently greatest among young adults, and they are likely to continue to enjoy the benefits of massage therapy as they age.

Earnings

Median hourly earnings of massage therapists, including gratuities earned, were $15.36 in May 2004. The middle 50 percent earned between $9.78 and $23.82. The lowest 10 percent earned less than $7.16, and the highest 10 percent earned more than $32.21. Generally, massage therapists earn 15 to 20 percent of their income as gratuities. For those who work in a hospital or other clinical setting, however, tipping is not common.

Related Occupations

Other workers in the health care industry who provide therapy to clients include physical therapists, physical therapists' assistants and aides, chiropractors, and workers in other occupations that use touch to aid healing or relieve stress.

Sources of Additional Information

General information on becoming a massage therapist is available from state regulatory boards.

For more information on becoming a massage therapist, contact:

- Associated Bodywork & Massage Professionals, 1271 Sugarbush Dr., Evergreen, CO 80439.
- American Massage Therapy Association, 500 Davis St., Suite 900, Evanston, IL 60201. Internet: http://www.amtamassage.org

For a directory of schools providing accredited massage therapy training programs, contact:

- Commission on Massage Therapy Accreditation, 1007 Church St., Suite 302, Evanston, IL 60201. Internet: http://www.comta.org
- Accrediting Commission of Career Schools and Colleges of Technology, 2101 Wilson Blvd., Suite 302, Arlington, VA 22201. Internet: http://www.accsct.org

Information on national testing and national certification is available from:

- National Certification Board for Therapeutic Massage and Bodywork, 1901 S. Meyers Rd., Suite 240, Oakbrook Terrace, IL 60181.

Material Moving Occupations

(O*NET 53-1021.00, 53-7011.00, 53-7021.00, 53-7031.00, 53-7032.01, 53-7032.02, 53-7033.00, 53-7041.00, 53-7051.00, 53-7061.00, 53-7062.01, 53-7062.02, 53-7062.03, 53-7063.00, 53-7064.00, 53-7071.01, 53-7071.02, 53-7072.00, 53-7073.00, 53-7081.00, 53-7111.00, 53-7121.00, and 53-7199.99)

Significant Points

- Job openings should be numerous because the occupation is very large and turnover is relatively high.
- Most jobs require little work experience or training.
- Pay is low, and the seasonal nature of the work may reduce earnings.

Nature of the Work

Material moving workers are categorized into two groups—operators and laborers. Operators use machinery to move construction materials, earth, petroleum products, and other heavy materials. Generally, they move materials over short distances—around construction sites, factories, or warehouses. Some move materials onto or off of trucks and ships. Operators control equipment by moving levers, wheels, and/or foot pedals; operating switches; or turning dials. They also may set up and inspect equipment, make adjustments, and perform minor maintenance or repairs. Laborers and hand material movers manually handle freight, stock, or other materials; clean vehicles, machinery, and other equipment; feed materials into or remove materials from machines or equipment; and pack or package products and materials.

Material moving occupations are classified by the type of equipment they operate or the goods they handle. Each piece of equipment requires different skills, as do different types of loads.

Industrial truck and tractor operators drive and control industrial trucks or tractors equipped to move materials around warehouses, storage yards, factories, or construction sites. A typical industrial truck, often called a forklift or lift truck, has a hydraulic lifting mechanism and forks for moving heavy and large objects. Industrial truck and tractor operators also may operate tractors that pull trailers loaded with materials, goods, or equipment within factories and warehouses or around outdoor storage areas.

Excavating and loading machine and dragline operators tend or operate machinery equipped with scoops, shovels, or buckets to dig and load sand, gravel, earth, or similar materials into trucks or onto conveyors. Construction and mining industries employ the majority of excavation and loading machine and dragline operators. *Dredge operators* excavate waterways, removing sand, gravel, rock, or other materials from harbors, lakes, rivers, and streams. Dredges are used primarily to maintain navigable channels but also are used to restore wetlands and other aquatic habitats; reclaim land; and create and maintain beaches. *Underground mining loading machine operators* use underground loading machines to load coal, ore, or rock into shuttles and mine cars or onto conveyors. Loading equipment may include power shovels, hoisting engines equipped with cable-drawn scraper or scoop, and machines equipped with gathering arms and conveyors.

Crane and tower operators work mechanical boom and cable or tower and cable equipment to lift and move materials, machinery, and other heavy objects. Operators extend and retract horizontally mounted booms and lower and raise hooks attached to load lines. Most operators are guided by other workers using hand signals or a radio. Operators position loads from an onboard console or from a remote console at the site. While crane and tower operators are noticeable at office building and other construction sites, the biggest group works in primary metal, metal fabrication, and transportation equipment manufacturing industries that use heavy, bulky materials. *Hoist and winch operators* control movement of cables, cages, and platforms to move workers and materials for manufacturing, logging, and other industrial operations. They work in positions such as derrick operators and hydraulic boom operators. Many hoist and winch operators are found in manufacturing or construction industries.

Pump operators tend, control, and operate power-driven pumps and manifold systems that transfer gases, oil, or other materials to vessels or equipment. They maintain the equipment to regulate the flow of materials according to a schedule set up by petroleum engineers and production supervisors. *Gas compressor and gas pumping station operators* operate steam, gas, electric motor, or internal combustion engine-driven compressors. They transmit, compress, or recover gases, such as butane, nitrogen, hydrogen, and natural gas. *Wellhead pumpers* operate power pumps and auxiliary equipment to produce flows of oil or gas from extraction sites.

Tank car, truck, and ship loaders operate ship-loading and -unloading equipment, conveyors, hoists, and other specialized material-handling equipment such as railroad tank car-unloading equipment. They may gauge or sample shipping tanks and test them for leaks. *Conveyor operators and tenders* control and tend conveyor systems that move materials to or from stockpiles, processing stations, departments, or vehicles. *Shuttle car operators* run diesel or electric-powered shuttle cars in underground mines, transporting materials from the working face to mine cars or conveyors.

Laborers and hand freight, stock, and material movers manually move materials and perform other unskilled general labor. These workers move freight, stock, and other materials to and from storage and production areas, loading docks, delivery vehicles, ships, and containers. Their specific duties vary by industry and work setting. In factories, they may move raw materials or finished goods between loading docks, storage areas, and work areas, as well as sort materials and supplies and prepare them according to their work orders. Specialized workers within this group include baggage and cargo handlers, who work in transportation industries, and truck loaders and unloaders.

Hand packers and packagers manually pack, package, or wrap a variety of materials. They may inspect items for defects, label cartons, stamp information on products, keep records of items packed, and stack packages on loading docks. This group also includes order fillers, who pack materials for shipment, as well as grocery store courtesy clerks. In grocery stores, they may bag groceries, carry packages to customers' cars, and return shopping carts to designated areas.

Machine feeders and offbearers feed materials into or remove materials from automatic equipment or machines tended by other workers.

Cleaners of vehicles and equipment clean machinery, vehicles, storage tanks, pipelines, and similar equipment using water and other cleaning agents, vacuums, hoses, brushes, cloths, and other cleaning equipment.

Refuse and recyclable material collectors gather refuse and recyclables from homes and businesses into their truck for transport to a dump, landfill, or recycling center. They lift and empty garbage cans or recycling bins by hand or operate a hydraulic lift truck that picks up and empties dumpsters. They work along scheduled routes.

Working Conditions

Material moving work tends to be repetitive and physically demanding. Workers may lift and carry heavy objects and stoop, kneel, crouch, or crawl in awkward positions. Some work at great heights and some work outdoors, regardless of weather and climate. Some jobs expose workers to fumes, odors, loud noises, harmful materials and chemicals, or dangerous machinery. To protect their eyes, respiratory systems, and hearing, these workers wear safety clothing, such as gloves, hardhats, and other safety devices. These jobs have become much less dangerous as safety equipment—such as overhead guards on lift trucks—has become common. Accidents usually can be avoided by observing proper operating procedures and safety practices.

Material movers generally work 8-hour shifts, though longer shifts also are not uncommon. In industries that work around the clock, material movers may work overnight shifts. Some do this because the establishment does not want to disturb customers during normal business hours. Refuse and recyclable material collectors often work shifts starting at 5 or 6 a.m. Some material movers work only during certain seasons, such as when the weather permits construction activity.

Training, Other Qualifications, and Advancement

Little work experience or training is required for most material moving occupations. Some employers prefer applicants with a high school diploma, but most simply require workers to be at least 18 years old and physically able to perform the work. For those jobs requiring physical exertion, employers may require that applicants pass a physical exam. Some employers also require drug testing or background checks before employment. Material movers often are younger than workers in other occupations, reflecting the limited training but significant physical requirements of many of these jobs. Material movers generally learn skills informally, on the job, from more experienced workers or their supervisors. Workers who handle toxic chemicals or use industrial trucks or other dangerous equipment must receive specialized training in safety awareness and procedures. Many of the training requirements are standardized through the U.S. Occupational Safety and Health Administration. This training is usually provided by the employer. Employers also must certify that each operator has received the training and evaluate each operator at least once every 3 years. For other operators, such as crane operators and those working with specialized loads, there are some training and apprenticeship programs, such as that offered by the International Union of Industrial Engineers, as well as certifying institutions, such as the National Commission for the Certification of Crane Operators. Some employers may require crane operators to be certified. Twelve states have laws requiring crane operators to be licensed. Licensing requirements typically include a written as well as a skills test to demonstrate that the licensee can operate a crane safely.

Material moving equipment operators need a good sense of balance, the ability to judge distances, and eye-hand-foot coordination. For jobs that involve dealing with the public, such as grocery store courtesy clerks, workers should be pleasant and courteous. Most jobs require basic arithmetic skills and the ability to read procedural manuals, to understand orders, and other billing documents. Mechanical aptitude and training in automobile or diesel mechanics can be helpful because some operators may perform basic maintenance on their equipment. Experience operating mobile equipment—such as tractors on farms or heavy equipment in the Armed Forces—is an asset. As material moving equipment becomes more advanced, workers will need to be increasingly comfortable with technology.

In many of these occupations, experience may allow workers to qualify or become trainees for jobs such as construction trades workers; assemblers or other production workers; motor vehicle operators; or vehicle and mobile equipment mechanics, installers, and repairers. In many workplaces, new employees gain experience in a material moving position before being promoted to a better paying and more highly skilled job. Some may eventually advance to become supervisors.

Employment

Material movers held 5.1 million jobs in 2004. They were distributed among the detailed occupations as follows:

Laborers and freight, stock, and material movers, hand	2,430,000
Packers and packagers, hand	877,000
Industrial truck and tractor operators	635,000
Cleaners of vehicles and equipment	347,000
First-line supervisors/managers of helpers, laborers, and material movers, hand	173,000
Refuse and recyclable material collectors	149,000
Machine feeders and offbearers	148,000
Excavating and loading machine and dragline operators	86,000
Conveyor operators and tenders	53,000

Crane and tower operators 44,000
Tank car, truck, and ship loaders 17,000
Wellhead pumpers 11,000
Pump operators, except wellhead pumpers 11,000
Hoist and winch operators 5,600
Gas compressor and gas pumping station operators 5,100
Loading machine operators, underground mining 4,300
Shuttle car operators 3,100
Dredge operators...2,500
All other material moving workers 58,000

About 29 percent of all material movers worked in the wholesale trade or retail trade industries. Another 22 percent worked in manufacturing; 14 percent in transportation and warehousing; 4 percent in construction and mining; and 15 percent in the employment services industry, on a temporary or contract basis. For example, companies that need workers for only a few days, to move materials or to clean up a site, may contract with temporary help agencies specializing in providing suitable workers on a short-term basis. A small proportion of material movers were self-employed.

Material movers work in every part of the country. Some work in remote locations on large construction projects such as highways and dams, while others work in factories, warehouses, or mining operations.

Job Outlook

Job openings should be numerous because the occupation is very large and turnover is relatively high—characteristic of occupations requiring little prior or formal training. Many openings will arise from the need to replace workers who transfer to other occupations or those who retire or leave the labor force for other reasons.

Employment in material moving occupations is projected to increase more slowly than the average for all occupations through 2014. Improvements in equipment, such as automated storage and retrieval systems and conveyors, will continue to raise productivity and moderate the demand for material movers.

Employment growth will stem from an expanding economy, especially in industries involved with the production, distribution, and sales of goods. Employment also will grow in the warehousing and storage industry as more firms contract out their warehousing functions to this industry. For example, a frozen food manufacturer may reduce its costs by outsourcing these functions to a refrigerated warehousing firm, which can more efficiently deal with the specialized storage needs of frozen food. Job growth for material movers depends on the growth or decline of employing industries and the type of equipment the workers operate or the materials they handle. For example, jobs in mining are expected to decline due to continued productivity increases within that industry. Job growth generally will be slower in large establishments, as they increasingly turn to automation for their material moving needs.

Both construction and manufacturing are very sensitive to changes in economic conditions, so the number of job openings in these industries will fluctuate. Although increasing automation will eliminate some routine tasks, new jobs will be created by the need to operate and maintain new equipment.

Earnings

Median hourly earnings of material moving workers in May 2004 were relatively low, as indicated by the following tabulation:

First-line supervisors/managers of helpers, laborers, and material movers, hand...................$18.40
Crane and tower operators 17.99
Pump operators, except wellhead pumpers 17.04
Wellhead pumpers 16.31
Hoist and winch operators 16.19
Tank car, truck, and ship loaders 15.59
Excavating and loading machine and dragline operators...15.37
Material moving workers, all other 13.87
Industrial truck and tractor operators.....................12.78
Refuse and recyclable material collectors 12.38
Conveyor operators and tenders 12.23
Machine feeders and offbearers 10.68
Laborers and freight, stock, and material movers, hand 9.67
Cleaners of vehicles and equipment 8.41
Packers and packagers, hand 8.25

Wages vary according to experience and job responsibilities. Wages usually are higher in metropolitan areas. Seasonal peaks and lulls in workload can affect the number of hours scheduled and, therefore, earnings. Certified crane operators tend to have a slightly higher hourly rate than those who are not certified.

Related Occupations

Other workers who operate mechanical equipment include construction equipment operators; machine setters, operators, and tenders—metal and plastic; rail transportation workers; and truck drivers and driver/sales workers. Other entry-level workers who perform mostly physical work are agricultural workers; building cleaning workers; construction laborers; forest, conservation, and logging workers; and grounds maintenance workers.

Sources of Additional Information

For information about job opportunities and training programs, contact local state employment service offices, building or construction contractors, manufacturers, and wholesale and retail establishments.

Information on safety and training requirements is available from:

- U.S. Department of Labor, Occupational Safety and Health Administration (OSHA), 200 Constitution Ave. NW, Washington, DC 20210. Internet: http://www.osha.gov

Information on industrial truck and tractor operators is available from:

- Industrial Truck Association, 1750 K St. NW, Suite 460, Washington, DC 20006. Internet: http://www.indtrk.org

Information on training and apprenticeships for industrial truck operators is available from:

- International Union of Industrial Engineers, 1125 17th St. NW, Washington, DC 20036. Internet: http://www.iuoe.org

Information on crane and derrick certification and licensure is available from:

- National Commission for the Certification of Crane Operators, 2750 Prosperity Ave., Suite 505, Fairfax, VA 22031. Internet: http://www.nccco.org

Medical and Health Services Managers

(O*NET 11-9111.00)

Significant Points

- Rapid employment growth is projected; job opportunities will be especially good in offices of health practitioners, general medical and surgical hospitals, home health care services, and outpatient care centers.
- Applicants with work experience in health care and strong business and management skills likely will have the best opportunities.
- Earnings are high, but long work hours are common.
- A master's degree is the standard credential for most positions, although a bachelor's degree is adequate for some entry-level positions in smaller facilities and in health information management.

Nature of the Work

Health care is a business and, like every other business, it needs good management to keep it running smoothly. Medical and health services managers, also referred to as *health care executives* or *health care administrators*, plan, direct, coordinate, and supervise the delivery of health care. Medical and health services managers include specialists and generalists. Specialists are in charge of specific clinical departments or services, while generalists manage or help manage an entire facility or system.

The structure and financing of health care are changing rapidly. Future medical and health services managers must be prepared to deal with evolving integrated health care delivery systems, technological innovations, an increasingly complex regulatory environment, restructuring of work, and an increased focus on preventive care. They will be called on to improve efficiency in health care facilities and the quality of the health care provided. Increasingly, medical and health services managers will work in organizations in which they must optimize efficiency of a variety of related services—for example, those ranging from inpatient care to outpatient follow-up care.

Large facilities usually have several assistant administrators to aid the top administrator and to handle daily decisions. Assistant administrators may direct activities in clinical areas such as nursing, surgery, therapy, medical records, or health information.

In smaller facilities, top administrators handle more of the details of daily operations. For example, many nursing home administrators manage personnel, finances, facility operations, and admissions and also have a larger role in resident care.

Clinical managers have training or experience in a specific clinical area and, accordingly, have more specific responsibilities than do generalists. For example, directors of physical therapy are experienced physical therapists, and most health information and medical record administrators have a bachelor's degree in health information or medical record administration. Clinical managers establish and implement policies, objectives, and procedures for their departments; evaluate personnel and work; develop reports and budgets; and coordinate activities with other managers.

Health information managers are responsible for the maintenance and security of all patient records. Recent regulations enacted by the federal government require that all health care providers maintain electronic patient records and that these records be secure. As a result, health information managers must keep up with current computer and software technology and with legislative requirements and developments. In addition, as patient data become more frequently used for quality management and in medical research, health information managers ensure that databases are complete, accurate, and available only to authorized personnel.

In group medical practices, managers work closely with physicians. Whereas an office manager might handle business affairs in small medical groups, leaving policy decisions to the physicians themselves, larger groups usually employ a full-time administrator to help formulate business strategies and coordinate day-to-day business.

A small group of 10 to 15 physicians might employ 1 administrator to oversee personnel matters, billing and collection, budgeting, planning, equipment outlays, and patient flow. A large practice of 40 to 50 physicians might have a chief administrator and several assistants, each responsible for different areas.

Medical and health services managers in managed care settings perform functions similar to those of their counterparts in large group practices, except that they could have larger staffs to manage. In addition, they might do more community outreach and preventive care than do managers of a group practice.

Some medical and health services managers oversee the activities of a number of facilities in health systems. Such systems might contain both inpatient and outpatient facilities and offer a wide range of patient services.

Working Conditions

Most medical and health services managers work long hours. Facilities such as nursing care facilities and hospitals operate around the clock, and administrators and managers may be called at all hours to deal with problems. They also may travel to attend meetings or inspect satellite facilities.

Some managers work in comfortable, private offices; others share space with other managers or staff. They may spend considerable time walking to consult with co-workers.

Training, Other Qualifications, and Advancement

Medical and health services managers must be familiar with management principles and practices. A master's degree in health services administration, long-term care administration, health sciences, public health, public administration, or business administration is the standard credential for most generalist positions in this field. However, a bachelor's degree is adequate for some entry-level positions in smaller facilities, at the departmental level within health care organizations, and in health information management. Physicians' offices and some other facilities may substitute on-the-job experience for formal education.

Bachelor's, master's, and doctoral degree programs in health administration are offered by colleges; universities; and schools of public health, medicine, allied health, public administration, and business administration. In 2005, 70 schools had accredited programs leading to the master's degree in health services administration, according to the Commission on Accreditation of Healthcare Management Education.

For persons seeking to become heads of clinical departments, a degree in the appropriate field and work experience may be sufficient early in their career. However, a master's degree in health services administration or a related field might be required to advance. For example, nursing service administrators usually are chosen from among supervisory registered nurses with administrative abilities and graduate degrees in nursing or health services administration.

Health information managers require a bachelor's degree from an accredited program and a Registered Health Information Administrator (RHIA) certification from the American Health Information Management Association. In 2005, there were 45 accredited bachelor's programs in health information management according to the Commission on Accreditation for Health Informatics and Information Management Education.

Some graduate programs seek students with undergraduate degrees in business or health administration; however, many graduate programs prefer students with a liberal arts or health profession background. Candidates with previous work experience in health care also may have an advantage. Competition for entry into these programs is keen, and applicants need above-average grades to gain admission. Graduate programs usually last between 2 and 3 years. They may include up to 1 year of supervised administrative experience and coursework in areas such as hospital organization and management, marketing, accounting and budgeting, human resources administration, strategic planning, law and ethics, biostatistics or epidemiology, health economics, and health information systems. Some programs allow students to specialize in one type of facility—hospitals, nursing care facilities, mental health facilities, or medical groups. Other programs encourage a generalist approach to health administration education.

New graduates with master's degrees in health services administration may start as department managers or as staff. The level of the starting position varies with the experience of the applicant and the size of the organization. Hospitals and other health facilities offer postgraduate residencies and fellowships, which usually are staff positions. Graduates from master's degree programs also take jobs in large medical group practices, clinics, mental health facilities, nursing care corporations, and consulting firms.

Graduates with bachelor's degrees in health administration usually begin as administrative assistants or assistant department heads in larger hospitals. They also may begin as department heads or assistant administrators in small hospitals or nursing care facilities.

All states and the District of Columbia require nursing care facility administrators to have a bachelor's degree, pass a licensing examination, complete a state-approved training program, and pursue continuing education. Some states also require licenses for administrators in assisted living facilities. A license is not required in other areas of medical and health services management.

Medical and health services managers often are responsible for millions of dollars' worth of facilities and equipment and hundreds of employees. To make effective decisions, they need to be open to different opinions and good at analyzing contradictory information. They must understand finance and information systems and be able to interpret data. Motivating others to implement their decisions requires strong leadership abilities. Tact, diplomacy, flexibility, and communication skills are essential because medical and health services managers spend most of their time interacting with others.

Medical and health services managers advance by moving into more responsible and higher paying positions, such as assistant or associate administrator, department head, or CEO, or by moving to larger facilities. Some experienced managers also may become consultants or professors of health care management.

Employment

Medical and health services managers held about 248,000 jobs in 2004. About 30 percent worked in private hospitals, and another 16 percent worked in offices of physicians or in nursing care facilities. The remainder worked mostly in home health care services, federal government health care facilities, ambulatory facilities run by state and local governments, outpatient care centers, insurance carriers, and community care facilities for the elderly.

Job Outlook

Employment of medical and health services managers is expected to grow faster than average for all occupations through 2014, as the health care industry continues to expand and diversify. Job opportunities will be especially good in offices of health practitioners, general medical and surgical hospitals, home health care services, and outpatient care centers. Applicants with work experience in the health care field and strong business and management skills should have the best opportunities. Competition for jobs at the highest management levels will be keen because of the high pay and prestige.

Managers in all settings will be needed to improve quality and efficiency of health care while controlling costs, as insurance companies and Medicare demand higher levels of accountability. Managers also will be needed to computerize patient records and to ensure their security as required by law. Additional demand for managers will stem from the need to recruit workers and increase employee retention, to comply with changing regulations, to implement new technology, and to help improve the health of their communities by emphasizing preventive care.

Hospitals will continue to employ the most medical and health services managers over the 2004–14 projection period. However, the number of new jobs created is expected to increase at a slower rate in hospitals than in many other industries because of the growing utilization of clinics and other outpatient care sites. Despite relatively slow employment growth, a large number of new jobs will be created because of the industry's large size. Medical and health services managers with experience in large facilities will enjoy the best job opportunities, as hospitals become larger and more complex.

Employment will grow fastest in practitioners' offices and in home health care agencies. Many services previously provided in hospitals will continue to shift to these sectors, especially as medical technologies improve. Demand in medical group practice management will grow as medical group practices become larger and more complex. Managers with specialized experience in a particular field, such as reimbursement, should have good opportunities.

Medical and health services managers also will be employed by health care management companies that provide management services to hospitals and other organizations, as well as to specific departments such as emergency, information management systems, managed care contract negotiations, and physician recruiting.

Earnings

Median annual earnings of medical and health services managers were $67,430 in May 2004. The middle 50 percent earned between $52,530 and $88,210. The lowest 10 percent earned less than $41,450, and the highest 10 percent earned more than $117,990. Median annual earnings in the industries employing the largest numbers of medical and health services managers in May 2004 were as follows:

Federal government	$87,200
General medical and surgical hospitals	71,280
Offices of physicians	61,320
Nursing care facilities	60,940
Home health care services	60,320

Earnings of medical and health services managers vary by type and size of the facility, as well as by level of responsibility. For example, the Medical Group Management Association reported that, in 2004, median salaries for administrators were $72,875 in practices with 6 or fewer physicians, $95,766 in practices with 7 to 25 physicians, and $132,955 in practices with 26 or more physicians.

According to a survey by *Modern Healthcare* magazine, median annual compensation in 2004 for hospital administrators of selected clinical departments was $76,800 in respiratory care, $81,100 in physical therapy, $87,700 in home health care, $88,800 in laboratory services, $90,200 in long-term care, $93,500 in medical imaging/diagnostic radiology, $94,400 in rehabilitation services, $95,200 in cancer treatment facilities, $96,200 in cardiology, $102,800 in nursing services, and $113,200 in pharmacies. Salaries also varied according to size of facility and geographic region.

According to a survey by the Professional Association of Health Care Office Management, total 2004 median compensation for office managers in specialty physicians' practices was $72,047 in gastroenterology, $66,946 in dermatology, $66,207 in cardiology, $64,543 in ophthalmology, $63,801 in obstetrics and gynecology, $62,545 in orthopedics, $58,595 in pediatrics, $52,211 in internal medicine, $50,924 in psychiatry, and $50,049 in family practice.

Related Occupations

Medical and health services managers have training or experience in both health and management. Other occupations requiring knowledge of both fields are insurance underwriters and social and community service managers.

Sources of Additional Information

Information about undergraduate and graduate academic programs in this field is available from:

- Association of University Programs in Health Administration, 2000 North 14th St., Suite 780, Arlington, VA 22201. Internet: http://www.aupha.org

For a list of accredited graduate programs in medical and health services administration, contact:

- Commission on Accreditation of Healthcare Management Education, 2000 North 14th St., Suite 780, Arlington, VA 22201. Internet: http://www.cahmeweb.org

For information about career opportunities in health care management, contact:

- American College of Healthcare Executives, One N. Franklin St., Suite 1700, Chicago, IL 60606-4425. Internet: http://www.healthmanagementcareers.org

For information about career opportunities in long-term care administration, contact:

- American College of Health Care Administrators, 300 N. Lee St., Suite 301, Alexandria, VA 22314. Internet: http://www.achca.org

For information about career opportunities in medical group practices and ambulatory care management, contact:

- Medical Group Management Association, 104 Inverness Terrace East, Englewood, CO 80112-5306. Internet: http://www.mgma.org

For information about medical and health care office managers, contact:

- Professional Association of Health Care Office Management, 461 East Ten Mile Rd., Pensacola, FL 32534-9712.

For information about career opportunities in health information management, contact:

- American Health Information Management Association, 233 N. Michigan Ave., Suite 2150, Chicago, IL 60601-5800. Internet: http://www.ahima.org

Medical Assistants

(O*NET 31-9092.00)

Significant Points

- About 6 out of 10 medical assistants work in offices of physicians.

- Some medical assistants are trained on the job, but many complete 1- or 2-year programs in vocational-technical high schools, postsecondary vocational schools, and community and junior colleges.
- Medical assistants is projected to be one of the fastest-growing occupations over the 2004–14 period.
- Job prospects should be best for medical assistants with formal training or experience, particularly those with certification.

Nature of the Work

Medical assistants perform administrative and clinical tasks to keep the offices of physicians, podiatrists, chiropractors, and other health practitioners running smoothly. They should not be confused with physician assistants, who examine, diagnose, and treat patients under the direct supervision of a physician.

The duties of medical assistants vary from office to office, depending on the location and size of the practice and the practitioner's specialty. In small practices, medical assistants usually are generalists, handling both administrative and clinical duties and reporting directly to an office manager, physician, or other health practitioner. Those in large practices tend to specialize in a particular area under the supervision of department administrators.

Medical assistants perform many administrative duties, including answering telephones, greeting patients, updating and filing patients' medical records, filling out insurance forms, handling correspondence, scheduling appointments, arranging for hospital admission and laboratory services, and handling billing and bookkeeping.

Clinical duties vary according to state law and include taking medical histories and recording vital signs, explaining treatment procedures to patients, preparing patients for examination, and assisting the physician during the examination. Medical assistants collect and prepare laboratory specimens or perform basic laboratory tests on the premises, dispose of contaminated supplies, and sterilize medical instruments. They instruct patients about medications and special diets, prepare and administer medications as directed by a physician, authorize drug refills as directed, telephone prescriptions to a pharmacy, draw blood, prepare patients for X rays, take electrocardiograms, remove sutures, and change dressings.

Medical assistants also may arrange examining room instruments and equipment, purchase and maintain supplies and equipment, and keep waiting and examining rooms neat and clean.

Ophthalmic medical assistants and *podiatric medical assistants* are examples of specialized assistants who have additional duties. Ophthalmic medical assistants help ophthalmologists provide eye care. They conduct diagnostic tests, measure and record vision, and test eye muscle function. They also show patients how to insert, remove, and care for contact lenses, and they apply eye dressings. Under the direction of the physician, ophthalmic medical assistants may administer eye medications. They also maintain optical and surgical instruments and may assist the ophthalmologist in surgery. Podiatric medical assistants make castings of feet, expose and develop X rays, and assist podiatrists in surgery.

Working Conditions

Medical assistants work in well-lighted, clean environments. They constantly interact with other people and may have to handle several responsibilities at once.

Most full-time medical assistants work a regular 40-hour week. Many work part time, evenings, or weekends.

Training, Other Qualifications, and Advancement

Most employers prefer graduates of formal programs in medical assisting. Such programs are offered in vocational-technical high schools, postsecondary vocational schools, and community and junior colleges. Postsecondary programs usually last either 1 year, resulting in a certificate or diploma, or 2 years, resulting in an associate degree. Courses cover anatomy, physiology, and medical terminology, as well as typing, transcription, recordkeeping, accounting, and insurance processing. Students learn laboratory techniques, clinical and diagnostic procedures, pharmaceutical principles, the administration of medications, and first aid. They study office practices, patient relations, medical law, and ethics. Accredited programs include an internship that provides practical experience in physicians' offices, hospitals, or other health care facilities.

Both the Commission on Accreditation of Allied Health Education Programs (CAAHEP) and the Accrediting Bureau of Health Education Schools (ABHES) accredit programs in medical assisting. In 2005, there were over 500 medical assisting programs accredited by CAAHEP and about 170 accredited by ABHES. The Committee on Accreditation for Ophthalmic Medical Personnel approved 17 programs in ophthalmic medical assisting and 2 programs in ophthalmic clinical assisting.

Formal training in medical assisting, while generally preferred, is not always required. Some medical assistants are trained on the job, although this practice is less common than in the past. Applicants usually need a high school diploma or the equivalent. Recommended high school courses include mathematics, health, biology, typing, bookkeeping, computers, and office skills. Volunteer experience in the health care field also is helpful.

Although medical assistants are not licensed, some states require them to take a test or a course before they can perform certain tasks, such as taking X rays or giving injections.

Employers prefer to hire experienced workers or certified applicants who have passed a national examination indicating that the medical assistant meets certain standards of competence. The American Association of Medical Assistants awards the Certified Medical Assistant credential; American Medical Technologists awards the Registered Medical Assistant credential; the American Society of Podiatric Medical Assistants awards the Podiatric Medical Assistant, Certified credential; and the Joint Commission on Allied Health Personnel in Ophthalmology awards credentials at three levels: Certified Ophthalmic Assistant; Certified Ophthalmic Technician; and Certified Ophthalmic Medical Technologist.

Medical assistants deal with the public; therefore, they must be neat and well groomed and have a courteous, pleasant manner. Medical assistants must be able to put patients at ease and explain physicians' instructions. They must respect the confidential nature of medical information. Clinical duties require a reasonable level of manual dexterity and visual acuity.

Medical assistants may be able to advance to office manager. They may qualify for a variety of administrative support occupations or may teach medical assisting. With additional education, some enter other health occupations, such as nursing and medical technology.

Employment

Medical assistants held about 387,000 jobs in 2004. About 6 out of 10 worked in offices of physicians; about 14 percent worked in public and private hospitals, including inpatient and outpatient facilities; and 11 percent worked in offices of other health practitioners, such as chiropractors, optometrists, and podiatrists. The rest worked mostly in outpatient care centers, public and private educational services, other ambulatory health care services, state and local government agencies, employment services, medical and diagnostic laboratories, and nursing care facilities.

Job Outlook

Employment of medical assistants is expected to grow much faster than average for all occupations through the year 2014 as the health care industry expands because of technological advances in medicine and the growth and aging of the population. Increasing utilization of medical assistants in the rapidly growing health care industry will further stimulate job growth. In fact, medical assistants is projected to be one of the fastest-growing occupations over the 2004–14 period.

Employment growth will be driven by the increase in the number of group practices, clinics, and other health care facilities that need a high proportion of support personnel, particularly the flexible medical assistant who can handle both administrative and clinical duties. Medical assistants work primarily in outpatient settings, a rapidly growing sector of the health care industry.

In view of the preference of many health care employers for trained personnel, job prospects should be best for medical assistants with formal training or experience, particularly for those with certification.

Earnings

The earnings of medical assistants vary, depending on their experience, skill level, and location. Median annual earnings of medical assistants were $24,610 in May 2004. The middle 50 percent earned between $20,650 and $28,930. The lowest 10 percent earned less than $18,010, and the highest 10 percent earned more than $34,650. Median annual earnings in the industries employing the largest numbers of medical assistants in May 2004 were:

Colleges, universities, and professional schools	$27,490
Outpatient care centers	25,360
General medical and surgical hospitals	25,160
Offices of physicians	24,930
Offices of other health practitioners	21,930

Related Occupations

Workers in other medical support occupations include dental assistants, medical records and health information technicians, medical secretaries, occupational therapist assistants and aides, pharmacy aides, and physical therapist assistants and aides.

Sources of Additional Information

Information about career opportunities and the Certified Medical Assistant exam is available from:

- American Association of Medical Assistants, 20 North Wacker Dr., Suite 1575, Chicago, IL 60606. Internet: http://www.aama-ntl.org

Information about career opportunities and the Registered Medical Assistant certification exam is available from:

- American Medical Technologists, 710 Higgins Rd., Park Ridge, IL 60068-5765.

Information about career opportunities, training programs, and certification for ophthalmic medical personnel is available from:

- Joint Commission on Allied Health Personnel in Ophthalmology, 2025 Woodlane Dr., St. Paul, MN 55125-2998. Internet: http://www.jcahpo.org/newsite/index.htm

Information about certification for podiatric assistants is available from:

- American Society of Podiatric Medical Assistants, 2124 South Austin Blvd., Cicero, IL 60804. Internet: http://www.aspma.org

For a list of educational programs in medical assisting accredited by the Commission on Accreditation of Allied Health Education Programs, contact:

- Commission on Accreditation of Allied Health Education Programs, 1361 Park St., Clearwater, FL 33756. Internet: http://www.caahep.org

A list of ABHES-accredited educational programs in medical assisting is available from:

- Accrediting Bureau of Health Education Schools, 7777 Leesburg Pike, Suite 314 N, Falls Church, VA 22043. Internet: http://www.abhes.org

Medical Records and Health Information Technicians

(O*NET 29-2071.00)

Significant Points

- Employment is expected to grow much faster than average.
- Job prospects should be very good; technicians with a strong background in medical coding will be in particularly high demand.
- Entrants usually have an associate degree; courses include anatomy, physiology, medical terminology, statistics, and computer science.
- This is one of the few health occupations in which there is little or no direct contact with patients.

Nature of the Work

Every time a patient receives health care, a record is maintained of the observations, medical or surgical interventions, and treatment outcomes. This record includes information that the patient provides concerning his or her symptoms and medical history, the results of examinations, reports of X rays and laboratory tests, diagnoses, and treatment plans. Medical records and health information technicians organize and evaluate these records for completeness and accuracy.

Technicians assemble patients' health information. They make sure that patients' initial medical charts are complete, that all forms are completed and properly identified and signed, and that all necessary information is in the computer. They regularly communicate with physicians and other health care professionals to clarify diagnoses or to obtain additional information.

Some medical records and health information technicians specialize in coding patients' medical information for insurance purposes. Technicians who specialize in coding are called *health information coders*, *medical record coders*, *coder/abstractors*, or *coding specialists*. These technicians assign a code to each diagnosis and procedure. They consult classification manuals and also rely on their knowledge of disease processes. Technicians then use computer software to assign the patient to one of several hundred "diagnosis-related groups," or DRGs. The DRG determines the amount for which the hospital will be reimbursed if the patient is covered by Medicare or other insurance programs using the DRG system. In addition to the DRG system, coders use other coding systems, such as those geared toward ambulatory settings or long-term care.

Some technicians also use computer programs to tabulate and analyze data to improve patient care, control costs, provide documentation for use in legal actions, respond to surveys, or use in research studies. For example, *cancer* (or tumor) *registrars* maintain facility, regional, and national databases of cancer patients. Registrars review patient records and pathology reports, assign codes for the diagnosis and treatment of different cancers and selected benign tumors. Registrars conduct annual follow-ups on all patients in the registry to track their treatment, survival, and recovery. Physicians and public health organizations then use this information to calculate survivor rates and success rates of various types of treatment, locate geographic areas with high incidences of certain cancers, and identify potential participants for clinical drug trials. Cancer registry data also is used by public health officials to target areas for the allocation of resources to provide intervention and screening.

Medical records and health information technicians' duties vary with the size of the facility where they work. In large to medium-sized facilities, technicians might specialize in one aspect of health information or might supervise health information clerks and transcriptionists while a medical records and health information administrator manages the department. In small facilities, a credentialed medical records and health information technician sometimes manages the department.

Working Conditions

Medical records and health information technicians usually work a 40-hour week. Some overtime may be required. In hospitals—where health information departments often are open 24 hours a day, 7 days a week—technicians may work day, evening, and night shifts.

Medical records and health information technicians work in pleasant and comfortable offices. This is one of the few health occupations in which there is little or no direct contact with patients. Because accuracy is essential in their jobs, technicians must pay close attention to detail. Technicians who work at computer monitors for prolonged periods must guard against eyestrain and muscle pain.

Training, Other Qualifications, and Advancement

Medical records and health information technicians entering the field usually have an associate degree from a community or junior college. In addition to general education, coursework includes medical terminology, anatomy and physiology, legal aspects of health information, coding and abstraction of data, statistics, database management, quality improvement methods, and computer science. Applicants can improve their chances of admission into a program by taking biology, chemistry, health, and computer science courses in high school.

Hospitals sometimes advance promising health information clerks to jobs as medical records and health information technicians, although this practice may be less common in the future. Advancement usually requires 2 to 4 years of job experience and completion of a hospital's in-house training program.

Most employers prefer to hire Registered Health Information Technicians (RHIT), who must pass a written examination offered by the American Health Information Management Association (AHIMA). To take the examination, a person must graduate from a 2-year associate degree program accredited by the Commission on Accreditation for Health Informatics and Information Management Education (CAHIIM). Technicians trained in non-CAHIIM-accredited programs or trained on the job are not eligible to take the examination. In 2005, CAHIIM accredited 184 programs for health information technicians.

Experienced medical records and health information technicians usually advance in one of two ways—by specializing or managing. Many senior technicians specialize in coding, particularly Medicare coding, or in cancer registry. Most coding and registry skills are learned on the job. Some schools offer certificates in coding as part of the associate degree program for health information technicians, although there are no formal degree programs in coding. For cancer registry, there were 11 formal 2-year certificate programs in 2005 approved by the National Cancer Registrars Association (NCRA). Some schools and employers offer intensive 1- to 2-week training programs in either coding or cancer registry. Once coders and registrars gain some on-the-job experience, many choose to become certified. Certifications in coding are available either from AHIMA or from the American Academy of Professional Coders. Certification in cancer registry is available from the NCRA.

In large medical records and health information departments, experienced technicians may advance to section supervisor, overseeing the work of the coding, correspondence, or discharge sections, for example. Senior technicians with RHIT credentials may become director or assistant director of a medical records and health information department in a small facility. However, in larger institutions, the director usually is an administrator with a bachelor's degree in medical records and health information administration.

Employment

Medical records and health information technicians held about 159,000 jobs in 2004. About 2 out of 5 jobs were in hospitals. The rest were mostly in offices of physicians, nursing care facilities, outpatient care centers, and home health care services. Insurance firms that deal in health matters employ a small number of health information technicians to tabulate and analyze health information. Public health departments also hire technicians to supervise data collection from health care institutions and to assist in research.

Job Outlook

Job prospects should be very good. Employment of medical records and health information technicians is expected to grow much faster than average for all occupations through 2014 because of rapid growth in the number of medical tests, treatments, and procedures that will be increasingly scrutinized by health insurance companies, regulators, courts, and consumers. Also, technicians will be needed to enter patient information into computer databases to comply with federal legislation mandating the use of electronic patient records.

Although employment growth in hospitals will not keep pace with growth in other health care industries, many new jobs will, nevertheless, be created. The majority of new jobs is expected in offices of physicians as a result of increasing demand for detailed records, especially in large group practices. Rapid growth also is expected in home health care services, outpatient care centers, and nursing and residential care facilities. Additional job openings will result from the need to replace technicians who retire or leave the occupation permanently.

Technicians with a strong background in medical coding will be in particularly high demand. Changing government regulations and the growth of managed care have increased the amount of paperwork involved in filing insurance claims. Additionally, health care facilities are having difficulty attracting qualified workers, primarily because of the lack of both formal training programs and sufficient resources to provide on-the-job training for coders. Job opportunities may be especially good for coders employed through temporary help agencies or by professional services firms.

Some cancer registrars may have difficulty finding open positions in their geographic area because of a limited number of registrars employed by health care facilities and low job turnover. However, when a position does become vacant, qualified cancer registrars have excellent prospects because of the limited number of trained registrars available for employment.

Earnings

Median annual earnings of medical records and health information technicians were $25,590 in 2004. The middle 50 percent earned between $20,650 and $32,990. The lowest 10 percent earned less than $17,720, and the highest 10 percent earned more than $41,760. Median annual earnings in the industries employing the largest numbers of medical records and health information technicians in 2004 were as follows:

General medical and surgical hospitals	$26,640
Nursing care facilities	26,330
Outpatient care centers	23,870
Offices of physicians	22,130

Related Occupations

Medical records and health information technicians need a strong clinical background to analyze the contents of medical records. Other workers who need knowledge of medical terminology, anatomy, and physiology but have little or no direct contact with patients include medical secretaries and medical transcriptionists.

Sources of Additional Information

Information on careers in medical records and health information technology, including a list of programs accredited by CAHIIM, is available from:

- American Health Information Management Association, 233 N. Michigan Ave., Suite 2150, Chicago, IL 60601-5800. Internet: http://www.ahima.org

Information on training and certification for medical coders is available from:

- American Academy of Professional Coders, P.O. Box 45855, Salt Lake City, UT 84145-0855.

Information on a career as a cancer registrar is available from:

- National Cancer Registrars Association, 1340 Braddock Pl. #203, Alexandria, VA 22314. Internet: http://www.ncra-usa.org

Medical Scientists

(O*NET 19-1041.00 and 19-1042.00)

Significant Points

- Most medical scientists work in research and development.
- Most medical scientists need a Ph.D. degree in a biological science; however, epidemiologists typically require a master's degree in public health or, in some cases, a Ph.D. or medical degree.
- Despite projected rapid job growth, competition is expected for most positions.

Nature of the Work

Medical scientists research human diseases in order to improve human health. Most medical scientists conduct biomedical research and development to advance knowledge of life processes and living organisms, including viruses, bacteria, and other infectious agents. Past research has resulted in advances in diagnosis, treatment, and prevention of many diseases. Basic medical research continues to provide the building blocks necessary to develop solutions to human health problems, such as vaccines and medicines. Medical scientists also engage in clinical investigation, technical writing, drug application review, patent examination, and related activities.

Medical scientists study biological systems to understand the causes of disease and other health problems and to develop treatments and research tools and techniques, many of which have medical applications. These scientists try to identify changes in a cell or in chromosomes that signal the development of medical problems, such as different types of cancer. For example, medical scientists involved in cancer research may formulate a combination of drugs that will lessen the effects of the disease. Medical scientists who are also physicians can administer these drugs to patients in clinical trials, monitor their reactions, and observe the results. Those who are not physicians normally collaborate with a physician who deals directly with patients. Medical scientists examine the results of clinical trials and, if necessary, adjust the dosage levels to reduce negative side effects or to try to induce even better results. In addition to developing treatments for health problems, medical scientists attempt to discover ways to prevent health problems, for example, by affirming the link between smoking and lung cancer or between alcoholism and liver disease.

Many medical scientists work independently in private industry, university, or government laboratories, often exploring new areas of research or expanding on specialized research that they began in graduate school. Medical scientists working in colleges and universities, hospitals, and nonprofit medical research organizations typically submit grant proposals to obtain funding for their projects. Colleges and universities, private industry, and federal government agencies, such as the National Institutes of Health and the National Science Foundation, contribute greatly to the support of scientists whose research proposals are determined to be financially feasible and to have the potential to advance new ideas or processes.

Medical scientists who work in applied research or product development use knowledge discovered through basic research to develop new drugs and medical treatments. They usually have less autonomy than basic medical researchers to choose the emphasis of their research, relying instead on market-driven forces arising from their firm's products and goals. Medical scientists doing applied research and product development in private industry may be required to express their research plans or results to nonscientists who are in a position to reject or approve their ideas; thus, they must understand the impact of their work on business. Scientists increasingly work as part of teams, interacting with engineers, scientists of other disciplines, business managers, and technicians.

Medical scientists who conduct research usually work in laboratories and use electron microscopes, computers, thermal cyclers, or a wide variety of other equipment. Some may work directly with individual patients or larger groups as they administer drugs and monitor and observe the patients during clinical trials. Medical scientists who are also physicians may administer gene therapy to human patients, draw blood, excise tissue, or perform other invasive procedures.

Some medical scientists work in managerial, consulting, or administrative positions, usually after spending some time doing research and learning about the firm, agency, or project. In the 1980s, swift advances in basic medical knowledge related to genetics and molecules spurred growth in the field of biotechnology. Medical scientists using this technology manipulate the genetic material of animals, attempting to make organisms more productive or resistant to disease. Research using biotechnology techniques, such as recombining DNA, has led to the discovery of important drugs, including human insulin and growth hormone. Many other substances not previously available in large quantities are now produced by biotechnological means; some may one day be useful in treating diseases such as Parkinson's or Alzheimer's. Today, many medical scientists are involved in the science of genetic engineering—isolating, identifying, and sequencing human genes and then determining their function. This work continues to lead to the discovery of the genes associated with specific diseases and inherited traits, such as certain types of cancer or obesity. These advances in biotechnology have opened up research opportunities in almost all areas of medical science.

Some medical scientists specialize in epidemiology. This branch of medical science investigates and describes the determinants of disease, disability, and other health outcomes and develops the means for prevention and control. Epidemiologists may study many different diseases, such as tuberculosis, influenza, or cholera, often focusing on epidemics.

Epidemiologists can be separated into two groups—research and clinical. Research epidemiologists conduct research in an effort to eradicate or control infectious diseases that affect the entire body, such as AIDS or typhus. Others may focus only on localized infections of the brain, lungs, or digestive tract, for example. Research epidemiologists work at colleges and universities, schools of public health, medical schools, and research and development services firms. For example, federal government agencies, such as the U.S. Department of Defense, may contract with a research firm's epidemiologists to evaluate the incidence of malaria in certain parts of the world. While some perform consulting services, other research epidemiologists may work as college and university faculty.

Clinical epidemiologists work primarily in consulting roles at hospitals, informing the medical staff of infectious outbreaks and providing containment solutions. These epidemiologists sometimes are referred to as infection control professionals, and some of them are also physicians. Epidemiologists who are not physicians often collaborate with physicians to find ways to contain diseases and outbreaks. In addition to traditional duties of studying and controlling diseases, clinical epidemiologists also may be required to develop standards and guidelines for the treatment and control of communicable diseases. Some clinical epidemiologists may work in outpatient settings.

Working Conditions

Medical scientists typically work regular hours in offices or laboratories and usually are not exposed to unsafe or unhealthy conditions. However, those scientists who work with dangerous organisms or toxic substances in the laboratory must follow strict safety procedures to avoid contamination. Medical scientists also spend time working in clinics and hospitals administering drugs and treatments to patients in clinical trials. On occasion, epidemiologists may be required to work evenings and weekends to attend meetings and hearings for medical investigations.

Some medical scientists depend on grant money to support their research. They may be under pressure to meet deadlines and to conform to rigid grant-writing specifications when preparing proposals to seek new or extended funding.

Training, Other Qualifications, and Advancement

A Ph.D. degree in a biological science is the minimum education required for most prospective medical scientists, except epidemiologists, because the work of medical scientists is almost entirely research oriented. A Ph.D. degree qualifies one to do research on basic life processes or on particular medical problems or diseases and to analyze and interpret the results of experiments on patients. Some medical scientists obtain a medical degree instead of a Ph.D., but may not be licensed physicians because they have not taken the state licensing examination or completed a residency program, typically because they prefer research to clinical practice. Medical scientists who administer drug or gene therapy to human patients, or who otherwise interact medically with patients—drawing blood, excising tissue, or performing other invasive procedures—must be licensed physicians. To be licensed, physicians must graduate from an accredited medical school, pass a licensing examination, and complete 1 to 7 years of graduate medical education. It is particularly helpful for medical scientists to earn both Ph.D. and medical degrees.

Students planning careers as medical scientists should have a bachelor's degree in a biological science. In addition to required courses in chemistry and biology, undergraduates should study allied disciplines, such as mathematics, engineering, physics, and computer science, or courses in their field of interest. Once they have completed undergraduate studies, they can then select a specialty area for their advanced degree, such as cytology, bioinformatics, genomics, or pathology. In addition to formal education, medical scientists usually spend several years in a postdoctoral position before they apply for permanent jobs. Postdoctoral work provides valuable laboratory experience, including experience in specific processes and techniques such as gene splicing, which is transferable to other research projects. In some institutions, the postdoctoral position can lead to a permanent job.

Medical scientists should be able to work independently or as part of a team and be able to communicate clearly and concisely, both orally and in writing. Those in private industry, especially those who aspire to consulting and administrative positions, should possess strong communication skills so that they can provide instruction and advice to physicians and other health care professionals.

The minimum educational requirement for epidemiology is a master's degree from a school of public health. Some jobs require a Ph.D. or medical degree, depending on the work performed. Epidemiologists who work in hospitals and health care centers often must have a medical degree with specific training in infectious diseases. Currently, about 140 infectious disease training programs exist in 42 states. Some employees in research epidemiology positions are required to be licensed physicians because they must administer drugs in clinical trials.

Epidemiologists who perform laboratory tests often require the knowledge and expertise of a licensed physician in order to administer drugs to patients in clinical trials. Epidemiologists who are not physicians frequently work closely with one.

Few students select epidemiology for undergraduate study. Undergraduates, nonetheless, should study biological sciences and should have a solid background in chemistry, mathematics, and computer science. Once a student is prepared for graduate studies, he or she can choose a specialty within epidemiology. For example, those interested in studying environmental epidemiology should focus on environmental coursework, such as water pollution, air pollution, or pesticide use. The core work of environmental studies includes toxicology and molecular biology, and students may continue with advanced coursework in environmental or occupational epidemiology. Other specialty areas that students can pursue include infectious process, infection control precautions, surveillance methodology, and outbreak investigation. Some epidemiologists begin their careers in other health care occupations, such as registered nurse and medical technologist.

The Association for Professionals in Infection Control and Epidemiology (APIC) offers continuing-education courses and certification programs in infection prevention and control and applied epidemiology. To become certified as an infection control professional, applicants are required by a certified board to pass an examination for a one-time fee. Certification is recommended for those seeking advancement and for those seeking to continually upgrade their knowledge in a rapidly evolving field.

Employment

Medical scientists held about 77,000 jobs in 2004. Epidemiologists accounted for only 4,800 of that total. In addition, many medical scientists held faculty positions in colleges and universities, but they are classified as college or university faculty.

About 24 percent of medical scientists were employed in government; 24 percent were employed in scientific research and development services firms; 14 percent were employed in pharmaceutical and medicine manufacturing; 9 percent were employed in private hospitals; and most of the remainder were employed in private educational services and ambulatory health care services.

Among epidemiologists, 50 percent were employed in government; 23 percent were employed in management, scientific, and technical consulting services; 12 percent were employed in scientific research and development services; and 8 percent were employed in private hospitals.

Job Outlook

Employment of medical scientists is expected to grow much faster than average for all occupations through 2014. Despite projected rapid job growth, doctoral degree holders can expect to face considerable competition for basic research positions. The federal government funds much basic research and development, including many areas of medical research. Recent budget increases at the National Institutes of Health have led to large increases in federal basic research and development expenditures, with the number of grants awarded to researchers growing in number and dollar amount. However, the increase in expenditures is expected to slow significantly over the 2004–14 projection period, resulting in a highly competitive environment for winning and renewing research grants. In addition, if the number of advanced degrees awarded continues to grow, applicants are likely to face even more competition.

Medical scientists enjoyed rapid gains in employment between the mid-1980s and mid-1990s—reflecting, in part, increased staffing requirements in new biotechnology companies. Job growth should be dampened somewhat as increases in the number of new biotechnology firms slow down and as existing firms merge or are absorbed by larger, more established biotechnology or pharmaceutical firms. However, much of the basic medical research done in recent years has resulted in new knowledge, including the isolation and identification of new genes. Medical scientists will be needed to take this knowledge to the next stage—understanding how certain genes function within an entire organism—so that gene therapies can be developed to treat diseases. Even pharmaceutical and other firms not solely engaged in biotechnology are expected to increasingly use biotechnology techniques, thus creating employment for medical scientists.

Expected expansion in research related to health issues such as AIDS, cancer, and Alzheimer's disease, along with treating growing threats such as the increase in antibiotic resistance, also should result in employment growth. Moreover, environmental conditions such as overcrowding and the increasing frequency of international travel will tend to spread existing diseases and give rise to new ones. Medical scientists will continue to be needed because they greatly contribute to the development of many treatments and medicines that improve human health.

Opportunities in epidemiology also should be highly competitive, as the number of available positions remains limited. However, an increasing focus on monitoring patients at hospitals and health care centers to ensure positive patient outcomes will contribute to job growth. In addition, a heightened awareness of bioterrorism and rare, but infectious, diseases such as West Nile Virus or severe acute respiratory syndrome (SARS) should spur demand for these workers. As hospitals enhance their infection control programs, many will seek to boost the quality and quantity of their staff. Besides job openings due to employment growth, additional openings will result as workers leave the labor force or transfer to other occupations.

Medical scientists and some epidemiologists are less likely to lose their jobs during recessions than are those in many other occupations because they are employed on long-term research projects. However, a recession could influence the amount of money allocated to new research and development, particularly in areas of risky or innovative medical research. A recession also could limit extensions or renewals of existing projects.

Earnings

Median annual earnings of medical scientists, except epidemiologists, were $61,320 in May 2004. The middle 50 percent of these workers earned between $44,120 and $86,830. The lowest 10 percent earned less than $33,030, and the highest 10 percent earned more than $114,360. Median annual earnings in the industries employing the largest numbers of medical scientists in May 2004 were:

Pharmaceutical and medicine manufacturing $76,800
Scientific research and development services..........65,110
General medical and surgical hospitals 55,410
Colleges, universities, and professional schools 45,600

Median annual earnings of epidemiologists were $54,800 in May 2004. The middle 50 percent earned between $45,320 and $67,160. The lowest 10 percent earned less than $36,130, and the highest 10 percent earned more than $82,310.

Related Occupations

Many other occupations deal with living organisms and require a level of training similar to that of medical scientists. These occupations include biological scientists, agricultural and food scientists, and health occupations such as physicians and surgeons, dentists, and veterinarians.

Sources of Additional Information

For a brochure entitled Is a Career in the Pharmaceutical Sciences Right for Me, contact:

- American Association of Pharmaceutical Scientists (AAPS), 2107 Wilson Blvd., Suite 700, Arlington, VA 22201.

For a career brochure entitled *A Million and One,* contact:

- American Society for Microbiology, Career Information—Education Department, 1752 N St. NW, Washington, DC 20036-2804. Internet: http://www.asm.org

For information on infectious diseases training programs, contact:

- Infectious Diseases Society of America, Guide to Training Programs, 66 Canal Center Plaza, Suite 600, Alexandria, VA 22314. Internet: http://www.idsociety.org

Information on obtaining a medical scientist position with the federal government is available from the Office of Personnel Management through USAJOBS, the federal government's official employment information system. This resource for locating and applying for job opportunities can be accessed through the Internet at http://www.usajobs.opm.gov or through an interactive voice response telephone system at (703) 724-1850 or TDD (978) 461-8404. These numbers are not toll free, and charges may result.

Medical Transcriptionists

(O*NET 31-9094.00)

Significant Points

- Job opportunities will be good.
- Employers prefer medical transcriptionists who have completed a postsecondary training program at a vocational school or community college.
- Many medical transcriptionists telecommute from home-based offices as employees or subcontractors for hospitals and transcription services or as self-employed independent contractors.

- About 4 out of 10 work in hospitals and another 3 out of 10 work in offices of physicians.

Nature of the Work

Medical transcriptionists listen to dictated recordings made by physicians and other health care professionals and transcribe them into medical reports, correspondence, and other administrative material. They generally listen to recordings on a headset, using a foot pedal to pause the recording when necessary, and key the text into a personal computer or word processor, editing as necessary for grammar and clarity. The documents they produce include discharge summaries, history and physical examination reports, operative reports, consultation reports, autopsy reports, diagnostic imaging studies, progress notes, and referral letters. Medical transcriptionists return transcribed documents to the physicians or other health care professionals who dictated them for review and signature or correction. These documents eventually become part of patients' permanent files.

To understand and accurately transcribe dictated reports into a format that is clear and comprehensible for the reader, medical transcriptionists must understand medical terminology, anatomy and physiology, diagnostic procedures, pharmacology, and treatment assessments. They also must be able to translate medical jargon and abbreviations into their expanded forms. To help identify terms appropriately, transcriptionists refer to standard medical reference materials—both printed and electronic; some of these are available over the Internet. Medical transcriptionists must comply with specific standards that apply to the style of medical records in addition to the legal and ethical requirements involved with keeping patient information confidential.

Experienced transcriptionists spot mistakes or inconsistencies in a medical report and check to correct the information. Their ability to understand and correctly transcribe patient assessments and treatments reduces the chance of patients receiving ineffective or even harmful treatments and ensures high-quality patient care.

Currently, most health care providers transmit dictation to medical transcriptionists using either digital or analog dictating equipment. The Internet has grown to be a popular mode for transmitting documentation. Many transcriptionists receive dictation over the Internet and are able to quickly return transcribed documents to clients for approval. Another increasingly popular method utilizes speech recognition technology, which electronically translates sound into text and creates drafts of reports. Reports are then formatted; edited for mistakes in translation, punctuation, or grammar; and checked for consistency and any possible medical errors. Transcriptionists working in areas with standardized terminology, such as radiology or pathology, are more likely to encounter speech recognition technology. However, use of speech recognition technology will become more widespread as the technology becomes more sophisticated.

Medical transcriptionists who work in physicians' offices may have other office duties, such as receiving patients, scheduling appointments, answering the telephone, and handling incoming and outgoing mail. Medical secretaries also may transcribe as part of their jobs. Court reporters have similar duties, but with a different focus. They take verbatim reports of speeches, conversations, legal proceedings, meetings, and other events when written accounts of spoken words are necessary for correspondence, records, or legal proof.

Working Conditions

The majority of these workers are employed in comfortable settings, such as hospitals, physicians' offices, transcription service offices, clinics, laboratories, medical libraries, government medical facilities, or their own homes. Many medical transcriptionists telecommute from home-based offices as employees or subcontractors for hospitals and transcription services or as self-employed independent contractors.

Work in this occupation presents hazards from sitting in the same position for long periods. Workers can suffer wrist, back, neck, or eye problems due to strain and risk repetitive motion injuries such as carpal tunnel syndrome. The constant pressure to be accurate and productive also can be stressful.

Many medical transcriptionists work a standard 40-hour week. Self-employed medical transcriptionists are more likely to work irregular hours—including part time, evenings, weekends, or on call at any time.

Training, Other Qualifications, and Advancement

Employers prefer to hire transcriptionists who have completed post-secondary training in medical transcription, which is offered by many vocational schools, community colleges, and distance-learning programs. Completion of a 2-year associate degree or 1-year certificate program—including coursework in anatomy, medical terminology, legal issues relating to health care documentation, and English grammar and punctuation—is highly recommended, but not always required. Many of these programs include supervised on-the-job experience. Some transcriptionists, especially those already familiar with medical terminology from previous experience as a nurse or medical secretary, become proficient through refresher courses and training.

The American Association for Medical Transcription (AAMT) awards the voluntary designation Certified Medical Transcriptionist (CMT) to those who earn a passing score on a certification examination. As in many other fields, certification is recognized as a sign of competence. Because medicine is constantly evolving, medical transcriptionists are encouraged to update their skills regularly. Every 3 years, CMTs must earn continuing education credits to be recertified.

In addition to understanding medical terminology, transcriptionists must have good English grammar and punctuation skills, as well as proficiency with personal computers and word processing software. Normal hearing acuity and good listening skills also are necessary. Employers require applicants to take pre-employment tests and usually prefer individuals with experience.

With experience, medical transcriptionists can advance to supervisory positions, home-based work, editing, consulting, or teaching. With additional education or training, some become medical records and health information technicians, medical coders, or medical records and health information administrators.

Employment

Medical transcriptionists held about 105,000 jobs in 2004. About 4 out of 10 worked in hospitals and another 3 out of 10 worked in offices of physicians. Others worked for business support services; medical and diagnostic laboratories; outpatient care centers; and offices of physical, occupational and speech therapists and audiologists.

Job Outlook

Job opportunities will be good. Employment of medical transcriptionists is projected to grow faster than the average for all occupations through 2014. Demand for medical transcription services will be spurred by a growing and aging population. Older age groups receive proportionately greater numbers of medical tests, treatments, and procedures that require documentation. A high level of demand for transcription services also will be sustained by the continued need for electronic documentation that can easily be shared among providers, third-party payers, regulators, consumers, and health information systems. Growing numbers of medical transcriptionists will be needed to amend patients' records, edit documents from speech recognition systems, and identify discrepancies in medical reports.

Contracting out transcription work overseas and advancements in speech recognition technology are not expected to significantly reduce the need for well-trained medical transcriptionists. Outsourcing transcription work abroad—to countries such as India, Pakistan, Philippines, and the Caribbean—has grown more popular as transmitting confidential health information over the Internet has become more secure; however, the demand for overseas transcription services is expected only to supplement the demand for well-trained domestic medical transcriptionists. In addition, reports transcribed by overseas medical transcription services usually require editing for accuracy by domestic medical transcriptionists before they meet domestic quality standards. Speech-recognition technology allows physicians and other health professionals to dictate medical reports to a computer that immediately creates an electronic document. In spite of the advances in this technology, the software has been slow to grasp and analyze the human voice, the English language, and the medical vernacular with all its diversity. As a result, there will continue to be a need for skilled medical transcriptionists to identify and appropriately edit the inevitable errors created by speech recognition systems and to create a final document.

Hospitals will continue to employ a large percentage of medical transcriptionists, but job growth there will not be as fast as in other industries. An increasing demand for standardized records should result in rapid employment growth in physicians' offices, especially in large group practices.

Earnings

Medical transcriptionists had median hourly earnings of $13.64 in May 2004. The middle 50 percent earned between $11.50 and $16.32. The lowest 10 percent earned less than $9.67, and the highest 10 percent earned more than $19.11. Median hourly earnings in the industries employing the largest numbers of medical transcriptionists in May 2004 were:

General medical and surgical hospitals	$13.83
Offices of physicians	13.40
Business support services	13.40

Compensation methods for medical transcriptionists vary. Some are paid based on the number of hours they work or on the number of lines they transcribe. Others receive a base pay per hour with incentives for extra production. Employees of transcription services and independent contractors almost always receive production-based pay. Independent contractors earn more than do transcriptionists who work for others, but independent contractors have higher expenses than their corporate counterparts, receive no benefits, and may face higher risk of termination than do employed transcriptionists.

Related Occupations

A number of other workers type, record information, and process paperwork. Among these are court reporters; human resources assistants, except payroll and timekeeping; receptionists and information clerks; and secretaries and administrative assistants. Other workers who provide medical support include medical assistants and medical records and health information technicians.

Sources of Additional Information

For information on a career as a medical transcriptionist, send a self-addressed, stamped envelope to:

- American Association for Medical Transcription, 100 Sycamore Ave., Modesto, CA 95354-0550. Internet: http://www.aamt.org

State employment service offices can provide information about job openings for medical transcriptionists.

Nursing, Psychiatric, and Home Health Aides

(O*NET 31-1011.00, 31-1012.00, and 31-1013.00)

Significant Points

- Home health aides is projected to be the fastest growing occupation through 2014.
- Numerous job openings and excellent job opportunities are expected.
- Most jobs are in nursing and residential care facilities, hospitals, and home health care services.
- Modest entry requirements, low pay, high physical and emotional demands, and lack of advancement opportunities characterize this occupation.

Nature of the Work

Nursing and psychiatric aides help care for physically or mentally ill, injured, disabled, or infirm individuals confined to hospitals, nursing care facilities, and mental health settings. Home health aides have duties that are similar, but they work in patients' homes or residential care facilities.

Nursing aides—also known as nursing assistants, certified nursing assistants, geriatric aides, unlicensed assistive personnel, orderlies, or hospital attendants—perform routine tasks under the supervision of nursing and medical staff. They answer patients' call lights; deliver messages; serve meals; make beds; and help patients to eat, dress, and bathe. Aides also may provide skin care to patients; take their temperature, pulse rate, respiration rate, and blood pressure; and help them to get into and out of bed and walk. They also may escort patients to operating and examining rooms, keep patients' rooms neat, set up equipment, store and move supplies, and assist with some procedures. Aides observe patients' physical, mental, and emotional conditions and report any change to the nursing or medical staff.

Nursing aides employed in nursing care facilities often are the principal caregivers, having far more contact with residents than do other members of the staff. Because some residents may stay in a nursing care facility for months or even years, aides develop ongoing relationships with them and interact with them in a positive, caring way.

Home health aides help elderly, convalescent, or disabled persons live in their own homes instead of in a health care facility. Under the direction of nursing or medical staff, they provide health-related services, such as administering oral medications. Like nursing aides, home health aides may check patients' pulse rate, temperature, and respiration rate; help with simple prescribed exercises; keep patients' rooms neat; and help patients to move from bed, bathe, dress, and groom. Occasionally, they change nonsterile dressings, give massages and alcohol rubs, or assist with braces and artificial limbs. Experienced home health aides also may assist with medical equipment such as ventilators, which help patients breathe.

Most home health aides work with elderly or disabled persons who need more extensive care than family or friends can provide. Some help discharged hospital patients who have relatively short-term needs.

In home health agencies, a registered nurse, physical therapist, or social worker usually assigns specific duties to and supervises home health aides, who keep records of the services they perform and record each patient's condition and progress. The aides report changes in a patient's condition to the supervisor or case manager.

Psychiatric aides, also known as mental health assistants or psychiatric nursing assistants, care for mentally impaired or emotionally disturbed individuals. They work under a team that may include psychiatrists, psychologists, psychiatric nurses, social workers, and therapists. In addition to helping patients to dress, bathe, groom themselves, and eat, psychiatric aides socialize with them and lead them in educational and recreational activities. Psychiatric aides may play games such as cards with the patients; watch television with them; or participate in group activities, such as sports or field trips. They observe patients and report any physical or behavioral signs that might be important for the professional staff to know. They accompany patients to and from examinations and treatment. Because they have such close contact with patients, psychiatric aides can have a great deal of influence on their patients' outlook and treatment.

Working Conditions

Most full-time aides work about 40 hours a week, but, because patients need care 24 hours a day, some aides work evenings, nights, weekends, and holidays. Many work part time. In 2004, 25 percent of aides worked part time compared with 16 percent of all workers. Aides spend many hours standing and walking, and they often face heavy workloads. Aides must guard against back injury because they may have to move patients into and out of bed or help them to stand or walk. Aides also may face hazards from minor infections and major diseases, such as hepatitis, but can avoid infections by following proper procedures.

Aides often have unpleasant duties, such as emptying bedpans and changing soiled bed linens. The patients they care for may be disoriented, irritable, or uncooperative. Psychiatric aides must be prepared to care for patients whose illness may cause violent behavior. While their work can be emotionally demanding, many aides gain satisfaction from assisting those in need.

Home health aides may go to the same patient's home for months or even years. However, most aides work with a number of different patients, each job lasting a few hours, days, or weeks. Home health aides often visit multiple patients on the same day.

Home health aides generally work alone, with periodic visits from their supervisor. They receive detailed instructions explaining when to visit patients and what services to perform. Aides are individually responsible for getting to patients' homes, and they may spend a good portion of the working day traveling from one patient to another. Because mechanical lifting devices available in institutional settings are seldom available in patients' homes, home health aides are particularly susceptible to injuries resulting from overexertion when they assist patients.

Training, Other Qualifications, and Advancement

In many cases, a high school diploma or equivalent is necessary for a job as a nursing or psychiatric aide. However, a high school diploma generally is not required for jobs as home health aides. Hospitals may require previous experience as a nursing aide or home health aide. Nursing care facilities often hire inexperienced workers, who must complete a minimum of 75 hours of mandatory training and pass a competency evaluation as part of a state-approved training program within 4 months of their employment. Aides who complete the program are known as certified nurse assistants (CNAs) and are placed on the state registry of nursing aides. Some states also require psychiatric aides to complete a formal training program. However, most psychiatric aides learn their skills on the job from experienced workers.

Nursing and psychiatric aide training is offered in high schools, vocational-technical centers, some nursing care facilities, and some community colleges. Courses cover body mechanics, nutrition, anatomy and physiology, infection control, communication skills, and resident rights. Personal care skills, such as how to help patients to bathe, eat, and groom themselves, also are taught.

Some employers provide classroom instruction for newly hired aides, while others rely exclusively on informal on-the-job instruction by a licensed nurse or an experienced aide. Such training may last from several days to a few months. Aides also may attend lectures, workshops, and in-service training.

The federal government has guidelines for home health aides whose employers receive reimbursement from Medicare. Federal law requires home health aides to pass a competency test covering a wide range of areas: communication; documentation of patient status and care provided; reading and recording of vital signs; basic infection-control procedures; basic bodily functions; maintenance of a healthy environment; emergency procedures; physical, emotional, and developmental characteristics of patients; personal hygiene and grooming; safe transfer techniques; normal range of motion and positioning; and basic nutrition.

A home health aide may receive training before taking the competency test. Federal law suggests at least 75 hours of classroom and practical training supervised by a registered nurse. Training and testing programs may be offered by the employing agency but must meet the standards of the Center for Medicare and Medicaid Services. State regulations for training programs vary.

The National Association for Home Care offers national certification for home health aides. The certification is a voluntary demonstration that the individual has met industry standards. Some states also require aides to be licensed.

Aides must be in good health. A physical examination, including state-regulated tests such as those for tuberculosis, may be required. A criminal background check also is usually required for employment.

Applicants should be tactful, patient, understanding, emotionally stable, and dependable and should have a desire to help people. They also should be able to work as part of a team; have good communication skills; and be willing to perform repetitive, routine tasks. Home health aides should be honest and discreet because they work in private homes. They also will need access to their own car or public transportation to reach patients' homes.

For some individuals, these occupations serve as entry-level jobs, as in the case of high school and college students who may work while also attending school. In addition, experience as an aide can help individuals decide whether to pursue a career in health care. Opportunities for advancement within these occupations are limited. Aides generally need additional formal training or education in order to enter other health occupations. The most common health care occupations for former aides are licensed practical nurse, registered nurse, and medical assistant.

Employment

Nursing, psychiatric, and home health aides held about 2.1 million jobs in 2004. Nursing aides held the most jobs—approximately 1.5 million. Home health aides held roughly 624,000 jobs and psychiatric aides held about 59,000 jobs. Around 42 percent of nursing aides worked in nursing care facilities, and another 27 percent worked in hospitals. Most home health aides—about 34 percent—were employed by home health care services. Others were employed in nursing and residential care facilities and social assistance agencies. Around 54 percent of all psychiatric aides worked in hospitals, primarily in psychiatric and substance abuse hospitals, although some also worked in the psychiatric units of general medical and surgical hospitals. Others were employed in state government agencies; residential mental retardation, mental health, and substance abuse facilities; outpatient care centers; and nursing care facilities.

Job Outlook

Numerous job openings for nursing, psychiatric, and home health aides will arise from a combination of fast employment growth and high replacement needs. High replacement needs in this large occupation reflect modest entry requirements, low pay, high physical and emotional demands, and lack of opportunities for advancement. For these same reasons, many people are unwilling to perform the kind of work required by the occupation, limiting the number of entrants. Many aides also leave the occupation to attend training programs for other health care occupations. Therefore, persons who are interested in, and suited for, this work should have excellent job opportunities.

Overall employment of nursing, psychiatric, and home health aides is projected to grow much faster than the average for all occupations through the year 2014, although individual occupational growth rates will vary. Home health aides is expected to be the fastest-growing occupation as a result of both growing demand for home services from an aging population and efforts to contain costs by moving patients out of hospitals and nursing care facilities as quickly as possible. Consumer preference for care in the home and improvements in medical technologies for in-home treatment also will contribute to much-faster-than-average employment growth for home health aides.

Nursing aide employment will not grow as fast as home health aide employment, largely because nursing aides are concentrated in slower-growing nursing care facilities and hospitals. Employment of nursing aides is expected to grow faster than the average for all occupations through 2014 in response to the long-term care needs of an increasing elderly population. Financial pressures on hospitals to discharge patients as soon as possible should boost admissions to nursing care facilities. As a result, job opportunities will be more numerous in nursing and residential care facilities than in hospitals. Modern medical technology also will drive demand for nursing aides because, as the technology saves and extends more lives, it increases the need for long-term care provided by aides.

Employment of psychiatric aides—the smallest of the three occupations—is expected to grow more slowly than the average for all occupations. Most psychiatric aides currently work in hospitals, but most job growth will be in residential mental health facilities and in home health care agencies. There is a long-term trend toward treating mental health patients outside of hospitals because it is more cost effective and allows patients to live more normal lives. Demand for psychiatric aides in residential facilities will rise in response to growth in the number of older persons—many of whom will require mental health services—but also as an increasing number of mentally disabled adults, who were formerly cared for by their elderly parents, seek care. Job growth also could be affected by changes in government funding of programs for the mentally ill.

Earnings

Median hourly earnings of nursing aides, orderlies, and attendants were $10.09 in May 2004. The middle 50 percent earned between $8.59 and $12.09 an hour. The lowest 10 percent earned less than $7.31, and the highest 10 percent earned more than $14.02 an hour. Median hourly earnings in the industries employing the largest numbers of nursing aides, orderlies, and attendants in May 2004 were as follows:

Employment services	$11.29
Local government	11.10
General medical and surgical hospitals	10.44
Nursing care facilities	9.86
Community care facilities for the elderly	9.56

Nursing and psychiatric aides in hospitals generally receive at least 1 week of paid vacation after 1 year of service. Paid holidays and sick leave, hospital and medical benefits, extra pay for late-shift work, and pension plans also are available to many hospital employees and to some nursing care facility employees.

Median hourly earnings of home health aides were $8.81 in May 2004. The middle 50 percent earned between $7.52 and $10.38 an hour. The lowest 10 percent earned less than $6.52, and the highest 10 percent earned more than $12.32 an hour. Median hourly earnings in the industries employing the largest numbers of home health aides in May 2004 were as follows:

Nursing care facilities	$9.11
Residential mental retardation, mental health, and substance abuse facilities	8.97
Home health care services	8.57
Community care facilities for the elderly	8.57
Individual and family services	8.47

Home health aides receive slight pay increases with experience and added responsibility. Usually, they are paid only for the time worked in the home, not for travel time between jobs. Most employers hire only on-call hourly workers and provide no benefits.

Median hourly earnings of psychiatric aides were $11.19 in May 2004. The middle 50 percent earned between $9.09 and $14.09 an hour. The lowest 10 percent earned less than $7.63, and the highest 10 percent earned more than $16.74 an hour. Median hourly earnings in the industries employing the largest numbers of psychiatric aides in May 2004 were as follows:

General medical and surgical hospitals	$11.31
Psychiatric and substance abuse hospitals	11.06
Residential mental retardation, mental health, and substance abuse facilities	9.37

Related Occupations

Nursing, psychiatric, and home health aides help people who need routine care or treatment. So do childcare workers, licensed practical and licensed vocational nurses, medical assistants, occupational therapist assistants and aides, personal and home care aides, physical therapist assistants and aides, and registered nurses.

Sources of Additional Information

Information about employment opportunities may be obtained from local hospitals, nursing care facilities, home health care agencies, psychiatric facilities, state boards of nursing, and local offices of the state employment service.

Information on licensing requirements for nursing and home health aides and lists of state-approved nursing aide programs are available from state departments of public health, departments of occupational licensing, boards of nursing, and home care associations.

Occupational Therapists

(O*NET 29-1122.00)

Significant Points

- Employment is projected to increase much faster than the average, as rapid growth in the number of middle-aged and elderly individuals increases the demand for therapeutic services.
- Beginning in 2007, a master's degree or higher in occupational therapy will be the minimum educational requirement.
- Occupational therapists are increasingly taking on supervisory roles, allowing assistants and aides to work more closely with clients under the guidance of a therapist, in an effort to reduce the cost of therapy.
- More than a quarter of occupational therapists work part time.

Nature of the Work

Occupational therapists (OTs) help people improve their ability to perform tasks in their daily living and working environments. They work with individuals who have conditions that are mentally, physically, developmentally, or emotionally disabling. They also help them to develop, recover, or maintain daily living and work skills. Occupational therapists help clients not only to improve their basic motor functions and reasoning abilities, but also to compensate for permanent loss of function. Their goal is to help clients have independent, productive, and satisfying lives.

Occupational therapists assist clients in performing activities of all types, ranging from using a computer to caring for daily needs such as dressing, cooking, and eating. Physical exercises may be used to increase strength and dexterity, while other activities may be chosen to improve visual acuity and the ability to discern patterns. For example, a client with short-term memory loss might be encouraged to make lists to aid recall, and a person with coordination problems might be assigned exercises to improve hand-eye coordination. Occupational therapists also use computer programs to help clients improve decisionmaking, abstract-reasoning, problem-solving, and perceptual skills, as well as memory, sequencing, and coordination—all of which are important for independent living.

Therapists instruct those with permanent disabilities, such as spinal cord injuries, cerebral palsy, or muscular dystrophy, in the use of adaptive equipment, including wheelchairs, orthotics, and aids for eating and dressing. They also design or make special equipment needed at home or at work. Therapists develop computer-aided adaptive equipment and teach clients with severe limitations how to use that equipment in order to communicate better and control various aspects of their environment.

Some occupational therapists treat individuals whose ability to function in a work environment has been impaired. These practitioners arrange employment, evaluate the work environment, plan work activities, and assess the client's progress. Therapists also may collaborate with the client and the employer to modify the work environment so that the work can be successfully completed.

Occupational therapists may work exclusively with individuals in a particular age group or with particular disabilities. In schools, for example, they evaluate children's abilities, recommend and provide therapy, modify classroom equipment, and help children participate as fully as possible in school programs and activities. A therapist may work with children individually, lead small groups in the classroom, consult with a teacher, or serve on a curriculum or other administrative committee. Early intervention therapy services are provided to infants and toddlers who have, or at the risking of having, developmental delays. Specific therapies may include facilitating the use of the hands, promoting skills for listening and following directions, fostering social play skills, or teaching dressing and grooming skills.

Occupational therapy also is beneficial to the elderly population. Therapists help the elderly lead more productive, active, and independent lives through a variety of methods, including the use of adaptive equipment. Therapists with specialized training in driver rehabilitation assess an individual's ability to drive using both clinical and on-the-road tests. The evaluations allow the therapist to make recommendations for adaptive equipment, training to prolong driving independence, and alternative transportation options. Occupational therapists also work with the client to asses the home for hazards and to identify environmental factors that contribute to falls.

Occupational therapists in mental health settings treat individuals who are mentally ill, mentally retarded, or emotionally disturbed. To treat these problems, therapists choose activities that help people learn to engage in and cope with daily life. Activities include time management skills, budgeting, shopping, homemaking, and the use of public transportation. Occupational therapists also may work with individuals who are dealing with alcoholism, drug abuse, depression, eating disorders, or stress-related disorders.

Assessing and recording a client's activities and progress is an important part of an occupational therapist's job. Accurate records are essential for evaluating clients, for billing, and for reporting to physicians and other health care providers.

Working Conditions

Occupational therapists in hospitals and other health care and community settings usually work a 40-hour week. Those in schools may participate in meetings and other activities during and after the school day. In 2004, more than a quarter of occupational therapists worked part time.

In large rehabilitation centers, therapists may work in spacious rooms equipped with machines, tools, and other devices generating noise. The work can be tiring, because therapists are on their feet much of the time. Those providing home health care services may spend time driving from appointment to appointment. Therapists also face hazards such as back strain from lifting and moving clients and equipment.

Therapists increasingly are taking on supervisory roles. Because of rising health care costs, third-party payers are beginning to encourage occupational therapist assistants and aides to take more hands-on responsibility. By having assistants and aides work more closely with clients under the guidance of a therapist, the cost of therapy should decline.

Training, Other Qualifications, and Advancement

Currently, a bachelor's degree in occupational therapy is the minimum requirement for entry into the field. Beginning in 2007, however, a master's degree or higher will be the minimum educational requirement. As a result, students in bachelor's-level programs must complete their coursework and fieldwork before 2007. All states, Puerto Rico, Guam, and the District of Columbia regulate the practice of occupational therapy. To obtain a license, applicants must graduate from an accredited educational program and pass a national certification examination. Those who pass the exam are awarded the title "Occupational Therapist Registered (OTR)." Some states have additional requirements for therapists who work in schools or early intervention programs. These requirements may include education-related classes, an education practice certificate, or early intervention certification requirements.

In 2005, 122 master's degree programs offered entry-level education, 65 programs offered a combined bachelor's and master's degree, and 5 offered an entry-level doctoral degree. Most schools have full-time programs, although a growing number are offering weekend or part-time programs as well. Bachelor's degree programs in occupational therapy are no longer offered because of the requirement for a master's degree or higher beginning in 2007. In addition, post baccalaureate certificate programs for students with a degree other than occupational therapy are no longer offered.

Occupational therapy coursework includes the physical, biological, and behavioral sciences and the application of occupational therapy theory and skills. The completion of 6 months of supervised fieldwork also is required.

Persons considering this profession should take high school courses in biology, chemistry, physics, health, art, and the social sciences. College admissions offices also look favorably at paid or volunteer experience in the health care field. Relevant undergraduate majors include biology, psychology, sociology, anthropology, liberal arts, and anatomy.

Occupational therapists need patience and strong interpersonal skills to inspire trust and respect in their clients. Patience is necessary because many clients may not show rapid improvement. Ingenuity and imagination in adapting activities to individual needs are assets. Those working in home health care services must be able to adapt to a variety of settings.

Employment

Occupational therapists held about 92,000 jobs in 2004. About 1 in 10 occupational therapists held more than one job. The largest number of jobs were in hospitals. Other major employers were offices of other health practitioners (including offices of occupational therapists), public and private educational services, and nursing care facilities. Some occupational therapists were employed by home health care services, outpatient care centers, offices of physicians, individual and family services, community care facilities for the elderly, and government agencies.

A small number of occupational therapists were self-employed in private practice. These practitioners saw clients referred by physicians or other health professionals or provided contract or consulting services to nursing care facilities, schools, adult day care programs, and home health care agencies.

Job Outlook

Employment of occupational therapists is expected to increase much faster than the average for all occupations through 2014. The impact of proposed federal legislation imposing limits on reimbursement for therapy services may adversely affect the job market for occupational therapists in the short run. However, over the long run, the demand for occupational therapists should continue to rise as a result of growth in the number of individuals with disabilities or limited function who require therapy services. The baby-boom generation's movement into middle age, a period when the incidence of heart attack and stroke increases, will spur demand for therapeutic services. Growth in the population 75 years and older—an age group that suffers from high incidences of disabling conditions—also will increase demand for therapeutic services. Driver rehabilitation and fall-prevention training for the elderly are emerging practice areas for occupational therapy. In addition, medical advances now enable more patients with critical problems to survive—patients who ultimately may need extensive therapy.

Hospitals will continue to employ a large number of occupational therapists to provide therapy services to acutely ill inpatients. Hospitals also will need occupational therapists to staff their outpatient rehabilitation programs.

Employment growth in schools will result from the expansion of the school-age population, the extension of services for disabled students, and an increasing prevalence of sensory disorders in children. Therapists will be needed to help children with disabilities prepare to enter special education programs.

Earnings

Median annual earnings of occupational therapists were $54,660 in May 2004. The middle 50 percent earned between $45,690 and $67,010. The lowest 10 percent earned less than $37,430, and the highest 10 percent earned more than $81,600. Median annual earnings in the industries employing the largest numbers of occupational therapists in May 2004 were:

Home health care services................................$58,720
Offices of other health practitioners.....................56,620
Nursing care facilities 56,570
General medical and surgical hospitals 55,710
Elementary and secondary schools 48,580

Related Occupations

Occupational therapists use specialized knowledge to help individuals perform daily living skills and achieve maximum independence. Other workers performing similar duties include audiologists, chiropractors, physical therapists, recreational therapists, rehabilitation counselors, respiratory therapists, and speech-language pathologists.

Sources of Additional Information

For more information on occupational therapy as a career, contact:

- American Occupational Therapy Association, 4720 Montgomery Lane, Bethesda, MD 20824-1220. Internet: http://www.aota.org

For information regarding the requirements to practice as an occupational therapist in schools, contact the appropriate occupational therapy regulatory agency for your state.

Office and Administrative Support Worker Supervisors and Managers

(O*NET 43-1011.01 and 43-1011.02)

Significant Points

- Most jobs are filled by promoting office or administrative support workers from within the organization.
- Office automation will cause employment in some office and administrative support occupations to grow slowly or even decline, resulting in slower-than-average growth among supervisors and managers.
- Applicants are likely to encounter keen competition because their numbers should greatly exceed the number of job openings.

Nature of the Work

All organizations need timely and effective office and administrative support to operate efficiently. Office and administrative support supervisors and managers coordinate this support. These workers are employed in virtually every sector of the economy, working in positions as varied as teller supervisor, customer services manager, or shipping and receiving supervisor.

Although specific functions of office and administrative support supervisors and managers vary significantly, they share many common duties. For example, supervisors perform administrative tasks to ensure that their staffs can work efficiently. Equipment and machinery used in their departments must be in good working order. If the computer system goes down or a fax machine malfunctions, the supervisors must try to correct the problem or alert repair personnel. They also request new equipment or supplies for their department when necessary.

Planning the work and supervising the staff are key functions of this job. To do these effectively, the supervisor must know the strengths and weaknesses of each member of the staff, as well as the results required from and time allotted to each job. Supervisors must make allowances for unexpected staff absences and other disruptions by adjusting assignments or performing the work themselves if the situation requires it.

After allocating work assignments and issuing deadlines, office and administrative support supervisors and managers oversee the work to ensure that it is proceeding on schedule and meeting established quality standards. This may involve reviewing each person's work on a computer—as in the case of accounting clerks—or listening to how a worker deals with customers—as in the case of customer services representatives. When supervising long-term projects, the supervisor may meet regularly with staff members to discuss their progress.

Office and administrative support supervisors and managers also evaluate each worker's performance. If a worker has done a good job, the supervisor indicates that in the employee's personnel file and may recommend a promotion or other award. Alternatively, if a worker is performing inadequately, the supervisor discusses the problem with the employee to determine the cause and helps the worker to improve his or her performance. This might require sending the employee to a training course or arranging personal counseling. If the situation does not improve, the supervisor may recommend a transfer, demotion, or dismissal.

Office and administrative support supervisors and managers usually interview and evaluate prospective employees. When new workers arrive on the job, supervisors greet them and provide orientation to acquaint them with their organization and its operating routines. Some supervisors may be actively involved in recruiting new workers—for example, by making presentations at high schools and business colleges. They also may serve as the primary liaisons between their offices and the general public through direct contact and by preparing promotional information.

Supervisors help train new employees in organization and office procedures. They may teach new employees how to use the telephone system and operate office equipment. Because most administrative support work is computerized, they also must teach new employees to use the organization's computer system. When new office equipment or updated computer software is introduced, supervisors train experienced employees to use it efficiently or, if this is not possible, arrange for their employees to receive special outside training.

Office and administrative support supervisors and managers often act as liaisons between the administrative support staff and the professional, technical, and managerial staff. This may involve implementing new company policies or restructuring the workflow in their departments. They also must keep their superiors informed of their progress and any potential problems. Often, this communication takes the form of research projects and progress reports. Because supervisors and managers have access to information such as their department's performance records, they may compile and present these data for use in planning or designing new policies.

Office and administrative support supervisors and managers also may have to resolve interpersonal conflicts among the staff. In organizations covered by union contracts, supervisors must know the provisions of labor-management agreements and run their departments accordingly. They also may meet with union representatives to discuss work problems or grievances.

Working Conditions

Office and administrative support supervisors and managers are employed in a wide variety of work settings, but most work in clean and well-lit offices that usually are comfortable.

Most office and administrative support supervisors and managers work a standard 40-hour week. However, because some organizations operate around the clock, supervisors may have to work nights, weekends, and holidays. Sometimes, supervisors rotate among the three 8-hour shifts in a workday; in other cases, shifts are assigned on the basis of seniority.

Training, Other Qualifications, and Advancement

Most firms fill office and administrative support supervisory and managerial positions by promoting office or administrative support workers from within their organizations. To become eligible for promotion to a supervisory position, administrative support workers must prove they are capable of handling additional responsibilities. When evaluating candidates, supervisors look for strong teamwork, problem-solving, leadership, and communication skills, as well as determination, loyalty, poise, and confidence. They also look for more specific supervisory attributes, such as the ability to organize and coordinate work efficiently, to set priorities, and to motivate others. Increasingly, supervisors need a broad base of office skills coupled with personal flexibility to adapt to changes in organizational structure and move among departments when necessary.

In addition, supervisors must pay close attention to detail to identify and correct errors made by the staff they oversee. Good working knowledge of the organization's computer system also is an advantage. Many employers require postsecondary training—in some cases, an associate or even a bachelor's degree.

Administrative support workers with potential supervisory abilities may be given occasional supervisory assignments. To prepare for full-time supervisory duties, workers may attend in-house training or take courses in time management, project management, or interpersonal relations.

Some office and administrative support supervisor positions are filled with people from outside the organization. These positions may serve as entry-level training for potential higher level managers. New college graduates may rotate through departments of an organization at this level to learn the work of the organization.

Employment

Office and administrative support supervisors and managers held 1.5 million jobs in 2004. Although jobs for office and administrative support supervisors and managers are found in practically every industry, the largest number are found in organizations with a large administrative support workforce, such as banks, wholesalers, government agencies, retail establishments, business service firms, health care facilities, schools, and insurance companies. Because of most organizations' need for continuity of supervision, few office and administrative support supervisors and managers work on a temporary or part-time basis.

Job Outlook

Like those seeking other supervisory and managerial occupations, applicants for jobs as office and administrative support worker supervisors and managers are likely to encounter keen competition because the number of applicants should greatly exceed the number of job openings. Employment is expected to grow more slowly than average for all occupations through 2014. Besides the job openings arising from growth, a large number of openings will stem from the need to replace workers who transfer to other occupations or leave this large occupation for other reasons.

Employment of office and administrative support supervisors and managers is determined largely by the demand for administrative support workers. New technology should increase office and administrative support workers' productivity and allow a wider variety of tasks to be performed by people in professional positions. These trends will cause employment in some administrative support occupations to grow slowly or even decline. As a result, supervisors will direct smaller permanent staffs—supplemented by increased use of temporary administrative support staff—and perform more professional tasks. Office and administrative support managers will coordinate the increasing amount of administrative work and make sure that the technology is applied and running properly. However, organizational restructuring should continue to reduce employment in some managerial positions, distributing more responsibility to office and administrative support supervisors.

Earnings

Median annual earnings of office and administrative support supervisors and managers were $41,030 in May 2004; the middle 50 percent earned between $31,860 and $53,110. The lowest paid 10 percent earned less than $25,190, while the highest paid 10 percent earned more than $67,800. In May 2004, median annual earnings in the industries employing the largest numbers of office and administrative support supervisors and managers were:

Insurance carriers	$49,610
Local government	42,100
State government	40,930
Offices of physicians	39,690
Depository credit intermediation	36,980

In addition to typical benefits, some office and administrative support supervisors and managers, particularly in the private sector, may receive additional compensation in the form of bonuses and stock options.

Related Occupations

Office and administrative support supervisors and managers must understand and sometimes perform the work of those whom they oversee, including bookkeeping, accounting, and auditing clerks; cashiers; communications equipment operators; customer service representatives; data entry and information processing workers; general office clerks; receptionists and information clerks; stock clerks and order fillers; order clerks; and tellers. Their supervisory and administrative duties are similar to those of other supervisors and managers.

Sources of Additional Information

For information related to a wide variety of management occupations, including educational programs and certified designations, contact:

- National Management Association, 2210 Arbor Blvd., Dayton, OH 45439. Internet: http://www.nma1.org
- International Association of Administrative Professionals, 10502 NW Ambassador Dr., P.O. Box 20404, Kansas City, MO 64195-0404. Internet: http://www.iaap-hq.org

Office Clerks, General

(O*NET 43-9061.00)

Significant Points

- Employment growth and high replacement needs in this large occupation will result in numerous job openings.
- Prospects should be best for those with knowledge of basic computer applications and office machinery as well as good communication skills.
- Part-time and temporary positions are common.

Nature of the Work

Rather than performing a single specialized task, general office clerks have responsibilities that often change daily with the needs of the specific job and the employer. Whereas some clerks spend their days filing or keyboarding, others enter data at a computer terminal. They also can be called on to operate photocopiers, fax machines, and other office equipment; prepare mailings; proofread documents; and answer telephones and deliver messages.

The specific duties assigned to a clerk vary significantly, depending on the type of office in which he or she works. An office clerk in a doctor's office, for example, would not perform the same tasks that a clerk in a large financial institution or in the office of an auto parts wholesaler would perform. Although both may sort checks, keep payroll records, take inventory, and access information, clerks also perform duties unique to their employer, such as organizing medications, making transparencies for a presentation, or filling orders received by fax machine.

Clerks' duties also vary by level of experience. Whereas inexperienced employees make photocopies, stuff envelopes, or record inquiries, experienced clerks usually are given additional responsibilities. For example, they may maintain financial or other records, set up spreadsheets, verify statistical reports for accuracy and completeness, handle and adjust customer complaints, work with vendors, make travel arrangements, take inventory of equipment and supplies, answer questions on departmental services and functions, or help prepare invoices or budgetary requests. Senior office clerks may be expected to monitor and direct the work of lower level clerks.

Working Conditions

For the most part, general office clerks work in comfortable office settings. Those on full-time schedules usually work a standard 40-hour week; however, some work shifts or overtime during busy periods. About 16 percent of clerks work part time. Many clerks also work in temporary positions.

Training, Other Qualifications, and Advancement

Although most office clerk jobs are entry-level administrative support positions, employers may prefer or require previous office or business experience. Employers usually require a high school diploma or equivalent, and some require basic computer skills, including familiarity with word processing software, as well as other general office skills.

Training for this occupation is available through business education programs offered in high schools, community and junior colleges, and postsecondary vocational schools. Courses in office practices, word processing, and other computer applications are particularly helpful.

Because general office clerks usually work with other office staff, they should be cooperative and able to work as part of a team. Employers prefer individuals who are able to perform a variety of tasks and satisfy the needs of the many departments within a company. In addition, applicants should have good communication skills, be detail-oriented, and adaptable.

General office clerks who exhibit strong communication, interpersonal, and analytical skills may be promoted to supervisory positions. Others may move into different, more senior administrative jobs, such as receptionist, secretary, or administrative assistant. After gaining some work experience or specialized skills, many workers transfer to jobs with higher pay or greater advancement potential. Advancement to professional occupations within an organization normally requires additional formal education, such as a college degree.

Employment

General office clerks held about 3.1 million jobs in 2004. Most are employed in relatively small businesses. Although they work in every sector of the economy, about 46 percent worked in local government; health care and social assistance; administrative and support services; finance and insurance; or professional, scientific, and technical services industries.

Job Outlook

Employment growth and high replacement needs in this large occupation will result in numerous job openings for general office clerks. In addition to those for full-time jobs, many job openings are expected for part-time and temporary general office clerks. Prospects should be best for those who have knowledge of basic computer applications and office machinery—such as fax machines, telephone systems, and scanners—and good writing and communication skills. As general administrative support duties continue to be consolidated, employers will increasingly seek well-rounded individuals with highly developed communication skills and the ability to perform multiple tasks.

Employment of general office clerks is expected to grow more slowly than average for all occupations through the year 2014. The employment outlook for these workers will be affected by the increasing use of technology, expanding office automation, and the consolidation of administrative support tasks. Automation has led to productivity gains, allowing a wide variety of duties to be performed by fewer office workers. However, automation also has led to a consolidation of administrative support staffs and a diversification of job responsibilities. This consolidation increases the demand for general office clerks because they perform a variety of administrative support tasks. It will become increasingly common within small businesses to find a single general office clerk in charge of all administrative support work.

Job opportunities may vary from year to year because the strength of the economy affects demand for general office clerks. Companies tend to employ more workers when the economy is strong. Industries least likely to be affected by economic fluctuations tend to be the most stable places for employment.

Earnings

Median annual earnings of general office clerks were $22,770 in May 2004; the middle 50 percent earned between $18,090 and $28,950 annually. The lowest 10 percent earned less than $14,530, and the highest 10 percent earned more than $35,810. Median annual salaries in the industries employing the largest numbers of general office clerks in May 2004 were:

Local government	$25,880
State government	24,970
Elementary and secondary schools	23,500
Colleges, universities, and professional schools	23,160
Employment services	20,910

Related Occupations

The duties of general office clerks can include a combination of bookkeeping, keyboarding, office machine operation, and filing. Other office and administrative support workers who perform similar duties include bookkeeping, accounting, and auditing clerks; communications equipment operators; customer service representatives; data entry and information processing workers; order clerks; receptionists and information clerks; secretaries and administrative assistants; stock clerks and order fillers; and tellers. Nonclerical entry-level workers include cashiers, counter and rental clerks; and food and beverage serving and related workers.

Sources of Additional Information

State employment service offices and agencies can provide information about job openings for general office clerks.

For information related to administrative occupations, including educational programs and certified designations, contact:

- International Association of Administrative Professionals, 10502 NW Ambassador Dr., P.O. Box 20404, Kansas City, MO 64195-0404. Internet: http://www.iaap-hq.org

Painters and Paperhangers

(O*NET 47-2141.00 and 47-2142.00)

Significant Points

- Employment prospects should be excellent due to the expected job growth, coupled with the large numbers of workers who retire or leave the occupation for other jobs.
- Most workers learn informally on the job as helpers, but training experts recommend completion of an apprenticeship program.
- Nearly one-half of all painters and paperhangers are self employed.

Nature of the Work

Paint and wall coverings make surfaces clean, attractive, and bright. In addition, paints and other sealers protect exterior surfaces from wear caused by exposure to the weather.

Painters apply paint, stain, varnish, and other finishes to buildings and other structures. They choose the right paint or finish for the surface to be covered, taking into account durability, ease of handling, method of application, and customers' wishes. Painters first prepare the surfaces to be covered so that the paint will adhere properly. This may require removing the old coat of paint by stripping, sanding, wire brushing, burning, or water and abrasive blasting. Painters also wash walls and trim to remove dirt and grease, fill nail holes and cracks, sandpaper rough spots, and brush off dust. On new surfaces, they apply a primer or sealer to prepare the surface for the finish coat. Painters also mix paints and match colors, relying on knowledge of paint composition and color harmony. In large paint shops or hardware stores, these functions are automated.

There are several ways to apply paint and similar coverings. Painters must be able to choose the right paint applicator for each job, depending on the surface to be covered, the characteristics of the finish, and other factors. Some jobs need only a good bristle brush with a soft, tapered edge; others require a dip or fountain pressure roller; still others can best be done using a paint sprayer. Many jobs need several types of applicators. The right tools for each job not only expedite the painter's work but also produce the most attractive surface.

When working on tall buildings, painters erect scaffolding, including "swing stages," scaffolds suspended by ropes, or cables attached to roof hooks. When painting steeples and other conical structures, they use a bosun's chair, a swing-like device.

Paperhangers cover walls and ceilings with decorative wall coverings made of paper, vinyl, or fabric. They first prepare the surface to be covered by applying "sizing," which seals the surface and makes the covering adhere better. When redecorating, they may first remove the old covering by soaking, steaming, or applying solvents. When necessary, they patch holes and take care of other imperfections before hanging the new wall covering.

After the surface has been prepared, paperhangers must prepare the paste or other adhesive. Then, they measure the area to be covered, check the covering for flaws, cut the covering into strips of the proper size, and closely examine the pattern in order to match it when the strips are hung. Much of this process can now be handled by specialized equipment.

The next step is to brush or roll the adhesive onto the back of the covering, if needed, and to then place the strips on the wall or ceiling, making sure the pattern is matched, the strips are hung straight, and the edges are butted together to make tight, closed seams. Finally, paperhangers smooth the strips to remove bubbles and wrinkles, trim the top and bottom with a razor knife, and wipe off any excess adhesive.

Working Conditions

Most painters and paperhangers work 40 hours a week or less; about one-fourth have variable schedules or work part time. Painters and paperhangers must stand for long periods, often working from scaffolding and ladders. Their jobs also require a considerable amount of climbing and bending. These workers must have stamina, because much of the work is done with their arms raised overhead. Painters often work outdoors but seldom in wet, cold, or inclement weather. Some painting jobs can leave a worker covered with paint.

Painters and paperhangers sometimes work with materials that are hazardous or toxic, such as when they are required to remove lead-based paints. In the most dangerous situations, painters work in a sealed self-contained suit to prevent inhalation of or contact with hazardous materials.

Training, Other Qualifications, and Advancement

Painting and paperhanging is learned mostly through on-the-job training and by working as a helper to an experienced painter. However, there are a number of formal and informal training programs that provide more thorough instruction and a better career foundation. In general, the more formal the training received the more likely the individual will enter the profession at a higher level. Besides apprenticeships, some workers gain skills by attending technical schools that offer training prior to employment. These schools can take about a year to complete. Others receive training through local vocational high schools. Applicants should have good manual dexterity and color sense. There are limited opportunities for informal training for paperhangers because there are fewer paperhangers and helpers are usually not required.

If available, apprenticeships are usually the best way to enter the profession. They generally provide a mixture of classroom instruction and on-the-job training. Apprenticeships for painters and paperhangers consist of 2 to 4 years of on-the-job training, supplemented by 144 hours of related classroom instruction each year. Apprentices or helpers generally must be at least 18 years old and in good physical condition. A high school education or its equivalent, with courses in mathematics, usually is required to enter an apprenticeship program. Apprentices receive instruction in color harmony, use and care of tools and equipment, surface preparation, application techniques, paint mixing and matching, characteristics of different finishes, blueprint reading, wood finishing, and safety.

Whether a painter learns the trade through a formal apprenticeship or informally as a helper, on-the-job instruction covers similar skill areas. Under the direction of experienced workers, trainees carry supplies, erect scaffolds, and do simple painting and surface preparation tasks while they learn about paint and painting equipment. As they gain experience, trainees learn to prepare surfaces for painting and paperhanging, to mix paints, and to apply paint and wall coverings efficiently and neatly. Near the end of their training, they may learn decorating concepts, color coordination, and cost-estimating techniques. In addition to learning craft skills, painters must become familiar with safety and health regulations so that their work complies with the law.

Painters and paperhangers may advance to supervisory or estimating jobs with painting and decorating contractors. Many establish their own painting and decorating businesses. For those who would like to advance, it is increasingly important to be able to communicate in both English and Spanish in order to relay instructions and safety precautions to workers with limited English skills; Spanish speaking workers make up a large part of the construction workforce in many areas. Painting contractors need good English skills in order to deal with clients and subcontractors.

Employment

Painters and paperhangers held about 486,000 jobs in 2004; most were painters. Around one-third of painters and paperhangers work for painting and wall covering contractors engaged in new construction, repair, restoration, or remodeling work. In addition, organizations that own or manage large buildings—such as apartment complexes—employ maintenance painters, as do some schools, hospitals, factories, and government agencies.

Self-employed independent painting contractors accounted for nearly one-half of all painters and paperhangers, significantly greater than the one in five of construction trades workers in general.

Job Outlook

Job prospects should be excellent because each year thousands of painters retire or leave for jobs in other occupations. There are no strict training requirements for entry into these jobs, so many people with limited skills work as painters or helpers for a short time and then move on to other types of work. Many fewer openings will arise for paperhangers because the number of these jobs is comparatively small.

In addition to the need to replace experienced workers who leave, new jobs will be created. Employment of painters is expected to grow as fast as average for all occupations through the year 2014, reflecting increases in the level of new construction and in the stock of buildings and other structures that require maintenance and renovation. The relatively short life of exterior paints as well as changing color trends will stir demand for painters. Painting is labor-intensive and not susceptible to technological changes that might make workers more productive and slow employment growth. Paperhangers should see slower than average employment growth as easy application materials and reduced demand for paperhanging services limits growth.

Jobseekers considering these occupations should expect some periods of unemployment, especially until they gain experience. Many construction projects are of short duration, and construction activity is cyclical and seasonal in nature. Remodeling, restoration, and maintenance projects, however, often provide many jobs for painters and paperhangers even when new construction activity declines. The most versatile painters and skilled paperhangers generally are best able to keep working steadily during downturns in the economy.

Earnings

In May 2004, median hourly earnings of painters, construction and maintenance, were $14.55. The middle 50 percent earned between $11.59 and $19.04. The lowest 10 percent earned less than $9.47, and the highest 10 percent earned more than $25.11. Median hourly earnings in the industries employing the largest numbers of painters in May 2004 were as follows:

Local government	$18.36
Residential building construction	15.09
Nonresidential building construction	14.97
Building finishing contractors	14.44
Employment services	11.31

In May 2004, median earnings for paperhangers were $15.73. The middle 50 percent earned between $12.23 and $20.71. The lowest 10 percent earned less than $9.57, and the highest 10 percent earned more than $26.58.

Earnings for painters may be reduced on occasion because of bad weather and the short-term nature of many construction jobs. Hourly wage rates for apprentices usually start at 40 to 50 percent of the rate for experienced workers and increase periodically.

Some painters and paperhangers are members of the International Brotherhood of Painters and Allied Trades. Some maintenance painters are members of other unions.

Related Occupations

Painters and paperhangers apply various coverings to decorate and protect wood, drywall, metal, and other surfaces. Other construction occupations in which workers do finishing work include carpenters; carpet, floor, and tile installers and finishers; drywall installers, ceiling tile installers, and tapers; painting and coating workers, except construction and maintenance; and plasterers and stucco masons.

Sources of Additional Information

For details about painting and paperhanging apprenticeships or work opportunities, contact local painting and decorating contractors, local trade organizations, a local of the International Union of Painters and Allied Trades, a local joint union-management apprenticeship committee, or an office of the state apprenticeship agency or employment service.

For information about the work of painters and paperhangers and training opportunities, contact:

- International Union of Painters and Allied Trades, 1750 New York Ave. NW, Washington, DC 20006. Internet: http://www.iupat.org
- Associated Builders and Contractors, Workforce Development Department, 4250 North Fairfax Dr., 9th Floor, Arlington, VA 22203. Internet: http://www.trytools.org
- National Center for Construction Education and Research, P.O. Box 141104, Gainesville, FL 32614-1104. Internet: http://www.nccer.org
- Painting and Decorating Contractors of America, 11960 Westline Industrial Drive, Suite 201, St. Louis, MO 63146-3209. Internet: http://www.pdca.org

Paralegals and Legal Assistants

(O*NET 23-2011.00)

Significant Points

- About 7 out of 10 work for law firms; others work for corporate legal departments and government agencies.
- Most entrants have an associate's degree in paralegal studies, or a bachelor's degree coupled with a certificate in paralegal studies.
- Employment is projected to grow much faster than average, as employers try to reduce costs by hiring paralegals to perform tasks formerly carried out by lawyers.
- Competition for jobs should continue; experienced, formally trained paralegals should have the best employment opportunities.

Nature of the Work

While lawyers assume ultimate responsibility for legal work, they often delegate many of their tasks to paralegals. In fact, paralegals—also called legal assistants—are continuing to assume a growing range of tasks in the nation's legal offices and perform many of the same tasks as lawyers. Nevertheless, they are still explicitly prohibited from carrying out duties that are considered to be the practice of law, such as setting legal fees, giving legal advice, and presenting cases in court.

One of a paralegal's most important tasks is helping lawyers prepare for closings, hearings, trials, and corporate meetings. Paralegals investigate the facts of cases and ensure that all relevant information is considered. They also identify appropriate laws, judicial decisions, legal articles, and other materials that are relevant to assigned cases. After they analyze and organize the information, paralegals may prepare written reports that attorneys use in determining how cases should be handled. Should attorneys decide to file lawsuits on behalf of clients, paralegals may help prepare the legal arguments, draft pleadings and motions to be filed with the court, obtain affidavits, and assist attorneys during trials. Paralegals also organize and track files of all important case documents and make them available and easily accessible to attorneys.

In addition to this preparatory work, paralegals perform a number of other vital functions. For example, they help draft contracts, mortgages, separation agreements, and instruments of trust. They also may assist in preparing tax returns and planning estates. Some paralegals coordinate the activities of other law office employees and maintain financial office records. Various additional tasks may differ, depending on the employer.

Paralegals are found in all types of organizations, but most are employed by law firms, corporate legal departments, and various government offices. In these organizations, they can work in many different areas of the law, including litigation, personal injury, corporate law, criminal law, employee benefits, intellectual property, labor law, bankruptcy, immigration, family law, and real estate. As the law has become more complex, paralegals have responded by becoming more specialized. Within specialties, functions often are broken down further so that paralegals may deal with a specific area. For example, paralegals specializing in labor law may concentrate exclusively on employee benefits.

The duties of paralegals also differ widely with the type of organization in which they are employed. Paralegals who work for corporations often assist attorneys with employee contracts, shareholder agreements, stock-option plans, and employee benefit plans. They also may help prepare and file annual financial reports, maintain corporate minutes' record resolutions, and prepare forms to secure loans for the corporation. Paralegals often monitor and review government regulations to ensure that the corporation is aware of new requirements and is operating within the law. Increasingly, experienced paralegals are assuming additional supervisory responsibilities such as overseeing team projects and serving as a communications link between the team and the corporation.

The duties of paralegals who work in the public sector usually vary within each agency. In general, paralegals analyze legal material for internal use, maintain reference files, conduct research for attorneys, and collect and analyze evidence for agency hearings. They may prepare informative or explanatory material on laws, agency regulations, and agency policy for general use by the agency and the public. Paralegals employed in community legal-service projects help the poor, the aged, and others who are in need of legal assistance. They file forms, conduct research, prepare documents, and, when authorized by law, may represent clients at administrative hearings.

Paralegals in small and medium-size law firms usually perform a variety of duties that require a general knowledge of the law. For example, they may research judicial decisions on improper police arrests or help prepare a mortgage contract. Paralegals employed by large law firms, government agencies, and corporations, however, are more likely to specialize in one aspect of the law.

Familiarity with computers use and technical knowledge have become essential to paralegal work. Computer software packages and the Internet are used to search legal literature stored in computer databases and on CD-ROM. In litigation involving many supporting documents, paralegals usually use computer databases to retrieve, organize, and index various materials. Imaging software allows paralegals to scan documents directly into a database, while billing programs help them to track hours billed to clients. Computer software packages also are used to perform tax computations and explore the consequences of various tax strategies for clients.

Working Conditions

Paralegals employed by corporations and government usually work a standard 40-hour week. Although most paralegals work year round, some are temporarily employed during busy times of the year and then are released when the workload diminishes. Paralegals who work for law firms sometimes work very long hours when they are under pressure to meet deadlines. Some law firms reward such loyalty with bonuses and additional time off.

These workers handle many routine assignments, particularly when they are inexperienced. As they gain experience, paralegals usually assume more varied tasks with additional responsibility. Paralegals do most of their work at desks in offices and law libraries. Occasionally, they travel to gather information and perform other duties.

Training, Other Qualifications, and Advancement

There are several ways to become a paralegal. The most common is through a community college paralegal program that leads to an associate's degree. The other common method of entry, mainly for those who already have a college degree, is through a program that leads to a certification in paralegal studies. A small number of schools also offer bachelor's and master's degrees in paralegal studies. Some employers train paralegals on the job, hiring college graduates with no legal experience or promoting experienced legal secretaries. Other entrants have experience in a technical field that is useful to law firms, such as a background in tax preparation for tax and estate practice or in criminal justice, nursing, or health administration for personal injury practice.

An estimated 1,000 colleges and universities, law schools, and proprietary schools offer formal paralegal training programs. Approximately 260 paralegal programs are approved by the American Bar Association (ABA). Although many programs do not require such approval, graduation from an ABA-approved program can enhance one's employment opportunities. The requirements for admission to these programs vary. Some require certain college courses or a bachelor's degree, others accept high school graduates or those with legal experience, and a few schools require standardized tests and personal interviews.

Paralegal programs include 2-year associate degree's programs, 4-year bachelor's degree programs, and certificate programs that can take only a few months to complete. Most certificate programs provide intensive and, in some cases, specialized paralegal training for individuals who already hold college degrees, while associate's and bachelor's degree programs usually combine paralegal training with courses in other academic subjects. The quality of paralegal training programs varies; the better programs usually include job placement services. Programs generally offer courses introducing students to the legal applications of computers, including how to perform legal research on the Internet. Many paralegal training programs also offer an internship in which students gain practical experience by working for several months in a private law firm, the office of a public defender or attorney general, a bank, a corporate legal department, a legal aid organization, or a government agency. Experience gained in internships is an asset when one is seeking a job after graduation. Prospective students should examine the experiences of recent graduates before enrolling in a paralegal program.

Although most employers do not require certification, earning a voluntary certificate from a professional society may offer advantages in the labor market. The National Association of Legal Assistants (NALA), for example, has established standards for certification requiring various combinations of education and experience. Paralegals who meet these standards are eligible to take a 2-day examination, given three times each year at several regional testing centers. Those who pass this examination may use the Certified Legal Assistant (CLA) designation. The NALA also offers an advanced paralegal certification for those who want to specialize in other areas of the law. In addition, the Paralegal Advanced Competency Exam, administered through the National Federation of Paralegal Associations, offers professional recognition to paralegals with a bachelor's degree and at least 2 years of experience. Those who pass this examination may use the Registered Paralegal (RP) designation.

Paralegals must be able to document and present their findings and opinions to their supervising attorney. They need to understand legal terminology and have good research and investigative skills. Familiarity with the operation and applications of computers in legal research and litigation support also is important. Paralegals should stay informed of new developments in the laws that affect their area of practice. Participation in continuing legal education seminars allows paralegals to maintain and expand their knowledge of the law.

Because paralegals frequently deal with the public, they should be courteous and uphold the ethical standards of the legal profession. The National Association of Legal Assistants, the National Federation of Paralegal Associations, and a few states have established ethical guidelines for paralegals to follow.

Paralegals usually are given more responsibilities and require less supervision as they gain work experience. Experienced paralegals who work in large law firms, corporate legal departments, or government agencies may supervise and delegate assignments to other paralegals and clerical staff. Advancement opportunities also include promotion to managerial and other law-related positions within the firm or corporate legal department. However, some paralegals find it easier to move to another law firm when seeking increased responsibility or advancement.

Employment

Paralegals and legal assistants held about 224,000 jobs in 2004. Private law firms employed 7 out of 10 paralegals and legal assistants; most of the remainder worked for corporate legal departments and various levels of government. Within the federal government, the U.S. Department of Justice is the largest employer, followed by the Social Security Administration and the U.S. Department of the Treasury. A small number of paralegals own their own businesses and work as freelance legal assistants, contracting their services to attorneys or corporate legal departments.

Job Outlook

Employment for paralegals and legal assistants is projected to grow much faster than average for all occupations through 2014. Employers are trying to reduce costs and increase the availability and efficiency of legal services by hiring paralegals to perform tasks formerly carried out by lawyers. Besides new jobs created by employment growth, additional job openings will arise as people leave the occupation. Despite projections of rapid employment growth, competition for jobs should continue as many people seek to go into this profession; however, experienced, formally trained paralegals should have the best employment opportunities.

Private law firms will continue to be the largest employers of paralegals, but a growing array of other organizations, such as corporate legal departments, insurance companies, real estate and title insurance firms, and banks hire paralegals. Corporations in particular are boosting their in-house legal departments to cut costs. Demand for paralegals also is expected to grow as an expanding population increasingly requires legal services, especially in areas such as intellectual property, health care, international law, elder issues, criminal law, and environmental law. Paralegals who specialize in areas such as real estate, bankruptcy, medical malpractice, and product liability should have ample employment opportunities. The growth of prepaid legal plans also should contribute to the demand for legal services. Paralegal employment is expected to increase as organizations presently employing paralegals assign them a growing range of tasks and as paralegals are increasingly employed in small and medium-size establishments. A growing number of experienced paralegals are expected to establish their own businesses.

Job opportunities for paralegals will expand in the public sector as well. Community legal-service programs, which provide assistance to the poor, elderly, minorities, and middle-income families, will employ additional paralegals to minimize expenses and serve the most people. Federal, state, and local government agencies, consumer organizations, and the courts also should continue to hire paralegals in increasing numbers.

To a limited extent, paralegal jobs are affected by the business cycle. During recessions, demand declines for some discretionary legal services, such as planning estates, drafting wills, and handling real estate transactions. Corporations are less inclined to initiate certain types of litigation when falling sales and profits lead to fiscal belt tightening. As a result, full-time paralegals employed in offices adversely affected by a recession may be laid off or have their work hours reduced. However, during recessions, corporations and individuals are more likely to face other problems that require legal assistance, such as bankruptcies, foreclosures, and divorces. Paralegals, who provide many of the same legal services as lawyers at a lower cost, tend to fare relatively better in difficult economic conditions.

Earnings

Earnings of paralegals and legal assistants vary greatly. Salaries depend on education, training, experience, the type and size of employer, and the geographic location of the job. In general, paralegals who work for large law firms or in large metropolitan areas earn more than those who work for smaller firms or in less populated regions. In addition to earning a salary, many paralegals receive bonuses. In May 2004, full-time wage and salary paralegals and legal assistants had median annual earnings, including bonuses, of $39,130. The middle 50 percent earned between $31,040 and $49,950. The top 10 percent earned more than $61,390, while the bottom 10 percent earned less than $25,360. Median annual earnings in the industries employing the largest numbers of paralegals in May 2004 were as follows:

Federal government	$59,370
Local government	38,260
Legal services	37,870
State government	34,910

Related Occupations

Among the other occupations that call for a specialized understanding of the law and the legal system, but do not require the extensive training of a lawyer, are law clerks; title examiners, abstractors, and searchers; claims adjusters, appraisers, examiners, and investigators, and occupational health and safety specialists and technicians.

Sources of Additional Information

General information on a career as a paralegal can be obtained from:

- Standing Committee on Paralegals, American Bar Association, 321 North Clark St., Chicago, IL 60610. Internet: http://www.abanet.org/legalservices/paralegals

For information on the Certified Legal Assistant exam, schools that offer training programs in a specific state, and standards and guidelines for paralegals, contact:

- National Association of Legal Assistants, Inc., 1516 South Boston St., Suite 200, Tulsa, OK 74119. Internet: http://www.nala.org

Information on a career as a paralegal, schools that offer training programs, job postings for paralegals, the Paralegal Advanced Competency Exam, and local paralegal associations can be obtained from:

- National Federation of Paralegal Associations, 2517 Eastlake Ave. East, Suite 200, Seattle, WA 98102. Internet: http://www.paralegals.org

Information on paralegal training programs, including the pamphlet *How to Choose a Paralegal Education Program*, may be obtained from:

- American Association for Paralegal Education, 19 Mantua Rd., Mt. Royal, NJ 08061. Internet: http://www.aafpe.org

Information on obtaining positions as occupational health and safety specialists and technicians with the federal government is available from the Office of Personnel Management through USAJOBS, the federal government's official employment information system. This resource for locating and applying for job opportunities can be accessed through the Internet at http://www.usajobs.opm.gov or through an interactive voice response telephone system at (703) 724-1850 or TDD (978) 461-8404. These numbers are not toll free, and charges may result.

Payroll and Timekeeping Clerks

(O*NET 43-3051.00 and 43-3051.00)

Significant Points

- Payroll and timekeeping clerks are found in every industry.
- Most employers prefer applicants with a high school diploma; computer skills are very desirable.
- Those who have completed a certification program, indicating that they can handle more complex payroll issues, will have an advantage in the job market.

Nature of the Work

Payroll and timekeeping clerks perform a vital function: ensuring that employees are paid on time and that their paychecks are accurate. If inaccuracies occur, such as monetary errors or incorrect amounts of vacation time, these workers research and correct the records. In addition, they may perform various other clerical tasks. Automated timekeeping systems that allow employees to enter the number of hours they have worked directly into a computer have eliminated much of the data entry and review by timekeepers and have elevated the job of payroll clerk. In offices that have not automated this function, however, payroll and timekeeping clerks still perform many of the traditional job functions.

The fundamental task of *timekeeping clerks* is distributing and collecting timecards each pay period. These workers review employee work charts, timesheets, and timecards to ensure that information is properly recorded and that records have the signatures of authorizing officials. In companies that bill for the time spent by staff, such as law or accounting firms, timekeeping clerks make sure that the hours recorded are charged to the correct job so that clients can be properly billed. These clerks also review computer reports listing timecards that cannot be processed because of errors, and they contact the employee or the employee's supervisor to resolve the problem. In addition, timekeeping clerks are responsible for informing managers and other employees about procedural changes in payroll policies.

Payroll clerks, also called payroll technicians, screen timecards for calculating, coding, or other errors. They compute pay by subtracting allotments, including federal and state taxes and contributions to retirement, insurance, and savings plans, from gross earnings. Increasingly, computers are performing these calculations and alerting payroll clerks to problems or errors in the data. In small organizations or for new employees whose records are not yet entered into a computer system, clerks may perform the necessary calculations manually. In some small offices, clerks or other employees in the accounting department process payroll.

Payroll clerks record changes in employees' addresses; close out files when workers retire, resign, or transfer; and advise employees on income tax withholding and other mandatory deductions. They also issue and record adjustments to workers' pay because of previous errors or retroactive increases. Payroll clerks need to follow changes in tax and deduction laws so they are aware of the most recent revisions. Finally, they prepare and mail earnings and tax-withholding statements for employees' use in preparing income tax returns.

In small offices, payroll and timekeeping duties are likely to be included in the duties of a general office clerk, a secretary, or an accounting clerk. However, large organizations employ specialized payroll and timekeeping clerks to perform these functions. In offices that have automated timekeeping systems, payroll clerks perform more analysis of the data, examine trends, and work with computer systems. They also spend more time answering employees' questions and processing unique data.

Working Conditions

Payroll and timekeeping clerks usually work in clean, pleasant, and comfortable office settings. Clerks usually work a standard 35- to 40-hour week; however, longer hours might be necessary during busy periods. Payroll and timekeeping clerks also may face stress at times, particularly from the pressure to meet deadlines.

Training, Other Qualifications, and Advancement

Most employers prefer applicants with a high school diploma or GED. Computer skills are very desirable. Payroll and timekeeping clerks learn their skills through a combination of on-the-job experience and informal training. Training also can be attained through programs in high schools, business schools, and community colleges. New workers receive training in payroll, timekeeping, personnel issues, workplace practices, and company policies.

Payroll and timekeeping clerks must be able to interact and communicate with individuals at all levels of the organization. In addition, clerks should demonstrate poise, tactfulness, and diplomacy and have a high level of interpersonal skills in order to handle sensitive and confidential situations.

Most organizations specializing in payroll and timekeeping offer classes intended to enhance the marketable skills of their members. Some organizations offer certification programs; completion of a certification program indicates competence and can enhance one's advancement opportunities. For example, the American Payroll

Association offers two levels of certification, the Fundamental Payroll Certification (FPC) and the Certified Payroll Professional (CPP). The FPC is open to all individuals who wish to demonstrate basic payroll competency. The more advanced CPP is available those who have been employed in the practice of payroll for at least 3 years and who have obtained the FPC within the last 18 months. Both require experience and a passing score on a comprehensive exam.

Employment

Payroll and timekeeping clerks held about 214,000 jobs in 2004. They can be found in every industry, but a growing number work for employment services companies as temporary employees or for accounting, tax preparation, bookkeeping, and payroll services firms, which increasingly are taking on the payroll function as a service to other companies. Approximately 18 percent of all payroll and timekeeping clerks worked part time in 2004.

Job Outlook

Employment of payroll and timekeeping clerks is expected to grow about as fast as average for all occupations through 2014. In addition to job growth, numerous job openings will arise each year as payroll and timekeeping clerks leave the labor force or transfer to other occupations. Those who have completed a certification program, indicating that they can handle more complex payroll issues, will have an advantage in the job market.

As entering and recording payroll and timekeeping information becomes more simplified, the job itself is becoming more complex, with companies now offering a greater variety of pension, 401(k), and other investment plans to their employees. Also, the growing use of garnishment of wages for child support is adding to the complexity. These developments will fuel the demand for payroll and timekeeping clerks, who will be needed to record and monitor such information.

Firms increasingly are outsourcing the payroll function. As a result, the best employment opportunities are expected to be in companies that specialize in payroll, including companies in the employment services industry and the accounting, tax preparation, bookkeeping, and payroll services industry. Many of these companies are data processing facilities, but accounting firms also are taking on the payroll function to supplement their accounting work.

The increasing use of computers will limit employment growth of payroll and timekeeping clerks. For example, automated time clocks, which calculate employee hours, allow large organizations to centralize their timekeeping duties in one location. At individual sites, employee hours increasingly are tracked by computer and verified by managers. This information is compiled and sent to a central office to be processed by payroll clerks. In addition, the growing use of direct deposit will reduce the need to draft paychecks, because these funds are transferred automatically each pay period. Also, more organizations are allowing employees to update their payroll records electronically. In smaller organizations, payroll and timekeeping duties are being assigned to secretaries, general office clerks, or accounting clerks. Furthermore, the greater complexity of the job, coupled with the automation of records that is simplifying data entry, is resulting in payroll professionals, not payroll and timekeeping clerks, doing more of the work.

Earnings

Salaries of payroll and timekeeping clerks may vary considerably. The region of the country, size of city, and type and size of establishment all influence salary levels. Also, the level of expertise required and the complexity and uniqueness of a clerk's responsibilities may affect earnings.

Median annual earnings of payroll and timekeeping clerks in May 2004 were \$30,350. The middle 50 percent earned between \$24,430 and \$36,930. The lowest 10 percent earned less than \$19,680, and the highest 10 percent earned more than \$44,270. Median annual earnings in the industries employing the largest numbers of payroll and timekeeping clerks in May 2004 were:

Management of companies and enterprises	$32,600
Elementary and secondary schools	32,390
Local government	31,620
Accounting, tax preparation, bookkeeping, and payroll services	29,040
Employment services	28,010

Some employers offer educational assistance to payroll and timekeeping clerks.

Related Occupations

Payroll and timekeeping clerks perform a vital financial function—ensuring that employees are paid on time and that their paychecks are accurate. In addition, they may perform various other office and administrative support duties. Other financial clerks include bill and account collectors; billing and posting clerks and machine operators; bookkeeping, accounting, and auditing clerks; gaming cage workers; procurement clerks; and tellers.

Sources of Additional Information

For general information about payroll and timekeeping clerks, contact:

- American Payroll Association, 660 North Main Ave., Suite 100, Suite 660, San Antonio, TX 78205-1217. Internet: http://www.americanpayroll.org
- WorldatWork, 14040 N. Northsight Blvd., Scottsdale, AZ 85260. Internet: http://www.worldatwork.org

Information on employment opportunities for payroll and timekeeping clerks is available from local offices of the state employment service.

Personal and Home Care Aides

(O*NET 39-9021.00)

Significant Points

- Job opportunities are expected to be excellent because of rapid growth in home health care and high replacement needs.

- Skill requirements are low, as is the pay.
- About 33 percent of personal and home care aides work part time; most aides work with a number of different clients, each job lasting a few hours, days, or weeks.

Nature of the Work

Personal and home care aides help elderly, disabled, ill, and mentally disabled persons live in their own homes or in residential care facilities instead of in health facilities. Most personal and home care aides work with elderly or physically or mentally disabled clients who need more extensive personal and home care than family or friends can provide. Some aides work with families in which a parent is incapacitated and small children need care. Others help discharged hospital patients who have relatively short-term needs.

Personal and home care aides—also called *homemakers, caregivers, companions*, and *personal attendants*—provide housekeeping and routine personal care services. They clean clients' houses, do laundry, and change bed linens. Aides may plan meals (including special diets), shop for food, and cook. Aides also may help clients get out of bed, bathe, dress, and groom. Some accompany clients to doctors' appointments or on other errands.

Personal and home care aides provide instruction and psychological support to their patients. They may advise families and patients on nutrition, cleanliness, and household tasks. Aides also may assist in toilet training a severely mentally handicapped child, or they may just listen to clients talk about their problems.

In home health care agencies, a registered nurse, physical therapist, or social worker assigns specific duties and supervises personal and home care aides. Aides keep records of services performed and of clients' condition and progress. They report changes in the client's condition to the supervisor or case manager. In carrying out their work, aides cooperate with health care professionals, including registered nurses, therapists, and other medical staff.

Working Conditions

The personal and home care aide's daily routine may vary. Aides may go to the same home every day for months or even years. However, most aides work with a number of different clients, each job lasting a few hours, days, or weeks. Aides often visit four or five clients on the same day.

Surroundings differ from case to case. Some homes are neat and pleasant, whereas others are untidy and depressing. Some clients are pleasant and cooperative; others are angry, abusive, depressed, or otherwise difficult.

Personal and home care aides generally work on their own, with periodic visits by their supervisor. They receive detailed instructions explaining when to visit clients and what services to perform for them. About one-third of aides work part time, and some work weekends or evenings to suit the needs of their clients.

Aides are individually responsible for getting to the client's home. They may spend a good portion of the working day traveling from one client to another. Because mechanical lifting devices that are available in institutional settings are seldom available in patients' homes, aides must be careful to avoid overexertion or injury when they assist clients.

Training, Other Qualifications, and Advancement

In some states, the only requirement for employment is on-the-job training, which generally is provided by most employers. Other states may require formal training, which is available from community colleges, vocational schools, elder care programs, and home health care agencies. The National Association for Home Care and Hospice (NAHC) offers national certification for personal and home care aides. Certification is a voluntary demonstration that the individual has met industry standards. Certification requires the completion of a standard 75-hour course and written exam developed by NAHC. Home care aides seeking certification are evaluated on 17 different skills by a registered nurse.

Personal and home care aides should have a desire to help people and not mind hard work. They should be responsible, compassionate, emotionally stable, and cheerful. In addition, aides should be tactful, honest, and discreet because they work in private homes. Aides also must be in good health. A physical examination, including state-mandated tests such as those for tuberculosis, may be required. A criminal background check also may be required for employment. Additionally, personal and home care aides are responsible for their own transportation to reach patients' homes.

Advancement for personal and home care aides is limited. In some agencies, workers start out performing homemaker duties, such as cleaning. With experience and training, they may take on personal care duties. Some aides choose to receive additional training to become nursing and home health aides, licensed practical nurses, or registered nurses. Some experienced personal and home care aides may start their own home care agency.

Employment

Personal and home care aides held about 701,000 jobs in 2004. The majority of jobs were in home health care services; individual and family services; residential care facilities; and private households. Self-employed aides have no agency affiliation or supervision and accept clients, set fees, and arrange work schedules on their own.

Job Outlook

Excellent job opportunities are expected for this occupation, because rapid employment growth and high replacement needs are projected to produce a large number of job openings.

Employment of personal and home care aides is projected to grow much faster than average for all occupations through the year 2014. The number of elderly people, an age group characterized by mounting health problems and requiring some assistance with daily activities, is projected to rise substantially. In addition to the elderly, other patients, such as the mentally disabled, will increasingly rely on home care. This trend reflects several developments, including efforts to contain costs by moving patients out of hospitals and nursing care facilities as quickly as possible; the realization that treatment can be more effective in familiar rather than clinical surroundings; and the development and improvement of medical technologies for in-home treatment.

In addition to job openings created by the increase in demand for these workers, replacement needs are expected to lead to many openings. The relatively low skill requirements, low pay, and high emotional demands of the work result in high replacement needs. For these same reasons, many people are reluctant to seek jobs in the occupation. Therefore, persons who are interested in and suited for this work—particularly those with experience or training as personal care, home health, or nursing aides—should have excellent job prospects.

Earnings

Median hourly earnings of personal and home care aides were $8.12 in May 2004. The middle 50 percent earned between $6.83 and $9.70 an hour. The lowest 10 percent earned less than $5.93, and the highest 10 percent earned more than $10.87 an hour. Median hourly earnings in the industries employing the largest numbers of personal and home care aides in May 2004 were as follows:

Residential mental retardation, mental health and substance abuse facilities	$9.09
Vocational rehabilitation services	8.76
Community care facilities for the elderly	8.49
Individual and family services	8.48
Home health care services	6.99

Most employers give slight pay increases with experience and added responsibility. Aides usually are paid only for the time they work in the home, not for travel time between jobs. Employers often hire on-call hourly workers and provide no benefits.

Related Occupations

Personal and home care aides combine the duties of caregivers and social service workers. Workers in related occupations that involve personal contact to help others include childcare workers; nursing, psychiatric, and home health aides; occupational therapist assistants and aides; physical therapist assistants and aides; and social and human service assistants.

Sources of Additional Information

Information about employment opportunities may be obtained from local hospitals, nursing care facilities, home health care agencies, psychiatric facilities, residential mental health facilities, social assistance agencies, and local offices of the state employment service.

Pharmacists

(O*NET 29-1051.00)

Significant Points

- Very good employment opportunities are expected for pharmacists.
- Earnings are high, but some pharmacists work long hours, nights, weekends, and holidays.
- Pharmacists are becoming more involved in making decisions regarding drug therapy and in counseling patients.
- A license is required; the prospective pharmacist must graduate from an accredited college of pharmacy and pass a state examination.

Nature of the Work

Pharmacists distribute drugs prescribed by physicians and other health practitioners and provide information to patients about medications and their use. They advise physicians and other health practitioners on the selection, dosages, interactions, and side effects of medications. Pharmacists also monitor the health and progress of patients in response to drug therapy to ensure the safe and effective use of medication. Pharmacists must understand the use, clinical effects, and composition of drugs, including their chemical, biological, and physical properties. Compounding—the actual mixing of ingredients to form powders, tablets, capsules, ointments, and solutions—is a small part of a pharmacist's practice, because most medicines are produced by pharmaceutical companies in a standard dosage and drug delivery form. Most pharmacists work in a community setting, such as a retail drugstore, or in a health care facility, such as a hospital, nursing home, mental health institution, or neighborhood health clinic.

Pharmacists in community and retail pharmacies counsel patients and answer questions about prescription drugs, including questions regarding possible side effects or interactions among various drugs. They provide information about over-the-counter drugs and make recommendations after talking with the patient. They also may give advice about the patient's diet, exercise, or stress management or about durable medical equipment and home health care supplies. In addition, they also may complete third-party insurance forms and other paperwork. Those who own or manage community pharmacies may sell non-health-related merchandise, hire and supervise personnel, and oversee the general operation of the pharmacy. Some community pharmacists provide specialized services to help patients manage conditions such as diabetes, asthma, smoking cessation, or high blood pressure. Some community pharmacists also are trained to administer vaccinations.

Pharmacists in health care facilities dispense medications and advise the medical staff on the selection and effects of drugs. They may make sterile solutions to be administered intravenously. They also assess, plan, and monitor drug programs or regimens. Pharmacists counsel hospitalized patients on the use of drugs and on their use at home when the patients are discharged. Pharmacists also may evaluate drug-use patterns and outcomes for patients in hospitals or managed care organizations.

Pharmacists who work in home health care monitor drug therapy and prepare infusions—solutions that are injected into patients—and other medications for use in the home.

Some pharmacists specialize in specific drug therapy areas, such as intravenous nutrition support, oncology (cancer), nuclear pharmacy (used for chemotherapy), geriatric pharmacy, and psychopharmacotherapy (the treatment of mental disorders by means of drugs).

Most pharmacists keep confidential computerized records of patients' drug therapies to prevent harmful drug interactions. Pharmacists are responsible for the accuracy of every prescription that is filled, but they often rely upon pharmacy technicians and pharmacy aides to assist them in the dispensing process. Thus, the pharmacist may delegate prescription-filling and administrative tasks and supervise their completion. Pharmacists also frequently oversee pharmacy students serving as interns in preparation for graduation and licensure.

Increasingly, pharmacists are pursuing nontraditional pharmacy work. Some are involved in research for pharmaceutical manufacturers, developing new drugs and therapies and testing their effects on people. Others work in marketing or sales, providing expertise to clients on a drug's use, effectiveness, and possible side effects. Some pharmacists work for health insurance companies, developing pharmacy benefit packages and carrying out cost-benefit analyses on certain drugs. Other pharmacists work for the government, public health care services, the armed services, and pharmacy associations. Finally, some pharmacists are employed full time or part time as college faculty, teaching classes and performing research in a wide range of areas.

Working Conditions

Pharmacists work in clean, well-lighted, and well-ventilated areas. Many pharmacists spend most of their workday on their feet. When working with sterile or dangerous pharmaceutical products, pharmacists wear gloves and masks and work with other special protective equipment. Many community and hospital pharmacies are open for extended hours or around the clock, so pharmacists may work nights, weekends, and holidays. Consultant pharmacists may travel to nursing homes or other facilities to monitor patients' drug therapy.

About 21 percent of pharmacists worked part time in 2004. Most full-time salaried pharmacists worked approximately 40 hours a week. Some, including many self-employed pharmacists, worked more than 50 hours a week.

Training, Other Qualifications, and Advancement

A license to practice pharmacy is required in all states, the District of Columbia, and all U.S. territories. To obtain a license, the prospective pharmacist must graduate from a college of pharmacy that is accredited by the Accreditation Council for Pharmacy Education (ACPE) and pass an examination. All states require the North American Pharmacist Licensure Exam (NAPLEX), which tests pharmacy skills and knowledge, and 43 states and the District of Columbia require the Multistate Pharmacy Jurisprudence Exam (MPJE), which tests pharmacy law. Both exams are administered by the National Association of Boards of Pharmacy. Pharmacists in the eight states that do not require the MJPE must pass a state-specific exam that is similar to the MJPE. In addition to the NAPLEX and MPJE, some states require additional exams unique to their state. All states except California currently grant a license without extensive reexamination to qualified pharmacists who already are licensed by another state. In Florida, reexamination is not required if a pharmacist has passed the NAPLEX and MPJE within 12 years of his or her application for a license transfer. Many pharmacists are licensed to practice in more than one state. Most states require continuing education for license renewal. Persons interested in a career as a pharmacist should check with individual state boards of pharmacy for details on examination requirements, license renewal requirements, and license transfer procedures.

In 2004, 89 colleges of pharmacy were accredited to confer degrees by the Accreditation Council for Pharmacy Education. Pharmacy programs grant the degree of Doctor of Pharmacy (Pharm.D.), which requires at least 6 years of postsecondary study and the passing of a state board of pharmacy's licensure examination. Courses offered at colleges of pharmacy are designed to teach students about all aspects of drug therapy. In addition, schools teach students how to communicate with patients and other health care providers about drug information and patient care. Students also learn professional ethics, how to develop and manage medication distribution systems, and concepts of public health. In addition to receiving classroom instruction, students in Pharm.D. programs spend about one-forth of their time learning in a variety of pharmacy practice settings under the supervision of licensed pharmacists. The Pharm.D. degree has replaced the Bachelor of Pharmacy (B.Pharm.) degree, which is no longer being awarded.

The Pharm.D. is a 4-year program that requires at least 2 years of college study prior to admittance, although most applicants have completed 3 years. Entry requirements usually include courses in mathematics and natural sciences, such as chemistry, biology, and physics, as well as courses in the humanities and social sciences. Approximately two-thirds of all colleges require applicants to take the Pharmacy College Admissions Test (PCAT).

In 2003, the American Association of Colleges of Pharmacy (AACP) launched the Pharmacy College Application Service, known as PharmCAS, for students who are interested in applying to schools and colleges of pharmacy. This centralized service allows applicants to use a single Web-based application and one set of transcripts to apply to multiple schools of pharmacy. A total of 43 schools participated in 2003.

In the 2003–04 academic year, 67 colleges of pharmacy awarded the master-of-science degree or the Ph.D. degree. Both degrees are awarded after the completion of a Pharm.D. degree and are designed for those who want more laboratory and research experience. Many master's and Ph.D. degree holders do research for a drug company or teach at a university. Other options for pharmacy graduates who are interested in further training include 1-year or 2-year residency programs or fellowships. Pharmacy residencies are postgraduate training programs in pharmacy practice and usually require the completion of a research study. There currently are more than 700 residency training programs nationwide. Pharmacy fellowships are highly individualized programs that are designed to prepare participants to work in a specialized area of pharmacy, such clinical practice or research laboratories. Some pharmacists who run their own pharmacy obtain a master's degree in business administration (MBA). Others may obtain a degree in public administration or public health.

Areas of graduate study include pharmaceutics and pharmaceutical chemistry (physical and chemical properties of drugs and dosage forms), pharmacology (effects of drugs on the body), toxicology and pharmacy administration.

Prospective pharmacists should have scientific aptitude, good communication skills, and a desire to help others. They also must be conscientious and pay close attention to detail, because the decisions they make affect human lives.

In community pharmacies, pharmacists usually begin at the staff level. In independent pharmacies, after they gain experience and secure the necessary capital, some become owners or part owners of pharmacies. Pharmacists in chain drugstores may be promoted to pharmacy supervisor or manager at the store level, then to manager at the district or regional level, and later to an executive position within the chain's headquarters.

Hospital pharmacists may advance to supervisory or administrative positions. Pharmacists in the pharmaceutical industry may advance in marketing, sales, research, quality control, production, packaging, or other areas.

Employment

Pharmacists held about 230,000 jobs in 2004. About 61 percent work in community pharmacies that are either independently owned or part of a drugstore chain, grocery store, department store, or mass merchandiser. Most community pharmacists are salaried employees, but some are self-employed owners. About 24 percent of salaried pharmacists work in hospitals. Others work in clinics, mail-order pharmacies, pharmaceutical wholesalers, home health care agencies, or the federal government.

Job Outlook

Very good employment opportunities are expected for pharmacists over the 2004–14 period because the number of job openings created by employment growth and the need to replace pharmacists who leave the occupation or retire are expected to exceed the number of degrees granted in pharmacy. Enrollments in pharmacy programs are rising as more students are attracted by high salaries and good job prospects. Despite this increase in enrollments, job openings should still be more numerous than those seeking employment.

Employment of pharmacists is expected to grow faster than the average for all occupations through the year 2014, because of the increasing demand for pharmaceuticals, particularly from the growing elderly population. The increasing numbers of middle-aged and elderly people—who use more prescription drugs than younger people—will continue to spur demand for pharmacists in all employment settings. Other factors likely to increase the demand for pharmacists include scientific advances that will make more drug products available, new developments in genome research and medication distribution systems, increasingly sophisticated consumers seeking more information about drugs, and coverage of prescription drugs by a greater number of health insurance plans and Medicare.

Community pharmacies are taking steps to manage an increasing volume of prescriptions. Automation of drug dispensing and greater employment of pharmacy technicians and pharmacy aides will help these establishments to dispense more prescriptions.

With its emphasis on cost control, managed care encourages the use of lower cost prescription drug distributors, such as mail-order firms and online pharmacies, for purchases of certain medications. Prescriptions ordered through the mail and via the Internet are filled in a central location and shipped to the patient at a lower cost. Mail-order and online pharmacies typically use automated technology to dispense medication and employ fewer pharmacists. If the utilization of mail-order pharmacies increases rapidly, job growth among pharmacists could be limited.

Employment of pharmacists will not grow as fast in hospitals as in other industries, because hospitals are reducing inpatient stays, downsizing, and consolidating departments. The number of outpatient surgeries is increasing, so more patients are being discharged and purchasing their medications through retail, supermarket, or mail-order pharmacies, rather than through hospitals. An aging population means that more pharmacy services will be required in nursing homes, assisted-living facilities, and home care settings. The most rapid job growth among pharmacists is expected in these 3 settings.

New opportunities are emerging for pharmacists in managed care organizations where they analyze trends and patterns in medication use, and in pharmacoeconomics—the cost and benefit analysis of different drug therapies. Opportunities also are emerging for pharmacists trained in research and disease management—the development of new methods for curing and controlling diseases. Pharmacists also are finding jobs in research and development and in sales and marketing for pharmaceutical manufacturing firms. New breakthroughs in biotechnology will increase the potential for drugs to treat diseases and expand the opportunities for pharmacists to conduct research and sell medications. In addition, pharmacists are finding employment opportunities in pharmacy informatics, which uses information technology to improve patient care.

Job opportunities for pharmacists in patient care will arise as cost-conscious insurers and health systems continue to emphasize the role of pharmacists in primary and preventive health care. Health insurance companies realize that the expense of using medication to treat diseases and various health conditions often is considerably less than the costs for patients whose conditions go untreated. Pharmacists also can reduce the expenses resulting from unexpected complications due to allergic reactions or interactions among medications.

Earnings

Median annual wage and salary earnings of pharmacists in May 2004 were $84,900. The middle 50 percent earned between $75,720 and $94,850 a year. The lowest 10 percent earned less than $61,200, and the highest 10 percent earned more than $109,850 a year. Median annual earnings in the industries employing the largest numbers of pharmacists in May 2004 were:

Department stores	$86,720
Grocery stores	85,680
Health and personal care stores	85,380
General medical and surgical hospitals	84,560
Other general merchandise stores	84,170

Related Occupations

Pharmacy technicians and pharmacy aides also work in pharmacies. Persons in other professions who may work with pharmaceutical compounds include biological scientists, medical scientists, and chemists and materials scientists. Increasingly, pharmacists are involved in patient care and therapy, work that they have in common with physicians and surgeons.

Sources of Additional Information

For information on pharmacy as a career, preprofessional and professional requirements, programs offered by colleges of pharmacy, and student financial aid, contact:

- American Association of Colleges of Pharmacy, 1426 Prince St., Alexandria, VA 22314. Internet: http://www.aacp.org

General information on careers in pharmacy is available from:

- American Society of Health-System Pharmacists, 7272 Wisconsin Ave., Bethesda, MD 20814. Internet: http://www.ashp.org
- National Association of Chain Drug Stores, 413 N. Lee St., P.O. Box 1417-D49, Alexandria, VA 22313-1480. Internet: http://www.nacds.org
- Academy of Managed Care Pharmacy, 100 North Pitt St., Suite 400, Alexandria, VA 22314. Internet: http://www.amcp.org
- American Pharmacists Association, 2215 Constitution Ave. NW, Washington, DC 20037-2985. Internet: http://www.aphanet.org

Information on the North American Pharmacist Licensure Exam (NAPLEX) and the Multistate Pharmacy Jurisprudence Exam (MPJE) is available from:

- National Association of Boards of Pharmacy, 1600 Feehanville Dr., Mount Prospect, IL 60056. Internet: http://www.nabp.net

State licensure requirements are available from each state's board of pharmacy. Information on specific college entrance requirements, curriculums, and financial aid is available from any college of pharmacy.

Pharmacy Technicians

(O*NET 29-2052.00)

Significant Points

- Job opportunities are expected to be good for full-time and part-time work, especially for those with certification or previous work experience.
- Many technicians work evenings, weekends, and holidays.
- About 7 out of 10 of jobs are in retail pharmacies, grocery stores, department stores, or mass retailers.

Nature of the Work

Pharmacy technicians help licensed pharmacists provide medication and other health care products to patients. Technicians usually perform routine tasks to help prepare prescribed medication for patients, such as counting tablets and labeling bottles. Technicians refer any questions regarding prescriptions, drug information, or health matters to a *pharmacist*.

Pharmacy aides work closely with pharmacy technicians. They often are clerks or cashiers who primarily answer telephones, handle money, stock shelves, and perform other clerical duties. Pharmacy technicians usually perform more complex tasks than do pharmacy aides, although in some states their duties and job titles may overlap.

Pharmacy technicians who work in retail or mail-order pharmacies have varying responsibilities, depending on state rules and regulations. Technicians receive written prescriptions or requests for prescription refills from patients. They also may receive prescriptions sent electronically from the doctor's office. They must verify that the information on the prescription is complete and accurate. To prepare the prescription, technicians must retrieve, count, pour, weigh, measure, and sometimes mix the medication. Then, they prepare the prescription labels, select the type of prescription container, and affix the prescription and auxiliary labels to the container. Once the prescription is filled, technicians price and file the prescription, which must be checked by a pharmacist before it is given to the patient. Technicians may establish and maintain patient profiles, prepare insurance claim forms, and stock and take inventory of prescription and over-the-counter medications.

In hospitals, nursing homes, and assisted-living facilities, technicians have added responsibilities, including reading patients' charts and preparing and delivering the medicine to patients. Still, the pharmacist must check the order before it is delivered to the patient. The technician then copies the information about the prescribed medication onto the patient's profile. Technicians also may assemble a 24-hour supply of medicine for every patient. They package and label each dose separately. The packages are then placed in the medicine cabinets of patients until the supervising pharmacist checks them for accuracy. The packages are then given to the patients.

Working Conditions

Pharmacy technicians work in clean, organized, well-lighted, and well-ventilated areas. Most of their workday is spent on their feet. They may be required to lift heavy boxes or to use stepladders to retrieve supplies from high shelves.

Technicians work the same hours that pharmacists work. These may include evenings, nights, weekends, and holidays, particularly in facilities, such as hospitals and retail pharmacies, that are open 24 hours a day. As their seniority increases, technicians often acquire increased control over the hours they work. There are many opportunities for part-time work in both retail and hospital settings.

Training, Other Qualifications, and Advancement

Although most pharmacy technicians receive informal on-the-job training, employers favor those who have completed formal training and certification. However, there are currently few state and no federal requirements for formal training or certification of pharmacy technicians. Employers who have insufficient resources to give on-the-job training often seek formally educated pharmacy technicians. Formal education programs and certification emphasize the technician's interest in and dedication to the work. In addition to the military, some hospitals, proprietary schools, vocational or technical colleges, and community colleges offer formal education programs.

Formal pharmacy technician education programs require classroom and laboratory work in a variety of areas, including medical and pharmaceutical terminology, pharmaceutical calculations, pharmacy recordkeeping, pharmaceutical techniques, and pharmacy law and ethics. Technicians also are required to learn medication names, actions, uses, and doses. Many training programs include internships, in which students gain hands-on experience in actual pharmacies. Students receive a diploma, a certificate, or an associate's degree, depending on the program.

Prospective pharmacy technicians with experience working as an aide in a community pharmacy or volunteering in a hospital may have an advantage. Employers also prefer applicants with strong customer service and communication skills, as well as those with experience managing inventories, counting tablets, measuring dosages, and using computers. Technicians entering the field need strong mathematics, spelling, and reading skills. A background in chemistry, English, and health education also may be beneficial. Some technicians are hired without formal training, but under the condition that they obtain certification within a specified period to retain their employment.

The Pharmacy Technician Certification Board administers the National Pharmacy Technician Certification Examination. This exam is voluntary in most states and displays the competency of the individual to act as a pharmacy technician. However, more states and employers are requiring certification as reliance on pharmacy technicians grows. Eligible candidates must have a high school diploma or GED and no felony convictions, and those who pass the exam earn the title of Certified Pharmacy Technician (CPhT). The exam is offered several times per year at various locations nationally. Employers—often pharmacists—know that individuals who pass the exam have a standardized body of knowledge and skills. Many employers also will reimburse the costs of the exam as an incentive for certification.

Certified technicians must be recertified every 2 years. Technicians must complete 20 contact hours of pharmacy-related topics within the 2-year certification period to become eligible for recertification. Contact hours are awarded for on-the-job training, attending lectures, and college coursework. At least 1 contact hour must be in pharmacy law. Contact hours can be earned from several different sources, including pharmacy associations, pharmacy colleges, and pharmacy technician training programs. Up to 10 contact hours can be earned when the technician is employed under the direct supervision and instruction of a pharmacist.

Successful pharmacy technicians are alert, observant, organized, dedicated, and responsible. They should be willing and able to take directions. They must be precise; details are sometimes a matter of life and death. Although a pharmacist must check and approve all their work, they should be able to work independently without constant instruction from the pharmacist. Candidates interested in becoming pharmacy technicians cannot have prior records of drug or substance abuse.

Strong interpersonal and communication skills are needed because pharmacy technicians interact daily with patients, co-workers, and health care professionals. Teamwork is very important because technicians often are required to work with pharmacists, aides, and other technicians.

Employment

Pharmacy technicians held about 258,000 jobs in 2004. About 7 out of 10 jobs were in retail pharmacies, either independently owned or part of a drugstore chain, grocery store, department store, or mass retailer. About 2 out of 10 jobs were in hospitals and a small proportion was in mail-order and Internet pharmacies, clinics, pharmaceutical wholesalers, and the federal government.

Job Outlook

Good job opportunities are expected for full-time and part-time work, especially for technicians with formal training or previous experience. Job openings for pharmacy technicians will result from the expansion of retail pharmacies and other employment settings and from the need to replace workers who transfer to other occupations or leave the labor force.

Employment of pharmacy technicians is expected to grow much faster than the average for all occupations through 2014 because as the population grows and ages, demand for pharmaceuticals will increase dramatically. The increased number of middle-aged and elderly people—who use more prescription drugs than younger people—will spur demand for technicians in all practice settings. With advances in science, more medications are becoming available to treat a greater number of conditions.

In addition, cost-conscious insurers, pharmacies, and health systems will continue to expand the role of technicians. As a result, pharmacy technicians will assume responsibility for some of the more routine tasks previously performed by pharmacists. Pharmacy technicians also will need to learn and master new pharmacy technology as it emerges. For example, robotic machines are being increasingly used to dispense medicine into containers; technicians must oversee the machines, stock the bins, and label the containers. Thus, while automation is increasingly incorporated into the job, it will not necessarily reduce the need for technicians.

Almost all states have legislated the maximum number of technicians who can safely work under a pharmacist at one time. In some states, technicians have assumed more medication-dispensing duties as pharmacists have become more involved in patient care, resulting in more technicians per pharmacist. Changes in these laws could directly affect employment.

Earnings

Median hourly earnings of wage and salary pharmacy technicians in May 2004 were $11.37. The middle 50 percent earned between $9.40 and $13.85. The lowest 10 percent earned less than $7.96, and the highest 10 percent earned more than $16.61. Median hourly earnings in the industries employing the largest numbers of pharmacy technicians in May 2004 were:

General medical and surgical hospitals $12.93
Grocery stores..11.77

Other general merchandise stores	11.11
Department stores	10.56
Health and personal care stores	10.51

Certified technicians may earn more. Shift differentials for working evenings or weekends also can increase earnings. Some technicians belong to unions representing hospital or grocery store workers.

Related Occupations

This occupation is most closely related to pharmacists and pharmacy aides. Workers in other medical support occupations include dental assistants, licensed practical and licensed vocational nurses, medical transcriptionists, medical records and health information technicians, occupational therapist assistants and aides, physical therapist assistants and aides, and surgical technologists.

Sources of Additional Information

For information on the Certified Pharmacy Technician designation, contact:

- Pharmacy Technician Certification Board, 2215 Constitution Ave. NW, Washington DC 20037-2985. Internet: http://www.ptcb.org

For a list of accredited pharmacy technician training programs, contact:

- American Society of Health-System Pharmacists, 7272 Wisconsin Ave., Bethesda, MD 20814. Internet: http://www.ashp.org

For pharmacy technician career information, contact:

- National Pharmacy Technician Association, P.O. Box 683148, Houston, TX 77268. Internet: http://www.pharmacytechnician.org

Physical Therapist Assistants and Aides

(O*NET 31-2021.00 and 31-2022.00)

Significant Points

- Employment is projected to increase much faster than average; physical therapist aides may face keen competition from the large pool of qualified applicants.
- Physical therapist assistants generally have an associate degree, but physical therapist aides usually learn skills on the job.
- About 60 percent of jobs are in hospitals or offices of physical therapists.

Nature of the Work

Physical therapist assistants and aides perform components of physical therapy procedures and related tasks selected by a supervising physical therapist. These workers assist physical therapists in providing services that help improve mobility, relieve pain, and prevent or limit permanent physical disabilities of patients suffering from injuries or disease. Patients include accident victims and individuals with disabling conditions such as low-back pain, arthritis, heart disease, fractures, head injuries, and cerebral palsy.

Physical therapist assistants perform a variety of tasks. Components of treatment procedures performed by these workers, under the direction and supervision of physical therapists, involve exercises, massages, electrical stimulation, paraffin baths, hot and cold packs, traction, and ultrasound. Physical therapist assistants record the patient's responses to treatment and report the outcome of each treatment to the physical therapist.

Physical therapist aides help make therapy sessions productive under the direct supervision of a physical therapist or physical therapist assistant. They usually are responsible for keeping the treatment area clean and organized and for preparing for each patient's therapy. When patients need assistance moving to or from a treatment area, aides push them in a wheelchair or provide them with a shoulder to lean on. Because they are not licensed, aides do not perform the clinical tasks of a physical therapist assistant.

The duties of aides include some clerical tasks, such as ordering depleted supplies, answering the phone, and filling out insurance forms and other paperwork. The extent to which an aide or an assistant performs clerical tasks depends on the size and location of the facility.

Working Conditions

The hours and days that physical therapist assistants and aides work vary with the facility and with whether they are full- or part-time employees. Many outpatient physical therapy offices and clinics have evening and weekend hours to help coincide with patients' personal schedules. About 30 percent of all physical therapist assistants and aides work part time.

Physical therapist assistants and aides need a moderate degree of strength because of the physical exertion required in assisting patients with their treatment. In some cases, assistants and aides need to lift patients. Constant kneeling, stooping, and standing for long periods also are part of the job.

Training, Other Qualifications, and Advancement

Physical therapist aides are trained on the job, but physical therapist assistants typically earn an associate degree from an accredited physical therapist assistant program. Not all states require licensure or registration in order for the physical therapist assistant to practice. The states that require licensure stipulate specific educational and examination criteria. Complete information on practice acts and regulations can be obtained from the state licensing boards. Additional requirements may include certification in cardiopulmonary resuscitation (CPR) and other first aid and a minimum number of hours of clinical experience.

According to the American Physical Therapy Association, there were 238 accredited physical therapist assistant programs in the United States as of 2004. Accredited physical therapist assistant programs are designed to last 2 years, or 4 semesters, and culminate in an associate degree. Programs are divided into academic study and hands on clinical experience. Academic coursework includes algebra, anatomy and physiology, biology, chemistry, and psychology. Many programs require that students complete a semester of anatomy and physiology and have certifications in CPR and other first aid even before they begin their clinical field experience. Both educators and prospective employers view clinical experience as integral to ensuring that students understand the responsibilities of a physical therapist assistant.

Employers typically require physical therapist aides to have a high school diploma, strong interpersonal skills, and a desire to assist people in need. Most employers provide clinical on-the-job training.

Employment

Physical therapist assistants and aides held about 101,000 jobs in 2004. Physical therapist assistants held about 59,000 jobs, physical therapist aides approximately 43,000. Both work with physical therapists in a variety of settings. About 60 percent of jobs were in hospitals or in offices of physical therapists. Others worked primarily in nursing care facilities, offices of physicians, home health care services, and outpatient care centers.

Job Outlook

Employment of physical therapist assistants and aides is expected to grow much faster than the average for all occupations through the year 2014. The impact of proposed federal legislation imposing limits on reimbursement for therapy services may adversely affect the short-term job outlook for physical therapist assistants and aides. However, over the long run, demand for physical therapist assistants and aides will continue to rise in accordance with the increasing number of individuals with disabilities or limited function. The growing elderly population is particularly vulnerable to chronic and debilitating conditions that require therapeutic services. These patients often need additional assistance in their treatment, making the roles of assistants and aides vital. The large baby boom generation is entering the prime age for heart attacks and strokes, further increasing the demand for cardiac and physical rehabilitation. In addition, future medical developments should permit an increased percentage of trauma victims to survive, creating added demand for therapy services.

Physical therapists are expected to increasingly utilize assistants to reduce the cost of physical therapy services. Once a patient is evaluated and a treatment plan is designed by the physical therapist, the physical therapist assistant can provide many aspects of treatment as prescribed by the therapist.

Physical therapist assistants and aides with prior experience working in a physical therapy office or other health care setting will have the best job opportunities. Physical therapist aides may face keen competition from the large pool of qualified individuals with a high school diploma.

Earnings

Median annual earnings of physical therapist assistants were $37,890 in May 2004. The middle 50 percent earned between $31,060 and $44,050. The lowest 10 percent earned less than $24,110, and the highest 10 percent earned more than $52,110. Median annual earnings in the industries employing the largest numbers of physical therapist aides in May 2004 were:

Nursing care facilities......................................$40,360
General medical and surgical hospitals 37,790
Offices of other health practitioners......................37,120

Median annual earnings of physical therapist aides were $21,380 in May 2004. The middle 50 percent earned between $17,990 and $26,310. The lowest 10 percent earned less than $15,380, and the highest 10 percent earned more than $33,550. Median annual earnings of physical therapist aides in May 2004 were $21,120 in general medical and surgical hospitals and $20,360 in offices of physical therapists.

Related Occupations

Physical therapist assistants and aides work under the supervision of physical therapists. Other workers in the health care field who work under similar supervision include dental assistants, medical assistants, occupational therapist assistants and aides, pharmacy aides, pharmacy technicians, and social and human service assistants.

Sources of Additional Information

Career information on physical therapist assistants and a list of schools offering accredited programs can be obtained from:

- The American Physical Therapy Association, 1111 North Fairfax St., Alexandria, VA 22314-1488. Internet: http://www.apta.org

Physical Therapists

(O*NET 29 1123.00)

Significant Points

- Employment is expected to increase much faster than the average, as growth in the number of individuals with disabilities or limited functioning spurs demand for therapy services.
- Job opportunities should be particularly good in acute hospital, rehabilitation, and orthopedic settings.
- After graduating from an accredited physical therapist educational program, therapists must pass a licensure exam before they can practice.
- Nearly 6 out of 10 physical therapists work in hospitals or in offices of physical therapists.

Nature of the Work

Physical therapists provide services that help restore function, improve mobility, relieve pain, and prevent or limit permanent physical disabilities of patients suffering from injuries or disease. They restore, maintain, and promote overall fitness and health. Their patients include accident victims and individuals with disabling conditions such as low-back pain, arthritis, heart disease, fractures, head injuries, and cerebral palsy.

Therapists examine patients' medical histories and then test and measure the patients' strength, range of motion, balance and coordination, posture, muscle performance, respiration, and motor function. They also determine patients' ability to be independent and reintegrate into the community or workplace after injury or illness. Next, physical therapists develop plans describing a treatment strategy, its purpose, and its anticipated outcome. Physical therapist assistants, under the direction and supervision of a physical therapist, may be involved in implementing treatment plans with patients. Physical therapist aides perform routine support tasks, as directed by the therapist.

Treatment often includes exercise for patients who have been immobilized and lack flexibility, strength, or endurance. Physical therapists encourage patients to use their own muscles to increase their flexibility and range of motion before finally advancing to other exercises that improve strength, balance, coordination, and endurance. The goal is to improve how an individual functions at work and at home.

Physical therapists also use electrical stimulation, hot packs or cold compresses, and ultrasound to relieve pain and reduce swelling. They may use traction or deep-tissue massage to relieve pain. Therapists also teach patients to use assistive and adaptive devices, such as crutches, prostheses, and wheelchairs. They also may show patients exercises to do at home to expedite their recovery.

As treatment continues, physical therapists document the patient's progress, conduct periodic examinations, and modify treatments when necessary. Besides tracking the patient's progress, such documentation identifies areas requiring more or less attention.

Physical therapists often consult and practice with a variety of other professionals, such as physicians, dentists, nurses, educators, social workers, occupational therapists, speech-language pathologists, and audiologists.

Some physical therapists treat a wide range of ailments; others specialize in areas such as pediatrics, geriatrics, orthopedics, sports medicine, neurology, and cardiopulmonary physical therapy.

Working Conditions

Physical therapists practice in hospitals, clinics, and private offices that have specially equipped facilities, or they treat patients in hospital rooms, homes, or schools.

In 2004, most full-time physical therapists worked a 40-hour week; some worked evenings and weekends to fit their patients' schedules. About 1 in 4 physical therapists worked part time. The job can be physically demanding because therapists often have to stoop, kneel, crouch, lift, and stand for long periods. In addition, physical therapists move heavy equipment and lift patients or help them turn, stand, or walk.

Training, Other Qualifications, and Advancement

All states require physical therapists to pass a licensure exam before they can practice, after graduating from an accredited physical therapist educational program.

According to the American Physical Therapy Association, there were 205 accredited physical therapist programs in 2004. Of the accredited programs, 94 offered master's degrees, and 111 offered doctoral degrees. All physical therapist programs seeking accreditation are required to offer degrees at the master's degree level and above, in accordance with the Commission on Accreditation in Physical Therapy Education.

Physical therapist programs start with basic science courses such as biology, chemistry, and physics and then introduce specialized courses, including biomechanics, neuroanatomy, human growth and development, manifestations of disease, examination techniques, and therapeutic procedures. Besides getting classroom and laboratory instruction, students receive supervised clinical experience. Among the courses that are useful when one applies to a physical therapist educational program are anatomy, biology, chemistry, social science, mathematics, and physics. Before granting admission, many professional education programs require experience as a volunteer in a physical therapy department of a hospital or clinic. For high school students, volunteering with the school athletic trainer is a good way to gain experience.

Physical therapists should have strong interpersonal skills in order to be able to educate patients about their physical therapy treatments. Physical therapists also should be compassionate and possess a desire to help patients. Similar traits are needed to interact with the patient's family.

Physical therapists are expected to continue their professional development by participating in continuing education courses and workshops. In fact, a number of states require continuing education as a condition of maintaining licensure.

Employment

Physical therapists held about 155,000 jobs in 2004. The number of jobs is greater than the number of practicing physical therapists, because some physical therapists hold two or more jobs. For example, some may work in a private practice, but also work part time in another health care facility.

Nearly 6 out of 10 physical therapists worked in hospitals or in offices of physical therapists. Other jobs were in home health care services, nursing care facilities, outpatient care centers, and offices of physicians.

Some physical therapists were self-employed in private practices, seeing individual patients and contracting to provide services in hospitals, rehabilitation centers, nursing care facilities, home health care agencies, adult day care programs, and schools. Physical therapists also teach in academic institutions and conduct research.

Job Outlook

Employment of physical therapists is expected to grow much faster than the average for all occupations through 2014. The impact of proposed federal legislation imposing limits on reimbursement for therapy services may adversely affect the short-term job outlook for physical therapists. However, over the long run, the demand for physical therapists should continue to rise as growth in the number of individuals with disabilities or limited function spurs demand for therapy services. Job opportunities should be particularly good in acute hospital, rehabilitation, and orthopedic settings, because the elderly receive the most treatment in these settings. The growing elderly population is particularly vulnerable to chronic and debilitating conditions that require therapeutic services. Also, the baby-boom generation is entering the prime age for heart attacks and strokes, increasing the demand for cardiac and physical rehabilitation. Further, young people will need physical therapy as technological advances save the lives of a larger proportion of newborns with severe birth defects.

Future medical developments also should permit a higher percentage of trauma victims to survive, creating additional demand for rehabilitative care. In addition, growth may result from advances in medical technology that could permit the treatment of more disabling conditions.

Widespread interest in health promotion also should increase demand for physical therapy services. A growing number of employers are using physical therapists to evaluate worksites, develop exercise programs, and teach safe work habits to employees in the hope of reducing injuries in the workplace.

Earnings

Median annual earnings of physical therapists were $60,180 in May 2004. The middle 50 percent earned between $50,330 and $71,760. The lowest 10 percent earned less than $42,010, and the highest 10 percent earned more than $88,580. Median annual earnings in the industries employing the largest numbers of physical therapists in May 2004 were:

Home health care services	$64,650
Nursing care facilities	61,720
Offices of physicians	61,270
General medical and surgical hospitals	60,350
Offices of other health practitioners	60,130

Related Occupations

Physical therapists rehabilitate persons with physical disabilities. Others who work in the rehabilitation field include audiologists, chiropractors, occupational therapists, recreational therapists, rehabilitation counselors, respiratory therapists, and speech-language pathologists.

Sources of Additional Information

Additional career information and a list of accredited educational programs in physical therapy are available from:

- American Physical Therapy Association, 1111 North Fairfax St., Alexandria, VA 22314-1488. Internet: http://www.apta.org

Physician Assistants

(O*NET 29-1071.00)

Significant Points

- Physician assistant programs usually last at least 2 years; admission requirements vary by program, but many require at least 2 years of college and some health care experience.
- All states require physician assistants to complete an accredited education program and to pass a national exam in order to obtain a license.
- Physician assistants rank among the fastest growing occupations, as physicians and health care institutions increasingly utilize physician assistants in order to contain costs.
- Job opportunities should be good, particularly in rural and inner city clinics.

Nature of the Work

Physician assistants (PAs) practice medicine under the supervision of physicians and surgeons. They should not be confused with medical assistants, who perform routine clinical and clerical tasks. PAs are formally trained to provide diagnostic, therapeutic, and preventive health care services, as delegated by a physician. Working as members of the health care team, they take medical histories, examine and treat patients, order and interpret laboratory tests and X rays, and make diagnoses. They also treat minor injuries, by suturing, splinting, and casting. PAs record progress notes, instruct and counsel patients, and order or carry out therapy. In 48 states and the District of Columbia, physician assistants may prescribe medications. PAs also may have managerial duties. Some order medical supplies or equipment and supervise technicians and assistants.

Physician assistants work under the supervision of a physician. However, PAs may be the principal care providers in rural or inner city clinics, where a physician is present for only 1 or 2 days each week. In such cases, the PA confers with the supervising physician and other medical professionals as needed and as required by law. PAs also may make house calls or go to hospitals and nursing care facilities to check on patients, after which they report back to the physician.

The duties of physician assistants are determined by the supervising physician and by state law. Aspiring PAs should investigate the laws and regulations in the states in which they wish to practice.

Many PAs work in primary care specialties, such as general internal medicine, pediatrics, and family medicine. Other specialty areas include general and thoracic surgery, emergency medicine, orthopedics, and geriatrics. PAs specializing in surgery provide preoperative and postoperative care and may work as first or second assistants during major surgery.

Working Conditions

Although PAs usually work in a comfortable, well lighted environment, those in surgery often stand for long periods, and others do considerable walking. Schedules vary according to the practice setting, and often depend on the hours of the supervising physician. The workweek of hospital-based PAs may include weekends, nights, or early morning hospital rounds to visit patients. These workers also may be on call. PAs in clinics usually work a 40-hour week.

Training, Other Qualifications, and Advancement

All states require that PAs complete an accredited, formal education program and pass a national exam to obtain a license. PA programs usually last at least 2 years and are full time. Most programs are in schools of allied health, academic health centers, medical schools, or 4-year colleges; a few are in community colleges, the military, or hospitals. Many accredited PA programs have clinical teaching affiliations with medical schools.

In 2005, more than 135 education programs for physician assistants were accredited or provisionally accredited by the American Academy of Physician Assistants. More than 90 of these programs offered the option of a master's degree, and the rest offered either a bachelor's degree or an associate degree. Most applicants to PA educational programs already have a bachelor's degree.

Admission requirements vary, but many programs require 2 years of college and some work experience in the health care field. Students should take courses in biology, English, chemistry, mathematics, psychology, and the social sciences. Many PAs have prior experience as registered nurses, while others come from varied backgrounds, including military corpsman/medics and allied health occupations such as respiratory therapists, physical therapists, and emergency medical technicians and paramedics.

PA education includes classroom instruction in biochemistry, pathology, human anatomy, physiology, microbiology, clinical pharmacology, clinical medicine, geriatric and home health care, disease prevention, and medical ethics. Students obtain supervised clinical training in several areas, including family medicine, internal medicine, surgery, prenatal care and gynecology, geriatrics, emergency medicine, psychiatry, and pediatrics. Sometimes, PA students serve one or more of these "rotations" under the supervision of a physician who is seeking to hire a PA. The rotations often lead to permanent employment.

All states and the District of Columbia have legislation governing the qualifications or practice of physician assistants. All jurisdictions require physician assistants to pass the Physician Assistant National Certifying Examination, administered by the National Commission on Certification of Physician Assistants (NCCPA) and open only to graduates of accredited PA education programs. Only those successfully completing the examination may use the credential "Physician Assistant-Certified." In order to remain certified, PAs must complete 100 hours of continuing medical education every 2 years. Every 6 years, they must pass a recertification examination or complete an alternative program combining learning experiences and a take-home examination.

Some PAs pursue additional education in a specialty such as surgery, neonatology, or emergency medicine. PA postgraduate educational programs are available in areas such as internal medicine, rural primary care, emergency medicine, surgery, pediatrics, neonatology, and occupational medicine. Candidates must be graduates of an accredited program and be certified by the NCCPA.

Physician assistants need leadership skills, self-confidence, and emotional stability. They must be willing to continue studying throughout their career to keep up with medical advances.

As they attain greater clinical knowledge and experience, PAs can advance to added responsibilities and higher earnings. However, by the very nature of the profession, clinically practicing PAs always are supervised by physicians.

Employment

Physician assistants held about 62,000 jobs in 2004. The number of jobs is greater than the number of practicing PAs because some hold two or more jobs. For example, some PAs work with a supervising physician, but also work in another practice, clinic, or hospital. According to the American Academy of Physician Assistants, about 15 percent of actively practicing PAs worked in more than one clinical job concurrently in 2004.

More than half of jobs for PAs were in the offices of physicians. About a quarter were in hospitals, public or private. The rest were mostly in outpatient care centers, including health maintenance organizations; the federal government; and public or private colleges, universities, and professional schools. A few were self-employed.

Job Outlook

Employment of PAs is expected to grow much faster than average for all occupations through the year 2014, ranking among the fastest growing occupations, due to anticipated expansion of the health care industry and an emphasis on cost containment, resulting in increasing utilization of PAs by physicians and health care institutions.

Physicians and institutions are expected to employ more PAs to provide primary care and to assist with medical and surgical procedures because PAs are cost-effective and productive members of the health care team. Physician assistants can relieve physicians of routine duties and procedures. Telemedicine—using technology to facilitate interactive consultations between physicians and physician assistants—also will expand the use of physician assistants. Job opportunities for PAs should be good, particularly in rural and inner city clinics, because those settings have difficulty attracting physicians.

Besides the traditional office-based setting, PAs should find a growing number of jobs in institutional settings such as hospitals, academic medical centers, public clinics, and prisons. Additional PAs may be needed to augment medical staffing in inpatient teaching hospital settings as the number of hours physician residents are permitted to work is reduced, encouraging hospitals to use PAs to supply some physician resident services. Opportunities will be best in states that allow PAs a wider scope of practice.

Earnings

Median annual earnings of physician assistants were $69,410 in May 2004. The middle 50 percent earned between $57,110 and $83,560. The lowest 10 percent earned less than $37,320, and the highest 10 percent earned more than $94,880. Median annual earnings of physician assistants in 2004 were $70,310 in general medical and surgical hospitals and $69,210 in offices of physicians.

According to the American Academy of Physician Assistants, median income for physician assistants in full-time clinical practice in 2004 was $74,264; median income for first-year graduates was $64,536. Income varies by specialty, practice setting, geographical location, and years of experience. Employers often pay for their employees' liability insurance, registration fees with the Drug Enforcement Administration, state licensing fees, and credentialing fees.

Related Occupations

Other health care workers who provide direct patient care that requires a similar level of skill and training include audiologists, occupational therapists, physical therapists, registered nurses, and speech-language pathologists.

Sources of Additional Information

For information on a career as a physician assistant, including a list of accredited programs, contact:

- American Academy of Physician Assistants Information Center, 950 North Washington St., Alexandria, VA 22314-1552. Internet: http://www.aapa.org

For eligibility requirements and a description of the Physician Assistant National Certifying Examination, contact:

- National Commission on Certification of Physician Assistants, Inc., 12000 Findley Rd., Suite 200, Duluth, GA 30097. Internet: http://www.nccpa.net

Physicians and Surgeons

(O*NET 29-1061.00, 29-1062.00, 29-1063.00, 29-1064.00, 29-1065.00, 29-1066.00, 29-1067.00, and 29-1069.99)

Significant Points

- Many physicians and surgeons work long, irregular hours; over one-third of full-time physicians worked 60 or more hours a week in 2004.
- Formal education and training requirements are among the most demanding of any occupation, but earnings are among the highest.
- Job opportunities should be very good, particularly in rural and low-income areas.
- New physicians are much less likely to enter solo practice and more likely to work as salaried employees of group medical practices, clinics, hospitals, or health networks.

Nature of the Work

Physicians and surgeons serve a fundamental role in our society and have an effect upon all our lives. They diagnose illnesses and prescribe and administer treatment for people suffering from injury or disease. Physicians examine patients, obtain medical histories, and order, perform, and interpret diagnostic tests. They counsel patients on diet, hygiene, and preventive health care.

There are two types of physicians: M.D.—Doctor of Medicine—and D.O.—Doctor of Osteopathic Medicine. M.D.s also are known as allopathic physicians. While both M.D.s and D.O.s may use all accepted methods of treatment, including drugs and surgery, D.O.s place special emphasis on the body's musculoskeletal system, preventive medicine, and holistic patient care. D.O.s are more likely than M.D.s to be primary care specialists although they can be found in all specialties. About half of D.O.s practice general or family medicine, general internal medicine, or general pediatrics.

Physicians work in one or more of several specialties, including, but not limited to, anesthesiology, family and general medicine, general internal medicine, general pediatrics, obstetrics and gynecology, psychiatry, and surgery.

Anesthesiologists. Anesthesiologists focus on the care of surgical patients and pain relief. Like other physicians, they evaluate and treat patients and direct the efforts of those on their staffs. Anesthesiologists confer with other physicians and surgeons about appropriate treatments and procedures before, during, and after operations. These critical care specialists are responsible for maintenance of the patient's vital life functions—heart rate, body temperature, blood pressure, breathing—through continual monitoring and assessment during surgery. They often work outside of the operating room, providing pain relief in the intensive care unit, during labor and delivery, and for those who suffer from chronic pain.

Family and general practitioners. Family and general practitioners are often the first point of contact for people seeking health care, acting as the traditional family doctor. They assess and treat a wide range of conditions, ailments, and injuries, from sinus and respiratory infections to broken bones and scrapes. Family and general practitioners typically have a patient base of regular, long-term visitors. Patients with more serious conditions are referred to specialists or other health care facilities for more intensive care.

General internists. General internists diagnose and provide nonsurgical treatment for diseases and injuries of internal organ systems. They provide care mainly for adults who have a wide range of problems associated with the internal organs, such as the stomach, kidneys, liver, and digestive tract. Internists use a variety of diagnostic techniques to treat patients through medication or hospitalization. Like general practitioners, general internists are commonly looked upon as primary care specialists. They have patients referred to them by other specialists, in turn referring patients to those and yet other specialists when more complex care is required.

General pediatricians. Providing care from birth to early adulthood, pediatricians are concerned with the health of infants, children, and teenagers. They specialize in the diagnosis and treatment of a variety of ailments specific to young people and track their patients' growth to adulthood. Like most physicians, pediatricians work with different health care workers, such as nurses and other physicians, to assess and treat children with various ailments, such as muscular dystrophy. Most of the work of pediatricians, however, involves treating day-to-day illnesses that are common to children—minor injuries, infectious diseases, and immunizations—much as a general practitioner treats adults. Some pediatricians specialize in serious medical conditions and pediatric surgery, treating autoimmune disorders or serious chronic ailments.

Obstetricians and gynecologists. Obstetricians and gynecologists (ob/gyns) are specialists whose focus is women's health. They are responsible for general medical care for women, but also provide care related to pregnancy and the reproductive system. Like general practitioners, ob/gyns are concerned with the prevention, diagnosis, and treatment of general health problems, but they focus on ailments specific to the female anatomy, such as breast and cervical cancer, urinary tract and pelvic disorders, and hormonal disorders. Ob/gyns also specialize in childbirth, treating and counseling women throughout their pregnancy, from giving prenatal diagnoses to delivery and postpartum care. Ob/gyns track the health of, and treat, both mother and fetus as the pregnancy progresses.

Psychiatrists. Psychiatrists are the primary caregivers in the area of mental health. They assess and treat mental illnesses through a combination of psychotherapy, psychoanalysis, hospitalization, and medication. Psychotherapy involves regular discussions with patients about their problems; the psychiatrist helps them find solutions through changes in their behavioral patterns, the exploration of their past experiences, and group and family therapy sessions. Psychoanalysis involves long-term psychotherapy and counseling for patients. In many cases, medications are administered to correct chemical imbalances that may be causing emotional problems. Psychiatrists may also administer electroconvulsive therapy to those of their patients who do not respond to, or who cannot take, medications.

Surgeons. Surgeons are physicians who specialize in the treatment of injury, disease, and deformity through operations. Using a variety of instruments, and with patients under general or local anesthesia, a surgeon corrects physical deformities, repairs bone and tissue after injuries, or performs preventive surgeries on patients with debilitating diseases or disorders. Although a large number perform general surgery, many surgeons choose to specialize in a specific area. One of the most prevalent specialties is orthopedic surgery: the treatment of the musculoskeletal system. Others include neurological surgery (treatment of the brain and nervous system), cardiovascular surgery, otolaryngology (treatment of the ear, nose, and throat), and plastic or reconstructive surgery. Like primary care and other specialist physicians, surgeons also examine patients, perform and interpret diagnostic tests, and counsel patients on preventive health care.

A number of other medical specialists, including allergists, cardiologists, dermatologists, emergency physicians, gastroenterologists, ophthalmologists, pathologists, and radiologists, also work in clinics, hospitals, and private offices.

Working Conditions

Many physicians—primarily general and family practitioners, general internists, pediatricians, ob/gyns, and psychiatrists—work in small private offices or clinics, often assisted by a small staff of nurses and other administrative personnel. Increasingly, physicians are practicing in groups or health care organizations that provide backup coverage and allow for more time off. These physicians often work as part of a team coordinating care for a population of patients; they are less independent than solo practitioners of the past.

Surgeons and anesthesiologists typically work in well-lighted, sterile environments while performing surgery and often stand for long periods. Most work in hospitals or in surgical outpatient centers. Many physicians and surgeons work long, irregular hours. Over one-third of full-time physicians and surgeons worked 60 hours or more a week in 2004. Only 8 percent of all physicians and surgeons worked part-time, compared with 16 percent for all occupations. Physicians and surgeons must travel frequently between office and hospital to care for their patients. Those who are on call deal with many patients' concerns over the phone and may make emergency visits to hospitals or nursing homes.

Training, Other Qualifications, and Advancement

Formal education and training requirements for physicians are among the most demanding of any occupation—4 years of undergraduate school, 4 years of medical school, and 3 to 8 years of internship and residency, depending on the specialty selected. A few medical schools offer combined undergraduate and medical school programs that last 6 rather than the customary 8 years.

Premedical students must complete undergraduate work in physics, biology, mathematics, English, and inorganic and organic chemistry. Students also take courses in the humanities and the social sciences. Some students volunteer at local hospitals or clinics to gain practical experience in the health professions.

The minimum educational requirement for entry into a medical school is 3 years of college; most applicants, however, have at least a bachelor's degree, and many have advanced degrees. There are 146 medical schools in the United States—126 teach allopathic medicine and award a Doctor of Medicine (M.D.) degree; 20 teach osteopathic medicine and award the Doctor of Osteopathic Medicine (D.O.) degree. Acceptance to medical school is highly competitive. Applicants must submit transcripts, scores from the Medical College Admission Test, and letters of recommendation. Schools also consider an applicant's character, personality, leadership qualities, and participation in extracurricular activities. Most schools require an interview with members of the admissions committee.

Students spend most of the first 2 years of medical school in laboratories and classrooms, taking courses such as anatomy, biochemistry, physiology, pharmacology, psychology, microbiology, pathology, medical ethics, and laws governing medicine. They also learn to take medical histories, examine patients, and diagnose illnesses. During their last 2 years, students work with patients under the supervision of experienced physicians in hospitals and clinics, learning acute, chronic, preventive, and rehabilitative care. Through rotations in internal medicine, family practice, obstetrics and gynecology, pediatrics, psychiatry, and surgery, they gain experience in the diagnosis and treatment of illness.

Following medical school, almost all M.D.s enter a residency—graduate medical education in a specialty that takes the form of paid on-the-job training, usually in a hospital. Most D.O.s serve a 12-month rotating internship after graduation and before entering a residency, which may last 2 to 6 years.

All states, the District of Columbia, and U.S. territories license physicians. To be licensed, physicians must graduate from an accredited medical school, pass a licensing examination, and complete 1 to 7 years of graduate medical education. Although physicians licensed in one state usually can get a license to practice in another without further examination, some states limit reciprocity. Graduates of foreign medical schools generally can qualify for licensure after passing an examination and completing a U.S. residency.

M.D.s and D.O.s seeking board certification in a specialty may spend up to 7 years in residency training, depending on the specialty. A final examination immediately after residency or after 1 or 2 years of practice also is necessary for certification by a member board of the American Board of Medical Specialists (ABMS) or the American Osteopathic Association (AOA). The ABMS represents 24 specialty boards, ranging from allergy and immunology to urology. The AOA has approved 18 specialty boards, ranging from anesthesiology to surgery. For certification in a subspecialty, physicians usually need another 1 to 2 years of residency.

A physician's training is costly. According to the Association of American Medical Colleges, in 2004 more than 80 percent of medical school graduates were in debt for educational expenses.

People who wish to become physicians must have a desire to serve patients, be self-motivated, and be able to survive the pressures and long hours of medical education and practice. Physicians also must have a good bedside manner, emotional stability, and the ability to make decisions in emergencies. Prospective physicians must be willing to study throughout their career in order to keep up with medical advances.

Employment

Physicians and surgeons held about 567,000 jobs in 2004; approximately 1 out of 7 was self-employed and not incorporated. About 60 percent of salaried physicians and surgeons were in office of physicians, and 16 percent were employed by private hospitals. Others practiced in federal, state, and local governments, including hospitals, colleges, universities, and professional schools; private colleges, universities, and professional schools; and outpatient care centers.

According to the American Medical Association (AMA), in 2003 about 2 out 5 physicians in patient care were in primary care, but not in a subspecialty of primary care (table 1).

Table 1. Percent distribution of physicians by specialty, 2003

	Percent
Total	100.0
Primary care	40.8
Family medicine and general practice	12.8
Internal medicine	15.1
Obstetrics & gynecology	5.3
Pediatrics	7.6
Specialties	59.2
Anesthesiology	5.4
Psychiatry	5.4
Surgical specialties, selected	14.6
All other specialties	33.9

Source: American Medical Association, Physician Characteristics and Distribution in the US, 2005.

A growing number of physicians are partners or salaried employees of group practices. Organized as clinics or as associations of physicians, medical groups can afford expensive medical equipment and realize other business advantages.

According to the AMA, the New England and Middle Atlantic states have the highest ratio of physicians to population; the South Central and Mountain states have the lowest. D.O.s are more likely than M.D.s to practice in small cities and towns and in rural areas. M.D.s tend to locate in urban areas, close to hospital and education centers.

Job Outlook

Employment of physicians and surgeons is projected to grow faster than average for all occupations through the year 2014 due to continued expansion of health care industries. The growing and aging population will drive overall growth in the demand for physician services, as consumers continue to demand high levels of care using the latest technologies, diagnostic tests, and therapies. In addition to employment growth, job openings will result from the need to replace physicians and surgeons who retire over the 2004–14 period.

Demand for physicians' services is highly sensitive to changes in consumer preferences, health care reimbursement policies, and legislation. For example, if changes to health coverage result in consumers facing higher out-of-pocket costs, they may demand fewer physician services. Demand for physician services may also be tempered by patients relying more on other health care providers—such as physician assistants, nurse practitioners, optometrists, and nurse anesthetists—for some health care services. In addition, new technologies will increase physician productivity. Telemedicine will allow physicians to treat patients or consult with other providers remotely. Increasing use of electronic medical records, test and prescription orders, billing, and scheduling will also improve physician productivity.

Opportunities for individuals interested in becoming physicians and surgeons are expected to be very good. Reports of shortages in some specialties or geographic areas should attract new entrants, encouraging schools to expand programs and hospitals to expand available residency slots. However, because physician training is so lengthy, employment change happens gradually. In the short term, to meet increased demand, experienced physicians may work longer hours, delay retirement, or take measures to increase productivity, such as using more support staff to provide services. Opportunities should be particularly good in rural and low-income areas, because some physicians find these areas unattractive due to less control over work hours, isolation from medical colleagues, or other reasons.

Unlike their predecessors, newly trained physicians face radically different choices of where and how to practice. New physicians are much less likely to enter solo practice and more likely to take salaried jobs in group medical practices, clinics, and health networks.

Earnings

Earnings of physicians and surgeons are among the highest of any occupation. According to the Medical Group Management Association's Physician Compensation and Production Survey, median total compensation for physicians in 2004 varied by specialty, as shown in table 2. Total compensation for physicians reflects the amount reported as direct compensation for tax purposes, plus all voluntary salary reductions. Salary, bonus and/or incentive payments, research stipends, honoraria, and distribution of profits were included in total compensation.

Table 2. Median total compensation of physicians by specialty, 2004

	Less than two years in specialty	Over one year in specialty
Anesthesiology	$259,948	$321,686
Surgery: General	228,839	282,504
Obstetrics/gynecology: General	203,270	247,348
Psychiatry: General	173,922	180,000
Internal medicine: General	141,912	166,420
Pediatrics: General	132,953	161,331
Family practice (without obstetrics)	137,119	156,010

Source: Medical Group Management Association, Physician Compensation and Production Report, 2005.

Self-employed physicians—those who own or are part owners of their medical practice—generally have higher median incomes than salaried physicians. Earnings vary according to number of years in practice, geographic region, hours worked, and skill, personality, and professional reputation. Self-employed physicians and surgeons must provide for their own health insurance and retirement.

Related Occupations

Physicians work to prevent, diagnose, and treat diseases, disorders, and injuries. Other health care practitioners who need similar skills and who exercise critical judgment include chiropractors, dentists, optometrists, physician assistants, podiatrists, registered nurses, and veterinarians.

Sources of Additional Information

For a list of medical schools and residency programs, as well as general information on premedical education, financial aid, and medicine as a career, contact:

- Association of American Medical Colleges, Section for Student Services, 2450 N St. NW, Washington, DC 20037-1126. Internet: http://www.aamc.org
- American Association of Colleges of Osteopathic Medicine, 5550 Friendship Blvd., Suite 310, Chevy Chase, MD 20815-7231. Internet: http://www.aacom.org

For general information on physicians, contact:

- American Medical Association, 515 N. State St., Chicago, IL 60610. Internet: http://www.ama-assn.org
- American Osteopathic Association, Division of Communications, 142 East Ontario St., Chicago, IL 60611. Internet: http://www.osteopathic.org

For information about various medical specialties, contact:

- American Board of Medical Specialties, 1007 Church St., Suite 404, Evanston, IL 60201-5913. Internet: http://www.abms.org
- American Society of Anesthesiologists, 520 N. Northwest Hwy., Park Ridge, IL 60068-2573. Internet: http://www.asahq.org
- American Academy of Family Physicians, Resident Student Activities Department, 11400 Tomahawk Creek Pkwy., Leawood, KS 66211-2672. Internet: http://fmignet.aafp.org
- American College of Physicians, 190 North Independence Mall West, Philadelphia, PA 19106. Internet: http://www.acponline.org
- American College of Obstetricians and Gynecologists, 409 12th St. SW, P.O. Box 96920, Washington, DC 20090-6920. Internet: http://www.acog.org
- American Academy of Pediatrics, 141 Northwest Point Blvd., Elk Grove Village, IL 60007-1098. Internet: http://www.aap.org
- American Psychiatric Association, 1000 Wilson Blvd., Suite 1825, Arlington, VA 22209-3901. Internet: http://www.psych.org
- American College of Surgeons, Division of Education, 633 North Saint Clair St., Chicago, IL 60611-3211. Internet: http://www.facs.org

Information on federal scholarships and loans is available from the directors of student financial aid at schools of medicine.

Information on licensing is available from state boards of examiners.

Pipelayers, Plumbers, Pipefitters, and Steamfitters

(O*NET 47-2151.00, 47-2152.01, 47-2152.02, and 47-2152.03)

Significant Points

- Job opportunities should be excellent because not enough people are seeking training.
- Pipelayers, plumbers, pipefitters, and steamfitters make up one of the largest and highest-paid construction occupations.

Nature of the Work

Most people are familiar with plumbers, who come to their home to unclog a drain or install an appliance. In addition to these activities, however, pipelayers, plumbers, pipefitters, and steamfitters install, maintain, and repair many different types of pipe systems. For example, some systems move water to a municipal water treatment plant and then to residential, commercial, and public buildings. Other systems dispose of waste, provide gas to stoves and furnaces, or provide for heating and cooling needs. Pipe systems in power plants carry the steam that powers huge turbines. Pipes also are used in manufacturing plants to move material through the production process. Specialized piping systems are very important in both pharmaceutical and computer-chip manufacturing.

Although pipelaying, plumbing, pipefitting, and steamfitting sometimes are considered a single trade, workers generally specialize in one of five areas. *Pipelayers* lay clay, concrete, plastic, or cast-iron pipe for drains, sewers, water mains, and oil or gas lines. Before laying the pipe, pipelayers prepare and grade the trenches either manually or with machines. After laying the pipe, they weld, glue, cement or otherwise join the pieces together. *Plumbers* install and repair the water, waste disposal, drainage, and gas systems in homes and commercial and industrial buildings. Plumbers also install plumbing fixtures—bathtubs, showers, sinks, and toilets—and appliances such as dishwashers and water heaters. *Pipefitters* install and repair both high- and low-pressure pipe systems used in manufacturing, in the generation of electricity, and in the heating and cooling of buildings. They also install automatic controls that are increasingly being used to regulate these systems. Some pipefitters specialize in only one type of system. *Steamfitters* install pipe systems that move liquids or gases under high pressure. *Sprinklerfitters* install automatic fire sprinkler systems in buildings.

Pipelayers, plumbers, pipefitters, and steamfitters use many different materials and construction techniques, depending on the type of project. Residential water systems, for example, incorporate copper, steel, and plastic pipe that can be handled and installed by one or two plumbers. Municipal sewerage systems, on the other hand, are made of large cast-iron pipes; installation normally requires crews of pipefitters. Despite these differences, all pipelayers, plumbers, pipefitters, and steamfitters must be able to follow building plans or blueprints and instructions from supervisors, lay out the job, and work efficiently with the materials and tools of their trade. Computers and specialized software are used to create blueprints and plan layouts.

When construction plumbers install piping in a new house, for example, they work from blueprints or drawings that show the planned location of pipes, plumbing fixtures, and appliances. Recently, plumbers have become more involved in the design process. Their knowledge of codes and the operation of plumbing systems can cut costs. They first lay out the job to fit the piping into the structure of the house with the least waste of material. Then they measure and mark areas in which pipes will be installed and connected. Construction plumbers also check for obstructions such as electrical wiring and, if necessary, plan the pipe installation around the problem.

Sometimes, plumbers have to cut holes in walls, ceilings, and floors of a house. For some systems, they may hang steel supports from ceiling joists to hold the pipe in place. To assemble a system, plumbers—using saws, pipe cutters, and pipe-bending machines—cut and bend lengths of pipe. They connect lengths of pipe with fittings, using methods that depend on the type of pipe used. For plastic pipe, plumbers connect the sections and fittings with adhesives. For copper pipe, they slide a fitting over the end of the pipe and solder it in place with a torch.

After the piping is in place in the house, plumbers install the fixtures and appliances and connect the system to the outside water or sewer lines. Finally, using pressure gauges, they check the system to ensure that the plumbing works properly.

Working Conditions

Pipefitters and steamfitters most often work in industrial and power plants. Plumbers work in commercial and residential settings where water and septic systems need to be installed and maintained. Pipelayers work outdoors, sometime in remote areas, as they build the pipelines that connect sources of oil, gas, and chemicals with the users of these materials. Sprinklerfitters work mostly in multistory buildings that require the use of sprinkler systems.

Because pipelayers, plumbers, pipefitters, and steamfitters frequently must lift heavy pipes, stand for long periods, and sometimes work in uncomfortable or cramped positions, they need physical strength as well as stamina. They also may have to work outdoors in inclement weather. In addition, they are subject to possible falls from ladders, cuts from sharp tools, and burns from hot pipes or soldering equipment.

Pipelayers, plumbers, pipefitters, and steamfitters engaged in construction generally work a standard 40-hour week; those involved in maintaining pipe systems, including those who provide maintenance services under contract, may have to work evening or weekend shifts, as well as be on call. These maintenance workers may spend quite a bit of time traveling to and from worksites.

Training, Other Qualifications, and Advancement

Pipelayers, plumbers, pipefitters, and steamfitters enter into the profession in a variety of ways. Most residential and industrial plumbers get their training in career and technical schools and community colleges and from on-the-job training. Pipelayers, plumbers, pipefitters, and steamfitters who work mainly for commercial enterprises are usually trained through formal apprenticeship programs.

Apprenticeship programs generally provide the most comprehensive training available for these jobs. They are administered by either union locals and their affiliated companies or by nonunion contractor organizations. Organizations that sponsor apprenticeships include: the United Association of Journeymen and Apprentices of the Plumbing and Pipefitting Industry of the United States and Canada; local employers of either the Mechanical Contractors Association of America, the National Association of Plumbing-Heating-Cooling Contractors, or the National Fire Sprinkler Association; the Associated Builders and Contractors; the National Association of Plumbing-Heating-Cooling Contractors; the American Fire Sprinkler Association, or the Home Builders Institute of the National Association of Home Builders.

Apprenticeships—both union and nonunion—consist of 4 or 5 years of on-the-job training, in addition to at least 144 hours per year of related classroom instruction. Classroom subjects include drafting and blueprint reading, mathematics, applied physics and chemistry, safety, and local plumbing codes and regulations. On the job, apprentices first learn basic skills, such as identifying grades and types of pipe, using the tools of the trade, and safely unloading materials. As apprentices gain experience, they learn how to work with various types of pipe and how to install different piping systems and plumbing fixtures. Apprenticeship gives trainees a thorough knowledge of all aspects of the trade. Although most pipelayers, plumbers, pipefitters, and steamfitters are trained through apprenticeship, some still learn their skills informally on the job.

Applicants for union or nonunion apprentice jobs must be at least 18 years old and in good physical condition. Apprenticeship committees may require applicants to have a high school diploma or its equivalent. Armed Forces training in pipelaying, plumbing, and pipefitting is considered very good preparation. In fact, persons with this background may be given credit for previous experience when entering a civilian apprenticeship program. Secondary or postsecondary courses in shop, plumbing, general mathematics, drafting, blueprint reading, computers, and physics also are good preparation.

Although there are no uniform national licensing requirements, most communities require plumbers to be licensed. Licensing requirements vary from area to area, but most localities require workers to pass an examination that tests their knowledge of the trade and of local plumbing codes.

With additional training, some pipelayers, plumbers, pipefitters, and steamfitters become supervisors for mechanical and plumbing contractors. Others, especially plumbers, go into business for themselves, often starting as a self-employed plumber working from home. Some eventually become owners of businesses employing many workers and may spend most of their time as managers rather than as plumbers. Others move into closely related areas such as construction management or building inspection.

Employment

Pipelayers, plumbers, pipefitters, and steamfitters constitute one of the largest construction occupations, holding about 561,000 jobs in 2004. About 1 in 2 worked for plumbing, heating, and air-conditioning contractors engaged in new construction, repair, modernization, or maintenance work. Others did maintenance work for a variety of industrial, commercial, and government employers. For example, pipefitters were employed as maintenance personnel in the petroleum and chemical industries, in which manufacturing operations require the moving of liquids and gases through pipes. More than 1 in 10 pipelayers, plumbers, pipefitters, and steamfitters were self-employed. Almost 1 in 3 pipelayers, plumbers, pipefitters, and steamfitters belonged to a union.

Jobs for pipelayers, plumbers, pipefitters, and steamfitters are distributed across the country in about the same proportion as the general population.

Job Outlook

Job opportunities are expected to be excellent, as demand for skilled pipelayers, plumbers, pipefitters, and steamfitters is expected to outpace the supply of workers trained in this craft. Many employers report difficulty finding potential workers with the right qualifications. In addition, many people currently working in these trades are expected to retire over the next 10 years, which will create additional job openings.

Employment of pipelayers, plumbers, pipefitters, and steamfitters is expected to grow about as fast as average for all occupations through the year 2014. Demand for plumbers will stem from new construction and building renovation. Bath remodeling, in particular, is expected to continue to grow and create more jobs for plumbers. In addition, repair and maintenance of existing residential systems will keep plumbers employed. Demand for pipefitters and steamfitters will be driven by maintenance activities for places having extensive systems of pipes, such as power plants, water and wastewater treatment plants, office buildings, and factories. Growth of pipelayer jobs will stem from the building of new water and sewer lines and pipelines to new oil and gas fields. Demand for sprinklerfitters will increase due to changes to state and local rules for fire protection in homes and businesses.

Traditionally, many organizations with extensive pipe systems have employed their own plumbers or pipefitters to maintain equipment and keep systems running smoothly. But, to reduce labor costs, many of these firms no longer employ full-time, in-house plumbers or pipefitters. Instead, when they need a plumber, they rely on workers provided under service contracts by plumbing and pipefitting contractors.

Construction projects generally provide only temporary employment. When a project ends, some pipelayers, plumbers, pipefitters, and steamfitters may be unemployed until they can begin work on a new project, although most companies are trying to limit these periods of unemployment in order to retain workers. In addition, the jobs of pipelayers, plumbers, pipefitters, and steamfitters are generally less sensitive to changes in economic conditions than jobs in other construction trades. Even when construction activity declines, maintenance, rehabilitation, and replacement of existing piping systems, as well as the increasing installation of fire sprinkler systems, provide many jobs for pipelayers, plumbers, pipefitters, and steamfitters.

Earnings

Pipelayers, plumbers, pipefitters, and steamfitters are among the highest paid construction occupations. In May 2004, median hourly earnings of pipelayers were $13.68. The middle 50 percent earned between $11.05 and $18.69. The lowest 10 percent earned less than $9.19, and the highest 10 percent earned more than $25.07. Also in May 2004, median hourly earnings of plumbers, pipefitters, and steamfitters were $19.85. The middle 50 percent earned between $15.01 and $26.67. The lowest 10 percent earned less than $11.62, and the highest 10 percent earned more than $33.72. Median hourly earnings in the industries employing the largest numbers of plumbers, pipefitters, and steamfitters in May 2004 were as follows:

Industry	Earnings
Natural gas distribution	$23.86
Nonresidential building construction	21.55
Building equipment contractors	19.85
Utility system construction	18.29
Local government	16.30

Apprentices usually begin at about 50 percent of the wage rate paid to experienced pipelayers, plumbers, pipefitters, and steamfitters. Wages increase periodically as skills improve. After an initial waiting period, apprentices receive the same benefits as experienced pipelayers, plumbers, pipefitters, and steamfitters.

Many pipelayers, plumbers, pipefitters, and steamfitters are members of the United Association of Journeymen and Apprentices of the Plumbing and Pipefitting Industry of the United States and Canada.

Related Occupations

Other occupations in which workers install and repair mechanical systems in buildings are boilermakers; electricians; elevator installers and repairers; heating, air-conditioning, and refrigeration mechanics and installers; industrial machinery installation, repair, and maintenance workers; millwrights; sheet metal workers; and stationary engineers and boiler operators. Other related occupations include construction managers and construction and building inspectors.

Sources of Additional Information

For information about apprenticeships or work opportunities in pipelaying, plumbing, pipefitting, and steamfitting, contact local plumbing, heating, and air-conditioning contractors; a local or state chapter of the National Association of Plumbing, Heating, and Cooling Contractors; a local chapter of the Mechanical Contractors Association; a local chapter of the United Association of Journeymen and Apprentices of the Plumbing and Pipefitting Industry of the United States and Canada; or the nearest office of your state employment service or apprenticeship agency.

For information about apprenticeship opportunities for pipelayers, plumbers, pipefitters, and steamfitters, contact:

- United Association of Journeymen and Apprentices of the Plumbing and Pipefitting Industry, 901 Massachusetts Ave. NW, Washington, DC 20001. Internet: http://www.ua.org

For more information about training programs for pipelayers, plumbers, pipefitters, and steamfitters, contact:

- Associated Builders and Contractors, Workforce Development Department, 4250 North Fairfax Dr., 9th Floor, Arlington, VA 22203. Internet: http://www.trytools.org
- Home Builders Institute, National Association of Home Builders, 1201 15th St. NW, Washington, DC 20005. Internet: http://www.hbi.org

For general information about the work of pipelayers, plumbers, and pipefitters, contact:

- Mechanical Contractors Association of America, 1385 Piccard Dr., Rockville, MD 20850. Internet: http://www.mcaa.org
- Plumbing-Heating-Cooling Contractors—National Association, 180 S. Washington St, Falls Church, VA 22040. Internet: http://www.phccweb.org
- National Center for Construction Education and Research, P.O. Box 141104, Gainesville, FL 32614-1104. Internet: http://www.nccer.org

For general information about the work of sprinklerfitters, contact:

- American Fire Sprinkler Association, Inc., 9696 Skillman St., Suite 300, Dallas, TX 75243-8264. Internet: http://www.firesprinkler.org
- National Fire Sprinkler Association, P.O. Box 1000, Patterson, NY 12563. Internet: http://www.nfsa.org

Police and Detectives

(O*NET 33-1012.00, 33-3021.01, 33-3021.02, 33-3021.03, 33-3021.04, 33-3021.05, 33-3031.00, 33-3051.01, 33-3051.02, 33-3051.03, and 33-3052.00)

Significant Points

- Police and detective work can be dangerous and stressful.
- Competition should remain keen for higher-paying jobs with state and federal agencies and police departments in affluent areas; opportunities will be better in local and special police departments that offer relatively low salaries or in urban communities where the crime rate is relatively high.
- Applicants with college training in police science or military police experience should have the best opportunities.

Nature of the Work

People depend on police officers and detectives to protect their lives and property. Law enforcement officers, some of whom are state or federal special agents or inspectors, perform these duties in a variety of ways, depending on the size and type of their organization. In most jurisdictions, they are expected to exercise authority when necessary, whether on or off duty.

Uniformed police officers have general law enforcement duties, including maintaining regular patrols and responding to calls for service. They may direct traffic at the scene of an accident, investigate a burglary, or give first aid to an accident victim. In large police departments, officers usually are assigned to a specific type of duty. Many urban police agencies are involved in community policing—a practice in which an officer builds relationships with the citizens of local neighborhoods and mobilizes the public to help fight crime.

Police agencies are usually organized into geographic districts, with uniformed officers assigned to patrol a specific area, such as part of the business district or outlying residential neighborhoods. Officers may work alone, but in large agencies, they often patrol with a partner. While on patrol, officers attempt to become thoroughly familiar with their patrol area and remain alert for anything unusual. Suspicious circumstances and hazards to public safety are investigated or noted, and officers are dispatched to individual calls for assistance within their district. During their shift, they may identify, pursue, and arrest suspected criminals; resolve problems within the community; and enforce traffic laws.

Public college and university police forces, public school district police, and agencies serving transportation systems and facilities are examples of special police agencies. These agencies have special geographic jurisdictions and enforcement responsibilities in the United States. Most sworn personnel in special agencies are uniformed officers; a smaller number are investigators.

Some police officers specialize in such diverse fields as chemical and microscopic analysis, training and firearms instruction, or handwriting and fingerprint identification. Others work with special units, such as horseback, bicycle, motorcycle or harbor patrol; canine corps; special weapons and tactics (SWAT); or emergency response teams. A few local and special law enforcement officers primarily perform jail-related duties or work in courts. Regardless of job duties or location, police officers and detectives at all levels must write reports and maintain meticulous records that will be needed if they testify in court.

Sheriffs and deputy sheriffs enforce the law on the county level. Sheriffs are usually elected to their posts and perform duties similar to those of a local or county police chief. Sheriffs' departments tend to be relatively small, most having fewer than 50 sworn officers. Deputy sheriffs have law enforcement duties similar to those of officers in urban police departments. Police and sheriffs' deputies who provide security in city and county courts are sometimes called bailiffs.

State police officers (sometimes called *state troopers* or *highway patrol officers*) arrest criminals statewide and patrol highways to enforce motor vehicle laws and regulations. State police officers are best known for issuing traffic citations to motorists. At the scene of accidents, they may direct traffic, give first aid, and call for emergency equipment. They also write reports used to determine the cause of the accident. State police officers are frequently called upon to render assistance to other law enforcement agencies, especially those in rural areas or small towns.

State law enforcement agencies operate in every state except Hawaii. Most full-time sworn personnel are uniformed officers who regularly patrol and respond to calls for service. Others work as investigators, perform court-related duties, or carry out administrative or other assignments.

Detectives are plainclothes investigators who gather facts and collect evidence for criminal cases. Some are assigned to interagency task forces to combat specific types of crime. They conduct interviews, examine records, observe the activities of suspects, and participate in raids or arrests. Detectives and state and federal agents and inspectors usually specialize in investigating one of a wide variety of violations, such as homicide or fraud. They are assigned cases on a rotating basis and work on them until an arrest and conviction occurs or until the case is dropped.

Fish and game wardens enforce fishing, hunting, and boating laws. They patrol hunting and fishing areas, conduct search and rescue operations, investigate complaints and accidents, and aid in prosecuting court cases.

The federal government maintains a high profile in many areas of law enforcement. *Federal Bureau of Investigation (FBI) agents* are the Government's principal investigators, and they are responsible for investigating violations of more than 200 categories of federal law and conducting sensitive national security investigations. Agents may conduct surveillance, monitor court-authorized wiretaps, examine business records, investigate white-collar crime, or participate in sensitive undercover assignments. The FBI investigates organized crime, public corruption, financial crime, fraud against the Government, bribery, copyright infringement, civil rights violations, bank robbery, extortion, kidnapping, air piracy, terrorism, espionage, interstate criminal activity, drug trafficking, and other violations of federal statutes.

U.S. Drug Enforcement Administration (DEA) agents enforce laws and regulations relating to illegal drugs. Not only is the DEA the lead agency for domestic enforcement of federal drug laws, it also has sole responsibility for coordinating and pursuing U.S. drug investigations abroad. Agents may conduct complex criminal investigations, carry out surveillance of criminals, and infiltrate illicit drug organizations using undercover techniques.

U.S. marshals and deputy marshals protect the federal courts and ensure the effective operation of the judicial system. They provide protection for the federal judiciary, transport federal prisoners, protect federal witnesses, and manage assets seized from criminal enterprises. They enjoy the widest jurisdiction of any federal law enforcement agency and are involved to some degree in nearly all federal law enforcement efforts. In addition, U.S. marshals pursue and arrest federal fugitives.

Bureau of Alcohol, Tobacco, Firearms, and Explosives agents regulate and investigate violations of federal firearms and explosives laws as well as federal alcohol and tobacco tax regulations.

The U.S. Department of State *Bureau of Diplomatic Security special agents* are engaged in the battle against terrorism. Overseas, they advise ambassadors on all security matters and manage a complex range of security programs designed to protect personnel, facilities, and information. In the United States, they investigate passport and visa fraud, conduct personnel security investigations, issue security clearances, and protect the Secretary of State and a number of foreign dignitaries. They also train foreign civilian police and administer a counter-terrorism reward program.

The *Department of Homeland Security* employs numerous law enforcement officers under several different agencies, including *Customs and Border Protection, Immigration and Customs Enforcement,* and the *U.S. Secret Service. U.S. Border Patrol agents* protect more than 8,000 miles of international land and water boundaries. Their missions are to detect and prevent the smuggling and unlawful entry of undocumented foreign nationals into the United States; to apprehend those persons violating the immigration laws; and to interdict contraband, such as narcotics.

Immigration inspectors interview and examine people seeking entrance to the United States and its territories. They inspect passports to determine whether people are legally eligible to enter the United States. Immigration inspectors also prepare reports, maintain records, and process applications and petitions for immigration or temporary residence in the United States.

Customs inspectors enforce laws governing imports and exports by inspecting cargo, baggage, and articles worn or carried by people, vessels, vehicles, trains, and aircraft entering or leaving the United States. These inspectors examine, count, weigh, gauge, measure, and sample commercial and noncommercial cargoes entering and leaving the United States. Customs inspectors seize prohibited or smuggled articles; intercept contraband; and apprehend, search, detain, and arrest violators of U.S. laws. *Customs agents* investigate violations, such as narcotics smuggling, money laundering, child pornography, and customs fraud, and they enforce the Arms Export Control Act. During domestic and foreign investigations, they develop and use informants; conduct physical and electronic surveillance; and examine records from importers and exporters, banks, couriers, and manufacturers. They conduct interviews, serve on joint task forces with other agencies, and get and execute search warrants.

Federal Air Marshals provide air security by fighting attacks targeting U.S. airports, passengers, and crews. They disguise themselves as ordinary passengers and board flights of U.S. air carriers to locations worldwide.

U.S. Secret Service special agents protect the President, Vice President, and their immediate families; Presidential candidates; former Presidents; and foreign dignitaries visiting the United States. Secret Service agents also investigate counterfeiting, forgery of Government checks or bonds, and fraudulent use of credit cards.

Other federal agencies employ police and special agents with sworn arrest powers and the authority to carry firearms. These agencies include the Postal Service, the Bureau of Indian Affairs Office of Law Enforcement, the Forest Service, and the National Park Service.

Working Conditions

Police and detective work can be very dangerous and stressful. In addition to the obvious dangers of confrontations with criminals, police officers and detectives need to be constantly alert and ready to deal appropriately with a number of other threatening situations. Many law enforcement officers witness death and suffering resulting from accidents and criminal behavior. A career in law enforcement may take a toll on their private lives.

Uniformed officers, detectives, agents, and inspectors are usually scheduled to work 40-hour weeks, but paid overtime is common. Shift work is necessary because protection must be provided around the clock. Junior officers frequently work weekends, holidays, and nights. Police officers and detectives are required to work at any time their services are needed and may work long hours during investigations. In most jurisdictions, whether on or off duty, officers are expected to be armed and to exercise their authority whenever necessary.

The jobs of some federal agents such as U.S. Secret Service and DEA special agents require extensive travel, often on very short notice. They may relocate a number of times over the course of their careers. Some special agents in agencies such as the U.S. Border Patrol work outdoors in rugged terrain for long periods and in all kinds of weather.

Training, Other Qualifications, and Advancement

Civil service regulations govern the appointment of police and detectives in most states, large municipalities, and special police agencies, as well as in many smaller jurisdictions. Candidates must be U.S. citizens, usually must be at least 20 years of age, and must meet rigorous physical and personal qualifications. In the federal government, candidates must be at least 21 years of age but less than 37 years of age at the time of appointment. Physical examinations for entrance into law enforcement often include tests of vision, hearing, strength, and agility. Eligibility for appointment usually depends on performance in competitive written examinations and previous education and experience. In larger departments, where the majority of law enforcement jobs are found, applicants usually must have at least a high school education, and some departments require a year or two of college coursework. Federal and state agencies typically require a college degree. Candidates should enjoy working with people and meeting the public.

Because personal characteristics such as honesty, sound judgment, integrity, and a sense of responsibility are especially important in law enforcement, candidates are interviewed by senior officers, and their character traits and backgrounds are investigated. In some agencies, candidates are interviewed by a psychiatrist or a psychologist or given a personality test. Most applicants are subjected to lie detector examinations or drug testing. Some agencies subject sworn personnel to random drug testing as a condition of continuing employment.

Before their first assignments, officers usually go through a period of training. In state and large local departments, recruits get training in their agency's police academy, often for 12 to 14 weeks. In small agencies, recruits often attend a regional or state academy. Training includes classroom instruction in constitutional law and civil rights, state laws and local ordinances, and accident investigation. Recruits also receive training and supervised experience in patrol, traffic control, use of firearms, self-defense, first aid, and emergency response. Police departments in some large cities hire high school graduates who are still in their teens as police cadets or trainees. They do clerical work and attend classes, usually for 1 to 2 years, at which point they reach the minimum age requirement and may be appointed to the regular force.

Police officers usually become eligible for promotion after a probationary period ranging from 6 months to 3 years. In a large department, promotion may enable an officer to become a detective or to specialize in one type of police work, such as working with juveniles. Promotions to corporal, sergeant, lieutenant, and captain usually are made according to a candidate's position on a promotion list, as determined by scores on a written examination and on-the-job performance.

Most states require at least two years of college study to qualify as a fish and game warden. Applicants must pass written and physical examinations and vision, hearing, psychological, and drug tests similar to those taken by other law enforcement officers. Once hired, officers attend a training academy lasting from 3 to 12 months, sometimes followed by further training in the field.

To be considered for appointment as an FBI agent, an applicant must be a graduate of an accredited law school or a college graduate with one of the following: a major in accounting, electrical engineering, or information technology; fluency in a foreign language; or three years of related full-time work experience. All new agents undergo 18 weeks of training at the FBI Academy on the U.S. Marine Corps base in Quantico, Virginia.

Applicants for special agent jobs with the U.S. Secret Service and the Bureau of Alcohol, Tobacco, and Firearms must have a bachelor's degree, a minimum of three years' related work experience, or a combination of education and experience. Prospective special agents undergo 11 weeks of initial criminal investigation training at the Federal Law Enforcement Training Center in Glynco, Georgia, and another 17 weeks of specialized training with their particular agencies.

Applicants for special agent jobs with the DEA must have a college degree with at least a 2.95 grade point average or specialized skills or work experience, such as foreign language fluency, technical skills, law enforcement experience, or accounting experience. DEA special agents undergo 14 weeks of specialized training at the FBI Academy in Quantico, Virginia.

U.S. Border Patrol agents must be U.S. citizens, be younger than 37 years of age at the time of appointment, possess a valid driver's license, and pass a three-part examination on reasoning and language skills. A bachelor's degree or previous work experience that demonstrates the ability to handle stressful situations, make decisions, and take charge is required for a position as a Border Patrol agent. Applicants may qualify through a combination of education and work experience.

Postal inspectors must have a bachelor's degree and 1 year of related work experience. It is desirable that they have one of several professional certifications, such as that of certified public accountant. They also must pass a background investigation, meet certain health requirements, undergo a drug screening test, possess a valid state driver's license, and be a U.S. citizen between 21 and 36 years of age when hired.

Law enforcement agencies are encouraging applicants to take postsecondary school training in law enforcement-related subjects. Many entry-level applicants for police jobs have completed some formal postsecondary education, and a significant number are college graduates. Many junior colleges, colleges, and universities offer programs in law enforcement or administration of justice. Other courses helpful in preparing for a career in law enforcement include accounting, finance, electrical engineering, computer science, and foreign languages. Physical education and sports are helpful in developing the competitiveness, stamina, and agility needed for many law enforcement positions. Knowledge of a foreign language is an asset in many federal agencies and urban departments.

Continuing training helps police officers, detectives, and special agents improve their job performance. Through police department academies, regional centers for public safety employees established by the states, and federal agency training centers, instructors provide annual training in self-defense tactics, firearms, use-of-force policies, sensitivity and communications skills, crowd-control techniques, relevant legal developments, and advances in law enforcement equipment. Many agencies pay all or part of the tuition for officers to work toward degrees in criminal justice, police science, administration of justice, or public administration and pay higher salaries to those who earn such a degree.

Employment

Police and detectives held about 842,000 jobs in 2004. About 80 percent were employed by local governments. State police agencies employed about 12 percent, and various federal agencies employed about 6 percent. A small proportion worked for educational services, rail transportation, and contract investigation and security services.

According to the U.S. Bureau of Justice Statistics, police and detectives employed by local governments primarily worked in cities with more than 25,000 inhabitants. Some cities have very large police forces, while thousands of small communities employ fewer than 25 officers each.

Job Outlook

The opportunity for public service through law enforcement work is attractive to many because the job is challenging and involves much personal responsibility. Furthermore, law enforcement officers in many agencies may retire with a pension after 25 or 30 years of service, allowing them to pursue a second career while still in their 40s or 50s. Because of relatively attractive salaries and benefits, the number of qualified candidates exceeds the number of job openings in federal law enforcement agencies and in most state police departments—resulting in increased hiring standards and selectivity by employers. Competition should remain keen for higher-paying jobs with state and federal agencies and police departments in more affluent areas. Opportunities will be better in local and special police departments, especially in departments that offer relatively low salaries or in urban communities where the crime rate is relatively high. Applicants with college training in police science, military police experience, or both should have the best opportunities.

Employment of police and detectives is expected to grow about as fast as the average for all occupations through 2014. A more security-conscious society and concern about drug-related crimes should contribute to the increasing demand for police services. However, employment growth will be hindered by reductions in federal hiring grants to local police departments and by expectations of low crime rates by the general public.

The level of government spending determines the level of employment for police and detectives. The number of job opportunities, therefore, can vary from year to year and from place to place. Layoffs, on the other hand, are rare because retirements enable most staffing cuts to be handled through attrition. Trained law enforcement officers who lose their jobs because of budget cuts usually have little difficulty finding jobs with other agencies. The need to replace workers who retire, transfer to other occupations, or stop working for other reasons will be the source of many job openings.

Earnings

Police and sheriff's patrol officers had median annual earnings of $45,210 in May 2004. The middle 50 percent earned between $34,410 and $56,360. The lowest 10 percent earned less than $26,910, and the highest 10 percent earned more than $68,880. Median annual earnings were $44,750 in federal government, $48,980 in state government, and $45,010 in local government.

In May 2004, median annual earnings of police and detective supervisors were $64,430. The middle 50 percent earned between $49,370 and $80,510. The lowest 10 percent earned less than $36,690, and the highest 10 percent earned more than $96,950. Median annual earnings were $86,030 in federal government, $62,300 in state government, and $63,590 in local government.

In May 2004, median annual earnings of detectives and criminal investigators were $53,990. The middle 50 percent earned between $40,690 and $72,280. The lowest 10 percent earned less than $32,180, and the highest 10 percent earned more than $86,010. Median annual earnings were $75,700 in federal government, $46,670 in state government, and $49,650 in local government.

Federal law provides special salary rates to federal employees who serve in law enforcement. Additionally, federal special agents and inspectors receive law enforcement availability pay (LEAP)—equal to 25 percent of the agent's grade and step—awarded because of the large amount of overtime that these agents are expected to work. For example, in 2005, FBI agents entered federal service as GS-10 employees on the pay scale at a base salary of $42,548, yet they earned about $53,185 a year with availability pay. They could advance to the GS-13 grade level in field nonsupervisory assignments at a base salary of $64,478, which was worth $80,597 with availability pay. FBI supervisory, management, and executive positions in grades GS-14 and GS-15 paid a base salary of about $76,193 and $89,625 a year, respectively, which amounted to $95,241 or $112,031 per year including availability pay. Salaries were slightly higher in selected areas where the prevailing local pay level was higher. Because federal agents may be eligible for a special law enforcement benefits package, applicants should ask their recruiter for more information.

According to the International City-County Management Association's annual Police and Fire Personnel, Salaries, and Expenditures Survey, average salaries for sworn full-time positions in 2004 were as follows:

	Minimum annual base salary	Maximum annual base salary
Police chief	$72,924	$92,983
Deputy chief	61,110	76,994
Police captain	60,908	75,497
Police lieutenant	56,115	67,580
Police sergeant	49,895	59,454
Police corporal	41,793	51,661

Total earnings for local, state, and special police and detectives frequently exceed the stated salary because of payments for overtime, which can be significant. In addition to the common benefits—paid vacation, sick leave, and medical and life insurance—most police and sheriffs' departments provide officers with special allowances for uniforms. Because police officers usually are covered by liberal pension plans, many retire at half pay after 25 or 30 years of service.

Related Occupations

Police and detectives maintain law and order, collect evidence and information, and conduct investigations and surveillance. Workers in related occupations include correctional officers, private detectives and investigators, and security guards and gaming surveillance officers.

Sources of Additional Information

Information about entrance requirements may be obtained from federal, state, and local law enforcement agencies.

For general information about sheriffs and to learn more about the National Sheriffs' Association scholarship, contact:

- National Sheriffs' Association, 1450 Duke St., Alexandria, VA 22314. Internet: http://www.sheriffs.org

Information about qualifications for employment as a FBI Special Agent is available from the nearest state FBI office. The address and phone number are listed in the local telephone directory. Internet: http://www.fbi.gov

Information on career opportunities, qualifications, and training for U.S. Secret Service Special Agents is available from the Secret Service Personnel Division at (202) 406-5800, (888) 813-8777, or (888) 813-USSS. Internet: http://www.treas.gov/usss

Information about qualifications for employment as a DEA Special Agent is available from the nearest DEA office, or call (800) DEA-4288. Internet: http://www.usdoj.gov/dea

Information about career opportunities, qualifications, and training to become a deputy marshal is available from:

- U.S. Marshals Service, Human Resources Division—Law Enforcement Recruiting, Washington, DC 20530-1000. Internet: http://www.usmarshals.gov

For information on operations and career opportunities in the U.S. Bureau of Alcohol, Tobacco, Firearms, and Explosives operations, contact:

- U.S. Bureau of Alcohol, Tobacco, Firearms, and Explosives Personnel Division, 650 Massachusetts Ave. NW, Room 4100, Washington, DC 20226. Internet: http://www.atf.treas.gov

Information about careers in U.S. Customs and Border Protection is available from:

- U.S. Customs and Border Protection, 1300 Pennsylvania Ave. NW, Washington, DC 20229. Internet: http://www.cbp.gov

Information about law enforcement agencies within the Department of Homeland Security is available from:

- U.S. Department of Homeland Security, Washington, DC 20528. Internet: http://www.dhs.gov

Property, Real Estate, and Community Association Managers

(O*NET 11-9141.00)

Significant Points

- Opportunities should be best for those with college degrees in business administration, real estate, or related fields and with professional designations.
- Good speaking, writing, computer, and financial skills, as well as an ability to tactfully deal with people, are essential.
- More than half of property, real estate, and community association managers are self-employed.

Nature of the Work

Buildings can be homes, stores, or offices to those who use them. To businesses and investors, properly managed real estate is a source of income and profits; to homeowners, it is a way to preserve and enhance resale values. Property, real estate, and community association managers maintain and increase the value of real estate investments. *Property and real estate managers* oversee the performance of income-producing commercial or residential properties and ensure that real estate investments achieve their expected revenues. *Community association managers* manage the common property and services of condominiums, cooperatives, and planned communities through their homeowners' or community associations.

When owners of apartments, office buildings, or retail or industrial properties lack the time or expertise needed for the day-to-day management of their real estate investments or homeowners' associations, they often hire a property or real estate manager or a community association manager. The manager is employed either directly by the owner or indirectly through a contract with a property management firm.

Generally, property and real estate managers handle the financial operations of the property, ensuring that rent is collected and that mortgages, taxes, insurance premiums, payroll, and maintenance bills are paid on time. In community associations, although homeowners pay no rent and pay their own real estate taxes and mortgages, community association managers must collect association dues. Some property managers, called *asset property managers*, supervise the preparation of financial statements and periodically report to the owners on the status of the property, occupancy rates, expiration dates of leases, and other matters.

Often, property managers negotiate contracts for janitorial, security, groundskeeping, trash removal, and other services. When contracts are awarded competitively, managers solicit bids from several contractors and advise the owners on which bid to accept. They monitor the performance of contractors and investigate and resolve complaints from residents and tenants when services are not properly provided. Managers also purchase supplies and equipment for the property and make arrangements with specialists for repairs that cannot be handled by regular property maintenance staff.

In addition to fulfilling these duties, property managers must understand and comply with provisions of legislation, such as the Americans with Disabilities Act and the Federal Fair Housing Amendment Act, as well as local fair housing laws. They must ensure that their renting and advertising practices are not discriminatory and that the property itself complies with all of the local, state, and federal regulations and building codes.

Onsite property managers are responsible for the day-to-day operations of a single property, such as an office building, a shopping center, a community association, or an apartment complex. To ensure that the property is safe and properly maintained, onsite managers routinely inspect the grounds, facilities, and equipment to determine whether repairs or maintenance is needed. In handling requests for repairs or trying to resolve complaints they meet not only with current residents, but also with prospective residents or tenants to show vacant apartments or office space. Onsite managers also are responsible for enforcing the terms of rental or lease agreements, such as rent collection, parking and pet restrictions, and termination-of-lease procedures. Other important duties of onsite managers include keeping accurate, up-to-date records of income and expenditures from property operations and submitting regular expense reports to the asset property manager or owners.

Property managers who do not work onsite act as a liaison between the onsite manager and the owner. They also market vacant space to prospective tenants through the use of a leasing agent or by advertising or other means, and they establish rental rates in accordance with prevailing local economic conditions.

Some property and real estate managers, often called *real estate asset managers*, act as the property owners' agent and adviser for the property. They plan and direct the purchase, development, and disposition of real estate on behalf of the business and investors. These managers focus on long-term strategic financial planning, rather than on day-to-day operations of the property.

In deciding to acquire property, real estate asset managers take several factors into consideration, such as property values, taxes, zoning, population growth, transportation, and traffic volume and patterns. Once a site is selected, they negotiate contracts for the purchase or lease of the property, securing the most beneficial terms. Real estate asset managers review their company's real estate holdings periodically and identify properties that are no longer financially profitable. They then negotiate the sale of, or terminate the lease on, such properties.

In many respects, the work of community association managers parallels that of property managers. They collect monthly assessments, prepare financial statements and budgets, negotiate with contractors, and help to resolve complaints. In other respects, however, the work of these managers differs from that of other residential property and real estate managers. Community association managers interact with homeowners and other residents on a daily basis. Hired by the volunteer board of directors of the association, they administer the daily affairs, and oversee the maintenance, of property and facilities that the homeowners own and use jointly through the association. They also assist the board and owners in complying with association and government rules and regulations.

Some associations encompass thousands of homes and employ their own onsite staff and managers. In addition to administering the associations' financial records and budget, managers may be responsible for the operation of community pools, golf courses, and community centers and for the maintenance of landscaping and parking areas. Community association managers also may meet with the elected boards of directors to discuss and resolve legal issues or disputes that may affect the owners, as well as to review any proposed changes or improvements by homeowners to their properties, to make sure that they comply with community guidelines.

Working Conditions

The offices of most property, real estate, and community association managers are clean, modern, and well lighted. However, many managers spend a major portion of their time away from their desks. Onsite managers in particular may spend a large portion of their workday away from their offices, visiting the building engineer, showing apartments, checking on the janitorial and maintenance staff, or investigating problems reported by tenants. Property and real estate managers frequently visit the properties they oversee, sometimes on a daily basis when contractors are doing major repair or renovation work. Real estate asset managers may spend time away from home while traveling to company real estate holdings or searching for properties to acquire.

Property, real estate, and community association managers often must attend evening meetings with residents, property owners, community association boards of directors, or civic groups. Not surprisingly, many managers put in long workweeks, especially before financial and tax reports are due and before board and annual meetings. Some apartment managers are required to live in the apartment complexes where they work so that they are available to handle any emergency that occurs, even when they are off duty. They usually receive compensatory time off for working nights or weekends. Many apartment managers receive time off during the week so that they are available on weekends to show apartments to prospective residents.

Training, Other Qualifications, and Advancement

Most employers prefer to hire college graduates for property management positions. Entrants with degrees in business administration, accounting, finance, real estate, public administration, or related fields are preferred, but those with degrees in the liberal arts also may qualify. Good speaking, writing, computer, and financial skills, as well as an ability to deal tactfully with people, are essential in all areas of property management.

Many people enter property management as onsite managers of apartment buildings, office complexes, or community associations or as employees of property management firms or community association management companies. As they acquire experience working under the direction of a property manager, they may advance to positions greater responsibility at larger properties. Those who excel as onsite managers often transfer to assistant property manager positions, in which they can acquire experience handling a broad range of property management responsibilities.

Previous employment as a real estate sales agent may be an asset to onsite managers because it provides experience that is useful in showing apartments or office space. In the past, those with backgrounds in building maintenance have advanced to onsite manager positions on the strength of their knowledge of building mechanical systems, but this path is becoming less common as employers place greater emphasis on administrative, financial, and communication abilities for managerial jobs.

Although many people entering jobs such as assistant property manager do so by having previously gained onsite management experience, employers increasingly are hiring inexperienced college graduates with bachelor's or master's degrees in business administration, accounting, finance, or real estate for these positions. Assistants work closely with a property manager and learn how to prepare budgets, analyze insurance coverage and risk options, market property to prospective tenants, and collect overdue rent payments. In time, many assistants advance to property manager positions.

The responsibilities and compensation of property, real estate, and community association managers increase as these workers manage more and larger properties. Most property managers, often called portfolio managers, are responsible for several properties at a time. As their careers advance, they gradually are entrusted with larger properties that are more complex to manage. Many specialize in the management of one type of property, such as apartments, office buildings, condominiums, cooperatives, homeowners' associations, or retail properties. Managers who excel at marketing properties to tenants might specialize in managing new properties, while those who are particularly knowledgeable about buildings and their mechanical systems might specialize in the management of older properties requiring renovation or more frequent repairs. Some experienced managers open their own property management firms.

Persons most commonly enter real estate asset manager jobs by transferring from positions as property managers or real estate brokers. Real estate asset managers must be good negotiators, adept at persuading and handling people, and good at analyzing data in order to assess the fair-market value of property or its development potential. Resourcefulness and creativity in arranging financing are essential for managers who specialize in land development.

Many employers encourage attendance at short-term formal training programs conducted by various professional and trade associations that are active in the real estate field. Employers send managers to these programs to improve their management skills and expand their knowledge of specialized subjects, such as the operation and maintenance of building mechanical systems, the enhancement of property values, insurance and risk management, personnel management, business and real estate law, community association risks and liabilities, tenant relations, communications, accounting and financial concepts, and reserve funding. Managers also participate in these programs to prepare themselves for positions of greater responsibility in property management. The completion of these programs, related job experience, and a satisfactory score on a written examination leads to certification, or the formal award of a professional designation, by the sponsoring association. (Some organizations offering such programs are listed as sources of additional information at the end of this statement.) In addition to seeking these qualifications, some associations require their members to adhere to a specific code of ethics. In a few states, community association managers must be licensed.

Managers of public housing subsidized by the federal government are required to be certified, but many property, real estate, and community association managers who work with all types of property choose to earn a professional designation voluntarily because it represents formal recognition of their achievements and status in the occupation. Real estate asset managers who buy or sell property are required to be licensed by the state in which they practice.

Employment

Property, real estate, and community association managers held about 361,000 jobs in 2004. More that one-third worked for real estate agents and brokers, lessors of real estate, or property management firms. Others worked for real estate development companies, government agencies that manage public buildings, and corporations with extensive holdings of commercial properties. More than half of property, real estate, and community association managers were self-employed.

Job Outlook

Employment of property, real estate, and community association managers is projected to increase about as fast as average for all occupations through the year 2014. In addition to job growth, a number of openings are expected to occur as managers transfer to other occupations or leave the labor force. Opportunities should be best for those with a college degree in business administration, real estate, or a related field and for those who attain a professional designation.

Job growth among onsite property managers in commercial real estate is expected to accompany the projected expansion of the real estate and rental and leasing industry. An increase in the nation's stock of apartments, houses, and offices also should require more property managers. Developments of new homes increasingly are being organized with community or homeowners' associations that provide community services and oversee jointly owned common areas requiring professional management. To help properties become more profitable or to enhance the resale values of homes, more commercial and residential property owners are expected to place their investments in the hands of professional managers.

The changing demographic composition of the population also should create more jobs for property, real estate, and community association managers. The number of older people will grow during the 2004–14 projection period, increasing the need for various types of suitable housing, such as assisted-living facilities and retirement communities. Accordingly, demand will rise for property and real estate managers to operate these facilities—especially those individuals who have a background in the operation and administrative aspects of running a health unit.

Earnings

Median annual earnings of salaried property, real estate, and community association managers were $39,980 in May 2004. The middle 50 percent earned between $27,190 and $59,360 a year. The lowest 10 percent earned less than $18,510, and the highest 10 percent earned more than $89,840 a year. Median annual earnings of salaried property, real estate, and community association managers in the largest industries that employed them in 2004 were as follows:

Local government	$51,980
Offices of real estate agents and brokers	40,000
Activities related to real estate	38,370
Lessors of real estate	34,300

Many resident apartment managers and onsite association managers receive the use of an apartment as part of their compensation package. Managers often are reimbursed for the use of their personal vehicles, and managers employed in land development often receive a small percentage of ownership in the projects that they develop.

Related Occupations

Property, real estate, and community association managers plan, organize, staff, and manage the real estate operations of businesses. Workers who perform similar functions in other fields include administrative services managers, education administrators, food service managers, lodging managers, medical and health services managers, real estate brokers and sales agents, and urban and regional planners.

Sources of Additional Information

For information about education and careers in property management, as well as information about professional designation and certification programs in both residential and commercial property management, contact:

- Institute of Real Estate Management, 430 N. Michigan Ave., Chicago, IL 60611. Internet: http://www.irem.org

For information on careers and certification programs in commercial property management, contact:

- Building Owners and Managers Institute, 1521 Ritchie Hwy., Arnold, MD 21012. Internet: http://www.bomi-edu.org

For information on careers and professional designation and certification programs in residential property management and community association management, contact:

- Community Associations Institute, 225 Reinekers Ln., Suite 300, Alexandria, VA 22314. Internet: http://www.caionline.org
- National Board of Certification for Community Association Managers, 225 Reinekers Lane, Suite 310, Alexandria, VA 22314. Internet: http://www.nbccam.org

Public Relations Specialists

(O*NET 27-3031.00)

Significant Points

- Although employment is projected to grow faster than average, keen competition is expected for entry-level jobs.
- Opportunities should be best for college graduates who combine a degree in public relations, journalism, or another communications-related field with a public relations internship or other related work experience.
- Creativity, initiative, and the ability to communicate effectively are essential.

Nature of the Work

An organization's reputation, profitability, and even its continued existence can depend on the degree to which its targeted "publics" support its goals and policies. Public relations specialists—also referred to as *communications specialists* and *media specialists*, among other titles—serve as advocates for businesses, nonprofit associations, universities, hospitals, and other organizations, and build and maintain positive relationships with the public. As managers recognize the importance of good public relations to the success of their organizations, they increasingly rely on public relations specialists for advice on the strategy and policy of such programs.

Public relations specialists handle organizational functions such as media, community, consumer, industry, and governmental relations; political campaigns; interest-group representation; conflict mediation; and employee and investor relations. They do more than "tell the organization's story." They must understand the attitudes and concerns of community, consumer, employee, and public interest groups and establish and maintain cooperative relationships with them and with representatives from print and broadcast journalism.

Public relations specialists draft press releases and contact people in the media who might print or broadcast their material. Many radio or television special reports, newspaper stories, and magazine articles start at the desks of public relations specialists. Sometimes the subject is an organization and its policies toward its employees or its role in the community. Often the subject is a public issue, such as health, energy, or the environment, and what an organization does to advance that issue.

Public relations specialists also arrange and conduct programs to keep up contact between organization representatives and the public. For example, they set up speaking engagements and often prepare speeches for company officials. These media specialists represent employers at community projects; make film, slide, or other visual presentations at meetings and school assemblies; and plan conventions. In addition, they are responsible for preparing annual reports and writing proposals for various projects.

In government, public relations specialists—who may be called press secretaries, information officers, public affairs specialists, or communication specialists—keep the public informed about the activities of agencies and officials. For example, public affairs specialists in the U.S. Department of State keep the public informed of travel advisories and of U.S. positions on foreign issues. A press secretary for a member of Congress keeps constituents aware of the representative's accomplishments.

In large organizations, the key public relations executive, who often is a vice president, may develop overall plans and policies with other executives. In addition, public relations departments employ public relations specialists to write, research, prepare materials, maintain contacts, and respond to inquiries.

People who handle publicity for an individual or who direct public relations for a small organization may deal with all aspects of the job. They contact people, plan and research, and prepare materials for distribution. They also may handle advertising or sales promotion work to support marketing efforts.

Working Conditions

Some public relations specialists work a standard 35- to 40-hour week, but unpaid overtime is common. Occasionally, they must be at the job or on call around the clock, especially if there is an emergency or crisis. Public relations offices are busy places; work schedules can be irregular and frequently interrupted. Schedules often have to be rearranged so that workers can meet deadlines, deliver speeches, attend meetings and community activities, and travel.

Training, Other Qualifications, and Advancement

There are no defined standards for entry into a public relations career. A college degree combined with public relations experience, usually gained through an internship, is considered excellent preparation for public relations work; in fact, internships are becoming vital to obtaining employment. The ability to communicate effectively is essential. Many entry-level public relations specialists have a college major in public relations, journalism, advertising, or communication. Some firms seek college graduates who have worked in electronic or print journalism. Other employers seek applicants with demonstrated communication skills and training or experience in a field related to the firm's business—information technology, health, science, engineering, sales, or finance, for example.

Many colleges and universities offer bachelor's and postsecondary degrees in public relations, usually in a journalism or communications department. In addition, many other colleges offer at least one course in this field. A common public relations sequence includes courses in public relations principles and techniques; public relations management and administration, including organizational development; writing, emphasizing news releases, proposals, annual reports, scripts, speeches, and related items; visual communications, including desktop publishing and computer graphics; and research, emphasizing social science research and survey design and implementation. Courses in advertising, journalism, business administration, finance, political science, psychology, sociology, and creative writing also are helpful. Specialties are offered in public relations for business, government, and nonprofit organizations.

Many colleges help students gain part-time internships in public relations that provide valuable experience and training. Membership in local chapters of the Public Relations Student Society of America (affiliated with the Public Relations Society of America) or in student chapters of the International Association of Business Communicators provides an opportunity for students to exchange views with public relations specialists and to make professional contacts that may help them find a job in the field. A portfolio of published articles, television or radio programs, slide presentations, and other work is an asset in finding a job. Writing for a school publication or television or radio station provides valuable experience and material for one's portfolio.

Creativity, initiative, good judgment, and the ability to communicate thoughts clearly and simply are essential in this occupation. Decision-making, problem-solving, and research skills also are important. People who choose public relations as a career need an outgoing personality, self-confidence, an understanding of human psychology, and an enthusiasm for motivating people. They should be competitive, yet able to function as part of a team and open to new ideas.

Some organizations, particularly those with large public relations staffs, have formal training programs for new employees. In smaller organizations, new employees work under the guidance of experienced staff members. Beginners often maintain files of material about company activities, scan newspapers and magazines for appropriate articles to clip, and assemble information for speeches and pamphlets. They also may answer calls from the press and the public, work on invitation lists and details for press conferences, or escort visitors and clients. After gaining experience, they write news releases, speeches, and articles for publication or plan and carry out public relations programs. Public relations specialists in smaller firms usually get all-around experience, whereas those in larger firms tend to be more specialized.

The Universal Accreditation Board accredits public relations specialists who are members of the Public Relations Society of America and who participate in the Examination for Accreditation in Public Relations process. This process includes both a readiness review and an examination, which are designed for candidates who have at least 5 years of full-time work or teaching experience in public relations and who have earned a bachelor's degree in a communications-related field. The readiness review includes a written submission by each candidate, a portfolio review, and dialogue between the candidate and a three-member panel. Candidates who successfully advance through readiness review and pass the computer-based examination earn the Accredited in Public Relations (APR) designation.

The International Association of Business Communicators (IABC) also has an accreditation program for professionals in the communications field, including public relations specialists. Those who meet all the requirements of the program earn the Accredited Business Communicator (ABC) designation. Candidates must have at least 5 years of experience and a bachelor's degree in a communications field and must pass written and oral examinations. They also must submit a portfolio of work samples demonstrating involvement in a range of communications projects and a thorough understanding of communications planning.

Employers may consider professional recognition through accreditation as a sign of competence in this field, which could be especially helpful in a competitive job market.

Promotion to supervisory jobs may come to public relations specialists who show that they can handle more demanding assignments. In public relations firms, a beginner might be hired as a research assistant or account coordinator and be promoted to account executive, senior account executive, account manager, and eventually vice president. A similar career path is followed in corporate public relations, although the titles may differ. Some experienced public relations specialists start their own consulting firms.

Employment

Public relations specialists held about 188,000 jobs in 2004. Public relations specialists are concentrated in service-providing industries such as advertising and related services; health care and social assistance; educational services; and government. Others worked for communications firms, financial institutions, and government agencies.

Public relations specialists are concentrated in large cities, where press services and other communications facilities are readily available and many businesses and trade associations have their headquarters. Many public relations consulting firms, for example, are in New York, Los Angeles, San Francisco, Chicago, and Washington, DC. There is a trend, however, for public relations jobs to be dispersed throughout the nation, closer to clients.

Job Outlook

Keen competition likely will continue for entry-level public relations jobs, as the number of qualified applicants is expected to exceed the number of job openings. Many people are attracted to this profession because of the high profile nature of the work. Opportunities should be best for college graduates who combine a degree in journalism, public relations, advertising, or another communications-related field with a public relations internship or other related work experience. Applicants without the appropriate educational background or work experience will face the toughest obstacles.

Employment of public relations specialists is expected to grow faster than average for all occupations through 2014. The need for good public relations in an increasingly competitive business environment should spur demand for public relations specialists in organizations of all types and sizes. The value of a company is measured not just by its balance sheet, but also by the strength of its relationships with those on whom it depends for its success. With the increasing demand for corporate accountability, more emphasis will be placed on improving the image of the client, as well as on building public confidence.

Employment in public relations firms should grow as firms hire contractors to provide public relations services rather than support full-time staff. In addition to those arising from employment growth, job opportunities should result from the need to replace public relations specialists who leave the occupation.

Earnings

Median annual earnings for salaried public relations specialists were $43,830 in May 2004. The middle 50 percent earned between $32,970 and $59,360; the lowest 10 percent earned less than $25,750, and the top 10 percent earned more than $81,120. Median annual earnings in the industries employing the largest numbers of public relations specialists in May 2004 were:

Advertising and related services	$50,450
Management of companies and enterprises	47,330
Business, professional, labor, political, and similar organizations	45,400
Local government	44,550
Colleges, universities, and professional schools	39,610

Related Occupations

Public relations specialists create favorable attitudes among various organizations, interest groups, and the public through effective communication. Other workers with similar jobs include advertising, marketing, promotions, public relations, and sales managers; demonstrators, product promoters, and models; news analysts, reporters, and correspondents; lawyers; market and survey researchers; sales representatives, wholesale and manufacturing; and police and detectives involved in community relations.

Sources of Additional Information

A comprehensive directory of schools offering degree programs, a sequence of study in public relations, a brochure on careers in public relations, and a $5 brochure entitled *Where Shall I Go to Study Advertising and Public Relations* are available from:

- Public Relations Society of America, Inc., 33 Maiden Lane, New York, NY 10038-5150. Internet: http://www.prsa.org

For information on accreditation for public relations professionals and the IABC Student Web site, contact:

- International Association of Business Communicators, One Hallidie Plaza, Suite 600, San Francisco, CA 94102.

Radiologic Technologists and Technicians

(O*NET 29-2034.01 and 29-2034.02)

Significant Points

- Job opportunities are expected to be favorable; some employers report difficulty hiring sufficient numbers of radiologic technologists and technicians.
- Formal training programs in radiography range in length from 1 to 4 years and lead to a certificate, an associate degree, or a bachelor's degree.
- Although hospitals will remain the primary employer, a greater number of new jobs will be found in physicians' offices and diagnostic imaging centers.

Nature of the Work

Radiologic technologists and technicians take X rays and administer nonradioactive materials into patients' bloodstreams for diagnostic purposes. Some specialize in diagnostic imaging technologies, such as computerized tomography (CT) and magnetic resonance imaging (MRI).

In addition to radiologic technologists and technicians, others who conduct diagnostic imaging procedures include cardiovascular technologists and technicians, diagnostic medical sonographers, and nuclear medicine technologists.

Radiologic technologists and technicians, also referred to as *radiographers*, produce X-ray films (radiographs) of parts of the human body for use in diagnosing medical problems. They prepare patients for radiologic examinations by explaining the procedure, removing articles such as jewelry, through which X rays cannot pass, and positioning patients so that the parts of the body can be appropriately radiographed. To prevent unnecessary exposure to radiation, these workers surround the exposed area with radiation protection devices, such as lead shields, or limit the size of the X-ray beam. Radiographers position radiographic equipment at the correct angle and height over the appropriate area of a patient's body. Using instruments similar to a measuring tape, they may measure the thickness of the section to be radiographed and set controls on the X-ray machine to produce radiographs of the appropriate density, detail, and contrast. They place the X-ray film under the part of the patient's body to be examined and make the exposure. They then remove the film and develop it.

Experienced radiographers may perform more complex imaging procedures. For fluoroscopies, radiographers prepare a solution of contrast medium for the patient to drink, allowing the radiologist (a physician who interprets radiographs) to see soft tissues in the body. Some radiographers, called *CT technologists*, operate CT scanners to produce cross-sectional images of patients. Radiographers who operate machines that use strong magnets and radio waves, rather than radiation, to create an image are called *MRI technologists*.

Radiologic technologists and technicians must follow physicians' orders precisely and conform to regulations concerning the use of radiation to protect themselves, their patients, and their co-workers from unnecessary exposure.

In addition to preparing patients and operating equipment, radiologic technologists and technicians keep patient records and adjust and maintain equipment. They also may prepare work schedules, evaluate purchases of equipment, or manage a radiology department.

Working Conditions

Most full-time radiologic technologists and technicians work about 40 hours a week. They may, however, have evening, weekend, or on-call hours. Opportunities for part time and shift work also are available.

Physical stamina is important, because technologists and technicians are on their feet for long periods and may lift or turn disabled patients. Technologists and technicians work at diagnostic machines, but also may perform some procedures at patients' bedsides. Some travel to patients in large vans equipped with sophisticated diagnostic equipment.

Although radiation hazards exist in this occupation, they are minimized by the use of lead aprons, gloves, and other shielding devices, as well as by instruments monitoring exposure to radiation. Technologists and technicians wear badges measuring radiation levels in the radiation area, and detailed records are kept on their cumulative lifetime dose.

Training, Other Qualifications, and Advancement

Preparation for this profession is offered in hospitals, colleges and universities, vocational-technical institutes, and the U.S. Armed Forces. Hospitals, which employ most radiologic technologists and technicians, prefer to hire those with formal training.

Formal training programs in radiography range in length from 1 to 4 years and lead to a certificate, an associate degree, or a bachelor's degree. Two-year associate degree programs are most prevalent.

Some 1-year certificate programs are available for experienced radiographers or individuals from other health occupations, such as medical technologists and registered nurses, who want to change fields or specialize in CT or MRI. A bachelor's or master's degree in one of the radiologic technologies is desirable for supervisory, administrative, or teaching positions.

The Joint Review Committee on Education in Radiologic Technology accredits most formal training programs for the field. The committee accredited 606 radiography programs in 2005. Radiography programs require, at a minimum, a high school diploma or the equivalent. High school courses in mathematics, physics, chemistry, and biology are helpful. The programs provide both classroom and clinical instruction in anatomy and physiology, patient care procedures, radiation physics, radiation protection, principles of imaging, medical terminology, positioning of patients, medical ethics, radiobiology, and pathology.

Federal legislation protects the public from the hazards of unnecessary exposure to medical and dental radiation by ensuring that operators of radiologic equipment are properly trained. Under this legislation, the federal government sets voluntary standards that the states may use for accrediting training programs and certifying individuals who engage in medical or dental radiography.

In 2005, 38 states certified radiologic technologists and technicians. Certification, which is voluntary, is offered by the American Registry of Radiologic Technologists. To be eligible for certification, technologists generally must graduate from an accredited program and pass an examination. Many employers prefer to hire certified radiographers. To be recertified, radiographers must complete 24 hours of continuing education every two years.

Radiologic technologists and technicians should be sensitive to patients' physical and psychological needs. They must pay attention to detail, follow instructions, and work as part of a team. In addition, operating complicated equipment requires mechanical ability and manual dexterity.

With experience and additional training, staff technologists may become specialists, performing CT scanning, angiography, and magnetic resonance imaging. Experienced technologists also may be promoted to supervisor, chief radiologic technologist, and, ultimately, department administrator or director. Depending on the institution, courses or a master's degree in business or health administration may be necessary for the director's position. Some technologists progress by leaving the occupation to become instructors or directors in radiologic technology programs; others take jobs as sales representatives or instructors with equipment manufacturers.

Employment

Radiologic technologists and technicians held about 182,000 jobs in 2004. More than half of all jobs were in hospitals. Most of the rest were in offices of physicians; medical and diagnostic laboratories, including diagnostic imaging centers; and outpatient care centers.

Job Outlook

Job opportunities are expected to be favorable. Some employers report difficulty hiring sufficient numbers of radiologic technologists and technicians. Imbalances between the demand for, and supply of, radiologic technologists and technicians should spur efforts to attract and retain qualified workers, such as improved compensation and working conditions. Radiologic technologists who also are experienced in more complex diagnostic imaging procedures, such as CT and MRI, will have better employment opportunities, brought about as employers seek to control costs by using multiskilled employees.

Employment of radiologic technologists and technicians is expected to grow faster than the average for all occupations through 2014, as the population grows and ages, increasing the demand for diagnostic imaging. Although health care providers are enthusiastic about the clinical benefits of new technologies, the extent to which they are adopted depends largely on cost and reimbursement considerations. For example, digital imaging technology can improve the quality of the images and the efficiency of the procedure, but remains expensive. Some promising new technologies may not come into widespread use because they are too expensive and third-party payers may not be willing to pay for their use.

Hospitals will remain the principal employer of radiologic technologists and technicians. However, a greater number of new jobs will be found in offices of physicians and diagnostic imaging centers. Health facilities such as these are expected to grow rapidly through 2014, due to the strong shift toward outpatient care, encouraged by third-party payers and made possible by technological advances that permit more procedures to be performed outside the hospital. Some job openings also will arise from the need to replace technologists and technicians who leave the occupation.

Earnings

Median annual earnings of radiologic technologists and technicians were $43,350 in May 2004. The middle 50 percent earned between $36,170 and $52,430. The lowest 10 percent earned less than $30,020, and the highest 10 percent earned more than $60,210. Median annual earnings in the industries employing the largest numbers of radiologic technologists and technicians in May 2004 were:

Medical and diagnostic laboratories	$46,620
General medical and surgical hospitals	43,960
Offices of physicians	40,290

Related Occupations

Radiologic technologists and technicians operate sophisticated equipment to help physicians, dentists, and other health practitioners diagnose and treat patients. Workers in related occupations include cardiovascular technologists and technicians, clinical laboratory technologists and technicians, diagnostic medical sonographers, nuclear medicine technologists, radiation therapists, and respiratory therapists.

Sources of Additional Information

For career information, send a stamped, self-addressed business-size envelope with your request to:

- American Society of Radiologic Technologists, 15000 Central Ave. S.E., Albuquerque, NM 87123-3917. Internet: http://www.asrt.org

For the current list of accredited education programs in radiography, write to:

- Joint Review Committee on Education in Radiologic Technology, 20 N. Wacker Dr., Suite 2850, Chicago, IL 60606-3182. Internet: http://www.jrcert.org

For information on certification, contact:

- American Registry of Radiologic Technologists, 1255 Northland Dr., St. Paul, MN 55120-1155. Internet: http://www.arrt.org

Real Estate Brokers and Sales Agents

(O*NET 41-9021.00 and 41-9022.00)

Significant Points

- Real estate brokers and sales agents often work evenings and weekends and usually are on call to suit the needs of clients.
- A license is required in every state and the District of Columbia.
- Although gaining a job may be relatively easy, beginning workers may face competition from well-established, more experienced agents and brokers in obtaining listings and in closing an adequate number of sales.
- Employment is sensitive to swings in the economy, especially interest rates; during periods of declining economic activity and increasing interest rates, the volume of sales and the resulting demand for sales workers fall.

Nature of the Work

One of the most complex and significant financial events in peoples' lives is the purchase or sale of a home or investment property. Because of this complexity and significance, people typically seek the help of real estate brokers and sales agents when buying or selling real estate.

Real estate brokers and sales agents have a thorough knowledge of the real estate market in their communities. They know which neighborhoods will best fit clients' needs and budgets. They are familiar with local zoning and tax laws and know where to obtain financing. Agents and brokers also act as intermediaries in price negotiations between buyers and sellers.

Real estate agents usually are independent sales workers who provide their services to a licensed real estate broker on a contract basis. In return, the broker pays the agent a portion of the commission earned from the agent's sale of the property. Brokers are independent businesspeople who sell real estate owned by others; they also may rent or manage properties for a fee. When selling real estate, brokers arrange for title searches and for meetings between buyers and sellers during which the details of the transactions are agreed upon and the new owners take possession of the property. A broker may help to arrange favorable financing from a lender for the prospective buyer; often, this makes the difference between success and failure in closing a sale. In some cases, brokers and agents assume primary responsibility for closing sales; in others, lawyers or lenders do. Brokers supervise agents who may have many of the same job duties. Brokers also supervise their own offices, advertise properties, and handle other business matters. Some combine other types of work, such as selling insurance or practicing law, with their real estate business.

Besides making sales, agents and brokers must have properties to sell. Consequently, they spend a significant amount of time obtaining listings—agreements by owners to place properties for sale with the firm. When listing a property for sale, agents and brokers compare the listed property with similar properties that recently sold, in order to determine a competitive market price for the property. Once the property is sold, both the agent who sold it and the agent who obtained the listing receive a portion of the commission. Thus, agents who sell a property that they themselves have listed can increase their commission.

Most real estate brokers and sales agents sell residential property. A small number—usually employed in large or specialized firms—sell commercial, industrial, agricultural, or other types of real estate. Every specialty requires knowledge of that particular type of property and clientele. Selling or leasing business property requires an understanding of leasing practices, business trends, and the location of the property. Agents who sell or lease industrial properties must know about the region's transportation, utilities, and labor supply. Whatever the type of property, the agent or broker must know how to meet the client's particular requirements.

Before showing residential properties to potential buyers, agents meet with them to get a feeling for the type of home the buyers would like. In this prequalifying phase, the agent determines how much the buyers can afford to spend. In addition, the agent and the buyer usually sign a loyalty contract which states that the agent will be the only one to show houses to buyers. An agent or broker then generates lists of properties for sale, their location and description, and available sources of financing. In some cases, agents and brokers use computers to give buyers a virtual tour of properties in which they are interested. With a computer, buyers can view interior and exterior images or floor plans without leaving the real estate office.

Agents may meet several times with prospective buyers to discuss and visit available properties. Agents identify and emphasize the most pertinent selling points. To a young family looking for a house, they may emphasize the convenient floor plan, the area's low crime rate, and the proximity to schools and shopping centers. To a potential investor, they may point out the tax advantages of owning a rental property and the ease of finding a renter. If bargaining over price becomes necessary, agents must follow their client's instructions carefully and may have to present counteroffers in order to get the best possible price.

Once both parties have signed the contract, the real estate broker or agent must make sure that all special terms of the contract are met before the closing date. For example, the agent must make sure that the mandated and agreed-upon inspections, including that of the home and termite and radon inspections, take place. Also, if the seller agrees to any repairs, the broker or agent must see that they are made. Increasingly, brokers and agents are handling environmental problems as well, by making sure that the properties they sell meet environmental regulations. For example, they may be responsible for dealing with lead paint on the walls. While loan officers, attorneys, or other persons handle many details, the agent must ensure that they are carried out.

Working Conditions

Advances in telecommunications and the ability to retrieve data about properties over the Internet allow many real estate brokers and sales agents to work out of their homes instead of real estate offices. Even with this convenience, much of the time of these workers is spent away from their desks—showing properties to customers, analyzing properties for sale, meeting with prospective clients, or researching the state of the market.

Agents and brokers often work more than a standard 40-hour week. They usually work evenings and weekends and are always on call to suit the needs of clients. Although the hours are long and frequently irregular, most agents and brokers have the freedom to determine their own schedule. Consequently, they can arrange their work so that they can have time off when they want it. Business usually is slower during the winter season.

Training, Other Qualifications, and Advancement

In every state and the District of Columbia, real estate brokers and sales agents must be licensed. Prospective agents must be high school graduates, be at least 18 years old, and pass a written test. The examination—more comprehensive for brokers than for agents—includes questions on basic real estate transactions and laws affecting the sale of property. Most states require candidates for the general sales license to complete between 30 and 90 hours of classroom instruction. Those seeking a broker's license need between 60 and 90 hours of formal training and a specific amount of experience selling real estate, usually 1 to 3 years. Some states waive the experience requirements for the broker's license for applicants who have a bachelor's degree in real estate.

State licenses typically must be renewed every 1 or 2 years; usually, no examination needs to be taken. However, many states require continuing education for license renewals. Prospective agents and brokers should contact the real estate licensing commission of the state in which they wish to work in order to verify the exact licensing requirements.

As real estate transactions have become more legally complex, many firms have turned to college graduates to fill positions. A large number of agents and brokers have some college training. College courses in real estate, finance, business administration, statistics, economics, law, and English are helpful. For those who intend to start their own company, business courses such as marketing and accounting are as significant as courses in real estate or finance.

Personality traits are equally as important as one's academic background. Brokers look for applicants who possess a pleasant personality, are honest, and present a neat appearance. Maturity, good judgment, trustworthiness, and enthusiasm for the job are required in order to encourage prospective customers in this highly competitive field. Agents should be well organized, be detail oriented, and have a good memory for names, faces, and business particulars.

Those interested in jobs as real estate agents often begin in their own communities. Their knowledge of local neighborhoods is a clear advantage. Under the direction of an experienced agent, beginners learn the practical aspects of the job, including the use of computers to locate or list available properties and identify sources of financing.

Many firms offer formal training programs for both beginners and experienced agents. Larger firms usually offer more extensive programs than smaller firms. More than a thousand universities, colleges, and junior colleges offer courses in real estate. At some, a student can earn an associate's or bachelor's degree with a major in real estate; several offer advanced degrees. Many local real estate associations that are members of the National Association of Realtors sponsor courses covering the fundamentals and legal aspects of the field. Advanced courses in mortgage financing, property development and management, and other subjects also are available.

Advancement opportunities for agents may take the form of higher rates of commission. As agents gain knowledge and expertise, they become more efficient in closing a greater number of transactions and increase their earnings. In many large firms, experienced agents can advance to sales manager or general manager. Persons who have received their broker's license may open their own offices. Others with experience and training in estimating property value may become real estate appraisers, and people familiar with operating and maintaining rental properties may become property managers. Experienced agents and brokers with a thorough knowledge of business conditions and property values in their localities may enter mortgage financing or real estate investment counseling.

Employment

In 2004, real estate brokers and sales agents held about 460,000 jobs; real estate sales agents held approximately 24 percent of these jobs. Many worked part time, combining their real estate activities with other careers. About 6 out of 10 real estate agents and brokers were self-employed. Real estate is sold in all areas, but employment is concentrated in large urban areas and in rapidly growing communities.

Most real estate firms are relatively small; indeed, some are one-person businesses. By contrast, some large real estate firms have several hundred agents operating out of numerous branch offices. Many brokers have franchise agreements with national or regional real estate organizations. Under this type of arrangement, the broker pays a fee in exchange for the privilege of using the more widely known name of the parent organization. Although franchised brokers often receive help in training sales staff and running their offices, they bear the ultimate responsibility for the success or failure of their firms.

Real estate brokers and sales agents are older, on average, than most other workers. Historically, many homemakers and retired persons were attracted to real estate sales by the flexible and part-time work schedules characteristic of the field. These individuals could enter, leave, and later return to the occupation, depending on the strength of the real estate market, their family responsibilities, or other personal circumstances. Recently, however, the attractiveness of part-time real estate work has declined, as increasingly complex legal and technological requirements are raising startup costs associated with becoming an agent.

Job Outlook

Employment of real estate brokers and sales agents is expected to grow about as fast as average for all occupations through the year 2014, because of the increasing housing needs of a growing population, as well as the perception that real estate is a good investment. Relatively low interest rates should continue to stimulate sales of real estate, resulting in the need for more agents and brokers. In addition, a large number of job openings will arise each year from the need to replace workers who transfer to other occupations or leave the labor force. However, job growth will be somewhat limited by the increasing use of technology, which is improving the productivity of agents and brokers. For example, prospective customers often can perform their own searches for properties that meet their criteria by accessing real estate information on the Internet. The increasing use of technology is likely to be more detrimental to part-time or temporary real estate agents than to full-time agents, because part-time agents generally are not able to compete with full-time agents who have invested in new technology. Changing legal requirements, such as disclosure laws, also may dissuade some who are not serious about practicing full time from continuing to work part time.

This occupation is relatively easy to enter and is attractive because of its flexible working conditions; the high interest in, and familiarity with, local real estate markets that entrants often have; and the potential for high earnings. Therefore, although gaining a job as a real estate agent or broker may be relatively easy, beginning agents and brokers may face competition from their well-established, more experienced counterparts in obtaining listings and in closing an adequate number of sales. Well-trained, ambitious people who enjoy selling—particularly those with extensive social and business connections in their communities—should have the best chance for success.

Employment of real estate brokers and sales agents often is sensitive to swings in the economy, especially interest rates. During periods of declining economic activity and increasing interest rates, the volume of sales and the resulting demand for sales workers falls. As a result, the earnings of agents and brokers decline, and many work fewer hours or leave the occupation altogether.

Earnings

The median annual earnings of salaried real estate sales agents, including commissions, were $35,670 in May 2004. The middle 50 percent earned between $23,500 and $58,110 a year. The lowest 10 percent earned less than $17,600, and the highest 10 percent earned more than $92,770. Median annual earnings in the industries employing the largest number of real estate sales agents in May 2004 were as follows:

Residential building construction	$54,770
Offices of real estate agents and brokers	37,970
Activities related to real estate	32,460
Lessors of real estate	25,840

Median annual earnings of salaried real estate brokers, including commission, were $58,720 in May 2004. The middle 50 percent earned between $33,480 and $99,820 a year. Median annual earning of real estate brokers were $61,550 in offices of real estate agents and brokers and $44,920 in activities related to real estate.

Commissions on sales are the main source of earnings of real estate agents and brokers. The rate of commission varies according to whatever the agent and broker agree on, the type of property, and its value. The percentage paid on the sale of farm and commercial properties or unimproved land is typically higher than the percentage paid for selling a home.

Commissions may be divided among several agents and brokers. When the property is sold, the broker or agent who obtained the listing usually shares the commission with the broker or agent who made the sale and with the firm that employs each of them. Although an agent's share varies greatly from one firm to another, often it is about half of the total amount received by the firm. Agents who both list and sell a property maximize their commission.

Income usually increases as an agent gains experience, but individual motivation, economic conditions, and the type and location of the property also affect earnings. Sales workers who are active in community organizations and in local real estate associations can broaden their contacts and increase their earnings. A beginner's earnings often are irregular, because a few weeks or even months may go by without a sale. Although some brokers allow an agent to draw against future earnings from a special account, the practice is not common with new employees. The beginner, therefore, should have enough money to live for about 6 months or until commissions increase.

Related Occupations

Selling expensive items such as homes requires maturity, tact, and a sense of responsibility. Other sales workers who find these character traits important in their work include insurance sales agents; retail salespersons; sales representatives, wholesale and manufacturing; and securities, commodities, and financial services sales agents. Although not involving sales, the work of property, real estate, and community association managers, as well as appraisers and assessors of real estate, requires an understanding of real estate.

Sources of Additional Information

Information on licensing requirements for real estate brokers and sales agents is available from most local real estate organizations or from the state real estate commission or board.

More information about opportunities in real estate is available on the Internet site of the following organization:

- National Association of Realtors. Internet: http://www.realtor.org

Receptionists and Information Clerks

(O*NET 43-4171.00)

Significant Points

- Good interpersonal skills are critical.
- A high school diploma or its equivalent is the most common educational requirement.
- Employment is expected to grow faster than average.

Nature of the Work

Receptionists and information clerks are charged with a responsibility that may have a lasting impact on the success of an organization:

making a good first impression. These workers often are the first representatives of an organization that a visitor may encounter, so good interpersonal skills—being courteous, professional, and helpful—are critical. Receptionists answer telephones, route and screen calls, greet visitors, respond to inquiries from the public, and provide information about the organization. Some receptionists are responsible for the coordination of all mail into and out of the office. In addition, receptionists contribute to the security of an organization by helping to monitor the access of visitors—a function that has become increasingly important since the terrorist attacks of September 11, 2001, heightened security concerns.

Whereas some tasks are common to most receptionists and information clerks, the specific responsibilities of receptionists vary with the type of establishment in which they work. For example, receptionists in hospitals and in doctors' offices may gather patients' personal and financial information and direct them to the proper waiting rooms. In corporate headquarters, receptionists may greet visitors and manage the scheduling of the board room or common conference area. In beauty or hair salons, by contrast, receptionists arrange appointments, direct customers to the hairstylist, and may serve as cashiers. In factories, large corporations, and government offices, they may provide identification cards and arrange for escorts to take visitors to the proper office. Those working for bus and train companies respond to inquiries about departures, arrivals, stops, and other related matters.

Increasingly, receptionists use multiline telephone systems, personal computers, and fax machines. Despite the widespread use of automated answering systems or voice mail, many receptionists still take messages and inform other employees of visitors' arrivals or cancellation of an appointment. When they are not busy with callers, most receptionists are expected to perform a variety of office duties, including opening and sorting mail, collecting and distributing parcels, transmitting and delivering facsimiles, updating appointment calendars, preparing travel vouchers, and performing basic bookkeeping, word processing, and filing.

Working Conditions

Receptionists who greet customers and visitors usually work in areas that are highly visible and designed and furnished to make a good impression. Most work stations are clean, well lighted, and relatively quiet. The work performed by some receptionists and information clerks may be tiring, repetitious, and stressful as many receptionists spend all day answering continuously ringing telephones and sometimes encounter difficult or irate callers. The work environment, however, may be very friendly and motivating for individuals who enjoy greeting customers face to face and making them feel comfortable.

Training, Other Qualifications, and Advancement

Although hiring requirements for receptionists and information clerks vary by industry, a high school diploma or its equivalent is the most common educational requirement. Good interpersonal skills and being technologically proficient also are important to employers. Receptionists and information clerks generally receive on-the-job training. However, employers often look for applicants who already possess certain skills, such as prior computer experience or answering telephones. Some employers also may prefer some formal office education or training. On the job, they learn how to operate the telephone system and computers. They also learn the proper procedures for greeting visitors and for distributing mail, faxes, and parcels.

Advancement for receptionists generally comes about either by transferring to a more responsible occupation or by being promoted to a supervisory position. Receptionists with especially strong computer skills may advance to a better paying job as a secretary or an administrative assistant.

Employment

Receptionists and information clerks held about 1.1 million jobs in 2004. More than 90 percent worked in service-providing industries. Among service-providing industries, health care and social assistance industries—including doctors' and dentists' offices, hospitals, nursing homes, urgent-care centers, surgical centers, and clinics—employed about one-third of all receptionists and information clerks. Manufacturing, wholesale and retail trade, government, and real estate industries also employed large numbers of receptionists and information clerks. More than 3 of every 10 receptionists and information clerks worked part time.

Job Outlook

Employment of receptionists and information clerks is expected to grow faster than the average for all occupations through 2014. This increase will result from rapid growth in service-providing industries—including physicians' offices, law firms, temporary help agencies, and consulting firms—where most are employed. In addition, turnover in this large occupation will create numerous openings as receptionists and information clerks transfer to other occupations or leave the labor force altogether. Opportunities should be best for persons with a wide range of clerical and technical skills, particularly those with related work experience.

Technology will have conflicting effects on the demand for receptionists and information clerks. The increasing use of voice mail and other telephone automation reduces the need for receptionists by allowing one receptionist to perform work that formerly required several. However, the increasing use of other technology has caused a consolidation of clerical responsibilities and growing demand for workers with diverse clerical and technical skills. Because receptionists and information clerks may perform a wide variety of clerical tasks, they should continue to be in demand. Further, they perform many tasks that are interpersonal in nature and are not easily automated, ensuring continued demand for their services in a variety of establishments.

Earnings

Median hourly earnings of receptionists and information clerks in May 2004 were $10.50. The middle 50 percent earned between $8.62 and $12.88. The lowest 10 percent earned less than $7.21, and the highest 10 percent earned more than $15.53. Median hourly earnings in the industries employing the largest number of receptionists and information clerks in May 2004 are shown below.

Offices of dentists	$12.37
General medical and surgical hospitals	11.07
Offices of physicians	10.92
Employment services	10.28
Personal care services	8.16

In 2005, the federal government typically paid salaries ranging from $22,937 to $27,818 a year to beginning receptionists with a high school diploma or 6 months of experience. The average annual salary for all receptionists employed by the federal government was about $29,185 in 2005.

Related Occupations

Receptionists deal with the public and often direct people to others who can assist them. Other workers who perform similar duties include dispatchers, secretaries and administrative assistants, and customer service representatives.

Sources of Additional Information

State employment offices can provide information on job openings for receptionists.

Recreation Workers

(O*NET 39-9032.00)

Significant Points

- Educational requirements for recreation workers range from a high school diploma to a graduate degree. Competition will remain keen for full-time career positions in recreation. The recreation field offers an unusually large number of part time and seasonal job opportunities.

Nature of the Work

People spend much of their leisure time participating in a wide variety of organized recreational activities, such as arts and crafts, the performing arts, camping, and sports. Recreation workers plan, organize, and direct these activities in local playgrounds and recreation areas, parks, community centers, religious organizations, camps, theme parks, and tourist attractions. Increasingly, recreation workers also are being found in workplaces, where they organize and direct leisure activities for employees.

Recreation workers hold a variety of positions at different levels of responsibility. *Recreation leaders*, who are responsible for a recreation program's daily operation, primarily organize and direct participants. They may lead and give instruction in dance, drama, crafts, games, and sports; schedule the use of facilities; keep records of equipment use; and ensure that recreation facilities and equipment are used properly. Workers who provide instruction and coach groups in specialties such as art, music, drama, swimming, or tennis may be called *activity specialists*. *Recreation supervisors* oversee recreation leaders and plan, organize, and manage recreational activities to meet the needs of a variety of populations. These workers often serve as liaisons between the director of the park or recreation center and the recreation leaders. Recreation supervisors with more specialized responsibilities also may direct special activities or events or oversee a major activity, such as aquatics, gymnastics, or performing arts. *Directors of recreation and parks* develop and manage comprehensive recreation programs in parks, playgrounds, and other settings. Directors usually serve as technical advisors to state and local recreation and park commissions and may be responsible for recreation and park budgets.

Camp counselors lead and instruct children and teenagers in outdoor-oriented forms of recreation, such as swimming, hiking, horseback riding, and camping. In addition, counselors provide campers with specialized instruction in subjects such as archery, boating, music, drama, gymnastics, tennis, and computers. In resident camps, counselors also provide guidance and supervise daily living and general socialization. *Camp directors* typically supervise camp counselors, plan camp activities or programs, and perform the various administrative functions of a camp.

Working Conditions

Recreation workers may work in a variety of settings—for example, a cruise ship, a woodland recreational park, a summer camp, or a playground in the center of a large urban community. Regardless of the setting, most recreation workers spend much of their time outdoors and may work in a variety of weather conditions. Recreation directors and supervisors, however, typically spend most of their time in an office, planning programs and special events. Directors and supervisors generally engage in less physical activity than do lower level recreation workers. Nevertheless, recreation workers at all levels risk suffering injuries during physical activities.

Many recreation workers work about 40 hours a week. People entering this field, especially camp counselors, should expect some night and weekend work and irregular hours. Many recreation jobs are seasonal.

Training, Other Qualifications, and Advancement

Educational requirements for recreation workers range from a high school diploma—or sometimes less for those seeking many summer jobs—to graduate degrees for some administrative positions in large public recreation systems. Full-time career professional positions usually require a college degree with a major in parks and recreation or leisure studies, but a bachelor's degree in any liberal arts field may be sufficient for some jobs in the private sector. In industrial recreation, or "employee services" as it is more commonly called, companies prefer to hire those with a bachelor's degree in recreation or leisure studies and a background in business administration.

Specialized training or experience in a particular field, such as art, music, drama, or athletics, is an asset for many jobs. Some jobs also require certification. For example, a lifesaving certificate is a prerequisite for teaching or coaching water-related activities. Graduates of associate's degree programs in parks and recreation, social work, and other human services disciplines also enter some career recreation positions. High school graduates occasionally enter career positions, but this is not common. Some college students work part time as recreation workers while earning degrees.

A bachelor's degree in a recreation-related discipline and experience are preferred for most recreation supervisor jobs and are required for higher level administrative jobs. However, an increasing number of recreation workers who aspire to administrative positions are obtaining master's degrees in parks and recreation, business administration, or public administration. Certification in the recreation field may be helpful for advancement. Also, many persons in other disciplines, including social work, forestry, and resource management, pursue graduate degrees in recreation.

Programs leading to an associate's or bachelor's degree in parks and recreation, leisure studies, or related fields are offered at several hundred colleges and universities. Many also offer master's or doctoral degrees in the field. In 2004, about 100 bachelor's degree programs in parks and recreation were accredited by the National Recreation and Park Association (NRPA). Accredited programs provide broad exposure to the history, theory, and practice of park and recreation management. Courses offered include community organization; supervision and administration; recreational needs of special populations, such as the elderly or disabled; and supervised fieldwork. Students may specialize in areas such as therapeutic recreation, park management, outdoor recreation, industrial or commercial recreation, or camp management.

The NRPA certifies individuals for professional and technical jobs. Certified Park and Recreation Professionals must pass an exam; earn a bachelor's degree with a major in recreation, park resources, or leisure services from a program accredited by the NRPA and the American Association for Leisure and Recreation; or earn a bachelor's degree and have at least 5 years of relevant full-time work experience. Continuing education is necessary to remain certified.

Persons planning recreation careers should be outgoing, good at motivating people, and sensitive to the needs of others. Excellent health and physical fitness are often required, due to the physical nature of some jobs. Volunteer experience, part-time work during school, or a summer job can lead to a full-time career as a recreation worker. As in many fields, managerial skills are needed to advance to supervisory or managerial positions.

Employment

Recreation workers held about 310,000 jobs in 2004, and many additional workers held summer jobs in the occupation. Of those with year-round jobs as recreation workers, about 35 percent worked for local governments, primarily in park and recreation departments. Around 11 percent of recreation workers were employed in civic and social organizations, such as the Boy Scouts or Girl Scouts or the Red Cross. Another 15 percent of recreation workers were employed by nursing and other personal care facilities.

The recreation field has an unusually large number of part-time, seasonal, and volunteer jobs, including summer camp counselors, craft specialists, and after-school and weekend recreation program leaders. In addition, many teachers and college students accept jobs as recreation workers when school is not in session. The vast majority of volunteers serve as activity leaders at local day camp programs, or in youth organizations, camps, nursing homes, hospitals, senior centers, and other settings.

Job Outlook

Competition will remain keen for career positions as recreation workers because the field attracts many applicants and because the number of career positions is limited compared with the number of lower level seasonal jobs. Opportunities for staff positions should be best for persons with formal training and experience gained in part-time or seasonal recreation jobs. Those with graduate degrees should have the best opportunities for supervisory or administrative positions. Job openings also will stem from the need to replace the large numbers of workers who leave the occupation each year.

Overall employment of recreation workers is expected to grow about as fast as the average for all occupations through 2014. People will spend more time and money on recreation, spurring growth in civic and social organizations and, to a lesser degree, state and local government. Much growth will be driven by retiring baby boomers, who, with more leisure time, high disposable income, and concern for health and fitness, are expected to increase their consumption of recreation services. Job growth also will be driven by rapidly increasing employment in nursing and residential care facilities. Employment growth may be inhibited, however, by budget constraints that local governments may face over the 2004–14 projection period.

The large number of temporary, seasonal jobs in the recreation field typically are filled by high school or college students, generally do not have formal education requirements, and are open to anyone with the desired personal qualities. Employers compete for a share of the vacationing student labor force, and although salaries in recreation often are lower than those in other fields, the nature of the work and the opportunity to work outdoors are attractive to many.

Earnings

In May 2004, median annual earnings of recreation workers who worked full time were $19,320. The middle 50 percent earned between $15,640 and $25,380. The lowest paid 10 percent earned less than $13,260, while the highest paid 10 percent earned $34,280 or more. However, earnings of recreation directors and others in supervisory or managerial positions can be substantially higher. Most public and private recreation agencies provide full-time recreation workers with typical benefits; part-time workers receive few, if any, benefits. In May 2004, median annual earnings in the industries employing the largest numbers of recreation workers were as follows:

Nursing care facilities....................................$20,660
Local government 19,650
Individual and family services 19,260
Other amusement and recreation industries 17,060
Civic and social organizations 16,950

Related Occupations

Recreation workers must exhibit leadership and sensitivity when dealing with people. Other occupations that require similar personal qualities include counselors, probation officers and correctional treatment specialists, psychologists, recreational therapists, and social workers.

Sources of Additional Information

For information on jobs in recreation, contact employers such as local government departments of parks and recreation, nursing and personal care facilities, the Boy Scouts or Girl Scouts, or local social or religious organizations.

For information on careers, certification, and academic programs in parks and recreation, contact:

- National Recreation and Park Association, Division of Professional Services, 22377 Belmont Ridge Rd., Ashburn, VA 20148-4501. Internet: http://www.nrpa.org

For career information about camp counselors, contact:

- American Camping Association, 5000 State Road 67 North, Martinsville, IN 46151-7902. Internet: http://www.acacamps.org

Registered Nurses

(O*NET 29-1111.00)

Significant Points

- Registered nurses constitute the largest health care occupation, with 2.4 million jobs.
- About 3 out of 5 jobs are in hospitals.
- The three major educational paths to registered nursing are a bachelor's degree, an associate degree, and a diploma from an approved nursing program.
- Registered nurses are projected to create the second largest number of new jobs among all occupations; job opportunities in most specialties and employment settings are expected to be excellent, with some employers reporting difficulty in attracting and retaining enough RNs.

Nature of the Work

Registered nurses (RNs), regardless of specialty or work setting, perform basic duties that include treating patients, educating patients and the public about various medical conditions, and providing advice and emotional support to patients' family members. RNs record patients' medical histories and symptoms, help to perform diagnostic tests and analyze results, operate medical machinery, administer treatment and medications, and help with patient follow-up and rehabilitation.

RNs teach patients and their families how to manage their illness or injury, including post-treatment home care needs, diet and exercise programs, and self-administration of medication and physical therapy. Some RNs also are trained to provide grief counseling to family members of critically ill patients. RNs work to promote general health by educating the public on various warning signs and symptoms of disease and where to go for help. RNs also might run general health screening or immunization clinics, blood drives, and public seminars on various conditions.

RNs can specialize in one or more patient care specialties. The most common specialties can be divided into roughly four categories—by work setting or type of treatment; disease, ailment, or condition; organ or body system type; or population. RNs may combine specialties from more than one area—for example, pediatric oncology or cardiac emergency—depending on personal interest and employer needs.

RNs may specialize by work setting or by type of care provided. For example, *ambulatory care nurses* treat patients with a variety of illnesses and injuries on an outpatient basis, either in physicians' offices or in clinics. Some ambulatory care nurses are involved in telehealth, providing care and advice through electronic communications media such as videoconferencing or the Internet. *Critical care nurses* work in critical or intensive care hospital units and provide care to patients with cardiovascular, respiratory, or pulmonary failure. *Emergency,* or *trauma, nurses* work in hospital emergency departments and treat patients with life-threatening conditions caused by accidents, heart attacks, and strokes. Some emergency nurses are flight nurses, who provide medical care to patients who must be flown by helicopter to the nearest medical facility. *Holistic nurses* provide care such as acupuncture, massage and aroma therapy, and biofeedback, which are meant to treat patients' mental and spiritual health in addition to their physical health. *Home health care nurses* provide at-home care for patients who are recovering from surgery, accidents, and childbirth. *Hospice and palliative care nurses* provide care for, and help ease the pain of, terminally ill patients outside of hospitals. *Infusion nurses* administer medications, fluids, and blood to patients through injections into patients' veins. *Long- term care nurses* provide medical services on a recurring basis to patients with chronic physical or mental disorders. *Medical-surgical nurses* provide basic medical care to a variety of patients in all health settings. *Occupational health nurses* provide treatment for job-related injuries and illnesses and help employers to detect workplace hazards and implement health and safety standards. *Perianesthesia nurses* provide preoperative and postoperative care to patients undergoing anesthesia during surgery. *Perioperative nurses* assist surgeons by selecting and handling instruments, controlling bleeding, and suturing incisions. Some of these nurses also can specialize in plastic and reconstructive surgery. *Psychiatric nurses* treat patients with personality and mood disorders. *Radiologic nurses* provide care to patients undergoing diagnostic radiation procedures such as ultrasounds and magnetic resonance imaging. *Rehabilitation nurses* care for patients with temporary and permanent disabilities. *Transplant nurses* care for both transplant recipients and living donors and monitor signs of organ rejection.

RNs specializing in a particular disease, ailment, or condition are employed in virtually all work settings, including physicians' offices, outpatient treatment facilities, home health care agencies, and hospitals. For instance, *addictions nurses* treat patients seeking help with alcohol, drug, and tobacco addictions. *Developmental disabilities nurses* provide care for patients with physical, mental, or behavioral disabilities; care may include help with feeding, controlling bodily functions, and sitting or standing independently. *Diabetes management nurses* help diabetics to manage their disease by teaching them proper nutrition and showing them how to test blood sugar levels and administer insulin injections. *Genetics nurses* provide early detection screenings and treatment of patients with genetic disorders, including cystic fibrosis and Huntington's disease. *HIV/AIDS nurses* care for patients diagnosed with HIV and AIDS. *Oncology nurses* care for patients with various types of cancer and may administer radiation and chemotherapies. Finally, *wound, ostomy, and continence nurses* treat patients with wounds caused by traumatic injury, ulcers, or arterial disease; provide post-operative care for patients with openings that allow for alternative methods of bodily waste elimination; and treat patients with urinary and fecal incontinence.

RNs specializing in treatment of a particular organ or body system usually are employed in specialty physicians' offices or outpatient care facilities, although some are employed in hospital specialty or critical care units. For example, *cardiac and vascular nurses* treat patients with coronary heart disease and those who have had heart surgery, providing services such as postoperative rehabilitation. *Dermatology nurses* treat patients with disorders of the skin, such as skin cancer and psoriasis. *Gastroenterology nurses* treat patients with digestive and intestinal disorders, including ulcers, acid reflux disease, and abdominal bleeding. Some nurses in this field also specialize in endoscopic procedures, which look inside the gastrointestinal tract using a tube equipped with a light and a camera that can capture images of diseased tissue. *Gynecology nurses* provide care to women with disorders of the reproductive system, including endometriosis, cancer, and sexually transmitted diseases. *Nephrology nurses* care for patients with kidney disease caused by diabetes, hypertension, or substance abuse. *Neuroscience nurses* care for patients with dysfunctions of the nervous system, including brain and spinal cord injuries and seizures. *Ophthalmic nurses* provide care to patients with disorders of the eyes, including blindness and glaucoma, and to patients undergoing eye surgery. *Orthopedic nurses* care for patients with muscular and skeletal problems, including arthritis, bone fractures, and muscular dystrophy. *Otorhinolaryngology nurses* care for patients with ear, nose, and throat disorders, such as cleft palates, allergies, and sinus disorders. *Respiratory nurses* provide care to patients with respiratory disorders such as asthma, tuberculosis, and cystic fibrosis. *Urology nurses* care for patients with disorders of the kidneys, urinary tract, and male reproductive organs, including infections, kidney and bladder stones, and cancers.

Finally, RNs may specialize by providing preventive and acute care in all health care settings to various segments of the population, including newborns (neonatology), children and adolescents (pediatrics), adults, and the elderly (gerontology or geriatrics). RNs also may provide basic health care to patients outside of health care settings in such venues as including correctional facilities, schools, summer camps, and the military. Some RNs travel around the United States and abroad providing care to patients in areas with shortages of medical professionals.

Most RNs work as staff nurses, providing critical health care services along with physicians, surgeons, and other health care practitioners. However, some RNs choose to become advanced practice nurses, who often are considered primary health care practitioners and work independently or in collaboration with physicians. For example, *clinical nurse specialists* provide direct patient care and expert consultations in one of many of the nursing specialties listed above. *Nurse anesthetists* administer anesthesia, monitor patient's vital signs during surgery, and provide post-anesthesia care. *Nurse midwives* provide primary care to women, including gynecological exams, family planning advice, prenatal care, assistance in labor and delivery, and neonatal care. *Nurse practitioners* provide basic preventive health care to patients, and increasingly serve as primary and specialty care providers in mainly medically underserved areas. The most common areas of specialty for nurse practitioners are family practice, adult practice, women's health, pediatrics, acute care, and gerontology; however, there are many other specialties. In most states, advanced practice nurses can prescribe medications.

Some nurses have jobs that require little or no direct patient contact. Most of these positions still require an active RN license. *Case managers* ensure that all of the medical needs of patients with severe injuries and illnesses are met, including the type, location, and duration of treatment. *Forensics nurses* combine nursing with law enforcement by treating and investigating victims of sexual assault, child abuse, or accidental death. *Infection control nurses* identify, track, and control infectious outbreaks in health care facilities; develop methods of outbreak prevention and biological terrorism responses; and staff immunization clinics. *Legal nurse consultants* assist lawyers in medical cases by interviewing patients and witnesses, organizing medical records, determining damages and costs, locating evidence, and educating lawyers about medical issues. *Nurse administrators* supervise nursing staff, establish work schedules and budgets, and maintain medical supply inventories. *Nurse educators* teach student nurses and also provide continuing education for RNs. *Nurse informaticists* collect, store, and analyze nursing data in order to improve efficiency, reduce risk, and improve patient care. RNs also may work as health care consultants, public policy advisors, pharmaceutical and medical supply researchers and salespersons, and medical writers and editors.

Working Conditions

Most RNs work in well-lighted, comfortable health care facilities. Home health and public health nurses travel to patients' homes, schools, community centers, and other sites. RNs may spend considerable time walking and standing. Patients in hospitals and nursing care facilities require 24-hour care; consequently, nurses in these institutions may work nights, weekends, and holidays. RNs also may be on call—available to work on short notice. Nurses who work in office settings are more likely to work regular business hours. About 23 percent of RNs worked part time in 2004, and 7 percent held more than one job.

Nursing has its hazards, especially in hospitals, nursing care facilities, and clinics, where nurses may care for individuals with infectious diseases. RNs must observe rigid, standardized guidelines to guard against disease and other dangers, such as those posed by radiation, accidental needle sticks, chemicals used to sterilize instruments, and anesthetics. In addition, they are vulnerable to back injury when moving patients, shocks from electrical equipment, and hazards posed by compressed gases. RNs who work with critically ill patients also may suffer emotional strain from observing patient suffering and from close personal contact with patients' families.

Training, Other Qualifications, and Advancement

In all states and the District of Columbia, students must graduate from an approved nursing program and pass a national licensing examination, known as the NCLEX-RN, in order to obtain a nursing license. Nurses may be licensed in more than one state, either by examination or by the endorsement of a license issued by another state. Currently 18 states participate in the Nurse Licensure Compact Agreement, which allows nurses to practice in member states without recertifying. All states require periodic renewal of licenses, which may involve continuing education.

There are three major educational paths to registered nursing: A bachelor's of science degree in nursing (BSN), an associate degree in nursing (ADN), and a diploma. BSN programs, offered by colleges and universities, take about 4 years to complete. In 2004, 674 nursing programs offered degrees at the bachelor's level. ADN programs, offered by community and junior colleges, take about 2 to 3 years to complete. About 846 RN programs in 2004 granted associate degrees. Diploma programs, administered in hospitals, last about 3 years. Only 69 programs offered diplomas in 2004. Generally, licensed graduates of any of the three types of educational programs qualify for entry-level positions as staff nurses.

Many RNs with an ADN or diploma later enter bachelor's programs to prepare for a broader scope of nursing practice. Often, they can find a staff nurse position and then take advantage of tuition reimbursement benefits to work toward a BSN by completing an RN-to-BSN program. In 2004, there were 600 RN-to-BSN programs in the United States. Accelerated master's degree programs in nursing also are available. These programs combine 1 year of an accelerated BSN program with 2 years of graduate study. In 2004, there were 137 RN-to-MSN programs.

Accelerated BSN programs also are available for individuals who have a bachelor's or higher degree in another field and who are interested in moving into nursing. In 2004, more than 165 of these programs were available. Accelerated BSN programs last 12 to 18 months and provide the fastest route to a BSN for individuals who already hold a degree.

Individuals considering nursing should carefully weigh the advantages and disadvantages of enrolling in a BSN program, because, if they do, their advancement opportunities usually are broader. In fact, some career paths are open only to nurses with a bachelor's or master's degree. A bachelor's degree often is necessary for administrative positions and is a prerequisite for admission to graduate nursing programs in research, consulting, and teaching, and all four advanced practice nursing specialties—clinical nurse specialists, nurse anesthetists, nurse midwives, and nurse practitioners. Individuals who complete a bachelor's receive more training in areas such as communication, leadership, and critical thinking, all of which are becoming more important as nursing care becomes more complex. Additionally, bachelor's degree programs offer more clinical experience in nonhospital settings. In 2004, 417 nursing schools offered master's degrees, 93 offered doctoral degrees, and 46 offered accelerated BSN-to-doctoral programs.

All four advanced practice nursing specialties require at least a master's degree. Most programs last about 2 years and require a BSN degree and some programs require at least 1 to 2 years of clinical experience as an RN for admission. In 2004, there were 329 master's and post-master's programs offered for nurse practitioners, 218 master's and post-master's programs for clinical nurse specialists, 92 programs for nurse anesthetists, and 45 programs for nurse midwives. Upon completion of a program, most advanced practice nurses become nationally certified in their area of specialty. In some states, certification in a specialty is required in order to practice that specialty.

All nursing education programs include classroom instruction and supervised clinical experience in hospitals and other health care facilities. Students take courses in anatomy, physiology, microbiology, chemistry, nutrition, psychology and other behavioral sciences, and nursing. Coursework also includes the liberal arts for ADN and BSN students.

Supervised clinical experience is provided in hospital departments such as pediatrics, psychiatry, maternity, and surgery. A growing number of programs include clinical experience in nursing care facilities, public health departments, home health agencies, and ambulatory clinics.

Nurses should be caring, sympathetic, responsible, and detail oriented. They must be able to direct or supervise others, correctly assess patients' conditions, and determine when consultation is required. They need emotional stability to cope with human suffering, emergencies, and other stresses.

Some RNs start their careers as licensed practical nurses or nursing aides, and then go back to school to receive their RN degree. Most RNs begin as staff nurses, and with experience and good performance often are promoted to more responsible positions. In management, nurses can advance to assistant head nurse or head nurse and, from there, to assistant director, director, and vice president. Increasingly, management-level nursing positions require a graduate or an advanced degree in nursing or health services administration. They also require leadership, negotiation skills, and good judgment.

Some nurses move into the business side of health care. Their nursing expertise and experience on a health care team equip them to manage ambulatory, acute, home-based, and chronic care. Employers—including hospitals, insurance companies, pharmaceutical manufacturers, and managed care organizations, among others—need RNs for health planning and development, marketing, consulting, policy development, and quality assurance. Other nurses work as college and university faculty or conduct research.

Foreign-educated nurses wishing to work in the United States must obtain a work visa. Applicants are required to undergo a review of their education and licensing credentials and pass a nursing certification and English proficiency exam, both conducted by the Commission on Graduates of Foreign Nursing Schools. (The commission is an immigration-neutral, nonprofit organization that is recognized internationally as an authority on credentials evaluation in the health care field.) Applicants from Australia, Canada (except Quebec), Ireland, New Zealand, and the United Kingdom are exempt from the language proficiency exam. In addition to these national requirements, most states have their own requirements.

Employment

As the largest health care occupation, registered nurses held about 2.4 million jobs in 2004. About 3 out of 5 jobs were in hospitals, in inpatient and outpatient departments. Others worked in offices of physicians, nursing care facilities, home health care services, employment services, government agencies, and outpatient care centers. The remainder worked mostly in social assistance agencies and educational services, public and private. About 1 in 4 RNs worked part time.

Job Outlook

Job opportunities for RNs in all specialties are expected to be excellent. Employment of registered nurses is expected to grow much faster than average for all occupations through 2014, and, because the occupation is very large, many new jobs will result. In fact, registered nurses are projected to create the second largest number of new jobs among all occupations. Thousands of job openings also will result from the need to replace experienced nurses who leave the occupation, especially as the median age of the registered nurse population continues to rise.

Much faster-than-average growth will be driven by technological advances in patient care, which permit a greater number of medical problems to be treated, and by an increasing emphasis on preventive care. In addition, the number of older people, who are much more likely than younger people to need nursing care, is projected to grow rapidly.

Employers in some parts of the country and in certain employment settings are reporting difficulty in attracting and retaining an adequate number of RNs, primarily because of an aging RN workforce and a lack of younger workers to fill positions. Enrollments in nursing programs at all levels have increased more rapidly in the past couple of years as students seek jobs with stable employment. However, many qualified applicants are being turned away because of a shortage of nursing faculty to teach classes. The need for nursing faculty will only increase as a large number of instructors nears retirement. Many employers also are relying on foreign-educated nurses to fill open positions.

Even though employment opportunities for all nursing specialties are expected to be excellent, they can vary by employment setting. For example, employment is expected to grow more slowly in hospitals—which comprise health care's largest industry—than in most other health care industries. While the intensity of nursing care is likely to increase, requiring more nurses per patient, the number of inpatients (those who remain in the hospital for more than 24 hours) is not likely to grow by much. Patients are being discharged earlier, and more procedures are being done on an outpatient basis, both inside and outside hospitals. Rapid growth is expected in hospital outpatient facilities, such as those providing same-day surgery, rehabilitation, and chemotherapy.

Despite the slower employment growth in hospitals, job opportunities should still be excellent because of the relatively high turnover of hospital nurses. RNs working in hospitals frequently work overtime and night and weekend shifts and also treat seriously ill and injured patients, all of which can contribute to stress and burnout. Hospital departments in which these working conditions occur most frequently—critical care units, emergency departments, and operating rooms—generally will have more job openings than other departments.

To attract and retain qualified nurses, hospitals may offer signing bonuses, family-friendly work schedules, or subsidized training. A growing number of hospitals also are experimenting with online bidding to fill open shifts, in which nurses can volunteer to fill open shifts at premium wages. This can decrease the amount of mandatory overtime that nurses are required to work.

More and more sophisticated procedures, once performed only in hospitals, are being performed in physicians' offices and in outpatient care centers, such as freestanding ambulatory surgical and emergency centers. Accordingly, employment is expected to grow much faster than average in these places as health care in general expands. However, RNs may face greater competition for these positions because they generally offer regular working hours and more comfortable working environments.

Employment in nursing care facilities is expected to grow faster than average because of increases in the number of elderly, many of whom require long-term care. In addition, the financial pressure on hospitals to discharge patients as soon as possible should produce more admissions to nursing care facilities. Job growth also is expected in units that provide specialized long-term rehabilitation for stroke and head injury patients, as well as units that treat Alzheimer's victims.

Employment in home health care is expected to increase rapidly in response to the growing number of older persons with functional disabilities, consumer preference for care in the home, and technological advances that make it possible to bring increasingly complex treatments into the home. The type of care demanded will require nurses who are able to perform complex procedures.

Generally, RNs with at least a bachelor's degree will have better job prospects than those without a bachelor's. In addition, all four advanced practice specialties—clinical nurse specialists, nurse practitioners, midwives, and anesthetists—will be in high demand, particularly in medically underserved areas such as inner cities and rural areas. Relative to physicians, these RNs increasingly serve as lower-cost primary care providers.

Earnings

Median annual earnings of registered nurses were $52,330 in May 2004. The middle 50 percent earned between $43,370 and $63,360. The lowest 10 percent earned less than $37,300, and the highest 10 percent earned more than $74,760. Median annual earnings in the industries employing the largest numbers of registered nurses in May 2004 were as follows:

Employment services	$63,170
General medical and surgical hospitals	53,450
Home health care services	48,990
Offices of physicians	48,250
Nursing care facilities	48,220

Many employers offer flexible work schedules, child care, educational benefits, and bonuses.

Related Occupations

Workers in other health care occupations with responsibilities and duties related to those of registered nurses are cardiovascular technologists and technicians; diagnostic medical sonographers; dietitians and nutritionists; emergency medical technicians and paramedics; licensed practical and licensed vocational nurses; massage therapists; medical and health services managers; nursing, psychiatric, and home health aides; occupational therapists; physical therapists; physician assistants; physicians and surgeons; radiologic technologists and technicians; respiratory therapists; and surgical technologists.

Sources of Additional Information

For information on a career as a registered nurse and nursing education, contact:

- National League for Nursing, 61 Broadway, New York, NY 10006. Internet: http://www.nln.org

For information on nursing career options, financial aid, and listings of BSN, graduate, and accelerated nursing programs, contact:

- American Association of Colleges of Nursing, 1 Dupont Circle NW, Suite 530, Washington, DC 20036. Internet: http://www.aacn.nche.edu

For additional information on registered nurses, including credentialing, contact:

- American Nurses Association, 8515 Georgia Ave., Suite 400, Silver Spring, MD 20910. Internet: http://nursingworld.org

For information on the NCLEX-RN exam and a list of individual states' boards of nursing, contact:

- National Council of State Boards of Nursing, 111 E. Wacker Dr., Suite 2900, Chicago, IL 60611. Internet: http://www.ncsbn.org

For information on obtaining U.S. certification and work visas for foreign-educated nurses, contact:

- Commission on Graduates of Foreign Nursing Schools, 3600 Market St., Suite 400, Philadelphia, PA 19104. Internet: http://www.cgfns.org

For a list of accredited clinical nurse specialist programs, contact:

- National Association of Clinical Nurse Specialists, 2090 Linglestown Rd., Suite 107, Harrisburg, PA 17110. Internet: http://www.nacns.org/cnsdirectory.shtml

For information on nurse anesthetists, including a list of accredited programs, contact:

- American Association of Nurse Anesthetists, 222 Prospect Ave., Park Ridge, IL 60068.

For information on nurse midwives, including a list of accredited programs, contact:

- American College of Nurse-Midwives, 8403 Colesville Rd., Suite 1550, Silver Spring, MD 20910. Internet: http://www.midwife.org

For information on nurse practitioners, including a list of accredited programs, contact:

- American Academy of Nurse Practitioners, P.O. Box 12846, Austin, TX 78711. Internet: http://www.aanp.org

Respiratory Therapists

(O*NET 29-1126.00 and 29-2054.00)

Significant Points

- Job opportunities will be very good, especially for therapists with cardiopulmonary care skills or experience working with infants.
- All states (except Alaska and Hawaii), the District of Columbia, and Puerto Rico require respiratory therapists to obtain a license.
- Hospitals will continue to employ the vast majority of respiratory therapists, but a growing number of therapists will work in other settings.

Nature of the Work

Respiratory therapists and *respiratory therapy technicians*—also known as respiratory care practitioners—evaluate, treat, and care for patients with breathing or other cardiopulmonary disorders. Practicing under the direction of a physician, respiratory therapists assume primary responsibility for all respiratory care therapeutic treatments and diagnostic procedures, including the supervision of respiratory therapy technicians. Respiratory therapy technicians follow specific, well-defined respiratory care procedures under the direction of respiratory therapists and physicians. In clinical practice, many of the daily duties of therapists and technicians overlap; furthermore, the two have the same education and training requirements. However, therapists generally have greater responsibility than technicians. For example, respiratory therapists will consult with physicians and other health care staff to help develop and modify individual patient care plans. Respiratory therapists also are more likely to provide complex therapy requiring considerable independent judgment, such as caring for patients on life support in intensive-care units of hospitals. In this description, the term *respiratory therapists* includes both respiratory therapists and respiratory therapy technicians.

Respiratory therapists evaluate and treat all types of patients, ranging from premature infants whose lungs are not fully developed to elderly people whose lungs are diseased. Respiratory therapists provide temporary relief to patients with chronic asthma or emphysema, as well as emergency care to patients who are victims of a heart attack, stroke, drowning, or shock.

To evaluate patients, respiratory therapists interview them, perform limited physical examinations, and conduct diagnostic tests. For example, respiratory therapists test patients' breathing capacity and determine the concentration of oxygen and other gases in patients' blood. They also measure patients' pH, which indicates the acidity or alkalinity of the blood. To evaluate a patient's lung capacity, respiratory therapists have the patient breathe into an instrument that measures the volume and flow of oxygen during inhalation and exhalation. By comparing the reading with the norm for the patient's age, height, weight, and sex, respiratory therapists can provide information that helps determine whether the patient has any lung deficiencies. To analyze oxygen, carbon dioxide, and pH levels, therapists draw an arterial blood sample, place it in a blood gas analyzer, and relay the results to a physician, who then may make treatment decisions.

To treat patients, respiratory therapists use oxygen or oxygen mixtures, chest physiotherapy, and aerosol medications. When a patient has difficulty getting enough oxygen into his or her blood, therapists increase the patient's concentration of oxygen by placing an oxygen mask or nasal cannula on the patient and set the oxygen flow at the level prescribed by a physician. Therapists also connect patients who cannot breathe on their own to ventilators that deliver pressurized oxygen into the lungs. The therapists insert a tube into the patient's trachea, or windpipe; connect the tube to the ventilator; and set the rate, volume, and oxygen concentration of the oxygen mixture entering the patient's lungs.

Therapists perform regular assessments of patients and equipment. If the patient appears to be having difficulty breathing or if the oxygen, carbon dioxide, or pH level of the blood is abnormal, therapists change the ventilator setting according to the doctor's orders or check the equipment for mechanical problems. In home care, therapists teach patients and their families to use ventilators and other life-support systems. In addition, therapists visit patients several times a month to inspect and clean equipment and to ensure its proper use. Therapists also make emergency visits if equipment problems arise.

Respiratory therapists perform chest physiotherapy on patients to remove mucus from their lungs and make it easier for them to breathe. For example, during surgery, anesthesia depresses respiration, so chest physiotherapy may be prescribed to help get the patient's lungs back to normal and to prevent congestion. Chest physiotherapy also helps patients suffering from lung diseases, such as cystic fibrosis, that cause mucus to collect in the lungs. Therapists place patients in positions that help drain mucus, and then vibrate the patients' rib cages and instruct the patients to cough.

Respiratory therapists also administer aerosols—liquid medications suspended in a gas that forms a mist which is inhaled—and teach patients how to inhale the aerosol properly to ensure its effectiveness.

In some hospitals, therapists perform tasks that fall outside their traditional role. Therapists' tasks are expanding into areas such as pulmonary rehabilitation, smoking cessation counseling, disease prevention, case management, and polysomnography—the diagnosis of breathing disorders during sleep, such as apnea. Respiratory therapists also increasingly treat critical care patients, either as part of surface and air transport teams or as part of rapid-response teams in hospitals.

Working Conditions

Respiratory therapists generally work between 35 and 40 hours a week. Because hospitals operate around the clock, therapists may work evenings, nights, or weekends. They spend long periods standing and walking between patients' rooms. In an emergency, therapists work under a great deal of stress. Respiratory therapists employed in home health care must travel frequently to the homes of patients.

Respiratory therapists are trained to work with hazardous gases stored under pressure. Adherence to safety precautions and regular maintenance and testing of equipment minimize the risk of injury. As in many other health occupations, respiratory therapists run the risk of catching an infectious disease, but carefully following proper procedures minimizes this risk.

Training, Other Qualifications, and Advancement

Formal training is necessary for entry into this field. Training is offered at the postsecondary level by colleges and universities, medical schools, vocational-technical institutes, and the Armed Forces. An associate's degree is required for entry into the field. Most programs award associate's or bachelor's degrees and prepare graduates for jobs as advanced respiratory therapists. A limited number of associate's degree programs lead to jobs as entry-level respiratory therapists. According to the Commission on Accreditation of Allied Health Education Programs (CAAHEP), 51 entry-level and 329 advanced respiratory therapy programs were accredited in the United States, including Puerto Rico, in 2005.

Among the areas of study in respiratory therapy are human anatomy and physiology, pathophysiology, chemistry, physics, microbiology, pharmacology, and mathematics. Other courses deal with therapeutic and diagnostic procedures and tests, equipment, patient assessment, cardiopulmonary resuscitation, the application of clinical practice guidelines, patient care outside of hospitals, cardiac and pulmonary rehabilitation, respiratory health promotion and disease prevention, and medical recordkeeping and reimbursement.

The National Board for Respiratory Care (NBRC) offers certification and registration to graduates of programs accredited by CAAHEP or the Committee on Accreditation for Respiratory Care (CoARC). Two credentials are awarded to respiratory therapists who satisfy the requirements: Registered Respiratory Therapist (RRT) and Certified Respiratory Therapist (CRT). Graduates from accredited entry-level or advanced-level programs in respiratory therapy may take the CRT examination. CRTs who were graduated from advanced-level programs and who meet additional experience requirements can take two separate examinations leading to the award of the RRT credential.

All states (except Alaska and Hawaii), the District of Columbia, and Puerto Rico require respiratory therapists to obtain a license. Passing the CRT exam qualifies respiratory therapists for state licenses. Also, most employers require respiratory therapists to maintain a cardiopulmonary resuscitation (CPR) certification. Supervisory positions and intensive-care specialties usually require the RRT or at least RRT eligibility.

Therapists should be sensitive to patients' physical and psychological needs. Respiratory care practitioners must pay attention to detail, follow instructions, and work as part of a team. In addition, operating advanced equipment requires proficiency with computers.

High school students interested in a career in respiratory care should take courses in health, biology, mathematics, chemistry, and physics. Respiratory care involves basic mathematical problem solving and an understanding of chemical and physical principles.

For example, respiratory care workers must be able to compute dosages of medication and calculate gas concentrations.

Respiratory therapists advance in clinical practice by moving from general care to the care of critically ill patients who have significant problems in other organ systems, such as the heart or kidneys. Respiratory therapists, especially those with bachelor's or master's degrees, also may advance to supervisory or managerial positions in a respiratory therapy department. Respiratory therapists in home health care and equipment rental firms may become branch managers. Some respiratory therapists advance by moving into teaching positions.

Employment

Respiratory therapists held about 118,000 jobs in 2004. More than 4 out of 5 jobs were in hospital departments of respiratory care, anesthesiology, or pulmonary medicine. Most of the remaining jobs were in offices of physicians or other health practitioners, consumer-goods rental firms that supply respiratory equipment for home use, nursing care facilities, and home health care services. Holding a second job is relatively common for respiratory therapists. About 13 percent held another job, compared with 5 percent of workers in all occupations.

Job Outlook

Job opportunities are expected to be very good, especially for respiratory therapists with cardiopulmonary care skills or experience working with infants. Employment of respiratory therapists is expected to increase faster than average for all occupations through the year 2014, because of substantial growth in the numbers of the middle-aged and elderly population—a development that will heighten the incidence of cardiopulmonary disease—and because of the expanding role of respiratory therapists in the early detection of pulmonary disorders, case management, disease prevention, and emergency care.

Older Americans suffer most from respiratory ailments and cardiopulmonary diseases such as pneumonia, chronic bronchitis, emphysema, and heart disease. As their numbers increase, the need for respiratory therapists will increase as well. In addition, advances in inhalable medications and in the treatment of lung transplant patients, heart attack and accident victims, and premature infants (many of whom are dependent on a ventilator during part of their treatment) will increase the demand for the services of respiratory care practitioners.

Although hospitals will continue to employ the vast majority of therapists, a growing number can expect to work outside of hospitals in home health care services, offices of physicians or other health practitioners, or consumer-goods rental firms.

Earnings

Median annual earnings of respiratory therapists were $43,140 in May 2004. The middle 50 percent earned between $37,650 and $50,860. The lowest 10 percent earned less than $32,220, and the highest 10 percent earned more than $57,580. In general medical and surgical hospitals, median annual earnings of respiratory therapists were $43,140 in May 2004.

Median annual earnings of respiratory therapy technicians were $36,740 in May 2004. The middle 50 percent earned between $30,490 and $43,830. The lowest 10 percent earned less than $24,640, and the highest 10 percent earned more than $52,280. Median annual earnings of respiratory therapy technicians employed in general medical and surgical hospitals were $36,990 in May 2004.

Related Occupations

Under the supervision of a physician, respiratory therapists administer respiratory care and life support to patients with heart and lung difficulties. Other workers who care for, treat, or train people to improve their physical condition include registered nurses, occupational therapists, physical therapists, and radiation therapists.

Sources of Additional Information

Information concerning a career in respiratory care is available from:

- American Association for Respiratory Care, 9425 N. MacArthur Blvd., Suite 100, Irving, TX 75063-4706. Internet: http://www.aarc.org

For a list of accredited educational programs for respiratory care practitioners, contact either of the following organizations:

- Commission on Accreditation for Allied Health Education Programs, 35 East Wacker Dr., Suite 1970, Chicago, IL 60601. Internet: http://www.caahep.org

Information on gaining credentials in respiratory care and a list of state licensing agencies can be obtained from:

- National Board for Respiratory Care, Inc., 8310 Nieman Rd., Lenexa, KS 66214-1579. Internet: http://www.nbrc.org

Retail Salespersons

(O*NET 41-2031.00)

Significant Points

- Good employment opportunities are expected because of the need to replace the large number of workers who leave the occupation each year.
- Most salespersons work evenings and weekends, particularly during sales and other peak retail periods.
- Employers look for people who enjoy working with others and who have tact, patience, an interest in sales work, a neat appearance, and the ability to communicate clearly.

Nature of the Work

Whether selling shoes, computer equipment, or automobiles, retail salespersons assist customers in finding what they are looking for and try to interest them in buying the merchandise. They describe a product's features, demonstrate its use, or show various models and colors. For some sales jobs, particularly those involving expensive and complex items, retail salespersons need special knowledge or skills. For example, salespersons who sell automobiles must be able to explain the features of various models, the manufacturers' specifications, the types of options and financing available, and the warranty.

Consumers spend millions of dollars every day on merchandise and often form their impression of a store by evaluating its sales force. Therefore, retailers stress the importance of providing courteous and efficient service to remain competitive. For example, when a customer wants an item that is not on the sales floor, the salesperson may check the stockroom, place a special order, or call another store to locate the item.

In addition to selling, most retail salespersons—especially those who work in department and apparel stores—make out sales checks; receive cash, checks, debit, and charge payments; bag or package purchases; and give change and receipts. Depending on the hours they work, retail salespersons may have to open or close cash registers. This work may include counting the money in the register; separating charge slips, coupons, and exchange vouchers; and making deposits at the cash office. Salespersons often are held responsible for the contents of their registers, and repeated shortages are cause for dismissal in many organizations.

Salespersons also may handle returns and exchanges of merchandise, wrap gifts, and keep their work areas neat. In addition, they may help stock shelves or racks, arrange for mailing or delivery of purchases, mark price tags, take inventory, and prepare displays.

Frequently, salespersons must be aware of special sales and promotions. They also must recognize security risks and thefts and know how to handle or prevent such situations.

Working Conditions

Most salespersons in retail trade work in clean, comfortable, well-lighted stores. However, they often stand for long periods and may need supervisory approval to leave the sales floor. They also may work outdoors if they sell items such as cars, plants, or lumber yard materials.

The Monday-through-Friday, 9-to-5 workweek is the exception rather than the rule in retail trade. Most salespersons work evenings and weekends, particularly during sales and other peak retail periods. The end-of-year holiday season is the busiest time for most retailers. As a result, many employers restrict the use of vacation time to some period other than Thanksgiving through the beginning of January.

The job can be rewarding for those who enjoy working with people. Patience and courtesy are required, especially when the work is repetitious and the customers are demanding.

Training, Other Qualifications, and Advancement

There usually are no formal education requirements for this type of work, although a high school diploma or the equivalent is preferred. Employers look for people who enjoy working with others and who have the tact and patience to deal with difficult customers. Among other desirable characteristics are an interest in sales work, a neat appearance, and the ability to communicate clearly and effectively. The ability to speak more than one language may be helpful for employment in communities where people from various cultures tend to live and shop. Before hiring a salesperson, some employers may conduct a background check, especially for a job selling high-priced items.

In most small stores, an experienced employee or the proprietor instructs newly hired sales personnel in making out sales checks and operating cash registers. In large stores, training programs are more formal and are usually conducted over several days. Topics generally discussed are customer service, security, the store's policies and procedures, and how to work a cash register. Depending on the type of product they are selling, employees may be given additional specialized training by manufacturers' representatives. For example, those working in cosmetics receive instruction on the types of products the store has available and for whom the cosmetics would be most beneficial. Likewise, salespersons employed by motor vehicle dealers may be required to participate in training programs designed to provide information on the technical details of standard and optional equipment available on new vehicle models. Since providing the best possible service to customers is a high priority for many employers, employees often are given periodic training to update and refine their skills.

As salespersons gain experience and seniority, they usually move to positions of greater responsibility and may be given their choice of departments in which to work. This often means moving to areas with potentially higher earnings and commissions. The highest earnings potential usually lies in selling "big-ticket" items—such as cars, jewelry, furniture, and electronic equipment—although doing so often requires extensive knowledge of the product and an extraordinary talent for persuasion.

Opportunities for advancement vary in small stores. In some establishments, advancement is limited because one person—often the owner—does most of the managerial work. In others, some salespersons are promoted to assistant managers. Large retail businesses usually prefer to hire college graduates as management trainees, making a college education increasingly important. However, motivated and capable employees without college degrees still may advance to administrative or supervisory positions in large establishments.

Retail selling experience may be an asset when one is applying for sales positions with larger retailers or in other industries, such as financial services, wholesale trade, or manufacturing.

Employment

Retail salespersons held about 4.3 million wage and salary jobs in 2004. They worked in stores ranging from small specialty shops employing a few workers to giant department stores with hundreds of salespersons. In addition, some were self-employed representatives of direct-sales companies and mail-order houses. The largest employers of retail salespersons are department stores, clothing and clothing accessories stores, building material and garden equipment and supplies dealers, other general merchandise stores, and motor vehicle and parts dealers.

This occupation offers many opportunities for part-time work and is especially appealing to students, retirees, and others seeking to supplement their income. However, most of those selling big-ticket items work full time and have substantial experience.

Because retail stores are found in every city and town, employment is distributed geographically in much the same way as the population.

Job Outlook

As in the past, employment opportunities for retail salespersons are expected to be good because of the need to replace the large number of workers who transfer to other occupations or leave the labor force each year. In addition, many new jobs will be created for retail salespersons as businesses seek to expand operations and enhance customer service. Employment is expected to grow about as fast as average for all occupations through the year 2014, reflecting rising retail sales stemming from a growing population. Opportunities for part-time work should be abundant, and demand will be strong for temporary workers during peak selling periods, such as the end-of-year holiday season. The availability of part-time and temporary work attracts many people seeking to supplement their income.

During economic downturns, sales volumes and the resulting demand for sales workers usually decline. Purchases of costly items, such as cars, appliances, and furniture, tend to be postponed during difficult economic times. In areas of high unemployment, sales of many types of goods decline. However, because turnover among retail salespersons is high, employers often can adjust employment levels simply by not replacing all those who leave.

Despite the growing popularity of electronic commerce, Internet sales have not decreased the need for retail salespersons. Retail stores commonly use an online presence to complement their in-store sales; there are very few Internet-only apparel and specialty stores. Retail salespersons will remain important in assuring customers that they will receive specialized service and in improving customer satisfaction, something Internet services cannot do. Therefore, the impact of electronic commerce on employment of retail salespersons is expected to be minimal.

Earnings

The starting wage for many retail sales positions is the federal minimum wage, which was $5.15 an hour in 2004. In areas where employers have difficulty attracting and retaining workers, wages tend to be higher than the legislated minimum.

Median hourly earnings of retail salespersons, including commissions, were $8.98 in May 2004. The middle 50 percent earned between $7.46 and $12.22 an hour. The lowest 10 percent earned less than $6.38, and the highest 10 percent earned more than $17.85 an hour. Median hourly earnings in the industries employing the largest numbers of retail salespersons in May 2004 were as follows:

Automobile dealers	$18.61
Building material and supplies dealers	10.85
Department stores	8.47
Other general merchandise stores	8.36
Clothing stores	8.17

Compensation systems vary by type of establishment and merchandise sold. Salespersons receive hourly wages, commissions, or a combination thereof. Under a commission system, salespersons receive a percentage of the sales they make. This system offers sales workers the opportunity to increase their earnings considerably, but they may find that their earnings strongly depend on their ability to sell their product and on the ups and downs of the economy. Employers may use incentive programs such as awards, banquets, bonuses, and profit-sharing plans to promote teamwork among the sales staff.

Benefits may be limited in smaller stores, but benefits in large establishments usually are comparable to those offered by other employers. In addition, nearly all salespersons are able to buy their store's merchandise at a discount, with the savings depending on the type of merchandise.

Related Occupations

Salespersons use sales techniques, coupled with their knowledge of merchandise, to assist customers and encourage purchases. Workers in other occupations who use these same skills include sales representatives, wholesale and manufacturing; securities, commodities, and financial services sales agents; counter and rental clerks; real estate brokers and sales agents; purchasing managers, buyers, and purchasing agents; insurance sales agents; sales engineers; and cashiers.

Sources of Additional Information

Information on careers in retail sales may be obtained from the personnel offices of local stores or from state merchants' associations.

General information about retailing is available from:

- National Retail Federation, 325 7th St. NW, Suite 1100, Washington, DC 20004.

Information about retail sales employment opportunities is available from:

- Retail, Wholesale, and Department Store Union, 30 East 29th St., 4th Floor, New York, NY 10016.

Information about training for a career in automobile sales is available from:

- National Automobile Dealers Association, Public Relations Department, 8400 Westpark Dr., McLean, VA 22102-3591. Internet: http://www.nada.org

Roofers

(O*NET 47-2181.00)

Significant Points

- Most roofers acquire their skills informally on the job; some roofers train through 3-year apprenticeship programs.
- Jobs openings for roofers should be plentiful because the work is hot, strenuous, and dirty, causing many individuals to leave for jobs in other construction trades.
- Demand for roofers is less susceptible to downturns in the economy than demand for other construction trades because most roofing work consists of repair and reroofing.

Nature of the Work

A leaky roof can damage ceilings, walls, and furnishings. To protect buildings and their contents from water damage, roofers repair and install roofs made of tar or asphalt and gravel; rubber or thermoplastic; metal; or shingles made of asphalt, slate, fiberglass, wood, tile, or other material. Repair and reroofing—replacing old roofs on existing buildings—makes up the majority of work for these workers.

There are two types of roofs—low- and steep-sloped. Roofs considered low-slope rise 4 inches per horizontal foot or less and steep-slope roofs increase more than 4 inches per horizontal foot. Most commercial, industrial, and apartment buildings have low-sloping roofs. Most houses have steep-sloped roofs. Some roofers work on both types; others specialize.

Most low-slope roofs are covered with several layers of materials. Roofers first put a layer of insulation on the roof deck. Over the insulation, they then spread a coat of molten bitumen, a tarlike substance. Next, they install partially overlapping layers of roofing felt—a fabric saturated in bitumen—over the surface. Roofers use a mop to spread hot bitumen over the surface and under the next layer. This seals the seams and makes the surface watertight. Roofers repeat these steps to build up the desired number of layers, called "plies." The top layer either is glazed to make a smooth finish or has gravel embedded in the hot bitumen to create a rough surface.

An increasing number of low-slope roofs are covered with a single-ply membrane of waterproof rubber or thermoplastic compounds. Roofers roll these sheets over the roof's insulation and seal the seams. Adhesive, mechanical fasteners, or stone ballast hold the sheets in place. The building must be of sufficient strength to hold the ballast. A small but growing number of flat-roofed buildings are now having "green" roofs installed. A "green" roof begins with a single or multi-ply waterproof system. After it is proven to be leak free, a root barrier is placed onto it, and then layers of soil, in which trees and grass are planted. Roofers are generally responsible for making sure the roof is watertight and can withstand the weight and water needs of the plantings.

Most residential steep-slope roofs are covered with shingles. To apply shingles, roofers first lay, cut, and tack 3-foot strips of roofing felt lengthwise over the entire roof. Then, starting from the bottom edge, they staple or nail overlapping rows of shingles to the roof. Workers measure and cut the felt and shingles to fit intersecting roof surfaces and to fit around vent pipes and chimneys. Wherever two roof surfaces intersect, or shingles reach a vent pipe or chimney, roofers cement or nail flashing-strips of metal or shingle over the joints to make them watertight. Finally, roofers cover exposed nailheads with roofing cement or caulking to prevent water leakage. Roofers who use tile, metal shingles, or shakes follow a similar process.

Because of their expertise in waterproofing roofs, some roofers also waterproof and damp-proof masonry and concrete walls and floors, including foundations. To prepare surfaces for waterproofing, they hammer and chisel away rough spots, or remove them with a rubbing brick, before applying a coat of liquid waterproofing compound. They also may paint or spray surfaces with a waterproofing material, or attach waterproofing membrane to surfaces. When damp-proofing, they usually spray a bitumen-based coating on interior or exterior surfaces. Roofers also install equipment that requires cutting through roofs, such as ventilation ducts and attic fans.

Working Conditions

Roofing work is strenuous. It involves heavy lifting, as well as climbing, bending, and kneeling. Roofers work outdoors in all types of weather, particularly when making repairs. However, they rarely work in very cold weather as ice can be treacherous. In northern states, roofing work is generally not performed during winter months.

Workers risk slips or falls from scaffolds, ladders, or roofs, or burns from hot bitumen, but safety precautions, if followed, can eliminate most accidents. In addition, roofs can become extremely hot during the summer, causing heat-related illnesses.

Training, Other Qualifications, and Advancement

Most roofers acquire their skills informally by working as helpers for experienced roofers and by taking some employer-provided classes. Safety training is one of the first classes that a worker takes. Trainees start by carrying equipment and material, and erecting scaffolds and hoists. Within 2 or 3 months, trainees are taught to measure, cut, and fit roofing materials and, later, to lay asphalt or fiberglass shingles. Because some roofing materials are used infrequently, it can take several years to get experience working on all the various types of roofing applications.

Some roofers train through 3-year apprenticeship programs administered by local union-management committees representing roofing contractors and locals of the United Union of Roofers, Waterproofers, and Allied Workers. The apprenticeship program generally consists of a minimum of 2,000 hours of on-the-job training annually, plus a minimum of 144 hours of classroom instruction a year in subjects such as tools and their use, arithmetic, and safety. On-the-job training for apprentices is similar to that for helpers, except that the apprenticeship program is more structured. Apprentices also learn to damp-proof and waterproof walls.

Good physical condition and good balance are essential for roofers, along with no fear of heights. A high school education, or its equivalent, is helpful, as are courses in mechanical drawing and basic mathematics. Most apprentices must be at least 18 years old. Experience with metal-working is helpful for workers who install metal roofing.

Roofers may advance to supervisor or estimator for a roofing contractor, or become contractors themselves.

Employment

Roofers held about 162,000 jobs in 2004. Almost all wage and salary roofers worked for roofing contractors. About 1 out of every 4 roofers was self-employed. Many self-employed roofers specialized in residential work.

Job Outlook

Job opportunities for roofers should be good through the year 2014, primarily because of the need to replace workers who leave the occupation. The proportion of roofers who leave the occupation each year is higher than in most construction trades—roofing work is hot, strenuous, and dirty, and a significant number of workers treat roofing as a temporary job until something better comes along. Some roofers leave the occupation to go into other construction trades.

Employment of roofers is expected to grow as fast as average for all occupations through 2014. Roofs deteriorate faster and are more susceptible to weather damage than most other parts of buildings and periodically need to be repaired or replaced. Roofing has a much higher proportion of repair and replacement work than most other construction occupations. As a result, demand for roofers is less susceptible to downturns in the economy than demand for other construction trades. In addition to repair and reroofing work on the growing stock of buildings, new construction of industrial, commercial, and residential buildings will add to the demand for roofers. Jobs should be easiest to find during spring and summer when most roofing is done.

Earnings

In May 2004, median hourly earnings of roofers were $14.83. The middle 50 percent earned between $11.54 and $19.80. The lowest 10 percent earned less than $9.41, and the highest 10 percent earned more than $25.59. The median hourly earnings of roofers in the foundation, structure, and building exterior contractors industry were $14.90 in May 2004.

Apprentices usually start at about 40 percent to 50 percent of the rate paid to experienced roofers and receive periodic raises as they acquire the skills of the trade. Earnings for roofers are reduced on occasion because poor weather limits the time they can work.

Some roofers are members of the United Union of Roofers, Waterproofers, and Allied Workers.

Related Occupations

Roofers use shingles, bitumen and gravel, single-ply plastic or rubber sheets, or other materials to waterproof building surfaces. Workers in other occupations who cover surfaces with special materials for protection and decoration include carpenters; carpet, floor, and tile installers and finishers; cement masons, concrete finishers, segmental pavers, and terrazzo workers; drywall installers, ceiling tile installers, and tapers; plasterers and stucco masons; and sheet metal workers.

Sources of Additional Information

For information about apprenticeships or job opportunities in roofing, contact local roofing contractors, a local chapter of the roofers union, a local joint union-management apprenticeship committee, or the nearest office of your state employment service or apprenticeship agency.

For information about the work of roofers, contact:

- National Roofing Contractors Association, 10255 W. Higgins Rd., Suite 600, Rosemont, IL 60018-5607. Internet: http://www.nrca.net
- United Union of Roofers, Waterproofers, and Allied Workers, 1660 L St. NW, Suite 800, Washington, DC 20036.

Sales Representatives, Wholesale and Manufacturing

(O*NET 41-4011.01, 41-4011.02, 41-4011.03, 41-4011.04, 41-4011.05, 41-4011.06, and 41-4012.00)

Significant Points

- Employment opportunities will be best for those with a college degree, the appropriate knowledge or technical expertise, and the personal traits necessary for successful selling. Job prospects for wholesale sales representatives will be better than those for manufacturing sales representatives, particularly in small firms.
- Earnings of sales representatives usually are based on a combination of salary and commissions.

Nature of the Work

Sales representatives are an important part of manufacturers' and wholesalers' success. Regardless of the type of product they sell, their primary duties are to interest wholesale and retail buyers and purchasing agents in their merchandise and to address clients' questions and concerns. Sales representatives represent one or several manufacturers or wholesale distributors by selling one product or a complementary line of products. Sales representatives demonstrate their products and advise clients on how using these products can reduce costs and increase sales. They market their company's products to manufacturers, wholesale and retail establishments, construction contractors, government agencies, and other institutions.

Depending on where they work, sales representatives have different job titles. Those employed directly by a manufacturer or wholesaler often are called *sales representatives. Manufacturers' agents* or *manufacturers' representatives* are self-employed sales workers or independent firms who contract their services to all types of manufacturing companies. Many of these titles, however, are used interchangeably.

Sales representatives spend much of their time traveling to and visiting with prospective buyers and current clients. During a sales call, they discuss the client's needs and suggest how their merchandise or services can meet those needs. They may show samples or catalogs that describe items their company stocks and inform customers about prices, availability, and ways in which their products can save money and boost productivity. Because a vast number of manufacturers and wholesalers sell similar products, sales representatives must emphasize any unique qualities of their products and services.

Manufacturers' agents or manufacturers' representatives might sell several complementary products made by different manufacturers and, thus, take a broad approach to their customers' business. Sales representatives may help install new equipment and train employees in its use. They also take orders and resolve any problems with or complaints about the merchandise.

Obtaining new accounts is an important part of the job. Sales representatives follow leads from other clients, track advertisements in trade journals, participate in trade shows and conferences, and may visit potential clients unannounced. In addition, they may spend time meeting with and entertaining prospective clients during evenings and weekends.

In a process that can take several months, sales representatives present their product to a customer and negotiate the sale. Aided by a laptop computer connected to the Internet, or other telecommunications device, they can make a persuasive audiovisual sales pitch and often can answer technical and nontechnical questions immediately.

Frequently, sales representatives who lack technical expertise work as a team with a technical expert. In this arrangement, the technical expert—sometimes a sales engineer—attends the sales presentation to explain the product and answer questions or concerns. The sales representative makes the preliminary contact with customers, introduces the company's product, and closes the sale. The representative is then able to spend more time maintaining and soliciting accounts and less time acquiring technical knowledge. After the sale, representatives may make followup visits to ensure that the equipment is functioning properly and may even help train customers' employees to operate and maintain new equipment. Those selling consumer goods often suggest how and where merchandise should be displayed. Working with retailers, they may help arrange promotional programs, store displays, and advertising.

Sales representatives have several duties beyond selling products. They analyze sales statistics; prepare reports; and handle administrative duties, such as filing expense account reports, scheduling appointments, and making travel plans. They read about new and existing products and monitor the sales, prices, and products of their competitors.

Manufacturers' agents who operate a sales agency also must manage their business. This requires organizational and general business skills, as well as knowledge of accounting, marketing, and administration.

Working Conditions

Some sales representatives have large territories and travel considerably. Because a sales region may cover several states, representatives may be away from home for several days or weeks at a time. Others work near their home base and travel mostly by car. Because of the nature of the work and the amount of travel, sales representatives may work more than 40 hours per week.

Although the hours are long and often irregular, most sales representatives have the freedom to determine their own schedule. Sales representatives often are on their feet for long periods and may carry heavy sample products, necessitating some physical stamina.

Dealing with different types of people can be stimulating but demanding. Sales representatives often face competition from representatives of other companies. Companies usually set goals or quotas that representatives are expected to meet. Because their earnings depend on commissions, manufacturers' agents are also under the added pressure to maintain and expand their clientele.

Training, Other Qualifications, and Advancement

The background needed for sales jobs varies by product line and market. Many employers hire individuals with previous sales experience who lack a college degree, but they increasingly prefer or require a bachelor's degree because job requirements have become more technical and analytical. Nevertheless, for some consumer products, factors such as sales ability, personality, and familiarity with brands are more important than educational background. On the other hand, firms selling complex, technical products may require a technical degree in addition to some sales experience. Many sales representatives attend seminars in sales techniques or take courses in marketing, economics, communication, or even a foreign language to provide the extra edge needed to make sales. In general, companies are looking for the best and brightest individuals who have the personality and desire to sell. Sales representatives need to be familiar with computer technology as computers are increasingly used in the workplace to place and track orders and to monitor inventory levels.

Many companies have formal training programs for beginning sales representatives lasting up to 2 years. However, most businesses are accelerating these programs to reduce costs and expedite the returns from training. In some programs, trainees rotate among jobs in plants and offices to learn all phases of production, installation, and distribution of the product. In others, trainees take formal classroom instruction at the plant, followed by on-the-job training under the supervision of a field sales manager.

New workers may get training by accompanying experienced workers on their sales calls. As they gain familiarity with the firm's products and clients, the new workers are given increasing responsibility until they are eventually assigned their own territory. As businesses experience greater competition, increased pressure is placed upon sales representatives to produce sales.

Sales representatives stay abreast of new products and the changing needs of their customers in a variety of ways. They attend trade shows at which new products and technologies are showcased. They also attend conferences and conventions to meet other sales representatives and clients and discuss new product developments. In addition, the entire sales force may participate in company-sponsored meetings to review sales performance, product development, sales goals, and profitability.

There are many certifications designed to raise standards and develop the skills of sales representatives, wholesale and manufacturing. A few examples are the Certified Professional Manufacturers' Representative, the Certified Sales Professional, and the Certified National Pharmaceutical Representative. Certification may involve completion of formal training and passing an examination.

Those who want to become sales representatives should be goal oriented, persuasive, and able to work well both independently and as part of a team. A pleasant personality and appearance, the ability to communicate well with people, and problem solving skills are highly valued. Patience and perseverance also are key to completing a sale, which can take several months.

Frequently, promotion takes the form of an assignment to a larger account or territory where commissions are likely to be greater. Experienced sales representatives may move into jobs as sales trainers, who instruct new employees on selling techniques and on company policies and procedures. Those who have good sales records and leadership ability may advance to higher level positions such as sales supervisor, district manager, or vice president of sales. In addition to advancement opportunities within a firm, some manufacturers' agents go into business for themselves. Others find opportunities in purchasing, advertising, or marketing research.

Employment

Manufacturers' and wholesale sales representatives held about 1.9 million jobs in 2004. About half of all salaried representatives worked in wholesale trade. Others were employed in manufacturing, retail trade, information, and construction. Because of the diversity of products and services sold, employment opportunities are available in every part of the country in a wide range of industries.

In addition to those working directly for a firm, many sales representatives are self-employed manufacturers' agents. They often form small sales firms and work for a straight commission based on the value of their own sales. Usually, however, manufacturers' agents gain experience and recognition with a manufacturer or wholesaler before becoming self-employed.

Job Outlook

Employment of sales representatives, wholesale and manufacturing, is expected to grow about as fast as average for all occupations through the year 2014, primarily because of continued growth in the variety and number of goods to be sold. Also, many job openings will result from the need to replace workers who transfer to other occupations or leave the labor force.

Prospective customers require sales workers to demonstrate or illustrate the particulars of a good or service. Computer technology makes sales representatives more effective and productive, for example, by allowing them to provide accurate and current information to customers during sales presentations.

Job prospects for sales representatives, wholesale and manufacturing, will be best for persons with the appropriate knowledge or technical expertise as well as the personal traits necessary for successful selling. Opportunities will be better for wholesale sales representatives than for manufacturing sales representatives because manufacturers are expected to continue contracting out sales duties to independent agents rather than using in-house or direct selling personnel. Agents are paid only if they sell, a practice that reduces the overhead cost to their clients. Also, by using an agent who usually contracts his or her services to more than one company, companies can share costs with the other companies involved with that agent. As their customers and manufacturers continue to merge with other companies, independent agents and other wholesale trade firms will, in response, also merge with each other to better serve their clients.

Although the demand for independent sales agents will increase over the 2004–14 projection period, the supply is expected to remain stable, or possibly decline, because of the difficulties associated with self-employment. This factor could lead to many opportunities for sales representatives to start their own independent sales agencies.

Those interested in this occupation should keep in mind that direct selling opportunities in manufacturing are likely to be best for products for which there is strong demand. Furthermore, jobs will be most plentiful in small wholesale and manufacturing firms because a growing number of these companies will rely on agents to market their products as a way to control their costs and expand their customer base.

Employment opportunities and earnings may fluctuate from year to year because sales are affected by changing economic conditions, legislative issues, and consumer preferences.

Earnings

Compensation methods vary significantly by the type of firm and the product sold. Most employers use a combination of salary and commissions or salary plus bonus. Commissions usually are based on the amount of sales, whereas bonuses may depend on individual performance, on the performance of all sales workers in the group or district, or on the company's performance.

Median annual earnings of sales representatives, wholesale and manufacturing, technical and scientific products, were $58,580, including commissions, in May 2004. The middle 50 percent earned between $41,660 and $84,480 a year. The lowest 10 percent earned less than $30,270, and the highest 10 percent earned more than $114,540 a year. Median annual earnings in the industries employing the largest numbers of sales representatives, technical and scientific products, in May 2004 were as follows:

Computer systems design and related services $70,220
Wholesale electronic markets and agents and brokers 65,990
Drugs and druggists' sundries merchant wholesalers 60,130
Professional and commercial equipment and supplies merchant wholesalers 59,080
Electrical and electronic goods merchant wholesalers 52,870

Median annual earnings of sales representatives, wholesale and manufacturing, except technical and scientific products, were $45,400, including commission, in May 2004. The middle 50 percent earned between $32,640 and $65,260 a year. The lowest 10 percent earned less than $24,070, and the highest 10 percent earned more than $92,740 a year. Median annual earnings in the industries employing the largest numbers of sales representatives, except technical and scientific products, in May 2004 were as follows:

Wholesale electronic markets and agents and brokers $50,680
Machinery, equipment, and supplies merchant wholesalers 46,030

Professional and commercial equipment and supplies merchant wholesalers 45,320
Grocery and related product wholesalers 44,210
Miscellaneous nondurable goods merchant wholesalers 40,240

In addition to their earnings, sales representatives usually are reimbursed for expenses such as transportation costs, meals, hotels, and entertaining customers. They often receive benefits such as health and life insurance, pension plan, vacation and sick leave, personal use of a company car, and frequent flyer mileage. Some companies offer incentives such as free vacation trips or gifts for outstanding sales workers.

Unlike those working directly for a manufacturer or wholesaler, manufacturers' agents are paid strictly on commission and usually are not reimbursed for expenses. Depending on the type of product or products they are selling, their experience in the field, and the number of clients they have, they can earn significantly more or less than those working in direct sales.

Related Occupations

Sales representatives, wholesale and manufacturing, must have sales ability and knowledge of the products they sell. Other occupations that require similar skills include advertising, marketing, promotions, public relations, and sales managers; insurance sales agents; purchasing managers, buyers, and purchasing agents; real estate brokers and sales agents; retail salespersons; sales engineers; and securities, commodities, and financial services sales agents.

Sources of Additional Information

Information on careers for manufacturers' representatives and agents is available from:

- Manufacturers' Agents National Association, One Spectrum Pointe, Suite 150, Lake Forest, CA 92630. Internet: http://www.manaonline.org
- Manufacturers' Representatives Educational Research Foundation, P.O. Box 247, Geneva, IL 60134. Internet: http://www.mrerf.org

Secretaries and Administrative Assistants

(O*NET 43-6011.00, 43-6012.00, 43-6013.00, and 43-6014.00)

Significant Points

- Numerous job openings will result from the need to replace workers who leave this very large occupation each year.
- Opportunities should be best for applicants with extensive knowledge of software applications.
- Increasing office automation and organizational restructuring will lead to slower than average growth in overall employment of secretaries and administrative assistants, but average growth is projected for legal and medical secretaries.

Nature of the Work

As the reliance on technology continues to expand in offices, the role of the office professional has greatly evolved. Office automation and organizational restructuring have led secretaries and administrative assistants to assume responsibilities once reserved for managerial and professional staff. Many secretaries and administrative assistants now provide training and orientation for new staff, conduct research on the Internet, and operate and troubleshoot new office technologies. In spite of these changes, however, the core responsibilities for secretaries and administrative assistants have remained much the same: Performing and coordinating an office's administrative activities and storing, retrieving, and integrating information for dissemination to staff and clients.

Secretaries and administrative assistants are responsible for a variety of administrative and clerical duties necessary to run an organization efficiently. They serve as information and communication managers for an office; plan and schedule meetings and appointments; organize and maintain paper and electronic files; manage projects; conduct research; and disseminate information by using the telephone, mail services, Web sites, and e-mail. They also may handle travel and guest arrangements.

Secretaries and administrative assistants are aided in these tasks by a variety of office equipment, such as fax machines, photocopiers, scanners, and videoconferencing and telephone systems. In addition, secretaries and administrative assistants often use computers to do tasks previously handled by managers and professionals: create spreadsheets; compose correspondence; manage databases; and create presentations, reports, and documents using desktop publishing software and digital graphics. They also may negotiate with vendors, maintain and examine leased equipment, purchase supplies, manage areas such as stockrooms or corporate libraries, and retrieve data from various sources. At the same time, managers and professionals have assumed many tasks traditionally assigned to secretaries and administrative assistants, such as keyboarding and answering the telephone. Because secretaries and administrative assistants often are not responsible for dictation and word processing, they have time to support more members of the executive staff. In a number of organizations, secretaries and administrative assistants work in teams to work flexibly and share their expertise.

Specific job duties vary with experience and titles. *Executive secretaries and administrative assistants*, for example, may perform fewer clerical tasks than do secretaries. In addition to arranging conference calls and scheduling meetings, they may handle more complex responsibilities such as conducting research, preparing statistical reports, training employees, and hiring and supervising other clerical staff.

Some secretaries and administrative assistants, such as legal and medical secretaries, perform highly specialized work requiring knowledge of technical terminology and procedures. For instance, *legal secretaries* prepare correspondence and legal papers such as summonses, complaints, motions, responses, and subpoenas under the supervision of an attorney or a paralegal. They also may review legal journals and assist with legal research—for example, by verifying quotes and citations in legal briefs. *Medical secretaries* transcribe dictation, prepare correspondence, and assist physicians or medical scientists with reports, speeches, articles, and conference proceedings. They also record simple medical histories, arrange for patients to be hospitalized, and order supplies. Most medical secretaries need to be familiar with insurance rules, billing practices, and hospital or laboratory procedures. Other technical secretaries who assist engineers or scientists may prepare correspondence, maintain their organization's technical library, and gather and edit materials for scientific papers.

Working Conditions

Secretaries and administrative assistants usually work in schools, hospitals, corporate settings, government agencies, or legal and medical offices. Their jobs often involve sitting for long periods. If they spend a lot of time keyboarding, particularly at a computer monitor, they may encounter problems of eyestrain, stress, and repetitive motion ailments such as carpal tunnel syndrome.

Office work can lend itself to alternative or flexible working arrangements, such as part-time work or telecommuting—especially if the job requires extensive computer use. About 19 percent of secretaries work part time and many others work in temporary positions. A few participate in job-sharing arrangements, in which two people divide responsibility for a single job. The majority of secretaries and administrative assistants, however, are full-time employees who work a standard 40-hour week.

Training, Other Qualifications, and Advancement

High school graduates who have basic office skills may qualify for entry-level secretarial positions. However, employers increasingly require extensive knowledge of software applications, such as word processing, spreadsheets, and database management.

Secretaries and administrative assistants should be proficient in keyboarding and good at spelling, punctuation, grammar, and oral communication. Employers also look for good customer service and interpersonal skills because secretaries and administrative assistants must be tactful in their dealings with people. Discretion, good judgment, organizational or management ability, initiative, and the ability to work independently are especially important for higher level administrative positions.

As office automation continues to evolve, retraining and continuing education will remain integral parts of secretarial jobs. Changes in the office environment have increased the demand for secretaries and administrative assistants who are adaptable and versatile.

Secretaries and administrative assistants may have to attend classes or participate in online education to learn how to operate new office technologies, such as information storage systems, scanners, the Internet, or new updated software packages. They also may assist in selecting and maintaining office equipment.

Secretaries and administrative assistants acquire skills in various ways. Training ranges from high school vocational education programs that teach office skills and keyboarding to 1- and 2-year programs in office administration offered by business schools, vocational-technical institutes, and community colleges. Many temporary placement agencies also provide formal training in computer and office skills. However, many skills tend to be acquired through on-the-job instruction by other employees or by equipment and software vendors. Specialized training programs are available for students planning to become medical or legal secretaries or administrative technology specialists. Bachelor's degrees and professional certifications are becoming increasingly important as business continues to become more global.

Testing and certification for proficiency in entry-level office skills is available through organizations such as the International Association of Administrative Professionals; National Association of Legal Secretaries (NALS), Inc.; and Legal Secretaries International, Inc. As secretaries and administrative assistants gain experience, they can earn several different designations. Prominent designations include the Certified Professional Secretary (CPS) and the Certified Administrative Professional (CAP), which can be earned by meeting certain experience or educational requirements and passing an examination. Similarly, those with 1 year of experience in the legal field, or who have concluded an approved training course and who want to be certified as a legal support professional, can acquire the Accredited Legal Secretary (ALS) designation through a testing process administered by NALS. NALS offers two additional designations: Professional Legal Secretary (PLS), considered an advanced certification for legal support professionals, and a designation for proficiency as a paralegal. Legal Secretaries International confers the Certified Legal Secretary Specialist (CLSS) designation in areas such as intellectual property, criminal law, civil litigation, probate, and business law to those who have 5 years of legal experience and pass an examination. In some instances, certain requirements may be waived.

Secretaries and administrative assistants generally advance by being promoted to other administrative positions with more responsibilities. Qualified administrative assistants who broaden their knowledge of a company's operations and enhance their skills may be promoted to senior or executive secretary or administrative assistant, clerical supervisor, or office manager. Secretaries with word processing or data entry experience can advance to jobs as word processing or data entry trainers, supervisors, or managers within their own firms or in a secretarial, word processing, or data entry service bureau. Secretarial and administrative support experience also can lead to jobs such as instructor or sales representative with manufacturers of software or computer equipment. With additional training, many legal secretaries become paralegals.

Employment

Secretaries and administrative assistants held about 4.1 million jobs in 2004, ranking among the largest occupations in the U.S. economy. The following tabulation shows the distribution of employment by secretarial specialty:

Secretaries, except legal, medical, and executive	1,934,000
Executive secretaries and administrative assistants	1,547,000
Medical secretaries	373,000
Legal secretaries	272,000

Secretaries and administrative assistants are employed in organizations of every type. Around 9 out of 10 secretaries and administrative assistants are employed in service providing industries, ranging from education and health care to government and retail trade. Most of the rest work for firms engaged in manufacturing or construction.

Job Outlook

Overall employment of secretaries and administrative assistants is expected to grow more slowly than average for all occupations over the 2004–14 period. In addition to those resulting from growth, numerous job openings will result from the need to replace workers who transfer to other occupations or leave this very large occupation for other reasons each year. Opportunities should be best for applicants with extensive knowledge of software applications, particularly experienced secretaries and administrative assistants.

Projected employment of secretaries and administrative assistants varies by occupational specialty. Employment growth in the health care and social assistance and legal services industries should lead to average growth for medical and legal secretaries. Employment of executive secretaries and administrative assistants is projected to grow average for all occupations. Growing industries—such as administrative and support services; health care and social assistance; educational services (private); and professional, scientific, and technical services—will continue to generate most new job opportunities. A decline in employment is expected for secretaries, except legal, medical, or executive; they account for about 47 percent of all secretaries and administrative assistants.

Increasing office automation and organizational restructuring will continue to make secretaries and administrative assistants more productive in coming years. Computers, e-mail, scanners, and voice message systems will allow secretaries and administrative assistants to accomplish more in the same amount of time. The use of automated equipment also is changing the distribution of work in many offices. In some cases, such traditional secretarial duties as keyboarding, filing, photocopying, and bookkeeping are being assigned to workers in other units or departments. Professionals and managers increasingly do their own word processing and data entry and handle much of their own correspondence rather than submit the work to secretaries and other support staff. Also, in some law and medical offices, paralegals and medical assistants are assuming some tasks formerly done by secretaries. As other workers assume more of these duties, there is a trend in many offices for professionals and managers to replace the traditional arrangement of one secretary per manager with secretaries and administrative assistants who support the work of systems, departments, or units. This approach often means that secretaries and administrative assistants assume added responsibilities and are seen as valuable members of a team, but it also contributes to the projected decline in the overall number of secretarial and administrative assistant positions.

Developments in office technology are certain to continue, and they will bring about further changes in the work of secretaries and administrative assistants. However, many secretarial and administrative duties are of a personal, interactive nature and, therefore, not easily automated. Responsibilities such as planning conferences, working with clients, and instructing staff require tact and communication skills. Because technology cannot substitute for these personal skills, secretaries and administrative assistants will continue to play a key role in most organizations.

Earnings

Median annual earnings of executive secretaries and administrative assistants were $34,970 in May 2004. The middle 50 percent earned between $28,500 and $43,430. The lowest 10 percent earned less than $23,810, and the highest 10 percent earned more than $53,460. Median annual earnings in the industries employing the largest numbers of executive secretaries and administrative assistants in May 2004 were:

Management of companies and enterprises $38,950
Local government 36,940
Colleges, universities, and professional schools 34,280
Employment services 31,620
State government 30,750

Median annual earnings of legal secretaries were $36,720 in May 2004. The middle 50 percent earned between $29,070 and $46,390. The lowest 10 percent earned less than $23,270, and the highest 10 percent earned more than $56,590. Medical secretaries earned a median annual salary of $26,540 in May 2004. The middle 50 percent earned between $21,980 and $32,690. The lowest 10 percent earned less than $19,140, and the highest 10 percent earned more than $39,140. Median annual earnings of secretaries, except legal, medical, and executive, were $26,110 in May 2004.

Salaries vary a great deal, however, reflecting differences in skill, experience, and level of responsibility. Certification in this field usually is rewarded by a higher salary.

Related Occupations

Workers in a number of other occupations type, record information, and process paperwork. Among them are bookkeeping, accounting, and auditing clerks; receptionists and information clerks; communications equipment operators; court reporters; human resources assistants, except payroll and timekeeping; computer operators; data entry and information processing workers; paralegals and legal assistants; medical assistants; and medical records and health information technicians. A growing number of secretaries and administrative assistants share in managerial and human resource responsibilities. Occupations requiring these skills include office and administrative support supervisors and managers; computer and information systems managers; administrative services managers; and human resources, training, and labor relations managers and specialists.

Sources of Additional Information

State employment offices provide information about job openings for secretaries and administrative assistants.

For information on the latest trends in the profession, career development advice, and the CPS or CAP designations, contact:

- International Association of Administrative Professionals, 10502 NW Ambassador Dr., P.O. Box 20404, Kansas City, MO 64195-0404. Internet: http://www.iaap-hq.org

Information on the CLSS designation can be obtained from:

- Legal Secretaries International Inc. Internet: http://www.legalsecretaries.org

Information on the ALS, PLS, and paralegal certifications are available from:

- National Association of Legal Secretaries, Inc., 314 East Third St., Suite 210, Tulsa, OK 74120. Internet: http://www.nals.org

Security Guards and Gaming Surveillance Officers

(O*NET 33-9031.00 and 33-9032.00)

Significant Points

- Opportunities for most jobs should be favorable, but competition is expected for higher-paying positions at facilities requiring longer periods of training and a high level of security, such as nuclear power plants and weapons installations.
- Because of limited formal training requirements and flexible hours, this occupation attracts many individuals seeking a second or part-time job.
- Some positions, such as those of armored car guards, are hazardous.

Nature of the Work

Guards, who are also called *security officers*, patrol and inspect property to protect against fire, theft, vandalism, terrorism, and illegal activity. These workers protect their employer's investment, enforce laws on the property, and deter criminal activity and other problems. They use radio and telephone communications to call for assistance from police, fire, or emergency medical services as the situation dictates. Security guards write comprehensive reports outlining their observations and activities during their assigned shift. They also may interview witnesses or victims, prepare case reports, and testify in court.

Although all security guards perform many of the same duties, their specific duties vary with whether the guard works in a "static" security position or on a mobile patrol. Guards assigned to static security positions usually serve the client at one location for a specified length of time. These guards must become closely acquainted with the property and people associated with it and must often monitor alarms and closed-circuit TV cameras. In contrast, guards assigned to mobile patrol duty drive or walk from location to location and conduct security checks within an assigned geographical zone. They may detain or arrest criminal violators, answer service calls concerning criminal activity or problems, and issue traffic violation warnings.

The security guard's job responsibilities also vary with the size, type, and location of the employer. In department stores, guards protect people, records, merchandise, money, and equipment. They often work with undercover store detectives to prevent theft by customers or employees, and they help apprehend shoplifting suspects prior to the arrival of the police. Some shopping centers and theaters have officers who patrol their parking lots to deter car thefts and robberies. In office buildings, banks, and hospitals, guards maintain order and protect the institutions' property, staff, and customers. At air, sea, and rail terminals and other transportation facilities, guards protect people, freight, property, and equipment. Using metal detectors and high-tech equipment, they may screen passengers and visitors for weapons and explosives, ensure that nothing is stolen while a vehicle is being loaded or unloaded, and watch for fires and criminals.

Guards who work in public buildings such as museums or art galleries protect paintings and exhibits by inspecting people and packages entering and leaving the building. In factories, laboratories, government buildings, data processing centers, and military bases, security officers protect information, products, computer codes, and defense secrets and check the credentials of people and vehicles entering and leaving the premises. Guards working at universities, parks, and sports stadiums perform crowd control, supervise parking and seating, and direct traffic. Security guards stationed at the entrance to bars and places of adult entertainment, such as nightclubs, prevent access by minors, collect cover charges at the door, maintain order among customers, and protect property and patrons.

Armored car guards protect money and valuables during transit. In addition, they protect individuals responsible for making commercial bank deposits from theft or bodily injury. When the armored car arrives at the door of a business, an armed guard enters, signs for the money, and returns to the truck with the valuables in hand. Carrying money between the truck and the business can be extremely hazardous; because of this risk, armored car guards usually wear bulletproof vests.

All security officers must show good judgment and common sense, follow directions and directives from supervisors, testify accurately in court, and follow company policy and guidelines. Guards should have a professional appearance and attitude and be able to interact with the public. They also must be able to take charge and direct others in emergencies or other dangerous incidents. In a large organization, the security manager often is in charge of a trained guard force divided into shifts; in a small organization, a single worker may be responsible for all security.

Gaming surveillance officers, also known as *surveillance agents,* and *gaming investigators* act as security agents for casino managers and patrons. Using primarily audio and video equipment in an observation room, they observe casino operations for irregular activities, such as cheating or theft, by either employees or patrons. They keep recordings that are sometimes used as evidence against alleged criminals in police investigations. Some casinos use a catwalk over one-way mirrors located above the casino floor to augment electronic surveillance equipment. Surveillance agents occasionally leave the surveillance room and walk the casino floor.

Working Conditions

Most security guards and gaming surveillance officers spend considerable time on their feet, either assigned to a specific post or patrolling buildings and grounds. Guards may be stationed at a guard desk inside a building to monitor electronic security and surveillance devices or to check the credentials of persons entering or leaving the premises. They also may be stationed at a guardhouse outside the entrance to a gated facility or community and may use a portable radio or cellular telephone that allows them to be in constant contact with a central station. The work usually is routine, but guards must be constantly alert for threats to themselves and the property they are protecting. Guards who work during the day may have a great deal of contact with other employees and members of the public. Gaming surveillance often takes place behind a bank of monitors controlling several cameras in a casino and thus can cause eyestrain.

Guards usually work at least 8-hour shifts for 40 hours per week and often are on call in case an emergency arises. Some employers have three shifts, and guards rotate to divide daytime, weekend, and holiday work equally. Guards usually eat on the job instead of taking a regular break away from the site. In 2004, 16% of guards worked part time, and many individuals held a second job as a guard to supplement their primary earnings.

Training, Other Qualifications, and Advancement

Most states require that guards be licensed. To be licensed as a guard, individuals must usually be at least 18 years old; pass a background check; and complete classroom training in such subjects as property rights, emergency procedures, and detention of suspected criminals. Drug testing often is required and may be random and ongoing.

Many employers of unarmed guards do not have any specific educational requirements. For armed guards, employers usually prefer individuals who are high school graduates or who hold an equivalent certification. Many jobs require a driver's license. For positions as armed guards, employers often seek people who have had responsible experience in other occupations.

Guards who carry weapons must be licensed by the appropriate government authority, and some receive further certification as special police officers, allowing them to make limited types of arrests while on duty. Armed guard positions have more stringent background checks and entry requirements than those of unarmed guards because of greater insurance liability risks. Compared with unarmed security guards, armed guards and special police typically enjoy higher earnings and benefits, greater job security, and more potential for advancement. Usually, they also are given more training and responsibility.

Rigorous hiring and screening programs consisting of background, criminal record, and fingerprint checks are becoming the norm in the occupation. Applicants are expected to have good character references, no serious police record, and good health. They should be mentally alert, emotionally stable, and physically fit to cope with emergencies. Guards who have frequent contact with the public should communicate well.

The amount of training guards receive varies. Training requirements are higher for armed guards because their employers are legally responsible for any use of force. Armed guards receive formal training in areas such as weapons retention and laws covering the use of force.

Many employers give newly hired guards instruction before they start the job and provide on-the-job training. An increasing number of states are making ongoing training a legal requirement for retention of certification. Guards may receive training in protection, public relations, report writing, crisis deterrence, and first aid, as well as specialized training relevant to their particular assignment.

The American Society for Industrial Security International has written voluntary training guidelines that are intended to provide regulating bodies consistent minimum standards for the quality of security services. These guidelines recommend that security guards receive at least 48 hours of training within the first 100 days of employment. The guidelines also suggest that security guards be required to pass a written or performance examination covering topics such as sharing information with law enforcement, crime prevention, handling evidence, the use of force, court testimony, report writing, interpersonal and communication skills, and emergency response procedures. In addition, they recommend annual training and additional firearms training for armed officers.

Guards who are employed at establishments placing a heavy emphasis on security usually receive extensive formal training. For example, guards at nuclear power plants undergo several months of training before being placed on duty—and even then, they perform their tasks only under close supervision. They are taught to use firearms, administer first aid, operate alarm systems and electronic security equipment, and spot and deal with security problems. Guards who are authorized to carry firearms may be periodically tested in their use.

Because many people do not stay long in this occupation, opportunities for advancement are good for those who are career security officers. Most large organizations use a military type of ranking that offers the possibility of advancement in both position and salary. Some guards may advance to supervisor or security manager positions. Guards with management skills may open their own contract security guard agencies. Pay rates vary substantially with the security level of the establishment, so there is also the opportunity to move to higher-paying jobs with increased experience and training.

In addition to possessing the keen observation skills required to perform their jobs, gaming surveillance officers and gaming investigators must have excellent verbal and writing abilities to document violations or suspicious behavior. They also need to be physically fit and have quick reflexes because they sometimes must detain individuals until local law enforcement officials arrive.

Gaming surveillance officers and investigators usually need some training beyond high school, but not a bachelor's degree; previous security experience is a plus. Several educational institutes offer certification programs. Training classes usually are conducted in a casino-like atmosphere and use surveillance camera equipment. Employers prefer either individuals with significant knowledge of casino operations through work experience or those with experience conducting investigations, such as former law enforcement officers.

Employment

Security guards and gaming surveillance officers held over 1.0 million jobs in 2004. Over half of all jobs for security guards were in investigation and security services, including guard and armored car services. These organizations provide security on a contract basis, assigning their guards to buildings and other sites as needed. Most other security officers were employed directly by educational services, hospitals, food services and drinking places, traveler accommodation (hotels), department stores, manufacturing firms, lessors of real estate (residential and nonresidential buildings), and governments. Guard jobs are found throughout the country, most commonly in metropolitan areas. Gaming surveillance officers worked primarily in gambling industries; traveler accommodation, which includes casino hotels; and local government. Gaming surveillance officers were employed only in those states and on those Indian reservations where gambling has been legalized.

A significant number of law enforcement officers work as security guards when they are off duty in order to supplement their incomes. Often working in uniform and with the official cars assigned to them, they add a high-profile security presence to the establishment with which they have contracted. At construction sites and apartment complexes, for example, their presence often deters crime.

Job Outlook

Opportunities for security guards and gaming surveillance officers should be favorable. Numerous job openings will stem from employment growth attributable to the demand for increased security and from the need to replace those who leave this large occupation each year. In addition to full-time job opportunities, the limited training requirements and flexible hours attract many persons seeking part-time or second jobs. However, competition is expected for higher-paying positions that require longer periods of training; these positions usually are found at facilities that require a high level of security, such as nuclear power plants or weapons installations.

Employment of security guards and gaming surveillance officers is expected to grow as fast as the average for all occupations through 2014 as concern about crime, vandalism, and terrorism continues to increase the need for security. Demand for guards also will grow as private security firms increasingly perform duties—such as providing security at public events and in residential neighborhoods—that were formerly handled by police officers. Casinos will continue to hire more surveillance officers as more states legalize gambling and as the number of casinos increases in states where gambling is already legal. In addition, casino security forces will employ more technically trained personnel as technology becomes increasingly important in thwarting casino cheating and theft.

Earnings

Median annual earnings of security guards were $20,320 in May 2004. The middle 50 percent earned between $16,640 and $25,510. The lowest 10 percent earned less than $14,390, and the highest 10 percent earned more than $33,270. Median annual earnings in the industries employing the largest numbers of security guards in May 2004 were as follows:

Elementary and secondary schools	$25,030
General medical and surgical hospitals	24,750
Local government	23,690
Traveler accommodation	21,710
Investigation and security services	19,030

Gaming surveillance officers and gaming investigators had median annual earnings of $25,840 in May 2004. The middle 50 percent earned between $20,430 and $33,790. The lowest 10 percent earned less than $17,710, and the highest 10 percent earned more than $42,420.

Related Occupations

Guards protect property, maintain security, and enforce regulations and standards of conduct in the establishments at which they work. Related security and protective service occupations include correctional officers, police and detectives, and private detectives and investigators.

Sources of Additional Information

Further information about work opportunities for guards is available from local security and guard firms and state employment service offices. Information about licensing requirements for guards may be obtained from the state licensing commission or the state police department. In states where local jurisdictions establish licensing requirements, contact a local government authority such as the sheriff, county executive, or city manager.

Social and Human Service Assistants

(O*NET 21-1093.00)

Significant Points

- While a bachelor's degree usually is not required, employers increasingly seek individuals with relevant work experience or education beyond high school.
- Employment is projected to grow much faster than average.
- Job opportunities should be excellent, particularly for applicants with appropriate postsecondary education, but pay is low.

Nature of the Work

Social and human service assistant is a generic term for people with a wide array of job titles, including human service worker, case management aide, social work assistant, community support worker, mental health aide, community outreach worker, life skill counselor, or gerontology aide. They usually work under the direction of workers from a variety of fields, such as nursing, psychiatry, psychology, rehabilitative or physical therapy, or social work. The amount of responsibility and supervision they are given varies a great deal. Some have little direct supervision; others work under close direction.

Social and human service assistants provide direct and indirect client services to ensure that individuals in their care reach their maximum level of functioning. They assess clients' needs, establish their eligibility for benefits and services such as food stamps, Medicaid, or welfare, and help to obtain them. They also arrange for transportation and escorts, if necessary, and provide emotional support. Social and human service assistants monitor and keep case records on clients and report progress to supervisors and case managers.

Social and human service assistants play a variety of roles in a community. They may organize and lead group activities, assist clients in need of counseling or crisis intervention, or administer a food bank or emergency fuel program. In halfway houses, group homes, and government-supported housing programs, they assist adults who need supervision with personal hygiene and daily living skills. They review clients' records, ensure that they take correct doses of medication, talk with family members, and confer with medical personnel and other caregivers to gain better insight into clients' backgrounds and needs. Social and human service assistants also provide emotional support and help clients become involved in their own well-being, in community recreation programs, and in other activities.

In psychiatric hospitals, rehabilitation programs, and outpatient clinics, social and human service assistants work with professional care providers, such as psychiatrists, psychologists, and social workers, to help clients master everyday living skills, communicate more effectively, and get along better with others. They support the client's participation in a treatment plan, such as individual or group counseling or occupational therapy.

Working Conditions

Working conditions of social and human service assistants vary. Some work in offices, clinics, and hospitals, while others work in group homes, shelters, sheltered workshops, and day programs. Many work under close supervision, while others work much of the time on their own, such as those who spend their time in the field visiting clients. Sometimes visiting clients can be dangerous even though most agencies do everything they can to ensure their workers' safety. Most work a 40-hour week, although some work in the evening and on weekends.

The work, while satisfying, can be emotionally draining. Understaffing and relatively low pay may add to the pressure. Turnover is reported to be high, especially among workers without academic preparation for this field.

Training, Other Qualifications, and Advancement

While a bachelor's degree usually is not required for entry into this occupation, employers increasingly seek individuals with relevant work experience or education beyond high school. Certificates or associate degrees in subjects such as social work, human services, gerontology, or one of the social or behavioral sciences meet most employers' requirements. Some jobs may require a bachelor's or master's degree in human services or a related field such as counseling, rehabilitation, or social work.

Human services degree programs have a core curriculum that trains students to observe patients and record information, conduct patient interviews, implement treatment plans, employ problem-solving techniques, handle crisis intervention matters, and use proper case management and referral procedures. General education courses in liberal arts, sciences, and the humanities also are part of the curriculum. Most programs offer the opportunity to take specialized courses related to addictions, gerontology, child protection, and other areas. Many degree programs require completion of a supervised internship.

Educational attainment often influences the kind of work employees may be assigned and the degree of responsibility that may be entrusted to them. For example, workers with no more than a high school education are likely to receive extensive on-the-job training to work in direct-care services, while employees with a college degree might be assigned to do supportive counseling, coordinate program activities, or manage a group home. Social and human service assistants with proven leadership ability, either from previous experience or as a volunteer in the field, often have greater autonomy in their work. Regardless of the academic or work background of employees, most employers provide some form of inservice training, such as seminars and workshops, to their employees.

There may be additional hiring requirements in group homes. For example, employers may require employees to have a valid driver's license or to submit to a criminal background investigation.

Employers try to select applicants who have a strong desire to help others, have effective communication skills, a strong sense of responsibility, and the ability to manage time effectively. Many human services jobs involve direct contact with people who are vulnerable to exploitation or mistreatment; therefore, patience, understanding, and a strong desire to help others are highly valued characteristics.

Formal education almost always is necessary for advancement. In general, advancement requires a bachelor's or master's degree in human services, counseling, rehabilitation, social work, or a related field. Typically, advancement brings case management, supervision, and administration roles.

Employment

Social and human service assistants held about 352,000 jobs in 2004. More than half worked in the health care and social assistance industries. One in three were employed by state and local governments, primarily in public welfare agencies and facilities for mentally disabled and developmentally challenged individuals.

Job Outlook

Job opportunities for social and human service assistants are expected to be excellent, particularly for applicants with appropriate postsecondary education. The number of social and human service assistants is projected to grow much faster than the average for all occupations between 2004 and 2014—ranking the occupation among the most rapidly growing. Many additional job opportunities will arise from the need to replace workers who advance into new positions, retire, or leave the workforce for other reasons. There will be more competition for jobs in urban areas than in rural areas, but qualified applicants should have little difficulty finding employment. Faced with rapid growth in the demand for social and human services many employers increasingly rely on social and human service assistants to undertake greater responsibility for delivering services to clients.

Opportunities are expected to be good in private social service agencies, which provide such services as adult day care and meal delivery programs. Employment in private agencies will grow as state and local governments continue to contract out services to the private sector in an effort to cut costs. Demand for social services will expand with the growing elderly population, who are more likely to need these services. In addition, more social and human service assistants will be needed to provide services to pregnant teenagers, the homeless, the mentally disabled and developmentally challenged, and substance abusers. Some private agencies have been employing more social and human service assistants in place of social workers, who are more educated and, thus, more highly paid.

Job training programs also are expected to require additional social and human service assistants. As social welfare policies shift focus from benefit-based programs to work-based initiatives there will be more demand for people to teach job skills to the people who are new to, or returning to, the workforce.

Residential care establishments should face increased pressures to respond to the needs of the mentally and physically disabled. Many of these patients have been deinstitutionalized and lack the knowledge or the ability to care for themselves. Also, more community-based programs and supportive independent-living sites are expected to be established to house and assist the homeless and the mentally and physically disabled. As substance abusers are increasingly being sent to treatment programs instead of prison, employment of social and human service assistants in substance abuse treatment programs also will grow.

The number of jobs for social and human service assistants in local governments will grow but not as fast as employment for social and human service assistants in other industries. Employment in the public sector may fluctuate with the level of funding provided by state and local governments. Also, some state and local governments are contracting out selected social services to private agencies in order to save money.

Earnings

Median annual earnings of social and human service assistants were $24,270 in May 2004. The middle 50 percent earned between $19,220 and $30,900. The top 10 percent earned more than $39,620, while the lowest 10 percent earned less than $15,480.

Median annual earnings in the industries employing the largest numbers of social and human service assistants in May 2004 were:

State government	$29,270
Local government	28,230
Individual and family services	23,400
Vocational rehabilitation services	21,770
Residential mental retardation, mental health and substance abuse facilities	20,410

Related Occupations

Workers in other occupations that require skills similar to those of social and human service assistants include social workers; counselors; childcare workers; occupational therapist assistants and aides; physical therapist assistants and aides; and nursing, psychiatric, and home health aides.

Sources of Additional Information

Information on academic programs in human services may be found in most directories of 2-year and 4-year colleges, available at libraries or career counseling centers.

For information on programs and careers in human services, contact:

- National Organization for Human Services, 5601 Brodie Lane, Suite 620-215, Austin, TX 78745. Internet: http://www.nohse.org
- Council for Standards in Human Services Education, Harrisburg Area Community College, Human Services Program, One HACC Dr., Harrisburg, PA 17110-2999. Internet: http://www.cshse.org

Information on job openings may be available from state employment service offices or directly from city, county, or state departments of health, mental health and mental retardation, and human resources.

Social Workers

(O*NET 21-1021.00, 21-1022.00, 21-1023.00, and 21-1029.99)

Significant Points

- About 9 out of 10 jobs are in health care and social assistance industries, as well as state and local government agencies.
- While a bachelor's degree is the minimum requirement, a master's degree in social work or a related field has become the standard for many positions.
- Employment is projected to grow faster than average.
- Competition for jobs is expected in cities, but opportunities should be good in rural areas.

Nature of the Work

Social work is a profession for those with a strong desire to help improve people's lives. Social workers help people function the best way they can in their environment, deal with their relationships, and solve personal and family problems. Social workers often see clients who face a life-threatening disease or a social problem, such as inadequate housing, unemployment, a serious illness, a disability, or substance abuse. Social workers also assist families that have serious domestic conflicts, sometimes involving child or spousal abuse.

Social workers often provide social services in health-related settings that now are governed by managed care organizations. To contain costs, these organizations emphasize short-term intervention, ambulatory and community-based care, and greater decentralization of services.

Most social workers specialize. Although some conduct research or are involved in planning or policy development, most social workers prefer an area of practice in which they interact with clients.

Child, family, and school social workers provide social services and assistance to improve the social and psychological functioning of children and their families and to maximize the family well-being and academic functioning of children. Some social workers assist single parents, arrange adoptions, or help find foster homes for neglected, abandoned, or abused children. In schools, they address such problems as teenage pregnancy, misbehavior, and truancy and advise teachers on how to cope with problem students. Increasingly, school social workers are teaching workshops to an entire class. Some social workers specialize in services for senior citizens, running support groups for family caregivers or for the adult children of aging parents, advising elderly people or family members about choices in areas such as housing, transportation, and long-term care, and coordinating and monitoring these services. Through employee assistance programs, they may help workers cope with job-related pressures or with personal problems that affect the quality of their work. Child, family, and school social workers typically work for individual and family services agencies, schools, or state or local governments. These social workers may be known as child welfare social workers, family services social workers, child protective services social workers, occupational social workers, or gerontology social workers.

Medical and public health social workers provide persons, families, or vulnerable populations with the psychosocial support needed to cope with chronic, acute, or terminal illnesses, such as Alzheimer's disease, cancer, or AIDS. They also advise family caregivers, counsel patients, and help plan for patients' needs after discharge by arranging for at-home services, from meals-on-wheels to oxygen equipment. Some work on interdisciplinary teams that evaluate certain kinds of patients—geriatric or organ transplant patients, for example. Medical and public health social workers may work for hospitals, nursing and personal care facilities, individual and family services agencies, or local governments.

Mental health and substance abuse social workers assess and treat individuals with mental illness or substance abuse problems, including abuse of alcohol, tobacco, or other drugs. Such services include individual and group therapy, outreach, crisis intervention, social rehabilitation, and training in skills of everyday living. They also may help plan for supportive services to ease patients' return to the community. Mental health and substance abuse social workers are likely to work in hospitals, substance abuse treatment centers, individual and family services agencies, or local governments. These social workers may be known as clinical social workers.

Other types of social workers include *social work planners and policymakers*, who develop programs to address such issues as child abuse, homelessness, substance abuse, poverty, and violence. These workers research and analyze policies, programs, and regulations. They identify social problems and suggest legislative and other solutions. They may help raise funds or write grants to support these programs.

Working Conditions

Full-time social workers usually work a standard 40-hour week; however, some occasionally work evenings and weekends to meet with clients, attend community meetings, and handle emergencies. Some, particularly in voluntary nonprofit agencies, work part time. Social workers usually spend most of their time in an office or residential facility, but also may travel locally to visit clients, meet with service providers, or attend meetings. Some may use one of several offices within a local area in which to meet with clients. The work, while satisfying, can be emotionally draining. Understaffing and large caseloads add to the pressure in some agencies. To tend to patient care or client needs, many hospitals and long-term care facilities are employing social workers on teams with a broad mix of occupations, including clinical specialists, registered nurses, and health aides.

Training, Other Qualifications, and Advancement

A bachelor's degree in social work (BSW) degree is the most common minimum requirement to qualify for a job as a social worker; however, majors in psychology, sociology, and related fields may qualify for some entry-level jobs, especially in small community agencies. Although a bachelor's degree is sufficient for entry into the field, an advanced degree has become the standard for many positions. A master's degree in social work (MSW) is typically required for positions in health settings and is required for clinical work as well. Some jobs in public and private agencies also may require an advanced degree, such as a master's degree in social services policy or administration. Supervisory, administrative, and staff training positions usually require an advanced degree. College and university teaching positions and most research appointments normally require a doctorate in social work (DSW or Ph.D.).

As of 2004, the Council on Social Work Education (CSWE) accredited 442 BSW programs and 168 MSW programs. The Group for the Advancement of Doctoral Education (GADE) listed 80 doctoral programs in social work (DSW or Ph.D.). BSW programs prepare graduates for direct service positions, such as caseworker, and include courses in social work values and ethics, dealing with a culturally diverse clientele, at-risk populations, promotion of social and economic justice, human behavior and the social environment, social welfare policy and services, social work practice, social research methods, and field education. Accredited BSW programs require a minimum of 400 hours of supervised field experience.

Master's degree programs prepare graduates for work in their chosen field of concentration and continue to develop the skills required to perform clinical assessments, manage large caseloads, take on supervisory roles, and explore new ways of drawing upon social services to meet the needs of clients. Master's programs last 2 years and include a minimum of 900 hours of supervised field instruction, or internship. A part-time program may take 4 years. Entry into a master's program does not require a bachelor's degree in social work, but courses in psychology, biology, sociology, economics, political science, and social work are recommended. In addition, a second language can be very helpful. Most master's programs offer advanced standing for those with a bachelor's degree from an accredited social work program.

All states and the District of Columbia have licensing, certification, or registration requirements regarding social work practice and the use of professional titles. Although standards for licensing vary by state, a growing number of states are placing greater emphasis on communications skills, professional ethics, and sensitivity to cultural diversity issues. Most states require two years (3,000 hours) of supervised clinical experience for licensure of clinical social workers. In addition, the National Association of Social Workers (NASW) offers voluntary credentials. Social workers with an MSW may be eligible for the Academy of Certified Social Workers (ACSW), the Qualified Clinical Social Worker (QCSW), or the Diplomate in Clinical Social Work (DCSW) credential, based on their professional experience. Credentials are particularly important for those in private practice; some health insurance providers require social workers to have them in order to be reimbursed for services.

Social workers should be emotionally mature, objective, and sensitive to people and their problems. They must be able to handle responsibility, work independently, and maintain good working relationships with clients and co-workers. Volunteer or paid jobs as a social work aide offer ways of testing one's interest in this field.

Advancement to supervisor, program manager, assistant director, or executive director of a social service agency or department is possible, but usually requires an advanced degree and related work experience. Other career options for social workers include teaching, research, and consulting. Some of these workers also help formulate government policies by analyzing and advocating policy positions in government agencies, in research institutions, and on legislators' staffs.

Some social workers go into private practice. Most private practitioners are clinical social workers who provide psychotherapy, usually paid for through health insurance or by the client themselves. Private practitioners must have at least a master's degree and a period of supervised work experience. A network of contacts for referrals also is essential. Many private practitioners split their time between working for an agency or hospital and working in their private practice. They may continue to hold a position at a hospital or agency in order to receive health and life insurance.

Employment

Social workers held about 562,000 jobs in 2004. About 9 out of 10 jobs were in health care and social assistance industries, as well as state and local government agencies, primarily in departments of health and human services. Although most social workers are employed in cities or suburbs, some work in rural areas. The following tabulation shows 2004 employment by type of social worker:

Child, family, and school social workers	272,000
Mental health and substance abuse social workers	116,000
Medical and public health social workers	110,000
Social workers, all other	64,000

Job Outlook

Competition for social worker jobs is expected in cities, where demand for services often is highest and training programs for social workers are prevalent. However, opportunities should be good in rural areas, which often find it difficult to attract and retain qualified staff. By specialty, job prospects may be best for those social workers with a background in gerontology and substance abuse treatment.

Employment of social workers is expected to increase faster than the average for all occupations through 2014. The rapidly growing elderly population and the aging baby boom generation will create greater demand for health and social services, resulting in particularly rapid job growth among gerontology social workers. Many job openings also will stem from the need to replace social workers who leave the occupation.

As hospitals continue to limit the length of patient stays, the demand for social workers in hospitals will grow more slowly than in other areas. Because hospitals are releasing patients earlier than in the past, social worker employment in home health care services is growing. However, the expanding senior population is an even larger factor. Employment opportunities for social workers with backgrounds in gerontology should be good in the growing numbers of assisted-living and senior-living communities. The expanding senior population also will spur demand for social workers in nursing homes, long-term care facilities, and hospices.

Strong demand is expected for substance abuse social workers over the 2004–14 projection period. Substance abusers are increasingly being placed into treatment programs instead of being sentenced to prison. Because of the increasing numbers of individuals sentenced to prison or probation who are substance abusers, correctional systems are increasingly requiring substance abuse treatment as a condition added to their sentencing or probation. As this trend grows, demand will increase for treatment programs and social workers to assist abusers on the road to recovery.

Employment of social workers in private social service agencies also will increase. However, agencies increasingly will restructure services and hire more lower paid social and human service assistants instead of social workers. Employment in state and local government agencies may grow somewhat in response to increasing needs for public welfare, family services, and child protection services; however, many of these services will be contracted out to private agencies. Employment levels in public and private social services agencies may fluctuate, depending on need and government funding levels.

Employment of school social workers also is expected to grow as expanded efforts to respond to rising student enrollments and continued emphasis on integrating disabled children into the general school population lead to more jobs. There could be competition for school social work jobs in some areas because of the limited number of openings. The availability of federal, state, and local funding will be a major factor in determining the actual job growth in schools.

Opportunities for social workers in private practice will expand, but growth may be somewhat hindered by restrictions that managed care organizations put on mental health services. The growing popularity of employee assistance programs is expected to spur demand for private practitioners, some of whom provide social work services to corporations on a contractual basis. However, the popularity of employee assistance programs will fluctuate with the business cycle, because businesses are not likely to offer these services during recessions.

Earnings

Median annual earnings of child, family, and school social workers were $34,820 in May 2004. The middle 50 percent earned between $27,840 and $45,140. The lowest 10 percent earned less than $23,130, and the top 10 percent earned more than $57,860. Median annual earnings in the industries employing the largest numbers of child, family, and school social workers in May 2004 were:

Elementary and secondary schools	$44,300
Local government	40,620
State government	35,070
Individual and family services	30,680
Other residential care facilities	30,550

Median annual earnings of medical and public health social workers were $40,080 in May 2004. The middle 50 percent earned between $31,620 and $50,080. The lowest 10 percent earned less than $25,390, and the top 10 percent earned more than $58,740. Median annual earnings in the industries employing the largest numbers of medical and public health social workers in May 2004 were:

General medical and surgical hospitals	$44,920
Home health care services	42,710
Local government	39,390
Nursing care facilities	35,680
Individual and family services	32,100

Median annual earnings of mental health and substance abuse social workers were $33,920 in May 2004. The middle 50 percent earned between $26,730 and $43,430. The lowest 10 percent earned less than $21,590, and the top 10 percent earned more than $54,180. Median annual earnings in the industries employing the largest numbers of mental health and substance abuse social workers in May 2004 were:

Psychiatric and substance abuse hospitals	$36,170
Local government	35,720
Outpatient care centers	33,220
Individual and family services	32,810
Residential mental retardation, mental health and substance abuse facilities	29,110

Median annual earnings of social workers, all other were $39,440 in May 2004. The middle 50 percent earned between $30,350 and $51,530. The lowest 10 percent earned less than $24,080, and the top 10 percent earned more than $62,720. Median annual earnings in the industries employing the largest numbers of social workers, all other in May 2004 were:

Local government	$42,570
State government	40,940
Individual and family services	32,280

About 1 out of 5 social workers is a member of a union. Many belong to the union associated with their place of employment.

Related Occupations

Through direct counseling or referral to other services, social workers help people solve a range of personal problems. Workers in occupations with similar duties include counselors, probation officers and correctional treatment specialists, psychologists, and social and human services assistants.

Sources of Additional Information

For information about career opportunities in social work and voluntary credentials for social workers, contact:

- National Association of Social Workers, 750 First St. NE, Suite 700, Washington, DC 20002-4241. Internet: http://www.socialworkers.org

For a listing of accredited social work programs, contact:

- Council on Social Work Education, 1725 Duke St., Suite 500, Alexandria, VA 22314-3457. Internet: http://www.cswe.org

Information on licensing requirements and testing procedures for each state may be obtained from state licensing authorities or from:

- Association of Social Work Boards, 400 South Ridge Pkwy., Suite B, Culpeper, VA 22701. Internet: http://www.aswb.org

Surgical Technologists

(O*NET 29-2055.00)

Significant Points

- Employment is expected to grow much faster than the average for all occupations through the year 2014.
- Job opportunities are expected to be good.
- Training programs last 9 to 24 months and lead to a certificate, diploma, or associate degree.
- Hospitals will continue to be the primary employer, although much faster employment growth is expected in offices of physicians and in outpatient care centers, including ambulatory surgical centers.

Nature of the Work

Surgical technologists, also called scrubs and surgical or operating room technicians, assist in surgical operations under the supervision of surgeons, registered nurses, or other surgical personnel. Surgical technologists are members of operating room teams, which most commonly include surgeons, anesthesiologists, and circulating nurses. Before an operation, surgical technologists help prepare the operating room by setting up surgical instruments and equipment, sterile drapes, and sterile solutions. They assemble both sterile and nonsterile equipment, as well as adjust and check it to ensure it is working properly. Technologists also get patients ready for surgery by washing, shaving, and disinfecting incision sites. They transport patients to the operating room, help position them on the operating table, and cover them with sterile surgical "drapes." Technologists also observe patients' vital signs, check charts, and assist the surgical team with putting on sterile gowns and gloves.

During surgery, technologists pass instruments and other sterile supplies to surgeons and surgeon assistants. They may hold retractors, cut sutures, and help count sponges, needles, supplies, and instruments. Surgical technologists help prepare, care for, and dispose of specimens taken for laboratory analysis and help apply dressings. Some operate sterilizers, lights, or suction machines, and help operate diagnostic equipment.

After an operation, surgical technologists may help transfer patients to the recovery room and clean and restock the operating room.

Working Conditions

Surgical technologists work in clean, well-lighted, cool environments. They must stand for long periods and remain alert during operations. At times they may be exposed to communicable diseases and unpleasant sights, odors, and materials.

Most surgical technologists work a regular 40-hour week, although they may be on call or work nights, weekends, and holidays on a rotating basis.

Training, Other Qualifications, and Advancement

Surgical technologists receive their training in formal programs offered by community and junior colleges, vocational schools, universities, hospitals, and the military. In 2005, the Commission on Accreditation of Allied Health Education Programs (CAAHEP) recognized more than 400 accredited programs. Programs last from 9 to 24 months and lead to a certificate, diploma, or associate degree. High school graduation normally is required for admission. Recommended high school courses include health, biology, chemistry, and mathematics.

Programs provide classroom education and supervised clinical experience. Students take courses in anatomy, physiology, microbiology, pharmacology, professional ethics, and medical terminology. Other studies cover the care and safety of patients during surgery, sterile techniques, and surgical procedures. Students also learn to sterilize instruments; prevent and control infection; and handle special drugs, solutions, supplies, and equipment.

Most employers prefer to hire certified technologists. Technologists may obtain voluntary professional certification from the Liaison Council on Certification for the Surgical Technologist by graduating from a CAAHEP-accredited program and passing a national certification examination. They may then use the Certified Surgical Technologist (CST) designation. Continuing education or reexamination is required to maintain certification, which must be renewed every 4 years.

Certification also may be obtained from the National Center for Competency Testing. To qualify to take the exam, candidates follow one of three paths: complete an accredited training program; undergo a 2-year hospital on-the-job training program; or acquire seven years of experience working in the field. After passing the exam, individuals may use the designation Tech in Surgery-Certified, TS-C (NCCT). This certification may be renewed every 5 years through either continuing education or reexamination.

Surgical technologists need manual dexterity to handle instruments quickly. They also must be conscientious, orderly, and emotionally stable to handle the demands of the operating room environment. Technologists must respond quickly and must be familiar with operating procedures in order to have instruments ready for surgeons without having to be told. They are expected to keep abreast of new developments in the field.

Technologists advance by specializing in a particular area of surgery, such as neurosurgery or open heart surgery. They also may work as circulating technologists. A circulating technologist is the "unsterile" member of the surgical team who prepares patients; helps with anesthesia; obtains and opens packages for the "sterile" persons to remove the sterile contents during the procedure; interviews the patient before surgery; keeps a written account of the surgical procedure; and answers the surgeon's questions about the patient during the surgery. With additional training, some technologists advance to first assistants, who help with retracting, sponging, suturing, cauterizing bleeders, and closing and treating wounds. Some surgical technologists manage central supply departments in hospitals, or take positions with insurance companies, sterile supply services, and operating equipment firms.

Employment

Surgical technologists held about 84,000 jobs in 2004. About 7 out of 10 jobs for surgical technologists were in hospitals, mainly in operating and delivery rooms. Other jobs were in offices of physicians or dentists who perform outpatient surgery and in outpatient care centers, including ambulatory surgical centers. A few, known as private scrubs, are employed directly by surgeons who have special surgical teams, like those for liver transplants.

Job Outlook

Employment of surgical technologists is expected to grow much faster than average for all occupations through the year 2014 as the volume of surgery increases. Job opportunities are expected to be good. The number of surgical procedures is expected to rise as the population grows and ages. The number of older people, including the baby boom generation, who generally require more surgical procedures, will account for a larger portion of the general population. Technological advances, such as fiber optics and laser technology, will permit an increasing number of new surgical procedures to be performed and also will allow surgical technologists to assist with a greater number of procedures.

Hospitals will continue to be the primary employer of surgical technologists, although much faster employment growth is expected in offices of physicians and in outpatient care centers, including ambulatory surgical centers.

grams consisting of up to 80 hours of classroom instruction before they are allowed to work. To qualify through either an exam or a training program, applicants must know local geography, motor vehicle laws, safe driving practices, and relevant regulations and display some aptitude for customer service. Some localities require an English proficiency test, usually in the form of listening comprehension; applicants who do not pass the English exam must take an English course in addition to any formal driving programs. Some classroom instruction includes route management, mapreading, and service for passengers with disabilities. Many taxicab or limousine companies sponsor applicants, giving them a temporary permit that allows them to drive before they have finished the training program and passed the test. Some jurisdictions, such as New York City, have discontinued this practice and now require driver applicants to complete the licensing process before operating a taxi or limousine.

Some taxi and limousine companies give new drivers on-the-job training. This training is typically informal and often lasts only about a week. Companies show drivers how to operate the taximeter and communications equipment and how to complete paperwork. Other topics covered may include driver safety and the best routes to popular sightseeing and entertainment destinations. Many companies have contracts with social service agencies and transportation services to transport elderly and disabled citizens in nonemergency situations. To support these services, new drivers may get special training in how to handle wheelchair lifts and other mechanical devices.

Taxi drivers and chauffeurs should be able to get along with many different types of people. They must be patient when waiting for passengers and when dealing with rude customers. It also is helpful for drivers to be tolerant and level-headed when driving in heavy and congested traffic. Drivers should be dependable since passengers expect to be picked up at a prearranged time and taken to the correct destination. To be successful, drivers must be responsible and self-motivated because they work with little supervision. Increasingly, companies encourage drivers to develop their own loyal customer base, so as to improve their business.

Many taxi drivers and chauffeurs are *lease drivers*. These drivers pay a daily, weekly, or monthly fee to the company allowing them to lease their vehicles. In the case of limousines, leasing also permits the driver access to the company's dispatch system. The fee also may include charges for vehicle maintenance, insurance, and a deposit on the vehicle. Lease drivers may take their cars home with them when they are not on duty.

Opportunities for advancement are limited for taxi drivers and chauffeurs. Experienced drivers may obtain preferred routes or shifts. Some advance to become lead drivers, who help to train new drivers, or to take dispatching and managerial positions. Many managers start their careers as drivers. Some people start their own limousine companies.

In small and medium-size communities, drivers sometimes are able to buy their own taxi, limousine, or other type of automobile and go into business for themselves. These independent owner-drivers require an additional permit allowing them to operate their vehicle as a company. Some big cities limit the number of operating permits. In these cities, drivers become owner-drivers by buying permits from owner-drivers who leave the business or by purchasing or leasing them from the city. Although many owner-drivers are successful, some fail to cover expenses and eventually lose their permits and automobiles. For both taxi and limousine service owners, good business sense and courses in accounting, business, and business arithmetic can help an owner-driver to be successful. Knowledge of mechanics enables owner-drivers to perform their own routine maintenance and minor repairs to cut expenses.

Employment

Taxi drivers and chauffeurs held about 188,000 jobs in 2004. About 27 percent of taxi drivers and chauffeurs were self-employed.

Job Outlook

Persons seeking jobs as taxi drivers and chauffeurs should encounter good opportunities because of the need to replace the many people who work in this occupation for short periods and then transfer to other occupations or leave the labor force. Opportunities for drivers vary greatly in terms of earnings, work hours, and working conditions, depending on economic and regulatory conditions. Opportunities should be best for persons with good driving records, good customer service instincts, and the ability to work flexible schedules.

Employment of taxi drivers and chauffeurs is expected to grow faster than the average for all occupations through the year 2014, as local and suburban travel increases. Employment growth also will stem from federal legislation requiring increased services for persons with disabilities. Rapidly growing metropolitan areas should offer the best job opportunities.

The number of job openings can fluctuate with the overall movements of the economy because the demand for taxi and limousine transportation depends on travel and tourism. During economic slowdowns, drivers seldom are laid off, but they may have to increase their work hours, and earnings may decline. When the economy is strong, job openings are numerous as many drivers transfer to other occupations. Extra drivers may be hired during holiday seasons as well as during peak travel and tourist times.

Earnings

Earnings of taxi drivers and chauffeurs vary greatly, depending on factors such as the number of hours worked, regulatory conditions, customers' tips, and geographic location. Median hourly earnings of salaried taxi drivers and chauffeurs, including tips, were $9.41 in May 2004. The middle 50 percent earned between $7.61 and $11.94 an hour. The lowest 10 percent earned less than $6.43, and the highest 10 percent earned more than $15.62 an hour. Median hourly earnings in the industries employing the largest numbers of taxi drivers and chauffeurs in May 2004 were:

Taxi and limousine service	$10.68
Other transit and ground passenger transportation	9.23
Traveler accommodation	8.48
Automobile dealers	8.45
Automotive equipment rental and leasing	8.25

Related Occupations

Other workers who have similar jobs include bus drivers and truck drivers and driver/sales workers.

Sources of Additional Information

Information on necessary permits and the registration of taxi drivers and chauffeurs is available from local government agencies that regulate taxicabs. Questions regarding licensing should be directed to your state motor vehicle administration. For information about work opportunities as a taxi driver or chauffeur, contact local taxi or limousine companies or state employment service offices.

For general information about the work of limousine drivers, contact:

- National Limousine Association, 49 South Maple Ave., Marlton, NJ 08053. Internet: http://www.limo.org

Teacher Assistants

(O*NET 25-9041.00)

Significant Points

- About 4 in 10 teacher assistants work part time.
- Educational requirements range from a high school diploma to some college training.
- Workers with experience in helping special education students, or who can speak a foreign language, will be especially in demand.

Nature of the Work

Teacher assistants provide instructional and clerical support for classroom teachers, allowing teachers more time for lesson planning and teaching. Teacher assistants tutor and assist children in learning class material using the teacher's lesson plans, providing students with individualized attention. Teacher assistants also supervise students in the cafeteria, schoolyard, and hallways, or on field trips. They record grades, set up equipment, and help prepare materials for instruction. Teacher assistants also are called teacher aides or instructional aides. Some assistants refer to themselves as paraeducators or paraprofessionals.

Some teacher assistants perform exclusively noninstructional or clerical tasks, such as monitoring nonacademic settings. Playground and lunchroom attendants are examples of such assistants. Most teacher assistants, however, perform a combination of instructional and clerical duties. They generally provide instructional reinforcement to children, under the direction and guidance of teachers. They work with students individually or in small groups—listening while students read, reviewing or reinforcing class lessons, or helping them find information for reports. At the secondary school level, teacher assistants often specialize in a certain subject, such as math or science. Teacher assistants often take charge of special projects and prepare equipment or exhibits, such as for a science demonstration. Some assistants work in computer laboratories, helping students using computers and educational software programs.

In addition to instructing, assisting, and supervising students, teacher assistants grade tests and papers, check homework, keep health and attendance records, do typing and filing, and duplicate materials. They also stock supplies, operate audiovisual equipment, and keep classroom equipment in order.

Many teacher assistants work extensively with special education students. As schools become more inclusive, integrating special education students into general education classrooms, teacher assistants in both general education and special education classrooms increasingly assist students with disabilities. Teacher assistants attend to a disabled student's physical needs, including feeding, teaching good grooming habits, or assisting students riding the school bus. They also provide personal attention to students with other special needs, such as those who speak English as a second language, or those who need remedial education. Teacher assistants help assess a student's progress by observing performance and recording relevant data.

While the majority of teacher assistants work in primary and secondary educational settings, others work in preschools and other child care centers. Often one or two assistants will work with a lead teacher in order to better provide the individual attention that young children require. In addition to assisting in educational instruction, they also supervise the children at play and assist in feeding and other basic care activities.

Teacher assistants also work with infants and toddlers who have developmental delays or other disabilities. Under the guidance of a teacher or therapist, teacher assistants perform exercises or play games to help the child develop physically and behaviorally. Some teacher assistants work with young adults to help them obtain a job or to apply for community services for the disabled.

Working Conditions

Approximately 4 in 10 teacher assistants work part time. However, even among full-time workers, about 16 percent work less than 40 hours per week. Most assistants who provide educational instruction work the traditional 9- to 10-month school year. Teacher assistants work in a variety of settings—including preschools, child care centers, and religious and community centers, where they work with young adults—but most work in classrooms in elementary, middle, and secondary schools. They also work outdoors supervising recess when weather allows, and they spend much of their time standing, walking, or kneeling.

Seeing students develop and gain appreciation of the joy of learning can be very rewarding. However, working closely with students can be both physically and emotionally tiring. Teacher assistants who work with special education students often perform more strenuous tasks, including lifting, as they help students with their daily routine. Those who perform clerical work may tire of administrative duties, such as copying materials or typing.

Training, Other Qualifications, and Advancement

Educational requirements for teacher assistants vary by state or school district and range from a high school diploma to some college training, although employers increasingly prefer applicants with some college training. Teacher assistants with instructional responsibilities usually require more training than do those who do not perform teaching tasks. Federal regulations require teacher assistants with instructional responsibilities in Title I schools—those with a large proportion of students from low-income households—to meet one of three requirements: hold a 2-year or higher degree, have a minimum of 2 years of college, or pass a rigorous state or local assessment. Many schools also require previous experience in working with children and a valid driver's license. Some schools may require the applicant to pass a background check.

A number of 2-year and community colleges offer associate degree or certificate programs that prepare graduates to work as teacher assistants. However, most teacher assistants receive on-the-job training. Those who tutor and review lessons with students must have a thorough understanding of class materials and instructional methods, and should be familiar with the organization and operation of a school. Teacher assistants also must know how to operate audio-visual equipment, keep records, and prepare instructional materials, as well as have adequate computer skills.

Teacher assistants should enjoy working with children from a wide range of cultural backgrounds, and be able to handle classroom situations with fairness and patience. Teacher assistants also must demonstrate initiative and a willingness to follow a teacher's directions. They must have good writing skills and be able to communicate effectively with students and teachers. Teacher assistants who speak a second language, especially Spanish, are in great demand for communicating with growing numbers of students and parents whose primary language is not English.

Advancement for teacher assistants—usually in the form of higher earnings or increased responsibility—comes primarily with experience or additional education. Some school districts provide time away from the job or tuition reimbursement so that teacher assistants can earn their bachelor's degrees and pursue licensed teaching positions. In return for tuition reimbursement, assistants are often required to teach a certain length of time for the school district.

Employment

Teacher assistants held almost 1.3 million jobs in 2004. Nearly 3 in 4 worked for state and local government education institutions, mostly at the preschool and elementary school level. Private schools, child care centers, and religious organizations employed most of the rest.

Job Outlook

Employment of teacher assistants is expected to grow about as fast as the average for all occupations through 2014. In addition to job openings stemming from employment growth, numerous openings will arise as assistants leave their jobs and must be replaced. Many assistant jobs require limited formal education and offer relatively low pay so each year many transfer to other occupations or leave the labor force to assume family responsibilities, to return to school, or for other reasons.

School enrollments are projected to increase only slowly over the next decade, but special education students and students for whom English is not their first language—the student populations for which teacher assistants are most needed—are expected to grow faster and increase as a share of the total school-age population. Legislation that requires students with disabilities and non-native English speakers to receive an education "equal" to that of other students, will continue to generate jobs for teacher assistants to accommodate these students' special needs. Children with special needs require much personal attention, and special education teachers, as well as general education teachers with special education students, rely heavily on teacher assistants.

The greater focus on quality and accountability that has been placed on education in recent years also is likely to lead to an increased demand for teacher assistants. Growing numbers of teacher assistants may be needed to help teachers prepare students for standardized testing and to provide extra assistance to students who perform poorly on standardized tests. This growth may be moderated, however, as schools are encouraged to allocate resources to hiring more full teachers for instructional purposes. An increasing number of after-school programs and summer programs also will create new opportunities for teacher assistants.

Opportunities for teacher assistant jobs are expected to be best for persons with at least 2 years of formal education after high school. Persons who can speak a foreign language should be in particular demand in school systems with large numbers of students whose families do not speak English at home. Demand is expected to vary by region of the country. Areas in which the population and school enrollments are expected to grow faster, such as many communities in the South and West, should have rapid growth in the demand for teacher assistants.

Earnings

Median annual earnings of teacher assistants in May 2004 were $19,410. The middle 50 percent earned between $15,410 and $24,320. The lowest 10 percent earned less than $13,010, and the highest 10 percent earned more than $29,220.

Full-time workers usually receive health coverage and other benefits. Teacher assistants who work part time ordinarily do not receive benefits.

In 2004, about 3 out of 10 teacher assistants belonged to unions—mainly the American Federation of Teachers and the National Education Association—which bargain with school systems over wages, hours, and the terms and conditions of employment.

Related Occupations

Teacher assistants who instruct children have duties similar to those of preschool, kindergarten, elementary, middle, and secondary school teachers, as well as special education teachers. However, teacher assistants do not have the same level of responsibility or training. The support activities of teacher assistants and their educational backgrounds are similar to those of childcare workers, library technicians, and library assistants. Teacher assistants who work with children with disabilities perform many of the same functions as occupational therapy assistants and aides.

Sources of Additional Information

For information on teacher assistants, including training and certification, contact:

- American Federation of Teachers, Paraprofessional and School Related Personnel Division, 555 New Jersey Ave. NW, Washington, DC 20001.
- National Education Association, Educational Support Personnel Division, 1201 16th Street, NW, Washington, DC 20036.

For information on a career as a teacher assistant, contact:

- National Resource Center for Paraprofessionals, 6526 Old Main Hill, Utah State University, Logan, UT 84322. Internet: http://www.nrcpara.org

Human resource departments of school systems, school administrators, and state departments of education also can provide details about employment opportunities and required qualifications for teacher assistant jobs.

Teachers—Postsecondary

(O*NET 25-1011.00, 25-1021.00, 25-1022.00, 25-1031.00, 25-1032.00, 25-1041.00, 25-1042.00, 25-1043.00, 25-1051.00, 25-1052.00, 25-1053.00, 25-1054.00, 25-1061.00, 25-1062.00, 25-1063.00, 25-1064.00, 25-1065.00, 25-1066.00, 25-1067.00, 25-1069.99, 25-1071.00, 25-1072.00, 25-1081.00, 25-1082.00, 25-1111.00, 25-1112.00, 25-1113.00, 25-1121.00, 25-1122.00, 25-1123.00, 25-1124.00, 25-1125.00, 25-1126.00, 25-1191.00, 25-1192.00, 25-1193.00, 25-1194.00, and 25-1199.99)

Significant Points

- Opportunities for postsecondary teaching jobs are expected to be good, but many new openings will be for part-time or non-tenure-track positions.
- Prospects for teaching jobs will be better and earnings higher in academic fields in which many qualified teachers opt for nonacademic careers, such as health specialties, business, and computer science, for example.
- Educational qualifications for postsecondary teacher jobs range from expertise in a particular field to a Ph.D., depending on the subject being taught and the type of educational institution.

Nature of the Work

Postsecondary teachers instruct students in a wide variety of academic and vocational subjects beyond the high school level that may lead to a degree or to improvement in one's knowledge or career skills. These teachers include college and university faculty, postsecondary career and technical education teachers, and graduate teaching assistants.

College and university faculty make up the majority of postsecondary teachers. They teach and advise more than 16 million full- and part-time college students and perform a significant part of our nation's research. Faculty also keep up with new developments in their field and may consult with government, business, nonprofit, and community organizations.

Faculty usually are organized into departments or divisions, based on academic subject or field. They usually teach several different related courses in their subject—algebra, calculus, and statistics, for example. They may instruct undergraduate or graduate students, or both. College and university faculty may give lectures to several hundred students in large halls, lead small seminars, or supervise students in laboratories. They prepare lectures, exercises, and laboratory experiments; grade exams and papers; and advise and work with students individually. In universities, they also supervise graduate students' teaching and research. College faculty work with an increasingly varied student population made up of growing shares of part-time, older, and culturally and racially diverse students.

Faculty keep abreast of developments in their field by reading current literature, talking with colleagues, and participating in professional conferences. They may also do their own research to expand knowledge in their field. They may perform experiments; collect and analyze data; and examine original documents, literature, and other source material. From this process, they arrive at conclusions, and publish their findings in scholarly journals, books, and electronic media.

Most college and university faculty extensively use computer technology, including the Internet; e-mail; CD-ROMs, and software programs, such as statistical packages. They may use computers in the classroom as teaching aids and may post course content, class notes, class schedules, and other information on the Internet. The use of e-mail, chat rooms, and other techniques has greatly improved communications between students and teachers and among students.

Some faculty use the Internet to teach courses to students at remote sites. These so-called "distance learning" courses are an increasingly popular option for non-traditional students such as working adults. While more convenient for students, faculty who teach these courses must be able to adapt existing courses to make them successful online or design a new course that takes advantage of the format.

Most faculty members serve on academic or administrative committees that deal with the policies of their institution, departmental matters, academic issues, curricula, budgets, equipment purchases, and hiring. Some work with student and community organizations. Department chairpersons are faculty members who usually teach some courses but have heavier administrative responsibilities.

The proportion of time spent on research, teaching, administrative, and other duties varies by individual circumstance and type of institution. Faculty members at universities normally spend a significant part of their time doing research; those in 4-year colleges, somewhat less; and those in 2-year colleges, relatively little. The teaching load, however, often is heavier in 2-year colleges and somewhat lighter at 4-year institutions. Full professors at all types of institutions usually spend a larger portion of their time conducting research than do assistant professors, instructors, and lecturers.

In addition to traditional 2- and 4-year institutions, an increasing number of faculty work in alternative schools or in programs that are aimed at providing career-related education for working adults. Courses are usually offered online or on nights and weekends. Faculty at these programs generally work part time and are only responsible for teaching, with little to no administrative and research responsibilities.

Postsecondary vocational education teachers, also known as *postsecondary career and technical education teachers,* provide instruction for occupations that require specialized training, but may not require a 4-year degree, such as welder, dental hygienist, X-ray technician, auto mechanic, and cosmetologist. Classes often are taught in an industrial or laboratory setting where students are provided hands-on experience. For example, welding instructors show students various welding techniques and essential safety practices, watch them use tools and equipment, and have them repeat procedures until they meet the specific standards required by the trade. Increasingly, career and technical education teachers are integrating academic and vocational curriculums so that students obtain a variety of skills that can be applied to the "real world."

Career and technical education teachers have many of the same responsibilities that other college and university faculty have. They must prepare lessons, grade papers, attend faculty meetings, and keep abreast of developments in their field. Career and technical education teachers at community colleges and career and technical schools also often play a key role in students' transition from school to work by helping to establish internship programs for students and by facilitating contact between students and prospective employers.

Graduate teaching assistants, often referred to as *graduate TAs*, assist faculty, department chairs, or other professional staff at colleges and universities by performing teaching or teaching-related duties. In addition to their work responsibilities, assistants have their own school commitments, as they are also students who are working towards earning a graduate degree, such as a Ph.D. Some teaching assistants have full responsibility for teaching a course—usually one that is introductory in nature—which can include preparation of lectures and exams, and assigning final grades to students. Others provide assistance to faculty members, which may consist of a variety of tasks such as grading papers, monitoring exams, holding office hours or help-sessions for students, conducting laboratory sessions, or administering quizzes to the class. Teaching assistants generally meet initially with the faculty member whom they are going to assist in order to determine exactly what is expected of them, as each faculty member may have his or her own needs. For example, some faculty members prefer assistants to sit in on classes, while others assign them other tasks to do during class time. Graduate teaching assistants may work one-on-one with a faculty member or, for large classes, they may be one of several assistants.

Working Conditions

Postsecondary teachers who work full time usually have flexible schedules. They must be present for classes, usually 12 to 16 hours per week, and for faculty and committee meetings. Most establish regular office hours for student consultations, usually 3 to 6 hours per week. Otherwise, teachers are free to decide when and where they will work, and how much time to devote to course preparation, grading, study, research, graduate student supervision, and other activities.

Some teach night and weekend classes. This is particularly true for teachers at 2-year community colleges or institutions with large enrollments of older students who have full-time jobs or family responsibilities. Most colleges and universities require teachers to work 9 months of the year, which allows them the time to teach additional courses, do research, travel, or pursue nonacademic interests during the summer and school holidays. Colleges and universities usually have funds to support research or other professional development needs of full time faculty, including travel to conferences and research sites.

About 3 out of 10 college and university faculty worked part time in 2004. Some part-timers, known as "adjunct faculty," have primary jobs outside of academia—in government, private industry, or nonprofit research—and teach "on the side." Others prefer to work part-time hours or seek full-time jobs but are unable to obtain them due to intense competition for available openings. Some work part time in more than one institution. Some adjunct faculty are not qualified for tenure-track positions because they lack a doctoral degree.

University faculty may experience a conflict between their responsibilities to teach students and the pressure to do research and publish their findings. This may be a particular problem for young faculty seeking advancement in 4-year research universities. Also, recent cutbacks in support workers and the hiring of more part-time faculty have put a greater administrative burden on full-time faculty. Requirements to teach online classes also have added greatly to the workloads of postsecondary teachers. Many find that developing the courses to put online, plus learning how to operate the technology and answering large amounts of e-mail, is very time-consuming.

Graduate TAs usually have flexibility in their work schedules like college and university faculty, but they also must spend a considerable amount of time pursuing their own academic coursework and studies. The number of hours that TAs work varies, depending on their assignments. Work may be stressful, particularly when assistants are given full responsibility for teaching a class; however, these types of positions allow graduate students the opportunity to gain valuable teaching experience. This experience is especially helpful for those graduate teaching assistants who seek to become faculty members at colleges and universities after completing their degree.

Training, Other Qualifications, and Advancement

The education and training required of postsecondary teachers varies widely, depending on the subject taught and educational institution employing them. Educational requirements for teachers are generally the highest at 4-year research universities while experience and expertise in a related occupation is the principal qualification at career and technical institutes.

Postsecondary teachers should communicate and relate well with students, enjoy working with them, and be able to motivate them.

They should have inquiring and analytical minds, and a strong desire to pursue and disseminate knowledge. Additionally, they must be self-motivated and able to work in an environment in which they receive little direct supervision.

Training requirements for postsecondary career and technical education teachers vary by state and by subject. In general, teachers need a bachelor's or higher degree, plus at least 3 years of work experience in their field. In some fields, a license or certificate that demonstrates one's qualifications may be all that is required. Teachers update their skills through continuing education, in order to maintain certification. They must also maintain ongoing dialogue with businesses to determine the most current skills needed in the workplace.

Four-year colleges and universities usually consider doctoral degree holders for full-time, tenure-track positions, but may hire master's degree holders or doctoral candidates for certain disciplines, such as the arts, or for part-time and temporary jobs. Most college and university faculty are in four academic ranks—professor, associate professor, assistant professor, and instructor. These positions usually are considered to be tenure-track positions. Most faculty members are hired as instructors or assistant professors. A smaller number of additional faculty members, called lecturers, are usually employed on contracts for a single academic term and are not on the tenure track.

In 2-year colleges, master's degree holders fill most full-time positions. However, in certain fields where there may be more applicants than available jobs, institutions can be more selective in their hiring practices. In these fields, master's degree holders may be passed over in favor of candidates holding Ph.Ds. Many 2-year institutions increasingly prefer job applicants to have some teaching experience or experience with distance learning. Preference also may be given to those holding dual master's degrees, especially at smaller institutions, because they can teach more subjects.

Schools and programs that provide education and training for working adults generally hire people who are experienced in the field to teach part time. A master's degree is also usually required.

Doctoral programs take an average of 6 years of full-time study beyond the bachelor's degree, including time spent completing a master's degree and a dissertation. Some programs, such as those in the humanities, may take longer to complete; others, such as those in engineering, usually are shorter. Candidates specialize in a subfield of a discipline—for example, organic chemistry, counseling psychology, or European history—but also take courses covering the entire discipline. Programs typically include 20 or more increasingly specialized courses and seminars plus comprehensive examinations on all major areas of the field. Candidates also must complete a dissertation—a written report on original research in the candidate's major field of study. The dissertation sets forth an original hypothesis or proposes a model and tests it. Students in the natural sciences and engineering usually do laboratory work; in the humanities, they study original documents and other published material. The dissertation is done under the guidance of one or more faculty advisors and usually takes 1 or 2 years of full-time work.

Some students, particularly those who studied in the natural sciences, spend additional years after earning their degree on postdoctoral research and study before taking a faculty position. Some Ph.D.s are able to extend postdoctoral appointments, or take new ones, if they are unable to find a faculty job. Most of these appointments offer a nominal salary.

Obtaining a position as a graduate teaching assistant is a good way to gain college teaching experience. To qualify, candidates must be enrolled in a graduate school program. In addition, some colleges and universities require teaching assistants to attend classes or take some training prior to being given responsibility for a course.

Although graduate teaching assistants usually work at the institution and in the department where they are earning their degree, teaching or internship positions for graduate students at institutions that do not grant a graduate degree have become more common in recent years. For example, a program called Preparing Future Faculty, administered by the Association of American Colleges and Universities and the Council of Graduate Schools, has led to the creation of many now-independent programs that offer graduate students at research universities the opportunity to work as teaching assistants at other types of institutions, such as liberal arts or community colleges. Working with a mentor, the graduate students teach classes and learn how to improve their teaching techniques. They may attend faculty and committee meetings, develop a curriculum, and learn how to balance the teaching, research, and administrative roles that faculty play. These programs provide valuable learning opportunities for graduate students interested in teaching at the postsecondary level, and also help to make these students aware of the differences among the various types of institutions at which they may someday work.

For faculty, a major step in the traditional academic career is attaining tenure. New tenure-track faculty usually are hired as instructors or assistant professors, and must serve a period—usually 7 years—under term contracts. At the end of the period, their record of teaching, research, and overall contribution to the institution is reviewed; tenure is granted if the review is favorable. Those denied tenure usually must leave the institution. Tenured professors cannot be fired without just cause and due process. Tenure protects the faculty's academic freedom—the ability to teach and conduct research without fear of being fired for advocating controversial or unpopular ideas. It also gives both faculty and institutions the stability needed for effective research and teaching, and provides financial security for faculty. Some institutions have adopted post-tenure review policies to encourage ongoing evaluation of tenured faculty.

The number of tenure-track positions is declining as institutions seek flexibility in dealing with financial matters and changing student interests. Institutions rely more heavily on limited term contracts and part-time, or adjunct, faculty, thus shrinking the total pool of tenured faculty. Limited-term contracts—typically 2 to 5 years—may be terminated or extended when they expire, but generally do not lead to the granting of tenure. In addition, some institutions have limited the percentage of faculty who can be tenured.

For most postsecondary teachers, advancement involves a move into administrative and managerial positions, such as departmental chairperson, dean, and president. At 4-year institutions, such advancement requires a doctoral degree. At 2-year colleges, a doctorate is helpful but not usually required, except for advancement to some top administrative positions.

Employment

Postsecondary teachers held nearly 1.6 million jobs in 2004. Most were employed in public and private 4-year colleges and universities and in 2-year community colleges. Other postsecondary teachers are employed by schools and institutes that specialize in training people in a specific field, such as technology centers or culinary schools, or work for businesses that provide professional development courses to employees of companies. Some career and technical education teachers work for state and local governments and job training facilities. The following tabulation shows postsecondary teaching jobs in specialties having 20,000 or more jobs in 2004:

Health specialties teachers	150,000
Graduate teaching assistants	143,000
Vocational education teachers	127,000
Business teachers	85,000
Art, drama, and music teachers	78,000
Biological science teachers	76,000
English language and literature teachers	69,000
Education teachers	60,000
Mathematical science teachers	53,000
Computer science teachers	45,000
Engineering teachers	42,000
Nursing instructors and teachers	41,000
Psychology teachers	37,000
Foreign language and literature teachers	27,000
Communications teachers	26,000
History teachers	24,000
Chemistry teachers	23,000
Philosophy and religion teachers	23,000

Job Outlook

Overall, employment of postsecondary teachers is expected to grow much faster than the average for all occupations through 2014. A significant proportion of these new jobs will be part-time positions. Job opportunities are generally expected to be very good—although they will vary somewhat from field to field—as numerous openings for all types of postsecondary teachers result from retirements of current postsecondary teachers and continued increases in student enrollments.

Projected growth in college and university enrollment over the next decade stems mainly from the expected increase in the population of 18- to 24-year-olds, who constitute the majority of students at postsecondary institutions, and from the increasing number of high school graduates who choose to attend these institutions. Adults returning to college to enhance their career prospects or to update their skills also will continue to create new opportunities for postsecondary teachers, particularly at community colleges and for-profit institutions that cater to working adults. However, many postsecondary educational institutions receive a significant portion of their funding from state and local governments, so expansion of public higher education will be limited by state and local budgets. Nevertheless, in addition to growth in enrollments, the need to replace the large numbers of postsecondary teachers who are likely to retire over the next decade will also create a significant number of openings. Many postsecondary teachers were hired in the late 1960s and the 1970s to teach members of the baby boom generation, and they are expected to retire in growing numbers in the years ahead.

Ph.D. recipients seeking jobs as postsecondary teachers will experience favorable job prospects over the next decade. While competition will remain tight for tenure-track positions at 4-year colleges and universities, there will be a considerable number of part-time or renewable, term appointments at these institutions and positions at community colleges available to them. Opportunities for master's degree holders are also expected to be favorable, as community colleges and other institutions that employ them, such as professional career education programs, are expected to experience considerable growth.

Opportunities for graduate teaching assistants are expected to be very good due to prospects for much higher undergraduate enrollments coupled with more modest graduate enrollment increases. Constituting almost 9 percent of all postsecondary teachers, graduate teaching assistants play an integral role in the postsecondary education system, and they are expected to continue to do so in the future.

One of the main reasons why students attend postsecondary institutions is to prepare themselves for careers, so the best job prospects for postsecondary teachers are likely to be in fields where job growth is expected to be strong over the next decade. These will include fields such as business, health specialties, nursing, and biological sciences. Community colleges and other institutions offering career and technical education have been among the most rapidly growing, and these institutions are expected to offer some of the best opportunities for postsecondary teachers.

Earnings

Median annual earnings of all postsecondary teachers in May 2004 were $51,800. The middle 50 percent earned between $36,590 and $72,490. The lowest 10 percent earned less than $25,460, and the highest 10 percent earned more than $99,980.

Earnings for college faculty vary according to rank and type of institution, geographic area, and field. According to a 2004–05 survey by the American Association of University Professors, salaries for full-time faculty averaged $68,505. By rank, the average was $91,548 for professors, $65,113 for associate professors, $54,571 for assistant professors, $39,899 for instructors, and $45,647 for lecturers. Faculty in 4-year institutions earn higher salaries, on average, than do those in 2-year schools. In 2004-05, faculty salaries averaged $79,342 in private independent institutions, $66,851 in public institutions, and $61,103 in religiously affiliated private colleges and universities. In fields with high-paying nonacademic alternatives—medicine, law, engineering, and business, among others—earnings exceed these averages. In others fields—such as the humanities and education—they are lower.

Many faculty members have significant earnings in addition to their base salary, from consulting, teaching additional courses, research, writing for publication, or other employment. In addition, many college and university faculty enjoy some unique benefits, including access to campus facilities, tuition waivers for dependents, housing and travel allowances, and paid sabbatical leaves. Part-time faculty usually have fewer benefits than full-time faculty.

Earnings for postsecondary career and technical education teachers vary widely by subject, academic credentials, experience, and region of the country. Part-time instructors usually receive few benefits.

Related Occupations

Postsecondary teaching requires the ability to communicate ideas well, motivate students, and be creative. Workers in other occupations that require these skills are teachers—preschool, kindergarten, elementary, middle, and secondary; education administrators; librarians; counselors; writers and editors; public relations specialists; and management analysts. Faculty research activities often are similar to those of scientists, as well as to those of managers and administrators in industry, government, and nonprofit research organizations.

Sources of Additional Information

Professional societies related to a field of study often provide information on academic and nonacademic employment opportunities. Special publications on higher education, such as *The Chronicle of Higher Education*, list specific employment opportunities for faculty. These publications are available in libraries.

For information on the Preparing Future Faculty program, contact:

- Council of Graduate Schools, One Dupont Circle, NW, Suite 430, Washington, DC 20036-1173. Internet: http://www.preparing-faculty.org

For information on postsecondary career and technical education teaching positions, contact state departments of career and technical education. General information on adult and career and technical education is available from:

- Association for Career and Technical Education, 1410 King St., Alexandria, VA 22314. Internet: http://www.acteonline.org

Teachers—Preschool, Kindergarten, Elementary, Middle, and Secondary

(O*NET 25-2011.00, 25-2012.00, 25-2021.00, 25-2022.00, 25-2023.00, 25-2031.00, and 25-2032.00)

Significant Points

- Public school teachers must have at least a bachelor's degree, complete an approved teacher education program, and be licensed.
- Many states offer alternative licensing programs to attract people into teaching, especially for hard-to-fill positions.
- Excellent job opportunities are expected as retirements, especially among secondary school teachers, outweigh slowing enrollment growth; opportunities will vary by geographic area and subject taught.

Nature of the Work

Teachers act as facilitators or coaches, using interactive discussions and "hands-on" approaches to help students learn and apply concepts in subjects such as science, mathematics, or English. They utilize "props" or "manipulatives" to help children understand abstract concepts, solve problems, and develop critical thought processes. For example, they teach the concepts of numbers or of addition and subtraction by playing board games. As the children get older, the teachers use more sophisticated materials, such as science apparatus, cameras, or computers.

To encourage collaboration in solving problems, students are increasingly working in groups to discuss and solve problems together. Preparing students for the future workforce is a major stimulus generating changes in education. To be prepared, students must be able to interact with others, adapt to new technology, and think through problems logically. Teachers provide the tools and the environment for their students to develop these skills.

Preschool, kindergarten, and elementary school teachers play a vital role in the development of children. What children learn and experience during their early years can shape their views of themselves and the world and can affect their later success or failure in school, work, and their personal lives. Preschool, kindergarten, and elementary school teachers introduce children to mathematics, language, science, and social studies. They use games, music, artwork, films, books, computers, and other tools to teach basic skills.

Preschool children learn mainly through play and interactive activities. *Preschool teachers* capitalize on children's play to further language and vocabulary development (using storytelling, rhyming games, and acting games), improve social skills (having the children work together to build a neighborhood in a sandbox), and introduce scientific and mathematical concepts (showing the children how to balance and count blocks when building a bridge or how to mix colors when painting). Thus, a less structured approach, including small-group lessons, one-on-one instruction, and learning through creative activities such as art, dance, and music, is adopted to teach preschool children. Play and hands-on teaching also are used by *kindergarten teachers*, but academics begin to take priority in kindergarten classrooms. Letter recognition, phonics, numbers, and awareness of nature and science, introduced at the preschool level, are taught primarily in kindergarten.

Most *elementary school teachers* instruct one class of children in several subjects. In some schools, two or more teachers work as a team and are jointly responsible for a group of students in at least one subject. In other schools, a teacher may teach one special subject—usually music, art, reading, science, arithmetic, or physical education—to a number of classes. A small but growing number of teachers instruct multilevel classrooms, with students at several different learning levels.

Middle school teachers and *secondary school teachers* help students delve more deeply into subjects introduced in elementary school and expose them to more information about the world. Middle and secondary school teachers specialize in a specific subject, such as English, Spanish, mathematics, history, or biology. They also can teach subjects that are career oriented. *Vocational education teachers*, also referred to as career and technical or career-technology teachers, instruct and train students to work in a wide variety of fields, such as health care, business, auto repair, communications, and, increasingly, technology. They often teach courses that are in high demand by area employers, who may provide input into the curriculum and offer internships to students. Many vocational teachers play an active role in building and overseeing these partnerships. Additional responsibilities of middle and secondary school teachers may include career guidance and job placement, as well as follow-ups with students after graduation.

Computers play an integral role in the education teachers provide. Resources such as educational software and the Internet expose students to a vast range of experiences and promote interactive learning. Through the Internet, students can communicate with other students anywhere in the world, allowing them to share experiences and differing viewpoints. Students also use the Internet for individual research projects and to gather information. Computers are used in other classroom activities as well, from solving math problems to learning English as a second language. Teachers also may use computers to record grades and perform other administrative and clerical duties. They must continually update their skills so that they can instruct and use the latest technology in the classroom.

Teachers often work with students from varied ethnic, racial, and religious backgrounds. With growing minority populations in most parts of the country, it is important for teachers to work effectively with a diverse student population. Accordingly, some schools offer training to help teachers enhance their awareness and understanding of different cultures. Teachers may also include multicultural programming in their lesson plans, to address the needs of all students, regardless of their cultural background.

Teachers design classroom presentations to meet students' needs and abilities. They also work with students individually. Teachers plan, evaluate, and assign lessons; prepare, administer, and grade tests; listen to oral presentations; and maintain classroom discipline. They observe and evaluate a student's performance and potential and increasingly are asked to use new assessment methods. For example, teachers may examine a portfolio of a student's artwork or writing in order to judge the student's overall progress. They then can provide additional assistance in areas in which a student needs help. Teachers also grade papers, prepare report cards, and meet with parents and school staff to discuss a student's academic progress or personal problems.

In addition to conducting classroom activities, teachers oversee study halls and homerooms, supervise extracurricular activities, and accompany students on field trips. They may identify students with physical or mental problems and refer the students to the proper authorities. Secondary school teachers occasionally assist students in choosing courses, colleges, and careers. Teachers also participate in education conferences and workshops.

In recent years, site-based management, which allows teachers and parents to participate actively in management decisions regarding school operations, has gained popularity. In many schools, teachers are increasingly involved in making decisions regarding the budget, personnel, textbooks, curriculum design, and teaching methods.

Working Conditions

Seeing students develop new skills and gain an appreciation of knowledge and learning can be very rewarding. However, teaching may be frustrating when one is dealing with unmotivated or disrespectful students. Occasionally, teachers must cope with unruly behavior and violence in the schools. Teachers may experience stress in dealing with large classes, heavy workloads, or old schools that are run down and lack many modern amenities. Accountability standards also may increase stress levels, with teachers expected to produce students who are able to exhibit satisfactory performance on standardized tests in core subjects. Many teachers, particularly in public schools, are also frustrated by the lack of control they have over what they are required to teach.

Teachers in private schools generally enjoy smaller class sizes and more control over establishing the curriculum and setting standards for performance and discipline. Their students also tend to be more motivated, since private schools can be selective in their admissions processes.

Teachers are sometimes isolated from their colleagues because they work alone in a classroom of students. However, some schools allow teachers to work in teams and with mentors to enhance their professional development.

Including school duties performed outside the classroom, many teachers work more than 40 hours a week. Part-time schedules are more common among preschool and kindergarten teachers. Although some school districts have gone to all-day kindergartens, most kindergarten teachers still teach two kindergarten classes a day. Most teachers work the traditional 10-month school year with a 2-month vacation during the summer. During the vacation break, those on the 10-month schedule may teach in summer sessions, take other jobs, travel, or pursue personal interests. Many enroll in college courses or workshops to continue their education. Teachers in districts with a year-round schedule typically work 8 weeks, are on vacation for 1 week, and have a 5-week midwinter break. Preschool teachers working in day care settings often work year round.

Most states have tenure laws that prevent public school teachers from being fired without just cause and due process. Teachers may obtain tenure after they have satisfactorily completed a probationary period of teaching, normally 3 years. Tenure does not absolutely guarantee a job, but it does provide some security.

Training, Other Qualifications, and Advancement

All 50 states and the District of Columbia require public school teachers to be licensed. Licensure is not required for teachers in private schools in most states. Usually licensure is granted by the State Board of Education or a licensure advisory committee. Teachers may be licensed to teach the early childhood grades (usually preschool through grade 3); the elementary grades (grades 1 through 6 or 8); the middle grades (grades 5 through 8); a secondary-education subject area (usually grades 7 through 12); or a special subject, such as reading or music (usually grades kindergarten through 12).

Requirements for regular licenses to teach kindergarten through grade 12 vary by state. However, all states require general education teachers to have a bachelor's degree and to have completed an approved teacher training program with a prescribed number of subject and education credits, as well as supervised practice teaching. Some states also require technology training and the attainment of a minimum grade point average. A number of states require that teachers obtain a master's degree in education within a specified period after they begin teaching.

Almost all states require applicants for a teacher's license to be tested for competency in basic skills, such as reading and writing, and in teaching. Almost all also require the teacher to exhibit proficiency in his or her subject. Many school systems are presently moving toward implementing performance-based systems for licensure, which usually require a teacher to demonstrate satisfactory teaching performance over an extended period in order to obtain a provisional license, in addition to passing an examination in their subject. Most states require continuing education for renewal of the teacher's license. Many states have reciprocity agreements that make it easier for teachers licensed in one state to become licensed in another.

Many states also offer alternative licensure programs for teachers who have a bachelor's degree in the subject they will teach, but who lack the necessary education courses required for a regular license. Many of these alternative licensure programs are designed to ease shortages of teachers of certain subjects, such as mathematics and science. Other programs provide teachers for urban and rural schools that have difficulty filling positions with teachers from traditional licensure programs. Alternative licensure programs are intended to attract people into teaching who do not fulfill traditional licensing standards, including recent college graduates who did not complete education programs and those changing from another career to teaching. In some programs, individuals begin teaching quickly under provisional licensure. After working under the close supervision of experienced educators for 1 or 2 years while taking education courses outside school hours, they receive regular licensure if they have progressed satisfactorily. In other programs, college graduates who do not meet licensure requirements take only those courses that they lack and then become licensed. This approach may take 1 or 2 semesters of full-time study. States may issue emergency licenses to individuals who do not meet the requirements for a regular license when schools cannot attract enough qualified teachers to fill positions. Teachers who need to be licensed may enter programs that grant a master's degree in education, as well as a license.

In many states, vocational teachers have many of the same requirements for teaching as their academic counterparts. However, because knowledge and experience in a particular field are important criteria for the job, some states will license vocational education teachers without a bachelor's degree, provided they can demonstrate expertise in their field. A minimum number of hours in education courses may also be required.

Licensing requirements for preschool teachers also vary by state. Requirements for public preschool teachers are generally more stringent than those for private preschool teachers. Some states require a bachelor's degree in early childhood education, while others require an associate's degree, and still others require certification by a nationally recognized authority. The Child Development Associate (CDA) credential, the most common type of certification, requires a mix of classroom training and experience working with children, along with an independent assessment of an individual's competence.

Private schools are generally exempt from meeting State licensing standards. For secondary school teacher jobs, they prefer candidates who have a bachelor's degree in the subject they intend to teach, or in childhood education for elementary school teachers. They seek candidates among recent college graduates as well as from those who have established careers in other fields. Private schools associated with religious institutions also desire candidates who share the values that are important to the institution.

In some cases, teachers of kindergarten through high school may attain professional certification in order to demonstrate competency beyond that required for a license. The National Board for Professional Teaching Standards offers a voluntary national certification. To become nationally accredited, experienced teachers must prove their aptitude by compiling a portfolio showing their work in the classroom and by passing a written assessment and evaluation of their teaching knowledge. Currently, teachers may become certified in a variety of areas, on the basis of the age of the students and, in some cases, the subject taught. For example, teachers may obtain a certificate for teaching English language arts to early adolescents (aged 11 to 15), or they may become certified as early childhood generalists. All states recognize national certification, and many states and school districts provide special benefits to teachers holding such certification. Benefits typically include higher salaries and reimbursement for continuing education and certification fees. In addition, many states allow nationally certified teachers to carry a license from one state to another.

The National Council for Accreditation of Teacher Education currently accredits teacher education programs across the United States. Graduation from an accredited program is not necessary to become a teacher, but it does make it easier to fulfill licensure requirements. Generally, 4-year colleges require students to wait until their sophomore year before applying for admission to teacher education programs. Traditional education programs for kindergarten and elementary school teachers include courses—designed specifically for those preparing to teach—in mathematics, physical science, social science, music, art, and literature, as well as prescribed professional education courses, such as philosophy of education, psychology of learning, and teaching methods. Aspiring secondary school teachers most often major in the subject they plan to teach while also taking a program of study in teacher preparation. Teacher education programs are now required to include classes in the use of computers and other technologies in order to maintain their accreditation. Most programs require students to perform a student-teaching internship.

Many states now offer professional development schools—partnerships between universities and elementary or secondary schools.

Students enter these 1-year programs after completion of their bachelor's degree. Professional development schools merge theory with practice and allow the student to experience a year of teaching firsthand, under professional guidance.

In addition to being knowledgeable in their subject, teachers must have the ability to communicate, inspire trust and confidence, and motivate students, as well as understand the students' educational and emotional needs. Teachers must be able to recognize and respond to individual and cultural differences in students and employ different teaching methods that will result in higher student achievement. They should be organized, dependable, patient, and creative. Teachers also must be able to work cooperatively and communicate effectively with other teachers, support staff, parents, and members of the community.

With additional preparation, teachers may move into positions as school librarians, reading specialists, instructional coordinators, or guidance counselors. Teachers may become administrators or supervisors, although the number of these positions is limited and competition can be intense. In some systems, highly qualified, experienced teachers can become senior or mentor teachers, with higher pay and additional responsibilities. They guide and assist less experienced teachers while keeping most of their own teaching responsibilities. Preschool teachers usually work their way up from assistant teacher, to teacher, to lead teacher—who may be responsible for the instruction of several classes—and, finally, to director of the center. Preschool teachers with a bachelor's degree frequently are qualified to teach kindergarten through grade 3 as well. Teaching at these higher grades often results in higher pay.

Employment

Preschool, kindergarten, elementary school, middle school, and secondary school teachers, except special education, held about 3.8 million jobs in 2004. Of the teachers in those jobs, about 1.5 million are elementary school teachers, 1.1 million are secondary school teachers, 628,000 are middle school teachers, 431,000 are preschool teachers, and 171,000 are kindergarten teachers. The majority work in local government educational services. About 10 percent work for private schools. Preschool teachers, except special education, are most often employed in child daycare services (61 percent), religious organizations (12 percent), local government educational services (9 percent), and private educational services (7 percent). Employment of teachers is geographically distributed much the same as the population.

Job Outlook

Job opportunities for teachers over the next 10 years will vary from good to excellent, depending on the locality, grade level, and subject taught. Most job openings will result from the need to replace the large number of teachers who are expected to retire over the 2004–14 period. Also, many beginning teachers decide to leave teaching after a year or two—especially those employed in poor, urban schools—creating additional job openings for teachers. Shortages of qualified teachers will likely continue, resulting in competition among some localities, with schools luring teachers from other states and districts with bonuses and higher pay.

Through 2014, overall student enrollments in elementary, middle, and secondary schools—a key factor in the demand for teachers—are expected to rise more slowly than in the past as children of the baby boom generation leave the school system. This will cause employment to grow as fast as the average for teachers from kindergarten through the secondary grades. Projected enrollments will vary by region. Fast-growing states in the West—particularly California, Idaho, Hawaii, Alaska, Utah, and New Mexico—will experience the largest enrollment increases. Enrollments in the South will increase at a more modest rate than in recent years, while those in the Northeast and Midwest are expected to hold relatively steady or decline. Teachers who are geographically mobile and who obtain licensure in more than one subject should have a distinct advantage in finding a job.

The job market for teachers also continues to vary by school location and by subject taught. Job prospects should be better in inner cities and rural areas than in suburban districts. Many inner cities—often characterized by overcrowded, ill-equipped schools and higher-than-average poverty rates—and rural areas—characterized by their remote location and relatively low salaries—have difficulty attracting and retaining enough teachers. Currently, many school districts have difficulty hiring qualified teachers in some subject areas—most often mathematics, science (especially chemistry and physics), bilingual education, and foreign languages. Increasing enrollments of minorities, coupled with a shortage of minority teachers, should cause efforts to recruit minority teachers to intensify. Also, the number of non-English-speaking students will continue to grow, creating demand for bilingual teachers and for those who teach English as a second language. Specialties that have an adequate number of qualified teachers include general elementary education, physical education, and social studies. Qualified vocational teachers also are currently in demand in a variety of fields at both the middle school and secondary school levels.

The number of teachers employed is dependent as well on state and local expenditures for education and on the enactment of legislation to increase the quality and scope of public education. At the federal level, there has been a large increase in funding for education, particularly for the hiring of qualified teachers in lower income areas. Also, some states are instituting programs to improve early childhood education, such as offering full day kindergarten and universal preschool. These last two programs, along with projected higher enrollment growth for preschool age children, will create many new jobs for preschool teachers, which are expected to grow much faster than the average for all occupations.

The supply of teachers is expected to increase in response to reports of improved job prospects, better pay, more teacher involvement in school policy, and greater public interest in education. In recent years, the total number of bachelor's and master's degrees granted in education has increased steadily. Because of a shortage of teachers in certain locations, and in anticipation of the loss of a number of teachers to retirement, many states have implemented policies that will encourage more students to become teachers. In addition, more teachers may be drawn from a reserve pool of career changers, substitute teachers, and teachers completing alternative certification programs.

Earnings

Median annual earnings of kindergarten, elementary, middle, and secondary school teachers ranged from $41,400 to $45,920 in May 2004; the lowest 10 percent earned $26,730 to $31,180; the top 10 percent earned $66,240 to $71,370. Median earnings for preschool teachers were $20,980.

According to the American Federation of Teachers, beginning teachers with a bachelor's degree earned an average of $31,704 in the 2003–04 school year. The estimated average salary of all public elementary and secondary school teachers in the 2003–04 school year was $46,597. Private school teachers generally earn less than public school teachers, but may be given other benefits, such as free or subsidized housing.

In 2004, more than half of all elementary, middle, and secondary school teachers belonged to unions—mainly the American Federation of Teachers and the National Education Association—that bargain with school systems over wages, hours, and other terms and conditions of employment. Fewer preschool and kindergarten teachers were union members—about 17 percent in 2004.

Teachers can boost their salary in a number of ways. In some schools, teachers receive extra pay for coaching sports and working with students in extracurricular activities. Getting a master's degree or national certification often results in a raise in pay, as does acting as a mentor. Some teachers earn extra income during the summer by teaching summer school or performing other jobs in the school system.

Related Occupations

Preschool, kindergarten, elementary school, middle school, and secondary school teaching requires a variety of skills and aptitudes, including a talent for working with children; organizational, administrative, and recordkeeping abilities; research and communication skills; the power to influence, motivate, and train others; patience; and creativity. Workers in other occupations requiring some of these aptitudes include teachers—postsecondary; counselors; teacher assistants; education administrators; librarians; childcare workers; public relations specialists; social workers; and athletes, coaches, umpires, and related workers.

Sources of Additional Information

Information on licensure or certification requirements and approved teacher training institutions is available from local school systems and state departments of education.

Information on the teaching profession and on how to become a teacher can be obtained from:

- Recruiting New Teachers, Inc., 385 Concord Ave., Suite 103, Belmont, MA 02478. Internet: http://www.recruitingteachers.org

Information on teachers' unions and education-related issues may be obtained from the following sources:

- American Federation of Teachers, 555 New Jersey Ave. NW, Washington, DC 20001.
- National Education Association, 1201 16th St. NW, Washington, DC 20036.

A list of institutions with accredited teacher education programs can be obtained from:

- National Council for Accreditation of Teacher Education, 2010 Massachusetts Ave. NW, Suite 500, Washington, DC 20036-1023. Internet: http://www.ncate.org

Information on alternative certification programs can be obtained from:

- National Center for Alternative Certification, 1901 Pennsylvania Ave. NW, Suite 201, Washington, DC 20006. Internet: http://www.teach-now.org

For information on vocational education and vocational education teachers, contact:

- Association for Career and Technical Education, 1410 King St., Alexandria, VA 22314. Internet: http://www.acteonline.org

For information on careers in educating children and issues affecting preschool teachers, contact either of the following organizations:

- National Association for the Education of Young Children, 1509 16th St. NW, Washington, DC 20036. Internet: http://www.naeyc.org
- Council for Professional Recognition, 2460 16th St. NW, Washington, DC 20009-3575. Internet: http://www.cdacouncil.org

Teachers—Self-Enrichment Education

(O*NET 25-3021.00)

Significant Points

- Part-time jobs, a lack of benefits, and self-employed workers are relatively common among self-enrichment teachers.
- Teachers should have knowledge and enthusiasm for their subject, but little formal training is required.
- Demand for self-enrichment courses is expected to rise as more people embrace lifelong learning and as growth continues in the numbers of retirees, who have more free time to take classes.

Nature of the Work

Self-enrichment teachers provide instruction in a wide variety of subjects that students take for personal enrichment or self-improvement. Some teach a series of classes that provide students with useful life skills, such as cooking, personal finance, and time management classes. Others provide group instruction intended solely for recreation, such as photography, pottery, and painting courses. Many others provide one-on-one instruction in a variety of subjects, including dance, singing, or playing a musical instrument. The instruction self-enrichment teachers provide seldom leads to a particular degree and attendance is voluntary, but dedicated, talented students sometimes go on to careers in the arts. Teachers who conduct courses on academic subjects in a non-academic setting, such as literature, foreign language, and history courses, are also included in this occupation.

Self-enrichment teachers provide instruction on a wide range of subjects, so they may have styles and methods of instruction that differ greatly. Most self-enrichment classes are relatively informal and not demanding of instructors. Some classes, such as pottery or sewing, may be largely hands-on, with the instructor demonstrating methods or techniques for the class, observing students as they attempt to do it themselves, and pointing out mistakes to students and offering suggestions to improve techniques. Other classes, such as those involving financial planning or religion and spirituality, may be more similar to a lecture in nature or rely more heavily on group discussions. Self-enrichment teachers may also teach classes offered through religious institutions, such as marriage preparation or classes in religion for children.

Many of the classes that self-enrichment educators teach are shorter in duration than classes taken for academic credit; some finish in 1 or 2 days to several weeks. These brief classes tend to be introductory in nature and generally focus on only one topic—for example, a cooking class that teaches students how to make bread. Some self-enrichment classes introduce children and youths to activities such as piano or drama, and may be designed to last anywhere from 1 week to several months.

Many self enrichment teachers provide one-on-one lessons to students. The instructor may only work with the student for an hour or two a week, but direct the student what they should practice in the interim until their next lesson. Many instructors work with the same students on a weekly basis for years and derive satisfaction from observing them mature and gain expertise. The most talented students may go on to paid careers as craft artists, painters, sculptors, dancers, singers, or musicians.

All self-enrichment teachers must prepare lessons beforehand and stay current in their fields. Many self enrichment teachers are self employed and provide instruction as a business. As such, they must collect any fees or tuition and keep records of students whose accounts are prepaid or in arrears. Although not a requirement for most types of classes, teachers may use computers and other modern technologies in their instruction or to maintain business records.

Working Conditions

Few self-enrichment education teachers are full time salaried workers. Most either work part time or are self-employed. Some have several part-time teaching assignments, but it is most common for teachers to have a full time job in another occupation, often related to the subject that they teach, in addition to their part-time teaching job. Although jobs in this occupation are primarily part time and pay is low, most teachers enjoy their work because it gives them the opportunity to share a subject they enjoy with others.

Many classes for adults are held in the evenings and on weekends in order to accommodate students who have a job or family responsibilities. Similarly, self-enrichment classes for children are usually held after school, on weekends, or during school vacations.

Students in self-enrichment programs attend by choice so they tend to be highly motivated and eager to learn. Students also often bring unique experiences of their own to classes, which can make teaching these students rewarding and satisfying. Self-enrichment teachers must have a great deal of patience, however, particularly when working with young children.

Training, Other Qualifications, and Advancement

The main qualification for self-enrichment teachers is expertise in their subject area, but requirements may vary greatly with both the type of class taught and the place of employment. In some cases, a portfolio of one's work may be required. For example, to secure a job teaching a photography course, an applicant would need to show examples of previous work. Some self-enrichment teachers are trained educators or other professionals who teach enrichment classes in their spare time. In many self-enrichment fields, however, instructors are simply experienced in the field, and want to share that experience with others.

In some disciplines, such as art or music, specific teacher training programs are available. Prospective dance teachers, for example, may complete programs that prepare them to instruct any number of types of dance—from ballroom dancing to ballet. In addition to knowledge of their subject, self-enrichment teachers should have good speaking skills and a talent for making the subject interesting. Patience and the ability to explain and instruct students at a basic level are important as well, particularly when one is working with children.

Opportunities for advancement in this profession are limited. Some part-time teachers are able to move into full-time teaching positions or program administrator positions, such as coordinator or director, when such vacancies occur. Experienced teachers may mentor new instructors.

Employment

Teachers of self-enrichment education held about 253,000 jobs in 2004. About 3 in 10 were self-employed. The largest numbers of teachers were employed by public and private educational institutions, religious organizations, and providers of social assistance and amusement and recreation services.

Job Outlook

Employment of self-enrichment education teachers is expected to grow faster than the average for all occupations through 2014. A large number of job openings is expected, due to both the growth of the occupation as well as to many existing teachers retiring or leaving their jobs for other reasons. New opportunities arise constantly in this occupation because many self-enrichment education jobs are short term and are often held as a second job.

The need for self-enrichment teachers is expected to grow as more people embrace lifelong learning and as course offerings expand. Self-enrichment education will also grow as a result of demographic changes. Retirees are one of the larger groups of participants in self enrichment education because they have more time for classes, and as the baby boomers begin to retire, demand for self enrichment education should grow. At the same time, the children of the baby boomer will be entering the age range of another large group of participants, young adults—who often are single and participate for the social as well as the educational experience.

Teachers who are knowledgeable in subjects that are not easily researched on the Internet and those that benefit from hands-on experiences, such as cooking, crafts, and the arts, will be in greater demand. Classes on self-improvement, personal finance, and computer and internet-related subjects are also expected to be popular.

Earnings

Median hourly earnings of self-enrichment teachers were $14.85 in May 2004. The middle 50 percent earned between $10.39 and $20.80. The lowest 10 percent earned less than $7.90, and the highest 10 percent earned more than $28.85. Self-enrichment teachers are generally paid by the hour or for each class that they teach.

Part-time instructors are usually paid for each class that they teach, and receive few benefits. Full-time teachers are generally paid a salary and may receive health insurance and other benefits.

Related Occupations

The work of self-enrichment teachers is closely related to that of other types of teachers, especially preschool, kindergarten, elementary school, middle school, and secondary school teachers. Self-enrichment teachers also teach a wide variety of subjects that may be related to the work done by those in many other occupations, such as dancers and choreographers; artists and related workers; musicians, singers, and related workers; recreation workers; and athletes, coaches, umpires, and related workers.

Sources of Additional Information

For information on employment of self-enrichment teachers, contact schools or local companies that offer self-enrichment programs.

Teachers—Special Education

(O*NET 25-2041.00, 25-2042.00, and 25-2043.00)

Significant Points

- All states require teachers to be licensed; licensing requires the completion of a teacher training program and at least a bachelor's degree, though many states require a master's degree.
- Excellent job prospects are expected due to rising enrollments of special education students and reported shortages of qualified teachers.
- Many states offer alternative licensure programs to attract people to these jobs who do not have the qualifications to become teachers under normal procedures.

Nature of the Work

Special education teachers work with children and youths who have a variety of disabilities. A small number of special education teachers work with students with mental retardation or autism, primarily teaching them life skills and basic literacy. However, the majority of special education teachers work with children with mild to moderate disabilities, using the general education curriculum, or modifying it, to meet the child's individual needs. Most special education teachers instruct students at the elementary, middle, and secondary school level, although some teachers work with infants and toddlers.

The various types of disabilities that qualify individuals for special education programs include specific learning disabilities, speech or language impairments, mental retardation, emotional disturbance, multiple disabilities, hearing impairments, orthopedic impairments, visual impairments, autism, combined deafness and blindness, traumatic brain injury, and other health impairments. Students are classified under one of the categories, and special education teachers are prepared to work with specific groups. Early identification of a child with special needs is an important part of a special education teacher's job. Early intervention is essential in educating children with disabilities.

Special education teachers use various techniques to promote learning. Depending on the disability, teaching methods can include individualized instruction, problem-solving assignments, and small-group work. When students need special accommodations in order to take a test, special education teachers see that appropriate ones are provided, such as having the questions read orally or lengthening the time allowed to take the test.

Special education teachers help to develop an Individualized Education Program (IEP) for each special education student. The IEP sets personalized goals for each student and is tailored to the student's individual needs and ability. When appropriate, the program includes a transition plan outlining specific steps to prepare students with disabilities for middle school or high school or, in the case of older students, a job or postsecondary study. Teachers review the IEP with the student's parents, school administrators, and the student's general education teacher. Teachers work closely with parents to inform them of their child's progress and suggest techniques to promote learning at home.

Special education teachers design and teach appropriate curricula, assign work geared toward each student's needs and abilities, and grade papers and homework assignments. They are involved in the students' behavioral, social, and academic development, helping the students develop emotionally, feel comfortable in social situations, and be aware of socially acceptable behavior. Preparing special education students for daily life after graduation also is an important aspect of the job. Teachers provide students with career counseling or help them learn routine skills, such as balancing a checkbook.

As schools become more inclusive, special education teachers and general education teachers are increasingly working together in general education classrooms. Special education teachers help general educators adapt curriculum materials and teaching techniques to meet the needs of students with disabilities. They coordinate the work of teachers, teacher assistants, and related personnel, such as therapists and social workers, to meet the individualized needs of the student within inclusive special education programs. A large part of a special education teacher's job involves interacting with others. Special education teachers communicate frequently with parents, social workers, school psychologists, occupational and physical therapists, school administrators, and other teachers.

Special education teachers work in a variety of settings. Some have their own classrooms and teach only special education students; others work as special education resource teachers and offer individualized help to students in general education classrooms; still others teach together with general education teachers in classes composed of both general and special education students. Some teachers work with special education students for several hours a day in a resource room, separate from their general education classroom. Considerably fewer special education teachers work in residential facilities or tutor students in homebound or hospital environments.

Special education teachers who work with infants usually travel to the child's home to work with the child and his or her parents. Many of these infants have medical problems that slow or preclude normal development. Special education teachers show parents techniques and activities designed to stimulate the infant and encourage the growth and development of the child's skills. Toddlers usually receive their services at a preschool where special education teachers help them develop social, self-help, motor, language, and cognitive skills, often through the use of play.

Technology is playing an increasingly important role in special education. Teachers use specialized equipment such as computers with synthesized speech, interactive educational software programs, and audiotapes to assist children.

Working Conditions

Special education teachers enjoy the challenge of working with students with disabilities and the opportunity to establish meaningful relationships with them. Although helping these students can be highly rewarding, the work also can be emotionally and physically draining. Many special education teachers are under considerable stress due to heavy workloads and administrative tasks. They must produce a substantial amount of paperwork documenting each student's progress and work under the threat of litigation against the school or district by students' parents if correct procedures are not followed or if the parents feel that their child is not receiving an adequate education, although recent legislation that has been passed is intended to reduce the burden of paperwork and the threat of litigation. The physical and emotional demands of the job cause some special education teachers to leave the occupation.

Some schools offer year-round education for special education students, but most special education teachers work only the traditional 10-month school year.

Training, Other Qualifications, and Advancement

All 50 states and the District of Columbia require special education teachers to be licensed. The state board of education or a licensure advisory committee usually grants licenses, and licensure varies by state. In some states, special education teachers receive a general education credential to teach kindergarten through grade 12. These teachers then train in a specialty, such as learning disabilities or behavioral disorders. Many states offer general special education licenses across a variety of disability categories, while others license several different specialties within special education.

For traditional licensing, all states require a bachelor's degree and the completion of an approved teacher preparation program with a prescribed number of subject and education credits and supervised practice teaching. However, many states require a master's degree in special education, involving at least 1 year of additional course work, including a specialization, beyond the bachelor's degree. Often a prospective teacher must pass a professional assessment test as well. Some states have reciprocity agreements allowing special education teachers to transfer their licenses from one state to another, but many others still require that experienced teachers reapply and pass licensing requirements to work in the state.

Many states also offer alternative routes to licensing, since there are not enough graduates from education programs to meet the needs of most schools. Alternative licensure programs are intended to attract people into teaching who do not fulfill traditional licensing standards, including recent college graduates who did not complete education programs and those changing from another career to teaching. Requirements vary by state, but generally require holding a bachelor's degree, successfully accomplishing a period of supervised preparation and induction, and passing an assessment test. In some programs, individuals begin teaching quickly under a provisional license and can obtain a regular license after teaching under the supervision of licensed teachers for a period of 1 to 2 years and completing required education courses.

Many colleges and universities across the United States offer programs in special education at the undergraduate, master's, and doctoral degree levels. Special education teachers usually undergo longer periods of training than do general education teachers. Most bachelor's degree programs are 4-year programs that include general and specialized courses in special education. However, an increasing number of institutions are requiring a 5th year or other graduate-level preparation. Among the courses offered are educational psychology, legal issues of special education, and child growth and development; programs also include courses imparting knowledge and skills needed for teaching students with disabilities. Some programs require specialization, while others offer generalized special education degrees or a course of study in several specialized areas. The last year of the program usually is spent student teaching in a classroom supervised by a certified teacher.

Special education teachers must be patient, able to motivate students, understanding of their students' special needs, and accepting of differences in others. Teachers must be creative and apply different types of teaching methods to reach students who are having difficulty learning. Communication and cooperation are essential skills, because special education teachers spend a great deal of time interacting with others, including students, parents, and school faculty and administrators.

Special education teachers can advance to become supervisors or administrators. They may also earn advanced degrees and become instructors in colleges that prepare others to teach special education. In some school systems, highly experienced teachers can become mentors to less experienced ones, providing guidance to those teachers while maintaining a light teaching load.

Employment

Special education teachers held a total of about 441,000 jobs in 2004. A great majority, about 90 percent, work in public schools. Another 6 percent work at private schools. Almost half work in elementary schools. A few worked for individual and social assistance agencies or residential facilities, or in homebound or hospital environments.

Job Outlook

Employment of special education teachers is expected to increase faster than the average for all occupations through 2014. Although student enrollments are expected to grow only slowly, additional positions for these workers will be created by continued increases in the number of special education students needing services, by legislation emphasizing training and employment for individuals with disabilities, and by educational reforms requiring higher standards for graduation. In addition to job openings resulting from growth, a large number of openings will result from the need to replace special education teachers who switch to teaching general education, change careers altogether, or retire. At the same time, many school districts report difficulty finding sufficient numbers of qualified teachers. As a result, special education teachers should have excellent job prospects.

The job outlook varies by geographic area and specialty. Although most areas of the country report difficulty finding qualified applicants, positions in inner cities and rural areas usually are more plentiful than job openings in suburban or wealthy urban areas. Student populations, in general, also are expected to increase more rapidly in certain parts of the country, such as the South and West, resulting in increased demand for special education teachers in those regions. In addition, job opportunities may be better in certain specialties—such as teachers who work with children with multiple disabilities or severe disabilities like autism—because of large increases in the enrollment of special education students classified under those categories. Legislation encouraging early intervention and special education for infants, toddlers, and preschoolers has created a need for early childhood special education teachers. Bilingual special education teachers and those with multicultural experience also are needed to work with an increasingly diverse student population.

The number of students requiring special education services has grown steadily in recent years as improvements in identification has allowed learning disabilities to be diagnosed at earlier ages. In addition, medical advances have resulted in more children surviving serious accidents or illnesses, but with impairments that require special accommodations. The percentage of foreign-born special education students also is expected to grow, as teachers become more adept in recognizing learning disabilities in that population. Finally, more parents are expected to seek special services for those of their children who have difficulty meeting the new, higher standards required of students.

Earnings

Median annual earnings in May 2004 of special education teachers who worked primarily in preschools, kindergartens, and elementary schools were $43,570. The middle 50 percent earned between $35,340 and $55,350. The lowest 10 percent earned less than $29,880, and the highest 10 percent earned more than $68,660.

Median annual earnings in May 2004 of middle school special education teachers were $44,160. The middle 50 percent earned between $35,650 and $57,070. The lowest 10 percent earned less than $30,230, and the highest 10 percent earned more than $74,230.

Median annual earnings in May 2004 of special education teachers who worked primarily in secondary schools were $45,700. The middle 50 percent earned between $36,920 and $59,340. The lowest 10 percent earned less than $30,860, and the highest 10 percent earned more than $73,190.

In 2004, about 62 percent of special education teachers belonged to unions—mainly the American Federation of Teachers and the National Education Association—that bargain with school systems over wages, hours, and the terms and conditions of employment.

In most schools, teachers receive extra pay for coaching sports and working with students in extracurricular activities. Some teachers earn extra income during the summer, working in the school system or in other jobs.

Related Occupations

Special education teachers work with students who have disabilities and special needs. Other occupations involved with the identification, evaluation, and development of students with disabilities include psychologists, social workers, speech-language pathologists, audiologists, counselors, teacher assistants, occupational therapists, recreational therapists, and teachers—preschool, kindergarten, elementary, middle, and secondary.

Sources of Additional Information

For information on professions related to early intervention and education for children with disabilities, listings of schools with special education training programs, information on teacher certification, and general information on related personnel issues, contact:

- The Council for Exceptional Children, 1110 N. Glebe Road, Suite 300, Arlington, VA 22201-5704. Internet: http://www.cec.sped.org
- National Center for Special Education Personnel & Related Service Providers, National Association of State Directors of Special Education, 1800 Diagonal Road, Suite 320, Alexandria, VA 22314. Internet: http://www.personnelcenter.org

To learn more about the special education teacher certification and licensing requirements in individual states, contact the state's department of education.

Top Executives

(O*NET 11-1011.01, 11-1011.02, and 11-1021.00)

Significant Points

- Keen competition is expected because the prestige and high pay attract a large number of qualified applicants.
- Top executives are among the highest paid workers; however, long hours, considerable travel, and intense pressure to succeed are common.

- The formal education and experience of top executives vary as widely as the nature of their responsibilities.

Nature of the Work

All organizations have specific goals and objectives that they strive to meet. Top executives devise strategies and formulate policies to ensure that these objectives are met. Although they have a wide range of titles—such as chief executive officer, chief operating officer, board chair, president, vice president, school superintendent, county administrator, or tax commissioner—all formulate policies and direct the operations of businesses and corporations, public sector organizations, nonprofit institutions, and other organizations.

A corporation's goals and policies are established by the *chief executive officer* in collaboration with other top executives, who are overseen by a board of directors. In a large corporation, the chief executive officer meets frequently with subordinate executives to ensure that operations are conducted in accordance with these policies. The chief executive officer of a corporation retains overall accountability; however, a *chief operating officer* may be delegated several responsibilities, including the authority to oversee executives who direct the activities of various departments and implement the organization's policies on a day-to-day basis. In publicly held and nonprofit corporations, the board of directors ultimately is accountable for the success or failure of the enterprise, and the chief executive officer reports to the board.

The nature of other high-level executives' responsibilities depends on the size of the organization. In large organizations, the duties of such executives are highly specialized. Some managers, for instance, are responsible for the overall performance of one aspect of the organization, such as manufacturing, marketing, sales, purchasing, finance, personnel, training, administrative services, computer and information systems, property management, transportation, or legal services.

In smaller organizations, such as independent retail stores or small manufacturers, a partner, owner, or general manager often is responsible for purchasing, hiring, training, quality control, and day-to-day supervisory duties.

Chief financial officers direct the organization's financial goals, objectives, and budgets. They oversee the investment of funds and manage associated risks, supervise cash management activities, execute capital-raising strategies to support a firm's expansion, and deal with mergers and acquisitions.

Chief information officers are responsible for the overall technological direction of their organizations. They are increasingly involved in the strategic business plan of a firm as part of the executive team. To perform effectively, they also need knowledge of administrative procedures, such as budgeting, hiring, and supervision. These managers propose budgets for projects and programs and make decisions on staff training and equipment purchases. They hire and assign computer specialists, information technology workers, and support personnel to carry out specific parts of the projects. They supervise the work of these employees, review their output, and establish administrative procedures and policies. Chief information officers also provide organizations with the vision to master information technology as a competitive tool.

Chief executives have overall responsibility for the operation of their organizations. Working with executive staff, they set goals and arrange programs to attain these goals. Executives also appoint department heads, who manage the employees who carry out programs. Chief executives also oversee budgets and ensure that resources are used properly and that programs are carried out as planned.

Chief executive officers carry out a number of other important functions, such as meeting with staff and board members to determine the level of support for proposed programs. In addition, they often nominate citizens to boards and commissions, encourage business investment, and promote economic development in their communities. To do all of these varied tasks effectively, chief executives rely on a staff of highly skilled personnel. Executives who control small companies, however, often do this work by themselves.

General and operations managers plan, direct, or coordinate the operations of companies or public and private sector organizations. Their duties include formulating policies, managing daily operations, and planning the use of materials and human resources, but are too diverse and general in nature to be classified in any one area of management or administration, such as personnel, purchasing, or administrative services. In some organizations, the duties of general and operations managers may overlap the duties of chief executive officers.

In addition to being responsible for the operational success of a company, top executives also are increasingly being held accountable for the accuracy of their financial reporting, particularly among publicly traded companies. For example, recently enacted legislation contains provisions for corporate governance, internal control, and financial reporting.

Working Conditions

Top executives typically have spacious offices and numerous support staff. General managers in large firms or nonprofit organizations usually have comfortable offices close to those of the top executives to whom they report. Long hours, including evenings and weekends, are standard for most top executives and general managers, although their schedules may be flexible.

Substantial travel between international, national, regional, and local offices to monitor operations and meet with customers, staff, and other executives often is required of managers and executives. Many managers and executives also attend meetings and conferences sponsored by various associations. The conferences provide an opportunity to meet with prospective donors, customers, contractors, or government officials and allow managers and executives to keep abreast of technological and managerial innovations.

In large organizations, job transfers between local offices or subsidiaries are common for persons on the executive career track. Top executives are under intense pressure to succeed; depending on the organization, this may mean earning higher profits, providing better service, or attaining fundraising and charitable goals. Executives in charge of poorly performing organizations or departments usually find their jobs in jeopardy.

Training, Other Qualifications, and Advancement

The formal education and experience of top executives vary as widely as the nature of their responsibilities. Many top executives have a bachelor's or higher degree in business administration or liberal arts. College presidents typically have a doctorate in the field in which they originally taught, and school superintendents often have a master's degree in education administration. A brokerage office manager needs a strong background in securities and finance, and department store executives generally have extensive experience in retail trade.

Some top executives in the public sector have a background in public administration or liberal arts. Others might have a background related to their jobs. For example, a health commissioner might have a graduate degree in health services administration or business administration.

Many top executive positions are filled from within the organization by promoting experienced, lower-level managers when an opening occurs. In industries such as retail trade or transportation, for instance, it is possible for individuals without a college degree to work their way up within the company and become managers. However, many companies prefer that their top executives have specialized backgrounds and, therefore, hire individuals who have been managers in other organizations.

Top executives must have highly developed personal skills. An analytical mind able to quickly assess large amounts of information and data is very important, as is the ability to consider and evaluate the relationships between numerous factors. Top executives also must be able to communicate clearly and persuasively. Other qualities critical for managerial success include leadership, self-confidence, motivation, decisiveness, flexibility, sound business judgment, and determination.

Advancement may be accelerated by participation in company training programs that impart a broader knowledge of company policy and operations. Managers also can help their careers by becoming familiar with the latest developments in management techniques at national or local training programs sponsored by various industry and trade associations. Managers who have experience in a particular field, such as accounting or engineering, may attend executive development programs to facilitate their promotion to an even higher level. Participation in conferences and seminars can expand knowledge of national and international issues influencing the organization and can help the participants develop a network of useful contacts.

General managers may advance to a top executive position, such as executive vice president, in their own firm or they may take a corresponding position in another firm. They may even advance to peak corporate positions such as chief operating officer or chief executive officer. Chief executive officers often become members of the board of directors of one or more firms, typically as a director of their own firm and often as chair of its board of directors. Some top executives establish their own firms or become independent consultants.

Employment

Top executives held about 2.3 million jobs in 2004. Employment by detailed occupation was distributed as follows:

General and operations managers 1,807,000
Chief executives 444,000
Legislators 66,000

Top executives are found in every industry, but service-providing industries, including government, employ 8 out of 10.

Job Outlook

Keen competition is expected for top executive positions because the prestige and high pay attract a large number of qualified applicants. Because this is a large occupation, numerous openings will occur each year as executives transfer to other positions, start their own businesses, or retire. However, many executives who leave their jobs transfer to other executive positions, a pattern that tends to limit the number of job openings for new entrants.

Experienced managers whose accomplishments reflect strong leadership qualities and the ability to improve the efficiency or competitive position of an organization will have the best opportunities. In an increasingly global economy, experience in international economics, marketing, information systems, and knowledge of several languages also may be beneficial.

Employment of top executives—including chief executives and general and operations managers—is expected to grow about as fast as average for all occupations through 2014. Because top managers are essential to the success of any organization, their jobs are unlikely to be automated or to be eliminated through corporate restructuring—trends that are expected to adversely affect employment of lower-level managers. Projected employment growth of top executives over the 2004–14 period varies by industry. For example, employment growth is expected to be much faster than average in professional, scientific, and technical services and in administrative and support services. However, employment is projected to decline in some manufacturing industries.

Earnings

Top executives are among the highest paid workers in the U.S. economy. However, salary levels vary substantially depending on the level of managerial responsibility; length of service; and type, size, and location of the firm. For example, a top manager in a very large corporation can earn significantly more than a counterpart in a small firm.

Median annual earnings of general and operations managers in May 2004 were $77,420. The middle 50 percent earned between $52,420 and $118,310. Because the specific responsibilities of general and operations managers vary significantly within industries, earnings also tend to vary considerably. Median annual earnings in the industries employing the largest numbers of general and operations managers in May 2004 were:

Computer systems design and related services $117,730
Management of companies and enterprises 99,670
Building equipment contractors...........................83,080
Depository credit intermediation 76,060
Local government 68,590

Median annual earnings of chief executives in May 2004 were $140,350; although chief executives in some industries earned considerably more.

Salaries vary substantially by type and level of responsibilities and by industry. According to a 2005 survey by Abbott, Langer, and Associates, the median income of chief executive officers in the nonprofit sector was $88,006 in 2005, but some of the highest paid made more than $700,000.

In addition to salaries, total compensation often includes stock options, dividends, and other performance bonuses. The use of executive dining rooms and company aircraft and cars, expense allowances, and company-paid insurance premiums and physical examinations also are among benefits commonly enjoyed by top executives in private industry. A number of chief executive officers also are provided with company-paid club memberships and other amenities.

Related Occupations

Top executives plan, organize, direct, control, and coordinate the operations of an organization and its major departments or programs. The members of the board of directors and lower-level managers also are involved in these activities. Many other management occupations have similar responsibilities; however, they are concentrated in specific industries or are responsible for a specific department within an organization. A few examples are administrative services managers; education administrators; financial managers; food service managers; and advertising, marketing, promotions, public relations, and sales managers. Legislators oversee their staffs and help set public policies in federal, state, and local governments.

Sources of Additional Information

For a variety of information on top executives, including educational programs, certification programs, and job listings, contact:

- American Management Association, 1601 Broadway, 6th Floor, New York, NY 10019. Internet: http://www.amanet.org
- International Public Management Association for Human Resources, 1617 Duke St., Alexandria, VA 22314. Internet: http://www.ipma-hr.org
- National Management Association, 2210 Arbor Blvd., Dayton, OH 45439. Internet: http://www.nma1.org

For information on executive financial management careers and certification, contact:

- Financial Executives International, 200 Campus Dr., P.O. Box 674, Florham Park, NJ 07932-0674. Internet: http://www.fei.org
- Financial Management Association International, College of Business Administration, University of South Florida, 4202 East Fowler Ave., BSN 3331, Tampa, FL 33620-5500. Internet: http://www.fma.org

Truck Drivers and Driver/Sales Workers

(O*NET 53-3031.00, 53-3032.01, 53-3032.02, and 53-3033.00)

Significant Points

- Job opportunities should be favorable.
- Competition is expected for jobs offering the highest earnings or most favorable work schedules.
- A commercial driver's license is required to operate most larger trucks.

Nature of the Work

Truck drivers are a constant presence on the nation's highways and interstates. They deliver everything from automobiles to canned food. Firms of all kinds rely on trucks to pick up and deliver goods because no other form of transportation can deliver goods door-to-door. Even if some goods travel most of the way by ship, train, or airplane, almost everything is carried by trucks at some point in its journey.

Before leaving the terminal or warehouse, truck drivers check the fuel level and oil in their trucks. They also inspect the trucks to make sure that the brakes, windshield wipers, and lights are working and that a fire extinguisher, flares, and other safety equipment are aboard and in working order. Drivers make sure their cargo is secure and adjust the mirrors so that both sides of the truck are visible from the driver's seat. Drivers report equipment that is inoperable, missing, or loaded improperly to the dispatcher.

Once under way, drivers must be alert in order to prevent accidents. Drivers can see farther down the road because large trucks seat them higher off the ground than other vehicles. This allows them to see the road ahead and select lanes that are moving more smoothly as well as giving them warning of any dangerous road conditions ahead of them.

The duration of runs vary according to the types of cargo and the destinations. Local drivers may provide daily service for a specific route or region, while other drivers make longer, intercity and interstate deliveries. Interstate and intercity cargo tends to vary from job to job more than local cargo. A driver's responsibilities and assignments change according to the type of loads transported and their vehicle's size.

New technologies are changing the way truck drivers work, especially long-distance truck drivers. Satellites and the Global Positioning System link many trucks with their company's headquarters. Troubleshooting information, directions, weather reports, and other important communications can be instantly relayed to the truck. Drivers can easily communicate with the dispatcher to discuss delivery schedules and courses of action in the event of mechanical problems. The satellite link also allows the dispatcher to track the truck's location, fuel consumption, and engine performance. Some drivers also work with computerized inventory tracking equipment. It is important for the producer, warehouse, and customer to know their product's location at all times so they can maintain a high quality of service.

Heavy truck and tractor-trailer drivers operate trucks or vans with a capacity of at least 26,000 pounds Gross Vehicle Weight (GVW). They transport goods including cars, livestock, and other materials in liquid, loose, or packaged form. Many routes are from city to city and cover long distances. Some companies use two drivers on very long runs—one drives while the other sleeps in a berth behind the cab. These "sleeper" runs can last for days, or even weeks. Trucks on sleeper runs typically stop only for fuel, food, loading, and unloading.

Some heavy truck and tractor-trailer drivers who have regular runs transport freight to the same city on a regular basis. Other drivers perform ad hoc runs because shippers request varying service to different cities every day.

The U.S. Department of Transportation requires that drivers keep a log of their activities, the condition of the truck, and the circumstances of any accidents.

Long-distance heavy truck and tractor-trailer drivers spend most of their working time behind the wheel, but also may have to load or unload their cargo. This is especially common when drivers haul specialty cargo, because they may be the only ones at the destination familiar with procedures or certified to handle the materials. Auto-transport drivers, for example, position cars on the trailers at the manufacturing plant and remove them at the dealerships. When picking up or delivering furniture, drivers of long-distance moving vans hire local workers to help them load or unload.

Light or delivery services truck drivers operate vans and trucks weighing less than 26,000 pounds GVW. They pick up or deliver merchandise and packages within a specific area. This may include short "turnarounds" to deliver a shipment to a nearby city, pick up another loaded truck or van, and drive it back to their home base the same day. These services may require use of electronic delivery tracking systems to track the whereabouts of the merchandise or packages. Light or delivery services truck drivers usually load or unload the merchandise at the customer's place of business. They may have helpers if there are many deliveries to make during the day, or if the load requires heavy moving. Typically, before the driver arrives for work, material handlers load the trucks and arrange items for ease of delivery. Customers must sign receipts for goods and pay drivers the balance due on the merchandise if there is a cash-on-delivery arrangement. At the end of the day drivers turn in receipts, payments, records of deliveries made, and any reports on mechanical problems with their trucks.

Some local truck drivers have sales and customer service responsibilities. The primary responsibility of *driver/sales workers*, or *route drivers*, is to deliver and sell their firm's products over established routes or within an established territory. They sell goods such as food products, including restaurant takeout items, or pick up and deliver items such as laundry. Their response to customer complaints and requests can make the difference between a large order and a lost customer. Route drivers may also take orders and collect payments.

The duties of driver/sales workers vary according to their industry, the policies of their employer, and the emphasis placed on their sales responsibility. Most have wholesale routes that deliver to businesses and stores, rather than to homes. For example, wholesale bakery driver/sales workers deliver and arrange bread, cakes, rolls, and other baked goods on display racks in grocery stores. They estimate how many of each item to stock by paying close attention to what is selling. They may recommend changes in a store's order or encourage the manager to stock new bakery products. Laundries that rent linens, towels, work clothes, and other items employ driver/sales workers to visit businesses regularly to replace soiled laundry. Their duties also may include soliciting new customers along their sales route.

After completing their route, driver/sales workers place orders for their next deliveries based on product sales and customer requests.

Working Conditions

Truck driving has become less physically demanding because most trucks now have more comfortable seats, better ventilation, and improved, ergonomically designed cabs. Although these changes make the work environment less taxing, driving for many hours at a stretch, loading and unloading cargo, and making many deliveries can be tiring. Local truck drivers, unlike long-distance drivers, usually return home in the evening. Some self-employed long-distance truck drivers who own and operate their trucks spend most of the year away from home.

Design improvements in newer trucks have reduced stress and increased the efficiency of long-distance drivers. Many newer trucks are equipped with refrigerators, televisions, and bunks.

The U.S. Department of Transportation governs work hours and other working conditions of truck drivers engaged in interstate commerce. A long-distance driver may drive for 11 hours and work for up to 14 hours including driving and non-driving duties—after having 10 hours off-duty. A driver may not drive after having worked for 60 hours in the past 7 days or 70 hours in the past 8 days unless they have taken at least 34 consecutive hours off-duty. Most drivers are required to document their time in a logbook. Many drivers, particularly on long runs, work close to the maximum time permitted because they typically are compensated according to the number of miles or hours they drive. Drivers on long runs face boredom, loneliness, and fatigue. Drivers often travel nights, holidays, and weekends to avoid traffic delays.

Local truck drivers frequently work 50 or more hours a week. Drivers who handle food for chain grocery stores, produce markets, or bakeries typically work long hours—starting late at night or early in the morning. Although most drivers have regular routes, some have different routes each day. Many local truck drivers, particularly driver/sales workers, load and unload their own trucks. This requires considerable lifting, carrying, and walking each day.

Training, Other Qualifications, and Advancement

State and federal regulations govern the qualifications and standards for truck drivers. All drivers must comply with federal regulations and any state regulations that are in excess of those federal requirements. Truck drivers must have a driver's license issued by the state in which they live, and most employers require a clean driving record. Drivers of trucks designed to carry 26,000 pounds or more—including most tractor-trailers, as well as bigger straight trucks—must obtain a commercial driver's license (CDL) from the state in which they live. All truck drivers who operate trucks transporting hazardous materials must obtain a CDL, regardless of truck size. In order to receive the hazardous materials endorsement a driver must be fingerprinted and submit to a criminal background check by the Transportation Security Administration. Federal regulations governing CDL administration allow for states to exempt farmers, emergency medical technicians, fire fighters, some military drivers, and snow and ice removers from the need for a CDL at the state's discretion. In many states a regular driver's license is sufficient for driving light trucks and vans.

To qualify for a CDL an applicant must have a clean driving record, pass a written test on rules and regulations, and then demonstrate that they can operate a commercial truck safely. A national database permanently records all driving violations committed by those with a CDL. A state will check these records and deny a CDL to those who already have a license suspended or revoked in another state. Licensed drivers must accompany trainees until they get their own CDL. A person may not hold more than one license at a time and must surrender any other licenses when a CDL is issued. Information on how to apply for a CDL may be obtained from state motor vehicle administrations.

Many states allow those who are as young as 18 years old to drive trucks within their borders. To drive a commercial vehicle between states one must be 21 years of age, according to the U.S. Department of Transportation (U.S. DOT), which establishes minimum qualifications for truck drivers engaging in interstate commerce. Federal Motor Carrier Safety Regulations—published by U.S. DOT—require drivers to be at least 21 years old and to pass a physical examination once every 2 years. The main physical requirements include good hearing, at least 20/40 vision with glasses or corrective lenses, and a 70-degree field of vision in each eye. Drivers may not be colorblind. Drivers must be able to hear a forced whisper in one ear at not less than 5 feet, with a hearing aid if needed. Drivers must have normal use of arms and legs and normal blood pressure. Drivers may not use any controlled substances, unless prescribed by a licensed physician. Persons with epilepsy or diabetes controlled by insulin are not permitted to be interstate truck drivers. Federal regulations also require employers to test their drivers for alcohol and drug use as a condition of employment, and require periodic random tests of the drivers while they are on duty. A driver must not have been convicted of a felony involving the use of a motor vehicle; a crime involving drugs; driving under the influence of drugs or alcohol; refusing to submit to an alcohol test required by a state or its implied consent laws or regulations; leaving the scene of a crime; or causing a fatality through negligent operation of a motor vehicle. All drivers must be able to read and speak English well enough to read road signs, prepare reports, and communicate with law enforcement officers and the public.

Many trucking operations have higher standards than those described here. Many firms require that drivers be at least 22 years old, be able to lift heavy objects, and have driven trucks for 3 to 5 years. Many prefer to hire high school graduates and require annual physical examinations. Companies have an economic incentive to hire less risky drivers, as good drivers use less fuel and cost less to insure.

Taking driver-training courses is a desirable method of preparing for truck driving jobs and for obtaining a CDL. High school courses in driver training and automotive mechanics also may be helpful. Many private and public vocational-technical schools offer tractor-trailer driver training programs. Students learn to maneuver large vehicles on crowded streets and in highway traffic. They also learn to inspect trucks and freight for compliance with regulations. Some programs provide only a limited amount of actual driving experience. Completion of a program does not guarantee a job. Those interested in attending a driving school should check with local trucking companies to make sure the school's training is acceptable. Some states require prospective drivers to complete a training course in basic truck driving before being issued their CDL. The Professional Truck Driver Institute (PTDI), a nonprofit organization established by the trucking industry, manufacturers, and others, certifies driver training courses at truck driver training schools that meet industry standards and Federal Highway Administration guidelines for training tractor-trailer drivers.

Drivers must get along well with people because they often deal directly with customers. Employers seek driver/sales workers who speak well and have self-confidence, initiative, tact, and a neat appearance. Employers also look for responsible, self-motivated individuals who are able to work well with little supervision.

Training given to new drivers by employers is usually informal, and may consist of only a few hours of instruction from an experienced driver, sometimes on the new employee's own time. New drivers may also ride with and observe experienced drivers before getting their own assignments. Drivers receive additional training to drive special types of trucks or handle hazardous materials. Some companies give 1 to 2 days of classroom instruction covering general duties, the operation and loading of a truck, company policies, and the preparation of delivery forms and company records. Driver/sales workers also receive training on the various types of products their company carries so that they can effectively answer questions about the products and more easily market them to their customers.

Although most new truck drivers are assigned to regular driving jobs immediately, some start as extra drivers—substituting for regular drivers who are ill or on vacation. Extra drivers receive a regular assignment when an opening occurs.

New drivers sometimes start on panel trucks or other small straight trucks. As they gain experience and show competent driving skills they may advance to larger, heavier trucks and finally to tractor-trailers.

The advancement of truck drivers generally is limited to driving runs that provide increased earnings, preferred schedules, or working conditions. Local truck drivers may advance to driving heavy or specialized trucks, or transfer to long-distance truck driving. Working for companies that also employ long-distance drivers is the best way to advance to these positions. Few truck drivers become dispatchers or managers.

Some long-distance truck drivers purchase trucks and go into business for themselves. Although some of these owner-operators are successful, others fail to cover expenses and go out of business. Owner-operators should have good business sense as well as truck driving experience. Courses in accounting, business, and business mathematics are helpful. Knowledge of truck mechanics can enable owner-operators to perform their own routine maintenance and minor repairs.

Employment

Truck drivers and driver/sales workers held about 3.2 million jobs in 2004. Of these workers, 451,000 were driver/sales workers and 2.8 million were truck drivers. Most truck drivers find employment in large metropolitan areas or along major interstate roadways where trucking, retail, and wholesale companies tend to have their distribution outlets. Some drivers work in rural areas, providing specialized services such as delivering newspapers to customers.

The truck transportation industry employed 25 percent of all truck drivers and driver/sales workers in the United States. Another 25 percent worked for companies engaged in wholesale or retail trade. The remaining truck drivers and driver/sales workers were distributed across many industries, including construction and manufacturing.

Around 9 percent of all truck drivers and driver/sales workers were self-employed. Of these, a significant number were owner-operators who either served a variety of businesses independently or leased their services and trucks to a trucking company.

Job Outlook

Job opportunities should be favorable for truck drivers. In addition to growth in demand for truck drivers, numerous job openings will occur as experienced drivers leave this large occupation to transfer to other fields of work, retire, or leave the labor force for other reasons. Jobs vary greatly in terms of earnings, weekly work hours, the number of nights spent on the road, and quality of equipment. There may be competition for the jobs with the highest earnings and most favorable work schedules.

Overall employment of truck drivers and driver/sales workers is expected to increase about as fast as the average for all occupations through the year 2014, due to growth in the economy and in the amount of freight carried by truck. Competing forms of freight transportation—rail, air, and ship transportation—still require trucks to move the goods between ports, depots, airports, warehouses, retailers, and final consumers who are not connected to these other modes of transportation. Demand for long-distance drivers will remain strong because they can transport perishable and time-sensitive goods more effectively than alternate modes of transportation. Job opportunities for truck drivers with local carriers will be more competitive than those with long-distance carriers because of the more desirable working conditions of local carriers.

Job opportunities may vary from year to year, since the output of the economy dictates the amount of freight to be moved. Companies tend to hire more drivers when the economy is strong and their services are in high demand. When the economy slows, employers hire fewer drivers or may lay off some drivers. Independent owner-operators are particularly vulnerable to slowdowns. Industries least likely to be affected by economic fluctuation, such as grocery stores, tend to be the most stable employers of truck drivers and driver/sales workers.

Earnings

Median hourly earnings of heavy truck and tractor-trailer drivers were $16.11 in May 2004. The middle 50 percent earned between $12.67 and $20.09 an hour. The lowest 10 percent earned less than $10.18, and the highest 10 percent earned more than $24.07 an hour. Median hourly earnings in the industries employing the largest numbers of heavy truck and tractor-trailer drivers in May 2004 were:

General freight trucking	$17.56
Grocery and related product wholesalers	17.32
Specialized freight trucking	15.61
Employment services	14.82
Cement and concrete product manufacturing	14.47

Median hourly earnings of light or delivery services truck drivers were $11.80 in May 2004. The middle 50 percent earned between $8.96 and $16.00 an hour. The lowest 10 percent earned less than $7.20, and the highest 10 percent earned more than $20.83 an hour. Median hourly earnings in the industries employing the largest numbers of light or delivery services truck drivers in May 2004 were:

Couriers	$17.94
General freight trucking	14.79
Grocery and related product wholesalers	12.44
Building material and supplies dealers	10.85
Automotive parts, accessories, and tire stores	8.07

Median hourly earnings of driver/sales workers, including commissions, were $9.66 in May 2004. The middle 50 percent earned between $6.94 and $14.59 an hour. The lowest 10 percent earned less than $5.96, and the highest 10 percent earned more than $19.81 an hour. Median hourly earnings in the industries employing the largest numbers of driver/sales workers in May 2004 were:

Drycleaning and laundry services	$14.67
Direct selling establishments	13.55
Grocery and related product wholesalers	12.36
Limited-service eating places	6.77
Full-service restaurants	6.59

Local truck drivers tend to be paid by the hour, with extra pay for working overtime. Employers pay long-distance drivers primarily by the mile. The per-mile rate can vary greatly from employer to employer and may even depend on the type of cargo they are hauling. Some long-distance drivers are paid a percent of each load's revenue. Typically, earnings increase with mileage driven, seniority, and the size and type of truck driven. Most driver/sales workers receive commissions based on their sales in addition to their hourly wages.

Most self-employed truck drivers are primarily engaged in long-distance hauling. Many truck drivers are members of the International Brotherhood of Teamsters. Some truck drivers employed by companies outside the trucking industry are members of unions representing the plant workers of the companies for which they work.

Related Occupations

Other driving occupations include ambulance drivers and attendants, except emergency medical technicians; bus drivers; and taxi drivers and chauffeurs. Another occupation involving sales duties is sales representatives, wholesale and manufacturing.

Sources of Additional Information

Information on truck driver employment opportunities is available from local trucking companies and local offices of the state employment service.

Information on career opportunities in truck driving may be obtained from:

- American Trucking Associations, Inc., 2200 Mill Rd., Alexandria, VA 22314. Internet: http://www.trucking.org

A list of certified tractor-trailer driver training courses may be obtained from:

- Professional Truck Driver Institute, 2200 Mill Rd., Alexandria, VA 22314. Internet: http://www.ptdi.org

Information on union truck driving can be obtained from:

- The International Brotherhood of Teamsters, 25 Louisiana Ave. NW, Washington, DC 20001.

Veterinary Technologists and Technicians

(O*NET 29-2056.00)

Significant Points

- Animal lovers get satisfaction in this occupation, but aspects of the work can be unpleasant, physically and emotionally demanding, and sometimes dangerous.
- Entrants generally complete a 2-year or 4-year veterinary technology program and must pass a state examination.
- Employment is expected to grow much faster than average.
- Keen competition is expected for jobs in zoos.

Nature of the Work

Owners of pets and other animals today expect state-of-the-art veterinary care. To provide this service, veterinarians use the skills of veterinary technologists and technicians, who perform many of the same duties for a veterinarian that a nurse would for a physician, including routine laboratory and clinical procedures. Although specific job duties vary by employer, there often is little difference between the tasks carried out by technicians and by technologists, despite some differences in formal education and training. As a result, most workers in this occupation are called technicians.

Veterinary technologists and technicians typically conduct clinical work in a private practice under the supervision of a veterinarian—often performing various medical tests along with treating and diagnosing medical conditions and diseases in animals. For example, they may perform laboratory tests such as urinalysis and blood counts, assist with dental prophylaxis, prepare tissue samples, take blood samples, or assist veterinarians in a variety of tests and analyses in which they often utilize various items of medical equipment, such as test tubes and diagnostic equipment. While most of these duties are performed in a laboratory setting, many are not. For example, some veterinary technicians obtain and record patients' case histories, expose and develop X rays, and provide specialized nursing care. In addition, experienced veterinary technicians may discuss a pet's condition with its owners and train new clinic personnel. Veterinary technologists and technicians assisting small-animal practitioners usually care for companion animals, such as cats and dogs, but can perform a variety of duties with mice, rats, sheep, pigs, cattle, monkeys, birds, fish, and frogs. Very few veterinary technologists work in mixed animal practices where they care for both small companion animals and larger, nondomestic animals.

Besides working in private clinics and animal hospitals, veterinary technologists and technicians may work in research facilities, where they may administer medications orally or topically, prepare samples for laboratory examinations, and record information on an animal's genealogy, diet, weight, medications, food intake, and clinical signs of pain and distress. Some may be required to sterilize laboratory and surgical equipment and provide routine postoperative care. At research facilities, veterinary technologists typically work under the guidance of veterinarians, physicians, and other laboratory technicians. Some veterinary technologists vaccinate newly admitted animals and occasionally are required to euthanize seriously ill, severely injured, or unwanted animals.

While the goal of most veterinary technologists and technicians is to promote animal health, some contribute to human health as well. Veterinary technologists occasionally assist veterinarians as they work with other scientists in medical-related fields such as gene therapy and cloning. Some find opportunities in biomedical research, wildlife medicine, the military, livestock management, or pharmaceutical sales.

Working Conditions

People who love animals get satisfaction from working with and helping them. However, some of the work may be unpleasant, physically and emotionally demanding, and sometimes dangerous. At times, veterinary technicians must clean cages and lift, hold, or restrain animals, risking exposure to bites or scratches. These workers must take precautions when treating animals with germicides or insecticides. The work setting can be noisy.

Veterinary technologists and technicians who witness abused animals or who euthanize unwanted, aged, or hopelessly injured animals may experience emotional stress. Those working for humane societies and animal shelters often deal with the public, some of whom might react with hostility to any implication that the owners are neglecting or abusing their pets. Such workers must maintain a calm and professional demeanor while they enforce the laws regarding animal care. In some animal hospitals, research facilities, and animal shelters, a veterinary technician is on duty 24 hours a day, which means that some may work night shifts. Most full-time veterinary technologists and technicians work about 40 hours a week, although some work 50 or more hours a week.

Training, Other Qualifications, and Advancement

There are primarily two levels of education and training for entry to this occupation: a 2-year program for veterinary technicians and a 4-year program for veterinary technologists. Most entry-level veterinary technicians have a 2-year degree, usually an associate's degree, from an accredited community college program in veterinary technology in which courses are taught in clinical and laboratory settings using live animals. About 15 colleges offer veterinary technology programs that are longer and that culminate in a 4-year bachelor's degree in veterinary technology. These 4-year colleges, in addition to some vocational schools, also offer 2-year programs in laboratory animal science. Approximately 5 schools offer distance learning.

In 2004, 116 veterinary technology programs in 43 states were accredited by the American Veterinary Medical Association (AVMA). Graduation from an AVMA-accredited veterinary technology program allows students to take the credentialing exam in any state in the country. Each state regulates veterinary technicians and technologists differently; however, all states require them to pass a credentialing exam following coursework. Passing the state exam assures the public that the technician or technologist has sufficient knowledge to work in a veterinary clinic or hospital. Candidates are tested for competency through an examination that includes oral, written, and practical portions and that is regulated by the State Board of Veterinary Examiners or the appropriate state agency. Depending on the state, candidates may become registered, licensed, or certified. Most states, however, use the National Veterinary Technician (NVT) exam. Prospects usually can have their passing scores transferred from one state to another, so long as both states utilize the same exam.

Employers recommend American Association for Laboratory Animal Science (AALAS) certification for those seeking employment in a research facility. AALAS offers certification for three levels of technician competence, with a focus on three principal areas—animal husbandry, facility management, and animal health and welfare. Those who wish to become certified must satisfy a combination of education and experience requirements prior to taking an exam. Work experience must be directly related to the maintenance, health, and well-being of laboratory animals and must be gained in a laboratory animal facility as defined by AALAS. Candidates who meet the necessary criteria can begin pursuing the desired certification on the basis of their qualifications. The lowest level of certification is Assistant Laboratory Animal Technician (ALAT), the second level is Laboratory Animal Technician (LAT), and the highest level of certification is Laboratory Animal Technologist (LATG). The examination consists of multiple-choice questions and is longer and more difficult for higher levels of certification, ranging from 2 hours for the ALAT to 3 hours for the LATG.

Persons interested in careers as veterinary technologists and technicians should take as many high school science, biology, and math courses as possible. Science courses taken beyond high school, in an associate's or bachelor's degree program, should emphasize practical skills in a clinical or laboratory setting. Because veterinary technologists and technicians often deal with pet owners, communication skills are very important. In addition, technologists and technicians should be able to work well with others, because teamwork with veterinarians is common. Organizational ability and the ability to pay attention to detail also are important.

Technologists and technicians usually begin work as trainees in routine positions under the direct supervision of a veterinarian. Entry-level workers whose training or educational background encompasses extensive hands-on experience with a variety of laboratory equipment, including diagnostic and medical equipment, usually require a shorter period of on-the-job training. As they gain experience, technologists and technicians take on more responsibility and carry out more assignments under only general veterinary supervision. Some eventually may become supervisors.

Employment

Veterinary technologists and technicians held about 60,000 jobs in 2004. Most worked in veterinary services. The remainder worked in boarding kennels, animal shelters, stables, grooming salons, zoos, and local, state, and federal agencies.

Job Outlook

Employment of veterinary technologists and technicians is expected to grow much faster than average for all occupations through the year 2014. Job openings also will stem from the need to replace veterinary technologists and technicians who leave the occupation over the 2004–14 period. Keen competition is expected for veterinary technologist and technician jobs in zoos, due to expected slow growth in zoo capacity, low turnover among workers, the limited number of positions, and the fact that the occupation attracts many candidates.

Pet owners are becoming more affluent and more willing to pay for advanced care because many of them consider their pet to be part of the family. This growing affluence and view of pets will spur employment growth for veterinary technologists and technicians. The number of dogs used as companion pets, which also drives employment growth, is expected to increase more slowly during the projection period than in the previous decade. However, the rapidly growing number of cats utilized as companion pets is expected to boost the demand for feline medicine and services, offsetting any reduced demand for veterinary care for dogs. The availability of advanced veterinary services, such as preventive dental care and surgical procedures, may provide opportunities for workers specializing in those areas. Biomedical facilities, diagnostic laboratories, wildlife facilities, humane societies, animal control facilities, drug or food manufacturing companies, and food safety inspection facilities will provide additional jobs for veterinary technologists and technicians. Furthermore, demand for these workers will stem from the desire to replace veterinary assistants with more highly skilled technicians and technologists in animal clinics and hospitals, shelters, kennels, and humane societies.

Employment of veterinary technicians and technologists is relatively stable during periods of economic recession. Layoffs are less likely to occur among veterinary technologists and technicians than in some other occupations because animals will continue to require medical care.

Earnings

Median hourly earnings of veterinary technologists and technicians were $11.99 in May 2004. The middle 50 percent earned between $9.88 and $14.56. The bottom 10 percent earned less than $8.51, and the top 10 percent earned more than $17.12.

Related Occupations

Others who work extensively with animals include animal care and service workers, veterinary assistants, and laboratory animal caretakers. Like veterinary technologists and technicians, they must have patience and feel comfortable with animals. However, the level of training required for these occupations is less than that needed by veterinary technologists and technicians. Veterinarians, who need much more formal education, also work extensively with animals, preventing, diagnosing, and treating their diseases, disorders, and injuries.

Sources of Additional Information

For information on certification as a laboratory animal technician or technologist, contact:

- American Association for Laboratory Animal Science, 9190 Crestwyn Hills Dr., Memphis, TN 38125. Internet: http://www.aalas.org

For information on careers in veterinary medicine and a listing of AVMA-accredited veterinary technology programs, contact:

- American Veterinary Medical Association, 1931 N. Meacham Rd., Suite 100, Schaumburg, IL 60173-4360. Internet: http://www.avma.org

Writers and Editors

(O*NET 27-3041.00, 27-3042.00, 27-3043.01, 27-3043.02, 27-3043.03, and 27-3043.04)

Significant Points

- Most jobs in this occupation require a college degree in communications, journalism, or English, although a degree in a technical subject may be useful for technical-writing positions.
- The outlook for most writing and editing jobs is expected to be competitive because many people are attracted to the occupation.
- Online publications and services are growing in number and sophistication, spurring the demand for writers and editors, especially those with Web experience.

Nature of the Work

Communicating through the written word, writers and editors generally fall into one of three categories. *Writers and authors* develop original fiction and nonfiction for books, magazines, trade journals, online publications, company newsletters, radio and television broadcasts, motion pictures, and advertisements. *Editors* examine proposals and select material for publication or broadcast. They review and revise a writer's work for publication or dissemination. *Technical writers* develop technical materials, such as equipment manuals, appendixes, or operating and maintenance instructions. They also may assist in layout work.

Most writers and editors have at least a basic familiarity with technology, regularly using personal computers, desktop or electronic publishing systems, scanners, and other electronic communications equipment. Many writers prepare material directly for the Internet. For example, they may write for electronic newspapers or magazines, create short fiction or poetry, or produce technical documentation that is available only online. Also, they may write text for Web sites. These writers should be knowledgeable about graphic design, page layout, and multimedia software. In addition, they should be familiar with interactive technologies of the Web so that they can blend text, graphics, and sound together.

Writers—especially of nonfiction—are expected to establish their credibility with editors and readers through strong research and the use of appropriate sources and citations. Sustaining high ethical standards and meeting publication deadlines are essential.

Creative writers, poets, and lyricists, including novelists, playwrights, and screenwriters, create original works—such as prose, poems, plays, and song lyrics—for publication or performance. Some works may be commissioned by a sponsor; others may be written for hire (on the basis of the completion of a draft or an outline).

Nonfiction writers either propose a topic or are assigned one, often by an editor or publisher. They gather information about the topic through personal observation, library and Internet research, and interviews. Writers then select the material they want to use, organize it, and use the written word to express ideas and convey information. Writers also revise or rewrite sections, searching for the best organization or the right phrasing. *Copy writers* prepare advertising copy for use by publication or broadcast media or to promote the sale of goods and services. *Newsletter writers* produce information for distribution to association memberships, corporate employees, organizational clients, or the public.

Freelance writers sell their work to publishers, publication enterprises, manufacturing firms, public relations departments, or advertising agencies. Sometimes, they contract with publishers to write a book or an article. Others may be hired to complete specific assignments, such as writing about a new product or technique.

Bloggers write for the Internet. Most bloggers write personal reflections on a subject of close personal or professional interest. Some blogs take the form of a personal diary; others read like reports from the field—first-hand, subjective accounts of an event or an activity. Most blogs are written for recreational reasons with little expectation of earning a fee; however, some blogs promote a business or support a cause and may generate interest or income through other activities.

Editors review, rewrite, and edit the work of writers. They may also do original writing. An editor's responsibilities vary with the employer and type and level of editorial position held. Editorial duties may include planning the content of books, technical journals, trade magazines, and other general-interest publications. Editors also decide what material will appeal to readers, review and edit drafts of books and articles, offer comments to improve the work, and suggest possible titles. In addition, they may oversee the production of the publications. In the book-publishing industry, an editor's primary responsibility is to review proposals for books and decide whether to buy the publication rights from the author.

Major newspapers and newsmagazines usually employ several types of editors. The *executive editor* oversees *assistant editors,* who have responsibility for particular subjects, such as local news, international news, feature stories, or sports. Executive editors generally have the final say about what stories are published and how they are covered. The *managing editor* usually is responsible for the daily operation of the news department. *Assignment editors* determine which reporters will cover a given story. *Copy editors* mostly review and edit a reporter's copy for accuracy, content, grammar, and style.

In smaller organizations, such as small daily or weekly newspapers or the membership or publications departments of nonprofit or similar organizations, a single editor may do everything or share responsibility with only a few other people. Executive and managing editors typically hire writers, reporters, and other employees. They also plan budgets and negotiate contracts with freelance writers, sometimes called "stringers" in the news industry. In broadcasting companies, *program directors* have similar responsibilities.

Editors and program directors often have assistants, many of whom hold entry-level jobs. These assistants, such as copy editors and *production assistants*, review copy for errors in grammar, punctuation, and spelling and check the copy for readability, style, and agreement with editorial policy. They suggest revisions, such as changing words and rearranging sentences, to improve clarity or accuracy. They also carry out research for writers and verify facts, dates, and statistics. Production assistants arrange page layouts of articles, photographs, and advertising; compose headlines; and prepare copy for printing. *Publication assistants* who work for publishing houses may read and evaluate manuscripts submitted by freelance writers, proofread printers' galleys, and answer letters about published material. Production assistants on small newspapers or in radio stations compile articles available from wire services or the Internet, answer phones, and make photocopies.

Technical writers put technical information into easily understandable language. They prepare operating and maintenance manuals, catalogs, parts lists, assembly instructions, sales promotion materials, and project proposals. Many technical writers work with engineers on technical subject matters to prepare written interpretations of engineering and design specifications and other information for a general readership. Technical writers also may serve as part of a team conducting usability studies to help improve the design of a product that still is in the prototype stage. They plan and edit technical materials and oversee the preparation of illustrations, photographs, diagrams, and charts.

Science and medical writers prepare a range of formal documents presenting detailed information on the physical or medical sciences. They convey research findings for scientific or medical professions and organize information for advertising or public relations needs. Many writers work with researchers on technical subjects to prepare written interpretations of data and other information for a general readership.

Working Conditions

Some writers and editors work in comfortable, private offices; others work in noisy rooms filled with the sound of keyboards and computer printers, as well as the voices of other writers tracking down information over the telephone. The search for information sometimes requires that writers travel to diverse workplaces, such as factories, offices, or laboratories, but many find their material through telephone interviews, the library, and the Internet.

Advances in electronic communications have changed the work environment for many writers. Laptop computers and wireless communications technologies allow growing numbers of writers to work from home and even on the road. The ability to e-mail, transmit, and download stories, research, or editorial review materials using the Internet allows writers and editors greater flexibility in where and how they complete assignments.

Some writers keep regular office hours, either to maintain contact with sources and editors or to establish a writing routine, but most writers set their own hours. Many writers, especially freelance writers, are paid per assignment; therefore, they work any number of hours necessary to meet a deadline. As a result, writers must be willing to work evenings, nights, or weekends to produce a piece acceptable to an editor or client by the publication deadline. Those who prepare morning or weekend publications and broadcasts also may regularly work nights and weekends.

While many freelance writers enjoy running their own businesses and the advantages of working flexible hours, most routinely face the pressures of juggling multiple projects with competing demands and the continual need to find new work in order to earn a living. Deadline pressures and long, erratic work hours—often part of the daily routine in these jobs—may cause stress, fatigue, or burnout; use of computers for extended periods may cause some individuals to experience back pain, eyestrain, or fatigue.

Training, Other Qualifications, and Advancement

A college degree generally is required for a position as a writer or editor. Although some employers look for a broad liberal arts background, most prefer to hire people with degrees in communications, journalism, or English. For those who specialize in a particular area, such as fashion, business, or law, additional background in the chosen field is expected. Knowledge of a second language is helpful for some positions.

Increasingly, technical writing requires a degree in, or some knowledge about, a specialized field—for example, engineering, business, or one of the sciences. In many cases, people with good writing skills can acquire specialized knowledge on the job. Some transfer from jobs as technicians, scientists, or engineers. Others begin as research assistants or as trainees in a technical information department, develop technical communication skills, and then assume writing duties.

Writers and editors must be able to express ideas clearly and logically and should love to write. Creativity, curiosity, a broad range of knowledge, self-motivation, and perseverance also are valuable.

Writers and editors must demonstrate good judgment and a strong sense of ethics in deciding what material to publish. Editors also need tact and the ability to guide and encourage others in their work.

For some jobs, the ability to concentrate amid confusion and to work under pressure is essential. Familiarity with electronic publishing, graphics, and video production equipment increasingly is needed. Use of electronic and wireless communications equipment to send e-mail, transmit work, and review copy often is necessary. Online newspapers and magazines require knowledge of computer software used to combine online text with graphics, audio, video, and animation.

High school and college newspapers, literary magazines, community newspapers, and radio and television stations all provide valuable, but sometimes unpaid, practical writing experience. Many magazines, newspapers, and broadcast stations have internships for students. Interns write short pieces, conduct research and interviews, and learn about the publishing or broadcasting business.

In small firms, beginning writers and editors hired as assistants may actually begin writing or editing material right away. Opportunities for advancement can be limited, however. Many writers look for work on a short-term, project-by-project basis. Many small or not-for-profit organizations either do not have enough regular work or cannot afford to employ writers on a full-time basis. However, they routinely contract out work to freelance writers.

In larger businesses, jobs usually are more formally structured. Beginners generally do research, fact checking, or copy editing. Advancement to full-scale writing or editing assignments may occur more slowly for newer writers and editors in larger organizations than for employees of smaller companies. Advancement often is more predictable, though, coming with the assignment of more important articles.

Advancement for freelancers often means working on larger, more complex projects for more money. Building a reputation and establishing a track record for meeting deadlines also makes it easier to get future assignments, as does instituting long-term freelance relationships with the same publications.

The growing popularity of blogs could allow some writers to get their work read; a few well-written blogs may garner some recognition for the author and may lead to a few paid pieces in other print or electronic publications. However, most bloggers do not earn much money writing their blogs.

Employment

Writers and editors held about 320,000 jobs in 2004. More than one-third were self-employed. Writers and authors held about 142,000 jobs; editors, about 127,000 jobs; and technical writers, about 50,000 jobs. About one-half of the salaried jobs for writers and editors were in the information sector, which includes newspaper, periodical, book, and directory publishers; radio and television broadcasting; software publishers; motion picture and sound-recording industries; Internet service providers, Web search portals, and data- processing services; and Internet publishing and broadcasting. Substantial numbers also worked in advertising and related services, computer systems design and related services, and public and private educational services. Other salaried writers and editors worked in computer and electronic product manufacturing; government agencies; religious organizations; and business, professional, labor, political, and similar organizations.

Jobs with major book publishers, magazines, broadcasting companies, advertising agencies, and public relations firms are concentrated in New York, Chicago, Los Angeles, Boston, Philadelphia, and San Francisco; however, many writers work elsewhere and travel regularly to meet with personnel at the headquarters. Jobs with newspapers, business and professional journals, and technical and trade magazines are more widely dispersed throughout the country.

Thousands of other individuals work as freelance writers, earning some income from their articles, books, and, less commonly, television and movie scripts. Most support themselves with income derived from other sources.

Job Outlook

Employment of writers and editors is expected to grow about as fast as the average for all occupations through the year 2014. The outlook for most writing and editing jobs is expected to be competitive because many people with writing or journalism training are attracted to the occupation.

Employment of salaried writers and editors for newspapers, periodicals, book publishers, and nonprofit organizations is expected to increase as demand grows for these publications. Magazines and other periodicals increasingly are developing market niches, appealing to readers with special interests. Businesses and organizations are developing newsletters and websites, and more companies are experimenting with publishing materials directly on the Internet. Online publications and services are growing in number and sophistication, spurring the demand for writers and editors, especially those with Web experience. Advertising and public relations agencies, which also are growing, should be another source of new jobs.

Opportunities should be best for technical writers and those with training in a specialized field. Demand for technical writers and writers with expertise in areas such as law, medicine, or economics is expected to increase because of the continuing expansion of scientific and technical information and the need to communicate it to others. Legal, scientific, and technological developments and discoveries generate demand for people to interpret technical information for a more general audience. Rapid growth and change in the high-technology and electronics industries result in a greater need for people to write users' guides, instruction manuals, and training materials. This work requires people who not only are technically skilled as writers, but also are familiar with the subject area.

In addition to job openings created by employment growth, some openings will arise as experienced workers retire, transfer to other occupations, or leave the labor force. Replacement needs are relatively high in this occupation; many freelancers leave because they cannot earn enough money.

Earnings

Median annual earnings for salaried writers and authors were $44,350 in May 2004. The middle 50 percent earned between

$31,720 and $62,930. The lowest 10 percent earned less than $23,330, and the highest 10 percent earned more than $91,260. Median annual earnings were $54,410 in advertising and related services and $37,010 in newspaper, periodical, book, and directory publishers.

Median annual earnings for salaried editors were $43,890 in May 2004. The middle 50 percent earned between $33,130 and $58,850. The lowest 10 percent earned less than $25,780, and the highest 10 percent earned more than $80,020. Median annual earnings of those working for newspaper, periodical, book, and directory publishers were $43,620.

Median annual earnings for salaried technical writers were $53,490 in May 2004. The middle 50 percent earned between $41,440 and $68,980. The lowest 10 percent earned less than $32,490, and the highest 10 percent earned more than $86,780. Median annual earnings in computer systems design and related services were $54,710.

According to the Society for Technical Communication, the median annual salary for entry level technical writers was $42,500 in 2004. The median annual salary for midlevel nonsupervisory technical writers was $51,500, and for senior nonsupervisory technical writers, $66,000.

Related Occupations

Writers and editors communicate ideas and information. Other communications occupations include announcers; interpreters and translators; news analysts, reporters, and correspondents; and public relations specialists.

Sources of Additional Information

For information on careers in technical writing, contact:

- Society for Technical Communication, Inc., 901 N. Stuart St., Suite 904, Arlington, VA 22203. Internet: http://www.stc.org

QUICK JOB SEARCH

Seven Steps to Getting a Good Job in Less Time

The Complete Text of a Results-Oriented Minibook

Millions of job seekers have found better jobs faster using the techniques in the *Quick Job Search.* So can you! The *Quick Job Search* covers the essential steps proven to cut job search time in half and is used widely by job search programs throughout North America. Topics include how to identify your key skills, define your ideal job, write a great resume quickly, use the most effective job search methods, get more interviews, and much more.

If you completed "Using the Job-Match Grid to Choose a Career" earlier in this book, the activities in this section will complement those efforts by helping you to define other skills you possess, focus your resume, and get a job quickly.

While it is a section in this book, the *Quick Job Search* is available from JIST Publishing as a separate booklet and in an expanded form as *Seven-Step Job Search.*

Quick Job Search Is Short, But It May Be All You Need

While *Quick Job Search* is short, it covers the basics on how to explore career options and conduct an effective job search. While these topics can seem complex, I have found some simple truths about looking for a job:

- If you are going to work, you might as well look for what you really want to do and are good at.
- If you are looking for a job, you might as well use techniques that will reduce the time it takes to find one—and that help you get a better job than you might otherwise.

That's what I emphasize in *Quick Job Search.*

Trust Me—Do the Worksheets. I know you will resist completing the worksheets. But trust me. They are worth your time. Doing them will give you a better sense of what you are good at, what you want to do, and how to go about getting it. You will also most likely get more interviews and present yourself better. Is this worth giving up a night of TV? Yes, I think so.

Once you finish this minibook and its activities, you will have spent more time planning your career than most people do. And you will know more than the average job seeker about finding a job.

Why Such a Short Book? I've taught job seeking skills for many years, and I've written longer and more detailed books than this one. Yet I have often been asked to tell someone, in a few minutes or hours, the most important things they should do in their career planning or job search. Instructors and counselors also ask the same question because they have only a short time to spend with folks they're trying to help. I've given this a lot of thought, and the seven topics in this book are the ones I think are most important to know.

This minibook is short enough to scan in a morning and conduct a more effective job search that afternoon. Granted, doing all the activities would take more time, but they will prepare you far better than scanning the book. Of course, you can learn more about all the topics it covers, but this minibook, *Quick Job Search,* may be all you need.

You can't just read about getting a job. The best way to get a job is to go out and get interviews! And the best way to get interviews is to make a job out of getting a job.

After many years of experience, I have identified just seven basic things you need to do that make a big difference in your job search. Each will be covered and expanded on in this minibook.

1. Identify your key skills.
2. Define your ideal job.
3. Learn the two most effective job search methods.
4. Create a superior resume and a portfolio.
5. Organize your time to get two interviews a day.
6. Dramatically improve your interviewing skills.
7. Follow up on all leads.

So, without further delay, let's get started!

STEP 1: Identify Your Key Skills and Develop a "Skills Language" to Describe Yourself

One survey of employers found that about 90 percent of the people they interviewed might have the required job skills, but they could not describe those skills and thereby prove that they could do the job they sought. They could not answer the basic question "Why should I hire you?"

Knowing and describing your skills is essential to doing well in interviews. This same knowledge is important to help you decide what type of job you will enjoy and do well. For these reasons, I consider identifying your skills a necessary part of a successful career plan or job search.

The Three Types of Skills

Most people think of their skills as job-related skills, such as using a computer. But we all have other types of skills that are important for success on a job—and that are important to employers. The following triangle arranges skills in three groups, and I think that this is a very useful way to consider skills.

Let's look at these three types of skills—self-management, transferable, and job-related—and identify those that are most important to you.

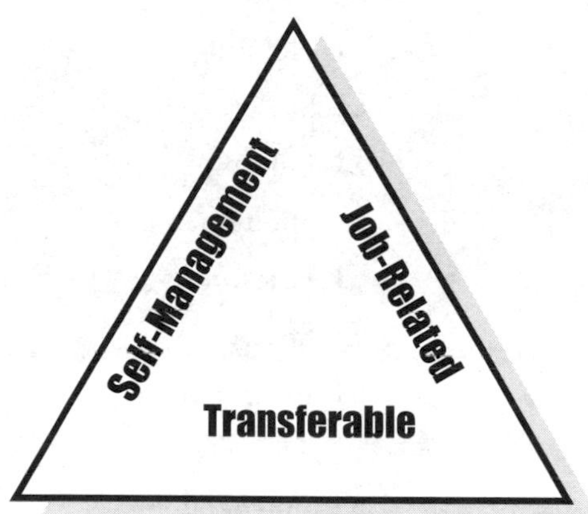

Quip

We all have thousands of skills. Consider the many skills required to do even a simple thing like ride a bike or bake a cake. But, of all the skills you have, employers want to know those key skills you have for the job they need done. You must clearly identify these key skills and then emphasize them in interviews.

Self-Management Skills

To begin identifying your skills, answer the question in the box that follows.

Your Good Worker Traits

Write down three things about yourself that you think make you a good worker. Think about what an employer might like about you or the way you work.

1. ______________________________
2. ______________________________
3. ______________________________

You just wrote down the most important things for an employer to know about you! They describe your basic personality and your ability to adapt to new environments. They are some of the most important skills to emphasize in interviews, yet most job seekers don't realize their importance—and don't mention them.

Review the Self-Management Skills Checklist that follows and put a check mark beside any skills you have. The key self-management skills listed first cover abilities that employers find particularly important. If one or more of the key self-management skills apply to you, mentioning them in interviews can help you greatly.

Self-Management Skills Checklist

Following are the key self-management skills that employers value highly. Place a check by those you already have.

- ❑ Have good attendance
- ❑ Get work done on time
- ❑ Am honest
- ❑ Get along with supervisor
- ❑ Arrive on time
- ❑ Get along with co-workers
- ❑ Follow instructions
- ❑ Am hard working/productive

(continued)

(continued)

Place a check by other self-management skills you have.

- ❑ Ambitious
- ❑ Mature
- ❑ Assertive
- ❑ Methodical
- ❑ Capable
- ❑ Modest
- ❑ Cheerful
- ❑ Motivated
- ❑ Competent
- ❑ Natural
- ❑ Conscientious
- ❑ Open-minded
- ❑ Creative
- ❑ Optimistic
- ❑ Culturally tolerant
- ❑ Original
- ❑ Decisive
- ❑ Patient
- ❑ Dependable
- ❑ Persistent
- ❑ Discreet
- ❑ Physically strong
- ❑ Eager
- ❑ Practical
- ❑ Efficient
- ❑ Problem-solving
- ❑ Energetic
- ❑ Proud of work
- ❑ Enthusiastic
- ❑ Quick to learn
- ❑ Expressive
- ❑ Reliable
- ❑ Flexible
- ❑ Resourceful
- ❑ Formal
- ❑ Responsible
- ❑ Friendly
- ❑ Results-oriented
- ❑ Good-natured
- ❑ Self-confident
- ❑ Helpful
- ❑ Sincere
- ❑ Humble
- ❑ Spontaneous
- ❑ Humorous
- ❑ Steady
- ❑ Imaginative
- ❑ Tactful
- ❑ Independent
- ❑ Team player
- ❑ Industrious
- ❑ Tenacious
- ❑ Informal
- ❑ Thrifty
- ❑ Intelligent
- ❑ Trustworthy
- ❑ Intuitive
- ❑ Versatile
- ❑ Loyal
- ❑ Well-organized

List the other self-management skills you have that have not been mentioned but you think are important to include.

____

____

____

After you finish checking the list, circle the five skills you feel are most important and write them in the box that follows.

Your Top Five Self-Management Skills

1. ______________________________
2. ______________________________
3. ______________________________

4. ______________________________

5. ______________________________

When thinking about their skills, some people find it helpful to complete the Essential Job Search Data Worksheet that starts on page 338. It organizes skills and accomplishments from previous jobs and other life experiences. Take a look at it and decide whether to complete it now or later.

Transferable Skills

We all have skills that can transfer from one job or career to another. For example, the ability to organize events could be used in a variety of jobs and may be essential for success in certain occupations. Your mission is to find a job that requires the skills you have and enjoy using.

It's not bragging if it's true. Using your new skills language may be uncomfortable at first, but employers need to learn about your skills. So practice saying positive things about the skills you have for the job. If you don't, who will?

Transferable Skills Checklist

Following are the key transferable skills that employers value highly. Place a check by those you already have. You may have used them in a previous job or in some non-work setting.

- ❑ Managing money/budgets
- ❑ Speaking in public
- ❑ Managing people
- ❑ Organizing/managing projects
- ❑ Meeting deadlines
- ❑ Using computers
- ❑ Meeting the public
- ❑ Writing well
- ❑ Negotiating

Place a check by the skills you have for working with data.

- ❑ Analyzing data
- ❑ Counting/taking inventory
- ❑ Auditing/checking for accuracy
- ❑ Investigating
- ❑ Budgeting
- ❑ Keeping financial records
- ❑ Calculating/computing
- ❑ Observing/inspecting
- ❑ Classifying data
- ❑ Paying attention to details
- ❑ Comparing/evaluating
- ❑ Researching/locating information
- ❑ Compiling/recording facts
- ❑ Synthesizing

Place a check by the skills you have for working with people.

- ❑ Administering
- ❑ Counseling people
- ❑ Being diplomatic
- ❑ Demonstrating
- ❑ Being kind
- ❑ Having insight
- ❑ Being outgoing
- ❑ Helping others
- ❑ Being patient
- ❑ Instructing others
- ❑ Being pleasant
- ❑ Interviewing people

(continued)

(continued)

- ❑ Being sensitive
- ❑ Listening
- ❑ Being sociable
- ❑ Persuading
- ❑ Being tactful
- ❑ Supervising
- ❑ Being tough
- ❑ Tolerating
- ❑ Caring for others
- ❑ Trusting
- ❑ Coaching
- ❑ Understanding
- ❑ Confronting others

Place a check by your skills in working with words and ideas.

- ❑ Being articulate
- ❑ Creating new ideas
- ❑ Being ingenious
- ❑ Designing
- ❑ Being inventive
- ❑ Editing
- ❑ Being logical
- ❑ Remembering information
- ❑ Communicating verbally
- ❑ Speaking publicly
- ❑ Corresponding with others
- ❑ Writing clearly

Place a check by the leadership skills you have.

- ❑ Being competitive
- ❑ Mediating problems
- ❑ Delegating
- ❑ Motivating people
- ❑ Directing others
- ❑ Motivating yourself
- ❑ Getting results
- ❑ Negotiating agreements
- ❑ Having self-confidence
- ❑ Planning events
- ❑ Influencing others
- ❑ Running meetings
- ❑ Making decisions
- ❑ Solving problems
- ❑ Making explanations
- ❑ Taking risks

Place a check by your creative or artistic skills.

- ❑ Appreciating music
- ❑ Expressing yourself
- ❑ Being artistic
- ❑ Performing/acting
- ❑ Dancing
- ❑ Playing instruments
- ❑ Drawing
- ❑ Presenting artistic ideas

Place a check by your skills for working with things.

- ❑ Assembling things
- ❑ Driving or operating vehicles
- ❑ Building things
- ❑ Operating tools/machines
- ❑ Constructing or repairing things

Add the other transferable skills you have that have not been mentioned but you think are important to include.

____

____

____

When you are finished, circle the five transferable skills you feel are most important for you to use in your next job and list them below.

YOUR TOP FIVE TRANSFERABLE SKILLS

1. ______________________________
2. ______________________________
3. ______________________________
4. ______________________________
5. ______________________________

Job-Related Skills

Job content or job-related skills are those you need to do a particular occupation. A carpenter, for example, needs to know how to use various tools. Before you select job-related skills to emphasize, you must first have a clear idea of the jobs you want. So let's put off developing your job-related skills list until you have defined the job you want—the topic that is covered next.

STEP 2: Define Your Ideal Job

Too many people look for a job without clearly knowing what they are looking for. Before you go out seeking a job, I suggest that you first define exactly what you want—not *just a job* but *the job.*

Most people think that a job objective is the same as a job title, but it isn't. You need to consider other elements of what makes a job satisfying for you. Then, later, you can decide what that job is called and what industry it might be in. You can compromise on what you consider your ideal job later if you need to.

EIGHT FACTORS TO CONSIDER IN DEFINING YOUR IDEAL JOB

As you try to define your ideal job, consider the following eight important questions. When you know what you want, your task then becomes finding a position that is as close to your ideal job as possible.

1. **What skills do you want to use?** From the skills lists in Step 1, select the top five skills that you enjoy using and most want to use in your next job.

   a.______________________________

   b.______________________________

   c.______________________________

   d.______________________________

   e.______________________________

(continued)

(continued)

2. **What type of special knowledge do you have?** Perhaps you know how to fix radios, keep accounting records, or cook food. Write down the things you know from schooling, training, hobbies, family experiences, and other sources. One or more of these knowledge areas could make you a very special applicant in the right setting.____________________

3. **With what types of people do you prefer to work?** Do you like to work with competitive people, or do you prefer hardworking folks, creative personalities, relaxed people, or some other types?____________________

4. **What type of work environment do you prefer?** Do you want to work inside, outside, in a quiet place, in a busy place, or in a clean or messy place; or do you want to have a window with a nice view? List the types of environments you prefer.____________________

5. **Where do you want your next job to be located—in what city or region?** If you are open to living and working anywhere, what would your ideal community be like? Near a bus line? Close to a childcare center?____________________

6. **What benefits or income do you hope to have in your next job?** Many people will take less money or fewer benefits if they like a job in other ways—or if they need a job quickly to survive. Think about the minimum you would take as well as what you would eventually like to earn. Your next job will probably pay somewhere in between.____________________

7. **How much and what types of responsibility are you willing to accept?** Usually, the more money you want to make, the more responsibility you must accept. Do you want to work by yourself, be part of a group, or be in charge? If you want to be in charge, how many people are you willing to supervise?

8. **What values are important or have meaning to you?** Do you have important values you would prefer to include in considering the work you do? For example, some people want to work to help others, clean up the environment, build structures, make machines work, gain power or prestige, or care for animals or plants. Think about what is important to you and how you might include this in your next job.____________________

Is It Possible to Find Your Ideal Job?

Can you find a job that meets all the criteria you just defined? Perhaps. Some people do. The harder you look, the more likely you are to find it. But you will likely need to compromise, so it is useful to know what is *most* important to include in your next job. Go back over your responses to the eight factors and mark a few of those that you would most like to have or include in your ideal job.

FACTORS I WANT IN MY IDEAL JOB

Write a brief description of your ideal job. Don't worry about a job title, or whether you have the experience, or other practical matters yet.____________________

How Can You Explore Specific Job Titles and Industries?

You might find your ideal job in an occupation you haven't considered yet. And, even if you are sure of the occupation you want, it may be in an industry that is unfamiliar to you. This combination of occupation and industry forms the basis for your job search, and you should consider a variety of options.

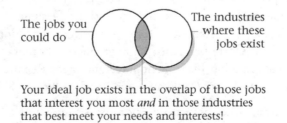

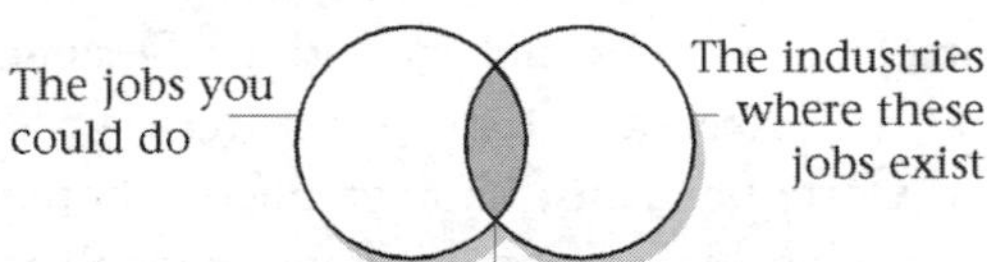

Your ideal job exists in the overlap of those jobs that interest you most *and* in those industries that best meet your needs and interests!

There are thousands of job titles, and many jobs are highly specialized, employing just a few people. While one of these more specialized jobs may be just what you want, most work falls within more general job titles that employ large numbers of people.

Review the Top Jobs in the Workforce

The list of job titles that follows was based on a list developed by the U.S. Department of Labor. It contains approximately 270 major jobs that employ about 90 percent of the U.S. workforce.

The job titles are organized within 16 major groupings called interest areas, presented in bold type. These groupings will help you quickly identify fields most likely to interest you. Job titles are presented in regular type within these groupings.

Begin with the interest areas that appeal to you most, and underline any job title that interests you. (Don't worry for now about whether you have the experience or credentials to do these jobs.) Then quickly review the remaining interest areas, underlining any job titles there that interest you. Note that some job titles are listed more than once because they fit into more than one interest area. When you have gone through all 16 interest areas, go back and circle the 5 to 10 job titles that interest you most. These are the ones you will want to research in more detail.

1. **Agriculture and Natural Resources:** Agricultural and Food Scientists; Agricultural Workers; Biological Scientists; Conservation Scientists and Foresters; Engineers; Farmers, Ranchers, and Agricultural Managers; Fishers and Fishing Vessel Operators; Forest, Conservation, and Logging Workers; Grounds Maintenance Workers; Material Moving Occupations; Pest Control Workers; Purchasing Managers, Buyers, and Purchasing Agents; Science Technicians.

2. **Architecture and Construction:** Architects, except Landscape and Naval; Boilermakers; Brickmasons, Blockmasons, and Stonemasons; Carpenters; Carpet, Floor, and Tile Installers and Finishers; Cement Masons, Concrete Finishers, Segmental Pavers, and Terrazzo Workers; Construction and Building Inspectors; Construction Equipment Operators; Construction Laborers; Construction Managers; Drafters; Drywall Installers, Ceiling Tile Installers, and Tapers; Electrical and Electronics Installers and Repairers; Electricians; Elevator Installers and Repairers; Glaziers; Hazardous Materials Removal Workers; Heating, Air-Conditioning, and Refrigeration Mechanics and Installers; Home Appliance Repairers; Insulation Workers; Landscape Architects; Line Installers and Repairers; Maintenance and Repair Workers, General; Material Moving Occupations; Painters and Paperhangers; Pipelayers, Plumbers, Pipefitters, and Steamfitters; Plasterers and Stucco Masons; Radio and Telecommunications Equipment Installers and Repairers; Roofers; Sheet Metal Workers; Structural and Reinforcing Iron and Metal Workers; Surveyors, Cartographers, Photogrammetrists, and Surveying Technicians.

3. **Arts and Communication:** Actors, Producers, and Directors; Advertising, Marketing, Promotions, Public Relations, and Sales Managers; Air Traffic Controllers; Announcers; Artists and Related Workers; Barbers, Cosmetologists, and Other Personal Appearance Workers; Broadcast and Sound Engineering Technicians and Radio Operators; Commercial and Industrial Designers; Communications Equipment Operators; Dancers and Choreographers; Dispatchers; Fashion Designers; Floral Designers; Graphic Designers; Interior Designers; Interpreters and Translators; Musicians, Singers, and Related Workers; News Analysts, Reporters, and Correspondents; Photographers; Photographic Process Workers and Processing Machine Operators; Precision Instrument and Equipment Repairers; Public Relations Specialists; Television, Video, and Motion Picture Camera Operators and Editors; Writers and Editors.

4. **Business and Administration:** Accountants and Auditors; Administrative Services Managers; Billing and Posting Clerks and Machine Operators; Bookkeeping, Accounting, and Auditing Clerks; Brokerage Clerks; Budget Analysts; Building Cleaning Workers; Communications Equipment Operators; Data Entry and Information Processing Workers; Engineering Technicians; File Clerks; Human Resources Assistants, except Payroll and Timekeeping; Human Resources, Training, and Labor Relations Managers

and Specialists; Management Analysts; Meeting and Convention Planners; Meter Readers, Utilities; Office and Administrative Support Worker Supervisors and Managers; Office Clerks, General; Operations Research Analysts; Payroll and Timekeeping Clerks; Postal Service Workers; Procurement Clerks; Production, Planning, and Expediting Clerks; Secretaries and Administrative Assistants; Shipping, Receiving, and Traffic Clerks; Stock Clerks and Order Fillers; Top Executives; Weighers, Measurers, Checkers, and Samplers, Recordkeeping.

5. **Education and Training:** Archivists, Curators, and Museum Technicians; Counselors; Education Administrators; Fitness Workers; Instructional Coordinators; Librarians; Library Assistants, Clerical; Library Technicians; Teacher Assistants; Teachers—Adult Literacy and Remedial Education; Teachers—Postsecondary; Teachers—Preschool, Kindergarten, Elementary, Middle, and Secondary; Teachers—Self-Enrichment Education; Teachers—Special Education.

6. **Finance and Insurance:** Advertising Sales Agents; Appraisers and Assessors of Real Estate; Bill and Account Collectors; Claims Adjusters, Appraisers, Examiners, and Investigators; Cost Estimators; Credit Authorizers, Checkers, and Clerks; Financial Analysts and Personal Financial Advisors; Financial Managers; Insurance Sales Agents; Insurance Underwriters; Interviewers; Loan Officers; Market and Survey Researchers; Securities, Commodities, and Financial Services Sales Agents; Tellers.

7. **Government and Public Administration:** Agricultural Workers; Court Reporters; Fire Fighting Occupations; Inspectors, Testers, Sorters, Samplers, and Weighers; Occupational Health and Safety Specialists and Technicians; Police and Detectives; Science Technicians; Tax Examiners, Collectors, and Revenue Agents; Top Executives; Urban and Regional Planners.

8. **Health Science:** Agricultural Workers; Animal Care and Service Workers; Athletic Trainers; Audiologists; Cardiovascular Technologists and Technicians; Chiropractors; Clinical Laboratory Technologists and Technicians; Dental Assistants; Dental Hygienists; Dentists; Diagnostic Medical Sonographers; Dietitians and Nutritionists; Licensed Practical and Licensed Vocational Nurses; Massage Therapists; Medical and Health Services Managers; Medical Assistants; Medical Records and Health Information Technicians; Medical Transcriptionists; Nuclear Medicine Technologists; Nursing, Psychiatric, and Home Health Aides; Occupational Therapist Assistants and Aides; Occupational Therapists; Opticians, Dispensing; Optometrists; Pharmacists; Pharmacy Aides; Pharmacy Technicians; Physical Therapist Assistants and Aides; Physical Therapists; Physician Assistants; Physicians and Surgeons; Podiatrists; Radiation Therapists; Radiologic Technologists and Technicians; Recreational Therapists; Registered Nurses; Respiratory Therapists; Science Technicians; Speech-Language Pathologists; Surgical Technologists; Veterinarians; Veterinary Technologists and Technicians.

9. **Hospitality, Tourism, and Recreation:** Athletes, Coaches, Umpires, and Related Workers; Barbers, Cosmetologists, and Other Personal Appearance Workers; Building Cleaning Workers; Chefs, Cooks, and Food Preparation Workers; Flight Attendants; Food and Beverage Serving and Related Workers; Food Processing Occupations; Food Service Managers; Gaming Services Occupations; Hotel, Motel, and Resort Desk Clerks; Lodging Managers; Recreation Workers; Reservation and Transportation Ticket Agents and Travel Clerks; Travel Agents.

10. **Human Service:** Child Care Workers; Counselors; Interviewers; Personal and Home Care Aides; Probation Officers and Correctional Treatment Specialists; Psychologists; Social and Human Service Assistants; Social Workers.

(continued)

(continued)

11. **Information Technology:** Coin, Vending, and Amusement Machine Servicers and Repairers; Computer and Information Systems Managers; Computer Operators; Computer Programmers; Computer Scientists and Database Administrators; Computer Software Engineers; Computer Support Specialists and Systems Administrators; Computer Systems Analysts; Computer, Automated Teller, and Office Machine Repairers.
12. **Law and Public Safety:** Correctional Officers; Emergency Medical Technicians and Paramedics; Fire Fighting Occupations; Job Opportunities in the Armed Forces; Judges, Magistrates, and Other Judicial Workers; Lawyers; Paralegals and Legal Assistants; Police and Detectives; Private Detectives and Investigators; Science Technicians; Security Guards and Gaming Surveillance Officers.
13. **Manufacturing:** Agricultural Workers; Aircraft and Avionics Equipment Mechanics and Service Technicians; Assemblers and Fabricators; Automotive Body and Related Repairers; Automotive Service Technicians and Mechanics; Bookbinders and Bindery Workers; Computer Control Programmers and Operators; Desktop Publishers; Diesel Service Technicians and Mechanics; Electrical and Electronics Installers and Repairers; Electronic Home Entertainment Equipment Installers and Repairers; Food Processing Occupations; Heavy Vehicle and Mobile Equipment Service Technicians and Mechanics; Home Appliance Repairers; Industrial Machinery Mechanics and Maintenance Workers; Industrial Production Managers; Inspectors, Testers, Sorters, Samplers, and Weighers; Jewelers and Precious Stone and Metal Workers; Machine Setters, Operators, and Tenders—Metal and Plastic; Machinists; Material Moving Occupations; Medical, Dental, and Ophthalmic Laboratory Technicians; Millwrights; Painting and Coating Workers, except Construction and Maintenance; Photographic Process Workers and Processing Machine Operators; Power Plant Operators, Distributors, and Dispatchers; Precision Instrument and Equipment Repairers; Prepress Technicians and Workers; Printing Machine Operators; Radio and Telecommunications Equipment Installers and Repairers; Semiconductor Processors; Small Engine Mechanics; Stationary Engineers and Boiler Operators; Textile, Apparel, and Furnishings Occupations; Tool and Die Makers; Water and Liquid Waste Treatment Plant and System Operators; Water Transportation Occupations; Welding, Soldering, and Brazing Workers; Woodworkers.
14. **Retail and Wholesale Sales and Service:** Advertising, Marketing, Promotions, Public Relations, and Sales Managers; Cashiers; Counter and Rental Clerks; Customer Service Representatives; Demonstrators, Product Promoters, and Models; Funeral Directors; Order Clerks; Property, Real Estate, and Community Association Managers; Purchasing Managers, Buyers, and Purchasing Agents; Real Estate Brokers and Sales Agents; Receptionists and Information Clerks; Retail Salespersons; Sales Engineers; Sales Representatives, Wholesale and Manufacturing; Sales Worker Supervisors.
15. **Scientific Research, Engineering, and Mathematics:** Actuaries; Atmospheric Scientists; Biological Scientists; Chemists and Materials Scientists; Drafters; Economists; Engineering and Natural Sciences Managers; Engineering Technicians; Engineers; Environmental Scientists and Hydrologists; Geoscientists; Mathematicians; Medical Scientists; Photographers; Physicists and Astronomers; Psychologists; Science Technicians; Social Scientists, Other; Statisticians; Surveyors, Cartographers, Photogrammetrists, and Surveying Technicians.
16. **Transportation, Distribution, and Logistics:** Aircraft Pilots and Flight Engineers; Bus Drivers; Cargo and Freight Agents; Couriers and Messengers; Material Moving Occupations; Postal Service Workers; Rail Transportation Occupations; Taxi Drivers and Chauffeurs; Truck Drivers and Driver/Sales Workers; Water Transportation Occupations.

You can find thorough descriptions for 100 job titles in the preceding list in this book.

You can find descriptions for all of these jobs in the Occupational Outlook Handbook, *published by the U.S. Department of Labor and also available from JIST.*

The New Guide for Occupational Exploration, *Fourth Edition, also provides more information on the interest areas used in this list. This book is published by JIST Works and describes about 1,000 major jobs, arranged within groupings of related jobs.*

Finally, "A Short List of Additional Resources" at the end of this minibook gives you resources for more job information.

Consider Major Industries

What industry you work in is often as important as the career field. For example, some industries pay much better than others, and others may simply be more interesting to you. A book titled *40 Best Fields for Your Career* contains very helpful reviews for each of the major industries mentioned in the following list. Many libraries and bookstores carry this book, as well as the U.S. Department of Labor's *Career Guide to Industries,* or you can find the information on the Internet at www.CareerOINK.com or at www.bls.gov/oco/cg/.

Underline industries that interest you, and then learn more about the opportunities they present. Jobs in most careers are available in a variety of industries, so consider what industries fit you best and focus your job search in these.

Agriculture and natural resources: Agriculture, forestry, and fishing; mining; oil and gas extraction.

Manufacturing, construction, and utilities: Aerospace product and parts manufacturing; chemical manufacturing, except drugs; computer and electronic product manufacturing; construction; food manufacturing; machinery manufacturing; motor vehicle and parts manufacturing; pharmaceutical and medicine manufacturing; printing; steel manufacturing; textile, textile products, and apparel manufacturing; utilities.

Trade: Automobile dealers, clothing, accessories, and general merchandise stores; grocery stores; wholesale trade.

Transportation: Air transportation; truck transportation and warehousing.

Information: Broadcasting; Internet service providers, Web search portals, and data processing services; motion picture and video industries; publishing, except software; software publishing; telecommunications.

Financial activities: Banking; insurance; securities, commodities, and other investments.

Professional and business services: Advertising and public relations; computer systems design and related services; employment services; management, scientific, and technical consulting services; scientific research and development services.

Education, health care, and social services: Child daycare services; educational services; health care; social assistance, except child care.

(continued)

(continued)

Leisure and hospitality: Art, entertainment, and recreation; food services and drinking places; hotels and other accommodations.

Government and advocacy, grantmaking, and civic organizations: Advocacy, grantmaking, and civic organizations; federal government; state and local government, except education and health care.

The Top Jobs and Industries That Interest You

Go back over the lists of job titles and industries. For numbers 1 and 2 below, list the jobs that interest you most. Then select the industries that interest you most, and list them below in number 3. These are the jobs and industries you should research most carefully. Your ideal job is likely to be found in some combination of these jobs and industries, or in more specialized but related jobs and industries.

1. The five job titles that interest you most

   a.______________________________

   b.______________________________

   c.______________________________

   d.______________________________

   e.______________________________

2. The five next most interesting job titles

   a.______________________________

   b.______________________________

   c.______________________________

   d.______________________________

   e.______________________________

3. The industries that interest you most

   a.______________________________

   b.______________________________

   c.______________________________

   d.______________________________

   e.______________________________

Is Self-Employment or Starting a Business an Option?

More than one in 10 workers are self-employed or own their own businesses. If these options interest you, consider them as well. Talk to people in similar roles to gather information and look for books and Web sites that provide information on options that are similar to those that interest you. A book titled *Best Jobs for the 21st*

Century (JIST Works) includes lists and descriptions of jobs with high percentages of self-employed. Also, the Small Business Administration's Web site at www.sba.gov is a good source of basic information on related topics.

SELF-EMPLOYMENT AREAS OF INTEREST

In the following space, write your current interest in self-employment or starting a business in an area related to your general job objective.

____

____

____

Can You Identify Your Job-Related Skills Now That You've Defined Your Ideal Job?

Earlier, I suggested that you should first define the job you want and then identify key job-related skills you have that support your ability to do that job. These are the job-related skills to emphasize in interviews.

So, now that you have determined your ideal job, you can pinpoint the job-related skills it requires. If you haven't done so, complete the Essential Job Search Data Worksheet on pages 338–342. Completing it will give you specific skills and accomplishments to highlight.

Yes, completing that worksheet requires time, but doing so will help you clearly define key skills to emphasize in interviews—when what you say matters so much. People who complete that worksheet will do better in their interviews than those who don't. After you complete the Essential Job Search Data Worksheet, you are ready to list your top five job-related skills.

Quip

It's a hassle, but... Completing the Essential Job Search Data Worksheet that starts on page 338 will help you define what you are good at—and remember examples of when you did things well. This information will help you define your ideal job and will be of great value in interviews. Look at the worksheet now, and promise to do it later today.

YOUR TOP FIVE JOB-RELATED SKILLS

List the top five job-related skills you think are most important. Include the job-related skills you have that you would most like to use in your next job.

1. ____
2. ____
3. ____
4. ____
5. ____

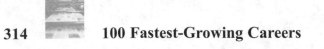

STEP 3: Use the Most Effective Methods to Find a Job in Less Time

Employer surveys have found that most employers don't advertise their job openings. They most often hire people they already know, people who find out about the jobs through word of mouth, or people who happen to be in the right place at the right time. Although luck plays a part in finding job openings, you can use the tips in this step to increase your luck.

Let's look at the job search methods that people use. The U.S. Department of Labor conducts a regular survey of unemployed people actively looking for work. Following are the results of their most recent findings.

Percentage of Unemployed People Who Use Various Job Search Methods

- **Contacted employer directly: 62.7%**
- **Sent out resumes/filled out applications: 54.5%**
- **Contacted public employment agency: 19.9%**
- **Placed or answered help wanted ads: 16.4%**
- **Contacted friends or relatives: 18%**
- **Contacted private employment agency: 7.7%**
- **Used other active search methods: 11.8%**

Source: U.S. Department of Labor, Current Population Survey

This step covers a number of job search methods. Most of the material is presented as information, with a few interactive activities. While each topic is short and reasonably interesting, taking a break now and then will help you absorb it all.

The survey shows that most people use more than one job search technique. For example, one person might read want ads, fill out applications, and ask friends for job leads. Others might send out resumes, contact everyone they know through previous jobs, and sign up at employment agencies.

But the survey covered only seven job search methods and asked only whether the job seeker did or did not use each method. The survey did not cover Internet job searches, nor did it ask whether a method actually worked in getting job offers.

Unfortunately, there hasn't been much conclusive recent research on the effectiveness of various job search methods. Most of what we know is based on older research and the observations of people who work directly with job seekers, such as professional resume writers and career counselors. I'll share what we do know about the effectiveness of job search methods in the content that follows.

Your job search objective. Almost everyone finds a job eventually, so your objective should be to find a good job in less time. The job search methods I emphasize in this minibook will help you do just that.

Get the Most Out of Less Effective Job Search Methods

The truth is that every job search method works for someone. But experience and research show that some methods are more effective than others are. Your task in the job search is to spend more of your time using more effective methods—and increase the effectiveness of all the methods you use.

So let's start by looking at some traditional job search methods and how you can increase their effectiveness. Only about one-third of all job seekers get their jobs using one of these methods, but you should still consider using them to some extent in your search. Later in the step, you'll read about the most effective methods, the ones you should devote the most time to in your search.

Newspaper and Internet Help Wanted Ads

Most jobs are never advertised, and only about 16 percent of all people get their jobs through the want ads. Everyone who reads the paper knows about these openings, so competition is fierce for the few advertised jobs.

The Internet also lists many job openings. But, as happens with newspaper ads, enormous numbers of people view these postings. Many job seekers make direct contact with employers via a company's Web site. Some people do get jobs through the bigger sites, so go ahead and apply. Just be sure to spend most of your time using more effective methods.

Filling Out Applications

Most employers require job seekers to complete an application form. Applications are designed to collect negative information, and employers use applications to screen people out. If, for example, your training or work history is not the best, you will often never get an interview, even if you can do the job.

Completing applications is a more effective approach for young and entry-level job seekers. The reason is that there is a shortage of workers for the relatively low-paying jobs typically sought by less-experienced job seekers. As a result, when trying to fill those positions, employers are more willing to accept a lack of experience or fewer job skills. Even so, you will get better results by filling out the application, if asked to do so, and then requesting an interview with the person in charge.

When you complete an application, make it neat and error-free, and do not include anything that could get you screened out. If necessary, leave a problem section blank. You can always explain situations in an interview.

Employment Agencies

There are three types of employment agencies. One is operated by the government and is free. The others, private employment agencies and temp agencies, are run as for-profit businesses and charge a fee to either you or an employer. Following are the advantages and disadvantages to using each.

The government employment service and One-Stop centers. Each state and province has a network of local offices to pay unemployment compensation, provide job leads, and offer other services—at no charge to you or to employers. The service's name varies by region. It may be called Job Service, Department of Labor, Unemployment Office, Workforce Development, or another name. Many of these offices are now also online, and some even require their users to sign up with a login and password to search for job leads and use other services on the Internet.

The Employment and Training Administration Web site at www.doleta.gov/uses gives you information on the programs provided by the government employment service, plus links to other useful sites. Another site, called America's Job Bank (www.ajb.dni.us), enables visitors to see all jobs that are listed with the government employment service and to search for jobs by region and other criteria. Canada's government Web site is at www.jobbank.gc.ca.

The government employment service lists only 5 to 10 percent of the available openings nationally, and only about 6 percent of all job seekers get their jobs there. Even so, visit your local office early in your job search. Find out whether you qualify for unemployment compensation and learn more about its services. Look into it—the price is right.

Private employment agencies. Private employment agencies are businesses that charge a fee either to you or to the employer who hires you. Fees can be from less than one month's pay to 15 percent or more of your annual salary. You will often see these agencies' ads in the help wanted section of the newspaper. Many have Web sites.

Be careful about using fee-based employment agencies. Recent research indicates that more people use and benefit from fee-based agencies than in the past. However, relatively few people who register with private agencies get a job through them.

If you use a private employment agency, ask for interviews with the employers who agree to pay the agency's fee. Do not sign an exclusive agreement or be pressured into accepting a job. Also, continue to actively look for your own leads. You can find these agencies in the phone book's yellow pages, and many state- or province-government Web sites offer lists of the private employment agencies in their states.

Temporary agencies. Temporary agencies offer jobs that last from several days to many months. They charge the employer an hourly fee, and then pay you a bit less and keep the difference. You pay no direct fee to the agency. Many private employment agencies now provide temporary jobs as well.

Temp agencies have grown rapidly for good reason. They provide employers with short-term help, and employers often use them to find people they might want to hire later. If the employers are dissatisfied, they can just ask the agency for different temp workers.

Temp agencies can help you survive between jobs and get experience in different work settings. Temp jobs provide a very good option while you look for long-term work, and you might get a job offer while working in a temp job. Holding a temporary job might even lead to a regular job with the same or a similar employer.

School and Other Employment Services

Only a small percentage of job seekers use school and other special employment services, probably because few job seekers have the service available to them. If you are a student or graduate, find out about any employment services at your school. Some schools provide free career counseling, resume-writing help, referrals to job openings, career interest tests, reference materials, Web sites listing job openings, and other services. Special career programs work with veterans, people with disabilities, welfare recipients, union members, professional groups, and many others. So check out these services and consider using them.

Mailing Versus Posting Resumes on the Internet

Many job search experts used to suggest that sending out lots of resumes was a great technique. That advice probably helped sell their resume books, but mailing resumes to people you do not know was never an effective approach. It very rarely works. A recent survey of 1,500 successful job seekers showed that only 2 percent found their positions through sending an unsolicited resume. The same is true for the Internet.

Although mailing your resume to strangers doesn't make much sense, posting it on the Internet might because

- It doesn't take much time.
- Many employers have the potential of finding your resume.
- You can post your resume on niche sites that attract only employers in your field.
- Your Internet resume is easily updated, allowing you to post your current accomplishments.
- You can easily link your resume to projects and Web sites that highlight your accomplishments.

Job searching on the Internet has its limitations, just like other methods. I'll cover resumes in more detail later and provide tips on using the Internet throughout this minibook.

Use the Two Job Search Methods That Work Best

The fact is that most jobs are not advertised, so how do *you* find them? The same way that about two-thirds of all job seekers do: networking with people you know (which I call making warm contacts) and directly contacting employers (which I call making cold contacts). Both of these methods are based on the job search rule you should know above all:

The Most Important Job Search Rule: Don't wait until the job opens before contacting the employer!

Employers fill most jobs with people they meet before a job is formally open. The trick is to meet people who can hire you before a job is formally available. Instead of asking whether the employer has any jobs open, I suggest that you say, *"I realize you may not have any openings now, but I would still like to talk to you about the possibility of future openings."*

Most Effective Job Search Method 1: Develop a Network of Contacts in Five Easy Stages

Studies find that 60 percent of all people located their jobs through a lead provided by a friend, a relative, or an acquaintance. That makes the people you know your number one source of job leads—more effective than all the traditional methods combined! Developing and using your contacts is called *networking,* and here's how it works:

1. **Make lists of people you know.** Make a thorough list of anyone you are friendly with. Then make a separate list of all your relatives. These two lists alone often add up to 25 to 100 people or more. Next, think of other groups of people that you have something in common with, such as former co-workers or classmates, members of your social or sports groups, members of your professional association, former employers, neighbors, and other groups. You might not know many of these people personally or well, but most will help you if you ask them.
2. **Contact each person in your list in a systematic way.** Obviously, some people will be more helpful than others, but any one of them might help you find a job lead.
3. **Present yourself well.** Begin with your friends and relatives. Call and tell them you are looking for a job and need their help. Be as clear as possible about the type of employment you want and the skills and qualifications you have. Look at the sample JIST Card and phone script later in this step for good presentation ideas.

Most jobs are never advertised because employers don't need to advertise or don't want to. Employers trust people referred to them by someone they know far more than they trust strangers. And most jobs are filled by referrals and people that the employer knows, eliminating the need to advertise. So, your job search must involve more than looking at ads.

4. **Ask your contacts for leads.** It is possible that your contacts will know of a job opening that interests you. If so, get the details and get right on it! More likely, however, they will not, so you should ask each person the Three Magic Networking Questions.

The Three Magic Networking Questions

- **Do you know of any openings for a person with my skills?**
  If the answer is "No" (which it usually is), then ask...
- **Do you know of someone else who might know of such an opening? If your contact does, get that name and ask for another one.**
  If he or she doesn't, ask...

(continued)

(continued)

- **Do you know of anyone who might know of someone else who might know of a job opening?**

  Another good way to ask this is "Do you know someone who knows lots of people?" *If all else fails, this will usually get you a name.*

5. **Contact these referrals and ask them the same questions.** From each person you contact, try to get two names of other people you might contact. Doing this consistently can extend your network of acquaintances by hundreds of people. Eventually, one of these people will hire you or refer you to someone who will!

If you are persistent in following these five steps, networking might be the only job search method you need. It works.

Dialing for dollars. The phone can get you more interviews per hour than any other job search tool. But it won't work unless you use it actively.

The phone book's yellow pages provide the most complete, up-to-date listing of potential job search targets you can get. It organizes them into categories that are very useful for job seekers. Just find a category that interests you, call each listing, and then contact employers listed there. All it takes is a 30-second phone call. Ask to speak with the hiring authority.

Most Effective Job Search Method 2: Contact Employers Directly

It takes more courage, but making direct contact with employers is a very effective job search technique. I call these cold contacts because people you don't know in advance will need to warm up to your inquiries. Two basic techniques for making cold contacts follow.

Use the yellow pages to find potential employers. Begin by looking at the index in the front of your phone book's yellow pages. For each entry, ask yourself, *"Would an organization of this kind need a person with my skills?"* If you answer *"Yes,"* then that organization or business type is a possible target. You can also rate "Yes" entries based on your interest, writing a "1" next to those that seem very interesting, a "2" next to those that you are not sure of, and a "3" next to those that aren't interesting at all.

Next, select a type of organization that got a "Yes" response and turn to that section of the yellow pages. Call each organization listed there and ask to speak to the person who is most likely to hire or supervise you—typically the manager of the business or a department head—not the personnel or human resources manager. A sample telephone script is included later in this section to give you ideas about what to say.

You can easily adapt this approach for use on the Internet by using sites such as www.yellowpages.com to get contacts anywhere in the world, or you can find phone and e-mail contacts on an employer's own Web site.

Drop in without an appointment. Another effective cold contact method is to just walk into a business or organization that interests you and ask to speak to the person in charge. Although dropping in is particularly effective in small businesses, it also works surprisingly well in larger ones. Remember to ask for an interview even if there are no openings now. If your timing is inconvenient, ask for a better time to come back for an interview.

Most Jobs Are with Small Employers

Businesses and organizations with fewer than 250 employees employ about 72 percent of all U.S. workers. Small organizations are also the source for around 75 percent of the new jobs created each year. They are simply too important to overlook in your job search! Many of them don't have personnel departments, which makes direct contacts even easier and more effective.

Create a Powerful Job Search Tool—the JIST Card®

Look at the sample cards that follow—they are JIST Cards, and they get results. Computer printed or even neatly written on a 3-by-5–inch card, JIST Cards include the essential information employers want to know.

A JIST Card Is a Mini Resume

JIST Cards have been used by thousands of job search programs and millions of people. Employers like their direct and timesaving format, and they have been proven as an effective tool to get job leads. Attach one to your resume. Give them to friends, relatives, and other contacts and ask them to pass them along to others who might know of an opening. Enclose them in thank-you notes after interviews. Leave one with employers as a business card. However you get them in circulation, you may be surprised at how well they work.

You can easily create JIST Cards on a computer and print them on card stock you can buy at any office supply store. Or have a few hundred printed cheaply by a local quick print shop. While they are often done as 3-by-5 cards, they can be printed in any size or format.

Sandy Nolan

Position: General Office/Clerical

Cell phone: (512) 232-9213

Email: snolan@aol.com

More than two years of work experience plus one year of training in office practices. Type 55 wpm, trained in word processing, post general ledger, have good interpersonal skills, and get along with most people. Can meet deadlines and handle pressure well.

Willing to work any hours.

Organized, honest, reliable, and hardworking.

Richard Straightarrow

Home: (602) 253-9678
Message: (602) 257-6643
E-mail: RSS@email.cmm

Objective: Electronics installation, maintenance, and sales

Four years of work experience plus a two-year A.S. degree in Electronics Engineering Technology. Managed a $360,000/year business while going to school full time, with grades in the top 25%. Familiar with all major electronic diagnostic and repair equipment. Hands-on experience with medical, consumer, communication, and industrial electronics equipment and applications. Good problem-solving and communication skills. Customer service oriented.

Willing to do what it takes to get the job done.

Self motivated, dependable, learn quickly.

A JIST Card Can Lead to an Effective Phone Script

The phone is an essential job search tool that can get you more interviews per hour than any other job search tool. But the technique won't work unless you use it actively throughout your search. After you have created your JIST Card, you can use it as the basis for a phone script to make warm or cold calls. Revise your JIST Card content so that it sounds natural when spoken, and then edit it until you can read it out loud in about 30 seconds. The sample phone script that follows is based on the content of a JIST Card. Use it to help you modify your own JIST Card into a phone script.

Overcome phone phobia! Making cold calls takes guts, but most people can get one or more interviews an hour using cold calls. Start by calling people you know and people they refer you to. Then try calls to businesses that don't sound very interesting. As you get better, call more desirable targets.

"Hello. My name is Pam Nykanen. I am interested in a position in hotel management. I have four years' experience in sales, catering, and accounting with a 300-room hotel. I also have an associate degree in hotel management, plus one year of experience with the Brady Culinary Institute. During my employment, I helped double revenues from meetings and conferences and increased bar revenues by 46 percent. I have good problem-solving skills and am good with people. I am also well-organized, hard working, and detail-oriented. When may I come in for an interview?"

With your script in hand, make some practice calls to warm or cold contacts. If making cold calls, contact the person most likely to supervise you. Then present your script just as you practiced it—without stopping.

Although the sample script assumes that you are calling someone you don't know, you can change it to address warm contacts and referrals. Making cold calls takes courage but works very well for many who are willing to do it.

Use the Internet in Your Job Search

The Internet has limitations as a job search tool. While many have used it to get job leads, it has not worked well for far more. Too many assume they can simply add their resume to resume databases, and employers will line up to hire them. Just like the older approach of sending out lots of resumes, good things sometimes happen, but not often.

I recommend two points that apply to all job search methods, including using the Internet:

- It is unwise to rely on just one or two methods in conducting your job search.
- It is essential that you use an active rather than a passive approach in your job search.

Use More Than One Job Search Method

I encourage you to use the Internet in your job search, but I suggest that you use it along with other techniques. Use the same sorts of job search techniques online as you do offline, including contacting employers directly and building up a network of personal contacts that can help you with your search.

Tips to Increase Your Effectiveness in Internet Job Searches

The following tips can increase the effectiveness of using the Internet in your job search:

- **Be as specific as possible in the job you seek.** This is important in using any job search method, and it's even more important in using the Internet in your job search. The Internet is enormous, so it is essential to be as focused as possible in your search. Narrow your job title or titles to be as specific as possible. Limit your search to specific industries or areas of specialization. Locate and use specialized job banks in your area of interest.

- **Have reasonable expectations.** Success on the Internet is more likely if you understand its limitations and strengths. For example, employers trying to find someone with skills in high demand, such as nurses, are more likely to use the Internet to recruit job candidates.
- **Limit your geographic options.** If you don't want to move or would move only to certain areas, state this preference on your resume and restrict your search to those areas. Many Internet sites allow you to view or search for only those jobs that meet your location criteria.
- **Create an electronic resume.** With few exceptions, resumes submitted on the Internet end up as simple text files with no graphic elements. Employers search databases of many resumes for those that include key words or meet other searchable criteria. So create a simple text resume for Internet use and include words that are likely to be used by employers searching for someone with your abilities. (See Step 4 for more on creating an electronic resume.)
- **Get your resume into the major resume databases.** Most Internet employment sites let you add your resume for free and then charge employers to advertise openings or to search for candidates. Although adding your resume to these databases is not likely to result in job offers, doing so allows you to use your stored resume to easily apply for positions that are posted at these sites. These easy-to-use sites often provide all sorts of useful information for job seekers.
- **Make direct contacts.** Visit the Web sites of organizations that interest you and learn more about them. Many post openings, allow you to apply online, offer information on benefits and work environment, or even provide access to staff who can answer your questions. Even if they don't, you can always search the site or e-mail a request for the name of the person in charge of the work that interests you and then communicate with that person directly.
- **Network.** You can network online, too, finding names and e-mail addresses of potential employer contacts or of other people who might know someone with job openings. Look at and participate in interest groups, professional association sites, alumni sites, chat rooms, e-mail discussion lists, and employer sites—these are just some of the many creative ways to network and interact with people via the Internet.

Check Out Career-Specific Sites First

Thousands of Internet sites provide lists of job openings and information on careers or education. Many have links to other sites that they recommend. Service providers such as America Online (www.aol.com) and the Microsoft Network (www.msn.com) have partnered with sites such as Careerbuilder.com to include career information and job listings plus links to other sites. Also check out www.jist.com and www.CareerOINK.com. Three additional career-related sites are Riley Guide at www.rileyguide.com, Monster.com at www.monster.com, America's Job Bank at www.ajb.dnl.us.

STEP 4: Write a Simple Resume Now and a Better One Later

Sending out resumes and waiting for responses is not an effective job-seeking technique. But, many employers *will* ask you for a resume, and it can be a useful tool in your job search. I suggest that you begin with a simple resume you can complete quickly. I've seen too many people spend weeks working on a resume when they could have been out getting interviews instead. If you want a better resume, you can work on it on weekends and evenings. So let's begin with the basics.

Tips for Creating a Superior Resume

The following tips make sense for any resume format:

- **Write it yourself.** It's okay to look at other resumes for ideas, but write yours yourself. Doing so will force you to organize your thoughts and background.
- **Make it error-free.** One spelling or grammar error will create a negative impressionist (see what I mean?). Get someone else to review your final draft for any errors. Then review it again because these rascals have a way of slipping in.
- **Make it look good.** Poor copy quality, cheap paper, bad type quality, or anything else that creates a poor appearance will turn off employers to even the best resume content. Get professional help with design and printing if necessary. Many professional resume writers and even print shops offer writing and desktop design services if you need help.
- **Be brief, be relevant.** Many good resumes fit on one page, and few justify more than two. Include only the most important points. Use short sentences and action words. If it doesn't relate to and support the job objective, cut it!
- **Be honest.** Don't overstate your qualifications. If you end up getting a job you can't handle, who does it help? And a lie can result in your being fired later.
- **Be positive.** Emphasize your accomplishments and results. A resume is no place to be too humble or to display your faults.
- **Be specific.** Instead of saying, "I am good with people," say, "I supervised four people in the warehouse and increased productivity by 30 percent." Use numbers whenever possible, such as the number of people served, percentage of sales increase, or amount of dollars saved.

You should also know that everyone feels that he or she is a resume expert. Whatever you do, someone will tell you that it's wrong. Remember that a resume is simply a job search tool.

You should never delay or slow down your job search because your resume is not good enough. The best approach is to create a simple and acceptable resume as quickly as possible and then use it. As time permits, create a better one if you feel you must.

Writing Chronological Resumes

Most resumes use a chronological format where the most recent experience is listed first, followed by each previous job. This arrangement works fine for someone with work experience in several similar jobs, but not as well for those with limited experience or for career changers.

Look at the two resumes for Judith Jones that follow. Both use the chronological approach.

The first resume would work fine for most job search needs. It could be completed in about an hour.

Notice that the second one includes some improvements. The first resume is good, but most employers would like the additional positive information in the improved resume.

Quip

Avoid the resume pile. Resume experts often suggest that a dynamite resume will jump out of the pile. This is old-fashioned advice. It assumes that you are applying to large organizations and for advertised jobs. Today most jobs are with small employers and are not advertised. To avoid joining that stack of resumes in the first place, look for job openings that others overlook.

Basic Chronological Resume Example

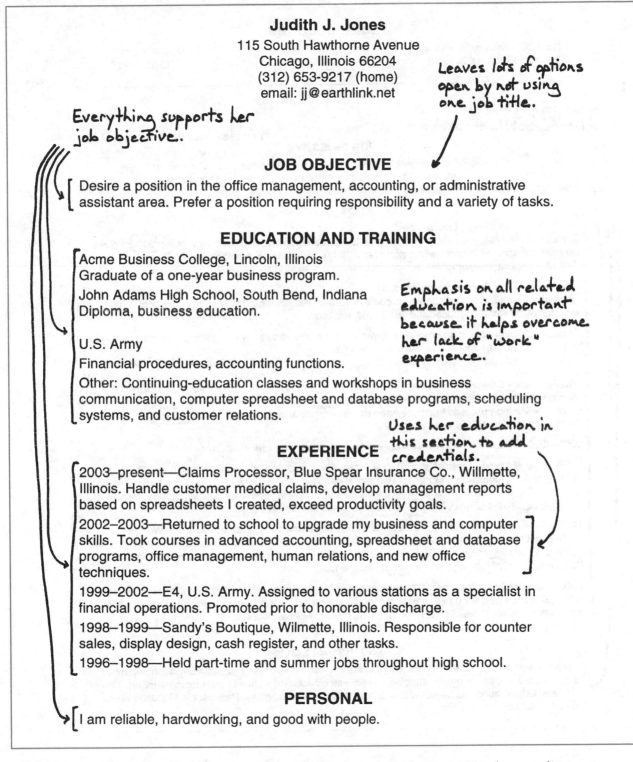

Judith J. Jones
115 South Hawthorne Avenue
Chicago, Illinois 66204
(312) 653-9217 (home)
email: jj@earthlink.net

Leaves lots of options open by not using one job title.

Everything supports her job objective.

JOB OBJECTIVE

Desire a position in the office management, accounting, or administrative assistant area. Prefer a position requiring responsibility and a variety of tasks.

EDUCATION AND TRAINING

Acme Business College, Lincoln, Illinois
Graduate of a one-year business program.

John Adams High School, South Bend, Indiana
Diploma, business education.

Emphasis on all related education is important because it helps overcome her lack of "work" experience.

U.S. Army
Financial procedures, accounting functions.

Other: Continuing-education classes and workshops in business communication, computer spreadsheet and database programs, scheduling systems, and customer relations.

Uses her education in this section to add credentials.

EXPERIENCE

2003–present—Claims Processor, Blue Spear Insurance Co., Willmette, Illinois. Handle customer medical claims, develop management reports based on spreadsheets I created, exceed productivity goals.

2002–2003—Returned to school to upgrade my business and computer skills. Took courses in advanced accounting, spreadsheet and database programs, office management, human relations, and new office techniques.

1999–2002—E4, U.S. Army. Assigned to various stations as a specialist in financial operations. Promoted prior to honorable discharge.

1998–1999—Sandy's Boutique, Wilmette, Illinois. Responsible for counter sales, display design, cash register, and other tasks.

1996–1998—Held part-time and summer jobs throughout high school.

PERSONAL

I am reliable, hardworking, and good with people.

I give some tips you can use when you write your simple chronological resume. Use the preceding resume as your guide.

Improved Chronological Resume Example

Judith J. Jones

115 South Hawthorne Avenue
Chicago, Illinois 66204

jj@earthlink.net
(312) 653-9217

Adds lots of details to reinforce skills throughout.

Provides more details here.

JOB OBJECTIVE

Seeking a position requiring excellent business management expertise in an office environment. Position should require a variety of skills, including office management, word processing, and spreadsheet and database application use.

EDUCATION AND TRAINING

Acme Business College, Lincoln, IL
Completed one-year program in Professional Office Management. Achieved GPA in top 30% of class. Courses included word processing, accounting theory and systems, advanced spreadsheet and database applications, graphics design, time management, and supervision.

John Adams High School, South Bend, IN
Graduated with emphasis on business courses. Earned excellent grades in all business topics and won top award for word-processing speed and accuracy.

Other: Continuing-education programs at own expense, including business communications, customer relations, computer applications, and sales techniques.

EXPERIENCE

Uses numbers to reinforce results.

2003–present—**Claims Processor, Blue Spear Insurance Company,** Wilmette, IL. Process 50 complex medical insurance claims per day, almost 20% above department average. Created a spreadsheet report process that decreased department labor costs by more than $30,000 a year. Received two merit raises for performance.

2002–2003—**Returned to business school to gain advanced office skills.**

1999–2002—**Finance Specialist (E4), U.S. Army.** Systematically processed more than 200 invoices per day from commercial vendors. Trained and supervised eight employees. Devised internal system allowing 15% increase in invoices processed with a decrease in personnel. Managed department with a budget equivalent of more than $350,000 a year. Honorable discharge.

1998–1999—**Sales Associate promoted to Assistant Manager, Sandy's Boutique,** Wilmette, IL. Made direct sales and supervised four employees. Managed daily cash balances and deposits, made purchasing and inventory decisions, and handled all management functions during owner's absence. Sales increased 26% and profits doubled during tenure.

1996–1998—**Held various part-time and summer jobs through high school while maintaining GPA 3.0/4.0.** Earned enough to pay all personal expenses, including car insurance. Learned to deal with customers, meet deadlines, work hard, and handle multiple priorities.

STRENGTHS AND SKILLS

Reliable, with strong work ethic. Excellent interpersonal, written, and oral communication and math skills. Accept supervision well, effectively supervise others, and work well as a team member. General ledger, accounts payable, and accounts receivable expertise. Proficient in Microsoft Word, Excel, and Outlook; WordPerfect.

Tips for Writing a Simple Chronological Resume

Follow these tips as you write a basic chronological resume:

- **Name.** Use your formal name (not a nickname).
- **Address and contact information.** Avoid abbreviations in your address and include your ZIP code. If you may move, use a friend's address or include a forwarding address. Most employers will not write to you, so provide reliable phone numbers and other contact options. Always include your area code in your phone number because you never know where your resume might travel. Make sure that you have an answering machine or voice mail, and record a professional-sounding message. Include alternative ways to reach you, such as a cell phone and e-mail address.
- **Job objective.** You should almost always have one, even if it is general. Notice how Judith Jones keeps her options open with her broad job objective in her basic resume on page 323. Writing "secretary" or "clerical" might limit her from being considered for other jobs.
- **Education and training.** Include any training or education you've had that supports your job objective. If you did not finish a formal degree or program, list what you did complete and emphasize accomplishments. If your experience is not strong, add details here such as related courses and extracurricular activities. In the two examples, Judith Jones puts her business schooling in both the education and experience sections. Doing this fills a job gap and allows her to present her training as equal to work experience.
- **Previous experience.** Include the basics such as employer name, job title, dates employed, and responsibilities—but emphasize specific skills, results, accomplishments, superior performance, and so on.
- **Personal data.** Do not include irrelevant details such as height, weight, and marital status or a photo. Current laws do not allow an employer to base hiring decisions on these points. Providing this information can cause some employers to toss your resume. You can include information about hobbies or leisure activities in a special section that directly supports your job objective. The first sample includes a Personal section in which Judith lists some of her strengths, which are often not included in a resume.
- **References.** Make sure that each reference will make nice comments about you and ask each to write a letter of recommendation that you can give to employers. You do not need to list your references on your resume. List them on a separate page and give it to employers who ask. If your references are particularly good, however, you can mention this somewhere—the last section is often a good place.

When you have a simple, errorless, and eye-pleasing resume, get on with your job search. There is no reason to delay! If you want to create a better resume in your spare time (evenings or weekends), use the name and contact information you currently have and improve the other sections of the resume.

Tips for an Improved Chronological Resume

Use these tips to improve your simple resume:

- **Job objective.** A poorly written job objective can limit the jobs an employer might consider you for. Think of the skills you have and the types of jobs you want to do; describe them in general terms. Instead of using a narrow job title such as "restaurant manager," you might write "manage a small to mid-sized business."
- **Education and training.** New graduates should emphasize their recent training and education more than those with a few years of related work experience would. A more detailed education and training section might include specific courses you took, and activities or accomplishments that support your job objective or reinforce your key skills. Include other details that reflect how hard you work, such as working your way through school or handling family responsibilities.
- **Skills and accomplishments.** Include those that support your ability to do well in the job you seek now. Even small details count. Maybe your attendance was perfect, you met a tight deadline, or you did the work of others during vacations. Be specific and include numbers—even if you have to estimate them. Judith's improved chronological resume example features more accomplishments and skills. Notice the impact of the numbers to reinforce results.
- **Job titles.** Past job titles may not accurately reflect what you did. For example, your job title may have been "cashier," but you also opened the store, trained new staff, and covered for the boss on vacations. Perhaps "head cashier and assistant manager" would be more accurate. Check with your previous employer if you are not sure.

(continued)

(continued)

- **Promotions.** If you were promoted or got good evaluations, say so—"cashier, promoted to assistant manager," for example. You can list a promotion to a more responsible job as a separate job if doing so results in a stronger resume.
- **Gaps in employment and other problem areas.** Employee turnover is expensive, so few employers want to hire people who won't stay or who won't work out. Gaps in employment, jobs held for short periods, or a lack of direction in the jobs you've held are all concerns for employers. So consider your situation and try to give an explanation of a problem area. Here are a few examples:

  2007—Continued my education at...

  2007—Traveled extensively throughout...

  2006 to present—Self-employed as barn painter and...

  2006—Took year off to have first child

  Use entire years to avoid displaying employment gaps you can't explain easily. If you had a few months of unemployment at the beginning of 2006 and then began a job in mid-2006, for example, you can list the job as "2006 to 2007."

Writing Skills and Combination Resumes

The skills resume emphasizes your most important skills, supported by specific examples of how you have used them. This type of resume allows you to use any part of your life history to support your ability to do the job you want.

While skills resumes can be very effective, creating them requires more work. And some employers don't like them because they can hide a job seeker's faults (such as job gaps, lack of formal education, or little related work experience) better than can a chronological resume. Still, a skills resume may make sense for you.

Look over the sample resumes that follow for ideas. Notice that one resume includes elements of a skills *and* a chronological resume. This so-called combination resume makes sense if your previous job history or education and training are positive. More resume examples appear at the end of this part.

Quip

Skip the negatives. Remember that a resume can get you screened out, but it is up to you to get the interview and the job. Cut out anything negative in your resume!

More Resume Examples

Find resume layout and presentation ideas in the four samples that follow.

The chronological resume sample on page 327 focuses on accomplishments through the use of numbers. While Jon's resume does not say so, it is obvious that he works hard and that he gets results.

The skills resume on page 328 is for a recent high school graduate whose only work experience was at a school office!

The combination resume on page 329 emphasizes Grant's relevant education and transferable skills because he has little work experience in the field.

The electronic resume on page 330 is appropriate for scanning or e-mail submission. It has a plain format that is easily read by scanners. It also has lots of key words that increase its chances of being selected when an employer searches a database.

A resume is not the most effective tool for getting interviews. A better approach is to make direct contact with those who hire or supervise people with your skills and ask them for an interview, even if no openings exist now. Then send a resume.

Use the information from your completed Essential Job Search Data Worksheet to write your resume.

The Chronological Resume to Emphasize Results

This simple chronological resume has few but carefully chosen words. It has an effective summary at the beginning, and every word supports his job objective.

Jon Feder

2140 Beach Road
Pompano Beach, Florida 20000

Phone: (222) 333-4444
E-mail: jfeder@com.com

Objective: Management position in a major hotel

He emphasizes results!

Summary of Experience: Three years of experience in sales, catering banquet services, and guest relations in a 75-room hotel. Doubled sales revenues from conferences and meetings. Increased dining room and bar revenues by 40%. Won prestigious national and local awards for increased productivity and services.

Experience:

Beachcomber Hotel, Pompano Beach, Florida
Assistant Manager
20XX to Present

Notice his use of numbers to increase the impact of the statements.

- Oversee a staff of 24, including dining room and bar, housekeeping, and public relations operations.
- Introduced new menus and increased dining room revenues by 40%. Awarded *Saveur* magazine's prestigious first place Hotel Cuisine award as a result of my selection of chefs.
- Attracted 58% more bar patrons by implementing Friday night Jazz at the Beach.

Beachcombers' Suites, Hollywood Beach, Florida
Sales and Public Relations
20XX to 20XX

Bullets here and above improve readability and emphasize key points.

- Doubled venues per month from weddings, conferences, and meetings.
- Chosen Chamber of Commerce Newcomer of the Year 20XX for the increase in business within the community.

Education:

Associate Degree in Hotel Management from Sullivan Technical Institute
Certificate in Travel Management from Phoenix University

While Jon had only a few years of related work experience, he used this resume to help him land a very responsible job in a large resort hotel.

The Skills Resume for Those with Limited Work Experience

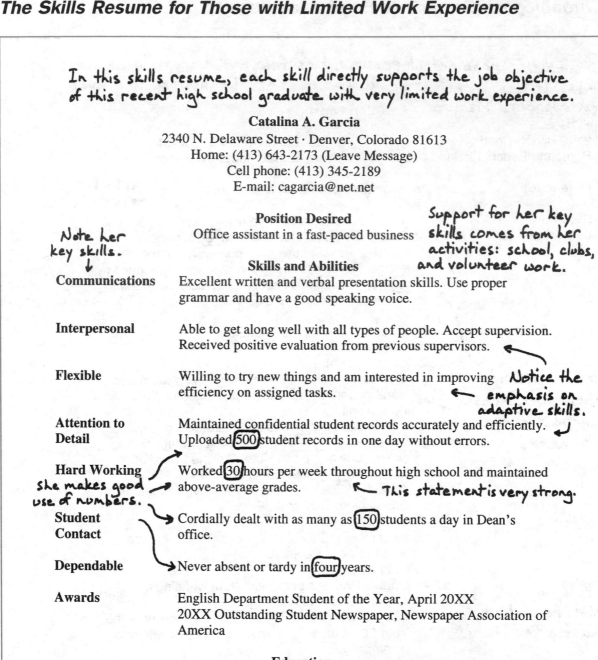

In this skills resume, each skill directly supports the job objective of this recent high school graduate with very limited work experience.

Catalina A. Garcia
2340 N. Delaware Street · Denver, Colorado 81613
Home: (413) 643-2173 (Leave Message)
Cell phone: (413) 345-2189
E-mail: cagarcia@net.net

Position Desired

Office assistant in a fast-paced business

Support for her key skills comes from her activities: school, clubs, and volunteer work.

Note her key skills.

Skills and Abilities

Communications Excellent written and verbal presentation skills. Use proper grammar and have a good speaking voice.

Interpersonal Able to get along well with all types of people. Accept supervision. Received positive evaluation from previous supervisors.

Flexible Willing to try new things and am interested in improving efficiency on assigned tasks.

Notice the emphasis on adaptive skills.

Attention to Detail Maintained confidential student records accurately and efficiently. Uploaded 500 student records in one day without errors.

Hard Working Worked 30 hours per week throughout high school and maintained above-average grades.

This statement is very strong.

She makes good use of numbers.

Student Contact Cordially dealt with as many as 150 students a day in Dean's office.

Dependable Never absent or tardy in four years.

Awards English Department Student of the Year, April 20XX
20XX Outstanding Student Newspaper, Newspaper Association of America

Education

Denver North High School. Took advanced English and communication classes. Member of student newspaper staff and FCCLA for four years. Graduated in top 30% of class.

Other

Girls' basketball team for four years. This taught me discipline, teamwork, how to follow instructions, and hard work. I am ambitious, outgoing, reliable, and willing to work.

Catalina's resume makes it clear that she is talented and hard working.

The Combination Resume for Those Changing Careers

Grant just finished computer programming school and has no work experience in the field. After listing the topics covered in the course, he summarized his employment experience, specifying that he earned promotions quickly. This would be attractive to any employer.

Grant Thomas

717 Carlin Court • Mendelein, IL 60000 • (555) 555-3333
E-mail: gthomas@com.com

Profile

- Outstanding student and tutor
- Winner of international computer software design competition three years
- Capable of being self-directed and independent, but also a team player
- Effective communicator, both orally and written
- Creative problem solver

Education and Training

M.S. in Software Engineering, Massachusetts Institute of Technology, Cambridge, MA
B.S. in Computer Engineering, California State University, Fullerton, CA
A rigorous education that focuses on topics such as

- Structure and interpretation of computer programs
- Circuits and electronics
- Signals and systems
- Computation structures
- Microelectronic devices and circuits
- Computer system engineering
- Computer language engineering
- Mathematics for computer science
- Analog electronics laboratory
- Digital systems laboratory

He includes important information that specifies topics he studied.

The work experiences support the job objective.

Highlights of Experience and Abilities

- Develop, create, and modify general computer applications software.
- Analyze user needs and develop software solutions.
- Confer with system analysts, computer programmers, and others.
- Modify existing software to correct errors.
- Coordinate software system installation and monitor equipment functioning to ensure specifications are met.
- Supervise work of programmers and technicians.
- Train customers and employees to use new and modified software.

Employment History

Software Specialist, First Rate Computers, Mendelein, IL 20XX – Present

- Technician and Customer and Employee Trainer throughout high school
- Promoted to software specialist and worked as a full-time telecommuting employee while completing the B.S. and M.S. degrees

References available on request

The Electronic Resume

Because this electronic format is to be scanned or e-mailed, it has no bold, bullets, or italics.

William Brown
409 S. Maish Road
Phoenix, AZ 50000

Phone message: (300) 444-5567

E-mail: wbrown@email.com

The many key words ensure that the employers' computer searches will select this resume.

OBJECTIVE

Store management career track in car audio store

==
SUMMARY OF SKILLS

Strategic planning, time management, team building, leadership, problem solving, quality customer service, conflict resolution, increasing productivity, confident, outgoing, high performing, aggressive sales

==
EXPERIENCE

Note the results statements and numbers used below.

Total of three years in sales

* SHIFT SUPERVISOR, Tech World, Audio Department, Phoenix, AZ, April 20XX to present: Promoted to Shift Supervisor of nine salespeople in three months. Responsible for strategic planning, time management, team building, leadership, problem solving, quality customer service, conflict resolution, and increasing productivity. Highest-selling team for three years.

* AUDIO SALESPERSON, Tech World, Audio Department, Phoenix, AZ, January 20XX to April 20XX: Arranged display, organized stockroom, sales to customers, and tracked inventory. Highest-selling staff member for three months.

==
EDUCATION AND TRAINING

Phoenix High School, top 40% of class

Additional training: Team Building, Franklin Time Management seminar, Team Building seminar

==
OTHER

* Installed audio systems in 10 cars: family, friends, and my own.

* Member of United States Autosound Association (USAA)

Use a Career Portfolio to Support Your Resume

Your resume is impressive, but there is another way that you can show prospective employers evidence of who you are and what you can do—a career portfolio.

What Is a Career Portfolio?

Unlike a resume, a career portfolio is a collection of documents that can include a variety of items. Here are some items you may want to place in your portfolio:

- Resume
- School transcripts
- Summary of skills
- Credentials, such as diplomas and certificates of recognition
- Reference letters from school officials and instructors, former employers, or co-workers
- List of accomplishments: Describe hobbies and interests that are not directly related to your job objective and are not included on your resume.
- Examples of your work: Depending on your situation, you can include samples of your art, photographs of a project, audiotapes, videotapes, images of Web pages you developed, and other media that can provide examples of your work.

Place each item on a separate page when you assemble your career portfolio.

Create a Digital Portfolio

A digital portfolio, also known as an electronic portfolio, contains all the information from your career portfolio in an electronic format. This material is then copied onto a CD-ROM or published on a Web site. With a digital portfolio, you can present your skills to a greater number of people than you can your paper career portfolio.

Your Career Portfolio

On the following lines, list the items you want to include in your career portfolio. Think specifically of those items that show your skills, education, and personal accomplishments.

____

____

____

____

____

____

____

____

____

____

STEP 5: Redefine What Counts as an Interview, and Then Get Two a Day

The average job seeker gets about five interviews a month—fewer than two a week. Yet many job seekers use the methods in this *Quick Job Search* to get two interviews a day. Getting two interviews a day equals 10 a week and 40 a month. That's 800 percent more interviews than the average job seeker gets. Who do you think will get a job offer quicker?

However, getting two interviews a day is nearly impossible unless you redefine what counts as an interview. If you define an interview in a different way, getting two a day is quite possible.

The New Definition of an Interview: Any face-to-face contact with someone who has the authority to hire or supervise a person with your skills—even if no opening exists at the time you talk with them.

If you use this new definition, it becomes *much* easier to get interviews. You can now interview with all sorts of potential employers, not just those who have job openings now. While most other job seekers look for advertised or actual openings, you can get interviews before a job opens up or before it is advertised and widely known. You will be considered for jobs that may soon be created but that others will not know about. And, of course, you can also interview for existing openings just as everyone else does.

Spending as much time as possible on your job search and setting a job search schedule are important parts of this Step.

Make Your Search a Full-Time Job

Job seekers average fewer than 15 hours a week looking for work. On average, unemployment lasts three or more months, with some people out of work far longer (for example, older workers and higher earners). My many years of experience researching job seeking indicate that the more time you spend on your job search each week, the less time you will likely remain unemployed.

Of course, using the more effective job search methods presented in this minibook also helps. Many job search programs that teach job seekers my basic approach of using more effective methods and spending more time looking have proven that these seekers often find a job in half the average time. More importantly, many job seekers also find better jobs using these methods.

So, if you are unemployed and looking for a full-time job, you should plan to look on a full-time basis. It just makes sense to do so, although many do not, or they start out well but quickly get discouraged. Most job seekers simply don't have a structured plan—they have no idea what they are going to do next Thursday. The plan that follows will show you how to structure your job search like a job.

Decide How Much Time You Will Spend Looking for Work Each Week and Day

First and most importantly, decide how many hours you are willing to spend each week on your job search. You should spend a minimum of 25 hours a week on hard-core job search activities with no goofing around. The following worksheet walks you through a simple but effective process to set a job search schedule for each week.

PLAN YOUR JOB SEARCH WEEK

1. How many hours are you willing to spend each week looking for a job?____________________
2. Which days of the week will you spend looking for a job?____________________
3. How many hours will you look each day?____________________
4. At what times will you begin and end your job search on each of these days?____________________

____

Create a Specific Daily Job Search Schedule

Having a specific daily schedule is essential because most job seekers find it hard to stay productive each day. The sample daily schedule that follows is the result of years of research into what schedule gets the best results. I tested many schedules in job search programs I ran, and this particular schedule worked best.

Consider using a schedule like this sample daily schedule. Why? Because it works.

A Sample Daily Schedule That Works

Time	*Activity*
7–8 a.m.	Get up, shower, dress, eat breakfast
8–8:15 a.m.	Organize work space, review schedule for today's interviews and promised follow-ups, check e-mail, update schedule as needed
8:15–9 a.m.	Review old leads for follow-up needed today; develop new leads from want ads, yellow pages, the Internet, warm contact lists, and other sources; complete daily contact list
9–10 a.m.	Make phone calls and set up interviews
10–10:15 a.m.	Take a break
10:15–11 a.m.	Make more phone calls, set up more interviews
11 a.m.–Noon	Send follow-up notes and do other office activities as needed
Noon–1 p.m.	Lunch break, relax
1–3 p.m.	Go on interviews, make cold contacts in the field
Evening	Read job search books, make calls to warm contacts not reachable during the day, work on a better resume, spend time with friends and family, exercise, relax

If you are not accustomed to using a daily schedule book or electronic planner, promise yourself to get a good one tomorrow. Choose one that allows for each day's plan on an hourly basis, plus daily to-do lists. Record your daily schedule in advance, and then add interviews as they come. Get used to carrying your planner with you and use it!

You can find a variety of computer programs or pocket-sized electronic schedulers to help organize your job search. If you don't use electronic tools, a simple schedule book and other paper systems will work just fine.

STEP 6: Dramatically Improve Your Interviewing Skills

Interviews are where the job search action is. You have to get them; then you have to do well in them. According to surveys of employers, most job seekers do not effectively present the skills they have to do the job. Even worse, most job seekers can't answer one or more problem questions.

This lack of performance in interviews is one reason why employers will often hire a job seeker who does well in the interview over someone with better credentials. The good news is that you can do simple things to dramatically improve your interviewing skills. This section will emphasize interviewing tips and techniques that make the most difference.

Your First Impression May Be the Only One You Make

Some research suggests that if the interviewer forms a negative impression in the first five minutes of an interview, your chances of getting a job offer approach zero. I know from experience that many job seekers can create a lasting negative impression within seconds.

Tips for Interviewing

Because a positive first impression is so important, I share these suggestions to help you get off to a good start:

- **Make a good impression before you arrive.** Your resume, e-mails, applications, and other written correspondence create an impression before the interview, so make them professional and error-free.
- **Do some homework on the organization before you go.** You can often get information on a business and on industry trends from the Internet or a library.
- **Dress and groom the same way the interviewer is likely to be dressed—but cleaner!** Employer surveys find that almost half of all people's dress or grooming creates an initial negative impression. So this is a big problem. If necessary, get advice on your interviewing outfits from someone who dresses well. Pay close attention to your grooming, too—little things do count.
- **Be early.** Leave in plenty of time to be a few minutes early to an interview.
- **Be friendly and respectful with the receptionist.** Doing otherwise will often get back to the interviewer and result in a quick rejection.
- **Follow the interviewer's lead in the first few minutes.** It's often informal small talk but very important for that person to see how you interact. This is a good time to make a positive comment on the organization or even something you see in the office.
- **Understand that a traditional interview is not a friendly exchange.** In a traditional interview situation, there is a job opening, and you will be one of several applicants for it. In this setting, the employer's task is to eliminate all applicants but one. The interviewer's questions are designed to elicit information that can be used to screen you out. And your objective is to avoid getting screened out. It's hardly an open and honest interaction, is it?

  Setting up interviews before an opening exists eliminates the stress of a traditional interview. In pre-interviews, employers are not trying to screen you out, and you are not trying to keep them from finding out stuff about you. Having said that, knowing how to answer questions that might be asked in a traditional interview is good preparation for any interview you face.
- **Be prepared to answer the tough interview questions.** Your answers to a few key problem questions may determine whether you get a job offer. There are simply too many possible interview questions to cover one by one. Instead, 10 basic questions cover variations of most other interview questions. So, if you can learn to answer the Top 10 Problem Interview Questions well, you will know how to answer most others.
- **Be prepared for the most important interview question of all.** "Why should I hire you?" is the most important question of all to answer well. Do you have a convincing argument why someone should hire you over someone else? If you don't, you probably won't get that job you really want. So think carefully about why someone should hire you and practice your response. Then make sure you communicate this in the interview, even if the interviewer never asks the question in a clear way.

Top 10 Problem Interview Questions

1. Why should I hire you?
2. Why don't you tell me about yourself?
3. What are your major strengths?
4. What are your major weaknesses?
5. What sort of pay do you expect to receive?
6. How does your previous experience relate to the jobs we have here?
7. What are your plans for the future?
8. What will your former employer (or references) say about you?
9. Why are you looking for this type of position, and why here?
10. Why don't you tell me about your personal situation?

Follow the Three-Step Process for Answering Interview Questions

I've developed a three-step process for answering interview questions. I know this might seem too simple, but the three-step process is easy to remember and can help you create a good answer to most interview questions. The technique has worked for thousands of people, so consider trying it.

1. **Understand what is really being asked.**

   Most questions are designed to find out about your self-management skills and personality, but interviewers are rarely this blunt. The employer's *real* question is often one or more of the following:

   - Can I depend on you?
   - Are you easy to get along with?
   - Are you a good worker?
   - Do you have the experience and training to do the job if we hire you?
   - Are you likely to stay on the job for a reasonable period of time and be productive?

   Ultimately, if you don't convince the employer that you will stay and be a good worker, it won't matter if you have the best credentials—he or she won't hire you.

2. **Answer the question briefly in a nondamaging way.** Present the facts of your particular work experience as advantages, not disadvantages. Many interview questions encourage you to provide negative information. One classic question I included in my list of Top 10 Problem Interview Questions was "What are your major weaknesses?" This is obviously a trick question, and many people are just not prepared for it.

   A good response is to mention something that is not very damaging, such as *"I have been told that I am a perfectionist, sometimes not delegating as effectively as I might."*

   But your answer is not complete until you continue with the next step.

3. **Answer the real question by presenting your related skills.** Base your answer on the key skills you have that support the job, and give examples to support these skills. For example, an employer might say to a recent graduate, *"We were looking for someone with more experience in this field. Why should we consider you?"* Here is one possible answer:

> *"I'm sure there are people who have more experience, but I do have more than six years of work experience, including three years of advanced training and hands-on experience using the latest methods and techniques. Because my training is recent, I am open to new ideas and am used to working hard and learning quickly."*

> In the previous example (about your need to delegate), a good skills statement might be

> *"I've been working on this problem and have learned to let my staff do more, making sure that they have good training and supervision. I've found that their performance improves, and it frees me up to do other things."*

Whatever your situation, learn to answer questions that present you well. It's essential to communicate your skills during an interview, and the three-step process can help you answer problem questions and dramatically improve your responses. It works!

How to Earn a Thousand Dollars a Minute

What do you do when the employer asks, "How much money would it take to get you to join our company?"

Tips on Negotiating Pay

Remember these few essential tips when it comes time to negotiate your pay:

- **The Number 1 Salary Negotiation Rule: The person who names a specific amount first loses.**
- **The only time to negotiate is after you have been offered the job.** Employers want to know how much you want to be paid so that they can eliminate you from consideration. They figure if you want too much, you won't be happy with their job and won't stay. And if you will take too little, they may think you don't have enough experience. So never discuss your salary expectations until an employer offers you the job.
- **If pressed, speak in terms of wide pay ranges.** If you are pushed to reveal your pay expectations early in an interview, ask the interviewer what the normal pay range is for this job. Interviewers will often tell you, and you can say that you would consider offers in this range.

  If you are forced to be more specific, speak in terms of a wide pay range. If you figure that the company will likely pay from $20,000 to $25,000 a year, for example, say that you would consider "any fair offer in the low to mid-twenties." This statement covers the employer's range and goes a bit higher. If all else fails, tell the interviewer that you would consider any reasonable offer.

  For this tip to work, you must know in advance what the job is likely to pay. You can get this information by asking people who do similar work, or from a variety of books and Internet sources of career information.
- **If you want the job, you should say so.** This is no time to be playing games.
- **Don't say "no" too quickly.** Never, ever turn down a job offer during an interview! Instead, thank the interviewer for the offer and ask to consider the offer overnight. You can turn it down tomorrow, saying how much you appreciate the offer and asking to be considered for other jobs that pay better or whatever. And it is okay to ask for additional pay or other concessions. But if you simply can't accept the offer, say why and ask the interviewer to keep you in mind for future opportunities. You just never know.

STEP 7: Follow Up on All Job Leads

It's a fact: People who follow up with potential employers and with others in their network get jobs more quickly than those who do not.

Rules for Effective Follow-Up

Here are four rules to guide you in your job search:

- **Send a thank-you note or e-mail to every person who helps you in your job search.**
- **Send the note within 24 hours after speaking with the person.**
- **Enclose JIST Cards with thank-you notes and all other correspondence.**
- **Develop a system to keep following up with good contacts.**

Thank-You Notes Make a Difference

Although thank-you notes can be e-mailed, most people appreciate and are more impressed by a mailed note. Here are some tips about mailed thank-you notes that you can easily adapt to e-mail use:

- You can handwrite or type thank-you notes on quality paper and matching envelopes.
- Keep the notes simple, neat, and error-free.
- Make sure to include a few copies of your JIST Card in the envelope.

Here is an example of a simple thank-you note.

April 5, XXXX

Mr. Kijek,

Thanks so much for your willingness to see me next Wednesday at 9 a.m. I know that I am one of many who are interested in working with your organization. I appreciate the opportunity to meet you and learn more about the position.

I've enclosed a JIST Card that presents the basics of my skills for this job and will bring my resume to the interview. Please call me if you have any questions at all.

Sincerely,

Bruce Vernon

Use Job Lead Cards to Follow Up

If you use contact management software, use it to schedule follow-up activities. But the simple paper system I describe here can work very well or can be adapted for setting up your contact management software.

- Use a simple 3-by-5–inch card to record essential information about each person in your network.
- Buy a 3-by-5–inch card file box and tabs for each day of the month.
- File the cards under the date you want to contact the person.
- Follow through by contacting the person on that date.

I've found that staying in touch with a good contact every other week can pay off big. Here's a sample card to give you ideas about creating your own.

ORGANIZATION: Mutual Health Insurance

CONTACT PERSON: Anna Tomey PHONE: 317-355-0216

SOURCE OF LEAD: Aunt Ruth

NOTES: 4/10 Called. Anna on vacation. Call back 4/15. 4/15 Interview set 4/20 at 1:30. 4/20 Anna showed me around. They use the same computers we used in school! (Friendly people.) Sent thank-you note and JIST Card, call back 5/1. 5/1 Second interview 5/8 at 9 a.m.!

In Closing

This is a short book, but it may be all you need to get a better job in less time. I hope this will be true for you, and I wish you well in your search. Remember this: You won't get a job offer because someone knocks on your door and offers one. Job seeking does involve luck, but you are more likely to have good luck if you are out getting interviews.

I'll close this minibook with a few final tips:

- **Approach your job search as if it were a job itself.** Create and stick to a daily schedule, and spend at least 25 hours a week looking.
- **Follow up on each lead you generate and ask each contact for referrals.**
- **Set out each day to schedule at least two interviews.** Remember the new definition of an interview—an interview includes talking to potential employers who don't have an opening now.
- **Send out lots of thank-you notes and JIST Cards.**
- **When you want the job, tell the employer that you want it and why you should be hired over everyone else.**

Don't get discouraged. There are lots of jobs out there, and someone needs an employee with your skills—your job is to find that someone.

I wish you luck in your job search and in your life.

Essential Job Search Data Worksheet

Take some time to complete this worksheet carefully. It will help you write your resume and answer interview questions. You can also photocopy it and take it with you to help complete applications and as a reference throughout your job search. Use an erasable pen or pencil to allow for corrections. Whenever possible, emphasize skills and accomplishments that support your ability to do the job you want. Use extra sheets as needed.

Your name______________________________

Date completed____

Job objective____

Key Accomplishments

List three accomplishments that best prove your ability to do the kind of job you want.

1. ____
2. ____
3. ____

Education and Training

Name of high school(s) and specific years attended____________________

Subjects related to job objective______________________________

Related extracurricular activities/hobbies/leisure activities____________________

Accomplishments/things you did well______________________________

Specific things you can do as a result______________________________

Schools you attended after high school, specific years attended, and degrees/certificates earned__________

Courses related to job objective______________________________

Related extracurricular activities/hobbies/leisure activities____________________

Accomplishments/things you did well______________________________

Specific things you can do as a result______________________________

Other Training

Include formal or informal learning, workshops, military training, skills you learned on the job or from hobbies—anything that will help support your job objective. Include specific dates, certificates earned, or other details as needed.______________________________

(continued)

(continued)

Work and Volunteer History

List your most recent job first, followed by each previous job. Military experience, unpaid or volunteer work, and work in a family business should be included here, too. If needed, use additional sheets to cover *all* significant paid or unpaid work experiences. Emphasize details that will help support your new job objective. Include numbers to support what you did: the number of people served over one or more years, number of transactions processed, percentage of sales increased, total inventory value you were responsible for, payroll of the staff you supervised, total budget responsible for, and so on. Emphasize results you achieved, using numbers to support them whenever possible. Mentioning these things on your resume and in an interview will help you get the job you want.

Job 1

Dates employed____________________

Name of organization____________________

Supervisor's name and job title____________________

Address____________________

Phone number/e-mail address/Web site____________________

What did you accomplish and do well?____________________

Things you learned; skills you developed or used____________________

Raises, promotions, positive evaluations, awards____________________

Computer software, hardware, and other equipment you used____________________

Other details that might support your job objective____________________

Job 2

Dates employed____________________

Name of organization____________________

Supervisor's name and job title____________________

Address____________________

Phone number/e-mail address/Web site____________________

What did you accomplish and do well?____________________

Things you learned; skills you developed or used____________________

Raises, promotions, positive evaluations, awards________________

____

Computer software, hardware, and other equipment you used________________

____

Other details that might support your job objective________________

____

Job 3

Dates employed________________

Name of organization________________

Supervisor's name and job title________________

Address________________

Phone number/e-mail address/Web site________________

What did you accomplish and do well?________________

____

Things you learned; skills you developed or used________________

____

Raises, promotions, positive evaluations, awards________________

____

Computer software, hardware, and other equipment you used________________

____

Other details that might support your job objective________________

____

References

Think of people who know your work well and will be positive about your work and character. Past supervisors are best. Contact them and tell them what type of job you want and your qualifications, and ask what they will say about you if contacted by a potential employer. Some employers will not provide references by phone, so ask them for a letter of reference in advance. If a past employer may say negative things, negotiate what they will say or get written references from others you worked with there.

Reference name________________

Position or title________________

Relationship to you________________

Contact information (complete address, phone number, e-mail address)________________

____

(continued)

(continued)

Reference name____________________

Position or title____________________

Relationship to you____________________

Contact information (complete address, phone number, e-mail address)____________________

____

Reference name____________________

Position or title____________________

Relationship to you____________________

Contact information (complete address, phone number, e-mail address)____________________

____

A Short List of Additional Resources

Thousands of books and countless Internet sites provide information on career subjects. Space limitations do not permit me to describe the many good resources available, so I list here some of the most useful ones. Because this is my list, I've included books I've written or that JIST publishes. You should be able to find these and many other resources at libraries, bookstores, and Web bookselling sites.

Resume and Cover Letter Books

My books. *The Quick Resume & Cover Letter Book* is one of the top-selling resume books at various large bookstore chains. It is very simple to follow, is inexpensive, has good design, and has good sample resumes written by professional resume writers. For more in-depth but still quick help, check out my two books in the *Help in a Hurry* series: *Same-Day Resume* (with advice on creating a simple resume in an hour and a better one later) and *15-Minute Cover Letter,* co-authored with Louise Kursmark (offering sample cover letters and tips for writing them fast and effectively).

Other books published by JIST. The following titles include many sample resumes written by professional resume writers, as well as good advice: *Amazing Resumes* by Jim Bright and Joanne Earl; *Cover Letter Magic* by Wendy S. Enelow and Louise M. Kursmark; the entire *Expert Resumes* series by Enelow and Kursmark; *Federal Resume Guidebook* by Kathryn Kraemer Troutman; *Gallery of Best Resumes, Gallery of Best Cover Letters,* and other books by David F. Noble; and *Résumé Magic* by Susan Britton Whitcomb.

Job Search and Interviewing Books

My books. You may want to check out my two books in the *Help in a Hurry* series: *Seven-Step Job Search* (even more tips and step-by-step guidance to cut your job search time in half) and *Next-Day Job Interview* (quick tips for preparing for a job interview at the last minute). *The Very Quick Job Search* is a thorough book with detailed advice and a "quick" section of key tips you can finish in a few hours. *Getting the Job You Really Want* includes many in-the-book activities and good career decision-making and job search advice.

Other books published by JIST. Titles include *Inside Secrets of Finding a Teaching Job* by Warner, Bryan, and Warner; *Insider's Guide to Finding a Job* by Wendy S. Enelow and Shelly Goldman; *Job Search Handbook for People with Disabilities* by Daniel J. Ryan; *Job Search Magic* and *Interview Magic* by Susan Britton Whitcomb; *Ultimate Job Search* by Richard H. Beatty; and *Over-40 Job Search Guide* by Gail Geary.

Books with Information on Jobs

The primary reference books. The *Occupational Outlook Handbook* is the source of job titles listed in this book. Published by the U.S. Department of Labor and updated every other year, the *OOH* covers about 90 percent of the workforce. The *O*NET Dictionary of Occupational Titles* book has descriptions for more than 1,000 jobs based on the O*NET (Occupational Information Network) database developed by the Department of Labor. The *Enhanced Occupational Outlook Handbook* includes the *OOH* descriptions plus more than 6,000 additional descriptions of related jobs from the O*NET and other sources. The *New Guide for Occupational Exploration* allows you to explore major jobs based on your interests.

Other books published by JIST. Here are a few good books that include job descriptions and helpful details on career options: *Overnight Career Choice, Best Jobs for the 21st Century, 50 Best Jobs for Your Personality, 40 Best Fields for Your Career, 200 Best Jobs for College Graduates,* and *300 Best Jobs Without a Four-Year Degree.*

Internet Resources

There are too many Web sites to list, but here are a few places you can start. A book by Anne Wolfinger titled *Best Career and Education Web Sites* gives unbiased reviews of the most helpful sites and ideas on how to use them. *Job Seeker's Online Goldmine,* by Janet Wall, lists the extensive free online job search tools from government and other sources. This book's job descriptions also include Internet addresses for related organizations. And www.jist.com lists recommended sites for career, education, and related topics, along with comments on each. Be aware that some Web sites provide poor advice, so ask your librarian, instructor, or counselor for suggestions on those best for your needs.

Other Resources

Libraries. Most libraries have the books mentioned here, as well as many other resources. Many also provide Internet access so that you can research online information. Ask the librarian for help finding what you need.

People. People who hold the jobs that interest you are one of the best career information sources. Ask them what they like and don't like about their work, how they got started, and the education or training needed. Most people are helpful and will give advice you can't get any other way.

Career Counseling. A good vocational counselor can help you explore career options. Take advantage of this service if it is available to you! Also consider a career-planning course or program, which will encourage you to be more thorough in your thinking.

Sample Resumes for Some of the Fastest-Growing Jobs

If you read the previous information, you know that I believe you should not depend on a resume alone in your job search. Even so, you will most likely need one, and you should have a good one.

Unlike some career authors, I do not preach that there is only one right way to do a resume. I encourage you to be an individual and to do what you think will work well for you. But I also know that some resumes are clearly better than others. The following pages contain some resumes that you can use as examples when preparing your own resume.

Each resume was written by a professional resume writer who is a member of one or more professional associations. These writers are highly qualified and hold various credentials. Most will provide help (for a fee) and welcome your contacting them (although this is not a personal endorsement).

The resumes appear in books published by JIST Works, including the following:

- *Best Resumes for College Students and New Grads* by Louise M. Kursmark
- *Expert Resumes for Computer and Web Jobs* by Wendy S. Enelow and Louise M. Kursmark
- *Expert Resumes for Health Care Careers* by Wendy S. Enelow and Louise M. Kursmark
- *Expert Resumes for Teachers and Educators* by Wendy S. Enelow and Louise M. Kursmark

- *Gallery of Best Resumes* by David F. Noble
- *Gallery of Best Resumes for People Without a Four-Year Degree* by David F. Noble

Contact Information for Resume Contributors

The following professional resume writers contributed resumes to this section. Their names are listed in alphabetical order. Each entry indicates which resume that person contributed.

Janet L. Beckstrom
President, Word Crafter
1717 Montclair Ave.
Flint, MI 48503
(800) 351-9818
E-mail: wordcrafter@voyager.net
Resume on page 354

Rosie Bixel
A Personal Scribe Résumé Writing & Design
4800 SW Macadam Ave., Suite 105
Portland, OR 97239
(503) 254-8262
E-mail: aps@bhhgroup.com
Resume on page 351

Arnold G. Boldt
Arnold-Smith Associates
625 Panorama Trail, Building One, Ste. 120C
Rochester, NY 14625
(585) 383-0350
E-mail: Arnie@ResumeSOS.com
www.ResumeSOS.com
Resume on page 353

LeRachel H. Buffkins
Writing for You, Inc.
14518 Cambridge Circle
Laurel, MD 20707
(301) 604-2048
E-mail: lbuffkins@writingforyouinc.com
www.writingforyouinc.com
Resume on pages 358–359

Diane Burns
Career Marketing Techniques
E-mail: diane@polishedresumes.com
www.polishedresumes.com
Resume on page 356

Kristie Cook
Absolutely Write
Olathe, KS
Resume on page 349

Daniel J. Dorotik, Jr.
100PercentResumes
5401 68th Street
Lubbock, TX 79424
(806) 783-9900
E-mail: dan@100percentresumes.com
www.100percentresumes.com
Resume on page 345

Debbie Ellis
Phoenix Career Group
(800) 876-5506
E-mail: debbie@phoenixcareergroup.com
www.phoenixcareergroup.com
Resume on page 357

MJ Feld
Careers by Choice, Inc.
205 East Main St., Suite 2-4
Huntington, NY 11743
(631) 673-5432
E-mail: mj@careersbychoice.com
www.careersbychoice.com
Resume on page 352

Wanda McLaughlin
President, Execuwrite
Chandler, AZ 85226
(480) 732-7966
E-mail: wanda@execuwrite.com
www.execuwrite.com
Resume on page 348

Jan Melnik
President, Absolute Advantage
P.O. Box 718
Durham, CT 06422
(860) 349-0256
E-mail: CompSPJan@aol.com
www.janmelnik.com
Resume on page 355

Meg Montford
President, Abilities Enhanced
P.O. Box 11823
Kansas City, MO 64138
(816) 767-1196
E-mail: meg@abilitiesenhanced.com
www.abilitiesenhanced.com
Resume on page 346

Don Orlando
The McLean Group
640 S. McDonough
Montgomery, AL 36104
(334) 264-2020
E-mail: yourcareercoach@aol.com
Resume on page 350

Jane Roqueplot
President/Owner, JaneCo's Sensible Solutions
194 N. Oakland Ave.
Sharon, PA 16146
(724) 342-0100
E-mail: jane@janecos.com
www.janecos.com
Resume on page 347

Accountants and Auditors

James M. Olson

9803 Clinton Avenue ▪ Houston, TX 77068
(281) 000-0000 ▪ name@msn.com

ACCOUNTANT

Detail-focused, highly ethical accounting professional with a BBA in Accounting and work experience demonstrating consistent achievement of organizational and fiscal objectives and goals. Able to pinpoint discrepancies and errors to prevent continuing and potentially unnecessary cost expenditures. Willing to accept responsibilities beyond immediate job duties and take on special projects at management request. Proficient in Excel, Access, other MS programs, J.D. Edwards, and proprietary software. ***Knowledge and skill areas include***

- Audits & Financial Statements
- Accounts Receivable/Payable
- Financial Reconciliations
- General Ledger Accounting
- Record/Systems Automation
- Financial Research Projects
- Strategic & Financial Analysis
- Audit Review Procedures
- Teamwork & Communication

Education

TEXAS UNIVERSITY, Houston, TX
Bachelor of Business Administration (BBA) in Accounting, 2000

Accounting G.P.A.: 3.5 / Member, Beta Alpha Psi—for Honors Accounting, Finance, and IT students

Relevant Experience

Accountant, CITY OF NAME, Anywhere, TX 2001–Present

Fully responsible for several core accounting functions within municipality of 200,000 residents, including preparing financial statements and monthly reports/reconciliations, analyzing expense reports, integrating technology to facilitate accounting tasks, and completing special research projects as needed. Assigned significant role in managing finances of WTMPA, organizing large bodies of financial data, and preparing all financial statements for 2001 and 2002 audits. ***Selected Accomplishments:***

- **Records Analysis & Error Identification**—Researched, identified, and helped resolve several large discrepancies in receivables and payables, all favorable to City of Name:
  - ***$100,000 in A/R account for City of Name's power purchases;***
  - ***$20,000 underpayment for A/R in General Fund Account;***
  - ***$10,000 excess in A/P for Internal Service funds.***
- **Policy Development**—Played key role in development of new travel policy, with projected elimination of problems previously stalling productivity of accounting and internal audit functions.
- **Financial Analysis**—Compiled analysis of franchise fees subsequently used by Assistant City Manager in evaluating potential effects of pending legislation.
- **Audit Review Compliance**—Prepared cash flow and financial statements for external auditors on 13 Internal Service and 10 Special Revenue funds, with zero notes from auditors on review documents.
- **Teamwork & Collaboration**—Coordinated project with legal division that revived dormant accounts and ensured proper disposition. Worked with Chief Accountant to construct new reporting model.
- **Technology Improvement**—Changed automatic accounting instruction table in J.D. Edwards system, leading to correction of multiple unnecessary entries and subsequent cost/time savings.

Collection Agent, CITYBANK, Irving, TX 1997–1998

Trained new employees on account software; prepared detailed financial/customer reports for management.

Manager, TANNING SALON, Irving, TX 1996–1997

Managed A/P, A/R, payroll, and other financial functions in addition to general management activities.

Barbers, Cosmetologists, and Other Personal Appearance Workers

LATONYA JEFFERSON
500 Maple Street, Apt. 103
Kansas City, Missouri 64134
(816) 555-1212
LaTonyaJefferson@email.com

HAIR STYLIST / COSMETOLOGIST

Accomplished professional dedicated to enhancing client appearance in areas of universal hair care. Proven skills in execution of perfect hair-coloring techniques. Builder of "totally satisfied" customer relationships. Peer mentor and public educator in all facets of cosmetology. Licensed in Kansas and Missouri. PC-competent in MS Word, Excel and the Internet. World traveler fluent in Spanish and French.

EXPERIENCE

HAIR COLOR SPECIALIST, Spectacular Salon and Day Spa, Mission, KS (6/99 to Present)
Serve 18 clients per day from diverse cultural backgrounds. Participate in hair-show demonstrations.

- Acknowledged for highest level of salon retail sales among 10 stylists.
- Achieved rank of Head Colorist after only two-year employment period.

ASSISTANT MAKEUP ARTIST, Monique's Boutique Fashion Show, Kansas City, MO (9/99)

- Performed makeup and color services for 30 models in this annual event.

EDUCATION

INSTRUCTOR TRAINING, Superior School of Hair Styling, Leawood, KS (1999 to 2000)

- Completed 300 of the 350 hours required for certification.

CERTIFICATE OF COMPLETION, Midwest College of Cosmetology, Blue Springs, MO (7/98)

- Pivot Point Curriculum
- Sales Woman of the Month — awarded seven times
- Perfect Attendance
- Selected courses: Hair Chemistry; Advanced Color; Production Makeup Artist

PROFESSIONAL TRAINING, Heartland College of Beauty Arts, Kansas City, MO (1995 to 1996)

- Outstanding Work Award — received three times
- Selected courses: Ethnic Hair Care; Hair Weaving and Extensions; Hair Color

Chefs, Cooks, and Food Preparation Workers

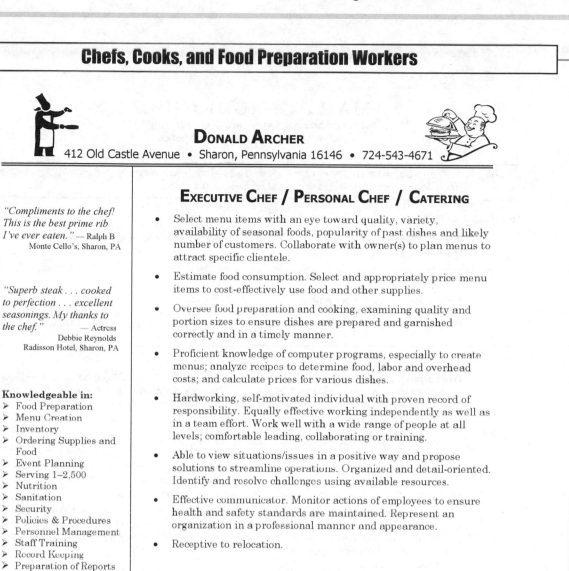

DONALD ARCHER
412 Old Castle Avenue • Sharon, Pennsylvania 16146 • 724-543-4671

"Compliments to the chef! This is the best prime rib I've ever eaten." — Ralph B
Monte Cello's, Sharon, PA

"Superb steak . . . cooked to perfection . . . excellent seasonings. My thanks to the chef." — Actress Debbie Reynolds
Radisson Hotel, Sharon, PA

Knowledgeable in:

- Food Preparation
- Menu Creation
- Inventory
- Ordering Supplies and Food
- Event Planning
- Serving 1–2,500
- Nutrition
- Sanitation
- Security
- Policies & Procedures
- Personnel Management
- Staff Training
- Record Keeping
- Preparation of Reports

Education

Culinary Arts
International Culinary Academy—Pittsburgh, Pennsylvania

Winner Institute of Arts & Sciences—Transfer, Pennsylvania

Food Competitions and Food Shows

Liberal Arts
Criminal Justice/ Pre-Law Course Work
Kent State University—Champion, Ohio

Executive Chef / Personal Chef / Catering

- Select menu items with an eye toward quality, variety, availability of seasonal foods, popularity of past dishes and likely number of customers. Collaborate with owner(s) to plan menus to attract specific clientele.
- Estimate food consumption. Select and appropriately price menu items to cost-effectively use food and other supplies.
- Oversee food preparation and cooking, examining quality and portion sizes to ensure dishes are prepared and garnished correctly and in a timely manner.
- Proficient knowledge of computer programs, especially to create menus; analyze recipes to determine food, labor and overhead costs; and calculate prices for various dishes.
- Hardworking, self-motivated individual with proven record of responsibility. Equally effective working independently as well as in a team effort. Work well with a wide range of people at all levels; comfortable leading, collaborating or training.
- Able to view situations/issues in a positive way and propose solutions to streamline operations. Organized and detail-oriented. Identify and resolve challenges using available resources.
- Effective communicator. Monitor actions of employees to ensure health and safety standards are maintained. Represent an organization in a professional manner and appearance.
- Receptive to relocation.

Experience

EXECUTIVE CHEF, Monte Cello's—*Sharon, Pennsylvania*
SOUS CHEF, Mr. D's Food Fair—*Brookfield, Ohio*
KITCHEN MANAGER, Sidetrack Inn—*Warren, Ohio*
STORE MANAGER, Pit Stop Pizza—*Cortland, Ohio*
GRILL AND SAUTÉ CHEF, Radisson Hotel—*Sharon, Pennsylvania*
PREP CHEF, Avalon Inn—*Howland, Ohio*
ASSISTANT MANAGER, Moovies, Inc.—*Cortland, Ohio*
PERSONAL SECURITY TECHNICIAN, Independent Contractor—*various locations*

Military

Military Police, 1984–1987, Honorable Discharge
United States Marine Corp.

Computer Software Engineers

MARY G. RODRIGUEZ

4411 East Maryland Avenue — Gilbert, AZ 85234
(480) 781-0710 — MRodriguez@aol.com

FOCUS Position as **Software Engineer** where B.S. Degree in Computer Science, experience in Object-Oriented Programming, and knowledge of Internet technology are desirable.

TECHNICAL EXPERTISE

Program Design / Development / Maintenance

Database & Network Administration

System Upgrades & Enhancements

Hardware & Software Evaluation / Support

Programming Languages / Platforms:
Java 1.2, C++, Visual C++, HTML, JCL, CICS, SQL, COBOL, Pascal, BASIC, NATURAL, FORTRAN, MS-DOS, Windows, UNIX

Software:
MS Office, CorelDRAW, Harvard Graphics, PageMaker, WordPerfect, Quattro Pro, Novell Network

RELATED EXPERIENCE

Programmer / Analyst STATE OF ARIZONA, Phoenix, AZ — 2002–2004
Used 4GL programming languages to develop interdepartmental programs. Analyzed data and wrote basic requirements documentation to create databases and programs. Assisted in training end users.
Achievements:
— Assisted in upgrading 20-system linked network in Novell.

Programmer ANALYTICAL RESEARCH, INC., Sacramento, CA — 2001–2002
Directly accountable for all facets of programming and system maintenance for market research company providing services for major travel and leisure accounts throughout the world, including America West Airlines, Lufthansa, United Airlines, and Ritz-Carlton Hotels.

Developed and implemented custom marketing research programs; administered 30,000+ database; coordinated user additions, deletions, and system back-up functions for Novell network. Participated in all phases of hardware and software upgrades, enhancements, and maintenance. Occasionally supervised temporary employees.
Achievements:
— Developed presentations for visual aids and company books utilizing a variety of graphic packages, including Harvard Graphics, CorelDRAW, ACROSS, and Windows.
— Managed 200+ slide presentations to major clients.
— Member of team that brought existing system, programs, and databases successfully into Y2K compliance.

Desktop Publisher ARTISTRY, INC., Los Angeles, CA — 1997–2000
Assisted customers in the development of visual graphic presentations for custom brochures and marketing materials. Determined client requirements, assisted in selection of special graphic designs and programs, and designed and processed orders.
Achievements:
— Developed strong skills in computer operations and creative design.

EDUCATION / TRAINING

B.S. in Computer Science, 2001 CALIFORNIA STATE UNIVERSITY, Northridge, CA
Emphasis: Software Engineering & Computer Mathematics

Java, Intermediate Java, C++, Visual C++ SCOTTSDALE COLLEGE, Scottsdale, AZ
— Currently attending
— Developed Mortgage Calculator utilizing Java applets

Computer Support Specialists and Systems Administrators

PENELOPE S. RICHARDS

4601 Arlington Drive, Baltimore, MD 21111
Home: (410) 521-4690
E-mail: oraclepro@hotmail.com

SUMMARY OF QUALIFICATIONS

- Computer Specialist with more than 8 years of experience in IT/IS.
- Praised by superiors for Oracle expertise, ability to work as a team member, and customer responsiveness.
- Proven oral and written communication skills; comfortable delivering presentations to large groups and training both technical and non-technical people in group settings as well as one-on-one.

TECHNICAL SKILLS

- Oracle
- PMRS
- HP900
- SunSPARC
- JAM
- Delphi
- Windows 98/NT/XP
- Novell NetWare
- Banyan
- TCP/IP
- Enterprise Technologies 4.0
- MS IIS
- UNIX
- FTP
- Telnet
- ARCserve
- TM1 Database
- ADP

EXPERIENCE

COMPUTER SPECIALIST **2002–Present**
Web Hosts Unlimited—Baltimore, MD
Perform system accounts maintenance; change TCP/IP protocols for security purposes and manage IP address changes under Internet Information Server (IIS); maintain active server pages (ASP); provide user support; back up TM1 database using ARCserve software; and monitor and install Microsoft security patches.

- Served as trouble desk coordinator, traveling on a moment's notice when necessary to provide onsite assistance.
- Wrote a database manual for onsite users to easily enhance the system and troubleshoot/solve problems.
- Recognized for outstanding performance.

COMPUTER SPECIALIST **1998–2002**
Market Researchers, Inc.—Washington, DC
Served as Lead Senior Computer Specialist for design, development, and implementation of two customized, complex database systems; worked as Lead Database Administrator (DBA) on and off site and trained Assistant DBAs; provided onsite user support in all areas of client/server software installation and upgrades.

- Designed, developed, tested, and maintained four Oracle Version 8 databases on a SunSPARC 2.0 server.
- Created, implemented, and maintained forms, reports, and program modules using JYACC JAM 6.3.
- Received Outstanding Performance award two years straight.
- Commended by the director for going the extra mile to troubleshoot and debug customized software for offsite operations systems.

COMPUTER SPECIALIST **1995–1998**
Onsite Marketing, Inc.—Washington, DC
Provided application software and database support; supervised 16 personnel; installed patches; verified nightly database changes were run and synchronized with Honolulu location; and assisted switching stations with transmission validity.

- Conducted application software training classes for new personnel.
- Participated on the qualification board for personnel as the senior software engineer.
- Recognized with outstanding performance award.

EDUCATION

Northern Virginia Community College–Alexandria, Virginia
Computer Technology, Effective Presentation

Engineers

Charles W. Morgan

861 Lem Morrison Drive ⌖ Auburn, Alabama 36830 ⌖ ☎ [334] 555-5555

What I bring to the Wastewater Department as an Entry-Level Civil Engineer:

- **Drive** to solve difficult problems—for the fun of doing it.
- **Discipline** to handle complex challenges well.
- Natural **aptitude** for advanced mathematics.

Education:

- B.S., **Civil Engineering,** Auburn University, Auburn, Alabama—2005

  Worked up to 20 hours a week for six semesters while carrying 15 credit hours. Athlete of the year every year from 2001 to 2005.

  Selected coursework:

  - Pipe and channel flow
  - Soils engineering
  - AutoCAD
  - Wastewater treatment
  - Open channel flow
  - Statistics
  - Water treatment
  - Technical and blueprint drawing
  - Environmental design
  - Engineering materials
  - Stormwater drainage design

Selected Examples of Problems Solved in Civil-Engineering Classes:

- Helped design town's entire drinking and wastewater plant. Contributed to 30-page report. Presented oral report before civil engineer with years of on-the-job experience. Got good grade—even though I hadn't taken a prerequisite course.
- Did extensive work to find the best site for a county landfill. Factored in major variables from elevation to soil type to climate. My written report well received.
- Reviewed hundreds of pages of stringent regulations to help design airport. Laid out three runways that met tough operational requirements.
- Analyzed three major engineering projects, parts of Denver International Airport. Demonstrated understanding of how engineering disciplines are integrated in the most challenging situations.

Basic Computer Literacy:

- AutoCAD; MS Windows, Excel, Word, and PowerPoint; Internet search tools

Relevant Work Experience:

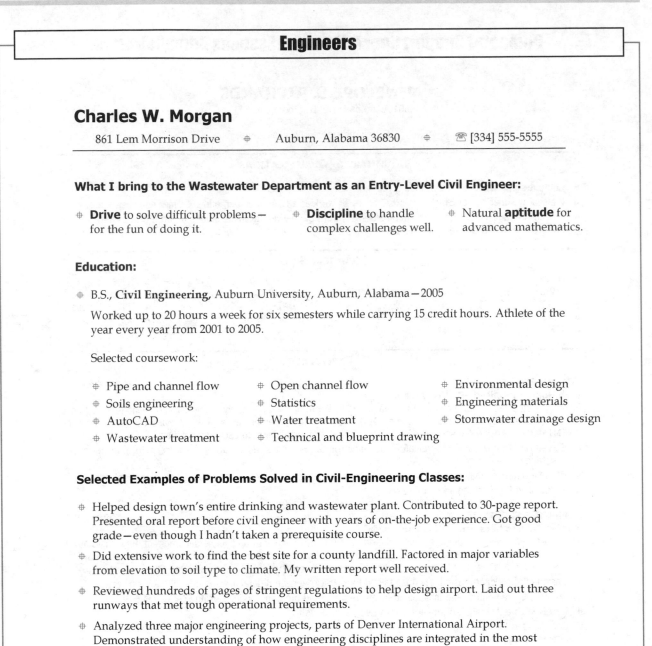

- Summer jobs, including work as a **construction assistant** for W.K. Charning Construction, Montgomery, Alabama

Food and Beverage Serving and Related Workers

Valerie W. Butler

333 S.E. Riveredge Drive • Vancouver, Washington 33333

222-222-2222 *cell* *home* 555-555-5555

Server

Professional Profile

Energetic and highly motivated ***Food Server*** with extensive experience in the food service industry. Expertise lies in working with the fine-dining restaurant, providing top-quality service, and maintaining a professional demeanor. Solid knowledge of the restaurant business, with strengths in excellent customer service and food and wine recommendations.

Get along well with management, coworkers, and customers. Well-developed communication skills. Known as a caring and intuitive "people person," with an upbeat and positive attitude. Highly flexible, honest, and punctual, with the ability to stay calm and focused in stressful situations. Committed to a job well done and a long-term career.

Outstanding Achievements & Recommendations

- Served notable VIP clientele, including clients associated with Murdock Charitable Trust.
- History of repeat and new customers requesting my service as their waitress.
- Known for creating an atmosphere of enjoyment and pleasure for the customer.

"...Valerie was warm, friendly, kind, and very efficient. We didn't feel rushed. She handled our requests, and we appreciated her genuine 'May I please you' attitude...."

Related Work History

Waitress • Banquets • Heathman Lodge • Vancouver, Washington • *2002–present*
Northwest seasonal cuisine.

Banquets • Dolce Skamania Lodge • Stevenson, Washington • *2001–2002*
Casual fine-dining restaurant.

Waitress • Hidden House • Vancouver, Washington • *1993–2001*
Exclusive fine-dining restaurant.

Waitress • Multnomah Falls Lodge Restaurant • Corbett, Oregon • *1992–1993*
Historic Columbia Gorge Falls restaurant serving authentic Northwestern cuisine.

Waitress • The Ahwahnee at Yosemite National Park • California • *1 year*
World-renowned, award-winning fine-dining restaurant—sister lodge to Timberline Lodge.

Graphic Designers

jason blue

433 darby drive, huntington, new york 11743 ♦ bluemagic@mail.net ♦ 555.555.5555

award-winning graphic designer

top-notch creative skills ... project management & production ... graphics business management

full advertising campaigns ♦ corporate identity/communication packages
business-to-business & business-to-consumer project design and management

brochures ♦ logos ♦ sales kits ♦ newsletters ♦ direct mail ♦ posters ♦ press kits ♦ sell sheets ♦ signage

professional experience

graphic designer, The Design Team, Northport, NY (2001–Present)

- Assess clients' needs and develop successful designs for promotional, marketing, and collateral materials across a wide variety of industries. Utilize an intuitive knack for appreciating clients' business goals as well as distinguishing clients' campaign from the competitive field.
- Establish rapport with clients, communicating vision of project with ease and passion. Through confident interpersonal interactions, secure sales and ensure clients' ultimate satisfaction with finished product.
- Meet client deadlines through judicious project management, orchestrating and coordinating milestones against timetables.
- Ensure profitability and competitiveness on projects through astute pricing of jobs.
- Evaluate and choose vendors for select outsourcing and materials purchasing. Credited with negotiating favorable prices, saving clients thousands of dollars.
- Brought in on several client projects requiring expert-level guidance. Provided consultation on conceptual and technical approaches, which ultimately allowed the client's in-house design staff to proceed with minimal supervision.

senior designer/art director, The Regional Letter, Melville, NY (1985–2001)

- Hired and supervised designers, interns, photographers, and freelance illustrators for Newsday's promotion & marketing department.
- Developed content-driven marketing programs that generated millions in new revenue for Newsday. Successes of these programs were noticed and subsequently rolled out as a model for all Tribune Media companies.
- Oversaw production scheduling and traffic management, ensuring that the tight weekly deadlines of the newspaper business were always met.
- Managed the department's budget for projects (allocation between departments, printing, studio rentals, and outside vendors).
- Designed special-events sections for the paper's city editions. Directed photo shoots and created illustrations to complement written material.
- Implemented new software/hardware and brought in products that enhanced the efficiency of the creative team. Trained staff on new technologies.

awards

Numerous Best of Long Island (BOLI) Ad Club Awards ♦ Art Directors' Club of New York Award ♦ Society of Illustrators Award ♦ NMA/Editor & Publisher Award ♦ 57th AGC Graphic Arts Award ♦ General Excellence Award, Newspaper Association of America

software proficiencies

Quark — Illustrator 10 — Photoshop — Acrobat — Flatbed scanning technology
Word for PCs and Macs

Physician Assistants

Lawrence A. Timmons

585-334-7305 | 24 Leonardo Drive, Rochester, New York 14624 | latpa@webtv.net

SUMMARY:

Physician's Assistant and Licensed Paramedic. Extensive training and field experience in Advanced Life Support and critical care. Twenty years' experience in active duty and management roles with suburban ambulance service.

EDUCATION:

May 2002

Bachelor of Science, Physician's Assistant
University of Rochester; Rochester, New York
GPA: 3.6 / Dean's List

Clinical Rotations:

- Critical Care Medicine
- Orthopaedics
- Internal Medicine
- Emergency Medicine
- General Surgery
- Family Medicine
- OB/Gyn
- Cardiology
- Psychiatry
- Pediatrics

May 1998

Associate of Applied Science, Liberal Arts,
Monroe Community College; Rochester, New York

CERTIFICATIONS:

Licensed Physician's Assistant (NYS)—1 yr.
Pediatric Advanced Life Support—7 yrs.
Advanced Trauma Life Support—3 yrs.
Licensed Paramedic (NYS)—7 yrs.
Advanced Cardiac Life Support—7 yrs.

RELEVANT EXPERIENCE:

2002–Present

Park Ridge Hospital Emergency Department; Rochester, New York
Physician's Assistant
Treat acute and non-acute patients in emergency department setting.

- Examine and evaluate incoming patients; diagnose and assess treatment options.
- Provide treatment and prescribe medications as necessary and appropriate.
- Admit patients to the hospital for further care as required.
- Suture lacerations and treat orthopedic injuries.
- Address needs of patients ranging from pediatric to geriatric.

1985–2001

Mendon Volunteer Ambulance Corps; Rochester, New York
Vice President / General Manager (2000–2001)
Directed day-to-day operations for suburban ambulance service responding to more than 4,500 calls per year. Responsibility for 130 paid and volunteer active-duty members.

- Appointed department heads responsible for Basic Life Support, Advanced Life Support, Logistics, Training, and Safety.
- Managed $450,000 operations budget.

EMT / Paramedic (1985–2001)

- Personally logged more than 5,000 hours of active duty time over 16 years.
- Served as Monroe/Livingston County Paramedic Preceptor for five years.

1994–2000

Flight Paramedic, Mercy Flight; Canandaigua, New York
Administered critical care to patients for air medical service covering 11-county region and responding to 500 calls per year.

- Responded to accident scenes in remote locations.
- Provided Advanced Life Support to patients as only care-giver aboard flight.

1993–Present

Trainer / Guest Lecturer
University of Buffalo and Monroe Community College Paramedic Training Programs.

Respiratory Therapists

ANGELA P. CARDOVA, CRT

1834 Highlands Dr.
Novi, MI 48375

248-555-3729
cardova@msn.com

PROFILE

- ✓ Over 8 years as Respiratory Therapist.
- ✓ Adult and pediatric care provider at emergency, critical, and subacute levels. Strong patient-assessment skills.
- ✓ Additional experience in home-care settings.

HIGHLIGHTS OF CLINICAL SKILLS

- ✓ Basic respiratory therapy
- ✓ Ventilator set-up and management (including high-frequency oscillator ventilators)
- ✓ Nasal CPAP therapy
- ✓ Arterial blood gas sampling and analysis
- ✓ Oxygen therapy
- ✓ Pulmonary function testing
- ✓ Extubation
- ✓ Weaning
- ✓ Protocol-driven therapy

CERTIFICATIONS

- ✓ Certified Respiratory Therapist/Registry-eligible (NBRC)
- ✓ BCLS (American Heart Assoc.)

EMPLOYMENT HISTORY

Respiratory Therapist: MERCY HOSPITAL • Livonia, Michigan 2002–Present

- Set up respiratory and related equipment in homes of recently discharged patients. Equipment includes:
  - ✓ Oxygen concentrator
  - ✓ Liquid oxygen
  - ✓ Oxygen conserving device
  - ✓ Nebulizer compressor
  - ✓ Apnea monitor
  - ✓ Ultrasonic nebulizer
  - ✓ Air compressor
  - ✓ Suction machine
  - ✓ CPAP fitting and set-up
- Perform respiratory assessments.
- Verify health benefits; maintain familiarity with Medicare guidelines.

Polysomnography Technician: OAKDALE HEALTH SYSTEM • Ypsilanti, Michigan 2001–2002

- Prepared for and monitored patients during sleep studies for evaluation of obstructive sleep apnea and other sleeping disorders.

Respiratory Therapist
HALMARK HOME HEALTH CARE CENTERS • Centerline, Michigan 1998–1999
ST. JOSEPH MERCY HOSPITAL • Ann Arbor, Michigan 1995–1998

EDUCATION

AAS in Respiratory Care: GRAND VALLEY STATE UNIVERSITY • Grand Rapids, Michigan 1995
Certified Medical Assistant Program: CLEARY COLLEGE • Ypsilanti, Michigan 1990

ACCOMPLISHMENTS

- ✓ Collaborated with other students to reactivate Zeta Phi Beta Sorority chapter at Grand Valley State University. Served as Chapter President for one year.

References available on request.

Retail Salespersons

Andrea J. Ruiz

4793 Hopewell Avenue
Meriden, CT 06450
(203) 555-1010 • ajruiz@aol.com

Qualifications Summary

Accomplished and motivated **Senior Retail Sales Associate** with 5+ years' exemplary experience and performance track record characterized by continued advancement into positions of increased visibility.

- Expert organizational skills, highly effective assessment and analytical skills, and key strategic planning ability.
- Broad range of operational experience includes sales, marketing, merchandising, sales analysis, public/vendor relations, markdowns, inventory control, and shrinkage.
- Strong leadership skills and ability to train new staff.
- PC skills include Windows, Excel, and Microsoft Word; bilingual (fluent in English and Spanish).

Core Competencies

- Dynamic Assortment-Building and Planning
- Quick Problem-Solving
- Accomplishment, Goal-Oriented Approach
- Merchandising Presentation Expertise
- Expert Negotiation Ability
- Key Decision-Making Skills
- Vendor Relation Skills
- Savvy Assessment Skills

Professional Experience

1999–Present J.C. PENNEY • Trumbull, CT
Senior Sales Associate *(promotion, 3/2000–Present)*

- Handle retail sales of Men's Sportswear; coordinate wardrobes and provide professional advice.
- Achieved "Selling Star for the Month" award, three consecutive months.
- Recipient of customer commendation letter and award pins recognizing exemplary customer service.
- Consistently exceed monthly goal for opening new customer charge accounts.
- Collaborate with Merchandising Manager in revamping department, coordinating fashion shows, and increasing traffic/exposure.

Sales Associate *(5/1999–3/2000)*

- Top producer in both American Woman and Ladies' Accessories departments.

1996–1999 LORD & TAYLOR • West Hartford, CT
Sales Associate *(part-time during academic year; full-time summers/vacations)*

- Ranked top floater among part-time staff; adept in quickly learning new departments.
- Named among top 3 sales associates in each department (Girls' Sportswear, Children's, Men's, Ladies', Home Boutique).

Education TRINITY COLLEGE • Hartford, CT
Bachelor of Art Degree, History *(1999)* — Concentrations: Design and Photography

- Recipient of Parson's award for outstanding leadership.

Continuing Professional Education *includes successful completion of corporate training programs in such topical areas as leadership/supervision, communication skills, mentoring, merchandising, motivational skills, and teamwork.*

Security Guards and Gaming Surveillance Officers

Allen Michaels

1290 River Walk Dr. ◆ Ocean City, MD 21045
(410) 884.5555 ◆ Email: allen@hotmail.com

SECURITY GUARD

Physical ◆ Industrial ◆ Facility ◆ Personal

EDUCATION

AA Degree in Business, Howard Community College, Maryland
February 2002

Self-defense Courses, Ocean City PD
1994 to Present

EXPERIENCE

University of Maryland Physics Laboratory, Baltimore, Maryland — 1998 to Present
Security Officer (DoD Contractor, SECRET Clearance)

- Manage two large security databases for 20,000 personnel (input and access information).
- Control the movement of property and personnel into and out of the facility. Verify government clearances and determine entry rights.
- Observe facilities for security violations.
- Respond to and investigate incidents and accidents; draft detailed reports.
- Escort visitors.
- Manage emergency calls and dispatch fire, police, or medical assistance as required.

Independent Contractor — 1994 to Present
Personal Protective Services & Trainer

- Accept independent contracts to protect individuals. Drive personal vehicles and monitor the activities of clients. Ensure that clients are not disturbed, harassed, or otherwise bothered in public locations.
- Install personal home security systems.
- Conduct one-to-one classes in self-defense techniques including the use of deadly force and such weapons/aids as pepper spray.

U.S. Army, Italy and Macedonia — 1994 to 1998
Security Guard

- Managed security requirements for a base: Controlled entry to and exit from restricted-access areas. Searched individuals, vehicles, and materials. Escorted authorized personnel.
- Effectively moved an arms room to the field. Inventoried, moved, and re-set up hundreds of line items of weapons worth over $5M. Operated and maintained 2.5-ton vehicles.
- Received recognition for superior performance of guard duty during the salvaging of Secretary Don White's plane in Macedonia.

Teachers—Preschool, Kindergarten, Elementary, Middle, and Secondary

H: 360-445-1256
210 Candlewood Court • Lacey, Washington 98509 • acellis@earthlink.com

OBJECTIVE

A position as an **Elementary School Teacher** that will utilize strong teaching abilities to create a nurturing, motivational, and stimulating learning environment to help children achieve their potential.

PROFILE

A highly motivated, enthusiastic, and dedicated educator who wants all children to be successful learners.
"**Believe** in the impossible"; continually research educational programs and procedures to benefit students.
Committed to creating a classroom atmosphere that is stimulating and encouraging to students.
Demonstrated ability to consistently individualize instruction, based on students' needs and interests.
Exceptional ability to establish cooperative, professional relationships with parents, staff, and administration.

EDUCATION

B.S. in Elementary Education, Troy State University, Dothan, Alabama — May 2005

- Summa Cum Laude • President's Honor List • Kappa Delta Phi
- National Collegiate Education Award Winner
- Who's Who Among Students in American Universities and Colleges
- Participated in the Test for Teaching Knowledge field project, 2001

A.A. in Arts and Sciences, Pierce College, Tacoma, Washington — 2001

CREDENTIALS

Elementary Education — Washington License (K–8)—Alabama License (K–6)

STUDENT TEACHING

Student Teacher—Grade 1, Harrand Creek Elementary School, Enterprise, Alabama — Fall 2004
Completed 200 hours of hands-on teaching in a first-grade classroom. Utilized children's literature to teach and reinforce reading, writing, grammar, and phonics. Coordinated and taught math lessons and activities. Collaborated with teacher in planning, preparing, and organizing thematic units. Observed the use of teaching techniques to meet the needs of visual, kinesthetic, and auditory learners for all subject areas. Assisted in the quarterly grading.

STUDENT INTERN EXPERIENCE (60 hours)

2nd Grade, Reading, Clover Park Elementary School, Dothan, Alabama
4th Grade, Reading, Science & Social Studies, Headland Elementary School, Dothan, Alabama
4th Grade, Math, EastGate Elementary School, Dothan, Alabama
5th Grade, Art & Social Studies, EastGate Middle School, Ozark, Alabama
1st Grade, Reading Tutor for student at-risk program, Troy State University, Alabama

RELATED EXPERIENCE

Director, Kinder-Care Learning Centers, Lacey, Washington — 1996 to 1998
Oversaw day-to-day operations of child care center for 65 children. Ensured all local, state, and federal rules and regulations were adhered to.

AFFILIATIONS

Member, National Council for Exceptional Children
Leader, Girl Scouts of America

Teachers—Special Education

DENNIS WATSON, SR.

5877 Anchor Way • Rockville, MD 20902 • (301) 495-1111 • dwatsonsr@yahoo.com

SPECIAL EDUCATION PROFESSIONAL

More than 15 years of classroom and field experience with the K–12 special-needs student population

- Educational knowledge and teaching skills include student-centered instruction, educational technology, parental involvement in student learning strategies, reflective teaching, critical-thinking instructional activities, individual learning plans, student motivation strategies, and active and meaningful learning activities.
- Proficiently implement principles, methods, and procedures for diagnosis, treatment, and rehabilitation of physical and mental dysfunctions, and for counseling and guidance.
- Experienced in curriculum and training design, teaching, and instruction for individuals and groups, and the measurement of training effects.
- Highly motivated and dedicated with a commitment to quality education; enforce rules for behavior to maintain order among the students.
- Characterized as a strong communicator with effective presentation skills.

HIGHLIGHTS OF QUALIFICATIONS

Individualized Education Programs (IEP) • Counseling • Curriculum Building
Testing & Assessment • Case Management • Training and Supervision
Organizational Development • Crisis Intervention

EDUCATION & CERTIFICATION

Master of Science, Special Education, with Emphasis on Collaborative Vocational Evaluation Training
George Washington University, Washington, D.C., 2004

Bachelor of Science, Special Education K–12
University of the District of Columbia, Washington, D.C., 1988

Teaching Certificate, K–12 Special Education, State of Maryland (Valid: 1998–2005)

TEACHING EXPERIENCE

Itinerant Special Education Resource Teacher
P.G. County Public Schools, Ace Road Special Education Office, 1999–Present

- Provide special education procedural and technical support to 11 school teams in reference to the assessment, identification, placement, and program review of students receiving special education services and support.
- Design and implement IEPs for developmentally disabled students; administer Woodcock-Johnson assessments for initial and re-evaluation referrals.

Dennis Watson, Sr. **Page 2**

- Communicate frequently with parents, social workers, school psychologists, occupational and physical therapists, school administrators, and other teachers.
- Initiate, plan, and coordinate programs such as the support group for parents of students with learning disabilities and attention-deficit disorder.
- Act as the designated Assistant Instructional Supervisor for Special Education designee at Multidisciplinary Team meetings per request.

Special Education Resource Teacher and Special Education Department Chair
P.G. County Public Schools, Spring Hill Middle School, 1995–1999

- Provided special education intensive resource instruction for 7th and 8th grade levels in the areas of Reading, Language Arts, and Social Studies.
- Supported the school staff by providing special education procedural and technical assistance in reference to the assessment, identification, placement, and program review of students receiving special education services.
- Developed IEPs and assisted with specific needs regarding implementation.
- Revised assessments for initial and reevaluation referrals.
- Coordinated placement of students with special needs into mainstream classes.

Special Education Learning Center Teacher
P.G. County Public Schools, Langley Park Elementary School, 1993–1995

- Instructed students in 4th, 5th, and 6th grade levels in the areas of Reading, Language Arts, Math, Science, and Social Studies.
- Designed curricula, assigned work geared toward each student's ability, and graded papers and homework assignments.
- Provided a highly structured academic environment using a variety of behavior management techniques.
- Facilitated the multidisciplinary team and weekly school instructional team meetings.

Special Education Learning Center Teacher
D.C. Public Schools, Garrison Elementary School, 1988–1993

- Instructed special-needs students on K–3rd grade levels in the areas of Reading, Language Arts, Math, Science, and Social Studies.
- Designed student IEPs and administered Brigance, Berry VMI, and Key Math assessments for initial and reevaluation referrals.
- Partnered with colleagues regarding curriculum modifications and behavior management strategies and techniques, as well as pre–referral intervention strategies.

ADDITIONAL PROFESSIONAL TRAINING

- P.G. County Public Schools:
  - Drug Awareness, 2000
  - MS Excel, 1999
  - Intro to Hispanic Culture, 1999
  - Teaching Students with Special Needs, 1996
- Trinity College Off-Campus, Teaching the Responsive Classroom, 1992
- D.C. Public Schools Teacher Training, Computer Literacy, 1989
- George Washington University, Technology in Special Education, 1988

Part IV

Important Trends in Jobs and Industries

In putting this section together, my objective was to give you a review of major labor market trends that will affect your career. To accomplish this, I included two excellent articles and two informative charts that originally appeared in U.S. Department of Labor publications.

The first article is "Tomorrow's Jobs." It provides a superb review of many trends affecting careers, the workforce, and the workplace. Read it for ideas on selecting a career path for the long term.

The second article is "Employment Trends in Major Industries." While you may not have thought much about it, the industry you work in is just as important as your occupational choice. This great article will help you learn about major trends affecting various industries.

The first chart, "High-Paying Occupations with Many Openings, Projected 2004–2014," shows median earnings for high-paying occupations that also have a large number of openings.

The second chart, "Large Metropolitan Areas That Had the Fastest Employment Growth, 2004–2005," lists areas of the U.S. that experienced a high rate of growth.

Tomorrow's Jobs

Making informed career decisions requires reliable information about opportunities in the future. Opportunities result from the relationships between the population, the labor force, and the demand for goods and services.

Population ultimately limits the size of the labor force—individuals working or looking for work—which constrains how much can be produced. Demand for various goods and services determines employment in the industries providing them. Occupational employment opportunities, in turn, result from demand for skills needed within specific industries. Opportunities for medical assistants and other healthcare occupations, for example, have surged in response to rapid growth in demand for health services.

Examining the past and projecting changes in these relationships is the foundation of the U.S. Department of Labor's Occupational Outlook Program. "Tomorrow's Jobs" presents highlights of Bureau of Labor Statistics projections of the labor force and occupational and industry employment that can help guide your career plans.

Population

Population trends affect employment opportunities in a number of ways. Changes in population influence the demand for goods and services. For example, a growing and aging population has increased the demand for health services. Equally important, population changes produce corresponding changes in the size and demographic composition of the labor force.

The U.S. civilian noninstitutional population is expected to increase by 23.9 million over the 2004–2014 period, at a slower rate of growth than during both the 1994–2004 and 1984–1994 periods (Chart 1). Continued growth will mean more consumers of goods and services, spurring demand for workers in a wide range of occupations and industries. The effects of population growth on various occupations will differ. The differences are partially accounted for by the age distribution of the future population.

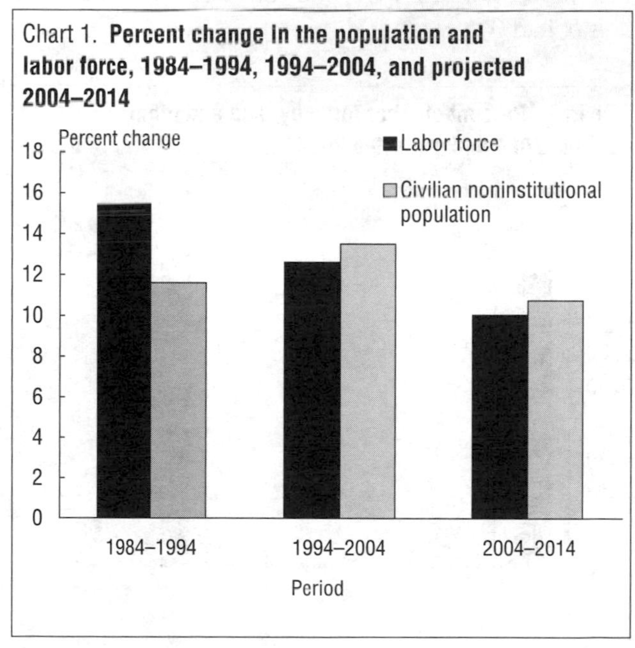

The youth population, aged 16 to 24, will grow 2.9 percent over the 2004–2014 period. As the baby boomers continue to age, the group aged 55 to 64 will increase by 36 percent or 10.4 million persons, more than any other group. The group aged 35 to 44 will decrease in size, reflecting the birth dearth following the baby boom generation.

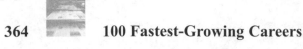

Minorities and immigrants will constitute a larger share of the U.S. population in 2014. The number of Hispanics is projected to continue to grow much faster than those of all other racial and ethnic groups.

Labor Force

Population is the single most important factor in determining the size and composition of the labor force—that is, people who are either working or looking for work. The civilian labor force is projected to increase by 14.7 million, or 10 percent, to 162.1 million over the 2004–2014 period.

The U.S. workforce will become more diverse by 2014. White, non-Hispanic persons will continue to make up a decreasing share of the labor force, falling from 70 percent in 2004 to 65.6 percent in 2014 (Chart 2). However, despite relatively slow growth, white, non-Hispanics will remain the largest group in the labor force in 2014. Asians are projected to account for an increasing share of the labor force by 2014, growing from 4.3 to 5.1 percent. Hispanics are projected to be the fastest growing of the four labor force groups, growing by 33.7 percent. By 2014, Hispanics will continue to constitute a larger proportion of the labor force than will blacks, whose share will grow from 11.3 percent to 12.0 percent.

The numbers of men and women in the labor force will grow, but the number of women will grow at a faster rate than the number of men. The male labor force is projected to grow by 9.1 percent from 2004 to 2014, compared with 10.9 percent for women. As a result, men's share of the labor force is expected to decrease from 53.6 to 53.2 percent, while women's share is expected to increase from 46.4 to 46.8 percent.

The youth labor force, aged 16 to 24, is expected to slightly decrease its share of the labor force to 13.7 percent by 2014. The primary working age group, between 25 and 54 years old, is projected to decline from 69.3 percent of the labor force in 2004 to 65.2 percent by 2014. Workers 55 and older, on the other hand, are projected to increase from 15.6 percent to 21.2 percent of the labor force between 2004 and 2014, due to the aging of the baby-boom generation (Chart 3).

Chart 2. **Percent of labor force by race and ethnic origin, 2004 and projected 2014**

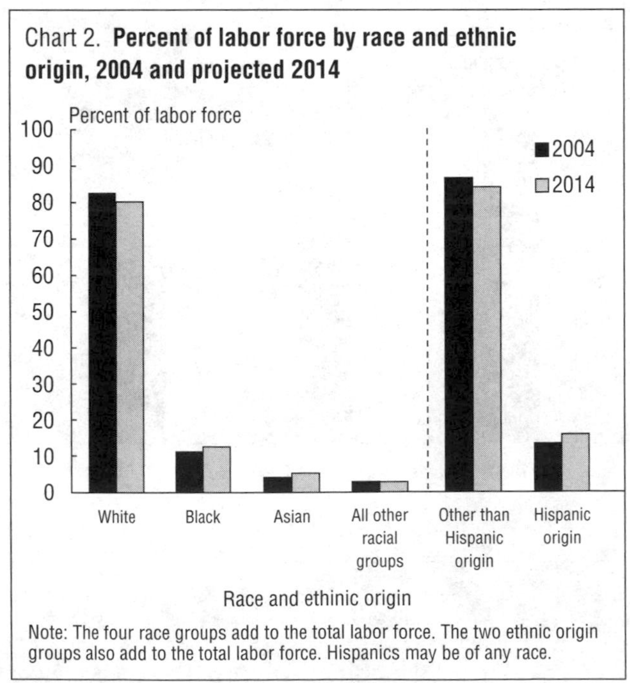

Note: The four race groups add to the total labor force. The two ethnic origin groups also add to the total labor force. Hispanics may be of any race.

Chart 3. **Percent of of labor force by age group, 2004 and projected 2014**

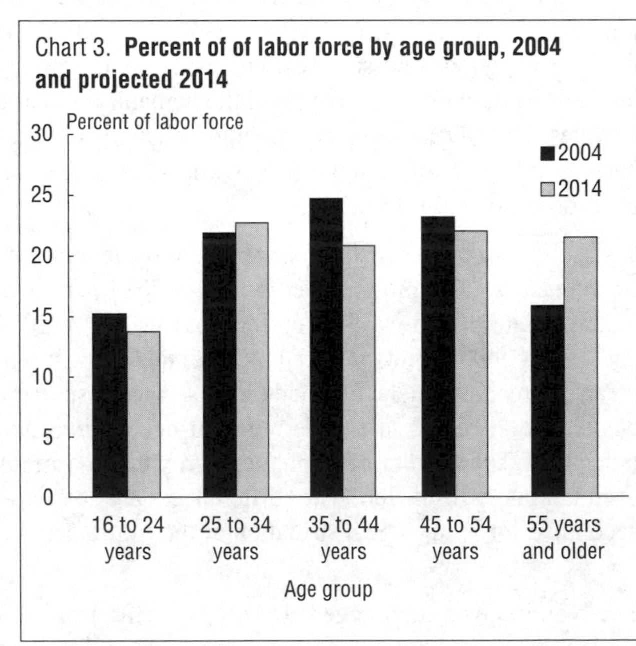

Employment

Total employment is expected to increase from 145.6 million in 2004 to 164.5 million in 2014, or by 13 percent. The 18.9 million jobs that will be added by 2014 will not be evenly distributed across major industrial and occupational groups. Changes in consumer demand, technology, and many other factors will contribute to the continually changing employment structure in the U.S. economy.

The following two sections examine projected employment change from both industrial and occupational perspectives. The industrial profile is discussed in terms of primary wage and salary employment. Primary employment excludes secondary jobs for those who hold multiple jobs. The exception is employment in agriculture, which includes self-employed and unpaid family workers in addition to wage and salary workers.

The occupational profile is viewed in terms of total employment—including primary and secondary jobs for wage and salary, self-employed, and unpaid family workers. Of the nearly 146 million jobs in the U.S. economy in 2004, wage and salary workers accounted for 133.5 million; self-employed workers accounted for 12.1 million; and unpaid family workers accounted for about 141,000. Secondary employment accounted for 1.7 million jobs. Self-employed workers held 9 out of 10 secondary jobs; wage and salary workers held most of the remainder.

Industry

Service-providing industries. The long-term shift from goods-producing to service-providing employment is expected to continue. Service-providing industries are expected to account for approximately 18.7 million of the 18.9 million new wage and salary jobs generated over the 2004–2014 period (Chart 4).

Education and health services. This industry supersector is projected to grow faster, 30.6 percent, and add more jobs than any other industry supersector. About 3 out of every 10 new jobs created in the U.S. economy will be in either the healthcare and social assistance or private educational services sectors.

Healthcare and social assistance—including private hospitals, nursing and residential care facilities, and individual and family services—will grow by 30.3 percent and add 4.3 million new jobs. Employment growth will be driven by increasing demand for healthcare and social assistance because of an aging population and longer life expectancies. Also, as more women enter the labor force, demand for childcare services is expected to grow. Private educational services will grow by 32.5 percent and add 898,000 new jobs through 2014. Rising student enrollments at all levels of education will create demand for educational services.

Professional and business services. This industry supersector, which includes some of the fastest-growing industries in the U.S. economy, will grow by 27.8 percent and add more than 4.5 million new jobs.

Employment in administrative and support and waste management and remediation services will grow by 31 percent and add 2.5 million new jobs to the economy by 2014. The fastest-growing industry in this sector will be employment services, which will grow by 45.5 percent and will contribute almost two-thirds of all new jobs in

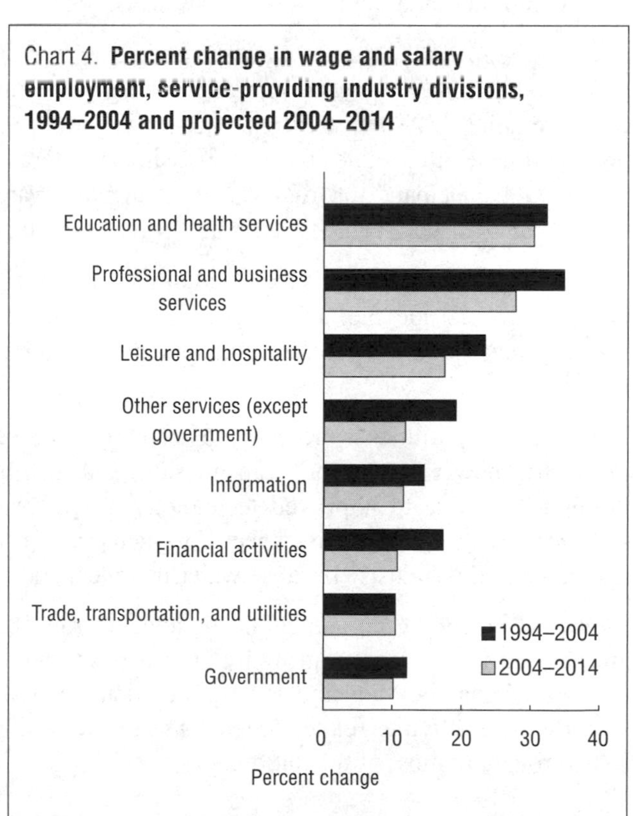
Chart 4. **Percent change in wage and salary employment, service-providing industry divisions, 1994–2004 and projected 2004–2014**

administrative and support and waste management and remediation services. Employment services ranks among the fastest-growing industries in the nation and is expected to be among those that provide the most new jobs.

Employment in professional, scientific, and technical services will grow by 28.4 percent and add 1.9 million new jobs by 2014. Employment in computer systems design and related services will grow by 39.5 percent and add almost one-fourth of all new jobs in professional, scientific, and technical services. Employment growth will be driven by the increasing reliance of businesses on information technology and the continuing importance of maintaining system and network security. Management, scientific, and technical consulting services also will grow very rapidly, by 60.5 percent, spurred by the increased use of new technology and computer software and the growing complexity of business.

Management of companies and enterprises will grow by 10.6 percent and add 182,000 new jobs.

Information. Employment in the information supersector is expected to increase by 11.6 percent, adding 364,000 jobs by 2014. Information contains some of the fast-growing computer-related industries such as software publishers; Internet publishing and broadcasting; and Internet service providers, Web search portals, and data processing services. Employment in these industries is expected to grow by 67.6 percent, 43.5 percent, and 27.8 percent, respectively. The information supersector also includes telecommunications; broadcasting; and newspaper, periodical, book, and directory publishers. Increased demand for residential and business land-line and wireless services, cable service, high-speed Internet connections, and software will fuel job growth among these industries.

Leisure and hospitality. Overall employment will grow by 17.7 percent. Arts, entertainment, and recreation will grow by 25 percent and add 460,000 new jobs by 2014. Most of these new job openings will come from the amusement, gambling, and recreation sector. Job growth will stem from public participation in arts, entertainment, and recreation activities—reflecting increasing incomes, leisure time, and awareness of the health benefits of physical fitness.

Accommodation and food services is expected to grow by 16.5 percent and add 1.8 million new jobs through 2014. Job growth will be concentrated in food services and drinking places, reflecting increases in population, dual-income families, and dining sophistication.

Trade, transportation, and utilities. Overall employment in this industry supersector will grow by 10.3 percent between 2004 and 2014. Transportation and warehousing is expected to increase by 506,000 jobs, or by 11.9 percent through 2014. Truck transportation will grow by 9.6 percent, adding 129,000 new jobs, while rail transportation is projected to decline. The warehousing and storage sector is projected to grow rapidly at 24.8 percent, adding 138,000 jobs. Demand for truck transportation and warehousing services will expand as many manufacturers concentrate on their core competencies and contract out their product transportation and storage functions.

Employment in retail trade is expected to increase by 11 percent, from 15 million to 16.7 million. Increases in population, personal income, and leisure time will contribute to employment growth in this industry, as consumers demand more goods. Wholesale trade is expected to increase by 8.4 percent, growing from 5.7 million to 6.1 million jobs.

Employment in utilities is projected to decrease by 1.3 percent through 2014. Despite increased output, employment in electric power generation, transmission, and distribution and natural gas distribution is expected to decline through 2014 due to improved technology that increases worker productivity. However, employment in water, sewage, and other systems is expected to increase 21 percent by 2014. Jobs are not easily eliminated by technological gains in this industry because water treatment and waste disposal are very labor-intensive activities.

Financial activities. Employment is projected to grow 10.5 percent over the 2004–2014 period. Real estate and rental and leasing is expected to grow by 16.9 percent and add 353,000 jobs by 2014. Growth will be due, in part, to increased demand for housing as the population grows. The fastest-growing industry in the financial activities supersector will be activities related to real estate, which will grow by 32.1 percent, reflecting the housing boom that persists throughout most of the nation.

Finance and insurance is expected to increase by 496,000 jobs, or 8.3 percent, by 2014. Employment in securities, commodity contracts, and other financial investments and related activities is expected to grow 15.8 percent by 2014, reflecting the increased number of baby boomers in their peak savings years, the growth of tax-favorable retirement plans, and the globalization of the securities markets. Employment in credit intermediation and related services, including banks, will grow by 5.4 percent and add about one-third of all new jobs within finance and insurance. Insurance carriers and related activities is expected to grow by 9.5 percent and add 215,000 new jobs by 2014. The number of jobs within agencies, brokerages, and other insurance-related activities is expected to grow about 19.4 percent, as many insurance carriers downsize their sales staffs and as agents set up their own businesses.

Government. Between 2004 and 2014, government employment, including that in public education and hospitals, is expected to increase by 10 percent, from 21.6 million to 23.8 million jobs. Growth in government employment will be fueled by growth in state and local educational services and the shift of responsibilities from the federal government to the state and local governments. Local government educational services is projected to increase 10 percent, adding 783,000 jobs. State government educational services is projected to grow by 19.6 percent, adding 442,000 jobs. Federal government employment, including the postal service, is expected to increase by only 1.6 percent as the federal government continues to contract out many government jobs to private companies.

Other services (except government). Employment will grow by 14 percent. More than 1 out of every 4 new jobs in this supersector will be in religious organizations, which is expected to grow by 11.9 percent. Other automotive repair and maintenance will be the fastest-growing industry at 30.7 percent. Also included among other services is personal care services, which is expected to increase by 19.5 percent.

Goods-producing industries. Employment in the goods-producing industries has been relatively stagnant since the early 1980s. Overall, this sector is expected to decline 0.4 percent over the 2004–2014 period. Although employment is expected to decline or increase more slowly than in the service-providing industries, projected growth among goods-producing industries varies considerably (Chart 5).

Construction. Employment in construction is expected to increase by 11.4 percent, from 7 million to 7.8 million. Demand for new housing and an increase in road, bridge, and tunnel construction will account for the bulk of job growth in this supersector.

Manufacturing. Employment change in manufacturing will vary by individual industry, but overall employment in this supersector will decline by 5.4 percent or 777,000 jobs. For example, employment in transportation equipment manufacturing is expected to grow by 95,000 jobs. Due to an aging population and increasing life expectancies, pharmaceutical and medicine manufacturing is expected to grow by 26.1 percent and add 76,000 jobs through 2014. However, productivity gains, job automation, and international competition will adversely affect employment in many other manufacturing industries. Employment in textile mills and apparel manufacturing will decline by 119,000 and 170,000 jobs, respectively. Employment in computer and electronic product manufacturing also will decline by 94,000 jobs through 2014.

Chart 5. **Percent change in wage and salary employment, goods-producing industry divisions, 1994–2004 and projected 2004–2014**

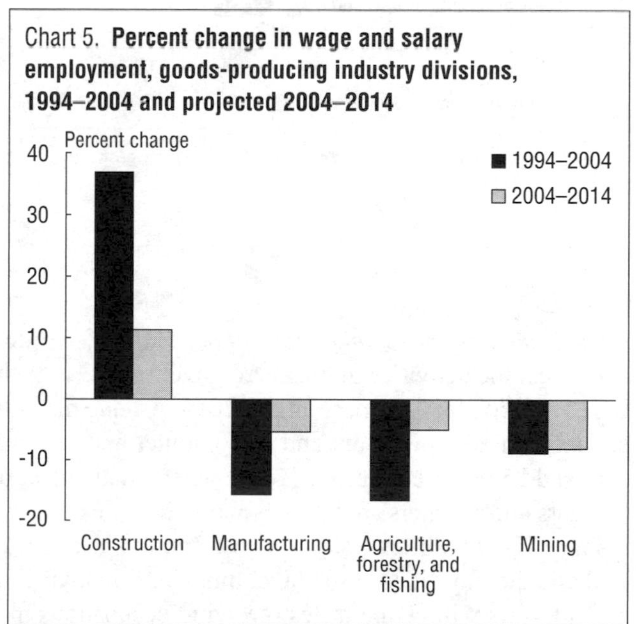

Agriculture, forestry, fishing, and hunting. Overall employment in agriculture, forestry, fishing, and hunting is expected to decrease by 5.2 percent. Employment is expected to continue to decline due to advancements in technology. The only industry within this supersector expected to grow is support activities for agriculture and forestry, which includes farm labor contractors and farm management services. This industry is expected to grow by 18.2 percent and add 19,000 new jobs.

Mining. Employment in mining is expected to decrease 8.8 percent, or by some 46,000 jobs, by 2014. Employment in coal mining and metal ore mining is expected to decline by 23.3 percent and 29.3 percent, respectively. Employment in oil and gas extraction also is projected to decline by 13.1 percent through 2014. Employment decreases in these industries are attributable mainly to technology gains that boost worker productivity, growing international competition, restricted access to federal lands, and strict environmental regulations that require cleaning of burning fuels.

Occupation

Expansion of service-providing industries is expected to continue, creating demand for many occupations. However, projected job growth varies among major occupational groups (Chart 6).

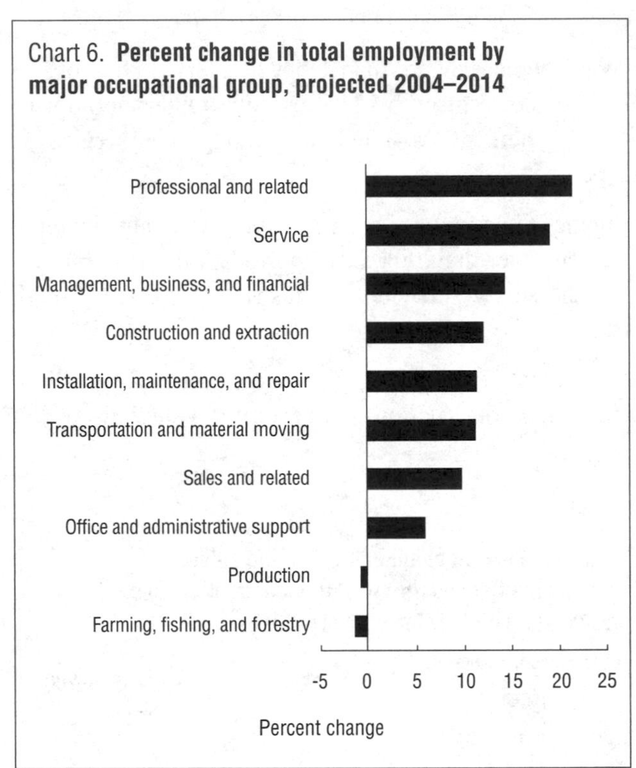

Professional and related occupations. Professional and related occupations will grow the fastest and add more new jobs than any other major occupational group. Over the 2004–2014 period, a 21.2-percent increase in the number of professional and related jobs is projected, which translates into 6 million new jobs. Professional and related workers perform a wide variety of duties, and are employed throughout private industry and government. About three-quarters of the job growth will come from three groups of professional occupations—computer and mathematical occupations; healthcare practitioners and technical occupations; and education, training, and library occupations—which will add 4.5 million jobs combined.

Service occupations. Service workers perform services for the public. Employment in service occupations is projected to increase by 5.3 million, or 19 percent, the second largest numerical gain and second highest rate of growth among the major occupational groups. Food preparation and serving related occupations are expected to add the most jobs among the service occupations, 1.7 million by 2014. However, healthcare support occupations are expected to grow the fastest, 33.3 percent, adding 1.2 million new jobs.

Management, business, and financial occupations. Workers in management, business, and financial occupations plan and direct the activities of business, government, and other organizations. Their employment is expected to increase by 2.2 million, or 14.4 percent, by 2014. Among managers, the numbers of preschool and childcare center/program educational administrators and of computer and information systems managers will grow the fastest, by 27.9 percent and 25.9 percent, respectively. General and operations managers will add the most new jobs, 308,000, by 2014. Farmers and ranchers are the only workers in this major occupational group whose numbers are expected to decline, losing 155,000 jobs. Among business and financial occupations, accountants and auditors and management analysts will add the most jobs, 386,000 combined. Employment, recruitment, and placement specialists and personal financial advisors will be the fastest-growing occupations in this group, with job increases of 30.5 percent and 25.9 percent, respectively.

Construction and extraction occupations. Construction and extraction workers construct new residential and commercial buildings, and also work in mines, quarries, and oil and gas fields. Employment of these workers is expected to grow 12 percent, adding 931,000 new jobs. Construction trades and related workers will account for more than three-fourths of these new jobs, 699,000, by 2014. Many extraction occupations will decline, reflecting overall employment losses in the mining and oil and gas extraction industries.

Installation, maintenance, and repair occupations. Workers in installation, maintenance, and repair occupations install new equipment and maintain and repair older equipment. These occupations will add 657,000 jobs by 2014, growing by 11.4 percent. Automotive service technicians and mechanics and general maintenance and repair workers will account for half of all new installation, maintenance, and repair jobs. The fastest growth rate will be among security and fire alarm systems installers, an occupation that is expected to grow 21.7 percent over the 2004–2014 period.

Transportation and material moving occupations. Transportation and material moving workers transport people and materials by land, sea, or air. The number of these workers should grow 11.1 percent, accounting for 1.1 million additional jobs by 2014. Among transportation occupations, motor vehicle operators will add the most jobs, 629,000. Material moving occupations will grow 8.3 percent and will add 405,000 jobs. Rail transportation occupations are the only group in which employment is projected to decline, by 1.1 percent, through 2014.

Sales and related occupations. Sales and related workers transfer goods and services among businesses and consumers. Sales and related occupations are expected to add 1.5 million new jobs by 2014, growing by 9.6 percent. The majority of these jobs will be among retail salespersons and cashiers, occupations that will add 849,000 jobs combined.

Office and administrative support occupations. Office and administrative support workers perform the day-to-day activities of the office, such as preparing and filing documents, dealing with the public, and distributing information. Employment in these occupations is expected to grow by 5.8 percent, adding 1.4 million new jobs by 2014. Customer service representatives will add the most new jobs, 471,000. Desktop publishers will be among the fastest-growing occupations in this group, increasing by 23.2 percent over the decade. However, due to rising productivity and increased automation, office and administrative support occupations also account for 11 of the 20 occupations with the largest employment declines.

Farming, fishing, and forestry occupations. Farming, fishing, and forestry workers cultivate plants, breed and raise livestock, and catch animals. These occupations will decline 1.3 percent and lose 13,000 jobs by 2014. Agricultural workers, including farmworkers and laborers, accounted for the overwhelming majority of new jobs in this group. The number of fishing and hunting workers is expected to decline, by 16.6 percent, while the number of logging workers is expected to increase by less than 1 percent.

Production occupations. Production workers are employed mainly in manufacturing, where they assemble goods and operate plants. Production occupations are expected to decline less than 1 percent, losing 79,000 jobs by 2014. Jobs will be created for many production occupations, including food processing workers; machinists; and welders, cutters, solderers, and brazers. Textile, apparel, and furnishings occupations, as well as assemblers and fabricators, will account for much of the job losses among production occupations.

Among all occupations in the economy, computer and healthcare occupations are expected to grow the fastest over the projection period (Chart 7). In fact, healthcare occupations make up 12 of the 20 fastest-growing occupations, while computer occupations account for 5 out of the 20 fastest-growing occupations in the economy. In addition to high growth rates, these 17 computer and healthcare occupations combined will add more than 1.8 million new jobs. High growth rates among computer and healthcare occupations reflect projected rapid growth in the computer and data processing and health services industries.

The 20 occupations listed in Chart 8 will account for 7.1 million jobs combined, over the 2004–2014 period. The occupations with the largest numerical increases cover a wider range of occupational categories than do those occupations with the fastest growth rates. Health occupations will account for some of these increases in employment,

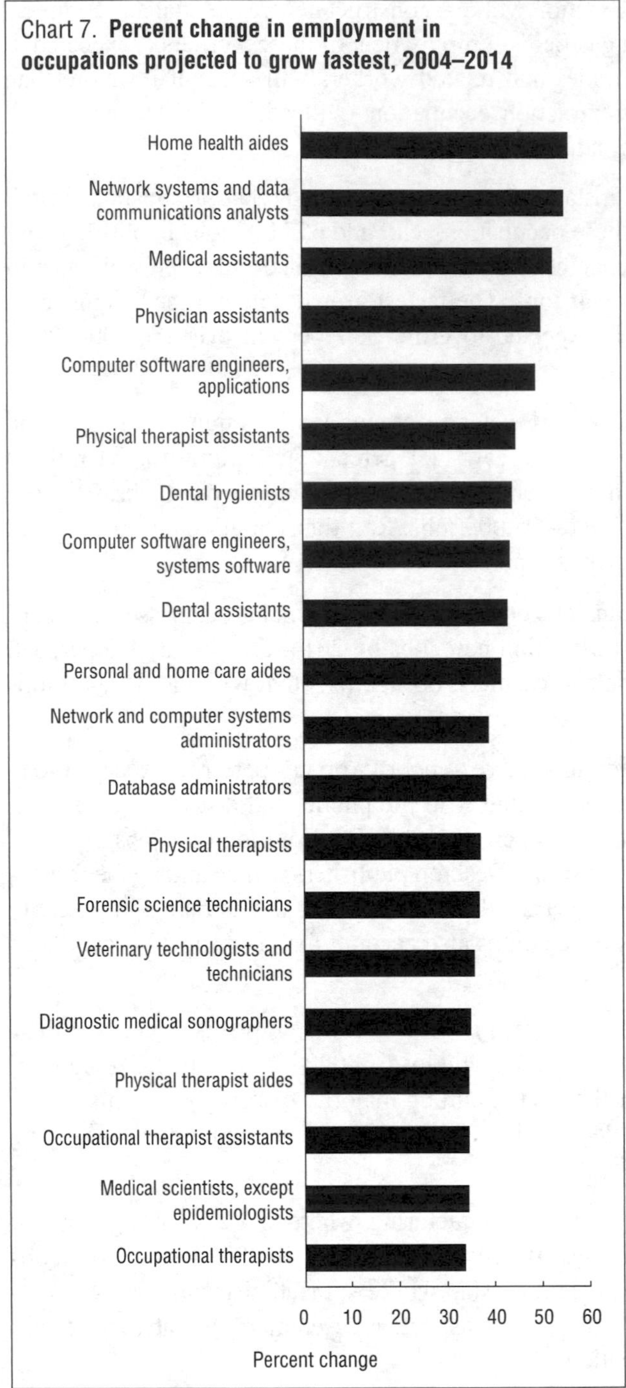

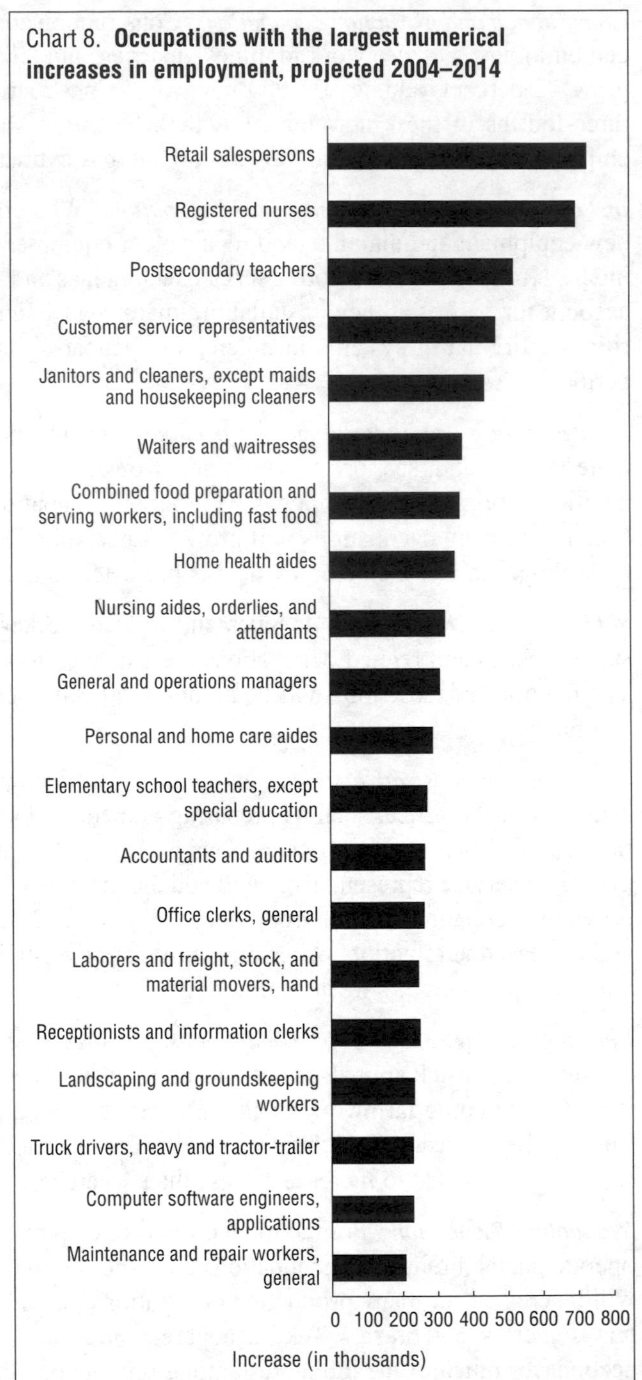

as well as occupations in education, sales, transportation, office and administrative support, and food service. Many of these occupations are very large, and will create more new jobs than will those with high growth rates. Only 3 out of the 20 fastest-growing occupations—home health aides, personal and home care aides, and computer software application engineers—also are projected to be among the 20 occupations with the largest numerical increases in employment.

Declining occupational employment stems from declining industry employment, technological advancements, changes in business practices, and other factors. For example, increased productivity and farm consolidations are expected to result in a decline of 155,000 farmers and ranchers over the 2004–2014 period (Chart 9).

The majority of the 20 occupations with the largest numerical decreases are office and administrative support and production occupations, which are affected by increasing plant and factory automation and the implementation of office technology that reduces the needs for these workers. For example, employment of word processors and typists is expected to decline due to the proliferation of personal computers, which allows other workers to perform duties formerly assigned to word processors and typists.

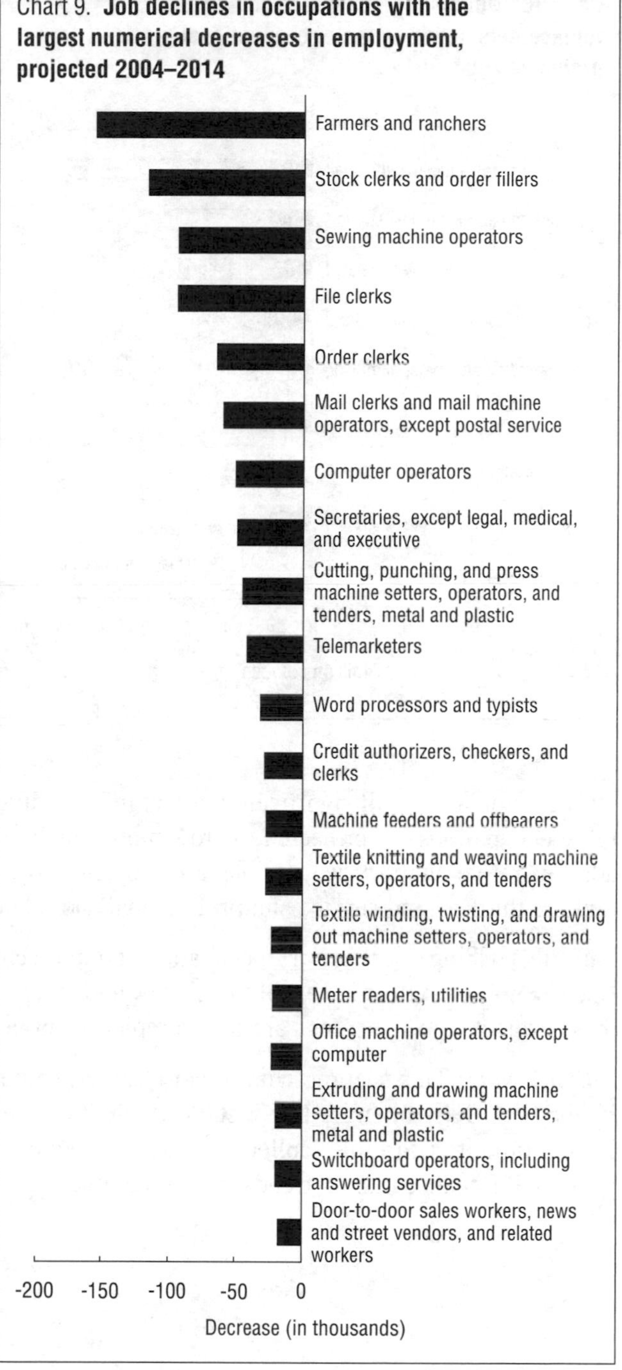

Education and Training

Among the 20 fastest-growing occupations, a bachelor's or associate degree is the most significant source of postsecondary education or training for 12 of them—network systems and data communications analysts; physician assistants; computer software engineers, applications; physical therapist assistants; dental hygienists; computer software engineers, systems software; network and computer systems administrators; database administrators; forensic science technicians; veterinary technologists and technicians; diagnostic medical sonographers; and occupational therapists assistants.

On-the-job training is the most significant source of postsecondary education or training for another 5 of the 20 fastest-growing occupations—physical therapist aides, medical assistants, home health aides, dental assistants, and personal and home care aides.

In contrast, on-the-job training is the most significant source of postsecondary education or training for 13 of the 20 occupations with the largest numerical increases; 6 of these 20 occupations have an associate or higher degree as the most significant source of postsecondary education or training. On-the-job training also is the most significant source of postsecondary education or training for all 20 of the occupations with the largest numerical decreases.

Total Job Openings

Job openings stem from both employment growth and replacement needs (Chart 10). Replacement needs arise as workers leave occupations. Some transfer to other occupations while others retire, return to school, or quit to assume household responsibilities. Replacement needs are projected to account for more than 60 percent of the

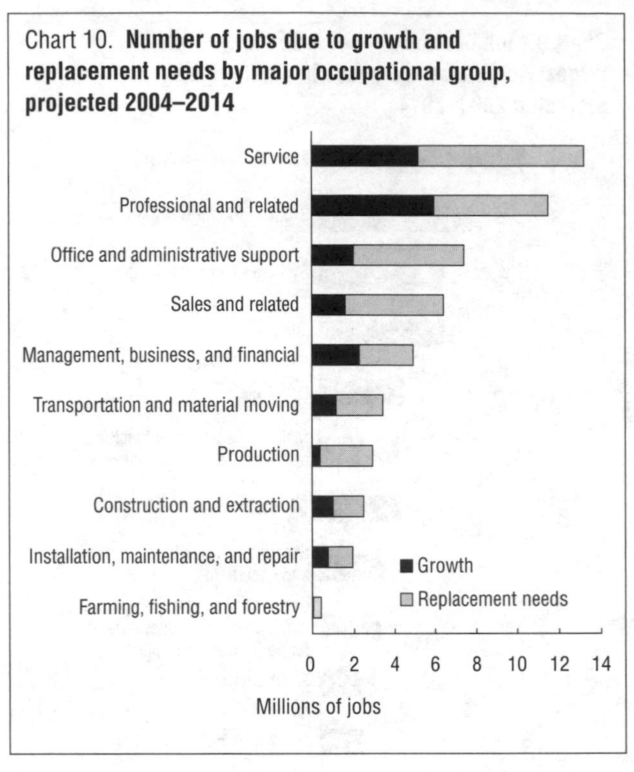
Chart 10. **Number of jobs due to growth and replacement needs by major occupational group, projected 2004–2014**

approximately 55 million job openings between 2004 and 2014. Thus, even occupations projected to experience slower-than-average growth or to decline in employment still may offer many job openings.

Professional and related occupations are projected to grow faster and add more jobs than any other major occupational group, with 6 million new jobs by 2014. Three-fourths of the job growth in professional and related occupations is expected among computer and mathematical occupations; healthcare practitioners and technical occupations; and education, training, and library occupations. With 5.5 million job openings due to replacement needs, professional and related occupations are the only major group projected to generate more openings from job growth than from replacement needs.

Service occupations are projected to have the largest number of total job openings, 13.2 million, reflecting high replacement needs. A large number of replacements will be necessary as young workers leave food preparation and service occupations. Replacement needs generally are greatest in the largest occupations and in those with relatively low pay or limited training requirements.

Office automation will significantly affect many individual office and administrative support occupations. Overall, these occupations are projected to grow more slowly than average, while some are projected to decline. Office and administrative support occupations are projected to create 7.5 million job openings over the 2004–2014 period, ranking third behind service and professional and related occupations.

Farming, fishing, and forestry occupations are projected to have the fewest job openings, approximately 286,000. Because job growth is expected to be slow, and levels of retirement and job turnover high, more than 95 percent of these projected job openings are due to replacement needs.

Editor's Note: This section, with minor changes, came from the *Occupational Outlook Handbook* and was written by the U.S. Department of Labor staff. Much of this section uses 2004 data, the most recent available at press time. By the time it is carefully collected and analyzed, data used by the U.S. Department of Labor is typically several years old. Because market trends tend to be gradual, this delay does not affect the material's usefulness.

Employment Trends in Major Industries

The U.S. economy can be broken down into numerous industries, each with its own set of characteristics. The Department of Labor has identified 45 industries that account for three-quarters of all workers. This section provides an overview of these industries and the economy as a whole.

Nature of the Industry

Industries are defined by the processes they use to produce goods and services. Workers in the United States produce and provide a wide variety of products and services and, as a result, the types of industries in the U.S. economy range widely—from agriculture, forestry, and fishing to aerospace manufacturing. Each industry has a unique combination of occupations, production techniques, inputs and outputs, and business characteristics. Understanding the nature of industries that interest you is important because it is this unique combination that determines working conditions, educational requirements, and the job outlook.

Industries consist of many different places of work, called establishments. Establishments are physical locations in which people work, such as the branch office of a bank, a gasoline service station, a school, a department store, or a plant that manufactures machinery. Establishments range from large factories and corporate office complexes employing thousands of workers to small community stores, restaurants, professional offices, and service businesses employing only a few workers. Establishments should not be confused with companies or corporations, which are legal entities. Thus, a company or corporation may have a single establishment or more than one establishment. Establishments that use the same or similar processes to produce goods or services are organized together into industries. Industries are, in turn, organized together into industry groups such as Information and Trade. These are further organized into industry subsectors and then ultimately into industry sectors. For the purposes of labor market analysis, the Bureau of Labor Statistics organizes industry sectors into industry supersectors. A company or corporation could own establishments classified in more than one industry, industry sector, or even industry supersector.

Each industry subsector is made up of a number of industry groups, which are, as mentioned, determined by differences in production processes. An easily recognized example of these distinctions is in the food manufacturing subsector, which is made up of industry groups that produce meat products, preserved fruits and vegetables, bakery items, and dairy products, among others. Each of these industry groups requires workers with varying skills and employs unique production techniques. Another example of these distinctions is found in utilities, which employs workers in establishments that provide electricity, natural gas, and water.

There are slightly more than 8 million private business establishments in the United States. Business establishments in the United States are predominantly small; 59.9 percent of all establishments employed fewer than 5 workers.

However, the medium-sized to large establishments employ a greater proportion of all workers. For example, establishments that employed 50 or more workers accounted for only 4.6 percent of all establishments, yet employed 56.3 percent of all workers. The large establishments—those with more than 500 workers—accounted for only 0.2 percent of all establishments, but employed 17.3 percent of all workers. Table 1 presents the percent distribution of employment according to establishment size.

The average size of these establishments varies widely across industries. Most establishments in the construction, wholesale trade, retail trade, finance and insurance, real estate and rental and leasing, and professional, scientific, and technical services industries are small, averaging fewer than 20 employees per establishment. However, wide differences within industries can exist. Hospitals, for example, employ an average of 724.9 workers, while physicians' offices employ an average of 10.1. Similarly, although there is an average of 14.3 employees per establishment for all of retail trade, department stores employ an average of 124.1 people but jewelry stores employ an average of only 5.8.

Establishment size can play a role in the characteristics of each job. Large establishments generally offer workers greater occupational mobility and advancement potential, whereas small establishments may provide their employees with broader experience by requiring them to assume a wider range of responsibilities. Also, small establishments are distributed throughout the nation—every locality has a few small businesses. Large establishments, in contrast, employ more workers and are less common, but they play a much more prominent role in the economies of the areas in which they are located.

Table 1. Percent distribution of nongovernment establishments and employment by establishment size

Establishment size (number of workers)	Establishments	Employment
Total	100.0	100.0
1 to 4	59.9	6.8
5 to 9	16.9	8.4
10 to 19	11.1	11.2
20 to 49	7.6	17.3
50 to 99	2.6	13.3
100 to 249	1.4	16.4
250 to 499	0.4	9.3
500 to 999	0.1	6.6
1,000 or more	0.1	10.7

Working Conditions

Just as the goods and services produced in each industry are different, working conditions vary significantly among industries. In some industries, the work setting is quiet, temperature-controlled, and virtually hazard-free, while other industries are characterized by noisy, uncomfortable, and sometimes dangerous work environments. Some industries require long workweeks and shift work, but standard 40-hour workweeks are common in many other industries. In still other industries, a lot of the jobs can be seasonal, requiring long hours during busy periods and abbreviated schedules during slower months. Production processes, establishment size, and the physical location of work usually determine these varying conditions.

One of the most telling indicators of working conditions is an industry's injury and illness rate. Overexertion, being struck by an object, and falls on the same level are among the most common incidents causing work-related injury or illness. In 2003, approximately 5.0 million nonfatal injuries and illnesses were reported across the various nongovernment industries. Among major industry divisions, manufacturing and construction tied for the highest rate of injury and illness—6.8 cases for every 100 full-time workers—while financial activities had the lowest rate—1.7 cases. About 5,700 work-related fatalities were reported in 2004; the most common events resulting in fatal injuries were transportation incidents, contact with objects and equipment, assaults and violent acts, and falls.

Work schedules are another important reflection of working conditions, and the operational requirements of each industry lead to large differences in hours worked and in part-time versus full-time status. In food services and drinking places, for example, fully 41.1 percent of employees worked part time in 2005 compared with only 1.7 percent in motor vehicles and motor vehicle equipment manufacturing. Table 2 presents industries having relatively high and low percentages of part-time workers.

Table 2. Part-time workers as a percent of total employment, selected industries

Industry	Percent part-time
All industries	17.4
Many part-time workers	
Food services and drinking places	41.1
Grocery stores	35.3
Clothing, accessory, and general merchandise stores	33.8
Arts, entertainment, and recreation	32.0
Child day care services	28.7
Motion picture and video industries	27.1
Social assistance	24.6
Educational services	21.9
Few part-time workers	
Pharmaceutical and medicine manufacturing	3.6
Utilities	3.2
Oil and gas extraction	3.2
Computer and electronic product manufacturing	2.8
Steel manufacturing	2.4
Mining	2.3
Aerospace product and parts manufacturing	1.9
Motor vehicles and parts manufacturing	1.7

The low proportion of part-time workers in some manufacturing industries often reflects the continuous nature of the production processes that makes it difficult to adapt the volume of production to short-term fluctuations in product demand. Once these processes are begun, it is costly to halt them; machinery must be tended and materials must be moved continuously. For example, the chemical manufacturing industry produces many different chemical products through controlled chemical reactions. These processes require chemical operators to monitor and adjust the flow of materials into and out of the line of production. Because production may continue 24 hours a day, 7 days a week under the watchful eyes of chemical operators who work in shifts, full-time workers are more likely to be employed. Retail trade and service industries, on the other hand, have seasonal cycles marked by various events that affect the hours worked, such as school openings or important holidays. During busy times of the year, longer hours are common, whereas slack periods lead to cutbacks in work hours and shorter workweeks. Jobs in these industries are generally appealing to students and others who desire flexible, part-time schedules.

Employment

The total number of jobs in the United States in 2004 was 145.6 million. This included 12.1 million self-employed workers, 141,000 unpaid workers in family businesses, and 133.5 million wage and salary jobs—including primary and secondary job holders. The total number of jobs is projected to increase to 164.5 million by 2014, and wage and salary jobs are projected to account for more than 152.1 million of them.

As shown in table 3, wage and salary jobs are the vast majority of all jobs, but they are not evenly divided among the various industries. Education, health, and social services had the largest number of jobs in 2004 with almost 28 million. Manufacturing, construction, and utilities had almost 21.9 million jobs, including 14.3 million manufacturing and 7.0 million construction jobs. The trade supersector was nearly as large, with about 20.7 million jobs, followed by professional and business services with 16.4 million jobs in 2004. Among the 45 industries, wage and salary employment ranged from only 156,200 in steel manufacturing to over 13 million in health services. The three largest industries—education services, health services, and food services and drinking places—together accounted for 34.7 million jobs, over one-quarter of the nation's wage and salary employment.

Table 3. Wage and salary employment, 2004, and projected change, 2004–14 (Employment in thousands)

	2004		2014		2004–2014	
Industry	Employment	Percent distribution	Employment	Percent distribution	Percent change	Employment change
All industries	133,478	100.0	152,093	100.0	13.9	18,615
Agriculture and natural resources	1,672	1.3	1,567	1.0	–6.3	–105
Agriculture, forestry, and fishing	1,149	0.9	1,090	0.7	–5.2	–60
Mining	207	0.2	180	0.1	–12.9	–27
Oil and gas extraction	316	0.2	297	0.2	–6.1	–19
Manufacturing, construction, and utilities	21,864	16.4	21,872	14.4	0.0	8
Aerospace product and parts manufacturing	444	0.3	480	0.3	8.2	36
Chemical manufacturing, except drugs	596	0.5	510	0.3	–14.4	–86
Computer and electronic product manufacturing	1,326	1.0	1,232	0.8	–7.1	–94
Construction	6,964	5.2	7,757	5.1	11.4	792
Food manufacturing	1,498	1.1	1,555	1.0	3.8	57
Machinery manufacturing	1,142	0.9	995	0.7	–12.8	–146
Motor vehicle and parts manufacturing	1,109	0.8	1,171	0.8	5.6	62
Pharmaceutical and medicine manufacturing	291	0.2	367	0.2	26.1	76
Printing	665	0.5	600	0.4	–9.8	–65
Steel manufacturing	156	0.1	135	0.1	–13.4	–21
Textile, textile product, and apparel manufacturing	701	0.5	380	0.2	–44.6	–321
Utilities	570	0.4	563	0.4	–1.3	–8
Trade	20,689	15.5	22,814	15.0	10.3	2,125
Automobile dealers	1,254	0.9	1,407	0.9	12.2	153
Clothing, accessory, and general merchandise stores	4,205	3.1	4,628	3.0	10.1	423
Grocery stores	2,447	1.8	2,607	1.7	6.6	160
Wholesale trade	5,655	4.2	6,131	4.0	8.4	476
Transportation	4,250	3.2	4,756	3.1	11.9	506
Air transportation	515	0.4	560	0.4	8.8	45
Truck transportation and warehousing	1,907	1.4	2,174	1.4	14.0	267

Industry	2004 Employment	2004 Percent distribution	2014 Employment	2014 Percent distribution	2004–2014 Percent change	2004–2014 Employment change
Information	3,138	2.4	3,502	2.3	11.6	364
Broadcasting	327	0.2	362	0.2	10.7	35
Motion picture and video industries	368	0.3	430	0.3	17.1	63
Publishing, except software	671	0.5	715	0.5	6.5	44
Software publishers	239	0.2	400	0.3	67.6	161
Telecommunications	1,043	0.8	975	0.6	–6.5	–68
Internet service providers, Web search portals, and data processing services	388	0.3	496	0.3	27.8	108
Financial activities	8,052	6.0	8,901	5.9	10.5	849
Banking	1,783	1.3	1,751	1.2	–1.8	–31
Insurance	2,260	1.7	2,476	1.6	9.5	215
Securities, commodities, and other investments	767	0.6	888	0.6	15.8	121
Professional and business services	16,414	12.3	20,980	13.8	27.8	4,566
Advertising and public relations services	425	0.3	520	0.3	22.4	95
Computer systems design and related services	1,147	0.9	1,600	1.1	39.5	453
Employment services	3,470	2.6	5,050	3.3	45.5	1,580
Management, scientific, and technical consulting services	779	0.6	1,250	0.8	60.5	471
Scientific research and development services	548	0.4	613	0.4	11.9	65
Education, health, and social services	27,973	21.0	34,399	22.6	23.0	6,426
Child day care services	767	0.6	1,062	0.7	38.4	295
Educational services	12,778	9.6	14,901	9.8	16.6	2,123
Health services	13,062	9.8	16,626	10.9	27.3	3,564
Social assistance, except child day care	1,365	1.0	1,810	1.2	32.6	445
Leisure and hospitality	12,479	9.3	14,694	9.7	17.7	2,215
Arts, entertainment, and recreation	1,833	1.4	2,293	1.5	25.1	460
Food services and drinking places	8,850	6.6	10,301	6.8	16.4	1,451
Hotels and other accommodations	1,796	1.3	2,100	1.4	16.9	304
Government and advocacy, grantmaking, and civic organizations	11,047	8.3	12,170	8.0	10.2	1,123
Advocacy, grantmaking, and civic organizations	1,231	0.9	1,410	0.9	14.5	179
Federal government	1,943	1.5	1,993	1.3	2.5	50
State and local government, except education and health	7,872	5.9	8,767	5.8	11.4	895

Note: May not add to totals due to omission of industries not covered.

Although workers of all ages are employed in each industry, certain industries tend to possess workers of distinct age groups. For the previously mentioned reasons, retail trade employs a relatively high proportion of younger workers to fill part-time and temporary positions. The manufacturing sector, on the other hand, has a relatively high median age because many jobs in the sector require a number of years to learn and perfect specialized skills that do not easily transfer to other firms. Also, manufacturing employment has been declining, providing fewer opportunities for younger workers to get jobs. As a result, one-fourth of the workers in retail trade were 24 years of age or younger in 2004, compared with only 8.2 percent of workers in manufacturing. Table 4 contrasts the age distribution of workers in all industries with the distributions in five very different industries.

Table 4. Percent distribution of wage and salary workers by age group, selected industries

Industry	Age group			
	16 to 24	25 to 44	45 to 64	65 and older
All industries	14	47	36	4
Computer systems design and related services	7	63	29	1
Educational services	9	42	45	3
Food services and drinking places	44	39	15	2
Telecommunications	8	56	34	2
Utilities	5	43	50	2

Employment in some industries is concentrated in one region of the country. Such industries often are located near a source of raw or unfinished materials upon which the industry relies. For example, oil and gas extraction jobs are concentrated in Texas, Louisiana, and Oklahoma; many textile mills and products manufacturing jobs are found in North Carolina, South Carolina, and Georgia; and a significant proportion of motor vehicle manufacturing jobs are located in Michigan and Ohio. On the other hand, some industries—such as grocery stores and educational services—have jobs distributed throughout the nation, reflecting the general population density.

Occupations in the Industry

The occupations found in each industry depend on the types of services provided or goods produced. For example, because construction companies require skilled trades workers to build and renovate buildings, these companies employ large numbers of carpenters, electricians, plumbers, painters, and sheet metal workers. Other occupations common to construction include construction equipment operators and mechanics, installers, and repairers. Retail trade, on the other hand, displays and sells manufactured goods to consumers. As a result, retail trade employs numerous retail salespersons and other workers, including more than three-fourths of all cashiers. Table 5 shows the industry sectors and the occupational groups that predominate in each.

Table 5. Industry sectors and their largest occupational group

Industry sector	Largest occupational group	Percent of industry wage and salary jobs
Agriculture, forestry, fishing, and hunting	Farming, fishing, and forestry occupations	61.1
Mining	Construction and extraction occupations	33.3
Construction	Construction and extraction occupations	66.2
Manufacturing	Production occupations	52.1
Wholesale trade	Sales and related occupations	24.7
Retail trade	Sales and related occupations	52.5
Transportation and warehousing	Transportation and material moving occupations	56.0
Utilities	Installation, maintenance, and repair occupations	25.6
Information	Professional and related occupations	29.1
Finance and insurance	Office and administrative support occupations	51.4
Real estate and rental and leasing	Sales and related occupations	22.7

Industry sector	Largest occupational group	Percent of industry wage and salary jobs
Professional, scientific, and technical services	Professional and related occupations	42.6
Management of companies and enterprises	Office and administrative support occupations	33.6
Administrative and support and waste management and remediation services	Office and administrative support occupations	23.2
Educational services, private	Professional and related occupations	59.6
Health care and social assistance	Professional and related occupations	42.6
Arts, entertainment, and recreation	Service occupations	57.2
Accommodation and food services	Service occupations	84.0
Government	Professional and related occupations	43.7

The occupational distribution clearly is influenced by the structure of its industries, yet there are many occupations, such as general managers or secretaries, that are found in all industries. In fact, some of the largest occupations in the U.S. economy are dispersed across many industries. For example, the group of professional and related occupations is among the largest in the nation while also experiencing the fastest growth rate. (See table 6.) Other large occupational groups include service occupations; office and administrative support occupations; sales and related occupations; and management, business, and financial occupations.

Table 6. Total employment and projected change by broad occupational group, 2004–14 (Employment in thousands)

Occupational group	Employment, 2004	Percent change, 2004–2014
Total, all occupations	145,612	13.0
Professional and related occupations	28,544	21.2
Service occupations	27,673	19.0
Office and administrative support occupations	23,907	5.8
Sales and related occupations	15,330	9.6
Management, business, and financial occupations	14,987	14.4
Production occupations	10,562	–0.1
Transportation and material moving occupations	10,098	11.1
Construction and extraction occupations	7,738	12.0
Installation, maintenance, and repair occupations	5,747	11.4
Farming, fishing, and forestry occupations	1,026	–1.3

Training and Advancement

Workers prepare for employment in many ways, but the most fundamental form of job training in the United States is a high school education. Better than 88 percent of the nation's workforce possessed a high school diploma or its equivalent in 2004. However, many occupations require more training, so growing numbers of workers pursue additional training or education after high school. In 2004, 28.7 percent of the nation's workforce reported having completed some college or an associate's degree as their highest level of education, while an additional 29.5 percent continued in their studies and attained a bachelor's or higher degree. In addition to these types of formal education, other sources of qualifying training include formal company-provided training, apprenticeships, informal on-the-job training, correspondence courses, Armed Forces vocational training, and non-work-related training.

The unique combination of training required to succeed in each industry is determined largely by the industry's production process and the mix of occupations it requires. For example, manufacturing employs many machine operators who generally need little formal education after high school, but sometimes complete considerable on-the-job training. In contrast, the educational services industry employs many types of teachers, most of whom require a bachelor's or higher degree. Training requirements by industry sector are shown in table 7.

Table 7. Percent distribution of workers by highest grade completed or degree received, by industry sector

Industry sector	High school diploma or less	Some college or associate degree	Bachelor's or higher degree
All industries	41.6	28.7	29.5
Agriculture, forestry, fishing, and hunting	64.3	21.4	14.2
Mining	60.4	21.8	17.8
Construction	64.7	24.5	10.8
Manufacturing	51.5	25.1	23.4
Wholesale trade	42.7	29.0	28.3
Retail trade	50.6	32.3	17.1
Transportation and warehousing	52.6	31.7	15.6
Utilities	38.7	34.1	27.0
Information	26.7	31.3	42.0
Finance and insurance	24.9	31.6	43.4
Real estate and rental and leasing	36.2	31.7	32.2
Professional, scientific, and technical services	14.4	25.1	60.6
Administrative and support and waste management services	55.3	28.4	16.3
Educational services	17.8	19.0	63.2
Health care and social assistance	30.6	34.8	34.7
Arts, entertainment, and recreation	39.5	31.8	28.6
Accommodation and food services	60.7	28.4	11.0

Persons with no more than a high school diploma accounted for about 64.7 percent of all workers in construction; 64.3 in agriculture, forestry, fishing, and hunting; 60.7 percent in accommodation and food services; 60.4 percent in mining; 51.5 percent in manufacturing; and 50.6 in retail trade. On the other hand, those who had acquired a bachelor's or higher degree accounted for 63.2 percent of all workers in private educational services; 60.6 percent in professional, scientific, and technical services; 43.4 percent in finance and insurance; and 42.0 percent in information.

Education and training also are important factors in the variety of advancement paths found in different industries. Each industry has some unique advancement paths, but workers who complete additional on-the-job training or education generally help their chances of being promoted. In much of the manufacturing sector, for example, production workers who receive training in management and computer skills increase their likelihood of being promoted to supervisory positions. Other factors that impact advancement and that may figure prominently in industries include the size of the establishments, institutionalized career tracks, and the mix of occupations. As a result, persons who seek jobs in particular industries should be aware of how these advancement paths and other factors may later shape their careers.

Earnings

Like other characteristics, earnings differ by industry, the result of a highly complicated process that reflects a number of factors. For example, earnings may vary due to the nature of occupations in the industry, average hours worked, geographical location, workers' average age, educational requirements, profits, and the degree of union representation of the workforce. In general, wages are highest in metropolitan areas to compensate for the higher cost of living. Also, as would be expected, industries that employ a large proportion of unskilled minimum-wage or part-time workers tend to have lower earnings.

The difference in earnings between the industries of software publishers and of food services and drinking places illustrates how various characteristics of industries can result in great differences in earnings. In software publishers, earnings of all wage and salary workers averaged $1,342 a week in 2004, while in food service and drinking places, earnings of all wage and salary workers averaged only $194 weekly. The difference is large primarily because software publishing establishments employ more higher-skilled, full-time workers, while food services and drinking places employ many lower-skilled workers on a part-time basis. In addition, most workers in software publishing are paid an annual salary, while many workers in food service and drinking places are paid a low hourly wage that is supplemented with money the workers receive as tips. Table 8 highlights the industries with the highest and lowest average weekly earnings.

Table 8. Average weekly earnings of production or nonsupervisory workers on private nonfarm payrolls, selected industries

Industry	Earnings
All industries	$529
Industries with high earnings	
Software publishers	1,342
Computer systems design and related services	1,136
Aerospace product and parts manufacturing	1,019
Scientific research and development services	1,006
Motor vehicle and parts manufacturing	925
Mining	909
Industries with low earnings	
Food manufacturing	510
Grocery stores	332
Arts, entertainment, and recreation	313
Hotels and other accommodations	302
Child day care services	299
Food services and drinking places	194

Employee benefits, once a minor addition to wages and salaries, continue to grow in diversity and cost. In addition to traditional benefits—paid vacations, life and health insurance, and pensions—many employers now offer various benefits to accommodate the needs of a changing labor force. Such benefits sometimes include childcare; employee assistance programs that provide counseling for personal problems; and wellness programs that encourage exercise, stress management, and self-improvement. Benefits vary among occupational groups, full- and part-time workers, public and private sector workers, regions, unionized and nonunionized workers, and small and large establishments. Data indicate that full-time workers and those in medium-sized and large establishments—those with 100 or more workers—usually receive better benefits than do part-time workers and those in smaller establishments.

Union representation of the workforce varies widely by industry, and it also may play a role in determining earnings and benefits. In 2004, about 13.8 percent of workers throughout the nation were union members or covered by union contracts. As table 9 demonstrates, union affiliation of workers varies widely by industry. Fully 50.0 percent of the workers in air transportation were union members, the highest rate of all the industries, followed by 37.6 percent in educational services, and 33.0 percent in iron and steel mills and steel product manufacturing. Industries with the lowest unionization rate include computer systems design and related services, 1.3 percent; food services and drinking places, 1.7 percent; and advertising and related services, 1.7 percent.

Table 9. Union members and other workers covered by union contracts as a percent of total employment, selected industries

Industry	Percent union members or covered by union contract
All industries	13.8
Industries with high unionization rates	
Air transportation	50.0
Educational services	37.6
Iron and steel mills and steel product manufacturing	33.0
Motor vehicles and motor vehicle equipment manufacturing	30.2
Industries with low unionization rates	
Banking and related activities	1.9
Advertising and related services	1.7
Food services and drinking places	1.7
Computer systems design and related services	1.3

Outlook

Total employment in the United States is projected to increase by about 14 percent over the 2004–2014 period. Employment growth, however, is only one source of job openings. The total number of openings in any industry also depends on the industry's current employment level and its need to replace workers who leave their jobs. Throughout the economy, replacement needs will create more job openings than will employment growth. Employment size is a major determinant of job openings—larger industries generally have larger numbers of workers who must be replaced and provide more openings. The occupational composition of an industry is another factor. Industries with high concentrations of professional, technical, and other jobs that require more formal education—occupations in which workers tend to leave their jobs less frequently—generally have fewer openings resulting from replacement needs. On the other hand, more replacement openings generally occur in industries with high concentrations of service, laborer, and other jobs that require little formal education and have lower wages because workers in these jobs are more likely to leave their occupations.

Employment growth is determined largely by changes in the demand for the goods and services provided by an industry, worker productivity, and foreign competition. Each industry is affected by a different set of variables that determines the number and composition of jobs that will be available. Even within an industry, employment may grow at different rates in different occupations. For example, changes in technology, production methods, and business practices in an industry might eliminate some jobs, while creating others. Some industries may be growing rapidly overall, yet opportunities for workers in occupations within those industries could be stagnant or even declining because they are adversely affected by technological change. Similarly, employment of some occupations may be declining in the economy as a whole, yet may be increasing in a rapidly growing industry.

Employment growth rates over the next decade will vary widely among industries. Agriculture and natural resources is the only sector in which all of the industries are expected to experience employment declines. Consolidation of farm land, increasing worker productivity, and depletion of wild fish stocks should continue to decrease employment in agriculture, forestry, and fishing. Employment in mining is expected to decline due to labor-saving technology while jobs in oil and gas extraction are expected to decrease with the continued reliance on foreign sources of energy.

Employment in manufacturing, construction, and utilities is expected to remain nearly unchanged as growth in construction is partially offset by declines in utilities and selected manufacturing industries. Growth in construction employment will stem from new factory construction as existing facilities are modernized; from new school construction, reflecting growth in the school-age population; and from infrastructure improvements, such as road and bridge construction. Employment declines are expected in chemical manufacturing, except drugs; machinery manufacturing; computer and electronic product manufacturing; printing; steel manufacturing; and textile, textile product, and apparel manufacturing. Textile, textile product, and apparel manufacturing is projected to lose about 321,200 jobs over the 2004–2014 period—more than any other manufacturing industry—due primarily to increasing imports replacing domestic products.

Employment gains are expected in some manufacturing industries. Small employment gains in food manufacturing are expected, as a growing and ever more diverse population increases the demand for manufactured food products. Employment growth in pharmaceutical and medicine manufacturing is expected, as sales of pharmaceuticals increase with growth in the population, particularly among the elderly, and with the introduction of new medicines to the market. Both food and pharmaceutical and medicine manufacturing also have growing export markets. Aerospace product and parts manufacturing and motor vehicle and parts manufacturing are both expected to have modest employment increases.

Growth in overall employment will result primarily from growth in service-providing industries over the 2004–2014 period, almost all of which are expected to have increasing employment. Job growth is expected to be led by health services and educational services, with large numbers of new jobs also in employment services, food services and drinking places, state and local government, and wholesale trade. When combined, these sectors will account for almost half of all new wage and salary jobs across the nation. Employment growth is expected in many other service-providing industries, but they will result in far fewer numbers of new jobs.

Health services will account for the most new wage and salary jobs, about 3.6 million over the 2004–2014 period. Population growth, advances in medical technologies that increase the number of treatable diseases, and a growing share of the population in older age groups will drive employment growth. Offices of physicians, the largest health care industry group, is expected to account for about 760,000 of these new jobs as patients seek more healthcare outside of the traditional inpatient hospital setting.

The educational services industry is expected to grow by nearly 17 percent over the 2004–2014 period, adding about 2.1 million new jobs. A growing emphasis on improving education and making it available to more children and young adults will be the primary factors contributing to employment growth. Employment growth at all levels of education is expected, particularly at the postsecondary level, as children of the baby boomers continue to reach college age, and as more adults pursue continuing education to enhance or update their skills.

Employment in one of the nation's fastest-growing industries—employment services—is expected to increase by more than 45 percent, adding another 1.6 million jobs over the 2004–2014 period. Employment will increase, particularly in temporary help services and professional employer organizations, as businesses seek new ways to make their workforces more specialized and responsive to changes in demand.

The food services and drinking places industry is expected to add almost 1.5 million new jobs over the 2004–2014 projection period. Increases in population, dual-income families, and dining sophistication will contribute to job growth. In addition, the increasing diversity of the population will contribute to job growth in food services and drinking places that offer a wider variety of ethnic foods and drinks.

Over 890,000 new jobs are expected to arise in state and local government, adding more than 11 percent over the 2004–2014 period. Job growth will result primarily from growth in the population and its demand for public services. Additional job growth will result as state and local governments continue to receive greater responsibility for administering federally funded programs from the federal government.

Wholesale trade is expected to add almost 480,000 new jobs over the coming decade, reflecting growth both in trade and in the overall economy. Most new jobs will be for sales representatives at the wholesale and manufacturing levels. However, industry consolidation and the growth of electronic commerce using the Internet are expected to limit job growth to 8.4 percent over the 2004–2014 period, less than the 14 percent projected for all industries.

Continual changes in the economy have far-reaching and complex effects on employment in industries. Job seekers should be aware of these changes, keeping alert for developments that can affect job opportunities in industries and the variety of occupations that are found in each industry.

Editor's Note: The preceding article was adapted from the Career Guide to Industries*, a publication of the U.S. Department of Labor. A book titled* 40 Best Fields for Your Career *(JIST Publishing) includes information from the* Career Guide to Industries *plus useful "best fields" lists and other helpful insights.*

High-Paying Occupations with Many Openings, Projected 2004–2014

Over the 2004–2014 decade, career choices abound for those seeking high earnings and lots of opportunities. High-paying occupations that are projected to have many openings are varied. This diverse group includes teachers, managers, and construction trades workers.

The job openings shown in the chart on the next page represent the total that are expected each year for workers who are either entering for the first time or moving from job to job within the occupation. The job openings result from each occupation's growth and from the need to replace workers who retire or leave the occupation permanently for some other reason.

Median earnings, such as those listed in the chart, indicate that half of the workers in an occupation made more than that amount, and half made less. The occupations in the chart ranked in the highest or second-highest earnings quartiles for 2004 median earnings. This means that median earnings for workers in these occupations were higher than the earnings for at least 50 percent of all occupations in 2004.

Most of these occupations had another thing going for them in 2004: low or very low unemployment. Workers in occupations that had higher levels of unemployment—carpenters and truck drivers—were more dependent on a strong economy or seasonal employment.

High-Paying Occupations with Many Openings, Projected 2004–2014

Occupation	Annual average job openings due to growth and total replacement needs, projected 2004–2014	Median annual earnings 2004
Postsecondary teachers	329,000	$54,160
Truck drivers, heavy and tractor-trailer	274,000	33,870
First-line supervisors/managers of retail sales workers	229,000	32,410
Registered nurses	229,000	53,640
Executive secretaries and administrative assistants	218,000	35,550
Carpenters	210,000	35,140
General and operations managers	208,000	79,300
Elementary school teachers, except special education	203,000	43,660
Business operations specialists, all other	193,000	53,880
Sales representatives, wholesale and manufacturing, except technical and scientific products	169,000	46,090
First-line supervisors/managers of office and administrative support workers	167,000	41,850
Accountants and auditors	157,000	51,310
Maintenance and repair workers, general	154,000	30,930
Secondary school teachers, except special and vocational education	107,000	46,120
Managers, all others	105,000	78,330
Painters, construction and maintenance	102,000	30,520
Farmers and ranchers	96,000	38,600
Automotive service technicians and mechanics	93,000	32,610
First-line supervisors/managers of production and operating workers	89,000	45,230
Computer support specialists	87,000	40,650

Source: U.S. Department of Labor, Office of Occupational Statistics and Employment Projections.

Large Metropolitan Areas That Had the Fastest Employment Growth, 2004–2005

The Sun Belt beamed for employment growth from 2004 to 2005, according to data from the Bureau of Labor Statistics. Between December 2004 and December 2005 (projected data), the Sun Belt was home to almost all the large metropolitan areas in the United States in which employment growth was highest. Total U.S. nonfarm payroll employment increased 1.2 percent over this period as the nation experienced a sluggish economy. As the chart on the next page shows, employment in nine of the metropolitan areas with at least 300,000 jobs in December 2004 grew by at least two and a half times the national rate over the same period—and one of them increased at more than five times the national rate.

But before packing your bags for one of these metropolitan areas, remember that these data do not show the variation in the kinds of jobs added.

Large Metropolitan Areas That Had the Fastest Employment Growth, 2004–2005

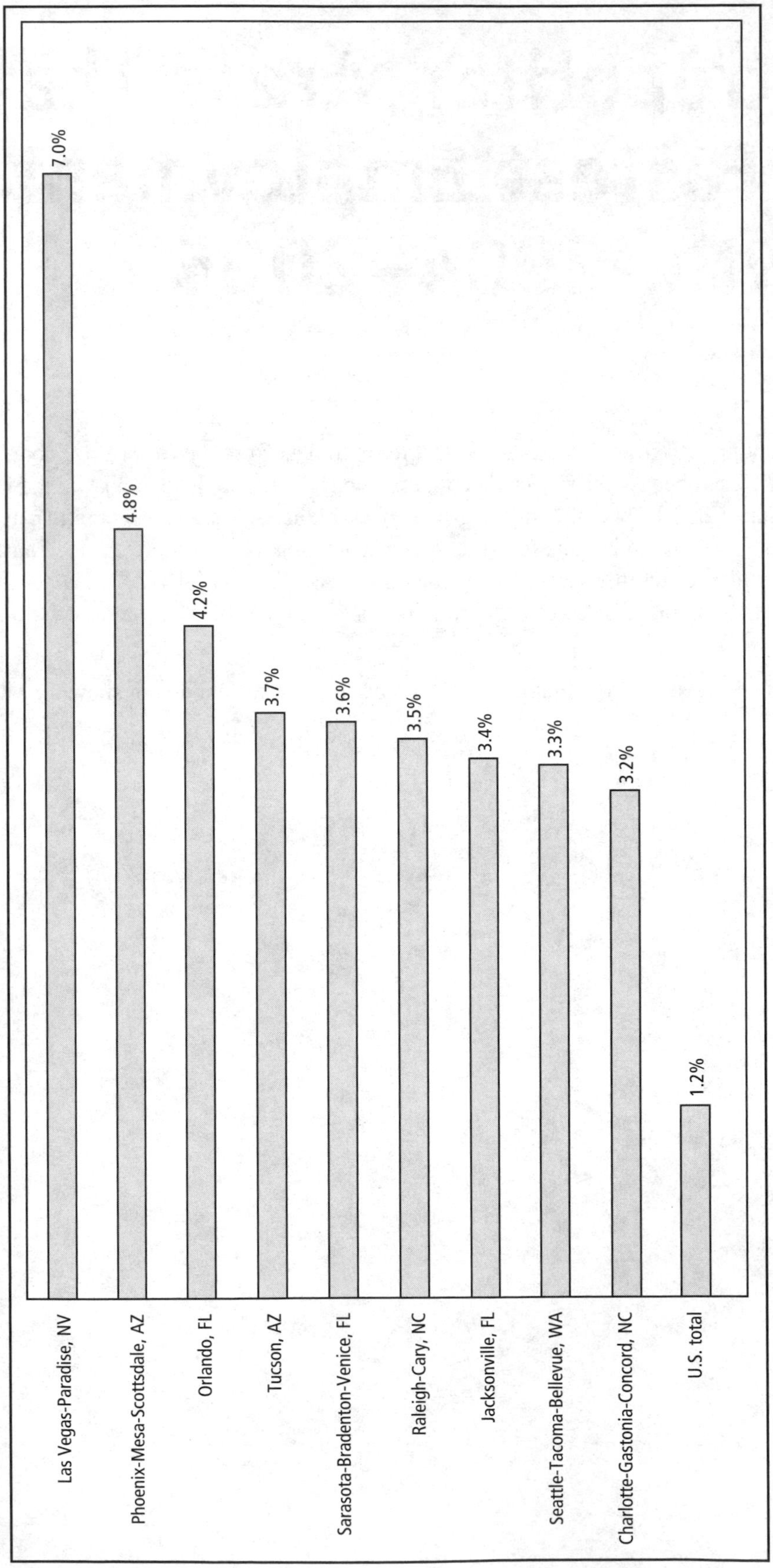

Las Vegas-Paradise, NV	7.0%
Phoenix-Mesa-Scottsdale, AZ	4.8%
Orlando, FL	4.2%
Tucson, AZ	3.7%
Sarasota-Bradenton-Venice, FL	3.6%
Raleigh-Cary, NC	3.5%
Jacksonville, FL	3.4%
Seattle-Tacoma-Bellevue, WA	3.3%
Charlotte-Gastonia-Concord, NC	3.2%
U.S. total	1.2%

Source: U.S. Department of Labor, Current Employment Statistics survey.

Index

A–B

accountants, 2, 27, 32–36, 345
administrative services managers, 4, 27, 36–38
advertising, marketing, promotions, public relations, and sales managers, 2, 27, 39–41
animal care and service workers, 3, 27, 41–44
applications, 315
athletes, coaches, umpires, and related workers, 3, 27, 44–47
auditors, 2, 27, 32–36, 345
automotive service technicians and mechanics, 3, 27, 47–51
barbers, cosmetologists, and other personal appearance workers, 3, 27, 51–53, 346
Best Jobs for the 21st Century, 14, 343
bill and account collectors, 2, 27, 53–54
bookkeeping, accounting, and auditing clerks, 4, 27, 55–56
building cleaning workers, 2, 27, 56–59
bus drivers, 3, 27, 59–62

C–E

career
  exploration, 7
  planning, 4, 6–7, 299–359
  portfolio, 331
carpenters, 3, 27, 62–64
cement masons, concrete finishers, segmental pagers, and terrazzo workers, 4, 27, 64–67
chefs, cooks, and food preparation workers, 3, 27, 67–71, 347
child care workers, 3, 27, 71–74
clinical laboratory technologists and technicians, 3, 27, 74–76
computer and information systems managers, 3, 27, 76–78
computer scientists and database administrators, 3, 27, 78–82
computer software engineers, 2, 27, 82–84, 348
computer support specialists and systems administrators, 2, 27, 84–87, 349
computer systems analysts, 2, 27, 87–90
counselors, 2, 27, 90–94
counter and rental clerks, 2, 27, 94–95
customer service representatives, 2, 95–98
demonstrators, product promoters, and models, 4, 27, 98–102
dental assistants, 2, 27, 102–103
dental hygienists, 3, 27, 103–105
earnings, 5, 380–382, 385–386
earnings section explained, 12, 25
education, 5–6, 371, 379–380
education administrators, 3, 27, 105–108
electricians, 4, 27, 108–111
emergency medical technicians and paramedics, 3, 27, 111–113
employment
  agencies, 315–316
  section explained, 11, 25
  totals, 365–371, 375–378
engineers, 4, 28, 113–122
Enhanced Occupational Outlook Handbook, 14, 343
Essential Job Search Data Worksheet, 338–342
Exploring Careers, 14

F–H

fastest-growing careers
  advice for evaluating, 4, 23–26
  list of, 2–4
  matching yourself to, 15–29
  by metropolitan areas, 387–388
  by occupational groups, 368–372
  selection process for this book, 1–2
  skills needed in, 27–29
financial analysts and personal financial advisors, 3, 28, 122–125
financial managers, 4, 28, 125–128
fire fighting occupations, 3, 28, 128–131
fitness workers, 2, 28, 131–133
food and beverage serving and related workers, 2, 28, 133–137, 351
food processing occupations, 4, 28, 137–140
gaming services occupations, 3, 28, 140–142
graphic designers, 4, 28, 143–145, 352
grounds maintenance workers, 2, 28, 145–148
hazardous materials removal workers, 4, 28, 148–150
heating, air-conditioning, and refrigeration mechanics and installers, 3, 28, 150–153
help wanted ads, 315
high-paying jobs with many openings, 385–386
hotel, motel, and resort desk clerks, 3, 28, 153–155
human resources assistants, except payroll and timekeeping, 4, 28, 155–157
human resources, training, and labor relations managers and specialists, 2, 28, 157–162

I–M

industries, 307, 311–312, 365–368, 373–384
instructional coordinators, 3, 28, 162–163
interviews, 332–336
JIST Cards, 319–320
Job-Match Grid, 15–29
job outlook section explained, 11–12, 25
job search, 8, 13, 299–359
lawyers, 4, 28, 163–167
licensed practical and licensed vocational nurses, 3, 28, 167–168
maintenance and repair workers, general, 3, 28, 169–170
management analysts, 3, 28, 170–173
market and survey researchers, 4, 28, 173–175
massage therapists, 4, 28, 175–178
material moving occupations, 4, 28, 178–181
medical and health services managers, 3, 28, 181–183
medical assistants, 2, 28, 183–185
medical records and health information technicians, 4, 28, 185–187
medical scientists, 3, 28, 187–190

medical transcriptionists, 3, 28, 190–192
metropolitan areas with fastest growth, 387–388

N–Q

nature of the work section explained, 9–10, 24
New Guide for Occupational Exploration, 14, 311, 343
networking, 317–318
nursing, psychiatric, and home health aides, 2, 28, 192–195
Occupational Outlook Handbook, iii, 9, 14, 311, 343
occupational therapists, 4, 28, 195–197
office and administrative support worker supervisors and managers, 4, 28, 197–199
office clerks, general, 4, 28, 199–201
O*NET codes explained, 9
*O*NET Dictionary of Occupational Titles,* 9, 14, 343
painters and paperhangers, 4, 28, 201–203
paralegals and legal assistants, 3, 28, 203–206
payroll and timekeeping clerks, 3, 29, 206–207
personal and home care aides, 2, 29, 207–209
pharmacists, 4, 29, 209–212
pharmacy technicians, 3, 29, 212–214
physical therapist assistants and aides, 3, 29, 214–215
physical therapists, 3, 29, 215–217
physician assistants, 3, 29, 217–219, 353
physicians and surgeons, 3, 29, 219–222
pipelayers, plumbers, pipefitters, and steamfitters, 3, 29, 222–225
police and detectives, 3, 29, 225–229
portfolio, 331
property, real estate, and community association managers, 4, 29, 229–232
public relations specialists, 3, 29, 232–235
Quick Job Search, 13, 299–359

R–T

radiologic technologists and technicians, 4, 29, 235–236
real estate brokers and sales agents, 4, 29, 237–239
receptionists and information clerks, 2, 29, 239–241
recreation workers, 3, 29, 241–243
registered nurses, 2, 29, 243–247
related occupations section explained, 13, 26
respiratory therapists, 4, 29, 247–249, 354
resume contributors, 344
resumes, 316, 321–331, 343–359
retail salespersons, 2, 29, 249–251, 355
roofers, 3, 29, 251–253
salary. *See* earnings
sales representatives, wholesale and manufacturing, 3, 29, 253–256
secretaries and administrative assistants, 4, 29, 256–259
security guards and gaming surveillance officers, 3, 29, 259–261, 356
skills
  checklists, 15–29, 301–304
  matching to careers, 15–29
  types of, 300–305
social and human service assistants, 2, 29, 261–263
social workers, 2, 29, 263–266
sources of additional information section explained, 13, 26
surgical technologists, 4, 29, 266–268
taxi drivers and chauffeurs, 3, 29, 268–271
teacher assistants, 3, 29, 271–273
teachers—postsecondary, 2, 29, 273–277
teachers—preschool, kindergarten, elementary, middle, and secondary, 2, 29, 277–281, 357
teachers—self-enrichment education, 2, 29, 281–283
teachers—special education, 3, 29, 283–285, 358–359
Tomorrow's Jobs, 363–372
top executives, 2, 29, 285–288
training, other qualifications, and advancement section explained, 10, 24–25
trends, 5–6, 361–388
truck drivers and driver/sales workers, 3, 29, 288–292

U–Z

veterinary technologists and technicians, 4, 29, 292–294
working conditions section explained, 10, 24
writers and editors, 3, 29, 294–297
Young Person's Occupational Outlook Handbook, 14

See us on the Web: www.jist.com

Young Person's Occupational Outlook Handbook, Fifth Edition

The Editors at JIST

Based on the *Occupational Outlook Handbook*, this text is ideal for helping young people explore careers. This book covers more than 270 jobs—each on one page—held by 88 percent of the workforce. It clusters job descriptions, making it easy to explore job options based on interest. It also makes direct connections between school subjects and the skills needed for jobs.

ISBN 1-59357-125-9 / Order Code LP-J1259

$19.95

College Majors Handbook with Real Career Paths and Payoffs, Second Edition

Neeta P. Fogg, Paul E. Harrington, and Thomas F. Harrington

The only book that provides information on the actual jobs and earnings of college graduates in 60 majors. Based on a U.S. Census Bureau study of 150,000 college graduates, this handbook offers the most accurate, helpful information available for making decisions on a college major—or what to do with a degree you have. Learn which majors are the best investment, the job and salary prospects for specific majors, and so much more.

ISBN 1-59357-074-0 / Order Code LP-J0740

$24.95

Job Seeker's Online Goldmine

A Step-by-Step Guidebook to Government and No-Cost Web Tools

Janet E. Wall, Ed.D.

Learn how to use little-known but powerful Internet tools that help you assess your career interests, research occupations and salary, do your resume, get a job, improve your skills, and plan and fund your education. These incredibly useful Web resources—sponsored by Uncle Sam and noncommercial entities—offer a goldmine of career- and education-related assistance.

ISBN 1-59357-294-8 / Order Code LP-J2948

$13.95

Guide to America's Federal Jobs, Third Edition

Bruce Maxwell and the Editors at JIST

This guide offers the most current information, step-by-step guidance, and helpful tips to be the best overall resource on federal employment. It includes summaries, Web addresses, and more for all agencies and departments, including the Department of Homeland Security. See examples and pay rates of real jobs. Obtain vital tips for applying online and using the federal jobs Web site most productively.

ISBN 1-59357-116-X / Order Code LP-J116X

$18.95

Call 1-800-648-JIST or Fax 1-800-JIST-FAX

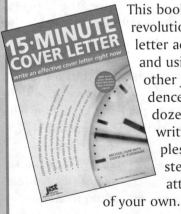